A BIRDER'S GUIDE TO ALASKA

by

George C. West

Copyright © 2002 by American Birding Association, Inc.
All rights reserved. No part of this publication may be reproduced, stored in a retrieval system, transmitted in any form or by any means, electronic, photocopying, or otherwise, without prior written permission of the publisher.
Library of Congress Catalog Number: 2002110390
ISBN Number: 1-878788-19-1

First Edition
1 2 3 4 5 6 7 8

Printed in the United States of America

Publisher
American Birding Association, Inc.
John Kricher, Chair, Publications Committee

Editor
Cindy Lippincott

Associate Editors
Bob Berman and Virginia Maynard

Layout and Typography
Cindy Lippincott; using CorelVENTURA, Windows version 8

Maps
Cindy Lippincott; using CorelDRAW, version 5

Cover Paintings
© George C. West, Birchside Studios, Green Valley, Arizona, *www.birchsidestudios.com*
front cover: *Smith's Longspur* from a photograph on the Denali Highway by Audubon L. Bakewell IV
back cover: *Red-faced and Pelagic Cormorants*

Cover Photograph
back cover: *Rock Ptarmigan*, photographed on Heintzleman Ridge of Thunder Mountain northwest of Juneau by Tim Schantz

Illustrations
© George C. West, Birchside Studios, Green Valley, Arizona, *www.birchsidestudios.com*

Distributed by
American Birding Association Sales
PO Box 6599
Colorado Springs, Colorado 80934-6599 USA
phone: (800) 634-7736 or (719) 578-0607
fax: (800) 590-2473 or (719) 578-9705
abasales@abasales.com

DEDICATION

This guide is dedicated to the memory of three highly influential Alaskan ornithologists and birders.

The first is **Laurence Irving**, former Director of the Naval Arctic Research Laboratory in Barrow, former Director of the Arctic Health Research Center in Anchorage, and former Director of the Institute of Arctic Biology at the University of Alaska Fairbanks. Larry was a widely known and respected environmental physiologist who became fascinated with birds relatively late in his career. However, his insights into ways of better understanding avian migration, distribution, and physiology led to many achievements and discoveries for birders. He was of the "old school," steeped in natural history but able to understand and give prudent advice on how to make modern physiological and biochemical methodology advance our knowledge of the biology of birds. He was my mentor at the Institute of Arctic Biology for many years and greatly influenced the way I viewed ornithology.

The second is **Malcolm E. "Pete" Isleib**, commercial fisherman for many years out of Cordova, and Alaska's premier birder for his too-short life. We visited Pete many times in the 1960s when he took us out in his fishing boat to the bars at the mouth of the Copper River to document the shorebird migration. He advised on many aspects of our studies in bird migration and made many major advances in our understanding of avian distribution in Alaska. He was a good friend and colleague.

The third is **Timothy J. Schantz**, a young and dedicated birder who also was taken away from the birding world far too early in his life. Tim took his birding seriously. Because he kept complete and accurate records of all his observations, his legacy has provided valuable information to this guide and will to other ornithologists and birders in the future. His personality and work as a guide were ideally blended, as one of his greatest gifts was assisting others to find and identify birds. Tim's dedication to birds, birders, and birding will be missed by all who might have enjoyed his enthusiasm when birding in Alaska

Acknowledgements and Contributors

In 1994, I published *A Birder's Guide to the Kenai Peninsula, Alaska* that was supported by the Pratt Museum in Homer, Alaska. At the same time, Nick Lethaby published *A Bird Finding Guide to Alaska* that covered 23 of the most popular sites. Both of these guides were in great demand and sold out within five years. By 2001, birders were calling and e-mailing to ask about a birder's guide to Alaska and an update of the Kenai guide. The American Birding Association acquired the rights to Lethaby's guide when Nick decided not to publish a second edition. Cindy Lippincott, who knew me from the early 1970s in Fairbanks, approached me on behalf of ABA to ask if I would consider authoring a guide covering the entire state, using Lethaby's and my books as a starting point. This volume is the result of about two years of effort to bring together a comprehensive guide to birding in Alaska.

Perhaps more than other regional birder's guides, this one required the specific knowledge, time, and energy of a large number of expert birders throughout the vast state of Alaska, as well as input from many birders who do not live in Alaska but who have birded there frequently over the years. Without the help of these birders and consultants, it would not have been possible to do justice to outlining the complexities of where to find birds in the 49th state. The contributors listed on pages v and vi wrote or helped to write chapters for the guide. Jeff Bouton, Terry Doyle, Steve Heinl, Paul Lehman, and Steve Zimmerman were especially helpful in many aspects of the guide in addition to their duties as chapter authors. The contributions of many other birders are recognized in the Acknowledgements following each chapter. Because contact information goes out of date so quickly, it is not included here. Many of these birders can be found in the latest edition of the ABA membership directory.

Cindy Lippincott encouraged the writing of this guide and ended up doing more than her fair share of the work in creating all the maps, editing every line, and keeping track of progress as chapters flew back and forth by e-mail. She and Bob Berman created the layout and managed to get all the information packed into this single volume along with some space for illustrations. Virginia Maynard copy-edited the manuscript and made many improvements. Their effort is greatly appreciated.

My thanks to all for your assistance in bringing this guide to the birding public.

I am continually thankful to my wife, Ellen, for her patience and support during the many long days I spent in the field, at the computer, and at the drawing table, working on this guide (and many other earlier guides).

CHAPTER AUTHORS

Audubon L. Bakewell IV — Owner and Naturalist-Guide, Paxson Alpine Tours and Cabins, Paxson, Alaska.

Larry Balch — Owner and leader, Attour, Inc. (tours for many years to Attu Island), Rockford, Illinois.

Melissa Cady — Wildlife Biologist, USDA Forest Service, Petersburg Ranger District, Petersburg, Alaska.

Edward Clark — Birder of all Alaska based in Fairbanks, Alaska.

Lana Creer-Harris — Nome birding expert since 1986. Formerly at the Nome Convention and Visitor Bureau, now residing at Spanish Fork, Utah.

Judy Dearborn — Birder of all Alaska based in Fairbanks, Alaska.

James DeWitt — Birder of interior Alaska based in Fairbanks, Alaska.

Nancy DeWitt — Executive Director, Alaska Bird Observatory, Fairbanks, Alaska.

Bob Dittrick — Owner, Wilderness Birding Adventures, Eagle River, Alaska.

Steve DuBois — Wildlife Biologist, Alaska Department of Fish and Game, Delta Junction, Alaska.

Cameron D. Eckert — Ecologist, birder, educator, and writer, Whitehorse, Yukon Territory.

Rick Ernst — Alaska birder based in Trapper Creek, Alaska.

Carmen Field — Biologist/Naturalist with the Alaska Department of Fish and Game, Homer, Alaska.

Delesta Fox — Alaska birder based in Anchorage, Alaska.

Cecily Fritz — Alaskan raptor specialist and Site Leader, Palmer, Alaska.

Steve Heinl — Birder of southeast Alaska, Alaska Department of Fish and Game, Ketchikan, Alaska.

James W. Helmericks — Owner and operator of Golden Plover Guiding Service, Colville Village, Alaska.

Sharon Kanareff — Birder and tour company owner in the Denali Borough, Alaska, now living in Olympia, Washington.

Aaron Lang — Birding guide from Eagle River, Alaska.

Keith Larson — Wildlife Biologist, U.S. Fish and Wildlife Service, Tetlin National Wildlife Refuge, now with Bird Studies Canada in Port Rowan, Ontario.

Paul Lehman — Birding guide, author, and editor with vast Alaskan experience, based at Cape May, New Jersey.

Will Lentz — Tour guide on the North Slope and Dalton Highway, based in Fairbanks, Alaska.

Robert MacDonald — Wildlife Biologist, U.S. Fish and Wildlife Service, Togiak National Wildlife Refuge, Dillingham, Alaska.

Richard MacIntosh — Alaska birder and biologist, National Marine Fisheries Service, Kodiak, Alaska.

Carol McIntyre — Wildlife Biologist, National Park Service, Denali National Park, Denali Park, Alaska.

Randy Meyers — Natural Resource Specialist, Bureau of Land Management, Kotzebue, Alaska.

Capt. Ed Murphy — Marine Pilot based in Homer, Alaska.

David K. Porter — Chief Ranger, Denali State Park, Trapper Creek, Alaska.

John Puschock — Biologist, USDA Forest Service, Seminole Ranger District, Umatilla, Florida (formerly at Kotzebue, Alaska).

Peg Robertsen — Wildlife Biologist, USDA Forest Service, Tofte Ranger District, Tofte, Minnesota (formerly at Wrangell, Alaska).

Susan E. Savage — Wildlife Biologist, Alaska Peninsula/Becharof National Wildlife Refuge, King Salmon, Alaska.

Timothy Schantz — Alaska guide and birder (deceased). Contributions of Tim's birding information was kindly provided by his brothers, Mike and Tom Schantz.

Nathan R. Senner — Alaska birder based in Anchorage, Alaska.

Stanley E. Senner — Executive Director, Audubon Alaska, National Audubon Society, Anchorage, Alaska.

Sean D. Smith — Director, World Birding Center/Texas Parks and Wildlife, Edinburg, Texas (formerly tour operator at Saint Paul, Pribilof Islands, Alaska).

Marlys E. Tedin — Birder living for many years in Sitka, Alaska.

Marjorie L. Ward — Birder living for many years in Sitka, Alaska.

Jim Williams — Associate Editor, *Birding*, American Birding Association, Webster, Wisconsin (many birding trips to Alaska).

Steven T. Zimmerman — Retired Assistant Regional Administrator, NOAA National Marine Fisheries Service; President, Juneau Audubon Society, Juneau, Alaska.

George West
Green Valley, Arizona
August 2002

TABLE OF CONTENTS

INTRODUCTION

Alaska! The word alone brings visions of Bluethroats and Arctic Warblers in every bush, of tundra filled with the cries of courting sandpipers and cackling ptarmigan, of swarms of half-a-million alcids swirling around an offshore island, of lines of shearwaters and fulmars with a smattering of storm-petrels and albatrosses, and of one Asian stray after another. These visions can become a reality if you are in the right place at the right time. But Alaska is enormous. From Attu at the western end of the Aleutian Island chain to Ketchikan in southeast, Alaska stretches over 2,350 miles, equivalent to the distance from California to Florida. From its northernmost point at Barrow to Amatignak Island at the southernmost arc of the Aleutian chain is 1,390 miles, or equivalent to driving from Fargo, North Dakota, to Brownsville, Texas.

Alaska's expansive and spectacular scenery includes several ranges of snow-capped mountains, each dissected with scores of active glaciers and culminating with Denali, at 20,320 feet the highest mountain in North America. There are tens of thousands of square miles of arctic tundra, boreal forest, lakes, rivers, streams, and bogs. Along Alaska's 33,904-mile coastline are fjords, bays, and biologically-rich estuaries, rocky, gravel, and sandy shores, and nutrient-laden mudflats ideal for migrating shorebirds. There are thousands of islands, from the extensive Aleutian chain to the maze of islands in southeast Alaska, many with inaccessible cliffs and slopes that support millions of nesting seabirds.

Some 469 species of birds are documented in Alaska and another 31 species have been seen, some with regularity, but have not been substantiated. Yet only some 627,000 people live in this vast state of 663,000 square miles and these mostly in its three largest cities—Anchorage, Fairbanks, and Juneau. This is about the same number of people living in the greater Tucson, Arizona, area. There are a few roads that connect cities and towns in southcentral and interior Alaska. Most of the other towns and villages are isolated by land travel, except by dogsled and snowmachine in winter, but are accessible by boat or aircraft or both in summer. Therefore, unlike birding in most of the rest of North America, you cannot simply get in your car and drive from one prime birding spot to the next. Rather, you must plan your trip carefully to reach your destinations by plane and/or boat and then find ground transportation from the airport or boat dock to your next birding adventure.

BIRDING IN ALASKA

Alaska's size and diversity of habitat present visiting birders with a great challenge. With so many species occurring in peripheral areas of the state, it is difficult to determine when and where to go to find a particular species. It is even harder to organize a visit as to exactly when and where you want to go. You cannot do it all in a single one- or two-week trip. By reading through this guide, you should be able to put together a series of venues that can be reached and birded in a relatively short time frame, depending on the species you are seeking or the places and scenery you wish to enjoy. If non-stop birding is your primary focus, for your initial visit it may be prudent to go with one of the nationally recognized birding-tour companies, all of which have long experience in Alaska. They will plan your trip, make all accommodation and tour arrangements, and make sure you experience the best of the birding opportunities in the areas they cover. If you go on your own, don't try to do it all in one trip. Select a few places and concentrate your efforts there to see all that those areas have to offer. Come back again to explore another region. Remember—to cover all of Alaska is equivalent to birding half of the Lower 48 states!

This guide does not treat all possible locations to bird in Alaska—to do so would create an even lengthier and heavier book. We have concentrated on those areas that can be reached by commercial transportation, including scheduled airline flights, trains, boats, and vehicles you can rent or bring with you. Also included are some significant birding spots accessible only by charter or private aircraft or boat. Although few visiting birders may ever reach these outposts—Forrester Island, Kelly Bar, Middleton Island, Arctic National Wildlife Refuge, Misty Fjords—Alaska's resident birders can use the logistical information to expand their birding destinations.

WHEN TO VISIT

Although the best birding season extends from the first of May until the end of September, birding at other times can be equally rewarding. We will concentrate on birding in the warmer months of the year, but this guide will also include suggestions for birders who come to Alaska in winter or, indeed, for the many Alaskan resident birders who don't hang up their binoculars come freeze-up! For each of your Alaskan adventures you will need to decide if you wish to view the arrival of waterfowl and seabirds in March and April or the impressive shorebird migration in the first two weeks of May. Perhaps you would enjoy the arrival of passerines in late May and early June, or the nesting peak of seabirds in July and early August. Equally impressive is the concentration of post-breeding birds in August and the fall migration in

September. From late October to March is the best time for wintering eiders and Long-tailed Ducks and perhaps a Gyrfalcon along the coast. Ross's Gull and juvenile Sharp-tailed Sandpipers, for example, usually are not seen until late September.

Most of the ducks and geese that arrive in April and May are familiar to birders from the Lower 48, but there may be vagrants like Baikal Teal, Tufted Duck, and Smew. Although seabirds begin to arrive in late April, they are not on the colonies in numbers until June and will remain on the rocky islands and surrounding oceans into September. Hundreds of thousands of shearwaters arrive from the southern hemisphere in mid-summer and spend their austral winter from the northern Gulf of Alaska into the Bering Sea, where they mix with the rarer northern species such as Short-tailed Albatross, Mottled Petrel, and Buller's Shearwater. Many interesting birds are found from winter into early spring, including Red-throated, Pacific, Common, and Yellow-billed Loons, Horned and Red-necked Grebes, Steller's, King, and Common Eiders, Harlequin Duck, flocks of scoters, Long-tailed Duck, Rock Sandpiper, and Snow Bunting. Accidentals in winter to the Kachemak Bay area, for example, include Emperor Goose, Slaty-backed Gull, Ivory Gull, White-throated Sparrow (rare to Alaska), McKay's Bunting, Brambling, and Purple and Cassin's Finches (rare to Alaska). June and July are probably the best months to plan a trip if you have not been to Alaska before—the roads have recovered from the spring thaw (frost heaves) and the water is calmer.

ALASKA BIRDING RESOURCES

To obtain current birding information you can subscribe to the Alaska Birds list on the web, or you can call one of the area-wide birding hot lines. To subscribe to the new Alaska state birding resource, go to *https://www.uaf.edu:8025/*. Scroll down the list and click on AlaskaBirds-L. You must submit your e-mail address and a password to sign up. Then, you can look at current sighting information from this address.

RECORDED HOT LINES

Upper Cook Inlet (Anchorage)	907-338-2473
Fairbanks	907-451-9213
Kachemak Bay (Homer)	907- 235-7337
Resurrection Bay (Seward)	907-224-2325
Juneau (spring–fall)	907-586-2591

MAPS, GUIDES, AND BIRDING TOURS

Alaska Birding — *https://www.uaf.edu:8025/*

Alaska Bird Checklists — *www.npwrc.usgs.gov/resource/othrdata/chekbirds/r7/alaska.htm*

Alaska Department of Fish and Game — *www.state.ak.us/adfg*

Alaska Department of Natural Resources Land Use Maps — *http://www.dnr.state.ak.us/mlw/planning/easmtatlas/index.htm*

Alaska Outdoor Guide — *www.alaskaoutdoorguide.com*

Alaska Public Lands Information Center — *www.nps.gov/aplic*

Alaska Search (any category) — *www.alaskasearch.com*

American Birding Association (sponsors birding tours) — *www.americanbirding.org*

Bell's Guide to Alaska — *www.alaskan.com/bells*

Bird Watching Tours of Anchorage — *www.anchoragebirding.com*

Borderland Tours (birding tours) — *www.borderland-tours.com*

Field Guides (birding tours) — *www.fieldguides.com*

High Lonesome Ecotours (birding tours) — *www.hilonesome.com*

U.S. Fish and Wildlife Service — *www.r7.fws.gov*

Victor Emanuel Nature Tours — *www.ventbird.com*

WINGS (birding tours) — *www.wingsbirds.com*

NOMENCLATURE AND SUBSPECIES

Bird names and taxonomic sequence follow the *ABA Checklist: Birds of the Continental United States and Canada*, Sixth Edition, 2002, which, in turn, follows American Ornithologists' Union *Check-list of North American Birds*, seventh edition, 1998, and its supplements. The older your field guide is, the more differences you will find between outdated common and scientific names and those currently accepted. You might benefit by investing in a recent field guide for your Alaska trip—try to choose one that illustrates the subspecies and other identifiable forms you'll find in Alaska.

With the advent of DNA technology adding to the knowledge gained from conventional genetic techniques and the traditional anatomical, morphological, physiological, and behavioral studies of birds, it is not surprising that it has become possible to differentiate among related populations of birds with greater accuracy. Often this had led to the designation of subspecies, and less often to splits of species into two or more full species. Western Alaska, especially the Aleutian and Bering Sea islands, are in close proximity to Siberia, so in the list of birds recorded for the state are many forms that come from eastern Asia. Most of these Asian subspecies belong to different subspecies than their North American relatives. In the *Annotated List of the Birds of Alaska*, page 474, mention is made of these Asiatic as well as other locally differentiated North American subspecies, especially when they can be distinguished by birders in the field by plumage, voice, or distribution. In the birding chapters that follow, it becomes awkward to write out the whole subspecies trinomial each time this distinction is required in listing the birds for a particular region. Instead, we have used the generally accepted common name. For example: *Spizella breweri taverneri* is recognized as Timberline Sparrow and will be referred to by that name in the birding chapters that follow. Subspecies names are from Clements (2000). Following is a list of the most commonly mentioned subspecies in this guide.

Tundra Bean Goose *Anser fabalis serrirostris*
Taiga Bean Goose *A.f. middendorffii*
Greater White-fronted Goose *Anser albifrons frontalis* and *A.a. gambelli*
Tule Goose *A.a. elgasi*
Aleutian Canada Goose *Branta canadensis leucopareia*
Cackling Canada Goose *B.c. minima*
Taverner's Canada Goose *B.c. taverneri*
Dusky Canada Goose *B.c. occidentalis*
Vancouver Canada Goose *B.c. fulva*
Lesser Canada Goose *B.c. parvipes*
Brant *Branta bernicla hrota*
Black Brant *B.b. nigricans*
Eurasian Green-winged Teal (Common Teal) *Anas crecca crecca*
Green-winged Teal *A.c. carolinensis*
Alaskan Red-tailed Hawk *Buteo jamaicensis alascensis*
Harlan's Hawk *B.j. harlani*
Western Red-tailed Hawk *B.j. calurus*
Eurasian Whimbrel *Numenius phaeopus variegatus*
Whimbrel *N.p. hudsonicus*
Pacific Dunlin *Calidris alpina pacifica*
Dunlin *C.a. arcticola*
Kamchatka Mew Gull *Larus canus kamtschatschensis*
Mew Gull *L.c. brachyrhynchus*
Herring Gull *Larus argentatus smithsonianus*
Vega Herring Gull *L.a. vegae*
(Eurasian) Common Tern *Sterna hirundo longipennis*
Red-shafted Flicker *Colaptes auratus cafer*
Yellow-shafted Flicker *C.a. auratus*
Horned Lark *Eremophila alpestris arcticola*
Flava Horned Lark *E.a. flava*
Barn Swallow *Hirundo rustica erythrogaster*

Palearctic Barn Swallow *H.r. rustica*
Asian Barn Swallow *H.r. gutturalis*
American Pipit *Anthus rubescens rubescens*
Japonicus American Pipit *A.r. japonicus*
Orange-crowned Warbler *Vermivora celata lutescens* – yellow-green form
Orange-crowned Warbler *V.c. celata* – gray-green form
Myrtle Warbler *Dendroica coronata coronata*
Audubon's Warbler *D.c. auduboni*
Timberline Sparrow *Spizella breweri taverneri*
Gambel's White-crowned Sparrow *Zonotrichia leucophrys gambelii*
Slate-colored Junco *Junco hyemalis hyemalis*
Oregon Junco *J.h. oreganus*

Subspecific names of species not in the above list are provided in the text. "Sooty" Fox Sparrows, for example, have many subspecies not generally recognized by subspecific common names. This is also the case for many races of Rock Ptarmigan, Winter Wren, and Song Sparrow. For information on the distribution of each of these subspecies in Alaska and their full scientific name, refer to the *Annotated List of the Birds of Alaska* on page 474. For field marks of subspecies, refer to one of the many current field guides.

Note: In July 2002, the American Ornithologists' Union split the nominate Common Snipe into two species—Common Snipe *Gallinago gallinago* and Wilson's Snipe *G. delicata*—both of which occur in Alaska. See page 494 for clarification of these species' ranges.

Where to Report Sightings

If you find a species far out of its normal range or not on the Alaska *state* checklist, send complete documentation (including a photograph if possible) to Daniel D. Gibson, Collections Manager, Birds, University of Alaska Museum, 907 Yukon Drive, Fairbanks, AK 99775-6960. If you find a bird out of season or not on a *regional* checklist, notify the Audubon Society or other birding organization listed for that region in this guide. (See *Organizations*, page 539.) If you are unable to make a local contact, you can contact this guide's author for assistance in reporting rarities; please correspond by e-mail if at all possible (*kbaybird@aol.com*).

Birding Ethics

The American Birding Association's *ABA Code of Birding Ethics* is on page 22. This sensible approach to birding will serve you and the birds well.

Everyone who enjoys birds and birding must always respect wildlife, its environment, and the rights of others. In any conflict of interest between birds and birders, the welfare of the birds and their environment comes first.

ALASKA AND ITS INHABITANTS

BIOGEOGRAPHIC REGIONS

Alaska can be divided roughly into six major biogeographic regions. **Northern Alaska** extends from the Brooks Range north to the Beaufort Sea and west to Point Hope. Much of the land area north of the Brooks Range is called the North Slope. As the land nears the coast, it flattens out and the annual freeze-and-thaw cycle of the tundra creates multi-sided polygons—some raised and some lowered and filled with water. This is ideal breeding habitat for many species of waterfowl and shorebirds. **Western Alaska** borders the Chukchi and Bering Seas south to the Kuskokwim River mouth and includes the Seward Peninsula and the islands in the Bering Sea. Seabirds, including the highest diversity of alcids anywhere, dominate the rocky coastal landscape in summer. **Southwest Alaska** includes the Alaska Peninsula and the Aleutian Islands. Coastal parts of both western and southwestern Alaska are only a few miles from Russia, so it is not surprising that these two regions host many Asian migrants and strays. Many of these species have colonized this western coastal and island region of Alaska, and some have penetrated far to the east on the mainland. The central part of the state is called the **Interior** and extends roughly from the Brooks Range south to the Alaska Range and east to the Yukon border. This region contains major glacial rivers like the Yukon, Tanana, and Kuskokwim that run through vast areas of unbroken boreal spruce forest to empty into the Bering Sea. Most of the Interior is underlain with permafrost, ground that is permanently frozen except in summer when the top layer thaws to produce wet bogs and lakes. The trees, mostly White and Black Spruce, Paper Birch, and Balsam Popular, are not commercially valuable, so the forests remain largely intact except for regularly occurring lightning-caused forest fires. Alpine tundra occurs on most of the higher elevations, permitting some tundra species to breed farther south than might be expected. The rivers run through flat and open country where millions of waterfowl and shorebirds nest, and through narrow rocky canyons ideal for many raptors.

From the Alaska Range south to the Gulf of Alaska is **Southcentral** or **Southcoastal Alaska**. This southern part of the state exclusive of the southeast panhandle is more populated, contains some farming country, and supports huge stretches of boreal forest of Sitka Spruce and Mountain and Western Hemlock. The coast's extensive mudflats provide critical habitat where nearly the entire world's populations of some shorebird species congregate on their way to breeding grounds in western and northern Alaska. **Southeast Alaska** is dominated by the northern extension of the Pacific Coastal Rain Forest, with large spruce, hemlock, and cedar trees favored by the timber industry. Remnants of the rain forest continue north and west to Turnagain Arm near Anchorage. The warmer climate and the many islands with their extensive coastlines, rivers, and forests entice bird species familiar in the Lower 48 states into Alaska.

GENERAL VEGETATION

There are many popular books on Alaskan wildflowers available in local bookstores. The most complete guide and key to Alaskan flora is by Hultén (1968), but it is a large, heavy book and is not suitable for field use. A good guide to trees and shrubs is by Viereck and Little (1972). A recent guide by Shaffer (2000) for southcentral Alaskan plants, including lichens, mosses, and liverworts, is a good one to consider (see *References* for these and other guides, page 560).

Arctic tundra is dominated by grasses and sedges, including the showy Arctic Cotton or Cottongrass (*Eriophorum* spp.) There are over 20 species of willow, other dwarf shrubs, and a multitude of dwarf flowers. Quaking Aspen (*Populus tremuloides*) and cottonwood (Balsam Poplar; *Populus balsamifera*) trees reach as far north in outposts as do spruce. The boreal forest transition and boreal forest biomes are dominated by White Spruce (*Picea glauca*) in drier areas and Black Spruce (*P. mariana*) and Larch (Tamarack; *Larix laricina*) in wet areas. Most areas containing stands of Black Spruce are underlain by permafrost (permanently frozen soil), at least north of the Alaska Range. The surface layers thaw in summer making access nearly impossible, but freeze again in winter. Cottonwood, Quaking Aspen, Paper or White Birch (*Betula papyrifera*), several species of willow (*Salix* spp), alder (*Alnus* spp), and many species of shrubs, grasses, sedges, and wildflowers are present throughout this region. The trees of the Pacific Coastal Rain Forest from Turnagain Arm to Valdez are primarily Sitka Spruce (*Picea sitchensis*) along with Western (*Tsuga heterophylla*) and Mountain (*T. mertensiana*) Hemlock. These species, along with Alaska Cedar (*Chamaecyparis nootkatensis*), present in Prince William Sound, form the deep forests of southeast Alaska islands. Other species enter farther south, including Lodgepole Pine (Shore Pine; *Pinus contorta*) in sandy areas, Pacific Silver Fir (*Abies amabilis*), Western Redcedar (*Thuja plicata*), Subalpine Fir (*Abies lasiocarpa*) at higher elevations, and Black Cottonwood (*Populus trichocarpa*) along rivers and streams.

In summer, you will find many species of wildflowers throughout the state. You will need a botanical guide to identify them. There are 215 species of grass, 155 species of sedge, and many species of orchid, lily, saxifrage, legume, mustard, crowfoot, pink, heath, figwort, and composite. Other than the grasses and sedges, the ericaceous plants are the most often encountered since many of them produce edible berries (Crowberry, Blueberry, and Lowbush Cranberry). The addition of Nagoonberry and Cloudberry makes birding around bogs a potential gourmet treat.

In the Interior, conspicuous flowers are Blue Bells, Monk's Hood, Larkspur, Lupine, Tundra Rose, Prickly Rose, and Fireweed. Farther south from Anchorage and on the Kenai Peninsula, the most conspicuous herb in open fields is Cow Parsnip, or *pushki,* with its large palmate leaves and white umbels. The tiny hairs on the stems release an acidic secretion that is activated on exposure to the sun and can be very irritating to the skin, so don't push through them with bare arms. In fall, Fireweed may cover the hillsides with a blanket of magenta. Woodland brush contains Devil's Club with its imposing spines.

MAMMALS AND OTHER ANIMALS

Moose — The one land mammal that you are most likely to encounter is Moose. These giants roam throughout the state except for the far northern and western tundra, the panhandle, and the Aleutian Islands. They reach the north coast of Alaska at the mouth of the Colville River where there is still some willow brush, their favorite winter diet. You are likely to meet Moose at any season anywhere along the road system or on hiking trails in the Interior and on the Kenai Peninsula. Cows with their one- to two-year-old calves are common, but mature bulls are seldom seen from the road. Moose can be dangerous, so read the Cautions on page 17.

Caribou are abundant on the North Slope, and there are herds in the Interior along the Tok Cutoff and the Denali Highway south to Kenai. **Reindeer** are the domesticated variety of Caribou and are herded by Native Alaskans on the Seward Peninsula and some Bering Sea islands. **Muskoxen** have been introduced on some of the Bering Sea islands and on the North Slope. **Dall's Sheep** are present at high elevations in the Brooks and Alaska Ranges and in some of the lower mountain ranges such as the Chugach around Anchorage. **Mountain Goats** are mostly confined to the coastal mountains and do not range much farther north or west than the shores of Cook Inlet and Kachemak Bay.

Brown Bears are present throughout the state. The largest individuals are on Kodiak Island and the Alaska Peninsula (formerly called big brown bear or Kodiak bear). In the Interior, these bears are referred to as grizzly bears. **Black Bears** also occur throughout Alaska except for the North Slope. **Polar Bears** are likely to be encountered only at Barrow. See Cautions on page 17 and in the Barrow chapter.

A complete list of the mammals that are known to occur in Alaska is in *Appendix E*, page 565. Common names for mammals mentioned in the text follow the University of Alaska Museum's checklist.

The only **amphibian** resident throughout most of Interior and southern Alaska is the Wood Frog. However, several other amphibians have invaded southeast Alaska, including several salamanders, toads, and frogs. **Reptiles** include rare occurrences in southeast Alaska of garter snakes (that may have been released from captivity) and sea turtles along the coast. For a complete list of amphibians and reptiles, see *Appendix E*, page 566.

Fishes — There are hundreds of species of marine fishes in Alaskan waters. Unless you do some fishing, you will not encounter very many species. Most people fish in saltwater for Pacific Halibut, but often catch other species, too. The five species of Pacific salmon spend most of their life in saltwater, but are usually seen, and caught, during their migration up freshwater streams to spawn. These species and others mentioned in the text are included in *Appendix E*, page 567.

Butterflies — While there are hundreds of butterfly species in Alaska, there is as yet no guide or checklist. Ken Philip in Fairbanks is the state's expert and plans to produce a checklist soon. In the meantime, consult two Canadian guides that include most if not all Alaskan species. See Layberry (1998) for interior butterflies and Guppy (2001) for southeast butterflies (*References*, page 560).

ALASKAN NATIVE CULTURES

Alaska is a mosaic of Native communities from the Tlingit and Haida of the southeast, the Aleuts of the Aleutian and Bering Sea islands, the Athabascans of the great Interior, the Nunamiut of the Brooks Range, the Yupik of western Alaska, to the Inuit of the Arctic coast (see inside front cover). These proud and resourceful people arrived in Alaska, primarily across the Bering land bridge, thousands of years ago. The influx of white men over the past centuries resulted in the decimation of many Natives through disease and armed conflict so that most of the diminished populations were concentrated in small areas at the periphery of white communities. This is no longer the case. Through the Alaska Native Land Claims Settlement Act of 1971, Alaska Natives enjoy full tribal independence. They own large areas of land, much of which is prime birding territory. Most Native peoples have made a great effort to retain their cultural heritage. Part of that heritage is the subsistence use of plants and animals for food, shelter, transportation, medicines, religious symbols, and many common items such as jewelry, twine, fishing lures, bird snares, traps, straws, eating and cooking utensils, and tools.

When you go into a Native village to bird, constantly keep in mind that you are a guest in the community. Perhaps you'll see the young boys practice their marksmanship by shooting local passerines, or you may find wild birds hung up to dry for food. Some of these may be the rare birds you are searching for! Do not chastise them or advise the children in any way. What they are doing is following their centuries-old customs and it is within the law. Respect Native ways and Native property. Do not trespass in yards or cemeteries. Keep away from subsistence supplies of drying fish and meat. Don't hesitate to ask questions and talk with the people, but ask if it is permissible to take photographs, or to look for a rare bird that you have seen on their land. But do these things only with expressed permission. Do not trespass on any land that is signed with no-trespassing signs. As is the case in parts of the Lower 48 states, some areas have already been closed to birders because of the negligence of a few birders who have violated the rights and wishes of private property owners. Please keep this in mind wherever you are birding in Alaska. Many Native villages are dry, i.e., no alcoholic beverages of any kind are allowed.

For a good introduction to Native uses of and knowledge about birds, see Russell and West (2002) in the *References*, page 560.

PLANNING YOUR TRIP

ALASKA TRAVEL RESOURCES

To get started, buy a current copy of *The Milepost*, updated and published annually by Morris Communications, Inc., and available at most bookstores. You may order it directly by e-mail at *books@themilepost.com* or by phone at 800-726-4707; *www.themilepost.com*. *The Milepost* gives you mile-by-mile listings of natural and man-made features along the contiguous road system in Alaska—including Southeast but not most bush locations such as Nome and Dillingham—and the highways and ferries that lead to the Alaska Highway through Canada. This includes gas stations, hotels, motels, gift shops, rest stops, RV parks, campgrounds, lakes, bridges, rivers, best fishing locations, places to stop to see a mountain top, and even litter barrels and significant bumps and dips in the roadbed. An additional helpful resource is the *Official State Guide and Vacation Planner* for Alaska, free from the State Division of Tourism (see web site, page 15).

Bell's Alaska Travel Guide offers another source of information about communities reachable by road, ferry, or commercial air travel (4133 19th Street #170, Lynden, WA 98264; 250-768-2426; e-mail *info@bellsalaska.com*; *www.bellsalaska.com*). There are data on accommodations, some road logs, National Park and National Forest information with links to web sites, along with trip-planning suggestions. You can order a copy of the published guide or view much of the information on their web site (see page 15). Detailed maps of the birding sites listed in this guide are included in the following chapters. However, you may wish to obtain topographic and land-use maps to assist in your travels and birding adventure from the *DeLorme Alaska Atlas and Gazetteer* (see *References* page 560) and from the State of Alaska, Department of Natural Resources online (see web sites, page 15).

PLANNING AHEAD

Once you have decided when to come to Alaska and where you'd like to bird or sightsee, give some serious thought to planning where you'll sleep if you're not camping or RVing and how you'll get around if you don't have your own vehicle. Throughout this guide you'll be reminded many times to book your critical reservations as far in advance as possible. This includes plane flights, ferry reservations, vehicle rentals, and accommodations in the busier tourist destinations such as Anchorage, Fairbanks, Denali, Kodiak, Homer, and Juneau. In well-known birding destinations that have very limited tourist facilities and no options for simply driving to the next town—Nome, Gambell, the Pribilofs, Wales, Barrow, and most bush villages—an independent traveler will often be competing with the tour companies for beds and vehicles. You can join one of these groups—and there are several that specialize in birding tours—or you can use the contacts and resources mentioned in this guide to help you plan a successful independent trip. The key to success is planning well ahead of your intended travel dates. Because of Alaska's size and uncertain weather, it is wise to plan a few "open" days between venues in case you are delayed.

HOW TO GET TO ALASKA

BY ROAD

Obtain a current copy of *The Milepost* (see above) for the most accurate and up-to-date mile-by-mile description of the several routes to reach Alaska and tour the state by car or RV. This book also notes the location of all campgrounds, parks, most lodges, gas stations, and restaurants, as well as scenic pullouts along the way. Hundreds of large and small display ads expand the travel information available. All routes from the south eventually lead—by road or by ferry—to the Alaska Highway that crosses the Yukon/Alaska border near Beaver Creek. The trip through Canada can be very rewarding, even though it is a long drive (Fairbanks is over 1,500 miles from Dawson Creek, BC). You can extend your Canadian bird list by stopping along the way (see page 141 on the Alaska Highway). Once inside Alaska, you will find many bogs and ponds, lakes, and rivers near the border to keep you busy for a week or more should you wish to take the time.

The paved and graded gravel roads in British Columbia, Yukon Territory, and Alaska are usually in good shape, but in summer there is always construction resulting in minor delays. Each year portions of the Alaska Highway are torn up, straightened out, or resurfaced. Make sure your vehicle is in good mechanical condition before leaving home. Repair facilities along the way, while now more available than in earlier years, are expensive and can result in serious delays if parts need to be ordered. Drive with care, as some roads lack shoulders, watch for numerous logging and semi-trucks and RVs that can slow you down, and keep a sharp eye out for Moose that can come up out of the roadside brush with alarming speed. Often a cow Moose is followed by one or two calves, so wait a minute before speeding on.

Although you may think that a four-wheel-drive vehicle would be better on Alaskan roads, you can get into trouble if you imagine you will be able to drive on the beach at low tide or on boggy ground in the backcountry. Once stuck, there are few people around to pull you out. Most good birding places can be easily reached by a short hike from a car safely parked above the high-tide line or on the edge of a gravel road.

BY AIR

Several major airlines fly from Seattle and a few other locations in the Lower 48 to Anchorage and Fairbanks. Some stop along the way in Canada or in Ketchikan, Sitka, Juneau, and up the coast, with flights usually terminating in Anchorage. Some of the smaller cities are also served by major air carriers, but most are connected to the major Alaska hubs by local commuter airlines. With these you can reach just about anywhere in the state. Since schedules and carriers change frequently, please check with your travel agent or on the web for the latest companies that provide air service to and within Alaska. In Anchorage and other major and some minor cities and towns, you can rent a car, a truck, or a van for local use (see individual sections of this guide).

BY SEA

The Alaska Marine Highway System consists of a fleet of ferries that serve the towns along the southern coast of Alaska. One fleet sails the Inside Passage from Bellingham, Washington, to Prince Rupert, BC, and to most of the cities along Alaska's panhandle, including Ketchikan, Wrangell, Petersburg, Sitka, Juneau, Skagway, and Haines (and some smaller communities). In summer, the M/V *Kennicott* sails across the Gulf of Alaska from Juneau to Seward and provides a unique opportunity to look for pelagic birds such as albatrosses and shearwaters (see page 453). Several ferries ply among the many coastal towns such as Valdez, Cordova, Whittier, Seward, Homer, Kodiak, and out the Alaska Peninsula to Dutch Harbor. There is no ferry connection between the end of the Inside Passage that terminates in Haines or Skagway and points farther west. To reach the coastal communities of Seward or Valdez, you will have to take the train (White Pass & Yukon Route) to Whitehorse and a bus or rental car from there, or rent a car and drive north, or bring your own car on the ferry. Contact the Alaska Marine Highway System for current schedules, which change with the season (907-272-7116; 907-465-3946; or within Alaska 800-642-0066). Their web address is *http://www.alaska.gov/ferry/*. Book your reservations well in advance, particularly if you wish to reserve a stateroom, if you are bringing your vehicle, or if you plan to make any overnight stops at Southeast towns.

CLIMATE AND WHAT TO BRING

Be prepared for cold, wet, and windy weather at all seasons, especially along the coast. In mid-summer, temperatures in the Interior may exceed 90°F, but most birders will encounter much cooler conditions. Temperatures rarely exceed 60° along the coast in summer; in winter, coastal temperatures average in the low 20°s, while it may plummet to -60° in the Interior near Fairbanks. Precipitation ranges from 10 to 20 inches per year, concentrated in fall and winter in the Arctic and the Interior. Along the northern coast of the Gulf of Alaska precipitation averages over 80 inches per year and along the panhandle, over 150 inches. In summer, bring a warm vest or sweater, a sturdy raincoat with hood or waterproof hat, and a knitted or fleece hat that will cover your ears. Gloves can make holding binoculars on shipboard or on the Bering Sea islands more comfortable. There is usually some wind, especially in the afternoon along the water. Hiking trails in the backcountry often require waterproof or water-resistant hiking boots. Hip-waders may be needed in some areas such as Barrow to reach the better birding areas. Dressing in layers is always recommended.

Boat trips in smaller craft often result in wet feet from spray and deck wash, but this does not apply to the larger charter vessels or the state ferries. Knee-high rubber boots are popular for getting around on the mudflats and standing on open boat decks. Seawater temperatures in summer near the coast may get as high as 55°F but are usually colder; in winter, seawater temperatures are below 40°and often below freezing as ice forms in sheltered bays and harbors.

In addition to the usual binoculars, a spotting scope is needed to scan offshore for seabirds and across the extensive mudflats for shorebirds. Never go into the backcountry in summer without bug repellent (see the Cautions on page 17).

Black-billed Magpie

RESOURCES FOR LOGISTICAL HELP

The area code for all of Alaska is 907. In the following chapters, if the area code is omitted, you can safely assume it is 907. Otherwise the area code (usually a toll-free area code) will be included.

Business contact information is provided throughout the guide for the convenience of the reader—information that might otherwise be difficult to find due to the remoteness of and low tourist interest in some of the locations covered. ABA and the author are not responsible for the quality of products and services mentioned in this guide. Also, mention of specific commercial accommodations and services does not imply ABA endorsement of these businesses to the exclusion of others providing the same or similar accommodations and services.

Following are a few general web sites to help you get oriented with Alaska's logistics. In addition, most of the guide's chapters include a *Logistics* section listing resources specific to that particular area.

Alaska Airlines — 800-252-7522 for reservations; *http://www.alaska-air.com.*

Alaska Department of Fish and Game — Box 25526, Juneau, AK 99802; 907-465-4100; *www.state.ak.us/adfg/adfghome.htm.*

Alaska Department of Natural Resources Land Use Maps — *http://www.dnr.state.ak.us/mlw/planning/easmtatlas/index.htm.*

Alaska Division of Tourism — Box 110809, Juneau, AK 99811; 907-465-2012; fax 907-465-3767; *http://www.dced.state.ak.us/tourism*; for a copy of the *Alaska State Vacation Planner*, contact the Alaska Travel Industry Association at 907-929-2200 ext. 201.

Alaska Lodging Guide — *www.alaska-lodging.com.*

Alaska Marine Highway System (state ferry) — Main office, 6858 Glacier Highway, Juneau, AK 99801; 800-642-0066; TDD 800-764-3779; fax 907-277-4829; *http://www.alaska.gov/ferry/.* Local Juneau phone 907-465-3941; local Anchorage phone 907-272-7116; local Kodiak phone 907-486-3800.

Alaska National Parks Accommodations Search — *www.nltours.com/denali/denalirooms.html.*

Alaska Natural History Association — PO Box 838, Denali Park, AK 99755; 907-274-8440; *www.alaskanha.org.* Local Anchorage: 750 West 2nd Avenue #100, Anchorage, AK 99501; 907-274-8440; fax 907-274-8343. Bookstores are located throughout the state.

Alaska Outdoor Guide — *www.alaskaoutdoorguide.com.*

Alaska Public Lands Information Center — 605 West 4th Avenue #104, Anchorage, AK 99501; 907-271-2737; *www.nps.gov/aplic.* In Fairbanks, 250 Cushman Street #1A, Fairbanks, AK 99701; 907-456-0527. In Ketchikan, Southeast Alaska Discovery Center, 50 Main Street,

Ketchikan; 907-228-6220. In Tok, PO Box 359, or Mile 1314 Alaska Highway, Tok, AK 99780; 907-883-5667.

Alaska Railroad — Passenger Services Department, Box 107500, Anchorage, AK 99510; 327 West Ship Creek Avenue, Anchorage, AK 99501; tollfree in Anchorage 800-544-0552; tollfree outside of Anchorage 800-478-2442; fax 907-265-2323; e-mail *reservations@akrr.com*; *http://www.alaskarailroad.com*. In Seward, 907-244-5552.

Alaska Search (any category) — *www.alaskasearch.com*.

Alaska State Parks — *http://www.dnr.state.ak.us/parks/directory.htm*.

Alaska Travel Guide — *www.alaska-travel.com*.

Alaska Visitor Center and Activities — *www.alaskavisitorcenter.com*.

BC Ferries — Main office, 1112 Fort Street, Victoria, BC V8V 4V2; recorded info 250-386-3431 in Victoria, 888-223-3779 in rest of BC; fax 250-381-5452; *www.bcferries.com*.

Bureau of Land Management — Alaska State Office, 222 West 7th Avenue #13, Anchorage, AK 99513; 907-271-5960. At the same address, Room 148, is BLM Public Information Center, open 8AM–3:34PM weekdays, closed holidays; *http://ak.blm.gov/directory.html*. In Fairbanks, 1150 University Avenue, 907-474-2200.

National Park Service — *www.nps.gov/*.

State of Alaska — *www.state.ak.us/*.

Tourism British Columbia — Box 9830 Stn Prov Govt, Victoria, BC V8W 9W5; 800-HELLOBC; *www.hellobc.com*.

Tourism Yukon — Box 2703, Whitehorse, YT Y1A 2C6 or 100 Hanson Street, 1st floor, Whitehorse; 867-667-5036; fax 867-667-3546; e-mail *vacation@gov.yk.ca*; *www.touryukon.com*.

U.S. Forest Service — Chugach National Forest: 3301 C Street, Anchorage, AK 99503; 907-743-9500; fax 907-743-9476; e-mail *mailroomr10chugach@fs.fed.us*; *www.fs.fed.us/r10/chugach*. Tongass National Forest: Box 21628, Juneau, AK 99802; 8465 Old Dairy Road, Juneau; 907-790-7419; *www.fs.fed.us/r10/tongass*. National site for reserving primitive wilderness cabins (*www.reserveusa.com*). Or call at 877-444-6777; say that you are looking for an Alaskan cabin to get a knowledgeable operator.

USGS Maps in Alaska — *http://rockyweb.cr.usgs.gov/public/acis/map_dealers/ak.html* There are about 30 dealers located throughout Alaska, many with web sites linked to this web site.

U.S. Fish and Wildlife Service — 1011 East Tudor Road, Anchorage, AK 99503; 786-3909; *Chuck_Young@fws.gov; www.r7.fws.gov.*

BIRDING CAUTIONS AND SAFETY

Although you may skip over the safety cautions in the owner's manual of your latest electronic appliance, please carefully read the following information. Some of these cautions may save your life. Others will make birding in Alaska a more pleasant experience.

WILD ANIMALS

Alaska is known for its wildness and for its abundance of wildlife. Many of the places you will visit are remote locations, with aircraft the only way to get to a hospital or an emergency-care facility. Your actions in relation to any wild animals you might encounter while birding can mean the difference between life and serious injury or even death. While it is unlikely that you will be attacked by an animal, it is better to know how best to avoid confrontation, and how to act if you do have an encounter. Different species require quite different behaviors on your part, and your safest course of action may not be the one you would choose intuitively.

MOOSE Most of these mammals are somewhat tolerant of humans. In winter, they may be in the middle of town looking for an ornamental tree to prune. In spring, they seek budding shrubs and flowers around houses where the snow has melted away. By summer, they have retreated to the forests, hillsides, and lakes, but are often encountered on hiking trails. If you see a Moose nearby while you are hiking, stop and find another way around it. Do not approach the animal for a photograph or a better look. While most Moose will move away if they sense your presence, cows with calves may not budge and are especially dangerous. Watch the ears and hackles (hairs on the back of the neck). If the ears flatten and the hackles are raised, back up and retreat slowly. Moose can move through deep woods with amazing speed—you cannot outrun a Moose.

BEARS It is unlikely that you will encounter a bear while birding. Nevertheless, Brown (includes grizzly) Bears are potentially dangerous, especially when a female is with cubs or protecting food caches. Here are some good ways to avoid a problem with Brown and Black Bears: • Avoid surprising bears by watching for bear signs such as scat and large footprints in the mud. • When you are hiking in dense brush or can't see around the next turn of the trail, it is smart to make some human noises such as singing, ringing a bell, or banging on metal, just to advertise that you are coming down the trail or through the alders. • Walk downwind (with the wind at your back) so your scent precedes you. • If you come across the carcass of an animal, back off and detour around as it might be a bear's cache. • When you become aware of a bear and it is aware of you, talk in a normal voice, wave your arms, and let it know you are a human. If the bear stands on its hind legs, it is to get a better look at you or to catch your scent. Stand your ground, shout, wave your arms, spread your jacket open, or if you are with others, stand together to appear larger. Do not try to get a little closer for a photograph! • Do not whistle, imitate bear sounds, or run away. Running triggers the predator-chase reflex. • Bears enjoy salmon, so from mid-June on, be especially cautious near rivers and streams. If you are camping make sure that you leave all of your food and toiletries in your car and not in your tent or in the open when you are away from the camp or at night. • If a bear starts walking toward you, drop your pack, coat, or some other piece of apparel that has your scent and back away slowly. Bears often make bluff charges that stop within ten feet of you. Hold your ground. You cannot outrun the bear. Yell and wave your arms. • If the bear attacks you, do not try to fight but curl up in a ball, face down with your hands and arms tightly locked in back of your neck. If you lie still and play dead, the bear may lose interest if it thinks that your threat to it has been eliminated. Remain motionless for as long as possible until the bear is well away from you.

Unlike other bear species, Polar Bears will hunt people for food. You cannot outrun them. You have to be protected by having a vehicle that can get you away from the area in a hurry if a bear starts stalking you. It is best to go with a guide to areas frequented by Polar Bears.

OTHER MAMMALS Muskox bulls can be dangerous if approached when they are guarding females and calves. It is highly unlikely you will be able to approach any of the other larger mammals, and rabies is not common in Alaska. However, it is never wise to hand-feed carnivores such as foxes.

BIRDS Do not climb trees to get a look at an eagle or hawk nest. Avoid approaching a jaeger or Arctic Tern nest on the tundra; you will be dive-bombed and can be injured on the head. Do not climb on sea cliffs to get a better photo of a nesting murre or auklet. Follow the *ABA Code of Birding Ethics* (page 22) regarding disturbance of birds and their habitats.

INSECTS Mosquitoes are a problem in summer throughout most of Alaska. The large *Culex* mosquitoes that overwinter as adults emerge in May and are immediately followed by the smaller, more abundant, and more aggressive mosquitoes through June. Black Flies or white-sox (*Simulium* spp) are in all areas with running water in July, and their tiny but aggressive No-see-um cousins remain active through September. Deer Flies and other Tabanid flies are most active in August. Some people use mosquito netting over their hats to cover the head and neck, but this makes binocular use difficult and should not be necessary if you use insect repellent with a high percentage of DEET. An alternative to large amounts of DEET is to treat your birding clothing with Permethrin and your skin with a 30-percent DEET product. If you're uncertain about which repellent or method is most effective, ask any Alaskan—everyone has a favorite approach or product.

PEOPLE Traveling birders often carry expensive and interesting gear—binoculars, spotting scope, camera, recording equipment, GPS, little computers—just the sort of things to tempt an otherwise honest human being. Keep your good stuff out of sight or locked up, or carry it with you when you leave your vehicle—a precaution you would take any place you travel. Be courteous and you will be rewarded with friendship—most Alaskans like to brag about their state and the wildlife. You may learn of a few good birding spots or hear some wild stories about their experiences. But also respect the people and their land. Do not trespass where the land is signed. Do not enter Native lands without permission. Permits for many areas are required and are mentioned in the appropriate chapters.

MOVING WATER AND MUD

TIDES Many places in Alaska have large tidal ranges where the high tide may be over 20 feet higher than the low tide six hours earlier. Low tides often reveal thousands of acres of mudflats with shorebirds feeding on them—or offer you a short-cut to get from one area on the shoreline to another. Two cautions are important: **Always know the stage of the tide**—whether it is on its way out, or in, and how high the next high tide will be. If you decide to bird on the flats at low tide, **work out a route of return to above the high-tide line** that will not require you to cross any low areas such as a tidal slough. These low areas will fill with the incoming tide and cut off your access to the beach. Some intertidal areas are filled with mud that will not support your weight. This is especially true around Turnagain Arm south of Anchorage, but is also the case wherever glacial silt accumulates. You may start out over this mud, slowly sink in, and not be able to pull your foot out. People have been drowned as the tide has risen over them as they were trapped in this "quick-mud."

BOATING Boating on Alaskan rivers and coastal waters is not the same as in most places in the Lower 48. If you have your canoe or skiff with you, make sure to observe all Coast Guard safety precautions before setting out on any body of water. Some of the larger lakes can be calm one minute and have white-caps the next. The water temperature is very cold and if you fall in without adequate protection (insulated survival suit), your chances of surviving hypothermia are slim. Large rivers such as the Yukon, Tanana, or Susitna are filled with glacial silt and can be especially dangerous. If you capsize, the silt will quickly fill your clothing and pull you under. There are many snags, deadheads, and sweepers along these rivers that are hard to avoid unless you have experience. Except for small lakes and clearwater streams, it is best to do your boating with an experienced operator.

Rough-legged Hawks

ABOUT THIS GUIDE

CURRENT ACCURACY

Lists of birds from any location are not fixed. These lists grow and become more accurate as more birders explore more territory in different seasons and document their sightings. Birds are rarely removed from a list. Because Alaska is so vast and relatively unexplored except for the few places covered in this guide, it is not surprising that species new to the state will be found with some frequency. Therefore, the checklists, annotated list, and regional lists of birds in the text will certainly slip out of date as soon as this guide goes to press. The same situation applies to directions to the birding sites and to information about accommodations and visitor services. Development has a way of altering habitat, making a once-prime birding spot the next shopping mall or subdivision.

Before any *ABA/Lane Birdfinding Guide* is published, reprinted, or revised, we do our best to check the accuracy of addresses, phone numbers, and web sites. When we ask you to let us know about changes that we should make when updating the guide, what we'd *really* like to hear about from you are changes to birding routes, birding sites, birding access, and things of that nature. Did we miss a productive, accessible site? Tell us about it! You can send an e-mail to *pubdir@aba.org* or a letter to Editor, ABA Birdfinding Guides, PO Box 6599, Colorado Springs, CO 80934. Don't forget to include information so we can contact you if more details are necessary.

It is inevitable that many of the resources and contacts listed here will change with time. We suggest that you give the ones we have listed here a try and if you are not successful, get on the web to search for the needed information.

HOW TO USE THIS GUIDE

The **Annotated List of the Birds of Alaska** beginning on page 474 and the **Checklists** to many of the most popular birding locations beginning on page 519 can help in planning your trip to Alaska. Look up the species you are most interested in finding and learn where they are most likely to be found or have been seen in the past.

HOW TO USE THE INDEX

All bird species and those subspecies whose names do not include the full-species name (see page 5 for examples), as well as many place names mentioned in the text, are indexed. The *Index* also includes the page number for all species listed in the *Annotated List of the Birds of Alaska*, which appears on pages 474–518. Within this page-range you will find the primary information about each species or subspecies in Alaska. Species (and a few subspecies) included in the *Checklists of Specific Locations in Alaska* are also indexed; to find them look for the last page number in the string of index numbers—it should fall between pages 519-538.

Each pair of facing-pages in the *Index* section contains an *Abbreviated Table of Contents* box. When you look up a bird name in the *Index*, it is followed by a string of numbers—the text pages on which the species or subspecies is mentioned. The *Abbreviated Table of Contents* box shows you the starting page numbers for the book's various chapters. You can avoid flipping back and forth to find out whether a species is mentioned for the area in which you're interested by turning only to those pages that fall within the page-range of the chapter covering that area. Try looking up Bluethroat, for example. You will readily see that it is mentioned in the Dalton Highway, Colville River Delta, Nome, Wales, Kotzebue, and Saint Lawrence Island chapters and no other chapters aside from the *Annotated List* and *Checklist*. This implies that you probably need to visit one of these places to have a good chance of seeing this bird. The *Abbreviated Table of Contents* has been included in all *ABA/Lane Birdfinding Guides* with indices, in case you have not noticed this feature before.

American Birding Association Code of Birding Ethics

Respect wildlife, its environment, and the rights of others.

Promote the welfare of birds and their environment.

Support the protection of important bird habitat.

Avoid stressing birds or exposing them to danger.

Limit methods of attracting birds.

Remain well back from nests, roosts, display areas, and feeding sites.

Keep habitat disturbance to a minimum.

Respect the law and the rights of others.

Ensure that feeders, nest structures, and other artificial bird environments are safe.

Maintain and clean feeders and nest structures regularly.

Keep birds safe from predation from cats and other domestic animals.

Group birding, whether organized or impromptu, requires special care.

Respect fellow birders. Share your knowledge, especially with beginners.

Document unethical birding behavior, intervene if prudent, and notify appropriate individuals or organizations.

Leaders should teach ethics through word and example.

Limit group impact on birds and their environment, and on others using the same area.

This ABA Code of Birding Ethics may be reprinted, reproduced, and distributed without restriction. Please acknowledge the role of ABA in developing and promoting this code.

ANCHORAGE

Nathan Senner

Anchorage is the only large metropolitan area in Alaska. About half of the state's population of around 650,000 lives there. Situated on a peninsula at the northeastern end of Cook Inlet, between Knik Arm to the north and Turnagain Arm to the south, it is an ideal place to start your birding adventure in Alaska. The waters around Anchorage are loaded with glacial silt that is either carried down to Cook Inlet by large river systems such as the Susitna, Matanuska, and Knik or that melts out of the many glaciers at the eastern end of Turnagain Arm. The silt creates a constantly shifting maze of mudflats and bars that makes ship navigation difficult, but some of the silt settles near shore and allows the establishment of marine invertebrates so crucial for migrating shorebirds. The water itself is not used by many other species due to its high silt content, so there is no reason to go out in a boat looking for pelagic birds here. Landbirds can be found in the city's many large greenbelts and parks, all surrounded by pristine wilderness, with easy access to places where many Alaskan specialties can be found. Metropolitan Anchorage has attracted a fair number of Asian rarities over the years.

In addition to the birding opportunities in the city and nearby areas, Anchorage connects to most of Alaska's modest road system. By heading out the Glenn Highway north and east you can make your way to Denali National Park, Fairbanks, or Valdez. By driving south on the Seward Highway you can reach Homer and Seward. In sum, Anchorage can provide you with a few days of excellent birding, or it can be the starting point for your trip around the state by car, train, or plane.

The Upper Cook Inlet hot line at 338-2473, sponsored by Anchorage Audubon Society, has up-to-date birding information. For general information about the city, stop at the Log Cabin Visitor Information Center downtown at 524 West 4th Avenue (at F Street). Anchorage has a full range of visitor facilities—hotels, motels, excellent restaurants, scads of malls and other shopping opportunities, many parks and an extensive trail system, all automotive and RV services, and medical facilities. Indeed, Anchorage is the regional supply center for most of Alaska south of the Alaska Range, and you can count on finding almost anything you need for your trip here rather than

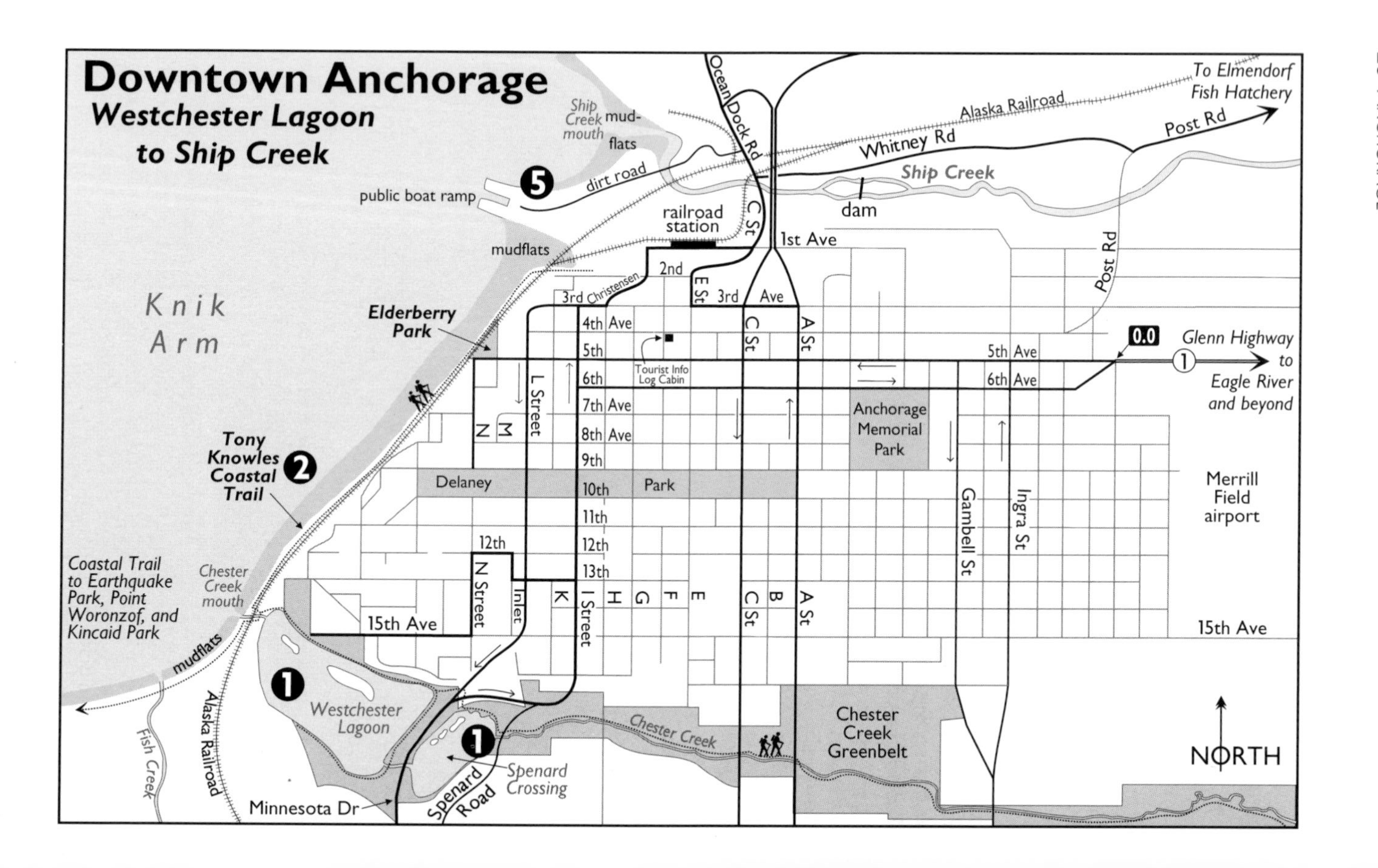
Downtown Anchorage
Westchester Lagoon
to Ship Creek
Ship Creek mouth
mud-flats
public boat ramp
dirt road
Ocean Dock Rd
Alaska Railroad
To Elmendorf Fish Hatchery
Post Rd
Whitney Rd
Ship Creek
dam
railroad station
C St
1st Ave
mudflats
2nd
3rd Christensen
E St
3rd
Ave
Post Rd
Knik Arm
Elderberry Park
4th Ave
5th
6th
7th Ave
8th Ave
9th
10th
11th
12th
13th
Tourist Info Log Cabin
C St
A St
0.0
Glenn Highway to Eagle River and beyond
5th Ave
6th Ave
L Street
M
N
Anchorage Memorial Park
Tony Knowles Coastal Trail
Delaney
Park
Gambell St
Ingra St
Merrill Field airport
12th
Coastal Trail to Earthquake Park, Point Woronzof, and Kincaid Park
Chester Creek mouth
N Street
Inlet
K
I Street
H
G
F
E
C St
B
A St
15th Ave
15th Ave
mudflats
Westchester Lagoon
Chester Creek
Chester Creek Greenbelt
NORTH
Fish Creek
Alaska Railroad
Minnesota Dr
Spenard Road
Spenard Crossing

carrying it all from home. During the busy summer tourist season, you *must* make hotel reservations well ahead of your intended arrival. The same advice applies to airplane, car rental, and tour reservations. If you come by air, you will land at Anchorage International Airport just west of the city. Your flight will probably swing in over Turnagain Arm and Cook Inlet before landing, giving you a fine view of how this beautiful city is laid out. Adjacent to the airport are two small lakes (Hood and Spenard) designated for use only by floatplanes. Although these can be busy, noisy places, you might get the first Barrow's Goldeneye, Mew Gull, or Arctic Tern of your trip there.

In the sections that follow, eight of the most productive and popular birding sites in the Anchorage Bowl are described, although there are many more places to visit if you have the time to do so. Check with Anchorage Audubon Society or a local book store for *Field Guide to Birding in Anchorage*, 3rd edition, by R.L. Scher, under revision in 2002.

WESTCHESTER LAGOON AND SPENARD CROSSING

From the airport, drive east on International Airport Road past Hood and Spenard Lakes on your left to the intersection of International Airport Road and Minnesota Drive. *All birding route directions will start from this intersection.* Turn left (north) onto Minnesota Drive toward downtown. You will pass through several intersections, the most important of which is Northern Lights Boulevard. After passing Northern Lights, the road goes downhill to a causeway between two lakes, Westchester Lagoon to the west and Spenard Crossing to the east. In combination, this is one of the best birding spots in Anchorage and the starting point for what can be either an hour of birding or a whole day. After passing the lakes, Minnesota Drive splits into northbound I Street and southbound L Street. From I Street, turn left (west) at the second traffic light onto 13th Avenue. Go straight through the light at L Street, turn right at a stop sign onto Inlet Place, and then left onto 12th Avenue at the next stop sign. After one block on 12th, turn left onto N Street. Turn right onto 15th Avenue at a stop sign. Continue west several blocks and the lagoon will be in front of you; park in either of the parking lots or on the street.

The lagoon holds an excellent variety of waterbirds from late April through fall freeze-up. Red-necked Grebes are conspicuous nesters, Common Loons are uncommon, but Pacific Loons are regular during migration, as are many dabbling and diving ducks, a number of which also breed in the area. At high tide during migration, hundreds of Hudsonian Godwits, Short-billed Dowitchers, and a smattering of other shorebird species roost on the islands in the middle of the lagoon. Search these flocks for Ruddy and Black Turnstones, Surfbird, Marbled Godwit (unusual), or even an Asian vagrant. Commonly seen are the Mew and Herring Gulls and Arctic Terns that nest on the island or nearby, with Glaucous-winged Gulls appearing toward the end of summer. During migration, look for Black-headed and Glaucous Gulls and Caspian Terns, all of which have shown up here a number of times. Eurasian Wigeon and Peregrine Falcon are regular migrants. In recent years a Yellow-headed Blackbird appeared on the island, and a Common Cuckoo was discovered in the woods behind the lagoon.

To reach Spenard Crossing, follow the paved trail east from Westchester Lagoon to two tunnels under Minnesota Drive. Head left at a fork in the trail to find the first tunnel. (The right fork will take you south on a trail leading between Minnesota Drive and Westchester Lagoon.) After a short distance pass through another tunnel to reach Spenard Crossing. This lake generally holds fewer birds, but it is often the first lake in spring and the last lake in fall to have open water. In April or late October it is worth visiting to look for the early-arriving or late-lingering ducks and gulls that tend to congregate there. Such rarities as Ring-billed and Slaty-backed Gulls have occurred, along with the more regular Eurasian Wigeons and Glaucous Gulls (early spring). If you want to explore Chester Creek Greenbelt to the east—an area particularly good for Boreal Chickadee—follow the bike trail as far as it suits you.

If your time is limited, it is far more worthwhile during the warm months (relatively speaking at least!) to head west from Westchester Lagoon to the paved **Tony Knowles Coastal Trail** along the shore of Cook Inlet. At the northeast corner of the lagoon, a right turn at the fork in the trail takes you toward downtown and Elderberry Park; a left turn leads toward Earthquake Park, the airport, and Kincaid Park. Either way, you will find excellent spots to view shorebirds from the trail (a spotting scope is helpful). Birders have found some gems along the Coastal Trail—Fork-tailed Storm-Petrel, Steller's Eider, and Terek Sandpiper. Granted, each of these species has shown up only once or twice, but it's worth keeping alert for the unexpected rarity. The best shorebird periods are the month of May (particularly the middle two weeks) and from the last week of June through early August; the majority of rarities were found during July. Typical migrants include Black-bellied Plover (rare in spring), American Golden-Plover (spring), Semipalmated (fall), Western, and Pectoral Sandpipers, Greater Yellowlegs, Whimbrel, Ruddy (spring) and Black (fall) Turnstones, Surfbird, and Sanderling. Arriving local breeders include Semipalmated Plover, Lesser Yellowlegs, Spotted Sandpiper, Hudsonian Godwit, Least Sandpiper, and Short-billed Dowitcher. In late summer waterfowl congregate along the shoreline in large numbers, while loons and sea ducks occasionally are seen on the inlet.

The forest bordering the back side of the trail can be very productive for the more common Anchorage Bowl species, including Alder Flycatcher, Black-capped and Boreal Chickadees, Hermit Thrush, Orange-crowned,

Yellow, Myrtle, Wilson's, and the occasional Blackpoll Warbler, as well as Savannah, Sooty Fox, and Lincoln's Sparrows. During fall migration (late August– early September), the Coastal Trail can be particularly good for large flocks of migrant passerines.

KINCAID PARK

At the west end of the Tony Knowles Coastal Trail is Kincaid Park, at 1,517 acres the second-largest of Anchorage's municipal parks. It can be reached on foot from downtown via the Coastal Trail (about nine miles) or by car. From the International Airport Road/Minnesota Drive intersection, drive south on Minnesota to Raspberry Road. Turn right (west) onto Raspberry, following it as it becomes Kincaid Road. This road ends in about five miles at a large chalet, the hub of an extensive cross-country ski/foot trail system. Trail maps are available at the chalet. The park is good throughout the year for boreal species, including Northern Goshawk, Spruce Grouse, Northern Saw-whet Owl, Three-toed Woodpecker, Boreal Chickadee, White-winged Crossbill, and Common Redpoll. In summer, add Pacific Loon (nesting on Little Campbell Lake on the east side of the park), Western Wood-Pewee, Alder Flycatcher, and Varied Thrush; in winter, add Bohemian Waxwing and Pine Grosbeak. Here you have a very profitable way to spend a few hours, either walking or cross-country skiing.

EARTHQUAKE AND ELDERBERRY PARKS

Starting from the northern terminus of the 11-mile-long Tony Knowles Coastal Trail and walking south (some locations are also accessible by car as described below), there is especially good shorebirding at Elderberry Park, at the mouth of Chester Creek (that drains Westchester Lagoon), at Fish Creek (south of the lagoon), on the shore below Earthquake Park, and at the marshes southwest of Point Woronzof.

To reach Elderberry Park from Westchester Lagoon, return to I Street, turn left, and drive north to 5th Avenue. Turn left (west), staying in the right lane (the other lanes force you to turn left again) down the hill. Toward the bottom of the hill, after the light at L Street, park in the small lot on the right and walk a short distance to the park.

You can get to the mouth of Fish Creek most easily by taking the path west along Westchester Lagoon, then south across a boardwalk over the marsh and through the tunnel under the railroad tracks to the Coastal Trail.

To go to 134-acre Earthquake Park from Minnesota and International Airport Road, take Minnesota north to Northern Lights Boulevard. Turn left (west) onto Northern Lights and follow it out to the last houses on the right, until the airport is visible on the left, where there is a small parking lot and a sign for the park on the right. The park commemorates the 1964 Good Friday earthquake that devastated much of downtown Anchorage. From the parking lot walk west a short distance on the bike trail, passing under the red steel arches to the area overlooking the inlet. Scan for shorebirds and Sandhill Cranes.

To get to Point Woronzof, you can either walk on the Coastal Trail west from Earthquake Park (one mile) or continue driving west on Northern Lights. The parking lot is on the right at the bottom of a hill.

SHIP CREEK

Ship Creek is located near the east end of the Coastal Trail, although you cannot get to the most productive viewing spots for shorebirds, gulls, and the occasional sea duck by following the trail. Instead, from Westchester Lagoon, backtrack to northbound I Street, or from the intersection of Minnesota Drive and International Airport Road, go north on Minnesota until the northbound lanes become I Street. Follow I Street to its end in another mile or so at 3rd Avenue. Turn right (east) one block to the traffic light and turn left (north) onto H Street (may be signed Christiensen Avenue). This street will wind around to the east and become 1st Avenue. At the stop sign, turn left (north) onto North C Street, and cross a low bridge to a stop sign at Whitney Road. (See map on page 26 for the route.)

The route is slightly different if you drive to Ship Creek from east or south of town. In this case, make your way to northbound A Street, which diverges from two-way C Street just north of Tudor Road (see map). Continue to the stop light at 3rd Avenue and A Street; turn left (west) onto 3rd Avenue, and continue west to a traffic light at E Street. Turn right (north) onto E Street, staying in the right lane as it bends right to cross 2nd Street, then left to 1st Street. You are now down the hill and on the flat area below the bridge buttress, traveling north. For 0.1 mile the street is called North C Street; the name changes to Ocean Dock Road at the intersection with Whitney Road, at the stop sign described in the last paragraph. Whitney Road leads east, and you will return to this intersection later.

For the moment continue north on Ocean Dock Road toward the port area. Take the first left possible, onto an unsigned dirt road that immediately crosses some railroad tracks. The mudflats and sedge flats along this dirt road are excellent for shorebirds, particularly on very high tides, when the birds are forced up toward the road. In addition to the usual shorebirds—Semipalmated Plover, Hudsonian Godwit, Ruddy and Black Turnstones, Surfbird, and Semipalmated, Western, and Least Sandpipers—both Baird's and Stilt Sandpipers have been seen here. By taking the dirt road all the way to the public boat launch, more mudflats will come into view on the south side of the parking lot. These are the same ones that are visible from the Coastal Trail, but this vantage point offers much better viewing when the tide is low—or when it is very high and the birds begin to come up onto the parking lot. In late fall, when there's little open water around, lingering gulls will congregate at the mouth of Ship Creek. This is often the best time to find Thayer's and Glaucous Gulls, in addition to the more typical Mew and Herring Gulls. Do not walk out on the mud!

After birding the mouth of the creek, head back to Ocean Dock Road, turn right, and at the stop sign turn left (east) onto Whitney Road. In a short distance you can pull off to the right and scan Ship Creek in both directions. During winter, ducks often congregate here, and American Dipper might be found year round. Continue driving east on Whitney Road, turning left (northeast) onto Post Road at a stop sign. After a mile, a concrete-lined, artificial pond on the right signed *Salmon Viewing Area* indicates that you are in the right place, so pull into the parking lot. (The gate into Elmendorf Air Force Base on Post Road is about 100 yards to the north.) This lake, and an adjacent smaller pond, are part of the **Elmendorf Fish Hatchery**. In winter, many ducks congregate here, including some semi-hardy birds such as Green-winged Teal, Greater Scaup, Bufflehead, and Common Merganser. Below the small dam here on Ship Creek is another good year-round place to look for American Dipper. Sometimes you can spot a dipper's nest on the fish weir. By turning back west on Post Road and then left (south) onto Reeve Boulevard (the first intersection), you can view the other hatchery pond.

ARCTIC VALLEY

From the intersection of Minnesota Drive and International Airport Road, drive north on Minnesota to 6th Avenue and turn right (east). This will become the Glenn Highway (Alaska Route 1). Take the highway east out of town to the first exit for Arctic Valley, one mile past Muldoon Road.

Anywhere along Arctic Valley Road past the golf course is excellent for most breeding landbirds in Anchorage, especially boreal species, including Spruce Grouse, Three-toed Woodpecker, Olive-sided Flycatcher, Townsend's Warbler, White-winged Crossbill, and, as the elevation increases, Golden-crowned Sparrow. From late February through early April, Arctic Valley Road might be the easiest place in the Anchorage Bowl to *hear* Boreal and Northern Saw-whet Owls. At the very top of the road is a small downhill ski area. Most of the interest up top for birders is during the summer, but after the snows accumulate, large flocks of all three species of ptarmigan often show up in the parking lots. Along the ridge tops in summer, nesting species are Golden Eagle, Willow and Rock Ptarmigan, Say's Phoebe, Horned Lark, American Pipit, and occasionally Townsend's Solitaire.

White-tailed Ptarmigan also nest around the higher peaks. During migration, this area can be good for watching raptors and passerines, including the occasional Northern Wheatear.

From Arctic Valley there are two choices: either continue northeast on the Glenn Highway toward Eagle River and Palmer (see the next chapters) and eventually the interior of the state, or head back into Anchorage.

HILLSIDE PARK

If you are coming into Anchorage on the Glenn Highway, follow the Seward Highway south at its intersection with 6th Avenue; here it is called Gambell. Or, if you are coming from Minnesota Drive and International Airport Road, take Minnesota north and exit east onto Tudor Road. Continue on Tudor to the New Seward Highway. Turn right and drive south to the one-lane Dimond Boulevard exit that immediately becomes four lanes. Move to either of the two left lanes in order to continue east on Dimond toward the mountains. Dimond will eventually turn into Abbott Road, taking you by Service High School. Past the high school go another mile until you see the parking lot for Hillside Park on the north. Almost any songbird that breeds in boreal forest habitat in the Anchorage area can be found at Hillside Park—from Spruce Grouse to Three-toed Woodpecker to Townsend's Warbler to White-winged Crossbill. Bohemian Waxwings have nested in some of the more boggy areas. Black-backed Woodpeckers have nested here a few times in recent years, most recently at a spot on the Lighted Loop Ski Trail called Coaches' Cut-Off (marked on the trail-system map). Hillside is good not only during the breeding season, but also throughout the winter, when finches and woodpeckers are often easier to find. The two most productive trails are Lighted Loop and Spencer Loop; neither is difficult walking and both can be followed for as long as one desires by taking some of the many spur trails in the park. By the time you visit, part of the Spencer Loop trail may have been usurped as an addition to the downhill ski area. A new chalet with public restrooms has already been built at the downhill ski site. Hillside Park's many map-signs will help to keep you oriented.

Hillside Park is part of a very large greenspace, the Campbell Tract. This city-owned corridor extends from Chugach State Park to Cook Inlet, more or less following the path of Campbell Creek. The whole corridor can be walked, but that would make for one very long day. On the east side of the parking area along Abbott Road a road leads into the downhill ski area where parking is also available. Trails from here connect back to the Hillside cross-country ski trails as well as running parallel to the downhill ski slope toward the South Fork of Campbell Creek, another good area for birding.

GLEN ALPS AND PROSPECT HEIGHTS

Chugach State Park is one of the largest state parks in the United States; the majority of it covers excellent alpine habitat. There are two easy entrances to the park, Glen Alps and Prospect Heights (parking fee $5 in 2001). To get to both from Hillside Park, continue east on Abbott Road, which soon veers south to become Hillside Drive. Drive south one mile to where Hillside turns right (west) to become O'Malley Road. After a short distance, turn left (south) back onto southbound Hillside Drive. Continue another mile until you can turn left (east) onto Upper Huffman Road.

If you are coming from the intersection of Minnesota Drive and International Airport Road, go north on Minnesota and exit right (east) onto Tudor Road. Continue on Tudor to the New Seward Highway, turn right, and drive south to Huffman Road. Exit right, cross over the highway heading east, and continue on Huffman Road and then onto Upper Huffman Road. At the fork of Sultana Drive and Toilsome Hill Drive a large road sign directs you to Prospect Heights or Glen Alps, so you must make a decision which to visit. If you decide on Prospect Heights, take the left fork onto Sultana Drive (there should be signs here for the park). If, instead, you decide on Glen Alps, go right at the fork onto Toilsome Hill Drive.

Both entrances offer excellent opportunities to reach alpine tundra, but from Prospect Heights a fairly strenuous hike is first required. If you wish to do this, the best trails are the ones leading to Wolverine Peak (10.5 miles round-trip). On the way up to the alpine you will pass through superb boreal forest that holds most breeding songbird species that occur in the Anchorage area. In the alpine tundra you will find many of the same species that are present at Arctic Valley, although Willow Ptarmigan is probably easier here; neither White-tailed nor Rock Ptarmigan should be expected routinely on the trail. Surfbirds have nested on Wolverine Peak and Townsend's Solitaires were seen there during the past few years.

The drive to Glen Alps is very steep and in winter should be undertaken only by vehicles with four-wheel drive or tire chains. Glen Alps provides easier access to tundra, but to reach the best areas, including places where Northern Wheatears have nested, a fairly strenuous hike is required. The best trail for alpine species from Glen Alps is Williwaw Lakes Trail, while the trail to Flattop is by far the most popular with tourists (on sunny summer days this trail can be very crowded). Although you are not that far from Anchorage, backcountry procedures must be remembered in both areas—bears and Moose are present, it is often cold and windy, and the weather can change with alarming rapidity. See Cautions in the *Introduction*, page 17.

POTTER MARSH

Aside from the Coastal Trail, Potter Marsh is probably the most productive birding site in the Anchorage Bowl. The locals are fond of driving down here to search for the first signs of spring, typified by the arrival of the many migrant waterfowl and a handful of nesting Arctic Terns. Over the years Potter Marsh has become so popular a destination that a boardwalk was built to encourage viewers not to slow down or park along the shoulder of the highway. Roadside parking and stopping regulations are now strictly enforced. It is well worth your while to visit the marsh.

If you are coming from either Glen Alps or Prospect Heights, return to Hillside Drive and head south. Follow the road for a couple miles as it turns west toward the coast, becoming Rabbit Creek Road. At the base of the mountains, turn left (southeast) onto the Old Seward Highway.

If you are coming from the intersection of Minnesota Drive and International Airport Road, go north on Minnesota and exit right (east) onto Tudor Road. Take Tudor to the New Seward Highway, turn right (south), drive about six miles, and exit to the right, following the signs to Rabbit Creek Road and Old Seward Highway. At the stop sign turn left (east) onto Rabbit Creek Road, go over the New Seward Highway, and continue for 0.6 mile. Turn right (south) onto the Old Seward Highway. This road takes you to the back side of Potter Marsh, where you can pull off at several places along the road to listen for songbirds—this stretch is particularly good for Yellow Warbler and Northern Waterthrush, as well as for Lincoln's and Golden-crowned Sparrows. Where the marsh is visible, look for Red-winged and Rusty Blackbirds, especially at the south end of the marsh. After about two miles, the Old Seward Highway intersects the New Seward Highway.

Turn right (toward Anchorage) on the highway to drive by the front side of the marsh. There are two pullouts along the road that must be used, as it is not safe (nor legal) to simply stop on the side of the road. From these pullouts many of the regular waterbirds such as Red-necked Grebe, Mew Gull, and Arctic Tern can be seen, in addition to breeding Pacific Loons, Canvasbacks, Red-necked Phalaropes, and Red-winged Blackbirds. During migration this is a good spot to get relatively close views of both Tundra and Trumpeter Swans as well as migrant raptors, including the occasional Short-eared Owl. You may also spot a few locally rare species, such as Pied-billed Grebe, Yellow Wagtail (accidental), and Common Yellowthroat. Bald Eagles nest in the trees at the north end of the marsh and in the trees to the east (near the old Rabbit Creek Inn). Pacific Loons nest at the south end of the marsh. On the west side of the highway, look in the ponds between the highway and the railroad grade for nesting Horned Grebes.

If you continue north along the highway, watch for the sign indicating the turn to reach the boardwalk you can see on your right. Turn right onto a short drive that leads to a parking lot and access to the boardwalk. From the boardwalk it is often easier to see both yellowlegs, Short-billed Dowitcher, Wilson's Snipe, and Red-necked Phalarope. Many birders stop at Potter Marsh as they head south on the Seward Highway to Girdwood, Portage, and the Kenai Peninsula (see Kenai Peninsula, page 267).

LOGISTICS

The area code for all telephone numbers is 907 unless otherwise indicated. Tourist and travel services (accommodations, restaurants, attractions, etc.) not listed below can be found in the latest edition of The Milepost. *Statewide travel and birding information services are listed under Logistics in the* Introduction, *page 15.*

For complete tourist information, contact the Log Cabin Visitor Information Center operated by the Anchorage Convention and Visitors Bureau. You can pick up maps and other tourist information at their three booths located at the airport or visit their log cabin at 524 West 4th Avenue (corner of F Street), Anchorage 99501; phone 276-4118; fax 278-5559; email *info@anchorage.net*; recorded phone message 276-3200; web site *http://www.anchorage.net*. It is imperative that you make reservations early for your stay in Anchorage or for your rental vehicle, as the town is inundated with tourists during summer.

If you plan to take the Alaska Railroad to Denali National Park or Fairbanks, be sure to make reservations in advance at 800-478-2442.

Chugach State Park headquarters is located at the Potter Section House on the Seward Highway just south of Potter Marsh. For information on the park call 345-5014, e-mail *chugstpk@alaska.net*, or visit their web site *http://www.dnr.state.ak.us/parks/units/chugach/*.

There is only one public campground in Anchorage (Centennial Camper Park, 8300 Glenn Highway; 343-6986), but you have a choice of several private RV parks. Again, make advance reservations. You can camp at Bird Creek at Milepost 101 on the Seward Highway and along the Portage Valley on the Portage Highway that leaves the Seward Highway at Milepost 78.9.

The best Anchorage-area map we've found is *Anchorage & Vicinity, Southcentral Alaska*, published by Todd Communications of Anchorage; 274-8633; *sales@toddcom.com*. Some of the other Road and Recreation maps published by Todd cover the Kenai Peninsula, Kachemak Bay, Matanuska Valley, and Parks Highway.

Anchorage Audubon Society can be reached at PO Box 101161, Anchorage 99510; *www.anchorageaudubon.org*. For recent bird sightings, call 338-2473.

Dale Fox, Bird Watching Tours of Anchorage, 248-7282; fax 248-7285; *www.anchoragebirding.com*.

ACKNOWLEDGEMENTS: Delesta Fox field-checked the Anchorage route and provided many clarifications and resources. Updates and birding notes from Jon Dunn are greatly appreciated.

Glenn Highway:

Eagle River to Palmer

Nathan Senner

Once you have fully pursued the birding opportunities in Anchorage, or are on your way north to other localities, the Eagle River and Matanuska-Susitna Valley areas provide a number of excellent places to bird.

Eagle River. To start your trek, turn onto the Glenn Highway (Alaska Route 1) heading east out of town (if you are downtown, the access is from eastbound 6th Avenue). About 15 miles out of Anchorage, you will see the first signs for Eagle River. Take the first exit, marked *Eagle River* and *Hiland Road*. Turn right at the stop sign, and right again at the traffic light onto Hiland Road. Take this road almost to its end, about 8 miles. Along the way look for signs directing you to Chugach State Park. Turn right on South Creek Road, turn right again on West River Drive, and cross the South Fork of Eagle River in order to reach the parking lot for Eagle Lakes Trail. The birding here is not spectacular, but you'll have a gorgeous hike and an introduction to the tundra/taiga ecotone that becomes more prevalent as you continue to travel farther north. Along with the usual boreal species, look for possible nesting Northern Shrike, Townsend's Solitaire, Pine Grosbeak, and White-winged Crossbill. Once you are out of the trees, you might spot Northern Harrier and Willow Ptarmigan, and maybe even a Short-eared Owl.

To continue on to other Eagle River sites, take Hiland Drive back to its intersection with Eagle River Loop road (the light at which you turned after leaving the Glenn Highway). Turn right onto Eagle River Loop and head into the town of Eagle River. At the second traffic light, Eagle River Road, turn right, following this road 11 miles to its end at the parking lot for **Eagle River Nature Center** (parking fee $5), the hub of miles of trails that lead into Chugach State Park, offering some of the best boreal forest birding in the region. In early spring, listen for Great Horned, Northern Hawk, Boreal, and Northern Saw-whet Owls. In summer, look for breeding American Kestrel (uncommon in Alaska), American Dipper, and Pine Grosbeak. Year round, you have a good chance for Downy, Hairy, Three-toed, and Black-backed Woodpeckers. In winter, the nature center's extensive array of feeders attracts many of the forest birds in good numbers, especially Pine Grosbeaks

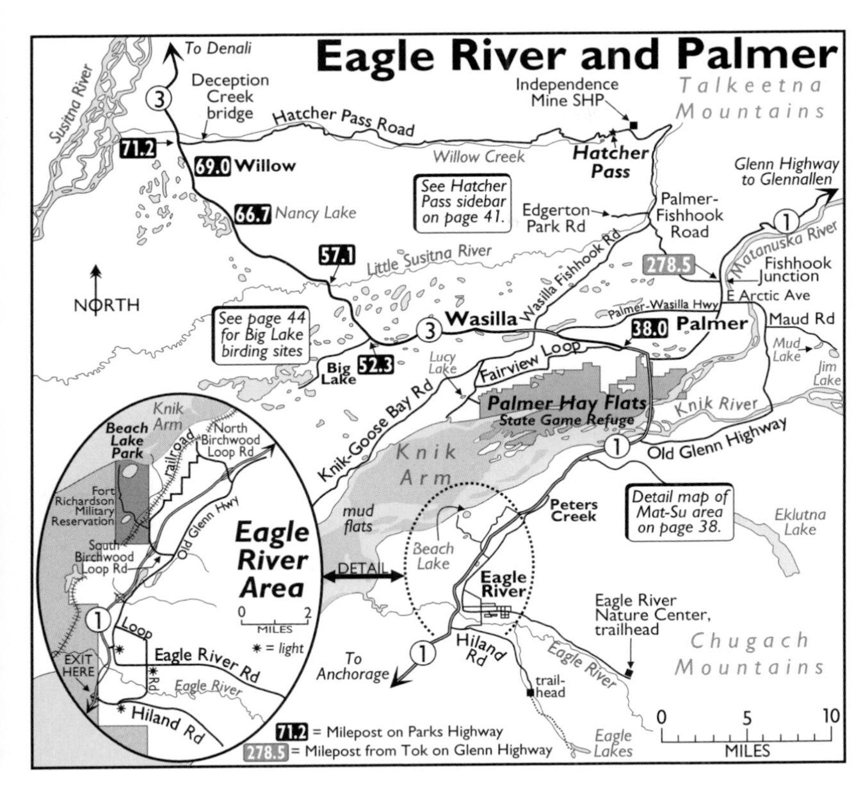

and Common and the occasional Hoary Redpoll. Bohemian Waxwings come to feed on the berries of the Mountain Ash trees.

When you leave the nature center, take Eagle River Road back into town. Go past the light where you turned to go to the nature center and drive into downtown Eagle River. When Eagle River Road ends at another light, turn left to go back to the Glenn Highway.

Continue north on the Glenn and take the next exit, South Birchwood Loop Road, turning left at the stop sign. Continue down this road and turn left at a sign for **Beach Lake Park**; the park is at the end of the road. As you bird the trails through more boreal forest, species of interest include nesting Western Wood-Pewee and Blackpoll Warbler, as well as very reclusive nesting Bohemian Waxwing and, on the lake, nesting Common Loon.

Return to the Glenn Highway and continue northeast for another 20 miles to the intersection of the Glenn and Parks Highways. Here you will need to decide whether you want to head toward Denali National Park and Fairbanks (left on the Parks Highway, Alaska Route 3, see page 42) or toward Glennallen and Valdez (continue straight on the Glenn toward Palmer). The Parks

Highway, including the Parks/Glenn Highway interchange here, is undergoing renovation and expansion; consequently, some aspects of the directions that follow might change. The Parks is now a four-lane, limited-access highway (with frontage roads) from the Parks/Glenn interchange north from this intersection. In summer 2002, construction to expand the Parks is scheduled to widen it to four lanes for another 4.25 miles, and by late 2003 the work should have reached the existing four-lane stretch along Wasilla Lake and into what is locally referred to as "Downtown Wasilla." There are plans to transform the Parks/Glenn intersection into a cloverleaf interchange, with work likely to begin in 2003. The current traffic light will be eliminated at that time, and you will then have to exit to the right to loop over the Glenn Highway to continue north on the Parks Highway.

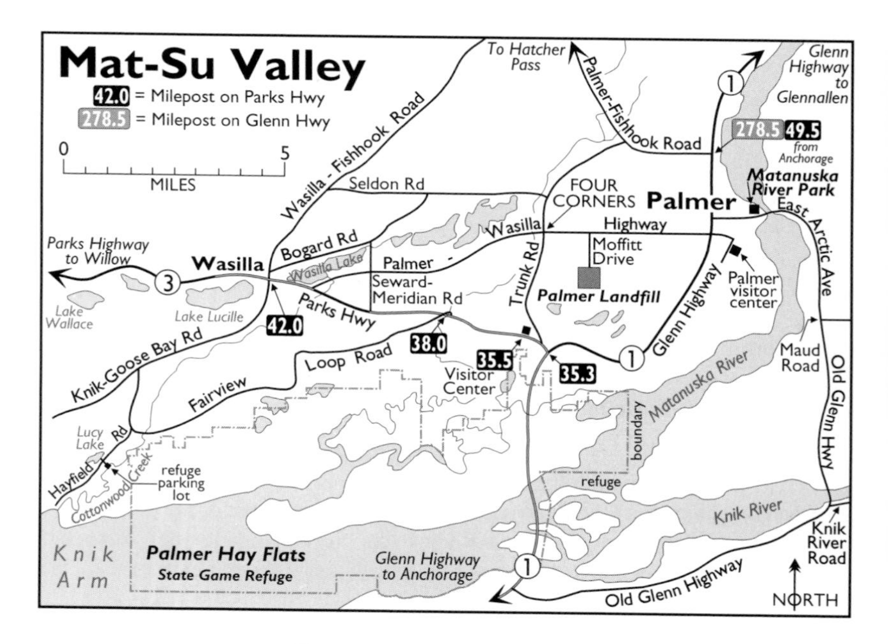

PALMER AREA

If you have a few free hours, you can explore three quite different, productive birding areas in Palmer, two reached by heading north on the Parks Highway, and the other found by traveling east on the Glenn Highway.

Palmer Hay Flats State Game Refuge. At the junction of the Parks and the Glenn Highways, follow the Parks Highway northwest, turning left (south) after about two miles onto Fairview Loop. This intersection is under construction and, when completed, you will exit the Parks Highway to the right, loop over the highway, and come down onto Fairview Loop. Follow that road for 9.6 miles to a T-intersection with Hayfield Road. Turn left here and continue for 1.3 miles, where you will see Lucy Lake Road on the right and an unnamed road on the left. Turn left onto the unnamed road. You also may see a sign, partly obscured by vegetation, designating the unmarked road as the public access for Palmer Hay Flats State Game Refuge. Follow the road as it winds down a hill and ends at a parking lot in about 0.4 mile. (*Warning:* in spring and after heavy rains this road can be very muddy and four-wheel drive may be necessary.) Mid-to-late April is the best time for birding here, but you will need knee-high boots or hip-waders then because of snowmelt and a high water-table at this time of year. Cross the footbridge to the left of the parking lot and meander to the right following a newly constructed path for four-wheelers. You should hear Sandhill Cranes in the distance. The area dries up in summer, but the tall grass provides lots of hiding places for some birds. A Sora, only the second record for Upper Cook Inlet, was heard here in summer 2001.

Palmer Hay Flats is probably the most productive waterfowl migration stopover and nesting area accessible in the greater Anchorage area. In spring (April–early May) large congregations of Greater White-fronted, Snow, and Canada Geese stop here, along with Sandhill Cranes and all the usual waterfowl that move through the area. Fall is dominated by ducks, though cranes also pass through in good numbers (*Caution*: the area is popular with duck hunters in fall.). The hay flats are good for American Golden-Plover and Pectoral Sandpiper in migration, and for Greater and Lesser Yellowlegs, Wilson's Snipe, and Red-necked Phalarope during breeding season. Be alert for a variety of migrating raptors, including Northern Harrier, Rough-legged Hawk, Peregrine Falcon, and Short-eared Owl.

Palmer Landfill. One popular place to bird in the Palmer area is the Palmer Landfill that often attracts strays such as Slaty-backed Gull, Common Grackle, and European Starling, in addition to the more common Mew, Glaucous-winged, Glaucous, and Herring Gulls and Black-billed Magpie. It is located just off the Palmer-Wasilla Highway, 1.1 miles east of Four Corners. Turn south from the Palmer-Wasilla Highway onto Moffitt Drive and follow this road for about one-half mile until you enter the landfill. To avoid paying the dump fee, tell the attendant that you are birding.

Palmer City. Coming from Anchorage, if you stay on the Glenn Highway rather than taking the Parks Highway, you will enter the town of Palmer. Turn right onto East Arctic Avenue and drive east out of town. The road becomes the Old Glenn Highway after several miles. In spring, any open field will hold geese, ducks, and cranes, so be on the lookout. Turn left into Matanuska River State Park just before the bridge to explore the woodland for warblers and other boreal nesters, especially Northern Waterthrush and Golden-crowned Sparrow. Continue driving east across the river and for another two miles and turn left onto Maud Road. After about two miles Maud Road becomes gravel and full of potholes; at 4.5 miles from the highway pull into a large parking area on the right. Mud Lake is visible from here and just a short walk down the hill. If you drive another 1.5 miles you come to the end of the road. Park here and walk down a short, rough road leading off to the right to Jim Lake. Both lakes are good for waterfowl in migration, including Trumpeter and Tundra Swans and Common and Barrow's Goldeneyes. Common Loons nest on Jim Lake, while Red-necked Grebes nest on both. Walk the woodland trail at Jim Lake to look for Northern Goshawk, American Kestrel, and Golden Eagle (along with Dall's Sheep) on the cliffs above the lake. Look for Calypso Orchids along the road, and be especially cautious for the many bears and Moose in this area.

Return to the Old Glenn, turning right toward Palmer. In spring, any open field will hold waterfowl and cranes, so always be alert.

You may return part way to Anchorage on the Old Glenn Highway. From Palmer, take East Arctic Avenue east across the Matanuska River and follow it as it bends south, passes Maud Road, becomes the Old Glenn Highway, and follows Bodenburg Creek to the Knik River. The Matanuska and Knik Rivers supply most of the glacial silt carried into Knik Arm of Cook Inlet. The Old Glenn turns west at its intersection with Knik River Road; the new Glenn Highway is about 10 miles farther.

LOGISTICS

The area code for all telephone numbers is 907 unless otherwise indicated. Tourist and travel services (accommodations, restaurants, attractions, etc.) not listed below can be found in the latest edition of The Milepost. *Statewide travel and birding information services are listed under Logistics in the* Introduction, *page 15.*

You can find accommodations, restaurants, and most other services in Eagle River. If Anchorage is too crowded for you, consider staying in Eagle River, Palmer, or Wasilla.

North Anchorage Visitor Information Center, Parkgate Building, 11723 Old Glenn Highway, Eagle River. Eagle River Nature Center, 694-2108; *www.ernc.org.*

There are public campgrounds at Eagle River and Eklutna, both off the Glenn Highway, the first at Milepost 10 (from Anchorage) and the second at Milepost 26.

Palmer is a small town with all the amenities necessary for a comfortable stay. Palmer and Wasilla are bedroom communities for Anchorage. However, you would be missing a unique slice of Alaskan history if you just whizzed on by without realizing how Palmer came to be the farming hub for Alaska—such a different orientation than the fishing-, logging-, mining-, and petroleum-driven origins so prevalent for non-Native settlements in the rest of the state. If you visit during the ten days prior to Labor Day, don't miss the annual Alaska State Fair.

ACKNOWLEDGEMENTS: Additional birding and other information for Palmer was provided by Bob Winckler for the Mat-Su Birders and Cecily Fritz. Nancy Faville reviewed the Hatcher Pass text and added some birding information.

very Blue Butterfly

HATCHER PASS

George West

The Hatcher Pass road (Palmer-Fishhook Road) leads into the alpine north of Palmer and Wasilla, then turns west to intersect the Parks Highway north of Willow. (See map on page 37.) The loop makes a pleasant day-trip from Anchorage, or an interesting deviation from your route whether you're heading north on the Parks toward Denali and Fairbanks or east on the Glenn toward Glennallen and beyond. The road is rarely closed by snow during the winter months; when it's open, the Pass is a popular cross-country skiing destination, and in summer you'll find parasailers.

Palmer-Fishhook Road leaves the Glenn Highway at Milepost 278.5 (49.5 miles from Anchorage). From the George Parks Highway (page 42), you can reach the western entrance to the Hatcher Pass road at Milepost 71.2.

Coming from the Glenn Highway, part of the Hatcher Pass road is paved and part is gravel, with paving activity an annual feature. Harlequin Ducks are common in the swift-moving Little Susitna River that parallels the lower section of the road. Harlequins can also be found on many of the ponds at higher elevations. Check for American Dipper in any quick-moving water, including around waterfalls. Seven miles up the road, turn left onto Edgerton Park Road and park along the bridge just beyond the turn. Dippers are common in the Little Susitna here as well, so if you don't see them right away, check underneath the bridge where they nest.

Independence Mine State Historical Park at Milepost 17 is worth a stop. You might find ptarmigan, Northern Wheatear, Wilson's Warbler, and other alpine species here. At Hatcher Pass summit, elevation 3,886 feet, you are 19.2 miles from the Glenn Highway and 31.8 miles from the Parks Highway. You can return the way you came or travel westward following Willow Creek to the Parks Highway. If you continue in this direction, look for an Osprey nest on top of a large power pole where the power-transmission lines cross the road 1.7 miles from the Parks Highway junction. Just west of here Deception Creek can be good for Bufflehead, mergansers, and local forest birds. There are primitive trails on both sides of the creek and on both sides of the road.

Parks Highway:

Glenn Highway Junction to Denali National Park

Rick Ernst and George West

The George Parks Highway (Alaska Route 3) leaves the Glenn Highway (Alaska Route 1) 35 miles northeast of Anchorage (Glenn Highway Milepost 35.3) and leads north to Fairbanks (358 miles from Anchorage). The road was named for George Parks, Alaska Territorial Governor from 1925–1933. A road was built many years ago from Fairbanks south to Denali (then McKinley) National Park, but it did not continue south to Anchorage—one either took the train from the park to Anchorage or drove across the Denali Highway to Paxson, down the Richardson to Glennallen, and into Anchorage on the Glenn—a very long drive, indeed. Another road led north from Anchorage to Talkeetna, but the gap between the two highways was not filled until 1971, when a bridge was completed over Hurricane Gulch near Milepost 174. The Anchorage- Fairbanks Highway was renamed the George Parks Highway in 1975. The route provides a good overview of interior boreal forest, riparian cottonwood, and alpine tundra. It is (in)famous for its Moose population, so be especially careful driving in the dim light of subarctic nights. You can often get better views of the summit of Denali (Mount McKinley) from stops along the Parks Highway than you can from within the National Park. Mileposts in the following text are given, as signed, from Anchorage (Milepost 0.0).

Parks Highway from Palmer to Willow

Only 0.1 mile up the hill from the junction of the Glenn and Parks Highways, Trunk Road exits right toward the Palmer-Wasilla Highway and access to the Palmer Landfill (see previous chapter and map on page 38). You might spot some birds in the farm fields along Trunk Road, but in general, it is better to continue north. You are in the Matanuska-Susitna Borough, an area locally known as Mat-Su. At Milepost 35.5, stop at the Mat-Su Visitor Center for information on accommodations and shopping in Wasilla, the next town north. If the visitor center is closed, check your copy of *The Milepost*. The turnoff to Palmer Hay Flats State Game Refuge on Fairview Loop Road is at Milepost 38 (see page 38).

Wasilla (Milepost 42) is a full-service community that serves in part as a bedroom community for Anchorage. There are several lakes along the highway (and on side roads) where you might find grebes, ducks, and gulls, but most are crowded with houses and public recreation activities. If you don't need to shop, get gas, or stay overnight, it is best to continue north.

Big Lake Road exits left (west) at Milepost 52.3 (see Big Lake sidebar on next page). The bridge over the Little Susitna River is at Milepost 57.1. This small river hosts runs of King and Silver Salmon that can be caught with salmon eggs, lures, or flies (make sure you have a license and salmon stamp or permit to comply with current regulations). Nancy Lake (Milepost 66.7) is a good place to camp and also to explore the lake in a small boat for loons, grebes, ducks, and shorebirds (species similar to those at Big Lake). The small community of Willow is just beyond at Milepost 69.

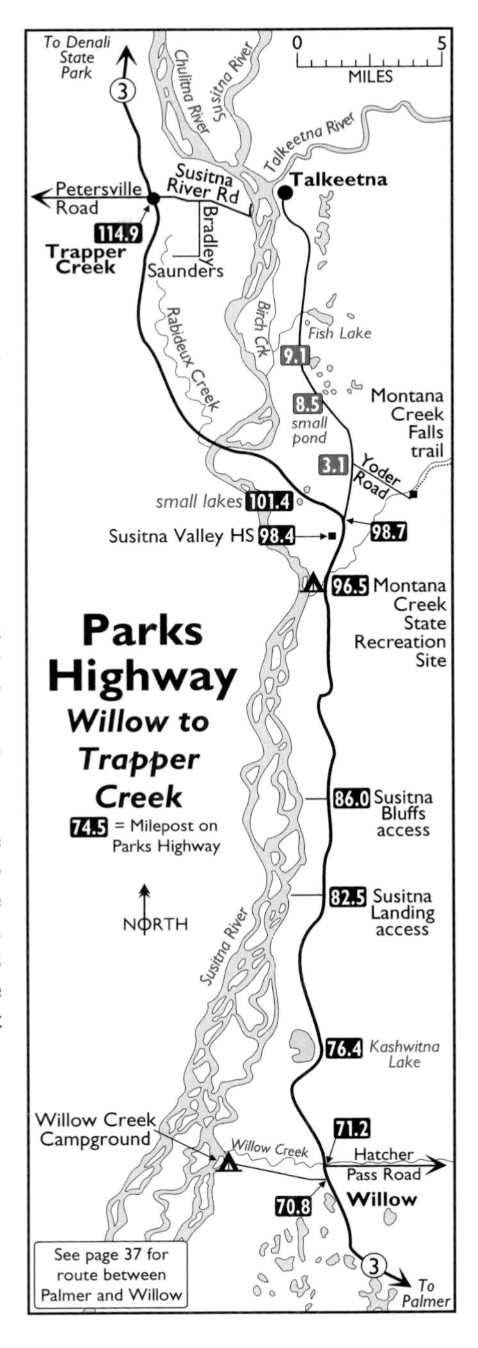

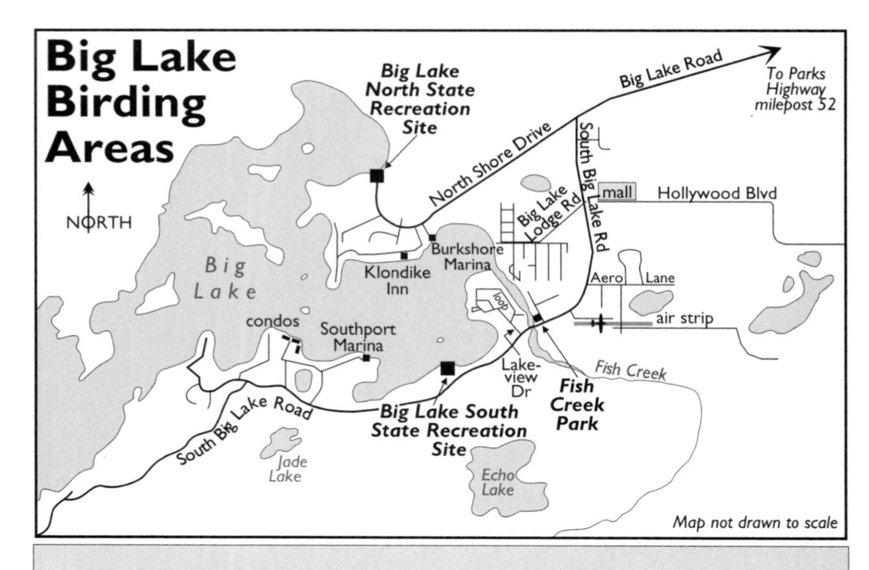

BIRDING AT BIG LAKE

Delesta Fox

Big Lake offers diversified habitat for raptors, shorebirds, and passerines. During summer weekends you are likely to find the town, parks, and lake somewhat crowded, so a weekday visit might produce more of the following species, in season. Look for Red-throated, Pacific, and Common Loons, Horned and Red-necked Grebes (spring and fall), Mallard, Surf and White-winged Scoters, Common and Barrow's Goldeneyes, Common and Red-breasted Mergansers, Bald Eagle, Northern Goshawk, Spruce Grouse, Sandhill Crane, Greater and Lesser Yellowlegs, Spotted Sandpiper, Bonaparte's, Mew, and Glaucous-winged Gulls, Arctic Tern, Great Horned Owl, Northern Hawk Owl, Great Gray Owl, Belted Kingfisher, Downy and Hairy Woodpeckers, Alder Flycatcher, Northern Shrike, Gray Jay, Black-billed Magpie, Common Raven, Tree and Violet-green Swallows, Black-capped and Boreal Chickadees, Red-breasted Nuthatch, Brown Creeper, American Dipper, Golden-crowned and Ruby-crowned Kinglets, Swainson's, Hermit, and Varied Thrushes, Orange-crowned and Myrtle Warblers, Northern Waterthrush, Wilson's Warbler, American Tree, Savannah, Fox, Song, Gambel's White-crowned, and Golden-crowned Sparrows, Slate-colored Junco, and Pine Grosbeak.

At Milepost 52 of the Parks Highway, take the well-marked turnoff to Big Lake. Go 3.6 miles on Big Lake Road to a fork just past the Tesoro gas station—North Shore Drive is straight ahead while South Big Lake Road curves off to the left.

North Shore Drive is approximately two miles long and offers three places to look for birds: Burkshore Marina has a large parking lot from which you can scope the southeast end of the lake. Scope for a pair of Common Loons from the left, in front of the Big Lake Lodge, to across the lake to the right near the condominiums, where you also may see several Pacific Loons. Red-necked Grebe, Mallard, and Common Merganser are found also in this section of the lake.

Continue on North Shore Drive a short way, watching for the Klondike Inn sign on the left. Drive to the end of this road to scope the area near the docks and boat-launch site for Common Loon, Red-necked Grebe, and Surf Scoter. Continue to the end of North Shore Drive to the Big Lake North State Recreation Site; camping and picnicking sites are available here. Scope the lake for the Common Loons. Red-necked Grebes nest to the left in the reeds, Bonaparte's Gulls, and Arctic Terns nest on the far shore between Petrovich Island (the island slightly to the left of the launch site) and the house (large, modified A-frame) on the far shore straight ahead. Walk through the campsites to listen for Black-capped and Boreal Chickadees, Ruby-crowned Kinglet, warblers, sparrows, and Slate-colored Junco.

Return to the fork and turn right onto South Big Lake Road. In 0.1 mile, you will come to a crossroad with the Big Lake Mall on the left. Turn right here onto Big Lake Lodge Road and drive to the shore to scope for the species mentioned above.

Return to South Big Lake Road, turn right, and drive past the airport and the school to Fish Creek Park on the right, where Bonaparte's Gulls and Arctic Terns often perch on the dam looking for small fish. Red-necked Grebes, Common and Barrow's Goldeneyes, and Common Mergansers can be seen in this creek. Walk across the bridge and turn right at the little red church to walk the loop road, listening for woodpeckers, warblers, Northern Waterthrush, sparrows, and juncos.

Continue for 0.2 mile to the Big Lake South State Recreation Site. Scope the area for the same pair of Common Loons that you looked for from Burkshore and the Big Lake Lodge. Listen for Downy and Hairy Woodpeckers, Black-capped and Boreal Chickadees, warblers, and sparrows.

Continue driving on South Big Lake Road another 0.3 mile to South Port Marina. Scope the lake to the left in front of the condominiums for Pacific and Common Loons and Red-necked Grebes. The Common Loons you've been searching for have been very successful in raising a chick in this area near the marina, their egg usually hatching between 3–6 July.

LOGISTICS

Big Lake Motel and Hanger Lounge—Mile 1.5 South Big Lake Road. Big Lake Mall—Mile 0.1 South Big Lake Road– grocery store, latte bar, restaurant, art gallery, T-shirt shop, etc.

Common Loon

WILLOW TO THE TALKEETNA CUTOFF

In Willow (Milepost 69.7) you can turn left (west) into the Willow Community Center and Library, located on the shore of Willow Lake, where you might find grebes, ducks, and Arctic Terns. You will see assorted passerines in the surrounding forest. The librarian can help you with any questions you may have about the area.

At Milepost 70.8, a left (west) turn and drive of about 3.5 miles will take you to Willow Creek Campground where the creek joins the Susitna River. In spring, the boreal forest is active with migrants passing through and birds claiming territories for the nesting season. Here you can find Ruby-crowned and Golden-crowned Kinglets, American Robin, Varied Thrush, Gambel's White-crowned Sparrow, and Slate-colored Junco, and, if you are lucky, Gray-cheeked, Swainson's, and Hermit Thrushes. Along the Susitna River, Bald Eagles and Herring Gulls can be seen feeding on spawned-out and dead salmon, though in early spring they may be feeding on the "hooligan" migration. These are a small smelt-like fish that migrate upstream in large numbers. Residents (permit required) use a net to dip for these fish to barbecue and enjoy their sweet meat. There are overnight camping and RV facilities at the campground—it's a nice place to spend some time birding.

In February–April 2002, a Great Spotted Woodpecker attended a feeder in the north Willow area—the first sighting of this species on the Alaskan mainland.

The turnoff to the Hatcher Pass road is at Milepost 71.2 (see page 41). The road may be closed at higher elevations due to snow cover until early July.

At Milepost 76.4 pull off at Kashwitna Lake for a great view of the Alaska Range and the "Sleeping Lady," Mount Susitna. Trumpeter Swans can be seen here in the fall, dipping and bobbing near the shore, oblivious to the cars and trucks whizzing by. You are paralleling the Susitna River to the west and can access it at several places: Susitna Landing at Milepost 82.5 and Susitna Bluffs at Milepost 86. You might enjoy a short boat ride on the Susitna to see areas less impacted by humans. If so, check out the riverboat services at those locations. The Susitna River is a large, braided, glacial river with its origins in the Alaska Range that flows into upper Cook Inlet northwest of Anchorage. Do not attempt to boat on this or any other glacial river unless you have experience. See Cautions in the *Introduction*, page 19.

As you head north on the Parks Highway, you will come to Montana Creek at Milepost 96.5. There is a state campground on the west side of the road, and from its parking lot you can walk to Montana Creek and the Susitna River. Watch for American Dippers on Montana Creek and shorebirds on the sandbars where the creek empties into the Susitna River.

As most birders know, birds will leave or become quiet when they hear someone approaching. One reliable way to view birds is to sit quietly in the woods to listen and wait for birds to show themselves. The trails behind Susitna Valley High School at Milepost 98.4 are good places for a pleasant bird walk and a quiet sit. Behind the school two large ball fields adjoin the running/ski-trail system. You may see and/or hear Alder Flycatcher, Ruby-crowned Kinglet, Brown Creeper, Varied Thrush, Gambel's White-crowned Sparrow, Slate-colored Junco, and other passerines on these trails. Some sections of the trail overlook Little Montana Lake, which has pairs of Common Loons, occasionally several majestic Trumpeter Swans, several species of ducks, Common Mergansers, and hovering Arctic Terns. Bonaparte's Gull and Belted Kingfisher are regular visitors to the lakes. If you don't have time to walk the school trails, stop at the pullout on the west side of the Parks Highway at Milepost 99.3 for a view of Montana and Little Montana Lakes.

THE TALKEETNA SPUR ROAD

At Milepost 98.7, just after the high school, turn northeast onto Talkeetna Spur Road. As you head toward Talkeetna there are several birding possibilities. At Mile 3.1 (distance from the turnoff) turn right onto Yoder Road, following this gravel road for three miles and crossing the bridge over Montana Creek. Immediately after crossing, turn to the left, to find the trailhead for the Montana Creek Falls Hiking Trail. You can take a six-hour round-trip hike to a spectacular falls on the Middle Fork of Montana Creek. The trail winds its way through boreal forest (White Spruce, Paper Birch, and alder), staying on the east side of the creek the whole way. On this hike you might encounter Ruby-crowned and Golden-crowned Kinglets, Swainson's and Gray-cheeked Thrushes, Myrtle Warbler, Lincoln's and Gambel's White-crowned Sparrows, and Slate-colored Junco. Keep an eye out for some of the raptors in the area—this is good habitat for the seldom-seen Northern Goshawk. Bald Eagles perch on trees next to the creek looking for lunch or on the gravel bars to eat spawned-out Red Salmon. At the end of the trail enjoy the reward of a 60-foot waterfall crashing into a clear, cold sparkling pool of water. This is the end of the line for the migrating King Salmon that lay their eggs in the creek. Some folks join the milling salmon for a quick dip in water that feels a few degrees away from being solid! Please remember to exercise extreme caution when hiking this trail because of the Brown Bears that come to feed on salmon. See Bear Cautions in the *Introduction*, page 17.

Return to the Spur Road and continue north toward Talkeetna. Ring-necked Ducks have been seen at the small pond to the east at Mile 8.5. At Mile 9.1, Fish Lake empties into Birch Creek, a good place for Lesser Scaup,

Bufflehead, Common and Barrow's Goldeneyes, and other waterbirds such as Common Merganser. Several years ago a Hooded Merganser was spotted in Fish Lake.

From here it's about five miles to Talkeetna. Go through the village and down Main Street to where it ends at the confluence of the Talkeetna and Susitna Rivers. You can walk onto the gravel bar to see Mew and Herring Gulls, and you might spot a Glaucous-winged Gull, as well as the many duck species that congregate here. Other birds that have been sighted in this area include Greater White-fronted Goose, Bald Eagle, Northern Goshawk, and Black-billed Magpie. The village may have several species of swallows, and a probable White Wagtail was seen here once. In 2001, a Black-backed Woodpecker was seen in the middle of town. Mainly, it is a great place to sit and watch the river flow by, with a great view of Denali looming in the distance.

TALKEETNA CUTOFF TO TRAPPER CREEK

Return to the Parks Highway and head north to Milepost 101.4, another set of small lakes on both sides of the road. The east lake—the one with the Beaver lodge—has been the home of a faithful pair of Trumpeter Swans that have nested here every summer for the past several years. If you are lucky they'll be out in plain view, though sometimes they are on the east end of the lake, where you'll need patience and binoculars to see them. Check the pond on the other side of the road, too—Northern Pintail, Green-winged Teal, Bufflehead, Common Goldeneye, and a swooping Northern Harrier have been spotted at this location. Don't forget to watch for the resident families of Beavers and Muskrats.

The next place to stop is on the north side of the Susitna River, just across the bridge. Drive down the rugged gravel road to a campground, a good picnic-lunch stop. Often you will see Bald Eagles, perched in trees, and several species of gulls. In spring the woods are full of nesting passerines. The campground is located below the bluffs where Rabideux Creek enters the Susitna River. There you can see and hear Greater Yellowlegs giving their scolding calls. Ducks come and go in the area, and Common Mergansers have been sighted there regularly. In early spring you can harvest the "fiddlehead" of the Ostrich Fern (*Matteuccia struthiopteris*) along Rabideux Creek where the creek crosses the Parks Highway about a mile north of the Susitna Bridge. (Always blanch the fiddleheads first, then fry them in butter for a real treat. Or steam them after washing to use in homemade potato soup. . .they are tasty!)

From here north toward Trapper Creek (Milepost 115) you pass muskeg vegetation interspersed with low hills and small streams. Keep your eyes open for Northern Harriers and Northern Hawk Owls or Bald Eagles circling as they look for dead salmon in the streams.

Two small ponds on the west side of the highway at Milepost 111.5 may hold some surprises—especially in early spring, when four species of ducks might be here, along with very noisy Wilson's Snipe and perhaps a nesting pair of Rusty Blackbirds. Sit quietly a while and you might see Beaver.

TRAPPER CREEK

If you happen to come to the Trapper Creek area sometime between 20 April–20 May, take a short side-trip to see an impressive congregation of Sandhill Cranes in a farm field. To get to the spot, turn right (east) from the Parks Highway onto Susitna River Road (East Petersville Road) at Milepost 114.8. Go about 1.5 miles, turn right onto Bradley Road, go about 0.5 mile to Saunders Road, and turn right again. About one-half mile down Saunders Road is a large 70-to-80-acre barley field. A group of the Pacific Flyway population of cranes makes a stop here on the way to breeding grounds on the Alaska Peninsula and Bristol Bay. The farmer is glad to have you come to look and asks only that you not go out into the field, but stay on Saunders Road. More than 200 cranes have landed here on occasion. It's a real treat to watch them dance and to hear their haunting unison calls. Since the 1960s when barley was first planted here, an increasing number of cranes have learned to use this spot as one of the refueling stations for their long journey. In a wet year when there are ponds in the field from melted snow, you can get an incredible variety of geese, ducks, and shorebirds stopping by to rest and feed.

If you follow Susitna River Road all the way east to the end (about 2.5 miles), you reach a slough of the Susitna River, a good place to see ducks, Bald Eagles, and shorebirds, depending on the season. A shy pair of American Dippers lives here, too. As you drive back on Susitna River Road watch the fields on both sides of the road. Standing water in spring has attracted Greater and Lesser Yellowlegs, Whimbrel, and other shorebirds. Other possibilities include Northern Hawk Owl, Merlin, American Pipit, and Lapland Longspur.

The junction of the Petersville Road is at Milepost 114.9 (see Petersville Road, page 51).

TRAPPER CREEK TO DENALI NATIONAL PARK

North of Trapper Creek the terrain becomes somewhat more hilly all the way to Denali State Park. (Refer to map on page 52.) This part of your trip holds the same species you have seen on your way up from Willow. At

Milepost 123.4 on the east side of the road a small lake has supported a pair of Pacific Loons over the years; it's worth a stop to check it out.

Denali State Park begins at Milepost 132.2 (see page 56). North of here are many places to stop and view Denali, to eat, to stay a while and enjoy the grandeur, or to charter a trip into the backcountry by horse, airplane, or helicopter. One of the best places to stop is at a large pullout at Milepost 135.2 on the west (left) side of the highway that offers great views of many of the higher peaks in the Alaska Range, including Denali—if the weather cooperates.

Hurricane Gulch Bridge is at Milepost 174, and most travelers stop to peer over the railing, though there is little birding potential here. The bridge is 260 feet over Hurricane Creek. There is a short trail for sightseers. Stop for another great view of the mountains at Milepost 183.2, also on the west side of the highway. At Milepost 196, the highway enters Broad Pass, an area at treeline and borderline alpine tundra. The summit of Broad Pass is at Milepost 201.4. In fall this is a good berry-picking spot, but not so great for birds. Check the tundra for American Golden-Plover and soaring Golden Eagles. Several lakes near the road might have loons, grebes, Trumpeter Swans, Canada Geese, and ducks. This area is not well birded, so your report of tundra birds here would be of interest.

As you descend from Broad Pass you are now in the Yukon River watershed. A small cluster of roadside businesses at Milepost 209.7 marks the western end of the Denali Highway (see page 115). A left turn here takes you into the small village of Cantwell, where there are a few motels and some stores (see *The Milepost* for a current listing). From Cantwell north to the entrance to Denali National Park at Milepost 237, you will encounter many lodges, cabins, hotels, and motels waiting for you. The closer you get to the park, the more necessary it is to have made advance reservations if you are planning a stay in this area. After leaving Cantwell, the highway parallels the Nenana River that enters the Tanana River at Nenana some 85 miles farther north. You might see Moose, Beaver, Red Fox, and possibly a Wolf along the road, but your chances for seeing large mammals and birds are much better in Denali National Park (see page 58).

LOGISTICS

Consult *The Milepost* for the current list of accommodations and other services along this stretch of the George Parks Highway.

Petersville Road and Denali State Park

David Porter

The Petersville Road

The Petersville Road stretches westward from Milepost 114.9 of the George Parks Highway in the heart of the community of Trapper Creek. The Susitna River Road runs east from this same intersection. All major services are available in Trapper Creek. These two local roads began their history just after the turn of the last century as the Cache Creek trail, then road, that connected Talkeetna, a gold mining supply town on the Alaska Railroad, with the mining district of the Peters and Dutch Hills. Access is much improved now, but the Susitna River still bars easy travel between Trapper Creek and Talkeetna. Take the Petersville Road to the west for better birding.

The first 3.1 miles of the Petersville Road is paved, with another 4 miles scheduled to be paved in summer 2002. Homestead hayfields on both sides of the road within the first 0.8 mile reflect the agricultural basis of the first settlers in Trapper Creek. These fields can be hot spots for spring shorebird migrants, especially in years with a late snowmelt farther north. Look for American Golden-Plover, Upland Plover (rare), and Whimbrel. Sandhill Cranes also use these fields, dancing in the spring and later feeding in pairs or small groups. A few pairs nest in the nearby bogs. (See previous chapter, page 49, for a nearby crane-viewing spot.)

The mixed, mature Paper Birch and White Spruce forest interspersed with houses along the first 1.5 miles offers opportunities to stop whenever something flits across the roadway. Here you can stop in the middle of the road and be taken for a local, but don't try this on the Parks Highway! This is one of the prime benefits of birding along the Petersville Road. The woods are alive early on summer mornings with Ruby-crowned Kinglets, Swainson's and Varied Thrushes, American Robins, Orange-crowned and Blackpoll Warblers, and Slate-colored Juncos. Check around the houses for Tree or Violet-green Swallows, and around the farmyards for oddities such as the Red-winged Blackbird that overwintered in the late 1980s.

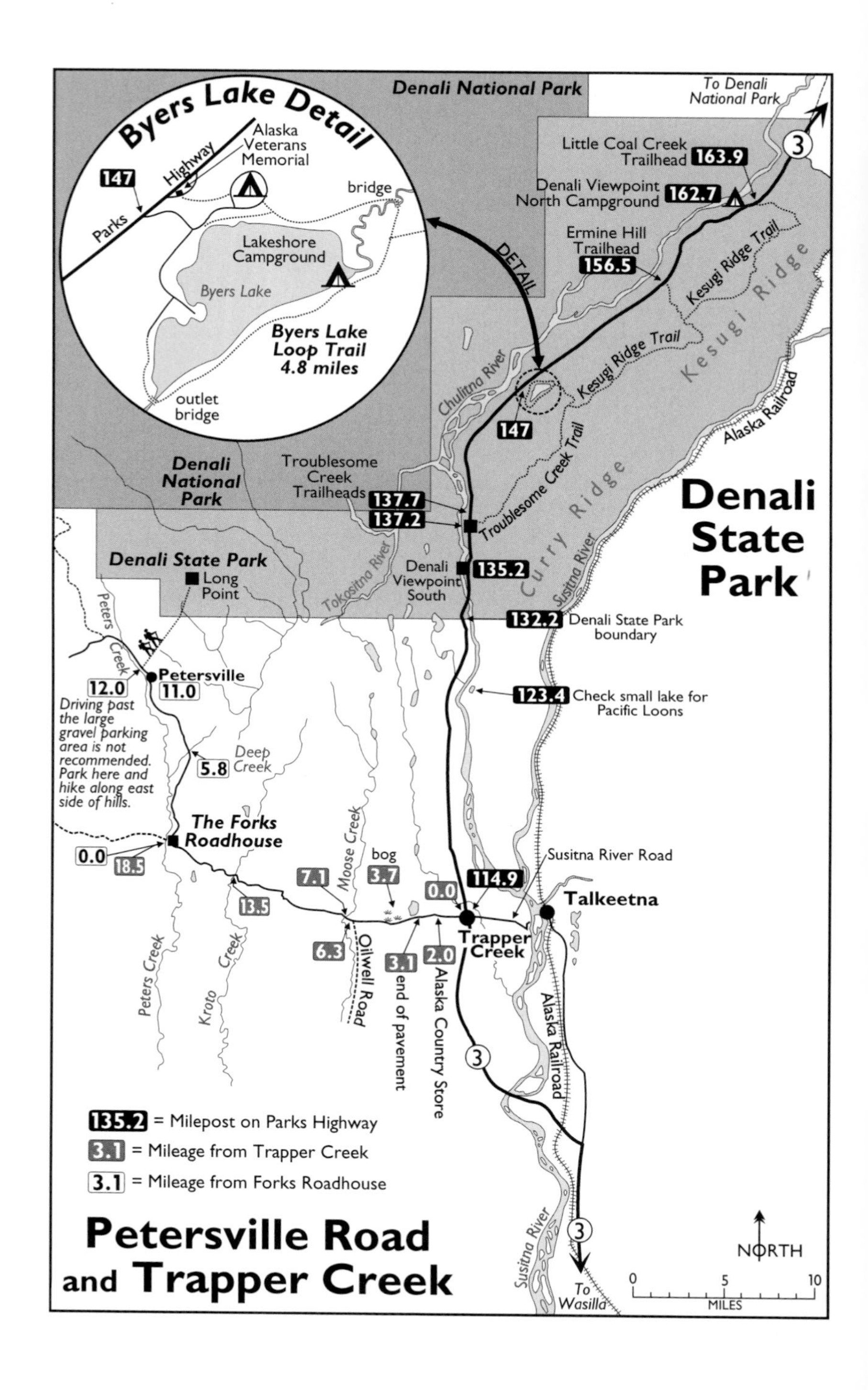
Petersville Road and Trapper Creek
Byers Lake Detail
Denali National Park
To Denali National Park
Alaska Veterans Memorial
147
Parks Highway
bridge
Lakeshore Campground
Byers Lake
Byers Lake Loop Trail 4.8 miles
outlet bridge
DETAIL
Little Coal Creek Trailhead 163.9
Denali Viewpoint North Campground 162.7
Ermine Hill Trailhead 156.5
Kesugi Ridge Trail
Kesugi Ridge
Chulitna River
Alaska Railroad
Troublesome Creek Trail
Troublesome Creek Trailheads 137.7 137.2
Denali State Park
Curry Ridge
Denali Viewpoint South 135.2
Tokositna River
Susitna River
Long Point
Peters Creek
132.2 Denali State Park boundary
Petersville 12.0 11.0
Driving past the large gravel parking area is not recommended. Park here and hike along east side of hills.
5.8 Deep Creek
123.4 Check small lake for Pacific Loons
The Forks Roadhouse
0.0 18.5
Moose Creek
bog 3.7
7.1
0.0
114.9
Susitna River Road
Talkeetna
13.5
6.3
Trapper Creek
Kroto Creek
Oilwell Road
3.1 end of pavement
2.0 Alaska Country Store
3
135.2 = Milepost on Parks Highway
3.1 = Mileage from Trapper Creek
3.1 = Mileage from Forks Roadhouse
To Wasilla
NORTH
0 5 10
MILES

If the tall White spruce are heavy with cones, look at the tops for flocks of White-winged Crossbills. If the Highbush Cranberries are still hanging on the shrubs at the end of winter, look for Pine Grosbeaks. When the dandelions bloom, scan the flocks of Common Redpolls for an uncommon Hoary Redpoll. Pine Siskins may be mixed in with the redpolls. Alder Flycatchers are common from early-to-mid-June to mid-August.

The Alaska Country Store at Mile 2.0 (distance from the Parks Highway) is the last chance to get supplies before heading west. The first small roadside bog, Mile 2.5, consists mostly of Sweet Gale rather than willow. Search edges of wet areas for Lincoln's Sparrow. Any open area from here to timberline and above may have a Savannah Sparrow.

The pavement ends at Mile 3.1, just 0.1 mile before the first lake overlook with a chance of waterbirds and also a great view of Denali and the Alaska Range. Trumpeter Swans sometimes paddle among the stones on the lake. This lake and adjacent bogs and fields attract species like Northern Harrier and Short-eared Owl. This is also a good spot for Wilson's Snipe and, in winter, Boreal Owl. Black-capped Chickadee and Red-breasted Nuthatch are also found here along with the occasional Boreal Chickadee that is found more commonly 30 miles north in Denali State Park. On a hayfield near here, a White-throated Sparrow set up a territory for three weeks in the mid-1990s.

At Mile 3.7 is the first of the big roadside bogs that increase in frequency and size as you go farther out the road. These bogs are good places to listen for Olive-sided Flycatcher. The Beaver pond at Mile 5.8 has Green-winged Teal and frequently Common Goldeneye. Anywhere along the road you may encounter Spruce Grouse picking up gravel. The junction at Mile 6.3 is Oilwell Road that heads south for six miles; birding opportunities along it are similar to those on this stretch of the main road. Moose Creek crosses the Petersville Road at Mile 7.1 and mixes Black Cottonwoods and Balsam Poplars into the habitat. Common Merganser and Gray-cheeked Thrush are sometimes found near the bridge.

Reflection Pond at Mile 10.6 is another good duck spot and usually has a pair of nesting Pacific Loons, whose success is limited some years by Bald Eagle predation on the chicks. Gray Jay, Black-billed Magpie, and Common Raven may be anywhere, but check especially around houses with moose-bone feeders or loose garbage. More ponds, colored in mid-summer with Yellow Pond Lilies, are at Miles 11.5 and 12.5—check them for Greater and Lesser Yellowlegs and Arctic Tern. Be sure to scan the tops of the scraggly Black Spruce along the margins of the swamps for perched Northern Hawk Owls. The large swamp on the north with the big glacial erratic at Mile 13.0 provides an open foreground to view Denali. Other species common to this area are Swainson's Thrush, Wilson's Warbler, Fox, Gambel's White-crowned, and Golden-crowned Sparrows.

Mile 13.5 is the Kroto Creek parking lot, the end of road maintenance in winter and the jumping-off spot for hundreds of winter-sport activists, primarily snowmachiners. The creek itself is another 0.2 mile and may have Spotted Sandpiper, Mew Gull, or American Dipper. The road narrows and gets bumpier from here on. You will pass more swamps and small ponds before the Peters Creek subdivision road junction at Mile 17.1. Stay on the main road. At Mile 17.3 a trail on the north leads to a winter lodge, so keep going, but definitely stop at The Forks Roadhouse (TFR), Mile 18.5.

Built in 1936, this historic roadhouse is *the* place for a lunch, a beer, a look at Alaskan history, and a current road report. The road turns north here and becomes worse, sometimes much worse, especially early in summer, so this may be as far as you want to take a two-wheel-drive vehicle. Usually by the second or third week in June, you can continue on with your rental vehicle. Before you head out, note the Cliff Swallow colony on the building. Alaskans are glad to tolerate the mess these birds make because of the mass of mosquitoes the swallows consume. Also, drive or walk the bumpy road 0.2 mile farther west to Peters Creek. The thick willow brush is sure to hold a Wilson's Warbler. This swift-flowing stream is popular with fishermen. There should be Mew Gulls as well as Bald Eagles when the salmon are in (first of July on). Harlequin Duck, Common Merganser, and Least Sandpiper are other possibilities. Check the tall cottonwoods for Downy or Hairy Woodpeckers. If you plan to camp, inquire about reports of bears in the area.

Mileages are now given with TFR as 0.0. At 0.9 mile north of TFR notice the semi-buried logs crosswise to the roadway. This is called corduroy, an early and still effective technique for crossing a wet stretch of trail or road. Deep Creek and the Beaver pond at Mile 5.8 are good places to linger for a while. The dense willow and nearby forest make it a very birdy spot, with several kinds of warblers, swallows, and waterbirds possible. This is also the closest reliable spot to Trapper Creek in which to locate Arctic Warbler. Listen for their long, monotone trill. Check the pond at Mile 6.7 for Common Goldeneye, and the small creeks and willow thickets at Miles 8.2 and 9.3 for singing Golden-crowned Sparrows. If the feeder is active at the house adjacent to the road at Mile 10.9, look for Gray Jay, Boreal and Black-capped Chickadees, Pine Grosbeak, and Red Squirrel. Mile 11.0 is the historic mining town of Petersville that had its heyday in the 1930s. Then, several hundred miners worked here and in the surrounding hills and creeks. Unfortunately, the buildings are not open to the public, so take your photos from the road and continue on.

There is a small ford at Mile 12.0. If you have made it this far with a two-wheel drive, you can probably safely cross the water. If not, park at the first wide spot just before the ford. Do not park in the roadway at any time as the hills beyond this point are still actively mined, and large equipment is trucked to the mines. There is a very large gravel-pad parking area that you can use on the west just 100 yards beyond the ford.

Beyond this point is The Canyon, where road conditions deteriorate even more. Within 0.3 mile, the puddles get seriously deep and wide, and the road narrows so that meeting any vehicle may mean that somebody has to back up. We suggest that you do not drive beyond this point. If you were to walk from the parking area at Mile 12, you would come to a fork 0.3 mile after the bridge over Peters Creek, at Mile 14.3. Left takes you toward the Cache Creek mining area, while right, after a major ford at Mile 15.1, takes you via right forks and many fords another three miles to the boundary of Denali State Park.

So, from the parking lot, we suggest leaving your vehicle and taking a vigorous yet rewarding hike into the alpine tundra. Hike up the rutted ATV/four-wheel-drive road that heads upward from the east side of the road across from the gravel pad. Don't be tempted to drive, as you may not make it to a turnaround spot. The pad is at an elevation of about 1,825 feet and the first major viewpoints you see on the near horizon to the north are about 2,800 feet. It is approximately two miles one-way of walking to these knobs. You can follow the ATV trail to the left that mostly stays on a dry, low rib as it climbs, or you can cut across a small drainage to the right on a muddier ATV trail. Your goal is to get above the alder and willow thickets and onto easier tundra walking. Just on the other side of these first knobs are several mountain tarns that make for reflective foregrounds when the nearby peaks of the Alaska Range, including Denali, are not obscured by clouds. Make sure you are not trying to find the bird that is making the harsh, loud chirp you hear everywhere; it is the alarm call of the Arctic Ground Squirrel.

American Golden-Plover

These thickets are thick with Golden-crowned Sparrows, while Savannah Sparrows are in the lower Dwarf Birch shrubs. Northern Harriers, Golden Eagles, and Long-tailed Jaegers patrol these hills as do Short-eared Owls (locally rare). Northern Wheatears are infrequently present. Shorebirds include

American Golden-Plover, Whimbrel, Surfbird, and Wilson's Snipe. If you want to go to the highpoint of this portion of the Peters Hills, it is another five miles one-way to Long Point, elevation 3,929 feet. White-tailed Ptarmigan sometimes are in the highest parts of these hills, while Willow Ptarmigan can be common lower down the slopes.

DENALI STATE PARK

Denali State Park (DSP; map on page 52) includes just over 325,000 acres of braided glacial streams, lowland forest, alpine tundra and bare mountaintops. These diverse, bird-rich habitats are truly wilderness, yet are also very accessible if you're willing to walk a bit. The George Parks Highway, Alaska Route 3, runs south and north through the park, bisecting it neatly in half. Along the highway, the park runs from Milepost 132.2 in the south to the railroad crossing at Milepost 169.1 to the north. It is also possible to enter DSP via the local train of the Alaska Railroad out of Talkeetna or Hurricane, but only if you want a trailless, brush-bashing experience.

If you are approaching the park from the north, be sure to scan the scraggly spruce tops in Broad Pass south of Cantwell, Milepost 210, for Northern Hawk Owls. If you are heading up from Anchorage, check the small lake on the east at Milepost 123.4 near the south entrance to DSP for occasional nesting Pacific Loons. Make sure that you move over to the right and stop or park well off the pavement as you bird the Parks Highway—most of the speeding traffic will not slow down for you.

The birding is best when you get out and walk or hike along the park trails. Trailheads and campgrounds are: Lower Troublesome at Milepost 137.2, Upper Troublesome at Milepost 137.7 (closed annually from mid-July through August because of potential bear problems), Alaska Veterans Memorial/Byers Lake Campground at Milepost 147.0, Ermine Hill at Milepost 156.5, and Little Coal Creek at Milepost 163.9. The last is the best route to the alpine. With an elevation gain of about 720 feet in 1.5 miles of hiking, you pop up above the timber and brush to be rewarded with spectacular views of Denali and the surrounding Alaska Range.

One of the most popular hikes is the Byers Lake Loop Trail. This 4.8-mile route begins and ends in Byers Lake Campground, involves very little up or down, and runs mostly adjacent to the lovely 0.5-by-1.5-mile lake. Some parts of the trail may be muddy, especially in early June and during the rains of August. Part of the trail, including the suspension bridge over Byers Creek near the north end of the lake, was built by the BLM in the early 1960s. The trail is also popular with both Black and Brown Bears, so heed the Bear Cautions given in the *Introduction* (page 17), especially in August when the Red Salmon are spawning along the eastern shore of the lake.

Trumpeter Swans have nested along the lake for years. In 2001, five cygnets were successfully raised. Rangers close the immediate area of the nest site, usually on the north end of the lake, in early June. Motorboats are prohibited, but canoes and kayaks can be rented. The swans, as well as the nesting Common Loons and Common Mergansers, should never be approached too closely. The lake occasionally attracts less-common birds, such as Long-tailed Duck (spring) or White-winged Scoter (summer). A Yellow-billed Loon was reported early in the summer in 1998.

The mature White Spruce and Paper (White) Birch forest along the lake is home to Black-capped and Boreal Chickadees, Brown Creeper, Swainson's Thrush, Myrtle Warbler, Fox Sparrow, and Slate-colored Junco. Any tapping should be checked out as there have been both Three-toed and Black-backed Woodpeckers in the area. Townsend's Warbler is relatively rare. The open swamp at the north end will probably have Greater Yellowlegs and Savannah Sparrow. Look down the creek while on the outlet bridge at the south end of the lake for Harlequin Duck or American Dipper. The most reliable site for dippers was the nest under Byers Creek bridge at Milepost 143.9, but summer-long construction in 2000 may have forced them to relocate.

For a more rigorous, multi-day hiking excursion with alpine birding opportunities try doing a loop between two trailheads. It is 17.3 miles from Little Coal Creek to Ermine Hill and about the same from Ermine Hill to Byers Lake. However, the up-and-down is more serious on the latter trail, including the appropriately named Whimbrel Hill. Other alpine possibilities include American Golden-Plover, nesting Surfbird, Long-tailed Jaeger, Horned Lark, Northern Wheatear, American Pipit, Wilson's Warbler, and Golden-crowned Sparrow. A fledged brood of Northern Hawk Owls was prominent along the forested portion of the Ermine Hill Trail for several weeks in 2000.

LOGISTICS

The area code for all telephone numbers is 907 unless otherwise indicated. Tourist and travel services (accommodations, restaurants, attractions, etc.) not listed below can be found in the latest edition of The Milepost. *Statewide travel and birding information services are listed under Logistics in the* Introduction, *page 15.*

Information is available on the Division of Parks and Outdoor Recreation website at *www.dnr.state.ak.us/parks/index.htm* or at Mat-Su/Copper River Basin Area Headquarters, HC 32 Box 6706, Wasilla, AK 99654; 745-3975; fax 745-0938.

Up-to-the-minute trail and birding information is available at the visitor center at the Alaska Veterans Memorial, Milepost 147.1 of the Parks Highway.

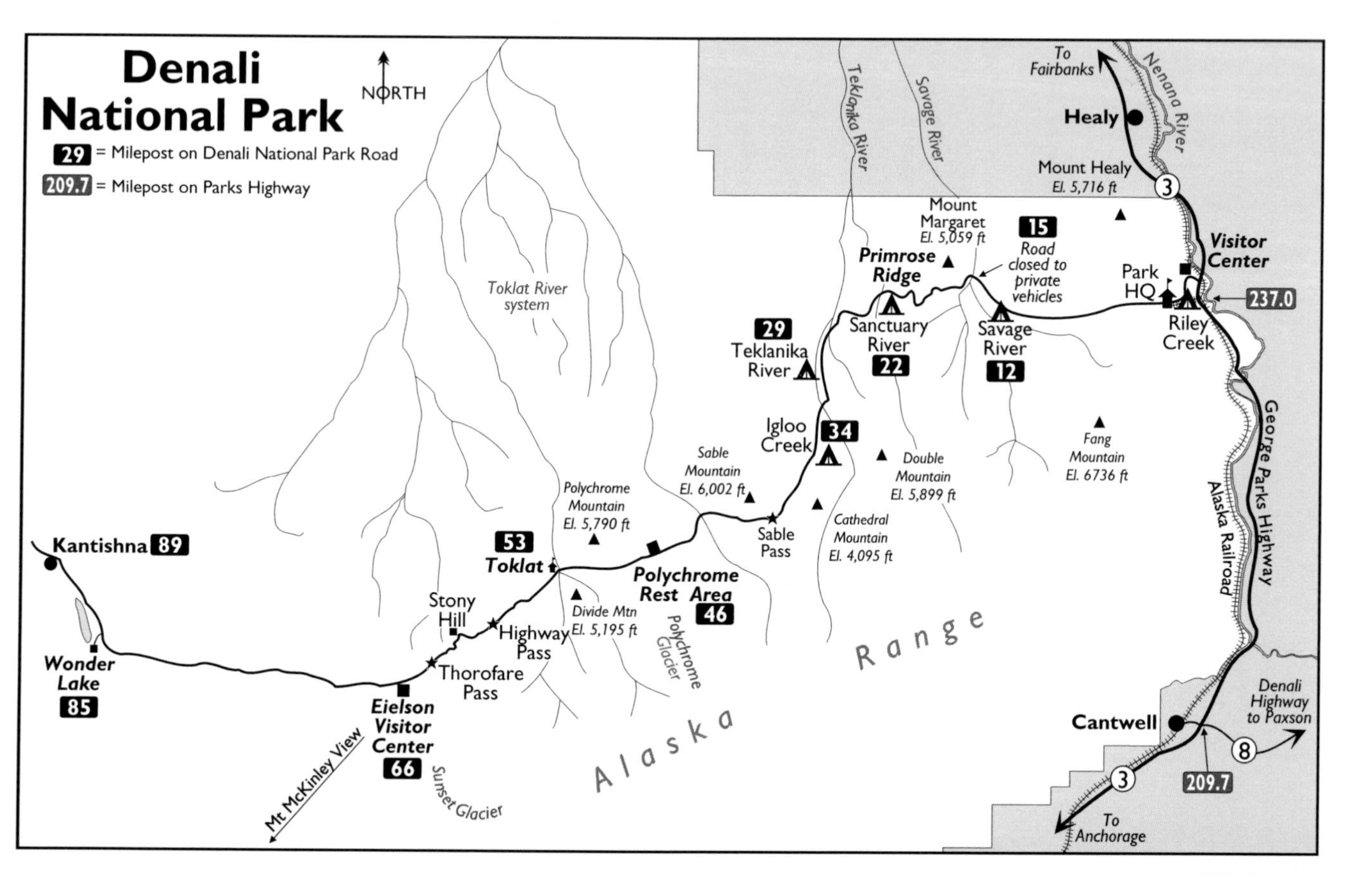
Denali National Park
NORTH
29 = Milepost on Denali National Park Road
209.7 = Milepost on Parks Highway
To Fairbanks
Healy
Nenana River
Teklanika River
Savage River
Mount Healy
El. 5,716 ft
3
Mount Margaret
El. 5,059 ft
15
Road closed to private vehicles
Visitor Center
Park HQ
Primrose Ridge
237.0
Riley Creek
29
Teklanika River
Sanctuary River
22
Savage River
12
Toklat River system
Igloo Creek
34
Sable Mountain
El. 6,002 ft
Double Mountain
El. 5,899 ft
Fang Mountain
El. 6736 ft
George Parks Highway
Alaska Railroad
Polychrome Mountain
El. 5,790 ft
Sable Pass
Cathedral Mountain
El. 4,095 ft
Kantishna 89
53
Toklat
Polychrome Rest Area
46
Stony Hill
Highway Pass
Divide Mtn
El. 5,195 ft
Polychrome Glacier
Range
Wonder Lake
85
Thorofare Pass
Eielson Visitor Center
66
Alaska
Denali Highway to Paxson
Cantwell
8
3
209.7
Mt McKinley View
Sunset Glacier
To Anchorage

DENALI NATIONAL PARK

Carol McIntyre and George West

One of every four tourists who comes to Alaska visits Denali National Park and Preserve. Originally established in 1917 as Mount McKinley National Park, and enlarged and renamed in 1980, Denali National Park and Preserve (Denali) encompasses nearly six million acres of a relatively pristine subarctic ecosystem. The park is designated as an International Biosphere Reserve under the United Nations Man and the Biosphere program. Denali offers some of the best wildlife viewing in Alaska. The most-visited portion of Denali is the road corridor north of the Alaska Range. Good birding, however, is also found on the south side of the Alaska Range along the Petersville Road and in adjacent Denali State Park (see previous chapter).

The Park and Preserve, which include habitats that rise from the Nenana River canyon through Black and White Spruce forests up to timberline and alpine tundra, provide some of the most spectacular scenery in Alaska. Most tourists hope to catch a glimpse of the highest mountain in North America, Mount McKinley at 20,320 feet, and some of the large mammals in the park. You can often get a good view of the mountain from several points along the George Parks Highway north of Trapper Creek. But the mountain is usually covered in clouds and is exposed to the top only about 10 percent of the time.

Conspicuous large mammals in the park include Caribou, Brown Bear, Dall's Sheep, and Moose. Arctic Ground Squirrel, Hoary Marmot, Red Fox, and Red Squirrel are also easy to find. If you are very lucky you will see Wolves. Even though most of the birds seen in Denali can be found elsewhere in Alaska, you would be remiss in not visiting the park. The combination of amazing scenery, opportunities to visit a variety of habitats with ease, and relatively good chances for seeing a diversity of subarctic breeding birds are good reasons to include a visit to Denali in your birding itinerary. You can gain access to the park in many ways, although the most often used method is a trip on one of the park shuttle or tour buses. You can also go backpacking, stay in a campground, or stay in a lodge in Kantishna, beyond Wonder Lake.

The original Denali National Park birdfinding guide said: "Denali National Park is the home of a fascinating assemblage of boreal birds. Those capable of withstanding the rigors of winter are joined in spring by a variety of migrants, forming a richly cosmopolitan avifauna. . . ." The following account is written for birders who will visit the park in summer. Those who may not have time for an extended stay in or around the park will be rewarded by at least riding the park bus, and more so by extending their stay and venturing beyond the park road. You will get the most from the park if you stay for a few days to watch these fantastic birds in this magnificent place. Here, as anywhere, birders should stay at least 100 yards away from nesting birds and recently fledged young.

A road permit is required to drive past the Savage River checkpoint on the Denali Park road. The park issues road permits to people who are camping at Teklanika Campground, allowing them to drive their vehicles only to the campground. The campgrounds at Igloo Creek and Wonder Lake are accessible only by bus; it is no longer possible to drive your vehicle to these campgrounds. The lodges in Kantishna transport their guests to and from Kantishna by private bus.

If you have time to take the bus ride *and* drive out to Savage, by all means do both, for the drive can be productive and allows you to set your own pace. Expanses of tundra and boreal forest occur along this route, along with a number of hiking trails. Northern Hawk Owl often can be found by carefully scanning the tops of spruce, especially those with dead limbs. The park naturalist at the Visitor Access Center or the bus drivers you might encounter at any of the bus stops are often up-to-speed on recent wildlife sightings along this stretch.

To continue past Savage River to reach the best birding locations, you are required to make reservations to take a shuttle bus . The bus driver will drop you off at any point along the road system all the way to Wonder Lake. You can be picked up by any other bus and move farther into the park, or catch a returning bus. You will not be able to bird well from the bus, as most tourists will be looking for mammals and a view of the mountain and not for birds (unless a ptarmigan flock is conspicuous by the road). The best birding areas are over a three-hour bus ride into the park, so you should plan either to stay the night in the Denali area after you leave the park or better yet, stay in a campground, backpack into the park, or reserve a place at a lodge in Kantishna. Otherwise, you will find that you have very little time to explore the best areas before you need to catch a return bus. Since the bus rides in and out of the park consume so much time, you should concentrate your birding efforts on just a few species. Some of the bus drivers are more knowledgeable about birds than others and will know where the most interesting species are. Inquire at the Visitor Access Center to find out which drivers might be most helpful in this respect.

Denali offers good birding throughout the summer, but do not go there before mid-June if you want to be sure of finding Arctic Warbler. It is also more likely that bad weather will cause access problems if you go before June, but some of the best birding is in early June. If you're planning a longer stay, consider purchasing *Birds of Denali* by McIntyre et al. (2002), an introduction to selected species, available at both visitor centers.

If you are not planning to visit Nome, Denali offers you a chance to see species such as Gyrfalcon, Long-tailed Jaeger, Northern Wheatear, and Arctic Warbler. It is also a good place to catch up with species like Willow and Rock Ptarmigan. All the areas mentioned are marked on the park maps, available free at headquarters, as well as on the map that accompanies this chapter. To find many of the species listed above, you need to bird in alpine tundra and on mountain ridges. Birds occur at very low densities in these habitats, so be prepared to spend several hours searching. Along the park road, this habitat occurs mainly from Sable Pass to the Eielson Visitor Center. However, many of these species, plus Rock and White-tailed Ptarmigan, American Golden-Plover, Whimbrel, Surfbird, and Lapland Longspur, can often be found on Primrose Ridge. If you are a strong walker, you can explore Primrose Ridge from the Savage River bridge area. Cross the Savage River Bridge and hike up to the top of Primrose Ridge on the west side of the Savage River. In this way, you can see many species without having to use the shuttle-bus system.

If you are prepared to catch the first bus of the day to Eielson Visitor Center, it is worth hiking up the Thorofare River, where Gyrfalcon and the very-high-altitude species like White-tailed Ptarmigan and Gray-crowned

Arctic Warbler

Rosy-Finch are possible. But, if you're not in top condition, it might not be possible for you to make this very long walk after riding the bus from the park entrance to Eielson Visitor Center, and still make it back to the entrance on the same day. Adventurous birders should consider a backpacking trip in this area. Thorofare Ridge or any of the higher elevations are good for high-altitude species. Gyrfalcons occur in the mountainous sections throughout Denali. For non-hikers, the best chances of seeing this species are near Polychrome, Stony Hill, and Eielson. A very reliable place to see one is the area south of the Polychrome bus stop. The most conspicuous raptor along the road is Golden Eagle, and you will have little trouble spotting one.

Since hunting is not allowed within the original park boundaries, ptarmigan are usually easier to find along the Denali Park road than elsewhere in the state. (Hunting is allowed in the expanded section of the park and preserve, but most of this area cannot be accessed with a car, except the Petersville Road.) Willow Ptarmigan are common in areas of tundra mixed with brushy willows. Males are conspicuous in May and early June, and after mid-June, family groups occur. You can often detect these by listening for the cheeping of the young chicks. Rock Ptarmigan occur higher up on Primrose Ridge, Cathedral Mountain, and other mountainous areas in the park. The ridges behind Eielson Visitor Center are a convenient place to look. White-tailed Ptarmigan reaches the northern limit of its range here, and is the most difficult of the three ptarmigan species to find. In summer, you usually will need to climb up above 4,000 feet to find one.

A number of shorebirds breed, including American Golden-Plover, Wandering Tattler, Upland Sandpiper, and Surfbird. To look for the first two species, it is necessary to climb up to alpine tundra. In contrast, Wandering Tattlers breed on gravelly streams such as Igloo Creek and the appropriately named Tattler Creek. Upland Sandpipers are very hard to find and do not occur here regularly. Long-tailed Jaegers nest on alpine tundra at several places in the park. A good area to look for them is around Stony Dome, between Highway Pass and Thorofare Pass. It is worth scanning for Northern Hawk Owls in tracts of spruce forest. Also look for them along the Parks Highway just south of the park entrance.

Other species inhabiting the spruce woods include Boreal and Black-capped Chickadees, Bohemian Waxwing, and White-winged Crossbill. Say's Phoebes are found in rocky areas between Polychrome Pass and Eielson Visitor Center—a pair sometimes nests at the visitor center itself. Another interior western species, Townsend's Solitaire, nests uncommonly in the park. It is best found by searching the upper reaches of streams at quite high elevation, where it prefers vertical faces that are often formed along creeks.

Two Old World species, Arctic Warbler and Northern Wheatear, can easily be found here. Northern Wheatears favor alpine areas and are often seen along the park road between Sable Pass and Eielson Visitor Center. Arctic Warblers breed in willow thickets and are easy to see after mid-June; Igloo Creek, between Tattler Creek and Igloo Creek Campground, is the classic location for them. However, Arctic Warblers may be seen easily in other areas of suitable habitat in the park. Generally, areas of taller willow scrub are preferred. The brushy willow habitat favored by Arctic Warblers is also attractive to American Tree Sparrows and Wilson's Warblers. Northern Shrikes occupy shrubby areas near the Toklat River. Lapland Longspurs favor alpine tundra habitat such as Primrose Ridge, Mount Wright, Stony Dome, and the ridges behind Eielson Visitor Center. Gray-crowned Rosy-Finch and Snow Bunting are high-altitude species, often discovered near permanent snowfields and along glaciers. You should plan to hike up to higher elevations such as upper Toklat River or Sunset or Sunrise Glaciers if you wish to see either one.

Past Eielson Visitor Center the habitat changes from mountainous to rolling tundra with scattered tundra ponds and Wonder Lake, a great area for waterfowl and waders. In mid-September visitors to Wonder Lake will be rewarded with marvelous opportunities to view migrating birds, especially Sandhill Cranes. The Kantishna Hills also offer great birding, with chances for Rock Ptarmigan, Surfbird, and other alpine nesters. Of course, adventuresome visitors will be rewarded with many great birding experiences by venturing off the park road!

LOGISTICS

The area code for all telephone numbers is 907 unless otherwise indicated. Tourist and travel services (accommodations, restaurants, attractions, etc.) not listed below can be found in the latest edition of The Milepost*. Statewide travel and birding information services are listed under Logistics in the* Introduction, *page 15.*

Access: You can easily drive to the park entrance from Anchorage (237 miles) or from Fairbanks (121 miles) on the George Parks Highway (Alaska Route 3) or take the Alaska Railroad train from Anchorage or Fairbanks. The train will stop to let you off or pick you up about anywhere along its route. Check with the railroad at 800-544-0552, or for Fairbanks at 800-895-7245, and for Anchorage at 800-478-2442. There are also several van-shuttles that run from Anchorage and Fairbanks to the park entrance—check *The Milepost* or the local Yellow Pages.

Denali National Park: The National Park Service web site is *www.nps.gov/dena/home/index.html*. The web site for the concessionaire at the park is *www.denalinationalpark.com*.

Accommodations: Although there are many places to stay around the park entrance, you *must* make reservations in advance. If you are planning to seriously bird the park, it might make sense to camp, or perhaps stay at one of the lodges at the western end of the Denali Park road or north or south of the park entrance. The following are suggestions: North Face Lodge / Camp Denali, 683-2290; *www.campdenali.com*. (Inquire about birding/natural history vacations). Kantishna

Roadhouse, 800-942-7420; *www.kantishnaroadhouse.com*. Denali Wilderness Lodge, *www.denaliwildernesslodge.com*; 800-541-9779. Denali Mountain Lodge, 683-2643. Denali Backcountry Lodge, 800-841-0692; *www.denalilodge.com*. Denali West Lodge, 888-607-5566; *www.denaliwest.com* (for those wanting to really get away; near Lake Minchumina; great birding). Denali Lakeside Lodging on Otto Lake near Healy several miles north of the park entrance, 683-2511; *www.alaskaone.com/denlakeside/*. Many other accommodations both north and south of the park entrance are listed in *The Milepost*.

Park and Tour Information: Denali Visitor Services at 683-2294 or *http://www.nps.gov/dena/home/index.html* are the best ways to obtain current information on getting into the park (buses, camping, etc., as well as current schedules of the buses and tours). You can and should book reservations for all tours and accommodations as far as possible in advance of your visit. Birders should plan to stay three nights in the Denali area in order to get a full day of birding in the park. The park is currently constructing a new visitor center that should be completed in 2005. In the meantime, stop at the Riley Creek entrance station to ask questions and pick up maps, guides, and other useful information.

You can get information about the park in advance, including the Denali bird guide, by writing to Alaska Natural History Association, PO Box 838, Denali Park, AK 99755; *www.alaskanha.org*. The Alaska Natural History Association also sells a checklist of birds for Denali. Their Anchorage contact information is ANHA, 750 West 2nd Avenue, Suite 100, Anchorage 99501; 274-8440.

Ask at the Riley Creek station or the visitor center about trips and stays in Kantishna beyone the western boundary of the park.

ACKNOWLEDGEMENTS: Forrest Davis added information about accessing the park by car and shuttle bus. Some birding information is from Lethaby (1994).

Willow Ptarmigan

PARKS HIGHWAY:

DENALI NATIONAL PARK TO FAIRBANKS

Sharon Kanareff

The section of the George Parks Highway from north of Denali National Park to Fairbanks boasts a wide variety of habitats that have been under-birded. The areas near the park can often be good alternatives if you don't have time to bird inside the park, and sometimes offer easier access and fewer crowds. As you near Fairbanks the sparrows, warblers, and raptors of the interior White and Black Spruce taiga and Paper Birch forests dominate.

The Nenana River canyon is a mile beyond the park entrance (Milepost 237.3). Home to the hotels, motels, restaurants, and gift shops that service the park's summer visitors, the area known locally as "the Canyon" also hosts the Interior's urban birds—Black-billed Magpies and Common Ravens. Recent years have seen a nesting Northern Goshawk pair, so watch raptors carefully here.

A series of small ponds just north of Bison Creek (Milepost 243.5) is good in spring for warblers and sparrows. Moose and their calves are often seen here at dawn and dusk, and the occasional Brown Bear frequents the area. Four miles north at Milepost 247 make a left turn onto Otto Lake Road. The Lions Club Park on Otto Lake (0.7 mile) provides a convenient viewpoint for a wide variety of waterfowl, including Red-throated Loon, grebes, swans, all three scoters, both goldeneyes, and Long-tailed Duck. Solitary Sandpiper and Wandering Tattler have frequented the shoreline, and Northern Waterthrush can sometimes be seen in the willows that surround the lake. You can rent a canoe at Otto Lake RV Park and Campground to paddle to the bird-rich coves at the far end of the lake. Most of the land surrounding this lake is privately owned.

Healy is just north of Otto Lake and is an excellent base for your park-area activities. Since 1918, Healy's history has been tied to the coal-mining industry. Today, Alaska's only commercial coal mine and the largest coal-fired steam plant in the state operate three miles east of town.

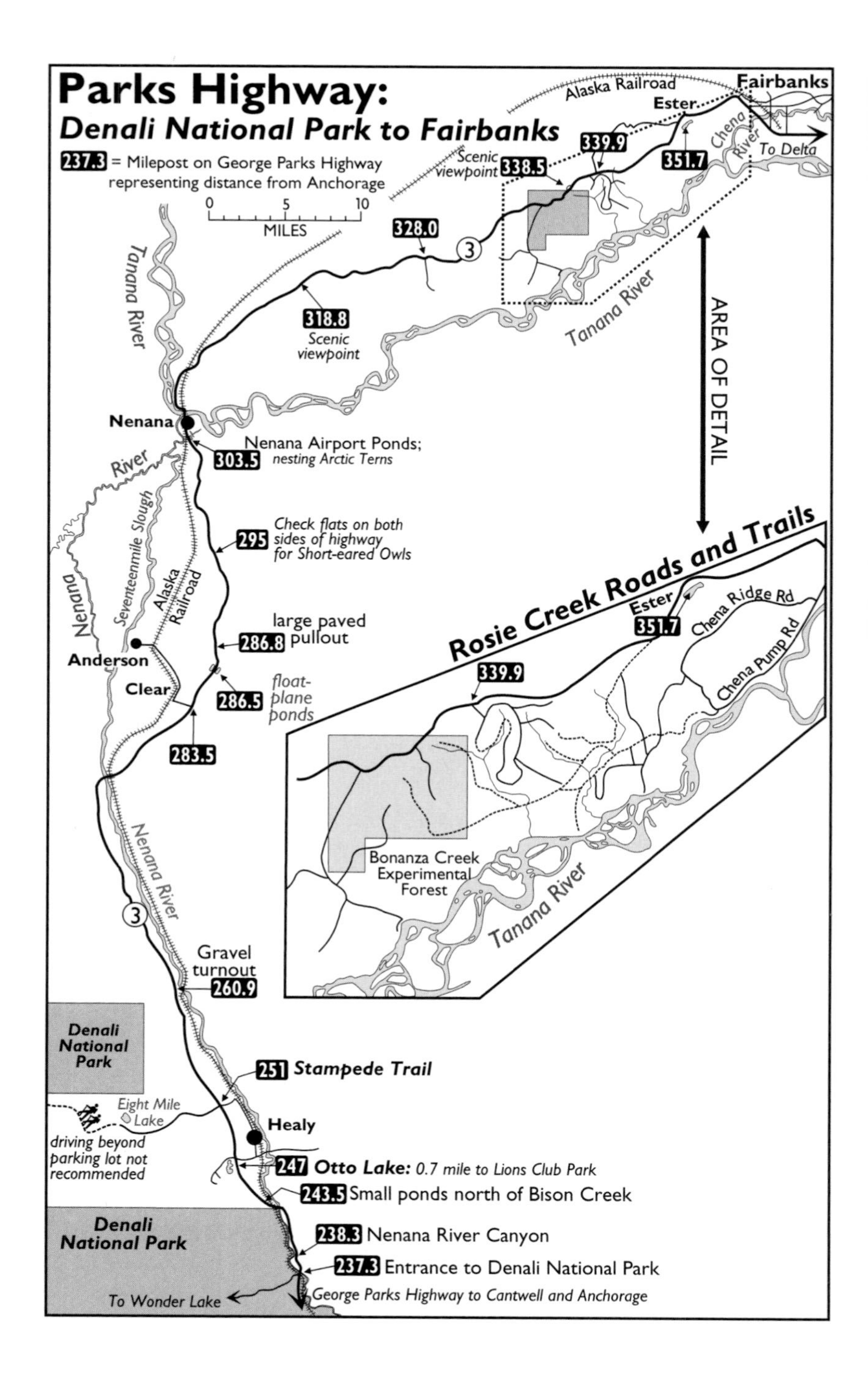

Parks Highway:
Denali National Park to Fairbanks
237.3 = Milepost on George Parks Highway representing distance from Anchorage
0 5 10
MILES
Alaska Railroad
Fairbanks
Ester
339.9
Scenic viewpoint 338.5
351.7
Chena River
To Delta
328.0
3
318.8 Scenic viewpoint
Tanana River
AREA OF DETAIL
Nenana
Nenana Airport Ponds;
303.5 nesting Arctic Terns
River
295 Check flats on both sides of highway for Short-eared Owls
Nenana
Seventeenmile Slough
Alaska Railroad
large paved
286.8 pullout
Anderson
Clear
286.5 float-plane ponds
283.5
Rosie Creek Roads and Trails
Ester
351.7
Chena Ridge Rd
Chena Pump Rd
339.9
Bonanza Creek Experimental Forest
Tanana River
Nenana River
3
Gravel turnout
260.9
Denali National Park
251 Stampede Trail
Eight Mile Lake
driving beyond parking lot not recommended
Healy
247 Otto Lake: 0.7 mile to Lions Club Park
243.5 Small ponds north of Bison Creek
Denali National Park
238.3 Nenana River Canyon
237.3 Entrance to Denali National Park
To Wonder Lake
George Parks Highway to Cantwell and Anchorage

Another place to explore Alaska's mining history is the Stampede Trail, a left turn at Milepost 251 on the Parks Highway. The trail follows the original route taken by the area's miners on their way to gold mines 90-some miles to the west at Kantishna, a settlement now surrounded by the park. In more recent times, the trail gained notoriety as the setting for the events detailed in Jon Krakauer's (1996) *Into the Wild*. Stampede Road, chip-sealed in 2001, winds through Panguingue Creek subdivision. Please observe the 25-mph speed limit. At Mile 4, the road narrows and becomes dirt and gravel. Watch for Willow Ptarmigan in the roadside ditches, and listen for Whimbrels calling from the willow tops. Upland Sandpipers and Long-tailed Jaegers regularly nest in the tundra from Mile 5 to the road's end at Eight Mile Lake. Wilson's Snipe actively display along this stretch in July. White-winged Crossbill and Northern Waterthrush are August regulars in the forested drainages leading to the lake. Northern Wheatears have been seen in the parking lot area, while Horned and Red-necked Grebes, White-winged Scoters, and Red-necked Phalaropes are often on Eight Mile Lake. In fall, swans, Greater White-fronted Geese, and Sandhill Cranes overnight there. Do not be tempted to drive the road past the parking lot—the tundra west of here has been known to strand even four-wheel-drive vehicles with winches except in winter when the ground is frozen.

Stampede Trail continues west of Eight Mile Lake, and you can make it a good day-hike if you want some exercise. It can produce species similar to those seen along the first 30 miles of the park road. Wear sturdy, waterproof boots and be wary—this stretch of trail occasionally hosts a Brown Bear family, and creeks frequently cross the trail as you work your way toward the Savage River (see Bear Cautions in the *Introduction*, page 17). The trail heads out west from the parking lot, passing by willow thickets alive with warblers and sparrows, crossing tundra, bogs, and passing through spruce forest that provides home for Spruce Grouse, Northern Hawk Owl, and, some years, Three-toed Woodpecker. Northern Harrier, American Kestrel, and Merlin can be seen on this hike, as well as nesting Solitary and Spotted Sandpipers. Alder and Hammond's Flycatchers and Say's Phoebe have been seen along the trail, while Bohemian Waxwing and Gray-cheeked Thrush are often highlights. Blackpoll Warbler and Northern Waterthrush stand out among the warblers, and the whole range of interior sparrow species can be found here. Arctic Warblers are possible in the tall willow brush. Semipalmated Plovers have nested in the sand-and-gravel areas along Fish Creek, and, as the creek begins to braid across the trail more frequently, watch for Barrow's Goldeneye and, in many years, nesting Harlequin Ducks.

Return to the Parks Highway and make a quick stop at the gravel turnout to the west at Milepost 260.9. Bank Swallows nest in the clay-and-sand banks in this area. The Beaver pond to the east by Rock Creek sometimes holds an interesting selection of small ducks.

Near Anderson (turn off at Milepost 283.5 – Anderson and Clear Air Force Base), the habitat turns to predominantly spruce taiga and birch forest. Ruffed Grouse often come to the highway to ingest the gravel. Anderson Riverside Park is 6 miles off the main highway and features riverside and rustic campsites. The park's 616 acres along the Nenana River can be a good place for warblers, sparrows, and the occasional Northern Hawk Owl.

Stop to check out the floatplane ponds on both sides of the road two miles north of the Anderson turnoff. These ponds have been home to nesting Horned Grebes and ducks, and swans use them early and late in the season. Park in the large, paved pullout at Milepost 286.8 or in the small, unpaved pullouts on both sides of the highway just before the ponds.

Short-eared Owls often work the flats on both sides of the highway near Milepost 295 and just south of Nenana between Mileposts 300 and 303. The Nenana airport ponds at Milepost 303.5 are worth a look—for many years Arctic Terns have nested just off the highway here. Nenana itself is noteworthy, not only as the port hub for the tugs and barges that supply the Interior's many isolated riverside villages, but also as the home of the Nenana Ice Classic, an annual event with cash prizes for those lucky folks who guess the exact day, hour, and minute that the ice will break up on the Tanana River. A large tripod is set on the river ice to the east (right side) of the bridge with a wire connecting the tripod to a clock in a shed on the riverbank. When the ice breaks up, the tripod begins to move downstream. This stretches the wire tight and stops the clock, freezing the time of the break-up.

Scenic viewpoints are frequent along the highway from Nenana to Fairbanks. A turnout at Milepost 318.8 features a good look at the bogs, creeks, and lakes that dot this area of the state. From the turnout at Milepost 338.5 you will get great views of the Tanana River to the southeast—and on rare occasions, Mount McKinley. Murphy Dome dominates the view to the west.

At Milepost 328 a dirt road leads to the south. This quiet logging road has been passable for passenger vehicles for the last several years. Northern Goshawk and Ruffed Grouse are seen here, as well as other typical forest species. Where the road crosses the high-voltage transmission intertie after two miles, you can stretch your legs by hiking the margins of the cleared swath for forest-peripheral and grassland birds.

At Milepost 339.9 is the turnoff to the Bonanza Creek Experimental Forest–Rosie Creek Burn. The unmarked turnoff to the east is just beyond the end of a guard rail. As you head in, the Bonanza Creek road system bears to the right, Rosie Creek's to the left. These are logging roads and are not well maintained, so drive with care. These roads can be extremely muddy in spring and often require a four-wheel-drive vehicle.

Bonanza Creek Experimental Forest is a predominantly old-growth White Spruce and Paper Birch forest unlike others in the Interior, interspersed with clearings from which to look for raptors and listen for woodpeckers and passerines. Great Horned, Great Gray, and Northern Hawk Owls, and Brown Creepers are seen here along with Northern Harrier, Sharp-shinned and Red-tailed Hawks, American Kestrel, and Merlin. Small numbers of shorebirds pass through the Tanana River flats below during spring.

Rosie Creek was the place to go for Black-backed Woodpecker right after the 1983 wildfire that scorched 8,000 acres in the area. Time has allowed regeneration of the brush and timber, and today the burn area is returning to use by the more common Interior species. You can reliably find many of the warblers and sparrows expected in this region, as well as Ruffed and Spruce

Northern Hawk Owl

Grouse. Some of the stands of unburned timber are good for Hammond's Flycatcher, Townsend's Warbler, and Boreal Chickadee as well as for owls.

The Ester ponds to the right at Milepost 351.7 recently have been widened and deepened and were practically dry in 2002. This former haven for nesting Horned Grebes and dabbling ducks will bear watching as its vegetation gets re-established. As you enter Fairbanks around Milepost 355, check out the University of Alaska Fairbanks agricultural fields to the north for Sandhill Cranes and Canada Geese grazing and massing to migrate south.

LOGISTICS

The area code for all telephone numbers is 907 unless otherwise indicated. Tourist and travel services (accommodations, restaurants, attractions, etc.) not listed below can be found in the latest edition of The Milepost. *Statewide travel and birding information services are listed under Logistics in the* Introduction, *page 15.*

Healy has a wide range of camping sites, B&Bs, hotels, motels, auto service stations, and a medical clinic. Many independent Denali Park visitors choose Healy for the value of its accommodations and proximity to the park. For more information visit the Greater Healy/Denali Chamber of Commerce log cabin at Mile 0.4 on the Healy Spur Road, call 683-4636, or visit the web site *www.denalichamber.com*.

Nenana offers an auto repair shop, restaurants and a variety of accommodations. For more visitor information call 832-9953, visit the log cabin at the junction of the Parks Highway and A Street, or visit the Nenana web site *www.mtaonline.net/~nenanacc/chamber/commercex.html*.

Between Nenana and Fairbanks are several places to catch an Alaskan meal: the Mondorosa at Milepost 308.8 boasts the "Best Hamburgers in Alaska;" Skinny Dick's Halfway Inn at Milepost 328 has its own charms. Ester hosts a hotel, RV park, two saloons, and several local and nationally known artists and their shops.

ACKNOWLEDGEMENTS: Rosie Creek Burn information is with reference to Springer (1993). Updates are from Nancy DeWitt, Kristin Bartecchi, and Edward Murphy. Rob Yaksich reviewed the text and added several suggestions of birding locations and species occurrence.

FAIRBANKS

Nancy DeWitt, Jim DeWitt, and George West

Fairbanks is Alaska's second largest city (population 32,200, areawide 85,000) and home of the University of Alaska Fairbanks. A product of the Gold Rush, Fairbanks has grown into a bustling trade and transportation center for interior and far northern Alaska. The University was established in 1917 as a College of Agriculture and School of Mines, but in 1922 it was reorganized and renamed the University. It is an internationally recognized research center for geophysics, arctic biology, marine science, and Native language studies, as well as a first-rate academic institution. The statewide offices of the University system are here and oversee the three main branches of the University in Fairbanks, Anchorage, and Juneau, as well as many community colleges in villages and towns throughout the state. A visit to the campus on the hill in College and to the University of Alaska Museum on the West Ridge will give you a good view of a modern university community, an afternoon of education and discovery at an excellent museum, and a sweeping panorama of the Tanana Flats southward to the Alaska Range. On a good day, you can see Denali (Mount McKinley) to the west and the three high peaks, Mounts Hayes, Hess, and Deborah, to the south.

Fairbanks is often overlooked by birders who either travel only as far north as Denali National Park or use Fairbanks as a transfer point for birding trips to the Brooks Range and the North Slope. Located in the central Tanana River valley, Fairbanks is part of the interior uplands of Alaska. It is bounded on the south by the Tanana River and on the north, west, and east by the low rolling hills of the Yukon-Tanana Uplands. The Chena River runs through the city. The immediate area offers a wide variety of habitats, including the sandbars of the Tanana River favored by gulls and terns, boggy taiga, mixed spruce-and-birch uplands, and alpine tundra.

The Alaska Bird Observatory has its headquarters in Fairbanks. This is a good place to stop and check with staff for the latest reports on rarities or Alaska specialties in the area and to learn more about their banding program and birding activities.

North of Fairbanks, the Steese Highway offers relatively easy access to the White Mountains and extensive alpine terrain (page 85). The Dalton Highway takes you all the way to the North Slope and Deadhorse (page 91). The George Parks (pages 42 and 65) and Richardson Highways (pages 100 and 107)

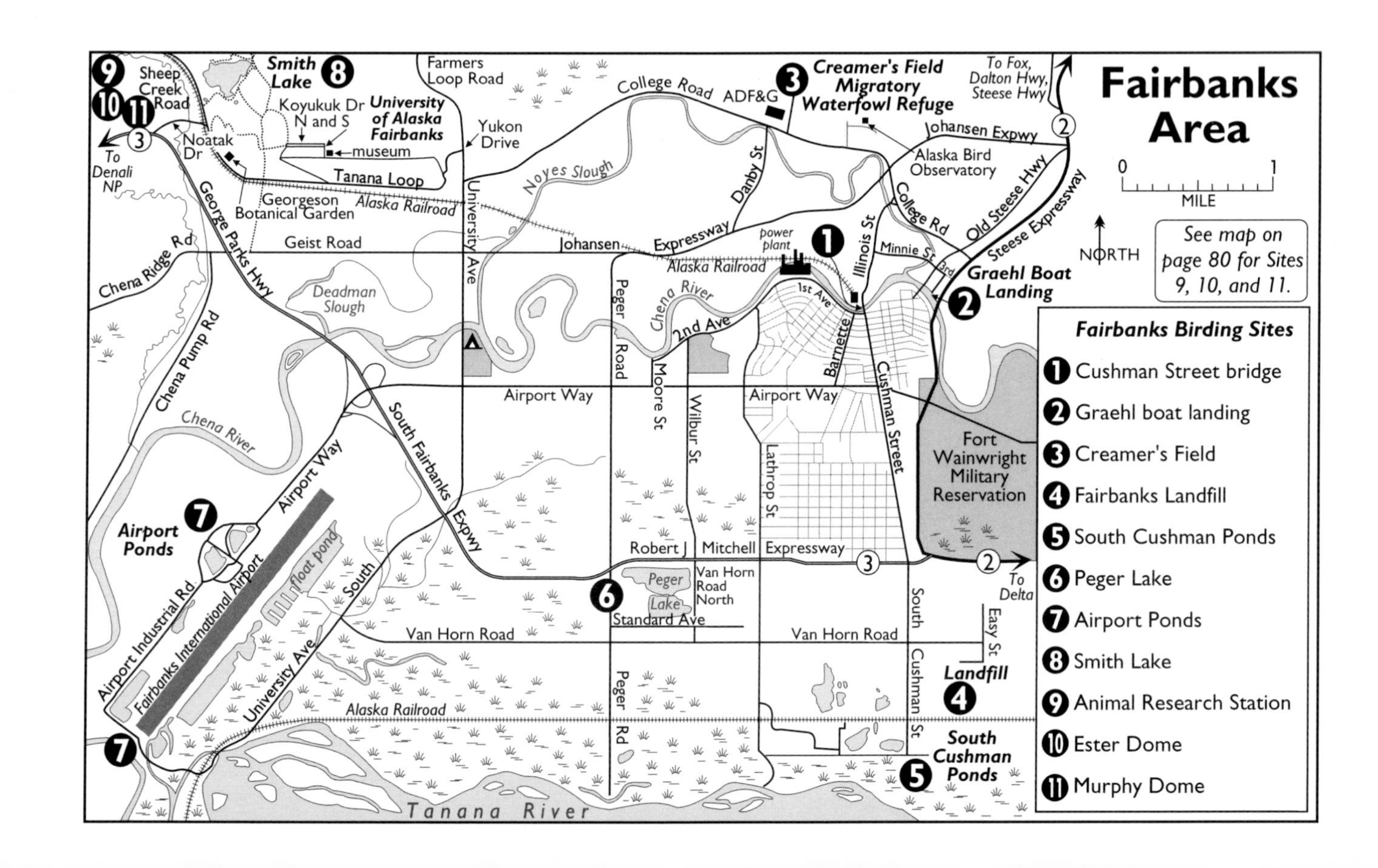

Fairbanks Area
0
1
MILE
NORTH
See map on page 80 for Sites 9, 10, and 11.
Fairbanks Birding Sites
1 Cushman Street bridge
2 Graehl boat landing
3 Creamer's Field
4 Fairbanks Landfill
5 South Cushman Ponds
6 Peger Lake
7 Airport Ponds
8 Smith Lake
9 Animal Research Station
10 Ester Dome
11 Murphy Dome
To Fox, Dalton Hwy, Steese Hwy
Johansen Expwy
Steese Expressway
Old Steese Hwy
Graehl Boat Landing
Alaska Bird Observatory
Creamer's Field Migratory Waterfowl Refuge
ADF&G
College Road
College Rd
Minnie St
3rd
Illinois St
Cushman Street
Barnette
1st Ave
power plant
Alaska Railroad
Chena River
2nd Ave
Fort Wainwright Military Reservation
To Delta
Easy St
Landfill
South Cushman Ponds
South
Cushman
St
Airport Way
Expressway
Van Horn Road
Lathrop St
Danby St
Wilbur St
Mitchell
Van Horn Road North
Robert J
Peger Lake
Standard Ave
Moore St
Peger Road
Peger Rd
Johansen
Noyes Slough
Yukon Drive
University Ave
Farmers Loop Road
University of Alaska Fairbanks
museum
Tanana Loop
South Fairbanks Expwy
Tanana River
Smith Lake
Koyukuk Dr N and S
Georgeson Botanical Garden
Geist Road
Deadman Slough
South University Ave
float pond
Fairbanks International Airport
George Parks Hwy
Noatak Dr
Sheep Creek Road
Chena Pump Rd
Chena Ridge Rd
Airport Ponds
Airport Industrial Rd
To Denali NP

lead you into the Alaska Range to the south and connect with the Alaska Highway to Canada (pages 141 and 159) and the Lower 48 states. Except for the Parks and Richardson Highways, most roads are paved for only 20 or 30 miles outside of Fairbanks, and then become gravel. The gravel roads are generally in good condition and can be driven in all kinds of weather. However, many car rental agencies do not permit you to drive their cars on gravel roads.

Migrant species generally begin their return to interior Alaska during late March and early April, peaking in May. Fall migration begins in August and continues into early October. All migration dates are dependent on prevailing weather; a late spring tends to concentrate the spring migration.

There are three birding loops around Fairbanks—all start from the Cushman Street bridge in downtown Fairbanks: North Fairbanks Loop including the Chena River and Creamer's Field, South Fairbanks Loop including the Borough Landfill, South Cushman Ponds, and the Airport Ponds, and West Fairbanks Loop including the University of Alaska, Smith Lake, and Ester and Murphy Domes.

NORTH FAIRBANKS LOOP

During winter, the Chena River below the Cushman Street bridge remains ice-free near the municipal power plant. A few hardy Mallards and Common Mergansers can usually be found here and are often hunted by Northern Goshawks.

In summer, the Graehl boat landing is a good starting point for a canoe trip down the Chena to the University Avenue bridge at the Chena River State Recreation campground. From the Cushman Bridge, travel north on Cushman Street (which turns into Illinois Street) and turn right on Minnie Street. Go past the first light (the road becomes 3rd Street at this point) and turn right on Forty Mile Avenue, which ends at the boat landing. The willows along the river are often loaded with Yellow Warblers in the spring. Bank Swallows nest in the bank across the river, and Belted Kingfishers are a common sighting. Townsend's Warblers and White-winged Crossbills are sometimes spotted in the tall spruce near the entrance to Noyes Slough, just downriver from the landing. If you are not canoeing, head for Creamer's Field.

Backtrack on Forty Mile Avenue, turn left onto 3rd Street, and then right onto the Old Steese Highway. Turn left onto College Road and drive about two miles to the intersection with Danby Street. Turn right (north) onto the frontage road in front of the Alaska Department of Fish and Game (ADF&G) office. Just beyond the stop sign is the south parking area for **Creamer's Field Migratory Waterfowl Refuge**, undoubtedly the best-known birding spot in Fairbanks. While operating Creamer's Dairy from the late 1920s until

1966, Charles Creamer cultivated large fields to feed his cows, and the fields attracted large numbers of migrating waterfowl and cranes. When the dairy went up for sale in 1966, local residents met to plan a way to purchase the property. Along with money raised by the community, the state legislature provided funds (25 percent) to match with the federal government's Pittman-Robertson funds (75 percent) to purchase the 250-acre farm. Management was given to the ADF&G. In 1970 an adjacent 1,500 acres of state land was added and the entire parcel was designated Creamer's Field Migratory Waterfowl Refuge in 1979. The ADF&G continues to grow grain to attract geese, ducks, and cranes. Grain is also spread on the ground during spring and fall migration to draw birds away from Fairbanks International and Fort Wainwright Airports.

In addition to the large fields, the 1,787-acre refuge includes a number of habitats, such as ponds, muskeg, mixed forest, and shrub land. Among the attractions at the refuge are a visitor center, two nature trails, and a bird-banding station operated by the Alaska Bird Observatory from May through September. The refuge presents year-round birding opportunities, with spring migration offering the greatest variety of birds (late April through late May). Several species commonly nest on the refuge, including Solitary Sandpiper, Wilson's Snipe, Alder and Hammond's Flycatchers, Myrtle Warbler, Savannah Sparrow, and Common Redpoll. A small number of breeding and subadult Sandhill Cranes remain on the refuge during summer. During fall migration, the annual Tanana Valley Sandhill Crane Festival is held during the last week of August to coincide with the spectacular number of cranes that stage at Creamer's Refuge. Winter is a good time to see Northern Goshawk, Boreal Chickadee, White-winged Crossbill, and Common Redpoll. Gyrfalcon, Willow Ptarmigan, and Northern Hawk Owl make rare appearances.

Adjacent to the south parking lot are several viewing platforms that provide good vantage points to scan the front field and two artificial ponds. A footpath parallels the road 0.25 mile to the barns and visitor center, passing two observation platforms for the front field. Be sure to scan the fields directly behind and west of the ADF&G building, as well. In addition to Canada Geese, Sandhill Cranes, and a variety of ducks, a number of interesting but less abundant species have been recorded in the fields during spring migration. These include Greater White-fronted Goose, Snow Goose, Black Brant, Trumpeter Swan, Eurasian Wigeon, Black-bellied Plover, Killdeer, Whimbrel, and Upland, Least, White-rumped, Baird's, Pectoral, Stilt, and Buff-breasted Sandpipers. A subadult Common Crane was seen here in 1958. Bald Eagle, Northern Harrier, and Peregrine Falcon are often seen hunting over the fields during spring and fall migration. The field may be very quiet in mid-summer. Tree and Violet-green Swallows nest in the numerous boxes in the fields, and Cliff Swallows nest on the old creamery building near the north parking area. The Rock Doves that hang around the barns are favorite targets for migrating Peregrine Falcons and resident Northern Goshawks. If water is present in the slough to the left of the barn during May, it is an excellent place to look for shorebirds.

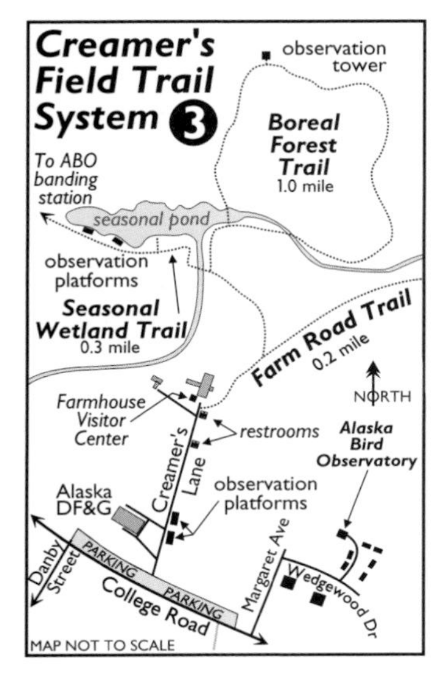

The visitor center, located in the original farmhouse for the dairy, is open daily between Memorial Day and Labor Day and on Saturdays year round; call 459-7307 (*www.creamersfield.org*) for current hours. The visitor center features displays about the dairy's history and the refuge's wildlife, trail guides, nature walk schedules, a notebook of recent wildlife sightings, a library, and a small gift shop. The center is operated by Friends of Creamer's Field, a nonprofit organization committed to promoting the history and wildlife of the refuge. They offer a series of impressive naturalist-led walks throughout the year.

If you are at the refuge when ABO has their mist nets open, get a map to their banding station from the visitor center or kiosk at the trailhead behind the restrooms near the barn. Take the Seasonal Wetland Trail 0.25 mile to the viewing platforms overlooking the seasonal pond. The pond typically holds water from late April until mid-June, when the frozen ground underneath thaws. Search for Horned and Red-necked Grebes, Blue-winged Teal, common dabbling ducks, Barrow's Goldeneye, Lesser Yellowlegs, Solitary Sandpiper, Bonaparte's Gull, and Rusty Blackbird. As the water recedes, the wetland attracts Alder Flycatcher, Yellow Warbler, Northern Waterthrush, and Lincoln's Sparrow. During fall migration, warblers and sparrows are plentiful here, and their presence often attracts Northern Shrikes and Sharp-shinned Hawks. A Northern Wheatear was spotted in 1998 singing in a willow next to a viewing platform.

Continue west along the trail, being sure to scan the field and its edges for Sharp-tailed Grouse and Savannah Sparrow. Large flocks of American Golden-Plovers and Lapland Longspurs are common in the spring. ABO's banding station is 150 yards beyond the end of the Seasonal Wetland Trail. Banding demonstrations are scheduled throughout the summer—call 451-7159 or check ABO's web site for a current schedule (*www.alaskabird.org*). There is no admission fee, but donations are encouraged. Visiting birders are welcome anytime, although banders may be too busy to chat during larger migration fallouts. Occasionally, an unusual bird shows up at the station, such as Northern Hawk Owl, Yellow-bellied Flycatcher, Arctic Warbler, or Golden-crowned Sparrow. The staff is usually happy to point out identification features of birds in the hand. They can often point you in the direction of other interesting species, such as a Ruffed Grouse on his drumming log, a Hammond's Flycatcher on territory, or nesting redpolls. Look for Great Horned Owls, woodpeckers, *Catharus* thrushes, and Fox Sparrows in the mixed woodland beyond the banding station. If the trail is dry north of the station, Harlan's Hawk, Olive-sided Flycatcher, Gray Jay, Bohemian Waxwing, and other boreal forest birds may be spotted.

Return to the bridge east of the seasonal pond to reach the Boreal Forest Trail. From here the trail makes a one-mile loop through the forest. As you pass through stands of Paper Birch, Quaking Aspen, and White and Black Spruce, watch and listen for Boreal Chickadee, Swainson's Thrush, Blackpoll Warbler, and Northern Waterthrush. A trail guide, available from the visitor center or the trailhead kiosk, describes the birds, mammals, vegetation, and geology found along the route. As you return to the visitor center, take a 0.25-mile side-trip to your left down the Farm Road Trail. A seasonal pond located beyond the first stand of trees is usually worth scanning for shorebirds and waterfowl during May and June. In spring 2002 a female Steller's Eider and a Wilson's Phalarope were discovered here. There is another pond at the end of the Farm Road Trail, but the trail is often impassable due to high water. Return to the Cushman Street bridge for the next birding loop in the Fairbanks area.

Common Redpoll (*left*) and Hoary Redpoll (*right*)

SOUTH FAIRBANKS LOOP

From the Cushman Street bridge, take First Avenue west to Barnette, turn left, and follow Barnette south to Airport Way. Go left (east) on Airport Way and then right (south) on Cushman Street. Follow Cushman south to Van Horn Road. Go left (east) on Van Horn Road to its intersection with Easy Street. Follow Easy Street south and then west to the gated entrance to the Borough Landfill (Monday–Friday 8–5, Saturday 9–5, Sunday 12–5). Ask permission at the scales to bird the landfill. Follow the staff's directions and stay out of the way of heavy equipment. In addition to hundreds of Common Ravens, watch for Bonaparte's, Mew, and Herring Gulls. Less commonly, Glaucous Gull and, rarely, Glaucous-winged Gull are seen. European Starlings—hardly special for most birders but rare in interior Alaska—were seen here in the 1980s but not in recent years.

Retrace your route to the intersection of South Cushman and Van Horn Road. Turn left on South Cushman and follow it south past the end of the pavement to the first of a series of gravel pits on the right side. The **South Cushman Ponds** are especially productive during spring migration. *Caution*: this is not the prettiest place in Alaska, and your birding experience may involve sharing the area with speeding gravel trucks, mud-boggers, target shooters, beer-drinking teenagers, and other exotics. Exercise common sense. The noise and traffic will be lowest early on weekday mornings. There are several steep access points from the built-up road down to the mudflats, many of which were blocked off in 2002. The areas can be muddy, and getting back out can be difficult. At a minimum, be in a 4x4 vehicle with high clearance if you try this. It is better to park your car and walk down to the flats.

Among the waterfowl, the common and numerous species during spring are Horned and Red-necked Grebes, Canada Goose, American Wigeon, Mallard, Northern Shoveler, Northern Pintail, Green-winged Teal, Canvasback, Ring-necked Duck, Greater and Lesser Scaup (Lesser predominating), Bufflehead, and Common Goldeneye. Regular but less-numerous species include Red-throated, Pacific, and Common Loons, Greater White-fronted Goose, Trumpeter and Tundra Swans (few individuals but conspicuous when present), Redhead, Surf and White-winged Scoters, Long-tailed Duck, Barrow's Goldeneye, and Common and Red-breasted Mergansers. Rare but regular are Blue-winged Teal, Gadwall, and Eurasian Wigeon. Snow Goose and Black Brant have also been seen here rarely.

After the end of May, waterfowl diversity drops, but there are a fair number of breeding waterfowl species, including the grebes, Canada Goose, American Wigeon, Mallard, Northern Shoveler, Northern Pintail,

Green-winged Teal, Canvasback, Ring-necked Duck, Greater and Lesser Scaup, Bufflehead, and Common Goldeneye.

The most abundant migrant shorebirds are Semipalmated and Pectoral Sandpipers, and Long-billed Dowitchers. Also common, but in lesser numbers, are American Golden-Plover, Hudsonian Godwit, Least and Baird's Sandpipers, and Red-necked Phalarope. You may get lucky and see a Black-bellied Plover in breeding plumage. Uncommon but regularly occurring species are Western and Stilt Sandpipers. There is a long list of rare species (but of regular, maybe annual, occurrence)—Upland Sandpiper, Whimbrel, Ruddy Turnstone, Sanderling, Dunlin, and Buff-breasted Sandpiper. Still rarer are Greater Yellowlegs, Sharp-tailed Sandpiper (one September record), Short-billed Dowitcher, and Wilson's Phalarope. The habitat is not optimal for Upland and Buff-breasted Sandpipers or Whimbrel—there are better areas in Fairbanks to see them. For the other rare species, however, South Cushman is *the* best spot in Fairbanks to locate them. You can also find Bonaparte's, Mew, and Herring Gulls, and Arctic Tern most of the spring and summer. Sabine's Gull was recorded on two occasions.

The swallow flocks often include all locally breeding species: Tree, Violet-green, Bank, Cliff, and occasionally Barn. Bank Swallows have bred in cut-banks in the area. The flats are a good place to see American Pipit, Lapland Longspur, and, occasionally, Horned Lark. Keep an eye out for raptors—scan the big cottonwoods and the sky for eagles. Northern Harrier, Sharp-shinned Hawk, Northern Goshawk, American Kestrel, Merlin, and Peregrine Falcon are all possible.

Continue south along South Cushman, turning right at the T-intersection and continuing west along the south side of the ponds. You can access the southerly margin of the ponds on foot at several points. The road will swing north again after about one-half mile. Near the turn, you can park and walk to the banks of the Tanana River along the road to your left. Do not block the gate. Take care along the banks of the river; it is deep, swift, full of glacial silt, and very cold. See Cautions in the *Introduction*, page 19. Nesting gulls are often on the gravel bars across the northernmost channel.

Continue north on the main dirt road. On your right, there are several places where you can get to the west side of the South Cushman Ponds, including the area beyond the motor-cross track. To the left is a dike running southwest toward the Tanana River. While it is possible to drive along the dike if the gate is open, it is safer and easier to walk it. On your right, watch for scoters, plovers, sandpipers, and phalaropes; on the left you may see geese, ducks, and cranes along the river banks. A Bald Eagle is possible in the trees across the river.

Backtrack to the intersection of South Cushman Street and Van Horn Road. Turn left and drive west along Van Horn Road about 1.5 miles to Van Horn Road North on the right. Turn right and follow this road to the intersection with Standard Avenue. On the left side is Peger Lake, another gravel pit. This large, deep gravel pit has the usual puddle ducks in the spring, but can also have Common Loon, and Surf, White-winged, and Black Scoters. Be careful not to trespass on developed lots.

Continue along Standard Avenue west to Peger Road. Turn left onto Peger Road and go south back to Van Horn Road. At the intersection turn right and continue west along Van Horn Road. During spring migration you may find shorebirds in the puddles and slough channels along the road past the end of the pavement. Van Horn Road ends at the junction with University Avenue South, which parallels the south side of Fairbanks International Airport. Obey all signs, and, in particular, do not enter the perimeter fence of the runways themselves. Turn left onto University Avenue South and follow it southwest. You will pass a series of sloughs and ponds that host waterfowl as well as Lesser Yellowlegs and Long-billed Dowitcher. Northern Harrier, American Kestrel, and American Golden-Plover may be present in the fields visible from the road. After the road crosses the railroad tracks, a number of side roads lead to more gravel pits, the river dike, and the Tanana River. If you have time, these are worth exploring.

As the road loops around the southwest end of the runways, the road changes to Airport Industrial Road and swings northeast, back onto pavement. Drive directly past the front of the passenger terminal and park in the gravel lot to the right, across from Evert's Air Fuel. The Airport Ponds, gravel pits on both sides of the airport exit road, are remarkably productive and are usually worth a careful look. All of the common migrants, particularly shorebirds, occur here. This seems to be the best local habitat for Stilt Sandpiper. It is also an excellent place to see Bonaparte's Gull and Arctic Tern up close, and a few pairs of Red-necked Grebes usually nest here. One or two male Ruddy Ducks are usually seen each spring. Be sure to scan flocks of wigeons with care, as there is occasionally a Eurasian Wigeon among them. In 1996 and 1997, Least Flycatchers nested in the aspens north of the west pond. Take Airport Road to Cushman Street and back to the bridge for the West Fairbanks Loop.

Red-necked Grebe

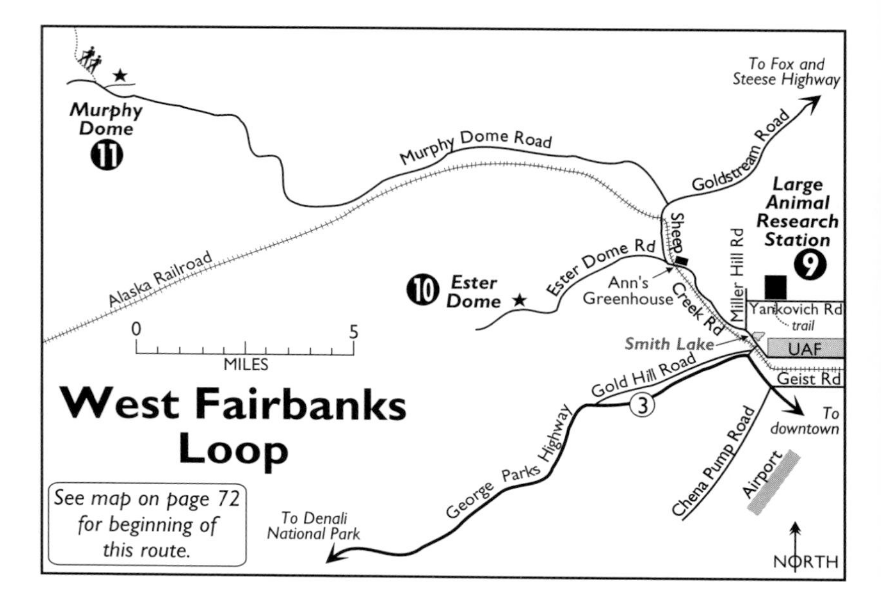

WEST FAIRBANKS LOOP

From the Cushman Street bridge in downtown Fairbanks, take First Avenue along the Chena River to Moore Street at Growden Park. The Chena can have a variety of ducks and shorebirds. Belted Kingfishers nest behind the Carlson Center in some years. In 1999, Great Horned Owls nested across the footbridge just west and downstream from Moore Street.

Turn left (south) on Moore Street to the intersection with Airport Way. Follow Airport Way to the interchange with the Parks Highway and take the right (northbound) exit. After the Geist Road interchange, watch the fields on the right. During spring and fall migration there may be many of the same birds as those seen at Creamer's Field. Northern Hawk Owls and Short-eared Owls are fairly common in this area. Follow the Parks Highway 1.3 miles to its intersection with Sheep Creek Road on the right.

University of Alaska Fairbanks Loop—Follow Sheep Creek Road across the Alaska Railroad tracks to the intersection with Noatak Drive and turn right. Watch the fields on your right for geese, cranes, and owls. On the left, you will pass the Georgeson Botanical Garden. Noatak ends at Tanana Loop. Turn left, uphill, and follow Tanana Loop to the top of the ridge. Park at the overlook on the left side of the road, across from the intersection with Yukon Drive, or along North or South Koyukuk Drives, across the street from the Geophysical Institute. Just behind the cross-country-skiing warm-up shack at Tanana Loop and North Koyukuk, you will find a ski trail leading west along the ridge away from the buildings. The trails are part of the Skarland Ski Trail system; you must use skis when the trails still have snow on them. During spring and summer, this area is very good for Boreal Chickadee, Varied Thrush, Townsend's Warbler, White-winged Crossbill, and other forest birds. Follow the trail west about one-quarter mile to a developed trail that goes downhill to your right. Take the first left into a large field. Follow the margin of the field in either direction to the opposite corner. A short trail from that corner will take you to the northeast side of Smith Lake.

Smith Lake is a shallow, marshy lake, and in both migration and breeding season it supports a wide variety of birds. The most common are Pacific and Common Loons, Horned and Red-necked Grebes, Canada Goose, Mallard, Blue-winged Teal, Northern Shoveler, Northern Pintail, Green-winged Teal, Canvasback, Ring-necked Duck, Greater and Lesser Scaup, Long-tailed Duck, and Bufflehead. Shorebirds include Semipalmated Plover, Lesser Yellowlegs, Pectoral Sandpiper, Long-billed Dowitcher, and Red-necked Phalarope. You may find Bonaparte's, Mew, and Herring Gulls and Arctic Tern. Passerines include Tree Swallow, Black-capped and Boreal Chickadees, Ruby-crowned Kinglet, Swainson's and Varied Thrushes, Lincoln's Sparrow, and Red-winged and Rusty Blackbirds. A Eurasian Wigeon was here in spring 2001.

Return to the parking lot, cross North Koyukuk, and walk the borders of the parking lot behind the Geophysical Institute. This area is one of the more reliable places for White-winged Crossbills. The chokecherry bushes in the islands of the parking lots between North and South Koyukuk Streets are a good location for Bohemian Waxwings when the fruit is ripe. Double back, by car, to the intersection of Sheep Creek Road and Tanana Loop.

Sheep Creek Road and the Large Animal Research Station (LARS). North of Sheep Creek Road a short, sometimes swampy trail leads to the southern margin of Smith Lake. Park at the junction of Sheep Creek and Noatak Drive and walk along the road about 200 yards to a large culvert and the beginning of the trail. This is a shorter route to view the lake, but it is sometimes very wet. See above for a description of possible species. Continue along Sheep Creek Road about one-quarter mile to its intersection with Miller Hill Road. Turn right and drive to the top of the ridge; turn right again onto Yankovich Road. About 0.2 mile east along Yankovich Road is a parking lot on the left for the University of Alaska Large Animal Research Station (LARS). Sandhill Cranes are common in these fields; Northern Harriers are sometimes seen. Reindeer and Muskoxen are usually visible in the fields north of the road.

Across the road is a trail into the University of Alaska Arboretum. This mature spruce-and-birch forest supports a wide variety of forest birds. Hammond's Flycatcher, Black-capped and Boreal Chickadees, Swainson's and Varied Thrushes, Bohemian Waxwing, Townsend's Warbler, and

White-winged Crossbill are fairly reliable. In most years, there is an active Northern Goshawk nest in the area.

Double back to Sheep Creek Road and continue west (right) along it. As the road rises and makes a curve to the left toward the Alaska Railroad tracks you will see a partially cleared area to the right, a good spot for Northern Hawk Owl. Across the railroad tracks and past Ann's Greenhouse is a junction on the left for Ester Dome Road. This is a moderately long, steep climb on a gravel road to one of the two highest hills (2,364 feet) around Fairbanks, with the dome just above tree line. Birding **Ester Dome** can be iffy. In the early morning and late evening twilight, grouse and ptarmigan might be common and, in migration, large flocks of migrating birds can move through. Drive all the way to the top, past the small forest of radio antennas, to the end of the road. A trail runs along the ridge top for about 2.5 miles (part of the Equinox Marathon Trail). This is one of the better spots to find Willow Ptarmigan and Ruffed Grouse.

Return to Sheep Creek Road and follow it northwest to **Murphy Dome** Road; turn left to go west about 25 miles to Murphy Dome, the highest point in the Fairbanks area. Murphy Dome at about 3,000 feet elevation is above the tree line and sometimes has alpine species that otherwise cannot be found closer than Twelvemile Summit on the Steese Highway, more than 85 miles northeast of Fairbanks (see page 85). About half of the road is gravel, normally in good condition. Birding on Murphy Dome is generally not as good as on Twelvemile or Eagle Summits, so go to Murphy Dome only if time or budget won't let you bird the Steese Highway. Murphy Dome is a U.S. Air Force facility; observe and obey signs. A four-wheeler trail runs west and gradually downhill from the end of the road. Listen and look for Willow and Rock Ptarmigan, Northern Wheatear, American Pipit, and Lapland Longspur.

LOGISTICS

The area code for all telephone numbers is 907 unless otherwise indicated. Tourist and travel services (accommodations, restaurants, attractions, etc.) not listed below can be found in the latest edition of The Milepost. *Statewide travel and birding information services are listed under Logistics in the* Introduction, *page 15.*

Fairbanks offers all of the traditional visitor amenities. Hotel rooms can be challenging to obtain during peak tourist season (Memorial Day through Labor Day), although bed-and-breakfasts will generally have some space. As with all of Alaska, it is necessary to make reservations for accommodations well in advance of your trip, especially during the peak season. There are many restaurants, gas stations, stores of all types, car rental agencies, and all the amenities of a large city.

Tours and attractions: You will enjoy an informative visit to the University of Alaska Museum on the West Ridge Campus of the University of Alaska Fairbanks. The museum is located at 907 Yukon Drive and there is an adjacent parking lot. For current hours, featured exhibits, and programs, call the museum at 474-7505; *www.uaf.edu/museum*. The ornithology collections are managed by Daniel D. Gibson.

Chena and Tanana River – For decades the Binkley family has operated a tour business that takes visitors down the clear-water Chena River onto the silt-laden Tanana River in paddlewheel-driven, flat-bottomed boats. Some boats hold several hundred people. The well-narrated tours take you to a Athabascan Indian camp on the Tanana where you are shown how Native people lived many years ago. This is not a birding trip, but you might see a few birds along the river anyway.

Fairbanks features the annual Tanana Valley Sandhill Crane Festival each August. This event celebrates the spectacular staging of Sandhill Crane in fall at Creamer's Field Migratory Waterfowl Refuge. Thousands of cranes feed and assemble before their long flight south. Activities include crane walks, children's activities, and workshops on photography, art, and bird identification.

Other useful local contacts:

Alaska Bird Observatory, *www.alaskabird.org* (Birding reports between April and September); 451-7159.

Alaska Department of Fish and Game, Creamer's Field, *http://www.state.ak.us/local/akpages/FISH.GAME/wildlife/region3/refuge3/creamers.htm*

Arctic Audubon Society — Birding hotline 451-9213; offers some local birding field trips and events; *www.arcticaudubon.org*.

Fairbanks Information — *www.alaskaone.com/fairbanks*.

Friends of Creamer's Field, 452-5162; Creamer's Field Visitor Center, 459-7307; *www.creamersfield.org*.

ACKNOWLEDGEMENTS:
Additional information and review of the chapter was provided by Philip Martin, Andrea Swingley, Mark Ross, Ken Russell, and John Wright. Richard Konz drove the routes to verify locations and accuracy of directions.

Red Squirrel

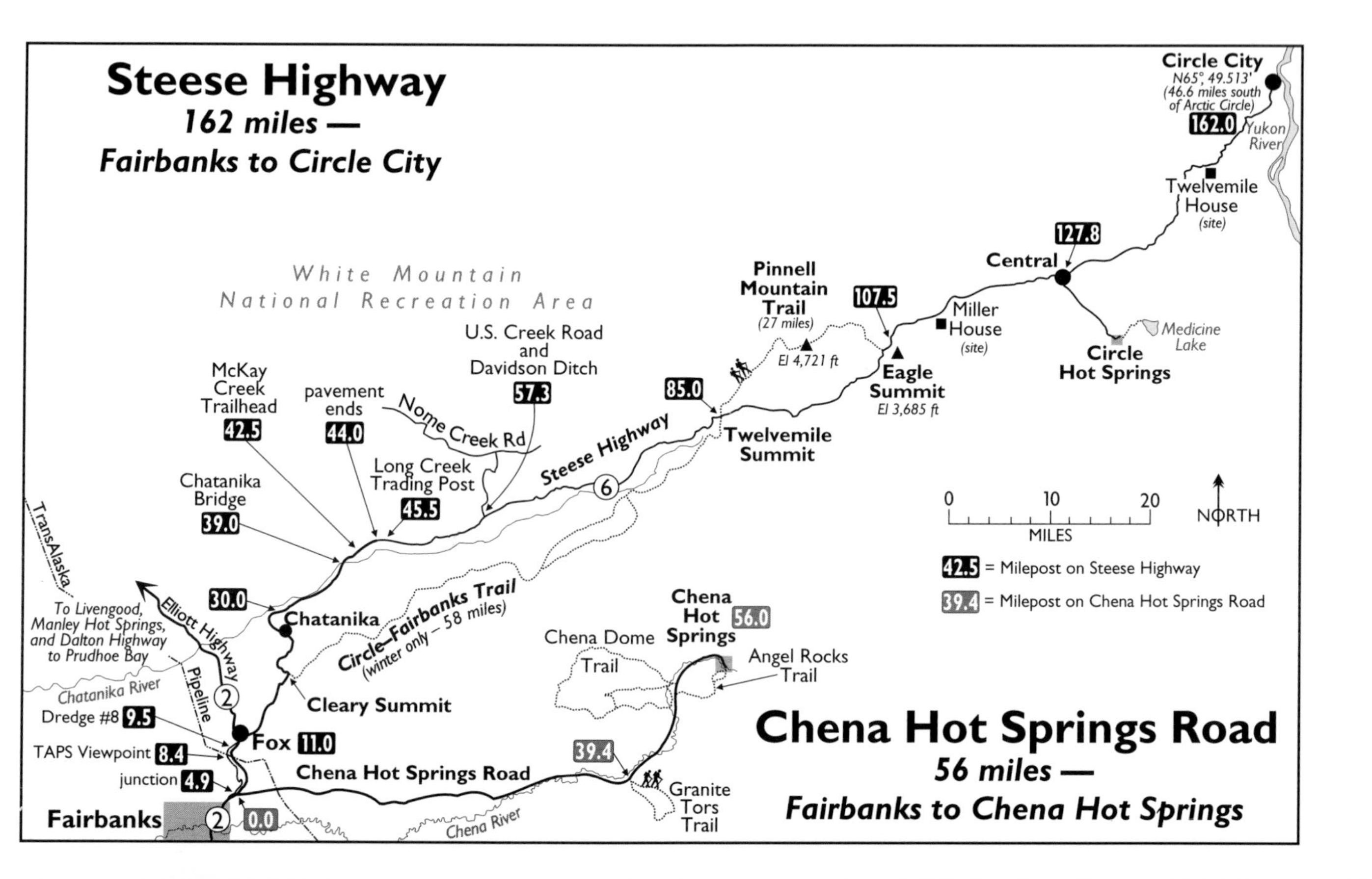
Steese Highway
162 miles —
Fairbanks to Circle City
White Mountain
National Recreation Area
Circle City
N65°, 49.513'
(46.6 miles south of Arctic Circle)
162.0
Yukon River
Twelvemile House
(site)
127.8
Central
Circle Hot Springs
Medicine Lake
Miller House
(site)
107.5
Eagle Summit
El 3,685 ft
Pinnell Mountain Trail
(27 miles)
El 4,721 ft
85.0
Twelvemile Summit
Steese Highway
6
U.S. Creek Road and Davidson Ditch
57.3
Nome Creek Rd
Long Creek Trading Post
45.5
pavement ends
44.0
McKay Creek Trailhead
42.5
Chatanika Bridge
39.0
30.0
Chatanika
Circle–Fairbanks Trail
(winter only – 58 miles)
Cleary Summit
TransAlaska
To Livengood, Manley Hot Springs, and Dalton Highway to Prudhoe Bay
Elliott Highway
2
Chatanika River
Pipeline
Dredge #8 9.5
TAPS Viewpoint 8.4
junction 4.9
Fox 11.0
Fairbanks
0.0
Chena Hot Springs Road
Chena River
39.4
Granite Tors Trail
Chena Dome Trail
Chena Hot Springs 56.0
Angel Rocks Trail
0 10 20
MILES
NORTH
42.5 = Milepost on Steese Highway
39.4 = Milepost on Chena Hot Springs Road
Chena Hot Springs Road
56 miles —
Fairbanks to Chena Hot Springs

STEESE HIGHWAY

George West

The Steese Highway (Alaska Routes 2 and 6) travels for 162 miles northeast from Fairbanks to Circle, a small Native community on the Yukon River. Although most of the highway passes through a combination of Quaking Aspen, Balsam Poplar, and Black and White Spruce forests, it also crosses two high passes that give easy access to alpine tundra. Since you can drive up to alpine tundra habitat here, this is a convenient place to look for species such as nesting Surfbird and Northern Wheatear. Unfortunately, some of the more sought-after mountain species found in Denali National Park, such as White-tailed Ptarmigan and Gray-crowned Rosy-Finch, do not occur here.

The Steese Highway leaves Fairbanks on its northeastern edge and takes you toward the town of Fox. Chena Hot Springs Road (see page 87) exits to the right at Milepost 4.9. There is easy access to an above-ground section of the TransAlaska Pipeline on the right side of the road at Milepost 8.4. At Milepost 9.5 you can exit to see one of the gold dredges (Dredge #8) that was used to excavate the stream courses for gold from 1927 to 1959. The small community of Fox is at Milepost 11, where Route 2 continues as the Elliott Highway (Livengood Road), leading to Manley (page 89) and the Dalton Highway to Prudhoe Bay (page 91). Take Route 6 to the right toward Central and Circle. At Milepost 16.5 pause at the Felix Pedro monument commemorating the first prospector to find gold in the area. This find in 1902 led to the founding of Fairbanks. The road climbs over Cleary Summit, site of two ski areas. Access to the historic Circle-Fairbanks Trail to the northeast (usable in winter only) can be reached about four miles past the summit. The snowmachine trail stretches 58 miles to Twelvemile Summit.

From Cleary Summit, the road descends into the Chatanika River valley. Chatanika Gold Camp is at Milepost 27.9. Another gold dredge (Dredge #3) is at Milepost 28.6, and the Chatanika Lodge is a colorful place to get a good meal. The University of Alaska operates the Poker Flat Research Range rocket launch facility at Milepost 29.5, designed primarily to study the northern lights (aurora borealis). There is no public access except on tours. Contact the Geophysical Institute at the University at 474-7558 for information. Numerous ponds along the way invite fishermen.

At Milepost 39 is a bridge and access to the Chatanika River at the Upper Chatanika River State Recreation Area. Here you may picnic, camp, fish for

Arctic Grayling, canoe 20 miles over to the Elliott Highway, or look for birds along the trails on the river bank. The Steese Highway passes mostly through Balsam Poplar and White Spruce forest, with some areas of permafrost-underlain Black Spruce stands. This mixed forest is not great birding habitat, but does hold species like Ruffed Grouse, Western Wood-Pewee, and Alder and Hammond's Flycatchers. You should also watch for Northern Hawk Owls that often perch on the tops of spruce trees. North of the Chatanika River crossing, start looking for Say's Phoebes that breed on some of the bridge structures where the highway crosses creeks. The McKay Creek Trailhead at Milepost 42.5 leads to over 200 miles of winter trails into the one-million-acre White Mountains National Recreation Area.

The pavement ends at Milepost 44. Groceries are available at Long Creek Trading Post at Milepost 45.4. At Milepost 57.3 you can see part of the historic Davidson Ditch, a 90-mile-long waterway built in 1929 that transported water from the Chatanika River to Fairbanks. Note the siphons that carried the water down into valleys and up again on the other side to the water-powered gold mining and processing operations in Fairbanks. U.S. Creek Road also turns off at Milepost 57.3 and runs seven miles to White Mountains National Recreation Area. You can camp here, pan for gold, or hike one of the trails into the boreal forest. Although we hesitate to mention it, there is an undocumented sighting of a Gray-headed Chickadee at the U.S. Creek campground, and a single bird was collected in 1980 near Sourdough Camp where McManus Creek empties into the Chatanika River. This is at about Milepost 70.

At Milepost 85 you come to **Twelvemile Summit** where the road climbs up into open tundra. From the parking lot on the right, walk part way up the 27-mile Pinnell Mountain National Recreation Trail to explore the high alpine ridges. It can be windy and cold here, so be prepared. About 20 minutes up the trail a rocky outcrop lies a few hundred yards off to the left. This outcrop lies directly above the parking lot and is easily visible from there. Check it carefully for Northern Wheatear, especially the scree slopes at its base. From here, hike the surrounding ridges. You should be prepared to spend at least several hours hiking, as bird life is sparse at this elevation. American Pipits and Horned Larks are common. In addition to Northern Wheatear, species of interest include Rock Ptarmigan, American Golden-Plover, Surfbird, Long-tailed Jaeger, and Lapland Longspur. Willow Ptarmigan, American Tree Sparrow, and Golden-crowned and Gambel's White-crowned Sparrows can be found slightly lower down; Golden Eagle and Merlin also occur here.

Eagle Summit (peak at Milepost 107.5, elevation 3,685 feet) is the best place for summer wildflowers, with many places to wander the alpine tundra. It should be easier to find Northern Wheatear here and, if you are lucky, nesting Surfbird. There is also the possibility of a Gyrfalcon. Rock Ptarmigan, American Pipit, Wilson's Warbler, American Tree Sparrow, Gambel's White-crowned and Golden-crowned Sparrows, and Lapland Longspur all nest in the brush on the slopes of these hills. If you happen to be on top of Eagle Summit on the summer solstice, you might witness the real midnight sun without crossing the Arctic Circle. Because of its elevation, Eagle Summit provides the only easily road accessible location to see the "sun that never sets" in the Alaskan summer. Otherwise you will have to drive the Dalton Highway or fly north of the Arctic Circle.

If you decide to go all the way to Eagle Summit, it is probably not worth spending time at Twelvemile Summit. You can continue on another 60 miles to Central, Circle Hot Springs, and Circle, but the birding there is no different than in other lower elevations in the Interior. Circle, on the banks of the Yukon River, is actually 46.6 miles below the Arctic Circle.

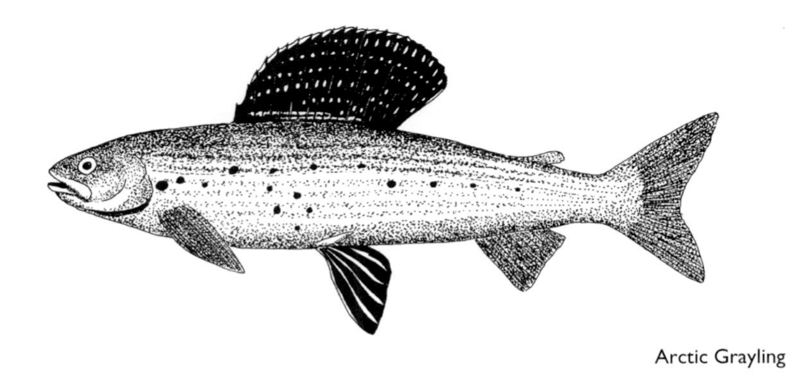

Arctic Grayling

CHENA HOT SPRINGS ROAD

George West and Nancy DeWitt

The Chena Hot Springs Road is a popular recreational road east of Fairbanks that follows the Chena River upstream to a private hot springs. Fishing, boating, and weekend camping are common all along the road. The road exits on the right side of the Steese Highway at Milepost 4.9 and leads 56 miles east to Chena Hot Springs near the upper Chena River. The Chena River State Recreation Area runs from Milepost 26.1 to Milepost 51 of this road. You are almost guaranteed to see Moose feeding on aquatic vegetation in the sloughs and oxbows of the Chena River during summer evenings. Along the way are many places to access the Chena River to fish for Arctic Grayling and look for birds. Any of the various campgrounds and trails are good bets for Boreal Chickadee, Townsend's Warbler, Common Redpoll, and White-winged Crossbill. Three-toed Woodpeckers are fairly common, and the area that burned in 2000 along the first few miles of the left fork of the Granite Tors Trail (Milepost 39.4) should have several woodpecker species feeding and nesting there. A large wildfire in 2002 enlarged the burned acreage, creating more woodpecker habitat.

Nest boxes can be seen along many of the roadside sloughs—they were erected for a study on goldeneyes, but several may be occupied by other ducks, American Kestrels, or Boreal Owls in spring. The boxes are closely monitored throughout the summer by the U.S. Fish and Wildlife Service and the Institute of Arctic Biology, University of Alaska Fairbanks. During June, Alder Flycatchers and Northern Waterthrushes sing in the wetter areas. Great Horned Owls are very common in the state recreation area. Great Gray Owls are occasionally seen or heard calling. Scan the Chena River for Harlequin Duck and American Dipper. Information for the three main hiking trails in the Recreation Area is available at each trailhead; hikers should expect to encounter steep terrain and mosquitoes. At the end of the Chena Hot Springs Road is a privately operated hot springs swimming pool facility and resort.

LOGISTICS

The area code for all telephone numbers is 907 unless otherwise indicated. Tourist and travel services (accommodations, restaurants, attractions, etc.) not listed below can be found in the latest edition of The Milepost. *Statewide travel and birding information services are listed under Logistics in the* Introduction, *page 15.*

Make sure you rent a car that is allowed to travel on gravel roads. Be sure the gas tank is full before you start out. It would be wise to carry sufficient food and water for a day's trip. Limited gas, food, and motel accommodations are available at Central (Milepost 127.8) and Circle (Milepost 162) if you decide to travel that far. Gas may be available at Chatanika and farther along the road, but don't count on it. Grocery stores may also be open along the road, but again, it is best to carry some food with you. You can take the side road to Circle Hot Springs that leaves the Steese at Milepost 127.8. This 8.3-mile gravel road leads to the Circle Hot Springs Resort where you can stay overnight, swim in the hot springs swimming pool, and get a hearty meal.

Circle Hot Springs Resort, 520-5113.

Chena Hot Springs Resort, *www.chenahotsprings.com*; 800-478-4681 or 451-8104.

ACKNOWLEDGEMENTS: Nancy DeWitt and Andrea Swingley provided many details and updated birding information. Some birding information is from Lethaby (1994).

ELLIOTT HIGHWAY

George West

Most people drive only the first part of the Elliott Highway (Alaska Route 2) to reach the Dalton Highway that leads north to Deadhorse and Prudhoe Bay (page 91). However, you may choose a shorter trip through the interior forests to a small village on the banks of Hot Springs Slough that feeds into the Tanana River downstream from Fairbanks. Birding along the Elliott Highway is little different from the back roads around Fairbanks or the Parks Highway between Fairbanks and Nenana. You will be able to find most of the regularly occurring passerines in the spruce, aspen, and cottonwoods along the road. At Manley Hot Springs you can bathe in the private hot springs and stay to dine in one of the oldest roadhouses in Alaska.

To reach the Elliott Highway, take the Steese Expressway (Alaska Route 2) out of Fairbanks (page 85) and drive 11 miles northeast to Fox. Here the road forks, the Steese bearing east and the Elliott continuing straight ahead. Look for an information sign about the Dalton Highway at the intersection. There are restaurants, gas stations, and other amenities in Fox. With your trip-odometer set on 0.0 at the intersection of the Steese and Elliott Highways, continue northwest on the Elliott, enjoying the 28 miles of pavement while it lasts. At Milepost 10.6 is Olnes Pond, where you can scan for grebes, loons, and ducks. At Milepost 11 the road crosses the Chatanika

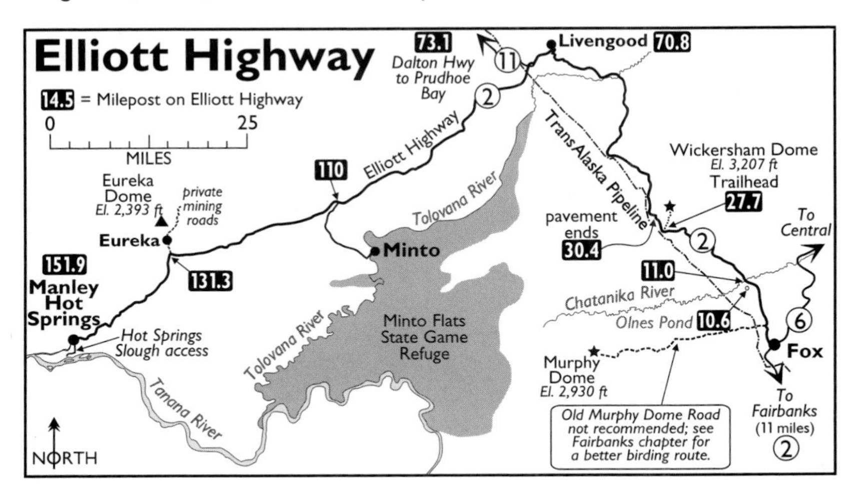

River, with access to the Lower Chatanika River State Recreation Area. You can camp here, fish for Arctic Grayling, or walk the banks of the river to look for warblers, waterthrushes, sparrows, and other birds. There are numerous pullouts along the road where you can safely stop to watch and listen for birds.

Two areas of alpine tundra are reachable from the Elliott Highway—Murphy Dome and Wickersham Dome. The road into Murphy Dome is rough and not recommended. See Fairbanks, page 82, for a better route. Wickersham Dome can be reached by stopping at the parking area at the Wickersham Dome Trailhead, Milepost 27.7. From here you can hike up the dome (elevation 3,207 feet) into the alpine tundra. However, the tundra area here is very limited and you will not find Northern Wheatears as you might at Eagle Summit on the Steese Highway. Wilson's Warbler, American Tree Sparrow, Golden-crowned Sparrow, and other forest-edge birds will be here. Berrypicking is excellent in the late summer and early fall, and Black Bears think so, too. The pavement ends at Milepost 30.4.

The gravel road from Milepost 30 to Milepost 73 winds northwest across hillsides and several streams. Some, such as the Tolovana, are good fly-fishing streams for Arctic Grayling. Since the construction of the Dalton Highway, several roadside businesses have emerged along the Elliott. The old mining town of Livengood is accessible at Milepost 70.8, but the area is all privately owned. At the junction of the Dalton Highway, Milepost 73.1, turn southwest to continue on the Elliott to Manley Hot Springs, 78.9 miles ahead. At Milepost 110 is the turnoff to the Athabascan village of Minto on the Tolovana River. You may drive this 11-mile road to the village where there is a gas station, lodging, and stores where you can purchase Native-crafted gifts. Many rare bird sightings in the Interior have been made at Minto Lakes, but you need a riverboat or floatplane to get to the area.

From the Minto junction, the road continues southwest, bypassing the road to Eureka at Milepost 131.3—this is a private mining area so there is no reason to detour here. Continue to Milepost 151.9 at the village of **Manley Hot Springs**. You may call the owner of the private hot springs baths if you would like to enjoy a mineral bath: 672-3171. You should stop at the Manley Roadhouse (672-3161), one of the oldest original roadhouses remaining from the gold rush era. For birding, you might prefer to continue to Hot Springs Slough on a 2.5-mile gravel road to the banks of the Tanana River. In summer, you can bird along the river bank and watch Native fish wheels in action as they slowly turn with the current of the silt-laden river. Salmon swimming upstream cannot see the wheel ahead and are scooped up in large wood-and-net baskets that also serve as the paddles that turn the fish wheel. The salmon are unceremoniously rotated over the top of the wheel and dumped into a holding tank on the upstream side of the wheel. Check at the roadhouse about chartering an aircraft in Manley for a trip into Minto Lakes.

DALTON HIGHWAY

Will Lentz

No road in Alaska has a more dramatic change along its length than the Dalton Highway. Beginning deep in the taiga some 70 miles north of Fairbanks and ending near the Arctic Ocean on the north coast, it traverses about 400 miles of nearly uninhabited land with unparalleled birding opportunities. The terrain includes boreal forest, alpine tundra, forested and bare-rock canyons, and high-arctic tundra. It crosses the continental divide and one of the largest rivers in North America, the Yukon.

SAFETY ON THE ROAD

The Dalton is gravel for its entire length, and although well maintained by the State of Alaska, it is far different from most North American highways. Its sole purpose is to service the oil industry on the North Slope, so there is a lot of heavy-truck traffic. If you elect to drive the road, be aware that most car-rental companies will not allow their vehicles on this road. If you take a private vehicle, be prepared for common mechanical difficulties such as flat tires, broken fan belt, chipped windshields, and the like. There is quite a bit of information available from the Alaska Public Lands Information Center about the Dalton and we strongly suggest that you do your homework.

If you're not interested in driving the Dalton in your own vehicle, you can sign up with a tour company that specializes in birding the highway. Smaller tour groups allow more flexibility to make frequent birding stops. It can be an added advantage to travel with someone who knows the ecology, landscape, and habits of the birds you seek.

FROM THE ELLIOTT HIGHWAY TO THE YUKON RIVER

The Dalton begins uneventfully as a fork in the Elliott Highway (previous chapter) at Milepost 73.1. Here, already 50 miles from the nearest services, you are deep in the taiga, and the road bobs in and out of a dozen valleys before you get to the Yukon. Watch for Northern Goshawks and Northern Hawk Owls as you drive. The owls are year-round residents and tend to be seen more frequently in the dense, stunted Black Spruce stands found on valley bottoms and on north-facing slopes.

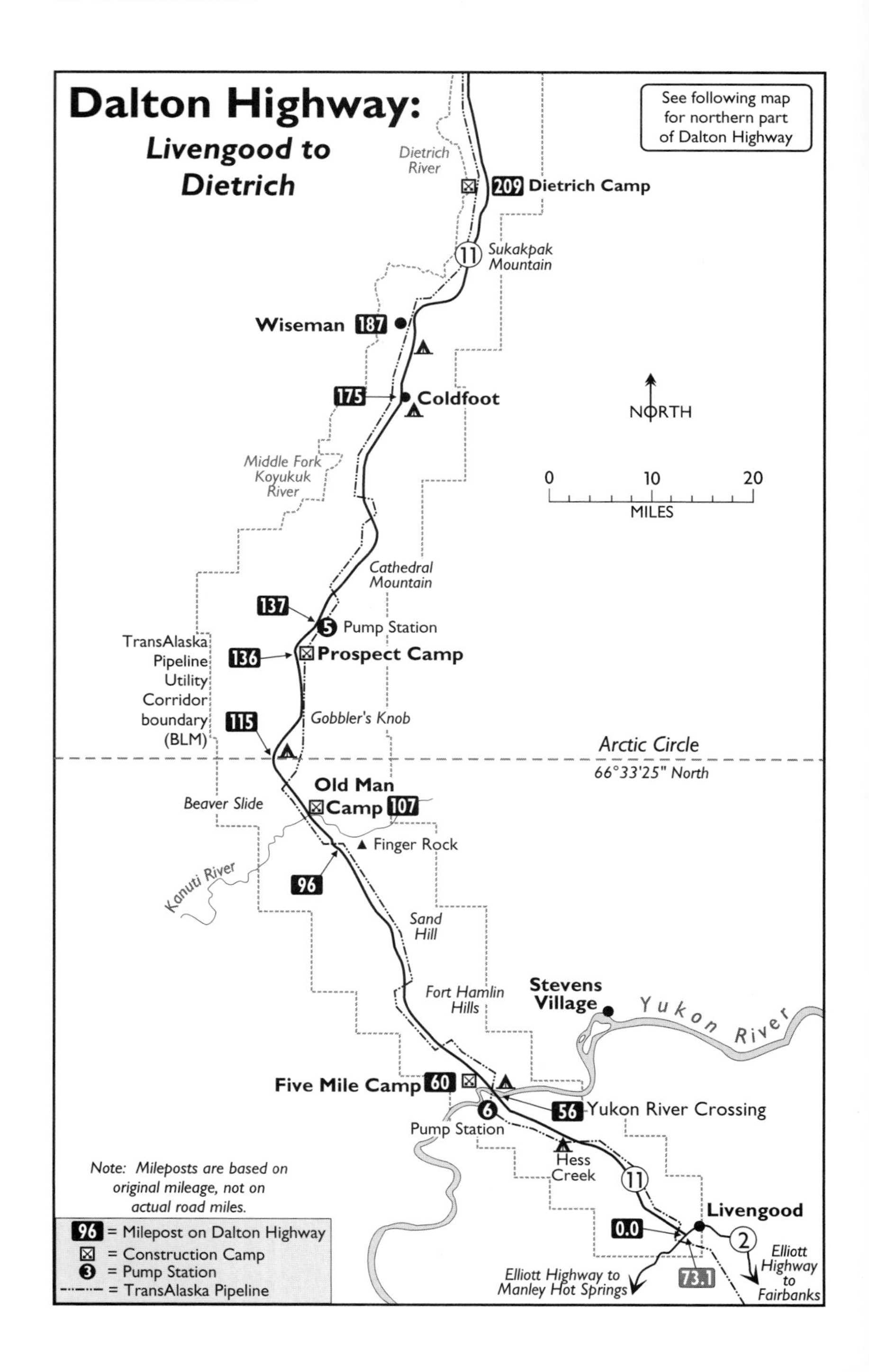

Dalton Highway:
Livengood to Dietrich
See following map for northern part of Dalton Highway
Dietrich River
209 Dietrich Camp
11 Sukakpak Mountain
Wiseman 187
175 Coldfoot
NORTH
0 10 20
MILES
Middle Fork Koyukuk River
Cathedral Mountain
137
5 Pump Station
TransAlaska Pipeline Utility Corridor boundary (BLM)
136 Prospect Camp
115
Gobbler's Knob
Arctic Circle
66°33'25" North
Old Man Camp 107
Beaver Slide
Finger Rock
Kanuti River
96
Sand Hill
Fort Hamlin Hills
Stevens Village
Yukon River
Five Mile Camp 60
56 Yukon River Crossing
6 Pump Station
Hess Creek
11
Livengood
0.0
2
73.1
Elliott Highway to Manley Hot Springs
Elliott Highway to Fairbanks
Note: Mileposts are based on original mileage, not on actual road miles.
96 = Milepost on Dalton Highway
= Construction Camp
3 = Pump Station
= TransAlaska Pipeline

A variety of boreal species can be found if you stop to take a short walk off the road. Most of the land in the utility corridor is state or federally owned. The pipeline right-of-way is leased by the Alyeska Pipeline Service Company that operates the TransAlaska Pipeline System (TAPS). Obey the no-trespassing and safety warnings around the pipeline and its access roads. There are still lots of roadside pulloffs, gravel pits, and fire-service roads that will get you away from the dusty, heavily-traveled main road.

Watch for Gray Jay, Black-capped and Boreal Chickadees, and Pine Grosbeak, as well as Ruffed and Spruce Grouse. Swainson's and Varied Thrushes, Orange-crowned Warbler, and Slate-colored Junco can be found in thickets near road-cuts and disturbed areas. Watch the tops of spruce trees for feeding White-winged Crossbills. Wildfires are a regular occurrence in Interior Alaska—search old burn areas for American Kestrel, Merlin, and Three-toed Woodpecker.

Just before reaching the Yukon River bridge at Milepost 56, you pass Pump Station 6, one of 12 pump stations on the TAPS from Prudhoe Bay to Valdez; you will see five on your way north to Deadhorse. The bridge over the Yukon is 2,000 feet long, inclined at a 5.5° angle, has a wood surface, and is the only permanent bridge across the river in Alaska.

As you descend into the Yukon valley you will notice a dramatic terrain change. Hills north of the river are granite domes, more rolling than the incised metamorphic terrain of the Tanana Uplands south of the river. This portion of the Yukon is known as The Canyon, a stark contrast to the Yukon Flats 30 miles upstream.

On the Yukon River and surrounding ponds, look for American Wigeon, Northern Shoveler, Northern Pintail, Bufflehead, and Common Goldeneye. Watch for Peregrine Falcons on the cliff faces. Inquire whether a boat excursion is available, so you can spend some time on the river.

It is possible to see Bald Eagles as they follow the salmon runs from late June until freeze-up. Mew Gulls and Common Ravens congregate near the river, as well. On the north bank of the Yukon is a small restaurant and service station. The open area of the parking lot on the north shore is frequented by Tree, Violet-green, Bank, and Cliff Swallows.

YUKON RIVER TO COLDFOOT

North of the Yukon the taiga begins to thin and a few Quaking Aspen parklands offer an interesting habitat, though it's not very birdy. If you do wander through these woods, watch for Black Bears.

At Milepost 60, Five Mile Camp, an abandoned construction camp, offers another chance for you to get off the main road into a bit of dense forest.

You gain altitude as you leave the Yukon River, peaking about 40 miles up the road near a granite outcropping called Finger Rock, Milepost 96. A nice pulloff here has an interpretive trail and a sweeping view of the Kanuti Valley. This is the most accessible alpine tundra you will encounter, so take a hike among the tors (granite formations) to enjoy the unique habitat. Watch for Northern Harrier and Whimbrel both here and in the valley below.

Different parts of the road were given colorful names the during construction of the pipeline. Just north of the Kanuti River is Old Man Camp (Milepost 107), a con- struction camp on a knoll of frost-cracked granitic sand. Beyond that a steep hill is known as Beaver Slide. Just before you reach the Arctic Circle (Milepost 115), you are back in the taiga.

Continue past Pump Station 5 in the Jim River Valley (Milepost 137). Shortly past here, the terrain changes slightly as you enter a part of Alaska that was glaciated during the most recent ice age. You are coming into the foothills of the Brooks Range, where you can stop at some of the many kettle lakes to scan for assorted waterfowl, including Horned Grebe.

Coldfoot (Milepost 175) is your next chance for a rest stop with services. Lesser Yellowlegs are often seen at the facilities here. During breeding season there is always a male or two calling from the short trees between the restaurant and the hotel.

Long-tailed Duck, Harlequin Duck, and Steller's Eider males (*top to bottom*)

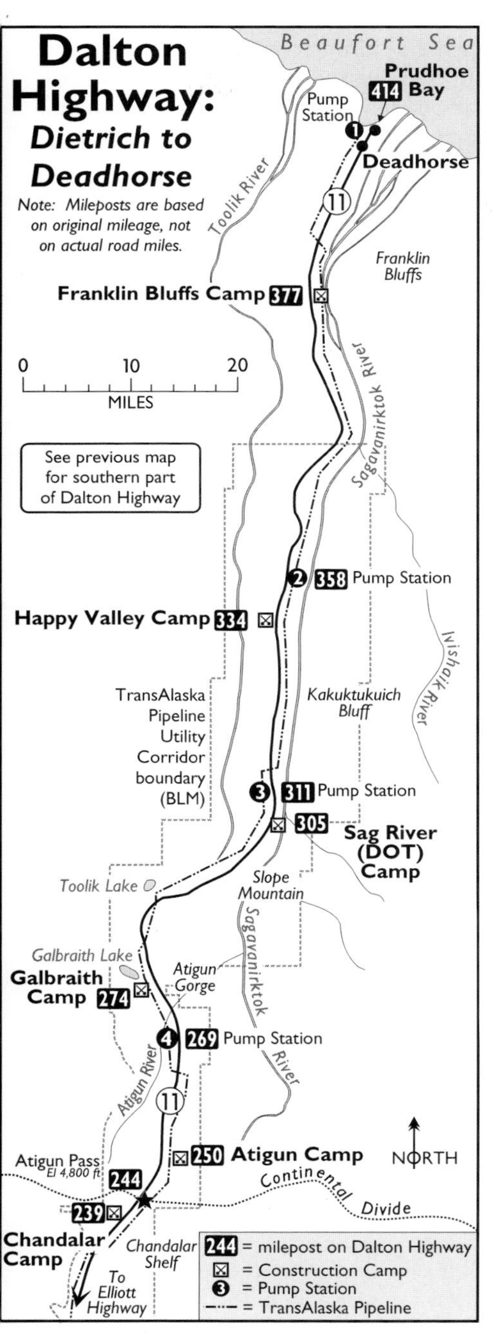

COLDFOOT TO DEADHORSE

North of Coldfoot the foothills begin to close in as you enter the heart of the Brooks Range. Golden Eagles and Peregrine Falcons nest on the cliffs. After a quick photo stop at the farthest north spruce tree, you climb out of the Dietrich Valley onto the Chandalar Shelf. Arctic Warblers can be found in the willow thickets here on the south slope of the Brooks Range. Watch for raptors and Common Ravens. Between here and the other side of Atigun Pass you may spot American Pipit and Hoary Redpoll.

After crossing the continental divide at Atigun Pass (Milepost 244) you will find yourself in a different world. At the bottom of this steep-sided valley watch for Northern Wheatear, Yellow Wagtail, Fox Sparrow, and Gray-crowned Rosy-Finch. Golden Eagle and Gyrfalcon ply the tundra for Arctic Ground Squirrel and lemmings. Brown Bears are common on the North Slope.

Once you leave Atigun Valley keep an eye out for Rough-legged Hawks (dark-phase common) and Gyrfalcons that nest on available cliffs such as Slope Mountain (near Sag River Camp, Milepost 305) and bluffs along the Sagavanirktok River. On dry upland slopes look for Willow Ptarmigan, Yellow Wagtail, Smith's Longspur, and

Gray-crowned Rosy-Finch in rocky areas. Ptarmigan tend to nest on slight elevations on the ground, usually with one side sheltered by sedge or dwarf willows. Since this is also the preferred ground for walking across the tundra, be prepared for a heart-stopping burst of feathers as the female explodes from her nest. Your foot will most likely be inches from where her brown-speckled eggs lie.

As you near the coast, the number and variety of species increase dramatically. This area is known as the North Slope. Once you drop out of the dry uplands, take a look around in thickets of dwarf willow for Bluethroats. Get familiar with their call because you will probably pick that up before you spot these shy, colorful birds. Jaegers, Glaucous Gull, Arctic Tern, and Common Raven often patrol the road and the Sagavanirktok River.

Several shorebird species are found here—American Golden-Plover and Stilt and Buff-breasted Sandpipers. Horned Lark, American Tree and Savannah Sparrows, Lapland and Smith's Longspurs, and Hoary Redpoll are here, too, and you'll have more opportunities for Northern Wheatear.

On this gently sloping plain, permafrost dominates the terrain. The ground is mostly defined in patterns of five- and six-sided polygons formed by ice action below the surface. Many of these disturbances hold water, forming a patchwork of ponds across the landscape. Shallow and relatively productive, this habitat is the magnet that draws birds to the Arctic Coastal Plain.

Plan to spend a good portion of your journey on the North Slope near the coast. Species such as Red-throated, Pacific, and Yellow-billed Loons, Spectacled Eider, and Red Phalarope nest here only near the coast. Tundra Swan, Northern Pintail, Green-winged Teal, Greater Scaup, Long-tailed Duck, Rock Ptarmigan, Long-billed Dowitcher, Wilson's Snipe, and Red-necked Phalarope become common. Greater White-fronted and Canada Geese can be seen easily, but Snow Geese and Black Brant are less likely because there are no staging areas or colonies near the road corridor.

Black-bellied Plovers and a suite of sandpipers—Semipalmated, Western, Baird's, Pectoral, and Buff-breasted—are present, but finding them may take some patience. With good luck you'll locate some of the rarer species, such as Spectacled Eider and Bar-tailed Godwit.

Either in the tundra of Finger Mountain or north of the Brooks Range you may have seen Parasitic or Long-tailed Jaegers, but you will have a far better chance for Pomarine near the coast. You will most certainly find Snow Buntings around the buildings of Deadhorse, where they often nest, as do Glaucous Gulls and Common Ravens.

Deadhorse (Milepost 414) is the last service area on the road, nearly 250 miles from Coldfoot. Accommodations are available in this oilfield service area, but reservations are a must during the tourist season. There is no public road access to the Arctic Ocean at Prudhoe Bay, and in order to get to the coast, you must sign up with a tour group. If you did not make arrangements in advance of your visit, inquire at the hotels about oilfield tours. Getting nearer the coast will increase your likelihood of finding Black Brant, Spectacled, King, and Common Eiders, and Sabine's or Ross's Gulls.

LOGISTICS

The area code for all telephone numbers is 907 unless otherwise indicated. Tourist and travel services (accommodations, restaurants, attractions, etc.) not listed below can be found in the latest edition of The Milepost. *Statewide travel and birding information services are listed under Logistics in the* Introduction, *page 15.*

There are no services between Fairbanks, Fox, and the Yukon River crossing. The only services along the Dalton Highway are at Yukon Crossing (Milepost 56; not in winter), Sixty-mile (Milepost 143; not in winter), Coldfoot (Milepost 175; limited services in winter), Wiseman (Milepost 187; limited services in winter), and Deadhorse (Milepost 414). Make sure your vehicle is in top shape. Carry two full-size spare tires on rims, a jack and other tools to aid in changing tires, spare fan belt, emergency flares, extra gas, oil, and windshield wiper fluid, and a CB radio to monitor channel 19.

Accommodations in Deadhorse include the Arctic Caribou Inn (659-2368 summer, 659-2449 winter) and the Arctic Oilfield Hotel (659-2614). Several of the many Deadhorse-based tour companies that will take you around the oil field and to the coast are advertised in *The Milepost*; you can get information about those currently operating from the Alaska Public Lands Information Center (APLIC) in Fairbanks (456-0527). There are scattered accommodations along the road. To find out which are open when you want to travel the Dalton, check the latest edition of *The Milepost* or call APLIC. You can get information and a brochure about the highway from any visitor center, BLM, or Public Lands office in the state. For current road conditions call Alaska Department of Transportation (456-7623) or check with APLIC.

There are no emergency medical services along the road. There are no banks or ATM machines. Most services accept major credit cards. Snacks are available at most service centers, but there are no full-service grocery stores. Cell phone service is not reliable beyond 35 miles north of Fairbanks until you reach Deadhorse. Bring insect repellent, rain gear, a first-aid kit, drinking water, warm clothes (even in summer), knee-high rubber boots, ready-to-eat food, camping gear, and a sleeping bag.

ACKNOWLEDGEMENTS: Dan Wetzel provided updates and added birding locations.

ARCTIC NATIONAL WILDLIFE REFUGE

Bob Dittrick

Birding the Arctic National Wildlife Refuge (ANWR) is a wilderness experience. The refuge, located in the extreme northeastern corner of Alaska, is accessible only by airplane, takes multiple days to visit, and requires the birder to be prepared with proper equipment and knowledge. This is Brown Bear country. Guided trips are recommended as the best way to bird this area.

Spectacular ANWR is notable for its nesting species, especially Gray-headed Chickadee, perhaps the least-seen nesting species in North America. Other nesting birds of interest include Red-throated and Yellow-billed Loons, Gyrfalcon, Peregrine Falcon, Surfbird, Pomarine, Parasitic, and Long tailed Jaegers, Snowy Owl, Arctic Warbler, Bluethroat, Northern Wheatear, Yellow Wagtail, and Smith's Longspur, as well as a variety of waterfowl and shorebirds, including Stilt and Buff-breasted Sandpipers.

Because of its wilderness nature, a visit to the refuge typically requires a 5-to-12-day backpack or river float. The Brooks Range's magnificent mountains bisect the refuge. Float trips normally start in the high-alpine tundra of the mountains, then traverse either down the south slope of the mountains into the boreal forest, or down the North Slope onto the vast coastal plain, then across a sea of arctic tundra to the Arctic Ocean. Backpack trips are limited only by the locations of airplane landing strips.

Gray-headed Chickadee (*top*) and Boreal Chickadee (*bottom*)

Typical Alaska boreal forest characterizes most of the habitat on the south side of the Brooks Range. This permafrost habitat has many ponds and lakes that are home to large numbers of waterfowl. Though birders seldom see Gray-headed Chickadees on the south side of the Brooks Range, this is their known habitat.

The high-arctic tundra is the dominant habitat of the treeless north side of the Brooks Range. Here, too, are multitudes of ponds and lakes. The rivers are braided remnants of past glacial periods that provide large gravel bars for nesting and staging shorebirds.

Generally, birding the refuge is best done between mid-June and mid-August; however, large concentrations of Snow Geese stage in the northeast portion of the refuge in September. September is, in essence, the beginning of winter. The birding season is short here. Beware that the world-class mosquito hatch is in July.

Gray-headed Chickadees have been seen in several locations on the north side of the Brooks Range, even though the north side is considered marginally in this species' range. The first nest was discovered in 1997; repeat visits since then have turned up other nesting activity. Due to the sensitive nature of this wilderness and potential problems of the cumulative effects associated with birders visiting a nest site, only a limited number of people are guided here each year.

LOGISTICS

The area code for all telephone numbers is 907 unless otherwise indicated. Tourist and travel services (accommodations, restaurants, attractions, etc.) not listed below can be found in the latest edition of The Milepost. *Statewide travel and birding information services are listed under Logistics in the* Introduction, *page 15.*

Access to the refuge is by air only. Flights to ANWR can be arranged with charter sir services from several different locations:

Fairbanks — Wright Air (474-0502; 800-478-0502).

Fort Yukon — Yukon Air Service, PO Box 84107, Fairbanks, AK 99708, 479-3993, June–September; PO Box 90, Fort Yukon, AK 99740, 662-2445, October–May; *yukonair@mosquitonet.com*. Arrange for scheduled air service from Fairbanks to Fort Yukon and Arctic Village and charter service into the refuge.

Coldfoot — Coyote Air Service, PO Box 60978, Fairbanks, AK 99706 (490-5995) winter; PO Box 9053, Coldfoot, AK 99701 (678-5995) summer.

Prudhoe Bay at Deadhorse and Kaktovik — Forty Mile Air (474-0018).

Bird Tours: Wilderness Birding Adventures, 5515 Wild Mountain Road, Eagle River, AK 99577; *www.wildernessbirding.com.*

For more information on the refuge, see *Organizations*, page 539 in this guide.

Richardson Highway:

Fairbanks to Delta Junction

Nancy DeWitt, Jim DeWitt, George West, and Steve DuBois

Fairbanks (Milepost 364) is at the north end of the Richardson Highway (Alaska Route 2) that begins in Valdez (Milepost 0) on the north shore of Prince William Sound. The TransAlaska Pipeline parallels the highway through most of its length and is visible at several points along the road. From Fairbanks to Delta, the road also parallels the Tanana River. In summer, Bald Eagles are common along with several species of raptors, puddle ducks, Lesser Yellowlegs, Spotted Sandpiper, Mew Gull, and passerines.

Five miles south of Fairbanks, Badger Road intersects the highway at Milepost 357.1. A side-trip of 6.9 miles on Badger Road is an alternate route to North Pole. The road parallels Badger Slough of the Chena River, occasionally visible from the road, and good for ducks, with Eurasian Wigeon occasionally seen along with assorted shorebirds and Belted Kingfisher.

If you bypass the Badger Road route and remain on the Richardson, you may see soaring Ospreys from near the Badger Road intersection for the next several miles. At Milepost 356.1 turn right (south) onto LuAnne Street. Take an immediate left onto the frontage road that parallels the highway. Go 0.3 mile and turn right onto Bethany Street, a gravel road. Continue on Bethany for 0.8 mile, past where the main road curves to the left and becomes O'Neal Avenue. Bethany narrows at this point and is often muddy, so you may need to walk from this intersection. It is a quarter-mile walk to the dike that parallels a large electrical transmission line. Scan the towers in both directions for an Osprey nest. Other birds possible on this walk are Red-tailed Hawk, Olive-sided Flycatcher, Boreal Chickadee, and Ruby-crowned Kinglet.

North Pole is 14.5 miles southeast of Fairbanks, and while not providing much in the way of birding, it is a target for young children who may wish to visit Santa Claus House. At Milepost 346.7 take the Laurence Road exit, well-marked with signs to Chena Lake Recreation Area. Drive east to the entrance (day-use fee $3 in 2001) and another 3 miles to the dam at the end of Main Road. The dam was built in the 1970s to control flood waters of the

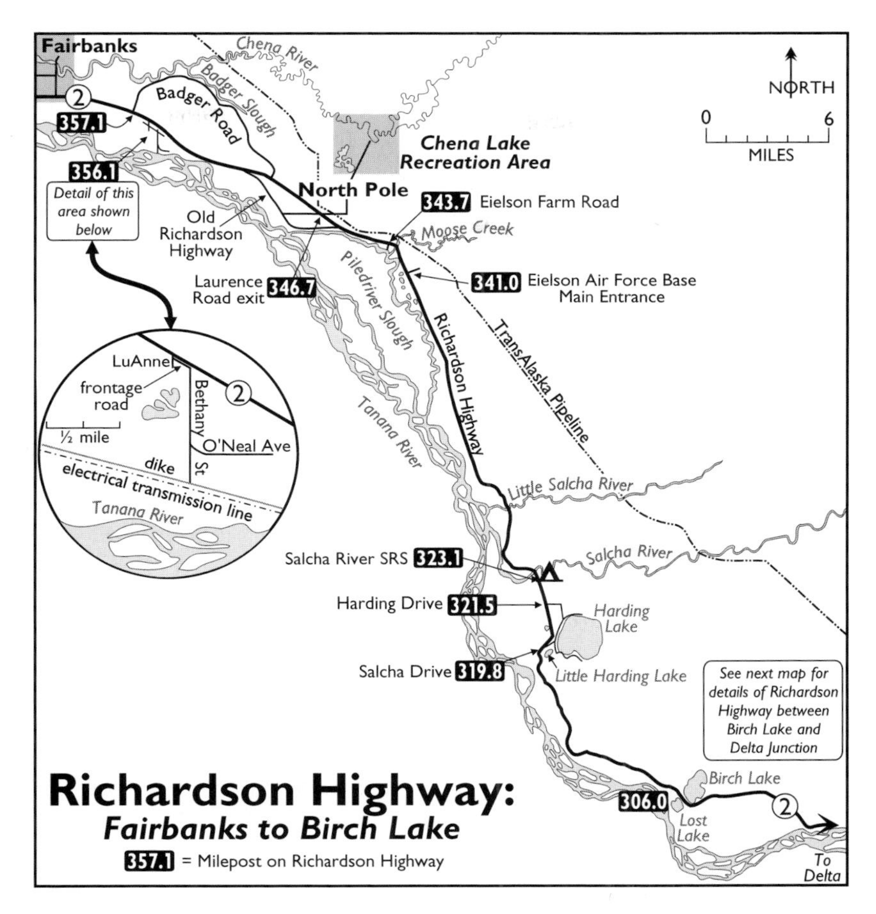

Chena River that in late summer 1967 devastated the city of Fairbanks, flooding many residences and businesses and causing millions of dollars of damage. The recreation area, while emphasizing picnicking, camping, and team sports, does have a large lake and the Chena River running through it. No motorized craft are allowed on the lakes (but they are permitted on the river), so birding from your canoe or kayak may be the best way for you to enjoy the area. In addition to some ducks (including possible scoters, Long-tailed Duck, and other diving ducks), Red-throated, Pacific, and Common Loons are found during migration and Horned Grebes nest here. The brush around the lakes supports a good variety of the local passerines such as flycatchers, chickadees, warblers, thrushes, and Rusty Blackbirds.

As you travel south along the Richardson, you can stop at several clearwater rivers that enter the Tanana from the northeast (Chena River in

Fairbanks, Moose Creek in North Pole, Little Salcha and Salcha Rivers at Salcha, and Shaw Creek near Delta Junction). Birding is best where these streams enter the Tanana River. Access to these river mouths is usually by way of rough dirt roads used by fishermen and hunters who launch their boats at these locations. It is best to walk rather than drive down these access roads, which may be muddy, rutted, or lack a turnaround area. Piledriver Slough is a clearwater river on the east side of the Tanana River and easily can be reached near Moose Creek at Milepost 343.7 (Eielson Farm Road).

After passing the entrance to Eielson Air Force Base at Milepost 341, scan the open areas on the south end of the runway for Merlin, American Golden-Plover, and Belted Kingfisher. The ponds to the west of the highway are also worth checking. Access is by several gravel roads that intersect the highway. Large "birds" in the form of military fighter jets, bombers, and transports can commonly be viewed from the highway as they land and take off on the runway on the east side of the highway.

Turn in to the Salcha River State Recreation Site (Milepost 323.1, Uphues Drive) to see this crystal-clear fishing and hunting stream. Vegetation in the large parking area is typical of the mature White Spruce-Paper Birch communities and provides nesting habitat for Townsend's Warblers.

At Milepost 321.5 turn left (east) at Harding Drive to visit Harding Lake, a very popular State Recreation Area, for picnicking, boating, and fishing. Here you should find Horned and Red-necked Grebes, Bald Eagle, Northern Harrier, many dabbling and diving ducks, Lesser Yellowlegs, Solitary and Spotted Sandpipers, Bonaparte's and Mew Gulls, Short-eared Owl, Belted Kingfisher, and Northern Waterthrush. Little Harding Lake, just south of Harding Lake, is better for birding. To go there directly from the Richardson, turn left at Salcha Drive at Milepost 319.8 and follow it to the intersection with the Harding Lake perimeter road. Turn right and drive about 0.8 mile to the Little Harding Lake sign. Watch for a trail on the right—it's about a one-quarter mile walk to the edge of the lake.

You can pull off the highway to the east to scan pretty Birch Lake at Milepost 306. Unless you get out on the water to explore the less-congested and less-developed far side of the lake, however, it is unlikely that you will see many birds except during late fall when waterfowl and, particularly, swans congregate here as the smaller lakes and ponds in the area freeze over.

At Mileposts 296.4 and 288.1, pull off at scenic parking areas if the weather will allow you to view the prominent peaks of the Alaska Range to the south (from east to west: Mount Hayes – 13,832 feet, Mount Hess – 11,940 feet, and Mount Deborah – 12,339 feet). The Milepost 288.1 pullout is directly adjacent to the Tanana River, where you can scan for Mew and Herring Gulls,

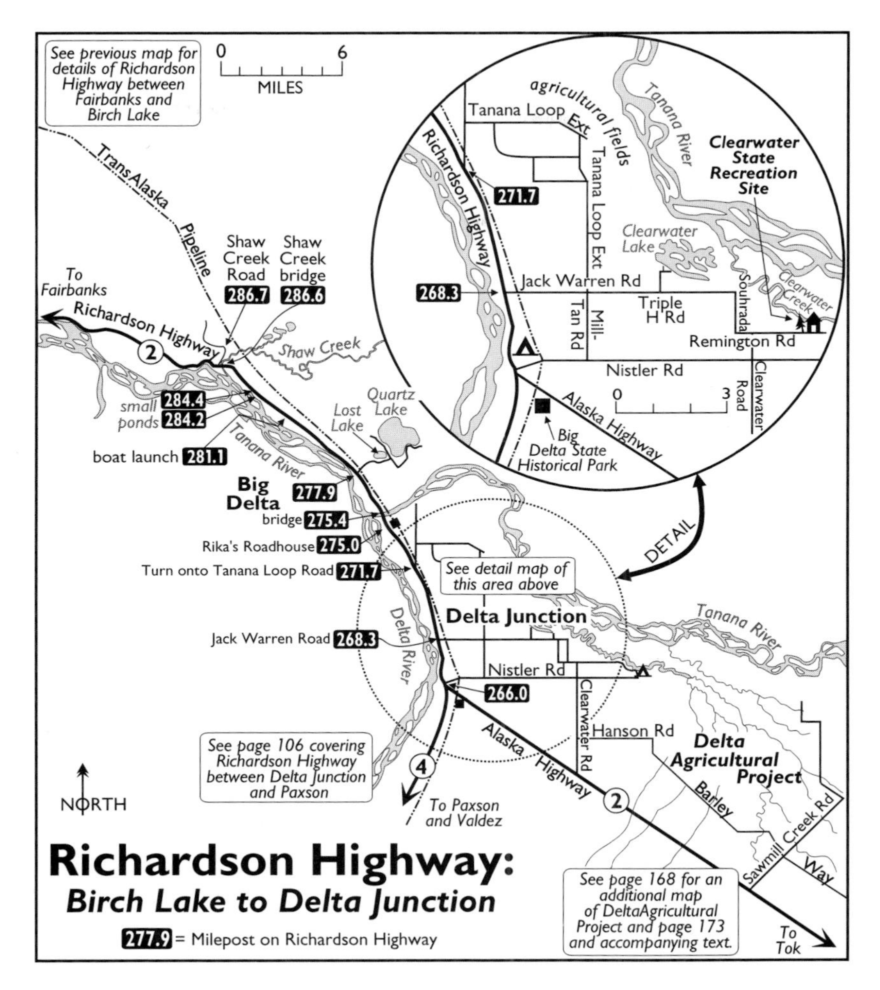

occasional Bald Eagles, and Peregrine Falcons that nest several miles downstream from this site and forage in the area.

Stop at two small ponds along the highway at Mileposts 284.4 and 284.2 for nesting dabbling ducks or to watch the Moose that feed here on aquatic vegetation during the summer. Willows surrounding the Milepost 284.4 pond also provide nesting habitat for Blackpoll Warblers. At Milepost 281.8, stop at a small undeveloped pullout on the right side of the road where local residents launch boats on the Tanana River. On the far bank of the river is a large cottonwood (Balsam Poplar) tree with an active Bald Eagle nest.

A gravel road on the left at Milepost 277.9 leads to Quartz Lake State Recreation Area. On the drive through the spruce forest to the park's two small lakes, Quartz and Lost Lakes, be alert for Spruce Grouse, particularly in the fall when they come to the roads to pick up grit. The lakes have developed campsites and picnic sites, and Quartz Lake provides good fishing for Rainbow Trout, landlocked Silver Salmon, and Arctic Char. There are stocked Rainbow Trout in Lost Lake. You can rent a boat at Quartz Lake to explore the vegetated portions of the lake margin.

Quartz Lake is a likely spot to look for Great Gray Owls in spring and to listen for singing Varied Thrushes. In late May during the ice break-up, look for Bald Eagle, Trumpeter Swan, and Surf and White-winged Scoters. Lost Lake is shallower and marshier than Quartz Lake, making it more attractive to ducks, including locally uncommon Blue-winged Teal and Ring-necked Duck. Red-throated and Pacific Loons, grebes, Northern Harrier, Lesser Yellowlegs, Solitary Sandpiper, Wilson's Snipe, and Arctic Tern all might be found here. Several good hiking trails traverse typical Interior boreal spruce forests. Black Bears are common in the area, so take appropriate precautions.

At Milepost 275.4, the Richardson crosses the Tanana River, providing you with a good look at the TransAlaska Pipeline suspended over the river. Shortly after crossing the bridge, birders can turn onto a dirt road on the right (west) or park in the large parking lot on the left (east) side of the highway and walk across the road. This is the confluence of the Delta and Tanana Rivers. Scope the bluffs across the Tanana for nesting Peregrine Falcons. From October through January, you may find a concentration of 10 to 15 Bald Eagles here, plus many Black-billed Magpies and Common Ravens feeding on a late run of Chum Salmon. American Dippers commonly overwinter in this area, since it has flowing water throughout the year.

Rika's Roadhouse at Big Delta State Historical Park (Milepost 275) has nice grounds in which to search for warblers. Northern Shrikes sometimes nest near the parking lot. Mew, Herring, and Glaucous-winged Gulls are often seen along the Tanana River. Look for Three-toed Woodpeckers in the spruce forest along the river.

At Milepost 271.7 turn left (east) onto Tanana Loop Road and then right on Tanana Loop Extension Road to view the extensive agricultural fields. As you drive by the many small farms interspersed with woodlands, you will see species similar to those discussed in detail in the Delta Agricultural Project sidebar (see page 173). Specialties along Tanana Loop Road include Pine Grosbeak and White-winged Crossbill. This is a good spot to see Northern Hawk Owl and to see or hear Great Horned, Great Gray, and Boreal Owls.

At Milepost 268.3, turn left (east) onto Jack Warren Road to visit Clearwater Lake and the Clearwater State Recreation Site. At Mile 10.2 of

Jack Warren Road (2.9 miles east of the Richardson Highway) you reach the intersection with Tanana Loop Extension Road mentioned above. Drive east on Jack Warren Road another 1.1 miles (4 miles total from the Richardson Highway) and turn left onto Triple H Road to get to Clearwater Lake. Triple H Road is gravel for the first 0.6 mile, then becomes an unimproved dirt road that can be extremely muddy during spring break-up and after heavy rains. After traveling 0.8 mile from Jack Warren Road, turn right onto Clearwater Avenue, taking the first turn to the left, marked with a small "landing" sign. Note that several feet beyond the landing road is a private driveway on the left that should be avoided. Continue along the landing road about 0.2 mile to an unimproved boat launch. Shallow, spring-fed Clearwater Lake is usually the first non-flowing water in the area to open in spring and the last to freeze in fall. As such, it attracts large numbers of early- and late-migrating waterfowl and swans. Waterfowl will begin arriving on the lake in early-to-mid-April and can still be seen in fall after most nearby waters have frozen.

Return to paved Jack Warren Road, and turn left. The road makes a 90-degree turn 1.8 miles east of Triple H Road and the name changes to Souhrada Road. Then it makes another 90-degree turn to the left, and in a mile, the name changes to Remington Road. Continue east an additional 3.7 miles to Clearwater State Recreation Site. This is an excellent camping location on spring-fed, crystal-clear Clearwater Creek. Without a boat, birders can hike along the river to look for occasional American Dippers and resident gull species. Occasionally in spring, Harlequin Ducks can be seen along the river. Clearwater Creek also provides excellent Arctic Grayling fishing, and there is a run of Silver Salmon in September.

Delta Junction (Milepost 266) lies at the intersection of the Richardson Highway and the Alaska Highway (page 159). This interior part of Alaska has much warmer and drier summers than the areas to the south and west and has some interior western species, most notably Sharp-tailed Grouse and Mountain Bluebird. In this part of the state, mixed woodlands host several species—such as Ruffed Grouse and Hammond's Flycatcher—not found in the Anchorage or Denali areas. To see both Sharp-tailed Grouse and Mountain Bluebirds, you will need to visit the Delta Agricultural Project (page 173).

LOGISTICS

The area code for all telephone numbers is 907 unless otherwise indicated. Tourist and travel services (accommodations, restaurants, attractions, etc.) not listed below can be found in the latest edition of The Milepost. *Statewide travel and birding information services are listed under Logistics in the* Introduction, *page 15.*

Delta Junction Chamber of Commerce, 895-5068 or 877-895-5068; *www.wildak.net/chamber/*. North Pole Chamber, 488-2242; *www.fairnet.org/npcc/*.

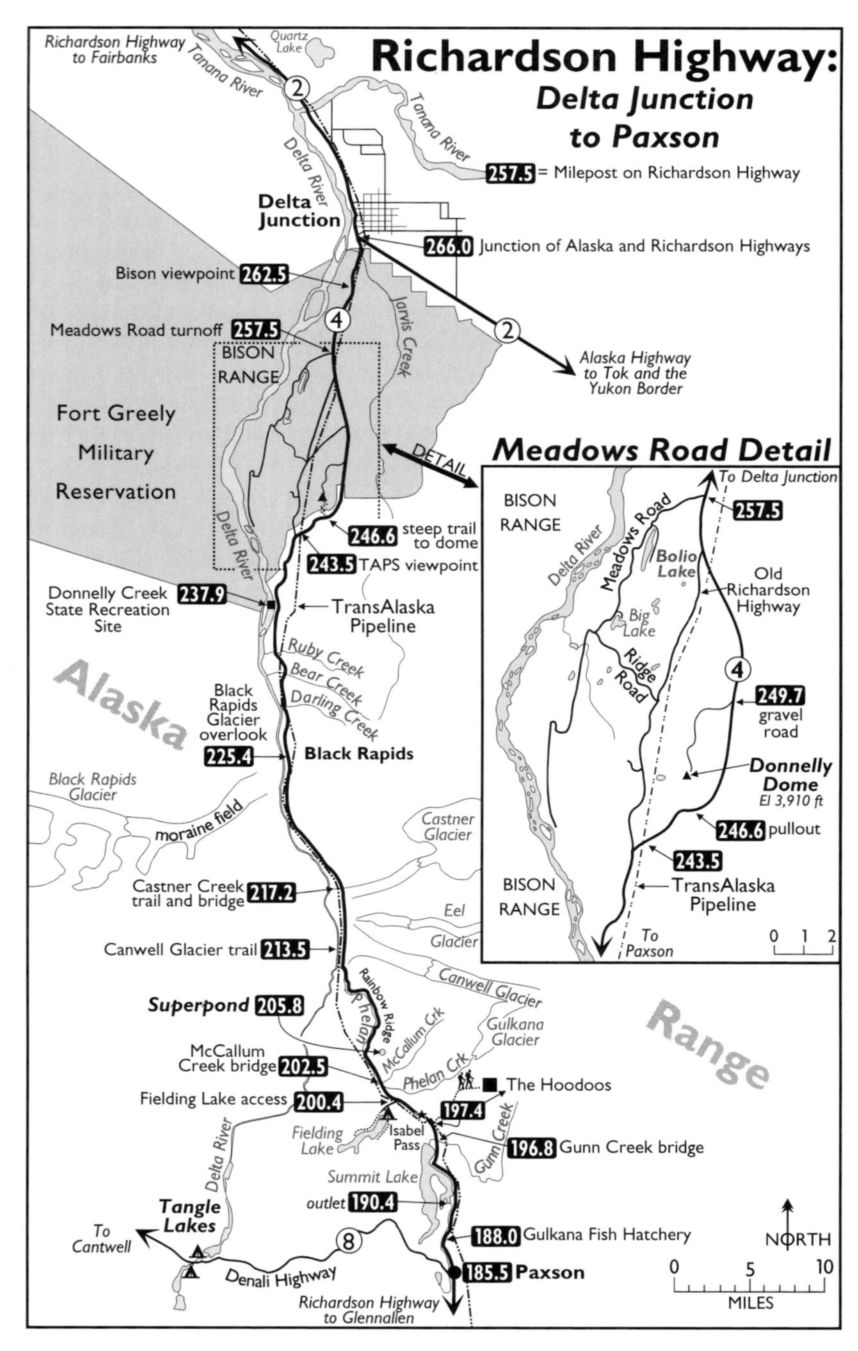
Richardson Highway: Delta Junction to Paxson
257.5 = Milepost on Richardson Highway
Richardson Highway to Fairbanks
Quartz Lake
Tanana River
Tanana River
Delta River
Delta Junction
266.0 Junction of Alaska and Richardson Highways
Bison viewpoint 262.5
Meadows Road turnoff 257.5
BISON RANGE
Jarvis Creek
Alaska Highway to Tok and the Yukon Border
Fort Greely Military Reservation
DETAIL
Delta River
246.6 steep trail to dome
243.5 TAPS viewpoint
Donnelly Creek State Recreation Site 237.9
TransAlaska Pipeline
Ruby Creek
Bear Creek
Darling Creek
Alaska
Black Rapids Glacier overlook 225.4
Black Rapids
Black Rapids Glacier
moraine field
Castner Glacier
Castner Creek trail and bridge 217.2
Eel Glacier
Canwell Glacier trail 213.5
Canwell Glacier
Rainbow Ridge
Phelan
Superpond 205.8
McCallum Crk
Gulkana Glacier
Range
McCallum Creek bridge 202.5
Phelan Crk
The Hoodoos
Fielding Lake access 200.4
197.4
Delta River
Fielding Lake
Isabel Pass
Gunn Creek
196.8 Gunn Creek bridge
Summit Lake
outlet 190.4
Tangle Lakes
To Cantwell
188.0 Gulkana Fish Hatchery
Denali Highway
185.5 Paxson
Richardson Highway to Glennallen
NORTH
0 5 10
MILES
Meadows Road Detail
To Delta Junction
BISON RANGE
257.5
Meadows Road
Delta River
Bolio Lake
Old Richardson Highway
Big Lake
Ridge Road
249.7 gravel road
Donnelly Dome
El 3,910 ft
246.6 pullout
243.5
BISON RANGE
TransAlaska Pipeline
To Paxson
0 1 2

Richardson Highway:

Delta Junction to Paxson

Jim DeWitt, Audubon L. Bakewell IV, and Steve DuBois

Delta Junction to Donnelly Creek

From Milepost 266 in Delta Junction, take the Richardson Highway (Alaska Route 4) south toward Paxson and Valdez. For the first few miles the road follows the east bank of the Delta River. At Milepost 262.5, stop at a pullout on the west for a view of the Delta's floodplain, where you might be able to spot Bison, descendants of a herd transplanted to the Delta area in the 1930s.

In 1999, a forest fire burned much of the spruce forest for the next 15 miles to the south, most of it on the Fort Greely Military Reservation. Burned areas such as this attract and support higher numbers of Three-toed and Black-backed Woodpeckers for a few years after the wildfire. In summer 2001, both species were seen from the highway along this stretch, so pull off the road occasionally to listen for their drumming and look for wood chips around the base of favored trees. Do not enter closed areas on Fort Greely.

At Milepost 257.5, turn right (west) onto Meadows Road. This gravel road is generally in good condition, but be aware if your rental car contract prohibits you from driving on any gravel roads. U.S. Army policy has allowed birding in this area without a special permit from Fort Greely, but that policy may change at any time. To be safe, phone the Fort Greely staff duty office at 873-4715 on weekdays for up-to-date information. If you are unable to get in touch with them, be aware that the army has a system of red warning flags to signify areas that are off limits along military roads in the area. If a red flag is flying, the area is closed to the public at that time. Respect all signs and closed areas on Fort Greely and yield to military vehicles.

The first one-half mile of Meadows Road traverses burned forest, where you should listen and watch for Three-toed and Black-backed Woodpeckers as well as some Northern Flickers that have also been seen here since the fire. About 1.2 miles along Meadow Road turn left onto an unsigned gravel road that skirts the eastern shore of Bolio Lake. This is one of the larger lakes in the Isabel Pass corridor through the Alaska Range and can hold surprisingly large numbers of migrating waterfowl. You should be able to find Red-necked Grebe, Trumpeter and Tundra Swans, American Wigeon, Northern Shoveler, Northern Pintail, Green-winged Teal, Canvasback, Redhead, Ring-necked Duck, Lesser Scaup, Surf and White-winged Scoters, Long-tailed Duck, Bufflehead, and Common Goldeneye on this lake. Some of these species remain to breed. Bolio Lake is also one of the best places in the area to find locally uncommon Gadwall and Blue-winged Teal. Look for migrating gulls, including Mew and Herring, as well as an occasional Pacific or Common Loon. In recent years, sportfishing activity seems to have impacted the number of loons found here. On the mudflats at the north and south ends of Bolio Lake you might turn up Lesser Yellowlegs, Long-billed Dowitcher, and other migrating shorebirds.

Double back to Meadows Road and turn left for 3.5 miles to Big Lake. Throughout this stretch watch for Golden Eagle and Red-tailed Hawk soaring overhead or perched on the utility poles. A poorly signed road on the left climbs a low ridge and then drops down to Big Lake, which holds many of the same species as Bolio Lake. If you don't have a four-wheel-drive vehicle, turn around at Big Lake and return to the Richardson Highway. If you do have four-wheel drive and the roads are in good shape, continue down Meadows Road. (*Caution*: if there is any snow around, don't try this; the upper slopes hold snow for a long time.) Watch for a left turn onto Ridge Road about 0.7 mile past Big Lake. This road climbs over a ridge locally known as Windy Ridge, the north shoulder of Donnelly Dome, and continues above tree line into alpine habitat where dozens of ponds dot the area. This is one of the better places to find Willow and Rock Ptarmigan, Upland Sandpiper, American Pipit, and Lapland Longspur. If the weather is clear, the view of the central Alaska Range is well worth the trek. If you continue along Ridge Road, it takes you to the old Richardson Highway; turn left to connect to the new Richardson Highway about five miles south of the Meadows Road junction.

Continue south on the Richardson along a stretch with very high numbers of nesting Gambel's White-crowned Sparrows and an occasional Upland Sandpiper. Caribou are common here, and you might see Moose feeding in the ponds along the road. In early morning or late evening in summer, be alert for Black and Brown Bears. At Milepost 249.7, about two miles into the five-mile straight stretch on the east side of Donnelly Dome, note the gravel road on the right. While sometimes closed to civilian traffic, this road leads part way up Donnelly Dome, giving you access to alpine tundra and a trail on the left through a gravel pit that leads to the top of Donnelly Dome via its north flank.

As the Richardson curves around the south end of Donnelly Dome and you approach the crest at Milepost 246.6, stop at a pullout on the right where Arctic Warblers and Hermit Thrushes have been seen in June and early July.

This is also a convenient starting point for the steeper but less brushy ascent of Donnelly Dome's eastern flank. You could spot a Golden Eagle about the steep rocks on the southwest slope of the Dome.

As you descend into Black Rapids Canyon, stop at Milepost 243.5 if you're interested in visiting a TransAlaska Pipeline interpretive viewpoint. At Milepost 241.3, a paved turnout on the west gives impressive views of some of the higher peaks in the central Alaska Range. Although these peaks are lower than the summits in Denali National Park, the Mount Hayes massif has summits ranging from 10,500 feet to Mount Hayes itself at 13,832 feet.

Twenty-eight miles south of Delta Junction, Milepost 243.3, you reach the Black Rapids Canyon valley floor and Donnelly Creek State Recreation Site. Though few birds other than Gray Jays are usually found in the camping area, the Beaver pond across the highway sometimes yields puddle ducks, Common and Barrow's Goldeneyes, and Belted Kingfisher.

BLACK RAPIDS CANYON

The Delta River flows north for about 80 miles from Tangle Lakes to the Tanana River through Black Rapids Canyon. Many of its tributaries are glacier-outlet streams, so the river carries extraordinary amounts of sediment. The silt deposited here since the last ice age has created an almost flat river-valley floor with the Delta's braided channels criss-crossing it. The drainage rises from about 1,400 feet at Donnelly Creek to around 3,300 feet at Isabel Pass. The glaciated peaks on the east side of the valley, where the road runs, climb to about 9,000 feet; those on the west side rise to 13,700 feet. It is a spectacular place! Black-billed Magpies are common in Black Rapids Canyon, and you may see them flying across the road or jumping up from a roadkill snack. Watch the tops of spruce trees throughout the canyon for Merlin and Northern Hawk Owl. Northern Shrikes are less commonly seen, but do occur on the valley floor. The thick spruce forests hold large numbers of White-winged Crossbills at times, so it's worth stopping along this stretch to listen for their melodious calls. The Delta River carries too heavy a load of glacial flour to support much life, so few waterbirds use the gravel bars. There are no salmon and virtually no other fish in these silty waters, making the north side of Isabel Pass less than ideal for Bald Eagles, but Golden Eagles are reasonably common as they hunt small mammals in the valley. Seedeaters sometimes forage in this area, increasing in numbers after plants start producing seeds. Willow and alder thickets can be very productive for thrushes and warblers, and Western Wood-Pewees have been fairly reliable between Donnelly Creek and Flood Creek. The Delta River valley also provides summer range for the Delta Bison herd, and any place that has a view of the river flats should be scanned for these introduced creatures. The small streams draining from the east into the Delta River are eroding down through the hanging valleys, some of which still have remnant glaciers. Active erosion chokes the canyons, so against your expectations the highway bridges over the creeks tend to be at the tops of hills. In early summer, the stream beds and river valley floors have spectacular fields of flowers.

From the Black Rapids Glacier overlook, Milepost 225.4, you can see that the glacier has retreated several miles up its canyon, while the low moraine hills immediately across the river are plain evidence of its rapid advance to within 300 meters of the viewpoint during the winter of 1936–1937. Scan the valley floor for Bison, and take the short trail (0.4 mile) that ends at a small pond. You won't see anything on the trail that you can't see elsewhere, but in good weather it's an interesting walk. At Milepost 217.2 you can take a longer walk up Castner Creek to the snout of Castner Glacier. Park at Castner Creek bridge and walk up the north side of the creek just over a mile for an excellent view of the exposed terminus of the glacier and the boil where the creek emerges from under the glacier. Be extremely careful if you climb on the glacier itself—the rocks and mud can thinly cover extremely slippery ice and the glacier surface itself is heavily crevassed. Your walk takes you through a mixed scrub-willow habitat with mature Black Spruce forest above the active wash areas. The higher, sandier gravel bars contain dens of Arctic Ground Squirrels, the preferred food of Golden Eagles and other raptors. Again, there are no unique birds along Castner Creek, but it's a nice walk.

Stop at Milepost 213.5, about one-half mile south of the Miller Creek bridge, the southernmost of three closely-grouped highway bridges. You'll make a left (east) turn into a gravel pit just past a pullout with a trash barrel. A two-track road, driveable only with a four-wheel-drive vehicle, begins at the south end of this gravel pit and climbs along an old channel of Miller Creek through a spectacular, narrow canyon on the north side of Rainbow Ridge, emerging near the snout of Canwell Glacier. If you don't have a 4x4 vehicle, it is a pleasant walk. Though the hike is worthwhile for the geology alone, this is also one of the best places in Black Rapids Canyon to see Golden Eagles, and you might even find a bonus Rock Ptarmigan on the narrow canyon's floor.

During fall migration in late August and September, passerines, especially Gambel's White-crowned and Golden-crowned Sparrows and Slate-colored Junco, rest in the canyon. On occasion, up to half a dozen Gyrfalcons have been tallied about the steep canyon walls. *Note*: Under no circumstances should you drive more than about two miles along this track. Stop at the point where the trail enters an alder thicket, even if you have four-wheel drive. At this point the trail narrows dramatically and there is no alternative to backing all the way out.

As you continue south on the highway, watch the tops of trees to the east for Merlin and Northern Hawk Owl, both fairly common between here and Fielding Lake. The highway now swings away from the Delta River to follow

Phelan Creek up to Isabel Pass. As you curve around the west end of Rainbow Ridge, scan the rock cliffs and talus slopes for Dall's Sheep that sometimes venture quite close to the road. In late summer they will move higher up the talus slopes of Rainbow Ridge. Bald Eagle, Red-tailed Hawk, and Golden Eagle are all fairly common in the Isabel Pass corridor. The talus slopes support Hoary Marmots, and if you're here during spring migration, watch for Snow Buntings. You can sometimes spot White-tailed Ptarmigan around Rainbow Ridge, especially on the open grassy slope at Milepost 207, particularly after a spring snowstorm.

The highway drops into the former streambed of Phelan Creek from Milepost 208 to Milepost 203. At Milepost 205.8, stop at the large Beaver pond visible on the east. Affectionately known as Superpond by Fairbanks birdathon teams, this spot has produced Long-tailed Duck, Common and Barrow's Goldeneyes, Red-breasted Merganser, Golden Eagle, Merlin, Belted Kingfisher, Western Wood-Pewee, Alder Flycatcher, Gray Jay, and Black-billed Magpie, as well as a wide assortment of the more-common ducks.

At McCallum Creek bridge, Milepost 202.5, park on the apron and walk up McCallum Creek on its north bank. After about a mile upstream of the crest of the low ridge on the left, watch for a trail that climbs up into the small valley to your left. Resist the temptation to use the TransAlaska Pipeline pad that is strictly off-limits to the public for security reasons. The small ponds in this valley support Red-necked and Red Phalaropes as well as the usual ducks and wading birds. Also at McCallum Creek bridge, you'll see a steep road climbing above tree line to a radio relay tower on the shoulder of one of the lower hills in Black Rapids Canyon. Although it's rather steep, you can hike up or take your four-wheel-drive vehicle. Listen for birds in the roadside brush as you start up the creek canyon. American Dipper, Myrtle Warbler, and Gambel's White-crowned Sparrow are found in the alder and willows along the creek. At the top, two ponds may hold phalaropes, ducks, and shorebirds. You might spot Willow and Rock Ptarmigan on the tundra and scree slopes above.

ISABEL PASS AND SUMMIT LAKE

The entrance road to Fielding Lake State Recreation Area is to the right (west) at Milepost 200.4. The lake, about two miles from the highway, is not an ideal birding site because its public road access is at the north end of a long, narrow lake oriented northeast-southwest. Even so, as one of the few large bodies of water in the vastness of the Alaska Range, it can yield some surprises, including a Sabine's Gull (August 1999). In migration good-sized rafts of ducks such as Surf Scoters can turn up, but these are usually more easily viewed at Summit Lake, a few miles farther south.

From Fielding Lake, the highway climbs quickly to Isabel Pass (Milepost 197.6) on the continental divide between the Yukon River drainage to the north and the Copper River drainage to the south. Just south of the pass, a gravel road heading east (Milepost 197.4) angles back north toward Gulkana Glacier, ending at the site of a 1970s TransAlaska Pipeline construction camp. In early April of each year, the Arctic Man snowmachine-skiing event happens here, giving rise to an ephemeral city of 6,000–8,000 energetic souls, their RVs and snowmachines almost outnumbering these Arctic men and women. This several-day disturbance has not cleared the area of birds, however, and Short-eared Owls have been found here several times in the last few years. Look for Gyrfalcons around the rock formations called the Hoodoos at the northeast end of the valley. You usually can find Willow Ptarmigan on the valley floor, especially in spring when they tee-up on the willows to call. The farther along you go, the more the road deteriorates. If road conditions permit and you are able to drive all the way up to the base of the Hoodoos, park there and walk the trail along the creek-bed just to the south and west of the rock formations. Along with the raptors mentioned earlier, Northern Harriers frequent this area. It also represents one of the more easterly known breeding locations for Arctic Warbler. Blackpoll Warblers and Golden-crowned Sparrows breed here, too. The birdiest portion of the foot trail is the first 1.5 miles.

Back on the Richardson, Milepost 196.8 marks the bridge over Gunn Creek, actually the headwaters of the Gulkana River. Stop a moment to look for Harlequin Duck and American Dipper along the riverbank. Summit Lake, a short distance farther on, usually keeps the majority of its ice until the last week of June or the first week of July, but the open areas are reliable for Lesser Scaup and the usual assortment of ducks. Less common, but still possible, are Red-throated, Pacific, and Common Loons, Trumpeter and Tundra Swans, and any of the scoters. You may see Arctic Terns patrolling the edges of the lake over any open water. Take advantage of the many pullouts along the road, as it snakes along the east shore of Summit Lake, to stop to look for waterfowl. Rarely, female and young White-tailed Ptarmigan are found just off the road in mid-to-late summer. There is a considerable Red Salmon run into Summit Lake; as a result, the lake is biologically far richer and more productive than similar lakes at an altitude of 3,210 feet at this latitude.

Summit Lake's outlet into the Gulkana River is accessible from a large interpretive pullout at Milepost 190.4. King Salmon first show up here in mid-June, and the Red Salmon begin to arrive in early July. The dying, spawned-out salmon attract large numbers of Bonaparte's, Mew, and Herring Gulls, along with graceful Arctic Terns. Most years Glaucous-winged Gulls come to join the feeding frenzy. Herring Gulls too gorged on salmon to fly are a fairly common sight. Bald Eagles, too, are anxious to take advantage of the seasonal abundance of salmon carcasses. During migration periods up to half a dozen Trumpeter Swans make use of the open water at this outlet.

A few miles downstream at Milepost 188 is the Gulkana River Hatchery. The area under the private bridge is a reliable spot for both American Dipper and Northern Waterthrush. Wandering Tattler and, in spring and early summer, Harlequin Duck are fairly common. Arctic Terns abound, fishing up and down the river. If you are lucky enough to be along this stretch of the river when the salmon smolt are moving downstream, you may see a kettle of birds of many species, all diving and swooping onto the river, moving downstream with the juvenile salmon. On occasion, Rough-legged Hawks occur in this section of the river during spring migration. This fast-flowing stretch of the Gulkana never freezes, even at sub-zero temperatures, allowing Bald Eagles to remain here well into early winter. In early November 2000, there were 110 Bald Eagles along the three miles of river north of Paxson, surviving on "rags"—the long-dead salmon carcasses. By late November fewer than five remained and none chose to overwinter with the few Mallards and American Dippers.

A few miles farther downstream is Paxson (Milepost 185.5). Watch the trees carefully in this area—for several years there has been a nesting pair of Merlins in the vicinity of the junction. In summer, the trees and shrubs here are reliable for Boreal Chickadee, Myrtle and Wilson's Warblers, Savannah, Fox, and Gambel's White-crowned Sparrows, and Slate-colored Junco, among others.

Even if you don't plan to bird the Denali Highway from Paxson, be sure to read the beginning of the Denali Highway chapter, page 115, that details the rich birding possibilities in the immediate Paxson area. Then turn to page 129 for the continuation of the Richardson Highway to Glennallen and Valdez.

LOGISTICS

The area code for all telephone numbers is 907 unless otherwise indicated. Tourist and travel services (accommodations, restaurants, attractions, etc.) not listed below can be found in the latest edition of The Milepost. *Statewide travel and birding information services are listed under Logistics in the* Introduction, *page 15.*

See also Denali Highway, page 127, and Richardson Highway: Paxson to Valdez, page 129, for more information about staying in the Paxson area.

ACKNOWLEDGEMENTS: Additional bird sighting information was provided by Jeff Bouton.

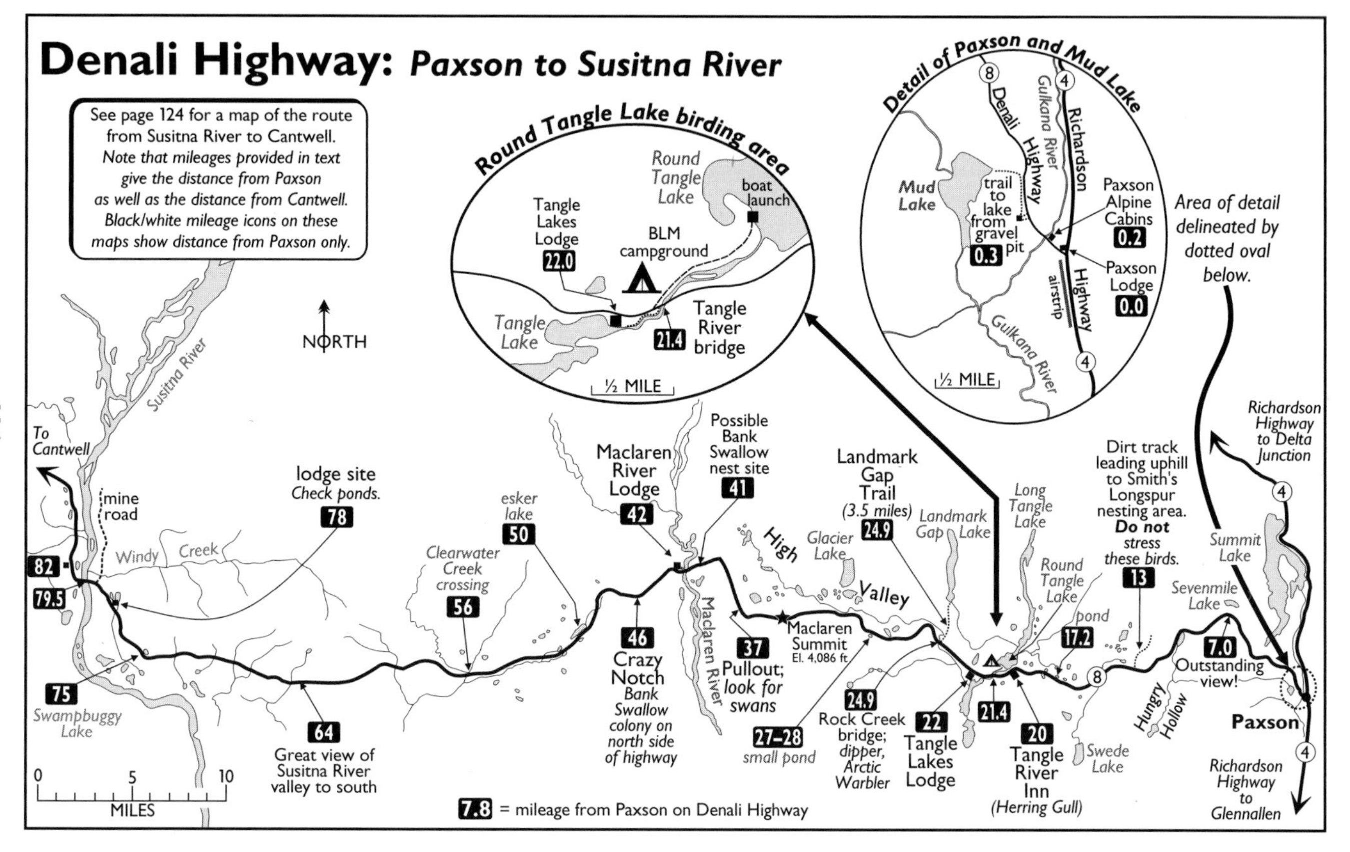
Denali Highway: Paxson to Susitna River
See page 124 for a map of the route from Susitna River to Cantwell.
Note that mileages provided in text give the distance from Paxson as well as the distance from Cantwell. Black/white mileage icons on these maps show distance from Paxson only.
NORTH
Round Tangle Lake birding area
Round Tangle Lake
boat launch
Tangle Lakes Lodge
22.0
BLM campground
Tangle Lake
21.4
Tangle River bridge
½ MILE
Detail of Paxson and Mud Lake
8
4
Denali Highway
Gulkana River
Richardson
Mud Lake
trail to lake from gravel pit
0.3
Paxson Alpine Cabins
0.2
Paxson Lodge
0.0
airstrip
Highway
Gulkana River
½ MILE
Area of detail delineated by dotted oval below.
Richardson Highway to Delta Junction
To Cantwell
Susitna River
mine road
lodge site
Check ponds.
78
Windy Creek
82
79.5
75
Swampbuggy Lake
64
Great view of Susitna River valley to south
Clearwater Creek crossing
56
esker lake
50
Maclaren River Lodge
42
46
Crazy Notch
Bank Swallow colony on north side of highway
Possible Bank Swallow nest site
41
Maclaren River
37
Pullout; look for swans
Maclaren Summit
El. 4,086 ft
27–28
small pond
High Valley
Glacier Lake
Landmark Gap Trail
(3.5 miles)
24.9
Landmark Gap Lake
24.9
Rock Creek bridge; dipper, Arctic Warbler
22
Tangle Lakes Lodge
21.4
Long Tangle Lake
Round Tangle Lake
20
Tangle River Inn
(Herring Gull)
pond
17.2
8
Swede Lake
Dirt track leading uphill to Smith's Longspur nesting area. Do not stress these birds.
13
Hungry Hollow
Sevenmile Lake
7.0
Outstanding view!
Summit Lake
4
Paxson
Richardson Highway to Glennallen
0 5 10
MILES
7.8 = mileage from Paxson on Denali Highway

THE DENALI HIGHWAY

Audubon L. Bakewell IV

The Denali Highway begins at Paxson, 186 miles north of Valdez on the Richardson Highway, and runs 135.5 miles west along the south flank of the Alaska Range. It joins the George Parks Highway at Cantwell, about 210 miles north of Anchorage. This account runs from east to west, so if you are planning to drive the highway from Cantwell, follow the route in reverse.

When the Denali Highway was completed in 1957, motorists gained access to McKinley (now Denali) National Park for the first time, previous access being only by the Alaska Railroad or small airplane. In 1972, when the George Parks Highway from Anchorage to Fairbanks was completed, it provided far easier access to the park, allowing the Denali Highway to revert to the desolate, backcountry status it has since maintained. Its stunning scenery and solitude are sufficient incentive for many visitors to challenge the Denali's unpaved and often rough surface, but the road is of particular interest to birders. The Denali provides one of the best accesses in Alaska to alpine tundra and the suite of birds nesting there—Gyrfalcon, all three ptarmigan, American Golden-Plover, Whimbrel, Long-tailed Jaeger, Lapland and Smith's Longspurs, and many others. Numerous streams, rivers, ponds, and lakes hold Trumpeter and Tundra Swans, Harlequin and many other ducks, and small numbers of shorebirds, including nesting Wandering Tattler. Birding along the highway will be described with reference to the seven substantially different habitat zones encountered as one travels from east to west.

SEASONS ALONG THE DENALI HIGHWAY

Winter season — The Denali is maintained from 15 May–1 October, and once the Alaska DOT maintenance trucks depart, snow accumulation quickly makes travel impossible by wheeled vehicles. In years of late onset of snowfall, travelers may be tempted to drive part or even all of the road, but this is strongly discouraged. As recently as 1998, a trio froze to death after their car became disabled. On the other hand, travel by snowmachine, dogsled, or cross-country skis can be a delightful and rewarding experience for the well-prepared birder.

In winter, bird species and numbers are few. Of note are Gyrfalcon, Willow and Rock Ptarmigan, Snowy Owl, and American Dipper. In early winter the Gulkana River only 0.2 mile from Paxson contains perhaps the highest inland concentration of Bald Eagles in Alaska—in early November 2000, over 110 adults were counted along the 3-mile stretch upstream from the Gulkana River bridge.

Spring season — Spring begins on the Denali Highway in mid-May when snowplows open the road and lasts until mid-June when, in most years, the lakes are mainly free of ice. Spring migration is extremely concentrated, with migratory raptors, shorebirds, inland gulls, Arctic Terns, warblers, and sparrows all seeming to arrive simultaneously in little more than three weeks' time. Most passerine appearances are firmly linked to insect hatches, and the migrants largely follow the watercourses leading up from the south. Along most of the highway, the road-opening activity provides the first snow-free areas of the season, where birds such as ptarmigan, Whimbrel, Short-eared Owl, Long-tailed Jaeger, American Pipit, various sparrows, and Lapland and Smith's Longspurs sometimes can be highly concentrated on the bare roadbed. As snows melt, the birds disperse to their tundra breeding grounds.

Summer season — The endless days of summer provide the solar energy necessary to sustain life in this landscape. Swarms of insects and rapidly growing vegetation are consumed by the birds as they quickly cycle through courtship, nesting, and rearing young. Prime birding time is the four weeks after mid-June. Arctic Warblers arrive around 10 June and are one of the commonest breeding birds found in the middle section of the highway. By the second half of July adult shorebirds are moving south, passerines have become silent and furtive, and most waterfowl are hiding as they molt. With exceptions, there is little pre-migration staging to observe at summer's end.

Fall season — Autumn is as brief as spring on the Denali. Most notable are the concentrations of Bald Eagles and an influx of maritime gulls that gather to feast on spawned-out salmon. Bohemian Waxwings may congregate in flocks exceeding 200. Fair-sized rafts of ducks representing all of Alaska's inland breeders and small concentrations of swans are present on lakes and ponds. By early October, few migrants remain.

BIRDING THE DENALI HIGHWAY

The following discussion concentrates on birds found from early May to mid-July. Mileages delineating the seven habitat zones are given in distances from both Paxson on the Richardson Highway and from Cantwell on the Parks Highway.

GULKANA RIVER ZONE

(Paxson 0–3 miles; Cantwell 132–135 miles)

The habitat for this section of highway is boreal forest and riparian brush. At Paxson Lodge, visitors occasionally may see and hear Merlins. In late summer, listen for them calling from the ridge across the Richardson Highway from the gasoline pumps. Common Ravens and Black-billed Magpies abound.

Merlins have nested for decades at Paxson Alpine Tours & Cabins (also called Denali Highway Cabins), Milepost 0.2, returning late in April each year. Feeders there host Boreal Chickadees year round. Other resident species include Downy and, more rarely, Hairy and Black-backed Woodpeckers, Bohemian Waxwing, Pine Grosbeak (rare in summer), and White-winged Crossbill. The Gulkana River bank opposite the cabins provides ideal perches for Bald Eagles, but only after the Merlins have migrated. Information about recent sightings is available at the office.

At Milepost 0.25, cross the Gulkana River. Harlequin Ducks normally are present in groups of three to eight from mid-May through early July; Wandering Tattlers persist a little longer. American Dippers occur through late June, then reappear in November and can be heard singing from the bridge all winter long, even at -35°F. Lesser Yellowlegs, Spotted Sandpiper, Mew Gull, Arctic Tern, Alder Flycatcher, Swainson's Thrush, Red Fox Sparrow, and Rusty Blackbird can be seen from the bridge or by walking the downstream bank. The more thickly wooded upstream bank is private property. An early May visit can be rewarded with waves of migrants concentrated on the riverbanks—Orange-crowned, Yellow, Myrtle, Blackpoll, and Wilson's Warblers, Fox and Gambel's White-crowned Sparrows, Rusty Blackbirds, and others stick to the stream's margins as they push northward. The steep gravel bank upstream from the bridge often has an active Belted Kingfisher nest.

Paxson Alpine Tours & Cabins runs three-hour wildlife-viewing float trips on summer evenings, drifting down the Gulkana River through the Paxson Wildlife Reserve and out onto Paxson Lake. Depending on the time of year, you might see Red-throated and Common Loons, ducks, Short-billed Dowitcher (rare), Wilson's Snipe, Bonaparte's, Mew, and Herring Gulls, Great Horned Owl, Varied Thrush, and Bohemian Waxwing, in addition to many of the species mentioned above.

At Milepost 0.3 (south side) are two accesses to a gravel pit. Take the westernmost entrance and look for a track that heads through the woods parallel to the Denali Highway, about 25 yards off the road. (Driving on the track is not recommended as there usually is at least one serious mud hole and turning around is difficult.) Walk this 500-yard trail to Mud Lake, listening for

Spruce Grouse

Black-capped and Boreal Chickadees, Ruby-crowned Kinglet, Swainson's, Hermit (occasional), and Varied Thrushes, Myrtle, Blackpoll, and Wilson's Warblers, and Pine Grosbeak. Alder Flycatchers favor the more open areas. Townsend's Solitaire is occasional here, mostly in autumn. Luck may bring you Ruffed or Spruce Grouse, and in late summer a juvenile Merlin might fly out to investigate you. As you approach the lake, listen for Wilson's Snipe and Lesser Yellowlegs that will almost certainly scold you from spruce-tops.

On the opposite edge of the lake, on a massive nest mound built up over decades to about fifteen feet wide by six feet high, is a Trumpeter Swan nest. At least one swan will be on the nest while the other gleans the lake's bottom nearby. A raft of assorted ducks—American Wigeon, Mallard, Northern Shoveler, Northern Pintail, Green-winged Teal, and Lesser Scaup—invariably follows the feeding swan, enjoying its protection and picking through what it has stirred up from the bottom. There usually is one pair of Common Loons on Mud Lake. In late autumn, just before freeze-up, Trumpeter Swans may be present in groups of up to six.

Back on the highway, the road quickly gains elevation. By Milepost 3 the spruce forest vanishes, giving way to tundra. Watch for Spruce Grouse before reaching tree line.

GLACIAL FORMATIONS—TANGLE LAKES ZONE

(Paxson 3–25 miles; Cantwell 110–132 miles)

The alpine tundra habitat here is dominated by Dwarf Birch and a variety of willows. Glacial geomorphological features abound. From Mileposts 3 through 7 the attention of even the most die-hard bird enthusiast is likely to be captured by the spectacle of the Alaska Range unfolding to the north. In good weather the view from Milepost 7 is one of the best Alaska has to offer. Be sure to look back to the southeast, where the great peaks of the Wrangell Mountains dominate the horizon. The enormous stratovolcano Mount Sanford (16,237 feet) is the almost perfectly symmetrical cone on the left.

There are birds here, too. The first Willow Ptarmigan for the westbound traveler may be spotted around Milepost 4. In spring they often are joined by Rock Ptarmigan that normally retreat to the cirques of Paxson Mountain shortly after the snow recedes. Arctic Warblers are present from mid-June. Gray-cheeked Thrush sightings increase, while those of Swainson's Thrushes decline. Gambel's White-crowned Sparrows continue, but are soon outnumbered by ubiquitous Savannah Sparrows. American Tree Sparrows are common. Snow Buntings linger here during autumn and spring. To the south between Mileposts 4 and 7 several great clefts appear in the west flank of Paxson Mountain, a few hundred yards off the roadway. This is prime raptor territory in spring and early summer, so scope the crags for Rough-legged Hawk, Golden Eagle, and Gyrfalcon, and scan closer to the road for Northern Harrier and Short-eared Owl.

The road drops to the level of Hungry Hollow draw at Milepost 10. To the north you'll see a number of bare rock knobs within one-half mile of the road, where Northern Wheatear has been reported. To the south a series of ponds hold the usual assortment of ducks and, often, Red-throated Loon. If swans are present, you might not be able to get close enough to determine whether they are Trumpeters or Tundras. Although this land is a stronghold of the Trumpeter Swan, a number of Tundra Swans occur on the Denali throughout the summer. The many ponds are increasingly visible as the road swings south and rises above the level of the draw.

You are now gaining elevation and entering Long-tailed Jaeger country, with several pairs nesting between Mileposts 11 and 15. It's not unusual to see them performing their aerial hijinks. Northern Harriers and Short-eared Owls also frequent this stretch.

The pullout at Milepost 13 is at the height of land for this stretch of road. To the south, the vast glacial outwash plain of Hungry Hollow affords a magnificent view of tundra, kettle holes, the Wrangell Mountains, and directly south, the Alphabet Range. When the road has just been opened and snows still blanket the land, the road surface here attracts American Pipits, American Tree, Savannah, Gambel's White-crowned, and Golden-crowned (rare) Sparrows, Lapland and Smith's Longspurs, and several other passerines. To the north is a dirt two-track leading uphill—do not drive up regardless of any fresh tracks you may see, but walk instead. The first 200 yards of this track pass through a thin copse of willow and cottonwood where Gray-cheeked and Swainson's Thrushes join American Tree, Savannah, Fox, and Gambel's White-crowned Sparrows. Arctic Warbler is possible; Blackpoll and Wilson's Warblers are there, too. Once you pass through the copse, watch for jaegers to the west and listen for American Golden-Plover and Whimbrel. The track mostly peters out when you reach a gravel pit/trash pile in about 300 yards. Gently sloping but wet tundra stretches to the north for about 500 yards to the base of a second hill. Walk the now-obscure trail in that direction. The area around the gravel pit is good for Horned Lark, and after that point Lapland Longspurs might be common. Farther on, in about 100–300 yards, you will reach a productive spot for Smith's Longspurs. *Note*: you may find yourself alone when you visit here, and the vastness of this land can make you think you are in untrammeled wilderness, but this is not the case. This location is probably the most-visited Smith's Longspur breeding site in the world—please act accordingly. The longspurs here are visited up to a half-dozen times each day during their very short breeding season. If you are lucky enough to view a Smith's, do not attempt to locate its nest or otherwise harass it during your viewing or photographing activities. Your actions not only directly stress the birds, but you can lead smart predators like Red Fox to the birds and their nests. Jaegers are also curious to investigate human presence and you may unwittingly clue them to the whereabouts of a meal. If this is a strong ptarmigan year, you might see some on your hike. Early in the season Rock Ptarmigan may be present along with the usual Willows.

If you have not yet spotted Long-tailed Jaegers, you have an opportunity to do so through to about Milepost 16. The pullout on the north at Milepost 16.8 overlooks a pond that usually holds a pair of Trumpeter Swans. A roadside pond begins at Milepost 17. Stop at the Milepost 17.2 pullout for possible American Wigeon, Mallard, Northern Shoveler, Northern Pintail, Green-winged Teal, Lesser Scaup, Bufflehead, Barrow's Goldeneye, Semipalmated Plover, Lesser Yellowlegs, Short-billed Dowitcher (rare), Wilson's Snipe, American Tree and Savannah Sparrows, and much more. An abbreviated esker forms a hill on the west end of the lake which used to be a good spot for Smith's Longspur, but the vegetation has grown up so much that few birds were found in 2001. However, it provides easy access and is worth examining. You might find an Arctic Warbler as your consolation prize.

The slope of Swede Mountain to the south at around Mileposts 18 to 19 provides enough protection for a reasonable stand of spruce to occur, attractive to a lone Bald Eagle that hunts the ducks in the stream that crosses the road at Milepost 18.4. Northern Harrier is the most often seen raptor both here and elsewhere along the highway.

The land directly behind Tangle River Inn, Milepost 20, is a near-certainty for spotting Herring Gulls, otherwise fairly uncommon in Interior Alaska except during late-summer salmon runs. At Milepost 20.1 a pullout overlooks Round Tangle Lake, the largest body of water directly on the Denali Highway, big enough to accommodate two or more pairs of Common Loons. The cove directly beneath the turnout provides shelter in some winds, and can be fruitful for waterfowl. Examine the wigeons as there was a Eurasian x American Wigeon hybrid present for much of summer 2000. This lake often holds fairly large rafts of ducks in autumn, including all three scoters. It is the last lake on the highway to freeze in the fall, and up to a dozen Trumpeter Swans might be present in early-to-mid-October. The gap through the Amphitheater Mountains to the north may serve as a modest flyway, because Northern Goshawk, uncommon in this sparsely-treed region, can occur here in autumn. Also watch for Gyrfalcon. Violet-green Swallows may be present with Tree Swallows here—both species occur along the highway's watercourses.

The road crosses the Tangle River at Milepost 21.4. Park at the BLM campground entryway adjacent to the bridge on the north side of the road and walk back to the bridge to scan the river for Harlequin Duck, Wandering Tattler, American Dipper, and Northern Waterthrush. Walk the trail upstream to the south looking for Swainson's, the occasional Hermit, and Gray-cheeked (uncommon) Thrushes in the thick vegetation. This is a good location for Fox and Golden-crowned Sparrows, otherwise uncommon on the eastern Denali Highway. Orange-crowned, Yellow, Myrtle, Blackpoll, and Wilson's Warblers are common in the willows. Walk or drive the campground access road downstream to the lake, keeping an eye out for the pair of Merlins that usually nests here.

The highway skirts the north shore of Tangle Lake, where Common and often Red-throated Loons may be found. At Tangle Lakes Lodge, Milepost 22, birders can rent canoes by the hour to paddle uplake (south) to explore sloughs and other backwaters, excellent places for viewing loons and other waterfowl. The mouth of Rock Creek, halfway uplake, is productive for Arctic Warbler and other warbler species. Say's Phoebes traditionally nest on one of the lodge outbuildings. Inquire at the lodge about recent sightings and report any of your own.

Between Mileposts 22 and 25 the road passes through fair Arctic Warbler territory. Landmark Gap, the prominent feature to the north, is inconsistently good for Gyrfalcon, as is the surrounding countryside. Park on the north just before or just after the bridge over Rock Creek, Milepost 24.9, to look for American Dippers. The knoll on the east side of the bridge is very good for Arctic Warblers. Landmark Gap Trail, departing from this point, leads 3.5 miles to the north to Landmark Gap Lake, an excellent pathway for those interested in walking through this tundra. Expect the usual suite of sparrows and warblers, plus Gray-cheeked Thrush. Do not attempt to drive the road unless you have four-wheel drive with off-road tires and a short wheelbase; even then, you will not be able to proceed faster than a walk.

HIGH VALLEY—MACLAREN SUMMIT ZONE

(Paxson 25–37 miles; Cantwell 98–110 miles)

To the west of Rock Creek, the road ramps up the edge of High Valley into a habitat of high alpine tundra and rocky slopes. This feature is about 1,000 feet higher than the surrounding countryside, high enough not to have been glaciated by the (latest) Wisconsin Ice Age. Consequently, this area lacks the relatively young glacial geomorphological features of adjacent lands to the east and west.

A small roadside pond on the south between Mileposts 27 and 28 is worth a stop to look for Red-necked Phalarope and Arctic Tern. Listen for Arctic Warblers; if you haven't yet found this species, the roadside willows along the ramp—from about Milepost 28 to 30—can be good. Golden Eagle, Gyrfalcon, Willow Ptarmigan, Short-eared Owl, and Northern Shrike also may occur. Red-necked Phalarope and Semipalmated Plover frequent the several ephemeral and permanent ponds on both sides of the road throughout this zone. As the highway rises to skirt the north flanks of Whistler and Maclaren Ridges, talus slopes and rock glacier-rubble reach to the road. This is territory for American Pipit, and Gray-cheeked Thrush may be abundant. Near Maclaren Summit, which occurs about 1.5 miles east of the DOT marker, the distance from the road to the top of Maclaren Ridge is only about 200 feet. Once the snow banks have nearly or completely vanished, it is a relatively easy and worthwhile scramble to reach skyline. From there, high tundra stretches gently to the south for about a dozen miles, prime breeding territory for most tundra nesters: Willow and Rock Ptarmigan, American Golden-Plover, Whimbrel, Long-tailed Jaeger, Lapland and Smith's Longspurs, and many more. The footing is relatively easy and the wildflower display in July is unsurpassed. If you have time, make a loop by hiking to the summit of Maclaren Ridge, then returning to the highway far down the road from where you started. Northern Wheatear is suspected of nesting here, but this has yet to be confirmed.

The road descends from High Valley on a several-mile-long ramp into the Maclaren River valley. At Milepost 37, stop at a well-used pullout near the top. Far below you is the river valley, where swans might be present in some of the many kettle holes, although they will be too distant to safely identify. Lapland and occasionally Smith's Longspurs have been seen near this turnout.

MACLAREN VALLEY—ESKER LAKES ZONE

(Paxson 37–64 miles; Cantwell 71–98 miles)

As you descend toward the Maclaren River, the alpine tundra is dotted with many small lakes. Some birds to watch for include Northern Harrier, Willow Ptarmigan, Short-eared Owl, and Alder Flycatcher. A roadside pond with a collapsing peat bank on the south side of the road at Milepost 41 held a Bank Swallow colony until 2001. The pond often has Red-necked Phalaropes. Cross the Maclaren River bridge at Milepost 42, where Cliff Swallows plaster their nests to the horizontal girders. The local Common Ravens have learned to prey on nestlings by walking along the girders and breaking open the mud nests. The small ponds adjacent to the Maclaren River can hold astonishing numbers of Trumpeter Swans. Late in September 2000, there were between 75 and 100 swans staging for migration in a pond upstream of the bridge and visible from the road at a point about one-quarter mile west of the bridge. Pass through Crazy Notch, watching for Short-eared Owls and listening for Arctic Warblers. At Milepost 46, a road-cut through an esker has a small Bank Swallow colony.

The road intermittently follows an esker ridge for the next six miles, flanked on both sides by a series of small lakes that are some of the most prolific breeding sites for puddle and diving ducks along the highway. Red-throated and Common Loons, Horned Grebes, and Long-tailed Ducks also are present, as are Trumpeter and, occasionally, Tundra Swans. The lake on the north side of Milepost 50 held a tantalizing duo of female Hooded Mergansers throughout July 1999, far north of their nearest confirmed breeding locations. The tall sedges and grasses by the streams and ponds here have Lincoln's Sparrows, uncommon elsewhere along the highway. Willow Ptarmigan occasionally are common on this stretch of road.

Clearwater Creek at Milepost 56 is worth checking for Wandering Tattler, American Dipper, Arctic Warbler, and Northern Waterthrush. West of the creek, the road follows the crest of the best-delineated esker of the entire highway, flanked by a small number of kettle holes that may hold the usual swans and ducks.

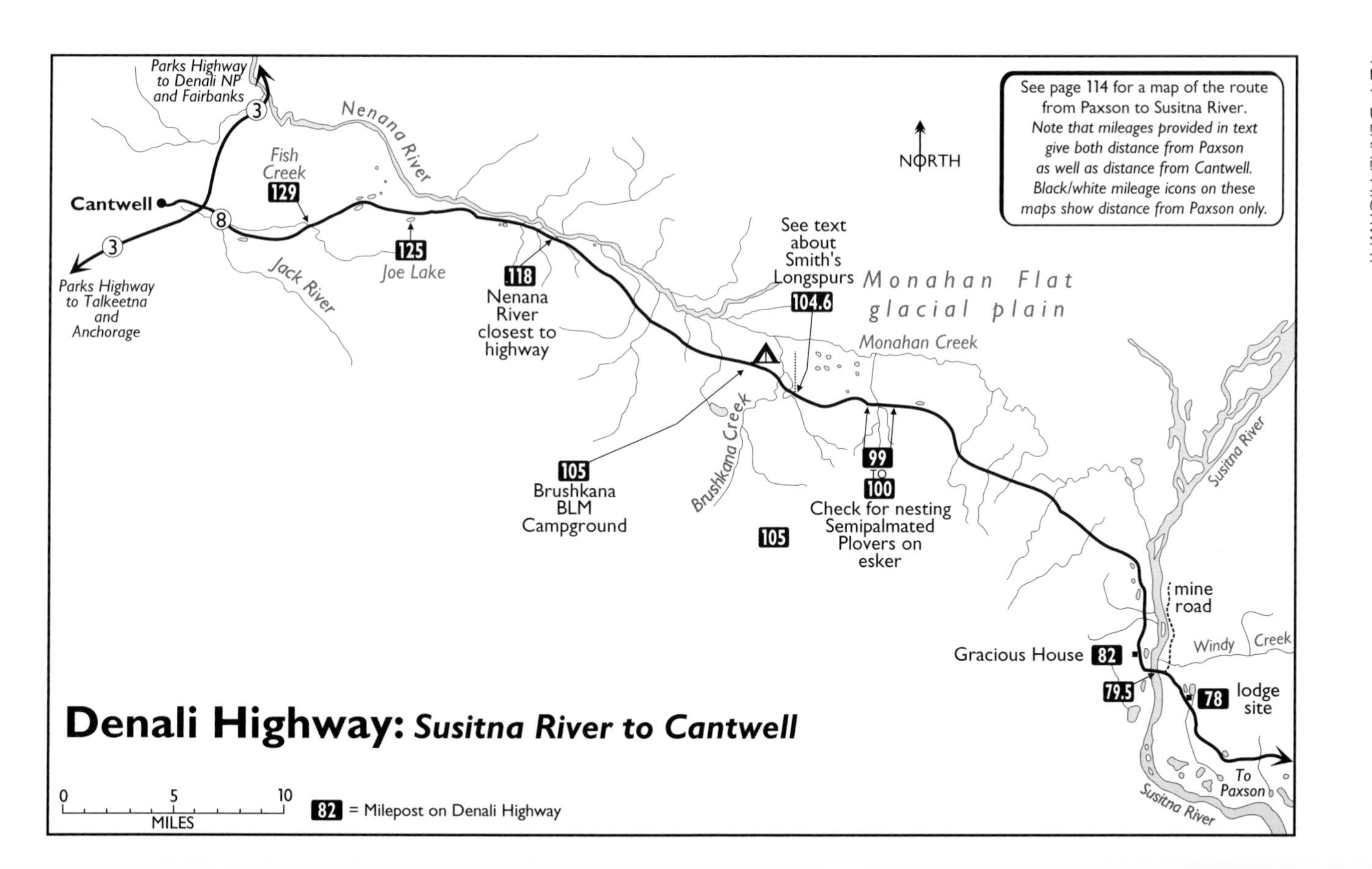

Denali Highway: *Susitna River to Cantwell*

CLEARWATER MOUNTAINS—SUSITNA VALLEY ZONE

(Paxson 64–92 miles; Cantwell 43–71 miles)

The highway veers south to swing around the Clearwater Mountains, an extension of the Alaska Range. The habitat changes as you drive from alpine tundra to boreal forest. Scan the flanks of the mountains for Golden Eagle and Gyrfalcon (rare). As the road rises again to the height of land at Milepost 64, you will have an extensive view to the south of the spruce-forested upper Susitna River valley. The road passes through the first moderate-sized spruce since leaving the Gulkana River at the highway's beginning. Look here for Ruffed and Spruce Grouse, Black-capped and Boreal Chickadees, Pine Grosbeak, and White-winged Crossbill. To the north, several roadside ponds between Mileposts 66 and 75 often carry small numbers of waterfowl. Travelers passing this way just after the road opens should scan the talus slopes for White-tailed Ptarmigan—this is one of the few places they very occasionally may be seen close to the highway. Two small lakes at Milepost 77–78, adjacent to a closed lodge, may hold Trumpeter or Tundra Swans.

Just short of the Susitna River, at Milepost 78.5, the gravel pit on the north side of the road leads to the Valdez Creek Mine road, one of the few driveable side roads along the highway, but you'll find the route almost devoid of birds. Red-necked Phalarope, swans, and ducks might be present in the roadside ponds along the Denali Highway east of the river.

Cross the Susitna at Milepost 79.5. The bridge affords an excellent view of the uppermost Susitna River valley and the glaciers that feed it, but the resultant silty waters hold little interest for birds. Nonetheless, the river course is a moderately important flyway, and late in the summer a small number of Sandhill Cranes occur here. Cliff Swallows nest on the bridge. West of the river and north of the highway is a good place to check for breeding Smith's Longspurs.

The two miles west of the river comprise one of the few consistent areas for Olive-sided Flycatcher along the highway, although even here their presence is occasional. Although there are numerous sites on the road that appear to be ideal habitat, this species is seen rarely. Gracious House is at Milepost 82. Check for Say's Phoebe about the buildings if you stop here for homemade pie or to spend the night.

MONAHAN FLAT ZONE

(Paxson 92–105 miles; Cantwell 30–43 miles)

A vast glacial plain stretches north from the highway to the base of the high peaks of the eastern Alaska Range for the next 15 miles. Upland Sandpiper is irregularly reported from here, and there are several parcels of terrain suitable for longspurs. Many of the waterbirds previously mentioned also occur here, but there are only a few bodies of open water within sight of the road. The esker upon which the highway is built at Mileposts 99–100 can produce nesting Semipalmated Plovers.

There are a number of sites for Smith's Longspur in this region. The most consistently productive are located a short distance east of the BLM campground by the Brushkana River, Milepost 105. Park at the turnout on the north side of the road just before descending the slope to the river, 0.4 mile before the campground on the river's west side. Put on rubber boots and walk directly north toward a large clearing with sparse trees on its far edge, listening for the longspur's distinctive call after about 400 yards. A smaller Smith's locale is reached by climbing the small slope adjacent to the campground's restrooms. This well-visited spot is hosting fewer and fewer birds each year, but if you are camping at Brushkana, it is worth checking out. Again (see Milepost 13 above), do not stress or endanger these birds.

NENANA RIVER VALLEY ZONE

(Paxson 105–135 miles; Cantwell 0–30 miles)

Upon leaving Monahan Flat, the highway enters intermittent spruce forest. If it is a good year for Northern Hawk Owls, you might see one anywhere along this westernmost stretch of the Denali. Northern Harriers also can be common here, and late in the summer Bohemian Waxwings might congregate here in flocks numbering in the hundreds. Spruce Grouse come down to the roadbed in search of grit, or perhaps the calcium chloride used to control dust. The Nenana River is visible from the road in many places as the highway drops close to river level near Milepost 118. Only a few sloughs here are suitable for waterfowl, but open areas should be scanned for Olive-sided Flycatchers. Check the gravel pit at Milepost 120 for nesting Bank Swallows, though they may not be present if DOT is working the pit. Joe Lake, on the south side of the road at Milepost 125, can be good for Horned Grebe and dabbling ducks, and Fish Creek at Milepost 129 is possible for Spotted Sandpiper. Belted Kingfisher may be present along the creek as it follows the highway in its final miles into Cantwell. The Denali Highway reaches the George Parks Highway (Alaska Route 3) 148 miles south of Fairbanks and 210 miles north of Anchorage.

LOGISTICS

The area code for all telephone numbers is 907 unless otherwise indicated. Statewide travel and birding information services are listed under Logistics in the Introduction, *page 15.*

Several lodges offer accommodations, meals, and other services (gas, towing) along the Denali Highway during the summer months. For your convenience they are all listed here; further details might be found in *The Milepost.* You can expect prices in this remote, highly-seasonal location to be higher than along the Richardson and Parks Highways.

Paxson Inn and Lodge (*Milepost 0.0*); 822-3330.

Paxson Alpine Tours & Cabins (a.k.a. Denali Highway Cabins) (*Milepost 0.2*), Audie Bakewell; 822-5972; *tours@denalihwy.com* or *cabins@ denalihwy.com*; web site *www.denalihwy.com*. Guided birding tours June–mid-July. Rental canoes and bicycles. Non-whitewater wildlife float trip through the Paxson Wildlife Reserve each summer evening, weather permitting.

Tangle River Inn (*Milepost 20*); 822-7304. Cabins and meals Tangle Lakes Lodge (*Milepost 22*), Alan and Susie Echols; 822-4202; *tanglelakes@starband.net*; web site *www.tanglelakeslodge.com*. Rental canoes for use on the Tangle Lakes. Maclaren River Lodge (*Milepost 42*); 822-7105. Gracious House (*Milepost 82*); 822-7307.

Cantwell — Accommodations in Cantwell include Backwoods Lodge, Cantwell Lodge, Denali Manor, and the Cantwell RV Park, all located west of the Parks Highway on a two-mile spur road that leads into Cantwell.

Please report sightings of local rarities to Audie Bakewell, including any Olive-sided Flycatcher or Northern Wheatear sightings.

ACKNOWLEDGEMENTS: This chapter is based on the forthcoming book *A Naturalist's Guide to North America's Most Beautiful Road* by Audie Bakewell. Richard Holmstrom added species information for the area around the Tangle Lakes. Notes by George West were incorporated into the text. Nancy DeWitt and Andrea Swingley of the Alaska Bird Observatory in Fairbanks kindly provided copies of Breeding Bird Survey results. Forrest Davis added some logistic information. Terry Doyle and Jon Dunn reviewed the chapter and provided additional birding notes.

Underwing Moth

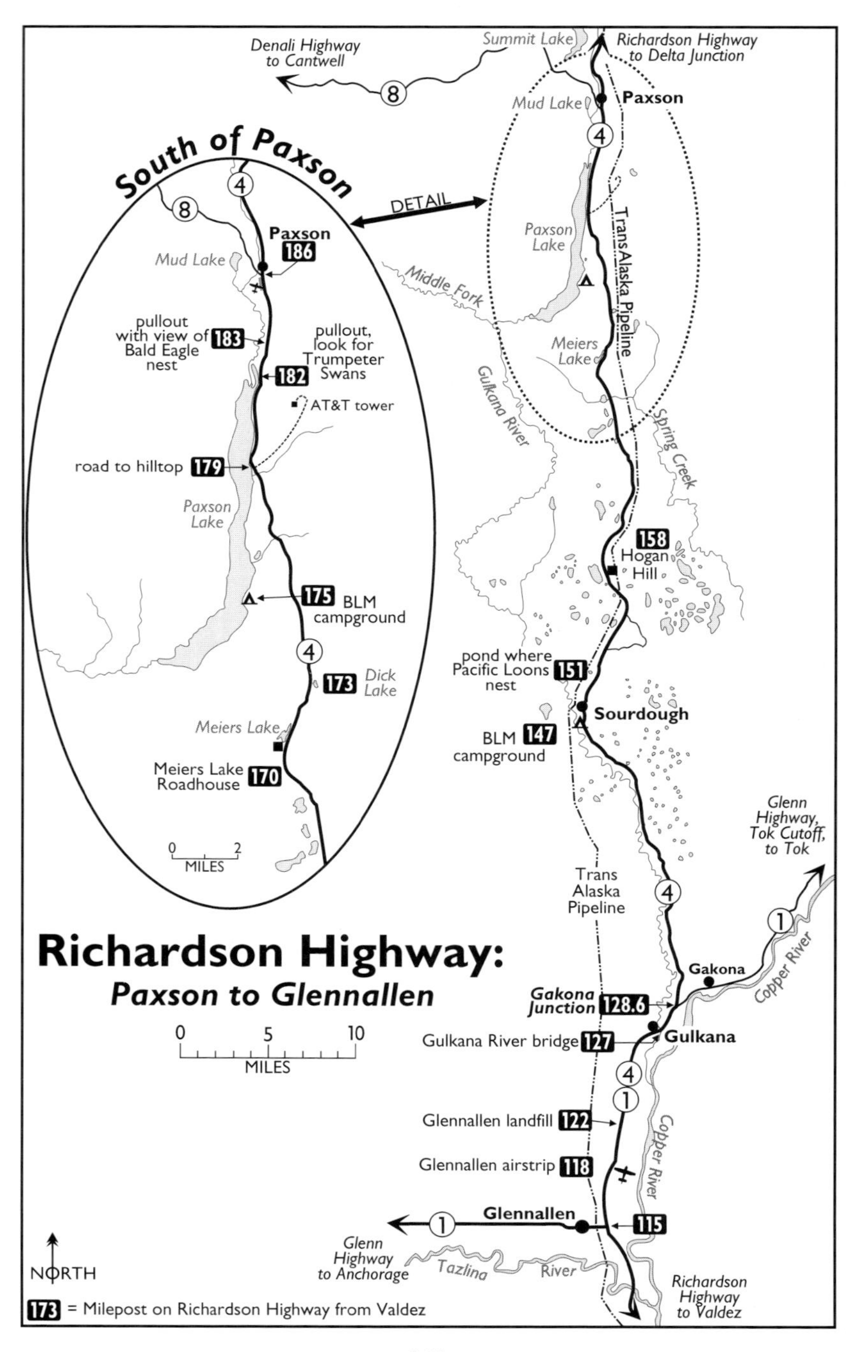

Richardson Highway:

Paxson to Glennallen

Richardson Highway:

Paxson to Glennallen

Audubon L. Bakewell IV, Jeff Bouton, and George West

Immediately south of the junction of the Richardson and Denali Highways at Paxson lies a grass airstrip on the west side of the road. This is worth scanning very early and very late in the season for Snow Buntings. There are often Bohemian Waxwings and Pine Grosbeaks in the adjacent spruce. A walk through the extensive trails between the airstrip and the Gulkana River can be productive for Boreal and Black-capped Chickadees, Varied and Swainson's Thrushes, Fox Sparrow, and, occasionally, Townsend's Solitaire.

The entire region south of the Denali and west of the Richardson Highways, as far south as Paxson Lake, is a wildlife preserve. This 20,000-acre Paxson Closed Area was set aside in 1958 as a preserve in order to allow Richardson Highway travelers the opportunity to see large animals from the highway. The Gulkana River creates a myriad of meanders, sloughs, and backwaters through this location, and the highway, slightly elevated on the flanks of the east Gulkana moraine, overlooks excellent habitat for Trumpeter Swan, Bald Eagle, Moose, and Beaver. A pullout at Milepost 183 is almost directly opposite a Bald Eagle nest, in continuous use since at least the mid-1970s. Scan the spruce tops just to the north of directly across the valley from this pullout; the nest is probably 600 yards away. Throughout the summer one or two pairs of Trumpeter Swans generally can be seen quite close to the highway. The usual assortment of dabbling ducks also occurs here: American Wigeon, Mallard, Northern Shoveler, and Green-winged Teal, an occasional Bufflehead, and Barrow's Goldeneye. The river hosts one of Alaska's largest Sockeye Salmon runs, and in August, when the fish are abundant, Bald Eagles, Herring and Glaucous-winged Gulls, and Common Ravens vie for the choice spots to gorge on the salmon.

There are two bays surrounding the influx of the Gulkana River that form the north end of Paxson Lake. One of them is visible from a pullout at Milepost 182. These shallow bays are very productive for Trumpeter Swan and Red-throated Loon. In autumn, medium-sized rafts of up to several hundred Greater and Lesser Scaup, three species of scoters, and dabbling

Great Horned Owl

ducks congregate here. The main body of the 12-mile-long lake holds several pairs of Common Loons. Arctic Terns are present until early August. You'll see several roads leading to the water's edge, but don't be tempted by them—all are private and trespassing is discouraged. Use only the highway pullouts and their associated trails. The exception is the public boat launch at the BLM Paxson Lake Campground at the south end of the lake (Milepost 175).

Well north of the campground, near Milepost 179, a broad gravel road to the east leads to the AT&T communications tower atop an unnamed peak. The three-mile drive is relatively easy and quite beautiful. The peak is 1,200 feet above the lake surface, and in clear weather provides magnificent views of the Alaska Range, the Wrangell Mountains, and the Chugach Mountains. The Black Spruce forest at the road's base provides fair opportunity for passerines, while the tundra at top is good for Willow Ptarmigan and, in spring, especially after a late snow, it may yield White-tailed Ptarmigan. Take a moderate hike to the obvious ridge east of the tower, where low tundra grasses attract Lapland and Smith's Longspurs. The very steep spur road to this ridge is for walking or four-wheel drive only. Return to the highway.

South from the BLM campground, the Richardson rises from White Spruce forest into Black Spruce bog. There are a number of lakes and ponds; the only sizable one is Dick Lake at Milepost 173, worth scanning for ducks and Horned Grebe. Alder Flycatcher is occasionally present here. Descend toward Meier's Lake, Milepost 172. The stream to the west contains numerous large stumps that are easily mistaken for Moose. Trumpeter Swans, however, often are present both there and in the lake. At Meier's Lake Roadhouse, Milepost 170, look for Northern Hawk Owl in the spruce-tops, or ask at the roadhouse whether there have been any sightings. Look for flocks of Sharp-tailed Grouse on the road in the high country near Meier's.

South from Meier's Lake the highway continues through spruce forest, climbing into alder forest along the flanks of Hogan Hill around Milepost 158. Check here for a population of Arctic Warblers. In June 1995, a Yellow-bellied Flycatcher and a Tennessee Warbler were found singing in this area. The Richardson then drops into many miles of Black Spruce bog. In good owl years Northern Hawk Owls should be present. Alder Flycatcher and Gray-cheeked and Swainson's Thrushes are common; Western Wood-Pewee is uncommon. There is a pulloff to the west at Milepost 151, where a two-acre pond traditionally has hosted a pair of Pacific Loons. Carefully heed the No Trespassing signs. There is no need to leave the public access to view the loons; transgressions will induce the owner to close it to all birders.

The entrance road to the BLM campground at Sourdough Creek is just south of some small buildings that mark the location of the former Sourdough Roadhouse at Milepost 147. The campground is one of the southernmost public access points to the Gulkana River, a Wild and Scenic River to the north. The land to the south is controlled by Ahtna, Inc., a Native corporation that has closed it to the public. The bridge across the now-large Gulkana River at Milepost 127 lets you view a backwater that often contains waterfowl.

The areas around the junction of the Tok Cutoff-Glenn Highway and Gakona (and a bit beyond) can be excellent for owls. Great Gray Owls might be seen in the mature deciduous stands of Balsam Poplar typically surrounded by open areas and some small spruce. Cruise the roads near dawn or dusk with your eyes wide open. Northern Hawk Owls are usually spotted in the tops of Black Spruce in low-lying areas during the day. Other species in the area from north of Gakona south to Gulkana include Sharp-tailed Grouse, Bank Swallow, Gray-cheeked and Swainson's Thrushes, Yellow and Blackpoll Warblers, and Northern Waterthrush.

The Glennallen landfill at Milepost 122 attracts Bald Eagles year round; immatures often roost near the highway. At Milepost 118, scan the extensive fields of the Gulkana airstrip for plovers and Upland Sandpiper. At Milepost 115, continue straight on the Richardson toward Valdez and Wrangell-Saint Elias National Park via the Richardson Highway (next chapter) or turn east on the Glenn Highway toward Palmer and Anchorage (page 184).

LOGISTICS

Tourist and travel services (accommodations, restaurants, attractions, etc.) can be found in the latest edition of The Milepost. *Statewide travel and birding information services are listed under Logistics in the* Introduction, *page 15.)*

Also see Denali Highway *Logistics* section, page 127.

ACKNOWLEDGEMENTS: Birding information from Tim Schantz's notes is appreciated. Terry Doyle reviewed the chapter and added birding notes.

RICHARDSON HIGHWAY:

GLENNALLEN TO VALDEZ

George West and Jeff Bouton

The Glenn Highway intersection with the Richardson Highway is at Milepost 115 of the Richardson. If you are turning west to Anchorage on Alaska Route 1, you will drive through the village of Glennallen, a small community with all the necessary services for a traveler.

Copper Center is at Milepost 105.1 as you drive south. You can bypass the town or go in for gas, a meal, or to spend the night. In 1992, a male Red-breasted Sapsucker, rare this far north, hit a window here and was brought to the National Park Service offices in Copper Center. As you head toward Valdez, look for Northern Hawk Owls, regular from here south.

At Milepost 91.1, the Old Edgerton Highway exits to the east toward Chitina and McCarthy (see next chapter). This road is not paved, so you may wish to continue south to Milepost 82.6 at Pippin Lake, where you can drive east on the paved Edgerton Highway (Alaska Route 10) to Chitina. Even if you do not plan to go all the way to Chitina or McCarthy on the Edgerton, consider driving east as far as Kenny Lake, where many rarities for interior Alaska have been recorded. Willow Lake, Milepost 87.7 of the Richardson, may be packed with loons, waterfowl, and Red-necked Phalaropes.

The Richardson continues south through the valleys of the Tonsina, Tiekel, and Tsina Rivers (all good for white-water kayaking). The road climbs slowly toward Thompson Pass. At Milepost 28.7, stop at Worthington Glacier State Recreation Site to drive up to and perhaps walk on the glacier. The road parallels Ptarmigan Creek as it heads to the pass. Throughout this area you will be in alpine tundra vegetation with willow brush and sedge meadows, good for White-tailed Ptarmigan, Northern Wheatear, Wilson's Warbler, and American Tree and Golden-crowned Sparrows. Thompson Pass, elevation 2,678 feet, crests at Milepost 26. As you begin your descent toward Valdez, stop at Blueberry Lake State Recreation Site, Milepost 24.1, for lunch or to camp overnight. A small pond here might have some waterfowl.

The highway drops into Keystone Canyon at Milepost 12.8 and parallels the Lowe River where you will find two spectacular waterfalls—Bridal Veil and Horsetail Falls. Trumpeter Swans nest in this area and might be easily observed from the highway in the small pools (Beaver-dammed offshoots) of the Lowe River. The road continues along the wide, braided Lowe River as it makes its way into Valdez. The turnoff to Robe Lake along the Robe River is at Milepost 4.7. This is a good fly-fishing stream in May and June. Typical forest birds may be seen along the road. The Richardson Highway officially ends at Old Valdez (Milepost 1), although the road continues west into the new town of Valdez.

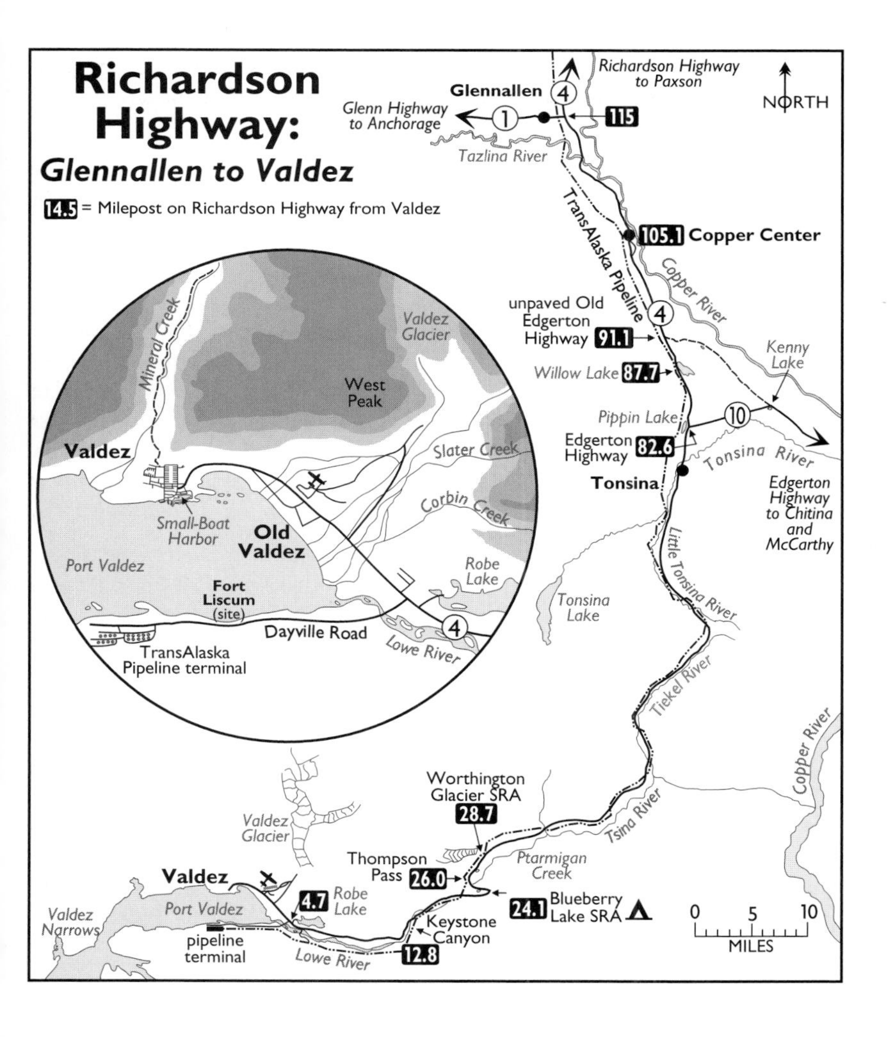

VALDEZ

The town most familiar to visitors to Prince William Sound is Valdez, site of the Alyeska Pipeline System's terminal port at the southern end of the TransAlaska Pipeline from Prudhoe Bay. The oil is loaded onto tankers here and shipped south to refineries in Washington and other places. Some comes north into Cook Inlet to refineries at Nikiski, north of the town of Kenai. Valdez is a modern fishing and shipping port with all the amenities you would expect from a small Alaskan town. The oil industry has dominated the town since 1968 when construction of the pipeline and terminal began.

You can get to Valdez by the Richardson Highway, by boat, by Alaska State ferry, or by plane. Valdez is 364 miles from Fairbanks on the Richardson or about 305 miles from Anchorage over the Glenn and Richardson Highways. You might come in on the Alaska State ferry from Cordova or Whittier and dock at the southern end of the city. Or you can take a scheduled commuter airline from Anchorage to the airport north of town. In any case, on a good day you will be impressed by the majesty of Valdez Arm, a giant fjord of water protected by 5,000-foot-high mountain peaks on both sides. However, be prepared for wet and windy weather that can occur any time of year, especially near the coastline.

There is a "new" Valdez and an Old Valdez. The latter was destroyed completely by the earthquake in 1964. A giant tidal wave (tsunami) roared into Valdez Arm and threw boats, people, and buildings high up on the shore; several people died here. The epicenter of the quake was very close to Valdez. Remnants of some buildings and docks can be seen if you drive the access road into the old town about four miles east on the highway. The new town was constructed after the earthquake and lacks the frontier character of the former old town.

Right outside Valdez in pristine Prince William Sound is Bligh Island, site of the grounding of the tanker *Exxon Valdez* in March 1989. The oil spill had a devastating impact on local bird, marine mammal, fish, and Native human populations. Millions of dollars of research has been conducted since then to document the impact of the oil spill and to determine whether each affected species has recovered or not. In general, most species have recovered. Some that were in decline before the spill, like Pigeon Guillemot and Marbled Murrelet, continue to decline. Bald Eagles, on the other hand, recovered quickly. Common Murres were heavily impacted throughout the spill area since most of the adult breeders were killed by the oil. After three or four years, younger murres began breeding, and the population is now almost back to its pre-spill numbers. Harlequin Ducks were severely impacted and have not recovered. Despite the clean-up efforts of Exxon and hundreds of volunteers, not all of the oil that hit the shores of Prince William Sound could

Red-necked Phalaropes

be removed. After a time of weathering, the oil was reduced to a tar, and finally to an almost solid state. The oil that seeped down among the rocks and gravel and could not be reached by the clean-up crews is still there, now solidified. Unfortunately, some toxic substances still dissolve from this tar into surrounding seawater. From there it enters the marine food chain and is taken up by plankton and, in turn, by clams and other mollusks. Harlequin Ducks feed on intertidal mollusks and thus ingest the toxic substances, and these, in some way, affect their ability to reproduce. Three good references on the spill are Lord (1992), Moskoff (2000), and Senner (1997) (See *References*, page 560).

Birding in Valdez is limited by access to the shoreline. Birds found here can also be found in other marine locations such as Homer, Seward, and Cordova, but if you are here for a while, following are some suggestions for birding the area.

By driving around Valdez near the docks and boat harbor and across the Lowe River on Dayville Road (about 7 miles east of Valdez) toward the pipeline terminal, you may turn up waterbirds, including loons, grebes, some sea ducks, Wandering Tattler, gulls, and alcids, including Pigeon Guillemot and Marbled Murrelet. Check especially near the small-boat harbor for the ubiquitous Bald Eagle, Parasitic Jaeger, Glaucous-winged Gull, and Northwestern Crow. Eagles nest on rock spires near the boat harbor, but the rocky terrain and sheer rock faces make for difficult footing and it is difficult to see much of the harbor from any vantage point due to the dense vegetation in the undeveloped areas. Aleutian Terns are often present, along with Arctic Terns, in late June and July. American Dippers are regular at the Crooked

Creek salmon-viewing pullout about one mile out of town. A second pullout for Pink and Silver Salmon spawning is 6.7 miles east of Valdez near the airport. Both areas provide you with a nice spectacle—the former in July and August and the latter area in August and September—as the streams fill with salmon.

Return to downtown Valdez and find Eagan Road west out of town. You will come into some mature Sitka Spruce with a Devil's Club understory along the shore of Mineral Creek. This is always an interesting spot, with Steller's Jay, Chestnut-backed Chickadee, Winter Wren, and Townsend's Warbler easily found. You might see a Rufous Hummingbird, as well. Access is difficult, and you need to try to find pulloffs away from private driveways, such as near the bridge over Mineral Creek. Walk along the side of the creek and the road. Walk the east bank of the stream down to where it meets Prince William Sound. Look for Black Brant that sometimes are on the sand flats in the small delta at the mouth of Mineral Creek, and for Harlequin Ducks and Black Oystercatchers.

LOGISTICS

The area code for all telephone numbers is 907 unless otherwise indicated. Tourist and travel services (accommodations, restaurants, attractions, etc.) not listed below can be found in the latest edition of The Milepost. *Statewide travel and birding information services are listed under Logistics in the* Introduction, *page 15.*

For information on the town of Valdez and local accommodations, contact the Valdez Convention and Visitor Bureau, PO Box 1603-ABA, Valdez, AK 99686; 835-2984 or 800-770-5954; *valdezak@alaska.net*; web site *www.alaskagold.com/valdez/index.html*.

Black Brant

EDGERTON HIGHWAY

George West

Perhaps the best reasons to travel the Edgerton Highway are to stop at Kenny Lake, site of several unusual waterfowl observations, to enjoy the scenery of the Wrangell-Saint Elias Mountain Range, and to explore the abandoned copper mine site at McCarthy at the end of the road.

The north turnoff—leading to the old Edgerton Highway—is at Milepost 91.1 of the Richardson Highway (Alaska Route 4). This gravel road joins the paved main highway in about 10 miles at Kenny Lake, and there is no particular reason to take this road except to vary your route. The junction of the paved Edgerton Highway (Alaska Route 10), Milepost 82.6, is 281 miles south of Fairbanks, 183 miles south of Delta Junction where the Alaska Highway (Route 2) joins the Richardson, and 32 miles south of the junction of Route 1, the Glenn Highway to Anchorage. The road is paved only to Chitina on the banks of the Copper River, where it becomes rough gravel for the next 58 miles to McCarthy. If you are short of time, travel at least to Kenny Lake, easily visible from the highway after about Milepost 5. All along the first five miles you get great looks at three of the highest peaks in the Wrangell Mountains—Mount Drum to the northeast at 12,010 feet, Mount Wrangell in the center at 14,163 feet, and Mount Blackburn to the east at 16,390 feet. Stop at the pullout with picnic tables on the shore of the lake at Milepost 7.7. Many unexpected birds have appeared at Kenny Lake, including Eurasian Wigeon, Cinnamon Teal, Ring-necked Duck, Wilson's Phalarope, and Yellow-bellied and Least Flycatchers.

The drive to Chitina is through typical interior Alaska spruce, alder, and cottonwood vegetation with associated birds. One good stop is pretty Liberty Falls State Recreation Site at Milepost 23.7. You can explore a road leading into the alpine past Liberty Falls on the right (west), a likely spot to look for White-tailed Ptarmigan.

If you are an Alaska resident, you can get a permit to accompany your fishing license in order to dip net for salmon in the Copper River south of Chitina between June and September. Fishing has been best along the old railroad grade that extends south along the Copper River to the Million Dollar Bridge east of Cordova (the road does not go through to Cordova). Birding is not the best here, however, as the railroad grade is carved into the mountainside with steep walls on one side and the rushing, silt-laden,

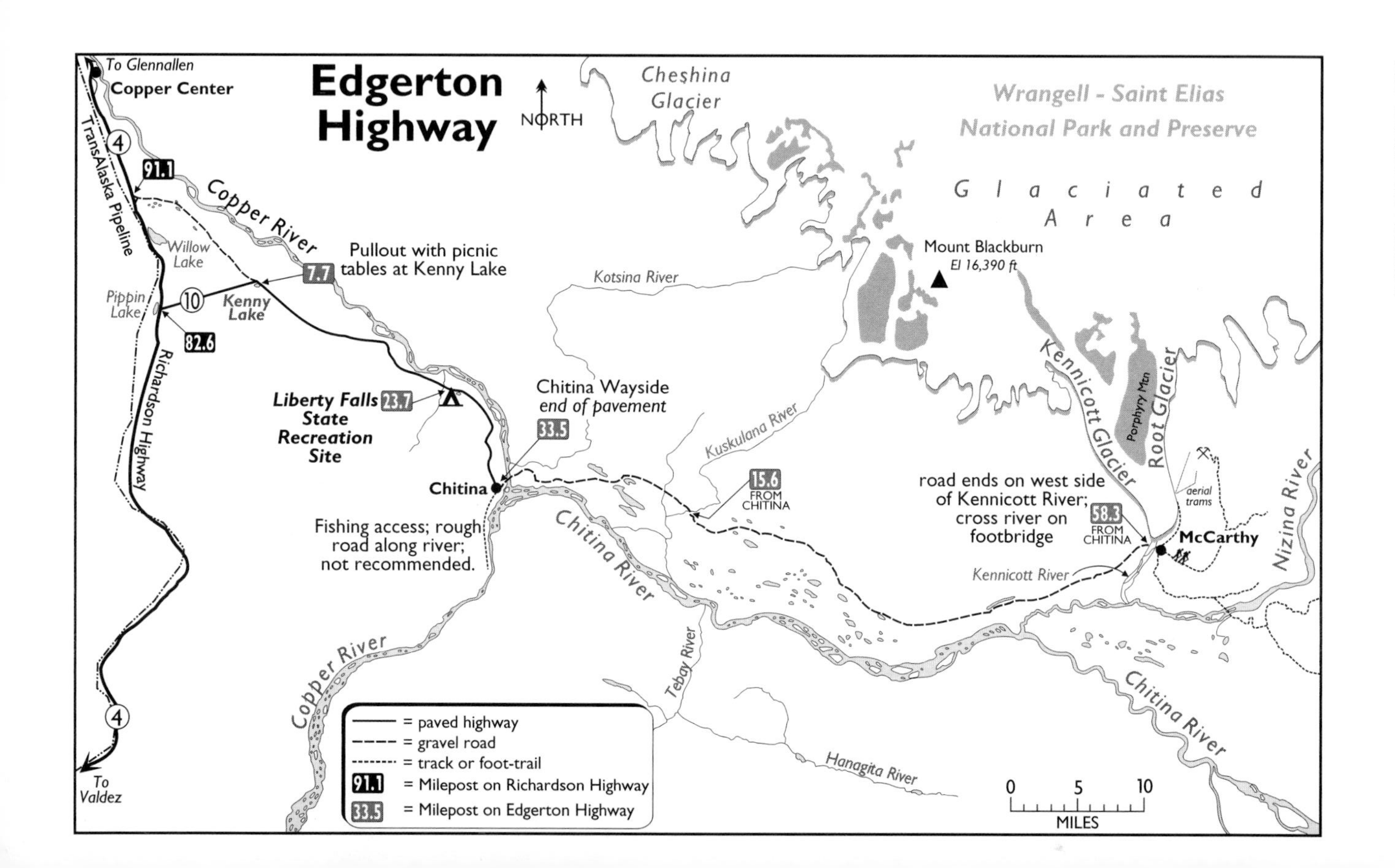
Edgerton Highway
NORTH
To Glennallen
Copper Center
4
91.1
TransAlaska Pipeline
Copper River
Willow Lake
Pippin Lake
10
Kenny Lake
82.6
7.7
Pullout with picnic tables at Kenny Lake
Richardson Highway
Liberty Falls State Recreation Site
23.7
Chitina
Fishing access; rough road along river; not recommended.
Chitina Wayside end of pavement
33.5
Kotsina River
Cheshina Glacier
Kuskulana River
15.6 FROM CHITINA
Chitina River
Tebay River
Hanagita River
Mount Blackburn
El 16,390 ft
Wrangell - Saint Elias National Park and Preserve
G l a c i a t e d A r e a
Kennicott Glacier
Porphyry Mtn
Root Glacier
aerial trams
McCarthy
road ends on west side of Kennicott River; cross river on footbridge
58.3 FROM CHITINA
Kennicott River
Nizina River
Chitina River
Copper River
4
To Valdez
= paved highway
= gravel road
= track or foot-trail
91.1 = Milepost on Richardson Highway
33.5 = Milepost on Edgerton Highway
0 5 10
MILES

dangerous Copper River on the other. It is recommended that you not drive your rental car along this "road" that can be very rough and dangerous.

Alder leaves and cones *Alnus crispa*

The ranger station for the Wrangell-Saint Elias National Park and Preserve is located in Chitina. The town also has a grocery store, gas station, restaurant, and motel. The pavement ends at Milepost 33.5. After passing the Chitina Wayside (restrooms) at Milepost 33.6, you can access the Copper River from a turnout at Milepost 34.1, but heed the warnings about boating in glacial rivers in the *Introduction*, page 19. The road crosses the Copper River on a modern bridge at Milepost 34.7, and reaches the junction of the McCarthy Road at Milepost 35.1. *Mileposts from here on indicate distance from Chitina.*

You will cross an old steel-trestle railroad bridge at Milepost 15.6. The bridge deck is 385 feet above the Kuskulana River. There are a few pullouts along this first section of the road, but after about 30 miles the road narrows, with heavy brush on both sides. Be cautious for bears in this area. After 50 miles, you will start seeing signs of civilization again as you approach McCarthy. The road ends at Milepost 58.3 at the Kennicott River. Pull in to the parking lot at Milepost 58.2, as you must walk across the bridge to reach McCarthy and get to the ruins of the Kennicott Copper Mine. You can walk up the hills above the mine buildings into the alpine to look for ptarmigan, Northern Wheatear, and other alpine species. But it is probably easier to do that elsewhere.

LOGISTICS

The area code for all telephone numbers is 907 unless otherwise indicated. Tourist and travel services (accommodations, restaurants, attractions, etc.) can be found in the latest edition of The Milepost. *Statewide travel and birding information services are listed under Logistics in the* Introduction, *page 15.*

There are several lodges and B&Bs in McCarthy.

ACKNOWLEDGEMENTS: Jeff Bouton provided details on where to find birds on this route.

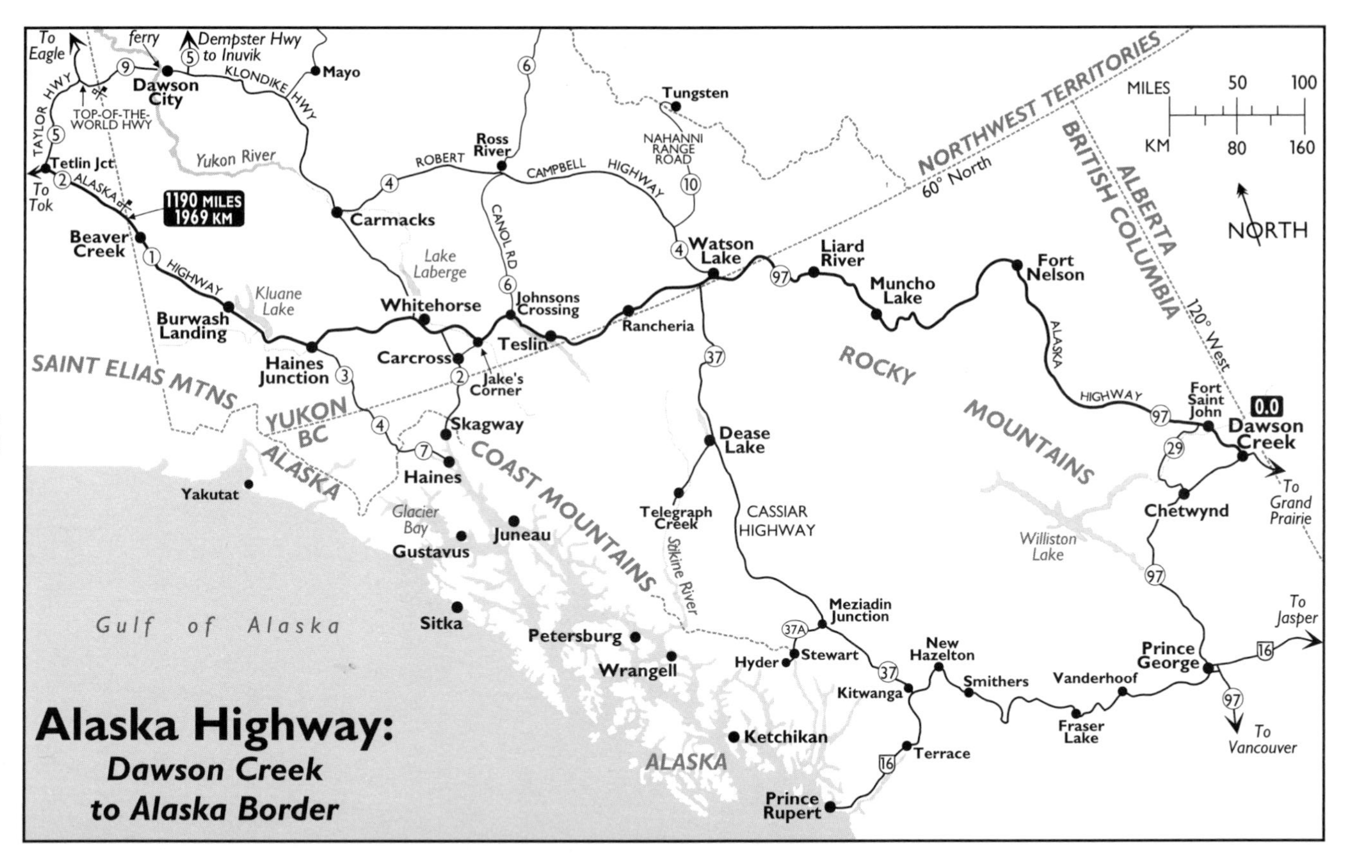

Alaska Highway:
Dawson Creek
to Alaska Border
MILES
50
100
KM
80
160
NORTH
NORTHWEST TERRITORIES
60° North
BRITISH COLUMBIA
ALBERTA
120° West
To Eagle
ferry
Dempster Hwy to Inuvik
Mayo
Dawson City
KLONDIKE HWY
TAYLOR HWY
TOP-OF-THE-WORLD HWY
Tungsten
NAHANNI RANGE ROAD
Yukon River
Ross River
ROBERT
CAMPBELL
HIGHWAY
Tetlin Jct
To Tok
ALASKA
1190 MILES
1969 KM
Beaver Creek
Carmacks
CANOL RD
Watson Lake
Liard River
Fort Nelson
HIGHWAY
Lake Laberge
Kluane Lake
Muncho Lake
Whitehorse
Johnsons Crossing
Burwash Landing
Rancheria
Teslin
Carcross
Haines Junction
Jake's Corner
ROCKY
SAINT ELIAS MTNS
YUKON
BC
Skagway
MOUNTAINS
Fort Saint John
0.0
Dawson Creek
Dease Lake
ALASKA
Haines
COAST MOUNTAINS
To Grand Prairie
Yakutat
Chetwynd
Telegraph Creek
Glacier Bay
Juneau
CASSIAR HIGHWAY
Gustavus
Williston Lake
Stikine River
Meziadin Junction
To Jasper
Gulf of Alaska
Sitka
Petersburg
Stewart
New Hazelton
Prince George
Hyder
Wrangell
Smithers
Vanderhoof
Kitwanga
Fraser Lake
To Vancouver
Ketchikan
Terrace
Prince Rupert

ALASKA HIGHWAY:

DAWSON CREEK TO ALASKA BORDER

Cameron D. Eckert

The Alaska Highway, also known as "the Alcan," runs 2,238 km/1,390 miles from Dawson Creek, British Columbia, across southern Yukon to Delta Junction, Alaska. From there it joins the Richardson Highway for the remaining 158km/98 miles to Fairbanks, Alaska. Built by the U.S. Army in 1942–1943 during World War II, it has been described as an engineering marvel that was completed in just eight months. Some travelers may feel that it has yet to be finished. Despite improvements over the years, the rougher sections still inspire feelings of what it was like 50 years ago. Nevertheless, the Alaska Highway traverses a remarkable and remote part of the continent and offers traveling birders a chance to experience the transition through the northern boreal forest to the doorstep of the subarctic.

Towns and settlements offer lodging, meals, automotive services, groceries, and camping at regular intervals along the highway. *The Milepost* has detailed information on services. Visitors will have no trouble using their credit cards in Canada and getting a fair exchange on the U.S. dollar. Two pieces of picture identification are required at border crossings, and travelers from outside Canada and the U.S. will need a passport. Safe travel along the highway requires moderate speed, good tires, and a proper spare. An extra can of gas is not needed unless extended off-road travel is planned. Always watch for wildlife on the highways. Common sense and courteous behavior are the best means for a safe trip.

The region's birdlife is reasonably well known, although there are still opportunities for discovery. Unfamiliar species, habitats, and song dialects provide visiting birders with plenty of surprises and chances to hone their skills. The Alaska Highway passes through the ranges of many species. A leisurely pace with frequent stops, especially as the habitat changes, is the best way to ensure that you don't miss common species such as Northern Goshawk, Spruce Grouse, Three-toed Woodpecker, or even Boreal Chickadee. Keep a keen eye on the spruce tops for Northern Hawk Owl and Great Gray Owl. The British Columbia section of the Alaska Highway is covered in greater detail in birdfinding guides by Mark (1984) and Taylor

(1993), with Eckert (2001), Finlay (2000), and Frisch (1987) providing additional information for the Yukon. Take advantage of local bird checklists (Eckert et al. 2001) to assess which species are expected, and document unusual sightings and breeding records. The Yukon Bird Club (see *Logistics* below) will ensure that such information is incorporated into the comprehensive Birds of the Yukon database. In this way, visitors can make a valuable contribution to knowledge of the region's birdlife. A bit of planning combined with a realistic pace will be rewarded with many memorable sightings and a substantial trip list.

Distances in this section of the guide are provided in kilometers and miles and both represent the actual distance traveled from Dawson Creek, BC, which is the zero mark. This does not correspond to either the physical kilometer posts or the historic mileage-markers along the Alaska Highway. Note that *The Milepost* publication provides distances using miles for the actual distance traveled, and kilometers for the physical kilometer posts (the two do not line up due to highway realignment over the years). The convention used here for direction along the highway is that "north" is headed toward Alaska and "south" is headed toward British Columbia. The locations described here will get you started on your trip of discovery, although you'll no doubt find countless other great places to go birding in this extraordinary region.

DAWSON CREEK, BC, TO WHITEHORSE, YUKON

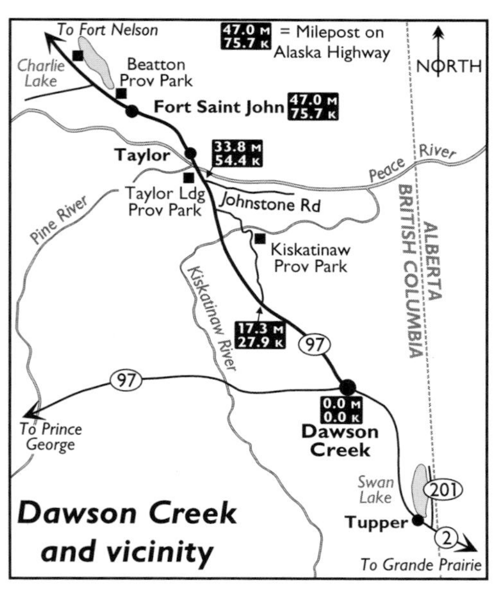

DAWSON CREEK, BC

The town of Dawson Creek is Milepost 0 of the Alaska Highway. The area is characterized by diverse habitats and ecosystems. Birders from British Columbia consider this to be an especially attractive region for a variety of localized species near the edge of their ranges. One of the best known birding locations is **Swan Lake Provincial Park**, located at the small town of Tupper, 37 km southeast of Dawson Creek on Highway 2. The park is a good location for a variety of songbirds. While this requires a detour from the Alaska Highway, it is worthwhile for those interested in observing Le Conte's and Nelson's Sharp-tailed Sparrows that are found near the park. Birdfinding guides by Mark (1984) and Taylor (1993) provide more detailed directions. To search for these sparrows go east from Tupper on Highway 2 for about 5 km/3.1 miles toward the Alberta border, turning left (north) onto Road 201 before crossing the BC/Alberta border. This road may not be suitable for vehicles such as RVs with a limited turning radius. Take Road 201 north across a set of railway tracks and then onward toward the southeast corner of Swan Lake. As the road bends to the east watch for a cutline on the west side of the road. Park here and walk along the cutline through the Quaking Aspen and watch for wet grassy meadows on the left which extend to the lakeshore. Both Le Conte's and Nelson's Sharp-tailed Sparrows breed in these meadows around the lake, with Le Conte's preferring slightly drier areas and Nelson's Sharp-tailed found in wetter areas. Nelson's Sharp-tailed is the rarer of the two species. Good luck, and you'll need your rubber boots!

KISKATINAW PROVINCIAL PARK, BC

The turnoff for Kiskatinaw Provincial Park is located on the right side (east) of the Alaska Highway at km 27.9/mile 17.3, and follows a 10 km/6-mile loop of the Old Alaska Highway which rejoins the main highway at km 34.8/mile 21.6. The park, located 4 km/2.5 miles down the loop road, offers overnight camping and access to the Kiskatinaw River. The riparian forests are home to Yellow-bellied Sapsucker, Gray and Blue Jays, and Black-capped and Boreal Chickadees. Black-throated Green and Bay-breasted Warblers are near the edge of their ranges here.

PEACE RIVER AND FORT SAINT JOHN, BC

The diverse and lush habitats of the Peace River (km 55.4/mile 34.4) north to the town of Fort Saint John (km 75.7/mile 47) make this a fascinating birding area. Species characteristic of the region include Eastern Phoebe, Philadelphia and Red-eyed Vireos, House Wren, numerous warblers including Cape May, Black-throated Green, Black-and-white, Ovenbird, Mourning, MacGillivray's, and Canada, as well as Western Tanager, Clay-colored Sparrow, Rose-breasted Grosbeak, and Baltimore Oriole. Three of the area's better known birding locations are Johnstone Road, Beatton Provincial Park, and Charlie Lake Provincial Park.

Johnstone Road (km 54.4/mile 33.8) is located on the right side (east) of the Alaska Highway about 1 km/0.6 mile south of the Peace River bridge (km 55.4/mile 34.4), which is 1 km/0.6 mile south of the town of Taylor (km 56.4/mile 35). Taylor Landing Provincial Park is located on the left side (west) of the Alaska Highway opposite Johnstone Road. Johnstone Road follows the Peace River through Quaking Aspen groves and riparian forests with good road conditions for about 5 km/3 miles. Beyond that point road conditions deteriorate, although birders can continue on foot. Species known in the area include Northern Goshawk, Philadelphia and Red-eyed Vireos, a wide variety of warblers, Clay-colored and White-throated Sparrows, Rose-breasted Grosbeak, and Baltimore Oriole.

Beatton Provincial Park (km 79.7/mile 49.5) is located on the right (east) about 4 km/2.5 miles north of Fort Saint John. Watch for the turnoff that leads 8 km/5 miles to the park. This park offers day use, camping, and a boat launch, with impressive stands of White Spruce and good views of Charlie Lake. A trail located at the edge of the playing field beyond the camping area and boat launch provides access to a mix of forest types including old-growth White Spruce. This is a good place to look for Three-toed and Black-backed Woodpeckers as well as a variety of songbirds.

Charlie Lake Provincial Park (km 86.9/mile 54) is on the right (east) about 11.4 km/7.1 miles north of Fort Saint John. The park offers day use, camping, and a boat launch. A trail leads 2 km/1.2 miles from the campground area to the lake. Scan the lake for Common Loon, Horned, Eared, and Western Grebes, Franklin's Gull, and Common Tern. The forested and wetland habitats are known for Bohemian Waxwing, Tennessee Warbler, White-throated Sparrow, and Rusty Blackbird.

Pileated Woodpecker

FORT NELSON, BC

The town of Fort Nelson (km 455.6/mile 283) is situated in a region known for its rich woodlands. The productive forest and wetland habitats are inhabited by a wide diversity of birds, including Broad-winged Hawk, Black Tern, Yellow-bellied Flycatcher, and various warblers. Two of the area's best known birding locations are Parker Lake and Kledo Creek.

Parker Lake Road (km 468.5/mile 291) is about 12.9 km/8 miles north of Fort Nelson. Watch for an unsigned dirt road on the left side (west) that leads to Parker Lake. Stop often along the road to check for songbirds, including Yellow-bellied Flycatcher in the open muskeg about half way down the road and Palm Warbler. The lake and shoreline habitats feature Sora, Wilson's Phalarope, Black Tern, and Swamp Sparrow. Why not take the canoe off the roof and spend the afternoon exploring the lakeside marshes?

Kledo Creek (km 512.6/mile 318.4), located about 57 km/35.4 miles north of Fort Nelson, features the rich forested habitats that are characteristic of the region. Species expected here include Least Flycatcher, Bay-breasted and Canada Warblers, Ovenbird, and White-throated Sparrow. As well, Connecticut Warbler and Clay-colored Sparrow have been reported from this location.

STONE MOUNTAIN PROVINCIAL PARK, BC

Stone Mountain Provincial Park (km 598.1/mile 371.5) features nearly 26,000 hectares/64,246 acres of stunning scenery, extraordinary landscapes, and remote wilderness. The Alaska Highway runs through the northern part of the park and provides access for camping, hiking, and birding. This is a rich area for wildlife—Woodland Caribou, Stone Sheep, and Moose often cross the highway, so drive with care. The best access to alpine habitats is from the microwave-tower road (km 601.3/mile 373.5) that starts west of the Summit Lake Lodge. Inquire at the gas station for directions if you have difficulty finding the microwave-tower road. Follow the road for 2.5 km/1.5 miles to the trailhead for Flower Springs Lake Trail and explore the trail by foot, or continue on another 4.5 km/2.8 miles to the microwave tower. Birds in the area include all three ptarmigan, American Tree and Golden-crowned Sparrows, and Gray-crowned Rosy-Finch.

LIARD RIVER HOTSPRINGS PROVINCIAL PARK, BC

Liard River Hotsprings Provincial Park (km 769.1/mile 477.7) offers overnight camping, with lodgings and a cafe at the adjacent Trapper Ray's Lodge. Liard Hotsprings is a very special place; plan to spend at least a night to enjoy both a dip in the hotsprings and the wonderful birding. The lush White Spruce and Paper Birch forests feature many species that are at the edge of their range and non-existent or very localized farther north. Such species commonly seen are Barred Owl, Pileated Woodpecker, Red-eyed Vireo, Magnolia and Black-and-white Warblers, Ovenbird, Western Tanager, and Rose-breasted Grosbeak. Other common species are Yellow-bellied Sapsucker, Warbling Vireo, Bohemian Waxwing, White-throated Sparrow, Red and White-winged Crossbills, and Pine Siskin. Greater and Lesser Yellowlegs and a variety of other shorebirds during migration are seen from the boardwalk across the hotsprings marsh.

Magnolia Warbler

WATSON LAKE, YUKON

The town of Watson Lake (km 986.8/mile 612.9), known as the "Gateway to the Yukon," is the first Yukon community north of the 60th parallel. It was established in 1940 as a support center for an airfield as part of Canada's Northwest Staging Route Program. For Yukon birders headed south, Watson Lake is the "Gateway to Eastern Songbirds." Species such as Pileated Woodpecker, Blue-headed Vireo, Magnolia Warbler, Western Tanager, Swamp and White-throated Sparrows, and Brewer's Blackbird reach the very western limit of their range in this area. Three of the better known birding locations are Hour Glass Creek, Wye Lake Park, and Watson Lake campground.

Hour Glass Creek flows from Hour Glass Lake and crosses the Alaska Highway about 5 km/3 miles south of Watson Lake's Signpost Forest. That is, just south of Watson Lake Campground Services (km 982.9/mile 610.5) and immediately south of the weigh station (km 982.7/mile 610.4) at the south end of town. The creek meanders through a broad wetland on the right side (upstream) of the highway and is a good place for Sora, Solitary Sandpiper, Common Nighthawk, Olive-sided and Alder Flycatchers, Blackpoll Warbler, Northern Waterthrush, Common Yellowthroat, and Lincoln's and Swamp Sparrows. Eastern Kingbird has been seen here. To bird the wetland you can either walk along the dry forest edge to the north or south of the wetland, or canoe upstream along the narrow marshy creek.

Wye Lake Park, located in the center of town just north of the junction of the Alaska Highway and Robert Campbell Highway, has a picnic area, marsh boardwalk, and trails. Pacific and Common Loons and Red-necked Grebes frequent the lake, and a variety of songbirds inhabits the surrounding forests and marshes, including Alder Flycatcher, Yellow Warbler, Common Yellowthroat, Western Tanager, Lincoln's Sparrow, and, rarely, Clay-colored Sparrow. In winter, an occasional covey of Willow Ptarmigan may be flushed from the shrubs.

Watson Lake campground (km 990.6/mile 615.3), 2 km/1.2 miles off the highway, offers camping, a boat launch, and a view of Watson Lake. Scan the lake for loons, grebes, and diving ducks. The forests host Spruce Grouse, Yellow-bellied Sapsucker, Three-toed Woodpecker, Swainson's Thrush, and White-winged Crossbill. Blue-headed Vireo has been seen here.

UPPER LIARD, YUKON

The village of Upper Liard (km 998.5/mile 620.2), located 11.7 km/7.3 miles north of Watson Lake, offers access to some of the Yukon's richest White Spruce forests along the Liard River. The best birding here is along the Albert Creek road (also known as Rancheria Loop Road) located about 2 km/1.3 miles north of the bridge over the Liard River. Go right on the Albert Creek road for about 1.6 km/1 mile, and bird the area around the marshy oxbow. Species regularly seen are Spruce Grouse, Yellow-bellied Sapsucker, Pileated Woodpecker, Western Wood-Pewee, Alder, Least, and Hammond's Flycatchers, Warbling Vireo, Swainson's and Varied Thrushes, Tennessee and Magnolia Warblers, American Redstart, Western Tanager, and Lincoln's and White-throated Sparrows. Both Rusty and Brewer's Blackbirds are found here. This is a particularly good area to watch for Great Gray Owl.

UPPER LIARD TO TESLIN, YUKON

The route between Upper Liard and Teslin passes through the Cassiar Mountains covering a wide range of habitats. Consider taking advantage of rest stops and birding opportunities at Little Rancheria Creek (km 1,042.3/mile 647.4), Big Creek rest area (km 1,048.3/mile 651.1), Lower Rancheria River (km 1,069.5/mile 664.3), Rancheria Falls Recreation Site and interpretive boardwalk (km 1,119.3/mile 695.2), Upper Rancheria River (km 1,124.9/mile 698.7), Swift River (km 1,130.5/mile 702.2), Partridge Creek (km 1,147.4/mile 712.7), Logjam Creek (km 1,171.9/mile 727.9), Smart River (km 1,184.6/mile 735.8), and Morley River day-use area (km 1,210.7/mile 752).

TESLIN, YUKON

The village of Teslin (km 1,249.4/mile 776) is located on the scenic shores of Teslin Lake at Nisutlin Bay. Teslin Lake is a great area for birds and many Yukon rarities have been recorded here, including Turkey Vulture, Clay-colored Sparrow, Lazuli Bunting, and Brambling. Scan the lake for Red-throated, Pacific, Common, and Yellow-billed Loons, with the latter being regular in fall. Horned and Red-necked Grebes and many species of waterfowl are common. During spring and summer, watch for Bonaparte's Mew, and Herring Gulls and Arctic Terns; migrant Thayer's and Glaucous Gulls occur in fall and often roost on top of the bridge over Nisutlin Bay. The shoreline and forest habitats are productive for songbirds, with Alder Flycatcher, Yellow Warbler, and Gambel's White-crowned Sparrow in the shrubs; Yellow-bellied Sapsucker, Least and Hammond's Flycatchers, Warbling Vireo, and Purple Finch in Quaking Aspen and Balsam Poplar forests; and Spruce Grouse, Three-toed Woodpecker, Boreal Chickadee, Golden-crowned Kinglet, and Townsend's Warbler in the older White Spruce forests. During migration, American Pipits, migrant sparrows, Lapland Longspurs, and Snow Buntings frequent roadsides.

TESLIN TO JAKE'S CORNER, YUKON

The highway between Teslin and Jake's Corner is peppered with good places to take a break from the trip and see some new birds. Consider stops at the Teslin Lake viewing platform (km 1,252.6/mile 778), Teslin Lake campground (km 1,264.2/mile 785.2), Ten Mile Creek (km 1,264.3/mile 785.3), Lone Tree Creek (km 1,270.1/mile 788.9), Deadman's Creek (km 1,279.3/mile 794.6), Robertson Creek (km 1,289.3/mile 800.8), Johnson's Crossing campground (km 1,302.3/mile 808.9), Little Teslin Lake (km 1,308.6/mile 812.8), Squanga Lake campground (km 1,321.8/mile 821), and Jake's Corner (km 1,347.2/mile 836.8).

CARCROSS, YUKON

The village of Carcross, nestled between Bennett Lake to the west and Nares Lake to the east, is exceptionally beautiful (refer to map on page 464). The side-trip to Carcross provides a wonderful scenic diversion that can be done as a loop that returns to the Alaska Highway at km 1,407.8/mile 874.4, just 14 km/8.7 miles south of Whitehorse. To reach Carcross, turn south on the Tagish road (Highway 8) from Jake's Corner (km 1,347.2/mile 836.8) and continue 55 km/34.2 miles to Carcross. Skagway, Alaska, is another 107 km/66.5 miles south along the South Klondike Highway. To return to the Alaska Highway from Carcross, go north about 50 km/31.1 miles on the South Klondike Highway (Highway 2). Three of the area's best-known birding locations are Nares Lake, Bennett Lake, and Montana Mountain.

Nares Lake on the east side of Carcross is an important spring staging area for waterfowl, shorebirds, and gulls. The best birding is typically from late April through early June, and again in fall. Dall's Sheep are often seen on the hills to the north and east of Nares Lake. Nares Lake can be viewed from the grassy airstrip immediately adjacent to the highway in Carcross, or drive south from Carcross along South Klondike Highway across the Nares River bridge and then take the first left about 1 km/0.6 mile south of the bridge. This road immediately swings north right along Nares Lake back toward the Nares River bridge.

Bennett Lake on the west side of Carcross is not as rich as Nares Lake but is certainly worth checking for loons, grebes, and waterfowl. There are two ways to bird Bennett Lake starting from the Carcross visitor center: Walk southwest from the visitor center along the beach and dunes, which continue about 2.5 km/1.6 miles to the outflow of the Watson River, or cross the footbridge adjacent to the visitor center across the Nares River and walk south along the train tracks.

Montana Mountain at Carcross is a spectacular birding attraction. A combination of driving and moderate hiking provides access to remote high-elevation (up to 2,000 m/6,000 ft) habitats which support species such as White-tailed Ptarmigan, Blue Grouse, Timberline Sparrow, and Gray-crowned Rosy-Finch. In the Yukon, Dusky Flycatchers are found breeding exclusively at or just below tree line and this species is common on Montana Mountain. It is a good idea to file an itinerary and return time with friends or officials whenever you explore remote areas such as Montana Mountain. This road is not suitable for vehicles such as RVs with a limited turning radius. To reach Montana Mountain, start at Carcross and head south on the South Klondike Highway (Highway 2) toward Skagway, which immediately takes you across the Nares River bridge. Take the first right immediately after the bridge onto a dirt road and continue a short distance (100 m/300 ft) to a T-junction where a right turn takes you back down to the Nares River and a left turn begins the ascent up Montana Mountain. The road may be impassable due to snow until late May but is usually clear by early June. Road conditions are poor but with care it is possible to drive a car about 10 km/6.3 miles to tree line where a rock slide makes it impossible to drive farther. At this point park and continue on foot. A hike along the road takes you past an old water tank converted into a Buddhist temple, an old mining camp and the crumbling remains of stone houses, to the top of the main road (the saddle). From here you can hike in any direction in search of high-alpine species. Blue Grouse inhabit the Subalpine Fir forests to tree line. Dusky Flycatcher and Golden-crowned Sparrow inhabit the tall shrubs at tree line, with Townsend's Solitaire and Hermit Thrush in the open coniferous forests along the creek. Timberline Sparrows favor dense, low shrubs and may be seen anywhere along the road above tree line. Willow Ptarmigan are common. Continue along the main road to the old Buddhist temple (water tower) on the right and check for Say's Phoebe. Continue past the temple to a fork in the road: stay left to keep on the main road or go right to make a small detour down to an old mining camp. Say's Phoebes nest in the old buildings and Timberline Sparrows inhabit the low shrubs around the camp. Return to the main road and continue on to the remains of the stone houses at the saddle. Golden Eagle, White-tailed Ptarmigan, Horned Lark, American Pipit, and Gray-crowned Rosy-Finch are regularly seen in this area. Just beyond the stone houses the main road ends and trails radiate in various directions. Any of the rocky slopes offer suitable habitat for White-tailed Ptarmigan and Gray-crowned Rosy-Finch. The ptarmigan tend to call, so don't ignore any grouse-like noises. Collared Pikas also call from the myriad rocky crevices.

Trumpeter Swan

MARSH LAKE, YUKON

Marsh Lake, situated along the Alaska Highway just north of Jake's Corner (km 1,347.2/mile 836.8), offers exceptional birding, particularly during spring migration when water levels are low and mudflats are exposed. The open lake and diverse shoreline habitats attract migrant loons, grebes, waterfowl, shorebirds, gulls, and passerines. The area has hosted many rarities, including King Eider, Bar-tailed Godwit, Little Stint, Sabine's Gull, and Black-legged Kittiwake. The tail-end of spring migration in late May features small numbers of Black Brant and a trickle of Parasitic Jaegers. Red-throated, Pacific, and Common Loons are common, while Yellow-billed Loons are rare but regular in spring and fall. The surrounding forests are home to Mountain Chickadee (rare and localized), Bohemian Waxwing, Pine Grosbeak, Purple Finch, and Red and White-winged Crossbills. Wetlands support breeding Sora, Lesser Yellowlegs, Least Sandpiper, Short-billed Dowitcher, Wilson's Snipe, Bonaparte's and Mew Gulls, Arctic Tern, Common Yellowthroat, Lincoln's Sparrow, and Rusty Blackbird. Take any opportunity to stop to scan the lake, especially at the Judas Creek subdivision and Lakeview Marina (km 1,368.5/mile 850), the pullout at historical milepost 883 (km 1,375.6/mile 854.4), Marsh Lake campground (km 1,384.4/mile 859.9), and the M'Clintock River bridge (km 1,386.4/mile 861.1). Take the first left north of the M'Clintock River bridge into the North M'Clintock subdivision (km 1,386.7/mile 861.3) that leads to a waterfowl-viewing facility known as **Swan Haven** overlooking M'Clintock Bay. During late April and early May, the bay hosts thousands of staging Trumpeter and Tundra Swans along with an enormous diversity of waterfowl and shorebirds. Eurasian Wigeon is regular in spring, and Mountain Chickadee has been seen at the birdfeeder here.

LEWES MARSH, YUKON

Lewes Marsh (km 1,396.4/mile 867.3) is an extensive wetland along the beginning of the Yukon River just north of Marsh Lake. From here, the Yukon River journeys 3,186 km/1,980 miles to the Bering Sea. Stop in the pullout on the right just before crossing the Yukon River bridge to scan the open water and mudflats (in spring) for waterfowl and shorebirds. To further explore Lewes Marsh, turn left immediately after crossing the bridge (if you are heading north). This road, known locally as Gunnar's Road, runs along Lewes Marsh for about 7 km/4.3 miles to a sawmill. This road may not be suitable for vehicles such as RVs with a limited turning radius. Stop at the many openings in the shrubs and mixed forest along the road to scan Lewes Marsh. In spring, migrant waterfowl and shorebirds occur in high numbers. Watch for Eurasian Wigeon among American Wigeon, and Harlequin Duck near the bridge. Shorebirds sweep through in high numbers in May, and just about every Yukon species may occur. High water levels in summer cover the mudflats and limit the birding, although Three-toed Woodpecker, Golden-crowned Kinglet, and a variety of other songbirds inhabit the surrounding forests. This would be an ideal opportunity to get some use out of a canoe that's spent too much time on top of the car. Mountain Chickadees frequent the feeders near the start of Gunnar's Road. Yellow-billed Loon occurs in fall, usually at or just downstream of the bridge.

WOLF CREEK, YUKON

Wolf Creek campground (km 1,411.6/mile 876.8), located 11.6 km/7.2 miles south of Whitehorse, offers day use, camping, and trails, and is a great place to view species that favor White Spruce forest. Trails lead from the northeast end of the campground along Wolf Creek and to the Yukon River. The White Spruce and Balsam Poplar forests and the deciduous shrubs along the creek are home to Spruce Grouse, Three-toed Woodpecker, Hammond's Flycatcher, Boreal Chickadee, Golden-crowned Kinglet, Bohemian Waxwing, Pine Grosbeak, Red and White-winged Crossbills, and Pine Siskin. Mountain Chickadee is rare in the area. In winter, American Dippers feed along fast-flowing stretches of Wolf Creek.

WHITEHORSE, YUKON

Whitehorse (km 1,423.2/mile 884) is the capital of the Yukon Territory. The downtown area and visitor information center are located off the highway, accessed by taking either the south access (Robert Service Way, km 1,423.2/mile 884) or the north access (Two Mile Hill, km 1,428.7/mile 887.4). Whitehorse is a vibrant and attractive city nestled in an extraordinary natural setting, making it hard to imagine how any traveler could resist its charm. So, why not take a break from the road and spend at least a night or two? Be sure to sample the wonderful bread at the Alpine Bakery located at the corner of 5th Avenue and Alexander Street. The brick-oven loaves are particularly tasty. The Whitehorse area features rich and diverse habitats with exceptional birding. Along with the many common breeders and migrants, Whitehorse has hosted an amazing string of rarities in recent years, including Taiga Bean Goose, Lesser Black-backed and Slaty-backed Gulls, Dusky Thrush, and Red-throated Pipit. A birding guide primarily devoted to Alaska, such as this one, cannot adequately cover this remarkable area. Additional birdfinding information is available through the sources and contacts listed in *Logistics* below. Bird checklists are available at the Alpine Bakery, Whitehorse Public Library (2071 2nd Avenue), Canadian Wildlife Service, and the Yukon Conservation Society. Visiting birders are welcome to contact the Yukon Bird Club for birdfinding tips and to report their sightings. Here are four of the most popular birding locations.

The **Yukon River Trail** offers a scenic and easy-paced birding walk right in downtown Whitehorse. The trail winds along the Yukon River through mixed Lodgepole Pine, White Spruce, and Quaking Aspen. There are numerous forks in the trail, but all the paths generally follow the river, making it difficult to get lost. To access the trail start at the historic riverboat SS *Klondike* in downtown Whitehorse and follow either of two directions: Take the pedestrian path along Robert Service Way upstream to Robert Service campground, or cross the bridge to Riverdale and take the trail immediately to the right when the bridge ends. From here, the trail follows the Yukon River about 2 km/1.3 miles upstream to the Whitehorse Fish Ladder and Schwatka Lake. Many points along the trail provide views of the river, with its gravel bars and mudflats. Watch for Harlequin Duck, Bald Eagle, Belted Kingfisher, Warbling Vireo, Black-capped and Boreal Chickadees, and Bohemian Waxwing. In summer, the islands host breeding Mew Gulls and Arctic Terns. Herring Gulls nest right at the power dam. American Dipper is common in winter.

Schwatka Lake is a convenient place to view waterbirds that usually occur on larger lakes. There are three ways to access Schwatka Lake: (1) Continue on the Yukon River Trail past the Whitehorse Fish Ladder to the dam at the south end of the trail, (2) follow Chadburn Lake Road which runs south from the fish ladder along Schwatka Lake, or (3) from the SS *Klondike*, take Robert Service Way out of downtown for 2.4 km/1.5 miles, past the Robert Service campground and take the first left past Yukon Electric to a T-junction. Go right at the T-junction and follow the road along the lake for 2 km/1.3 miles to a fork. Stay left at the fork to continue along the lake for 0.5 km/0.3 mile to a dead end. A right at the fork swings up the hill to the Alaska Highway via Miles Canyon. During migration Schwatka Lake hosts loons, grebes, and diving ducks. While Pacific and Common Loons are most common, Red-throated and Yellow-billed (fall) Loons also occur. Check the surrounding woods for Ruffed Grouse, Three-toed Woodpecker, Boreal Chickadee, Red-breasted Nuthatch, Golden-crowned and Ruby-crowned Kinglets, Townsend's Solitaire, Pine Grosbeak, and White-winged Crossbill.

McInytre Creek wetlands provide very important habitat to diverse communities of birds and other wildlife. It is well known to local birders as a great place to view species that are difficult to find elsewhere. To reach McIntyre Creek wetlands, take the Alaska Highway north from Two Mile Hill for 3 km/1.9 miles and turn left onto Fish Lake Road (at km 1,431.9/mile 889.4). Follow Fish Lake Road, stopping at Pumphouse Pond (km 3/mile 1.9), and then on to the wetlands (km 3.5/mile 2.2) at the junction of Fish Lake Road and Copper Haul Road (not marked by a road sign). Turn left onto Copper Haul Road to the interpretive overlook just off Fish Lake Road. Park here and explore the area by foot. White Spruce and Balsam Poplar forest, scattered dead trees throughout the wetland, and lush shrubs create exceptional habitat for a diverse and abundant songbird community. Watch for Hammond's Flycatcher, Boreal Chickadee, Golden-crowned and Ruby-crowned Kinglets, Warbling Vireo, Varied Thrush, Bohemian Waxwing, Townsend's and Blackpoll Warblers, and Red-winged and Rusty Blackbirds. Breeding shorebirds include Lesser Yellowlegs, Solitary and Spotted Sandpipers, and Wilson's Snipe.

Fish Lake and **Mount McIntyre** offer an opportunity to experience the area's birdlife in a truly impressive setting. To reach Fish Lake, continue along Fish Lake Road from McIntyre Creek wetlands for about 12 km/7.5 miles to the end. Hikers can reach the alpine habitats of Mount McIntyre from the Fish Lake Road. It is a good idea to file an itinerary and return time with friends or officials whenever you explore remote areas such as Mount McIntyre. While Dusky Flycatcher is most common at tree line, it also can be found in open shrubby habitats just below tree line along the Fish Lake Road from 2.4 km/1.5 miles to 4.8 km/3 miles past the junction with the Copper Haul Road. To reach the alpine habitats, watch for a small dirt trail located on the left side of the road about 10.8 km/6.8 miles past the Copper Haul Road (about 1.2 km/0.8 mile before Fish Lake). It is moderately-paced hike or bike ride of about 4 km/2.5 miles up this trail to tree line, continuing another 1.6 km/1 mile beyond tree line to a fork. From the fork go left or right to explore the tree line gullies. A right turn leads about 3 km/4.8 miles to the summit, while the left branch takes you across the open alpine and tree line habitats and eventually leads about 8.5 km/5.3 miles back down the mountain to the south end of the Copper Haul Road with another 3.7 km/2.3 miles to the Alaska Highway. However, this route can be confusing. Scan Fish Lake for loons, grebes, diving ducks, Bonaparte's Gulls, and Arctic Terns. In winter, small coveys of Willow Ptarmigan inhabit the dense willows around the lake, and American Dippers occur on Fish Creek. Check the subalpine shrubs for Willow Ptarmigan, Dusky Flycatcher, Townsend's Solitaire, and American Tree, Timberline, and Golden-crowned Sparrows. The alpine tundra at the summit is inhabited by Rock Ptarmigan, American Pipit, Horned Lark, and Savannah Sparrow.

Olive-sided Flycatcher

WHITEHORSE, YUKON, TO ALASKA BORDER

KUSAWA LAKE, YUKON

The Kusawa Lake road (km 1,493/mile 927.3), located on the left side (west) of the highway, leads 24 km/15 miles to Kusawa Lake campground. The campground offers day use, camping, and a boat launch. Boaters should keep in mind that the wind and waves can whip up quite quickly on Kusawa Lake. Upland Sandpiper and Northern Hawk Owl are sometimes seen between the Alaska Highway and a wetland about 1 km/0.6 mile from the turnoff. Species seen regularly include Common Loon, Olive-sided Flycatcher, Western Wood-Pewee, Bohemian Waxwing, with Three-toed Woodpecker and Boreal Chickadee in the older White Spruce forests.

PINE LAKE, YUKON

Pine Lake campground (km 1,578.8/mile 980.6) offers day use, camping, and a boat launch. This scenic boreal lake can be enjoyed from a shoreline boardwalk trail through diverse and productive habitats. It is an ideal lake for exploring by canoe. Scan the lake for loons, grebes, waterfowl, as well as Bonaparte's and Mew Gulls. Common forest birds include Northern Goshawk, Three-toed and Black-backed Woodpeckers, Gray Jay, Ruby-crowned Kinglet, Bohemian Waxwing, and Blackpoll Warbler. Brown Creeper, a Yukon rarity, is found here.

HAINES JUNCTION, YUKON

The village of Haines Junction (km 1,585.9/mile 985) is set against the stunning Saint Elias Mountains and is surrounded by exceptional beauty. Be sure to stop in at the Kluane National Park visitor center for local and backcountry information, and to get tips on birding and wildlife viewing areas. As well, visitors should inquire about any special requirements for visiting the park. Black-backed Woodpecker and Northern Hawk Owl are fairly common in the area.

The Dezadeash River Trail offers an easy-paced 3.5 km/2.2-mile walk along varied riparian habitats. To access the trail go south from Haines Junction a few hundred meters along the Haines Highway (Highway 3) toward Haines, Alaska (see page 457), and turn right into the parking area just before crossing the Dezadeash River bridge. Common species along the trail are Spotted Sandpiper, Western Wood-Pewee, Blackpoll Warbler, Northern Waterthrush, and Fox and Lincoln's Sparrows. Least Flycatcher, at the edge of its range here, may be found in the groves of Quaking Aspen.

BEAR CREEK SUMMIT, YUKON

Bear Creek Summit (km 1,610.2/mile 1,000.1; elevation 1,004 m/3,294 ft) is one of the highest points on the Alaska Highway. It offers access to the subalpine with a trail leading to higher-elevation alpine habitats. Birds seen in the area include Peregrine Falcon, all three ptarmigan, Northern Hawk Owl, Townsend's Solitaire, American Tree, Timberline, and Golden-crowned Sparrows.

SULPHUR LAKE, YUKON

Sulphur Lake (km 1,619.7/mile 1,006) is accessed by a small dirt road on the right side (north) of the highway. The lake hosts high numbers of waterfowl, especially during migration and the late summer (prebasic) molt. Eurasian Wigeon has been seen in spring, and Bald Eagles nest around the lake. Common forest birds include Spruce Grouse, Three-toed and Black-backed Woodpeckers, and White-winged Crossbill. With the next campground just 50 km/31 miles north, this would be a good place to take the canoe off the top of the car and enjoy an afternoon of paddling and exploring.

KLUANE LAKE AND KLUANE NATIONAL PARK, YUKON

Travelers heading north get their first glimpse of Kluane Lake from Boutillier Summit (km 1,641.9/mile 1,019.8; elevation 1,003 m/3,293 ft). Kluane Lake stretches 74 km/46 miles and is the largest lake in the Yukon. Small settlements along the highway offer gas, lodging, and camping. This is a landscape of enormous beauty with wonderful opportunities for hiking, wildlife viewing, and birding. Time spent exploring the high country will be rewarded with species such as all three ptarmigan, Long-tailed Jaeger, Northern Wheatear, Timberline Sparrow, Smith's Longspur, and Gray-crowned Rosy-Finch. One of the best locations for these species is the Burwash Uplands, which requires a well-planned hike. Direction to the uplands and information on backcountry hiking are available at the visitor centers in Haines Junction and at Sheep Mountain. Sharp-tailed Grouse may be seen along the highway north of Kluane Lake, particularly in the Duke River area.

SHEEP MOUNTAIN, YUKON

Sheep Mountain (km 1,656.4/mile 1,028.8) is the first stop after crossing the Slim's River bridge. The visitor center has telescopes for viewing usually easy-to-see Dall's Sheep. The interpretive staff can point you to a nearby moderately-paced trail that leads to subalpine habitats on Sheep Mountain. Species seen along the trail include Townsend's Solitaire and Swainson's and Varied Thrushes. Subalpine species include Timberline and Golden-crowned Sparrows. The Soldiers Summit Trail (km 1,659.4/mile 1,030.7) just to the north also offers a moderately-paced hike with good sheep viewing.

SHEEP MOUNTAIN TO BEAVER CREEK, YUKON

There are many scenic stops along the Alaska Highway from Sheep Mountain, along Kluane Lake and north to Beaver Creek. The Bayshore Inn's (km 1,662.4/mile 1,033) restaurant has a deck with a bird feeder and a fantastic view of Kluane Lake. Cottonwood RV Park (km 1,666.2/mile 1,034.9) offers camping and services in an attractive wooded setting. Congdon Creek campground (km 1,674.2/mile 1,039.9) on the shore of Kluane Lake has an easy interpretive trail, and camping amidst the songs of Olive-sided Flycatcher, Western Wood-Pewee, Ruby-crowned Kinglet, and Swainson's Thrush. Destruction Bay (km 1692.9/mile 1,051.5) is a small highway community with basic services and an occasional Mountain Bluebird. Burwash Landing (km 1,709/mile 1061.5) offers gas, groceries, lodging, and the Kluane Museum with its highly-rated wildlife display. The Duke River area (km 1,717.9/mile 1,067) is one of the best places in the Yukon for Sharp-tailed Grouse and Upland Sandpiper; check the small dirt road on the right just before crossing the Duke River bridge (heading north), although areas for turning around are limited, especially for larger RVs. Lake Creek campground (km 1,801.3/mile 1,118.8) is not well known for birds. Pickhandle Lake (km 1,812.4/mile 1,125.7) is located down a short gravel road on the left (west) and has a viewing platform with interpretive panels overlooking a wetland. Snag Junction campground (km 1,859.9/mile 1,155.2) offers basic camping, with lakeside serenades by Common Loons, Red-necked Grebes, Bonaparte's Gulls, and Great Horned Owls.

Beaver Creek (km 1,881.3/mile 1,168.5) is the last Yukon settlement before the U.S. customs (km 1,915.6/mile 1,189.8) entry point to Alaska. Note that there is a time-zone change (Alaska is one hour earlier), speed limits and distance markers are now in miles, and Alaska requires headlights to be on at all times.

LOGISTICS

Many suggestions for accommodations are given in the text. More accommodations, restaurants, service stations, stores, parks, and campgrounds are detailed in the latest edition of *The Milepost*. The following are useful contacts for birders along the Alaska Highway in Canada.

Yukon Bird Club, PO Box 31054, Whitehorse, Yukon Y1A 5P7; 867-667-4630 or 867-667-6703, *ybc@yknet.yk.ca; www.yukonweb.com/community/ybc/*.

Yukon Conservation Society, 302 Hawkings Street, Whitehorse, Yukon, Y1A 1X6; 867- 668-5678, fax 867-668-6637; *office@ycs.yk.ca*; *www.yukonconservation.org*.

Canadian Wildlife Service, 91782 Alaska Highway, Whitehorse, Yukon, Y1A 5B7; 867-667-3931.

Yukon Department of Tourism, 1st Floor, 100 Hanson Street, Whitehorse, Yukon, or PO Box 2703, Whitehorse, Yukon, Y1A 2C6; 867-667-5036, fax 867-667-3546; *vacation@gov.yk.ca*; *www.touryukon.com*.

CASSIAR HIGHWAY

If you have come north through British Columbia from western Washington, you may decide to join the Alaska Highway west of Watson Lake via the Cassiar Highway. While this guide does not treat birding along the Cassiar, you are encouraged to consider birding Stewart, BC, and Hyder, AK, about 40 miles west of the Cassiar from Meziadin Junction (see page 471). The Cassiar is still more primitive than the Alaska Highway, but is being developed annually. As of 2001, there was still a stretch of about 100 miles of gravel north of Meziadin Junction that may give pause to some motorists, especially those driving RVs and in stormy weather when the road may get muddy. There is great birding all along the road, so it is well worth it to make the trip. The Cassiar arrives on the Alaska Highway 21 km/13 miles west of Watson Lake. See *The Milepost* for the latest conditions and accommodations along this highway.

Alaska Highway:

Yukon Border to Delta Junction

Keith Larson

The eastern interior of Alaska is a fantastic place for birders, with over 190 species of birds recorded. Many of these birds are breeders at the end of their long migration routes (Surfbird, Long-tailed Jaeger, and Smith's Longspur) or northern specialties (Rock Ptarmigan and Boreal Chickadee). The Upper Tanana River Valley and eastern Yukon-Tanana Uplands of eastern interior Alaska comprise part of the boreal forest biome. From Delta Junction north to the Yukon River and east to the Canadian border, this region's habitats include vast Black Spruce and White Spruce forests, enormous wetland complexes, glacial river valleys, and alpine tundra totaling many thousands of acres.

Access is generally limited to those areas adjacent to the Alaska, Taylor (page 175), and Top-of-the-World Highways (page 179). These roads are very narrow compared to those in the Lower 48 states and are often damaged by frost-heaving action during the long winters and by thawing of permafrost in the summer. From September to November freezing rain and snow can be expected. During the short summer, construction crews work incessantly to patch up or even replace the many sections of damaged highway. There are hundreds of pullouts, gravel pits, and waysides—never more than a few miles apart—where you can safely pull off to look for birds. Be sure to park completely off the highway. The Alaska Highway carries heavy truck traffic year round and many tour buses and large RVs during the tourist season.

Some birders will explore the waterways and other remote areas by plane, boat, snowmachine, or on foot, although these options often require extensive backcountry experience and knowledge of local conditions. Check locally before launching your craft or setting off crosscountry, or better yet, go with an experienced guide.

In the Interior, warm summer days and long periods of daylight make for great birding. Extreme cold temperatures and long periods of darkness—a challenge for Christmas Bird counters—characterize winter conditions. Understanding the timing of migration, breeding, and species-specific habitat needs are essential to locating many target species. For example,

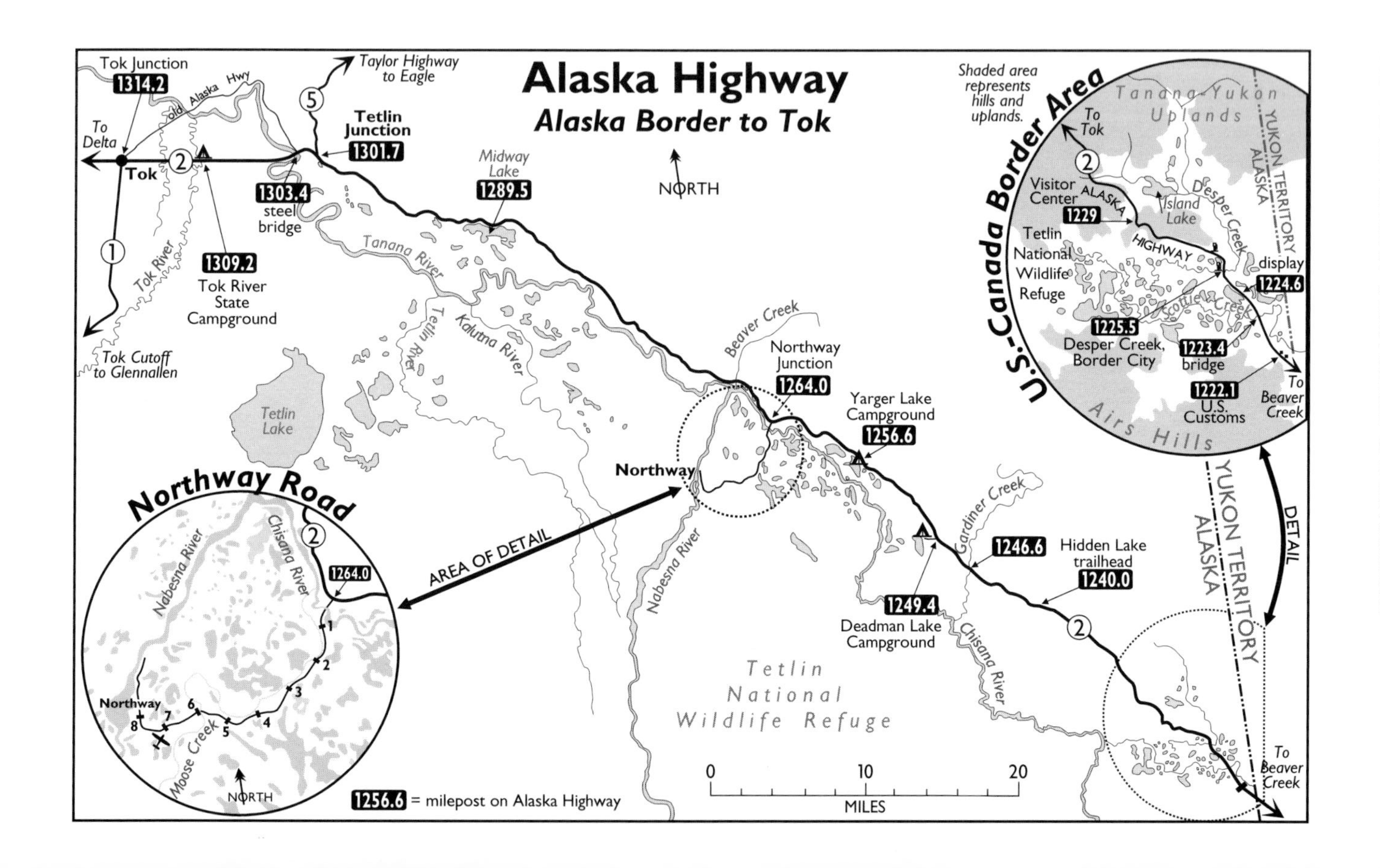

Alaska Highway
Alaska Border to Tok
NORTH
Tok Junction
1314.2
Old Alaska Hwy
To Delta
Tok
Taylor Highway to Eagle
Tetlin Junction
1301.7
1303.4
steel bridge
1309.2
Tok River State Campground
Tok River
Tok Cutoff to Glennallen
Midway Lake
1289.5
Tanana River
Tetlin River
Kalutna River
Tetlin Lake
Beaver Creek
Northway Junction
1264.0
Yarger Lake Campground
1256.6
Northway
Nabesna River
Gardiner Creek
1246.6
Hidden Lake trailhead
1240.0
1249.4
Deadman Lake Campground
Chisana River
Tetlin National Wildlife Refuge
0
10
20
MILES
YUKON TERRITORY
ALASKA
DETAIL
To Beaver Creek
Shaded area represents hills and uplands.
U.S.-Canada Border Area
Tanana-Yukon Uplands
To Tok
Visitor Center
ALASKA HIGHWAY
1229
Island Lake
Desper Creek
Tetlin National Wildlife Refuge
display
1224.6
Scottie Creek
1225.5
Desper Creek, Border City
1223.4
bridge
1222.1
U.S. Customs
To Beaver Creek
Airs Hills
YUKON TERRITORY
ALASKA
Northway Road
Nabesna River
Chisana River
1264.0
Northway
Moose Creek
NORTH
AREA OF DETAIL
1256.6 = milepost on Alaska Highway

long-distance migrants such as Alder Flycatcher that arrive around 1 June may spend only 45 days on their breeding grounds (tall alder and willow shrub).

The region's predominant habitats are Black Spruce and White Spruce with Quaking Aspen and Paper Birch in disturbed areas and well-drained south-facing slopes, Balsam Poplar (cottonwood) along rivers, and Black Spruce and Larch muskeg bogs underlain with permafrost in the lowlands.

However, the most productive habitat in terms of overall number and diversity of birds is wet, tall, willow-and-alder shrub. Some of the more extensive areas of this habitat occur along the Northway Road (page 166), at Dry Lake, and along the Taylor Highway (page 175). Early successional burns caused by summer lightning-sparked wildfires are also a good place to find this habitat.

Spring migration (late April to early June) is the best time for birding. From mid-May to early June, summer-resident breeders are busy setting up territories, and migrants (e.g., Rough-legged Hawk, Long-tailed Duck, American Golden-Plover, Semipalmated and Pectoral Sandpipers, Horned Lark, Lapland Longspur, and Snow Bunting) are attracted to abundant stopover habitats, especially the seasonally flooded locations. In spring unusual migrants such as Snow Goose and Buff-breasted Sandpiper (very rare) may stop over in the Interior, primarily due to poor weather conditions, on their way to northern breeding grounds. However, other vagrants are often found in June and early July. By July, birding is limited to summer-resident breeders, most of which are no longer singing, and it is the height of the mosquito season. Fall brings beautiful autumn colors, rain, and large flocks of migratory waterfowl and cranes, with a limited number of shorebirds.

Of the 191 documented species in this region, 116 are known breeders. During winter, only 6 of the 38 recorded species are considered common. A year-list here will easily top 100 species, and will include Trumpeter Swan, Sandhill Crane, Lesser Yellowlegs, Solitary and Spotted Sandpipers, Bonaparte's and Mew Gulls, Northern Hawk Owl, Alder Flycatcher, Northern Shrike, Gray Jay, Boreal Chickadee, Mountain Bluebird, Townsend's Solitaire, Gray-cheeked Thrush, Blackpoll Warbler, Golden-crowned Sparrow, Red-winged and Rusty Blackbirds, and Common Redpoll.

From year to year irruptive species—normally rare-to-uncommon or common species found in unusually large numbers such as Red-breasted Nuthatch, Pine Grosbeak, Common Redpoll, and Pine Siskin—appear in this region. Waterfowl from the North American prairie regions such as Gadwall and Blue-winged Teal are also found in this region's wetlands. Species hard to find elsewhere in Alaska—Ruddy Duck, Sharp-tailed Grouse, American Coot, Yellow-bellied Sapsucker, Yellow-bellied Flycatcher, Chipping Sparrow, Timberline Sparrow, and Red-winged Blackbird—are regular breeders found in small numbers. In addition, the area's eastern proximity accounts for a relatively high number of extralimital Alaska records.

Spring (late April–early June) and fall (late July–early October) migration are some of the best periods to bird the Alaska Highway. During late March and early April, roadside gravel patches attract flocks of Snow Buntings and, in May, small numbers of Horned Larks interspersed within large flocks of Lapland Longspurs. American Pipits and several species of sparrows, especially Gambel's White-crowned Sparrow, can be abundant. During May, September, and October thousands of migrating Trumpeter and Tundra Swans and Sandhill Cranes fly overhead. During May and late September–early October, watch utility poles for Rough-legged and Red-tailed (usually Harlan's) Hawks and check along the roadside for hunting Northern Harrier, Northern Hawk Owl, and Short-eared Owl. As lakes and rivers break-up (spring) and freeze-up (fall), waterfowl concentrate in this open water.

BIRDING THE ALASKA HIGHWAY

Alaska Route 2 is a paved two-lane road with little or no shoulder. It begins at the U.S.-Canada border, continuing to Tok Junction, and ending at Delta Junction. The highway first passes through Black Spruce muskeg, then climbs the southern edge of the Yukon-Tanana Uplands, and parallels the glacial Tanana River. The road is kept open throughout the year.

The route begins at 0.3 mile before the U.S. Customs station at the Welcome-to-Alaska wayside, Milepost 1221.8 (distance from Dawson Creek, BC). From here Tok Junction is 93 miles and Delta Junction 200 miles west of the border. Across the highway is a nice lake and marsh system where waterfowl congregate during migration, some remaining to breed. For the next 60 miles the Alaska Highway follows the northern boundary of Tetlin National Wildlife Refuge.

Immediately after U.S. Customs there is an extensive creek-and-marsh complex on the north. Scattered small, slow-growing Black Spruce and tall willow-shrub line the lakes and Scottie Creek. Look for Northern Harrier and Short-eared Owl perched or flying close to the ground in search of prey. During spring migration waterfowl such as American Wigeon, Green-winged Teal, Canvasback, Redhead (rare), Ring-necked Duck, Lesser Scaup, Bufflehead, and Barrow's Goldeneye abound in these wetlands. Red-winged Blackbirds and other birds unusual in Alaska are occasionally found here.

A sign for Tetlin NWR at Milepost 1222.5 indicates that the Alaska Highway forms the northern boundary for this 730,000-acre refuge. Since 1980 refuge staff and volunteers have documented 191 species of birds in the Upper Tanana Valley. These lands were established as a refuge because of the significant wetlands used by breeding waterfowl populations. In 1982 the first recorded Trumpeter Swan nest was located in the valley. Since then the recovering population has reached a high of 1,277 swans, including 103 breeding pairs with young in 2000.

At Milepost 1223.4 the highway crosses Scottie Creek. Look for Cliff Swallows nesting under bridges spanning this and other creeks. On the southwest side is a pullout where canoes or other small boats can be launched. The creek is lined with tall willow shrub and White Spruce. Here, Bald Eagles, various waterfowl, Spotted Sandpipers, and shrub-nesting passerines such as Yellow Warbler and Alder Flycatcher can be found. Scottie Creek has attracted many unusual-to-Alaska species, including early records of Yellow-bellied Sapsucker, Tennessee Warbler, Lark Sparrow, and Western Meadowlark.

The road continues west through a broad valley dominated by Black Spruce muskeg. To the north the Yukon-Tanana Uplands are blanketed with spruce and deciduous trees. To the south are the Airs Hills, the northern foothills of the Alaska Range. At Milepost 1224.6 Tetlin NWR has a boreal wetlands interpretive display overlooking Highway Lake. Look for Beaver lodges around the edges of the lake, and for Pacific Loons and other diving waterfowl that are common here.

Watch for Northern Hawk Owl or Short-eared Owl on the spruce tops as you drive along. Desper Creek is crossed at Milepost 1225.5. A boat launch and parking area is on the southeast side of the creek. On the other side is Border City gas station, RV park, and convenience store. Noisy Lesser Yellowlegs often harass human intruders along these waters in summer. Several hundred Cliff Swallows nest under the eaves of the gas station. Just to the west is a lake complex where Pacific Loons nest annually. Bonaparte's Gulls nest semi-colonially in the spruce. In June 1992 a Western Meadowlark was found singing here. The road now climbs the southern slopes of the Yukon-Tanana Uplands. Numerous roadside pullouts offer grand views of the Alaska Range. At Milepost 1226.0 is the last gas station for the next 38 miles. Habitats here are dominated by spruce forest, Black Spruce muskeg, and aspen or birch in disturbed areas. Watch for Moose and Caribou crossing the highway.

An overlook and Tetlin NWR interpretive display, *Corridors for Passage*, is at Milepost 1227.8. One mile farther is the refuge visitor center, open from the end of May through August, where you can get maps, information on road conditions, wildfires, and campgrounds, or use the restrooms. Look for possible Yellow-bellied Flycatchers in the tall shrubs around the building. A first Alaska record of Lark Sparrow and a stray Black Turnstone were spotted here.

The wetlands south of the highway form a mosaic of thaw lakes and small streams. This landscape is characterized by tall White Spruce and Paper Birch woodland, willow shrub lining the waterways, and Black Spruce muskeg. These rich habitats are inhabited by Pacific Loon, Horned and Red-necked Grebes, Trumpeter Swan, waterfowl, including Gadwall, Blue-winged Teal, and Ring-necked Duck, Osprey, Bald Eagle, Semipalmated Plover, Lesser Yellowlegs, Solitary and Spotted Sandpipers, Bonaparte's and Mew Gulls, Western Wood-Pewee, Alder Flycatcher, Swainson's and Hermit Thrushes, Orange-crowned and Yellow Warblers, Northern Waterthrush, Chipping, Fox, and Lincoln's Sparrows, and Rusty Blackbird.

Along the forested edge of the highway look for Red-tailed Hawk, American Kestrel, Yellow-shafted Flicker, Gray Jay, Boreal Chickadee, Ruby-crowned Kinglet, Bohemian Waxwing, Myrtle Warbler, and Common Redpoll. At Milepost 1236.2, a lake on the north usually has nesting Buffleheads and an active Beaver lodge. Here the highway begins to cut through hillsides of glacial loess (dunes of fine sand deposited by strong winds during the last ice age). These dunes are evident until Milepost 1301.7 where the Taylor Highway meets the Alaska Highway at Tetlin Junction.

On the south at Milepost 1240.0 is a trailhead for Hidden Lake that is stocked with Rainbow Trout for sportfishing. The mile-long trail leads through Black Spruce muskeg and White Spruce/aspen woodland habitats. You'll need waterproof boots during summer and plenty of mosquito repellent in July and August. Milepost 1243.7 offers a forested overlook and picnic area with great views of the Nutzotin Mountains (Alaska Range) and an interpretive display discussing the role of wildfire in the boreal forest.

Gardiner Creek (Milepost 1246.6) is known for its good Arctic Grayling fishing and is generally a good spot to camp. In many years, Soras have been heard calling from wetlands along the south side of the highway between here and Northway Junction (Milepost 1264).

An excellent spot for camping and birding is Tetlin NWR's Deadman Lake campground, Milepost 1249.4. The 1.2-mile road to the campground is on the south side of the highway. Camping is free and during summer the refuge offers nightly interpretive programs on regional cultural and natural history. The campground is predominately Black and White Spruce woodland with aspen on drier slopes. It has a boat launch, pier, pull-in campsites, outhouses, picnic tables, and an observation deck on the lake. After break-up in May, migratory waterfowl stop over—look for Long-tailed Ducks. In summer, breeding American Wigeon, Green-winged Teal, Ring-necked Duck, Lesser Scaup, Surf and White-winged Scoters, Bufflehead, and Barrow's Goldeneye are here. A canoe or kayak is useful for exploring the far reaches of this lake. A three-mile hike across spruce muskeg leads to Ten Mile Lake, where Yellow-bellied Sapsuckers were found in recent years.

At Milepost 1250.2 is a pullout and picnic area. White Spruce and aspen are the dominant vegetation, making this a good place for Boreal Chickadee and Gray Jay. Two miles farther, Milepost 1252.2, is Tetlin NWR's *Solar Basin* interpretative wayside.

American Kestrel

On the north at Milepost 1256.3, just before the Alaska State DOT station, is a Bank Swallow colony. Look for these colonies along any cut-bank in the highway or rivers in this region. Violet-green Swallows and Belted Kingfishers also nest in these cut-banks.

Yarger Lake campground at Milepost 1256.6 offers camping, picnic tables, boat launch, outhouses, and summer interpretative programs. This is an excellent place to camp and watch the abundant waterfowl during spring migration. Pacific and Common Loons, Horned and Red-necked Grebes, Surf and White-winged Scoters, Long-tailed Duck, and Common Merganser are possible in spring, summer, and fall. Lesser Yellowlegs and Spotted Sandpiper breed along the shores on this and other interior lakes. During summer look for Ruddy Duck, Sora, and American Coot. This is the most reliable location for Sora in central Alaska; June, when they are calling, is the best month. A Black-headed Gull was seen once.

At Eliza Lake, Milepost 1259, you can pull into a driveway on the north side of the highway to view the lake. A spotting scope is needed to fully search the lake as it is some distance from the highway. Eliza Lake had Black Terns in June 1994 and July 1996. Trumpeter Swans nest here. Beyond Eliza Lake to the west is an old lodge north of the highway where a Black-backed Wagtail made a surprise two-day appearance in late June 1990.

At Milepost 1263.1 the old Wrangell View gas station is a great place to pull off and view the Alaska Range. One mile farther west is Northway Junction, Milepost 1264. The Northway Road heads directly south across the Chisana River and through a large wetland basin (*see Northway Road sidebar on next page*). At the junction are a gas station, RV park, laundry, and grocery store.

The highway drops down the side of the hill and parallels the Chisana River to its confluence with the Nabesna River. Both rivers originate in the

THE NORTHWAY ROAD

Keith Larson

The Northway road is one of the best birding spots in eastern interior Alaska. The 9-mile-long road crosses the Chisana River, several smaller creeks, and curves around many lakes and ponds on its way to the primarily Native village of Northway. The main habitats are Black Spruce muskeg and White Spruce, Balsam Poplar, and Quaking Aspen woodlands. Northern Hawk Owl, Ruby-crowned Kinglet, Swainson's Thrush, American Robin, Myrtle Warbler, and Fox Sparrow usually occupy the woodland habitats. The entire road is lined with willow shrub that should be inspected for Alder Flycatcher, Yellow Warbler, Northern Waterthrush, and Lincoln's and Gambel's White-crowned Sparrows. Most of the local breeding birds are easy to find from the road.

At Milepost 1264, Alaska Highway, turn south onto the Northway road. Reset your trip-odometer to 0.0. The Natives living along the road and at Northway village are the primary users of this narrow, two-lane gravel road. Please drive and bird courteously to ensure that access privileges for future birders won't be compromised. Drive slowly, and when you stop get as far to the right as possible. Be respectful of the local residents by giving them ample room to pass your vehicle, by not stopping in front of their homes (their dogs will bark continuously), and by birding only from the road to avoid entering private property. (Read the paragraphs about Native Cultures in the *Introduction*, page 10.) Please turn around at Mile 8.5 before entering Northway village.

At Mile 0.3 from the junction, the Chisana River bridge hosts a colony of Cliff Swallows. On the northeast side of the river Tetlin National Wildlife Refuge maintains a boat launch and parking area. At Mile 0.5 the first lake to the right usually has nesting Horned Grebes or Buffleheads. Look overhead and listen for Wilson's Snipe and Bonaparte's Gull.

A large lake complex on the right between Miles 1.6 to 1.8 is a good spot for Red-necked Grebe, Canvasback, Ring-necked Duck, Lesser Scaup, Bufflehead, Barrow's Goldeneye, Bald Eagle, Mew Gull, and Arctic Tern. Opposite the lakes Common Yellowthroats were heard in Balsam Poplar snags and tall willow shrub.

Moose Creek parallels the road at Mile 2.0, and the road crosses Fish Camp Creek at Mile 2.6. On the left after the creek is a series of lakes that are largely mudflats in spring (late April to early June), where shorebirds such as Semipalmated Plover, Killdeer, Lesser Yellowlegs, Solitary, Spotted, and Least Sandpipers are seen. In July and August glacial runoff floods these mudflats. Listen for Northern Waterthrush in the shrubs lining the lakes.

Lakes at Miles 3.2 and 3.4 are good for waterfowl, and the low meadow on the right at Mile 4.5 might hold a Great Gray Owl. At Mile 6.2 another lake on the right is the best place to start searching for Red-winged Blackbird. Stop at the Northway Airport, Miles 6.4 to 7.0, to inspect the grassy fields for Killdeer and the shrubs for Chipping and Savannah Sparrows. On the right behind the warehouse, fire station, and FAA buildings are several lakes where Canvasback, Redhead, and Red-necked Phalarope are seen. Ruddy Ducks are recorded here annually. Continue birding to Mile 8.5, where you should turn around before entering Northway village.

Wrangell Mountains as glaciers and the milky-brown color of the water is from suspended glacial sediments created by the erosion and melting processes of glaciers. The combined river is called the Tanana and is one of the Interior's largest river systems. A pullout at Milepost 1269.0 has an interpretive display on the Gold Rush Centennial.

Trumpeter Swans occasionally nest on ponds in typical Black Spruce muskeg at Milepost 1272.7. The interpretative display here covers pond ecology and mosquitoes.

The highway continues to roll through spruce, aspen, and birch woodlands paralleling the Tanana River. On the south at Milepost 1289.5 is Midway Lake, an excellent place to break out the spotting scope and watch Pacific Loon, Horned Grebe, Trumpeter Swan, many species of ducks, Bonaparte's and Mew Gulls, and Arctic Tern. A pair of Bald Eagles is frequently seen overhead during summer months. Red-winged Blackbirds usually inhabit the islands of vegetation in the middle of the lake. Black Terns and Yellow-bellied Flycatchers have been found here.

As you continue west, evidence of wildfires scars the hillsides for the next several miles on the north. During August these hills are covered with Fireweed, giving an appearance of a sea of purple. Cavity-nesting species such as American Kestrel, Yellow-shafted Flicker, and Tree and Violet-green Swallows are possible. Post-burn stands of White Spruce are a good place to look for Three-toed and Black-backed Woodpeckers. Listen for them flaking bark rather than drumming.

Tetlin Junction, Milepost 1301.7, is the junction of the Alaska Highway and the Taylor Highway (see Taylor Highway, page 175). A pullout on the south at Milepost 1302.7 is a popular place for RVs to dry-camp. Below the pullout a large lake has nesting Pacific Loons and other waterfowl. Look for Moose feeding along the edges of the lake.

The highway crosses the Tanana River steel bridge at Milepost 1303.4. Large flocks of Cliff Swallows swarm the bridge trusses during summer. Just past the bridge at Milepost 1303.6 stop at a large pullout to search the tall willow-shrub for Alder Flycatcher, Yellow Warbler, and Fox Sparrow. From the Tanana River to Tok Junction large sections of burned and unburned Black Spruce muskeg warrant close scrutiny for Northern Harrier, Northern Goshawk, Sharp-tailed Grouse, Northern Hawk Owl, Short-eared Owl, Yellow-shafted Flicker, Three-toed and Black-backed Woodpeckers, and shrub species such as Lincoln's Sparrow (wet areas) and Gambel's White-crowned Sparrow.

During spring and fall migration (late April–early June, late June–early September) waterfowl and shorebirds congregate in the gravel pit about 100 yards north of the highway at Milepost 1306.6. You can drive the short access

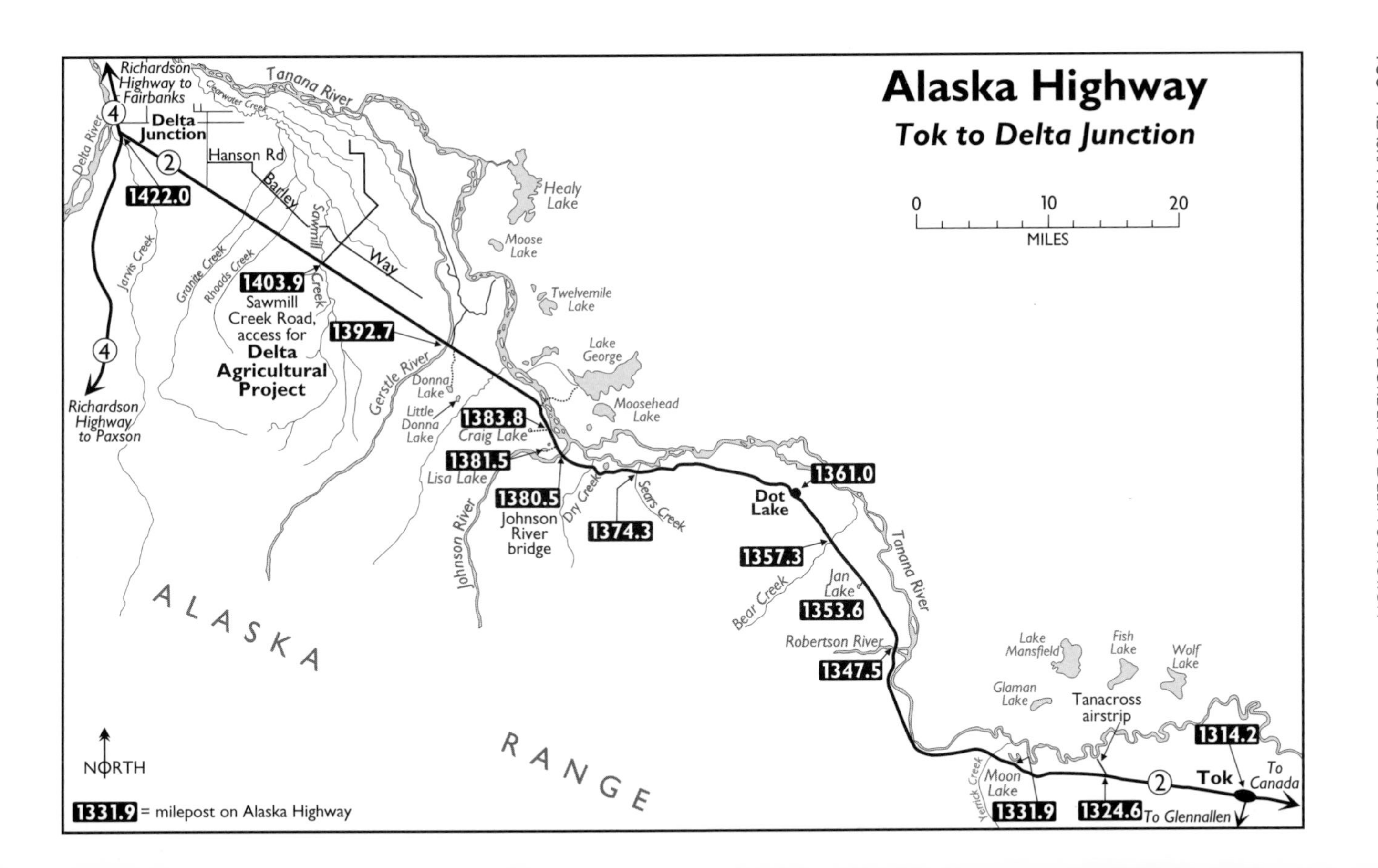
Alaska Highway
Tok to Delta Junction
0
10
20
MILES
Richardson Highway to Fairbanks
4
Delta Junction
Delta River
Tanana River
Clearwater Creek
Hanson Rd
Barley
Sawmill
Creek
Way
2
1422.0
Jarvis Creek
Granite Creek
Rhoads Creek
1403.9
Sawmill Creek Road, access for
Delta Agricultural Project
1392.7
Gerstle River
Donna Lake
Little Donna Lake
Richardson Highway to Paxson
Healy Lake
Moose Lake
Twelvemile Lake
Lake George
Moosehead Lake
1383.8
Craig Lake
1381.5
Lisa Lake
1380.5
Johnson River bridge
Johnson River
Dry Creek
Sears Creek
1374.3
1361.0
Dot Lake
1357.3
Bear Creek
Jan Lake
1353.6
Tanana River
Robertson River
1347.5
Lake Mansfield
Fish Lake
Wolf Lake
Glaman Lake
Tanacross airstrip
1314.2
Tok
To Canada
Yerrick Creek
Moon Lake
1331.9
1324.6
To Glennallen
ALASKA RANGE
NORTH
1331.9 = milepost on Alaska Highway

road, but *do not* drive down into the pit. Look for Sandhill Crane, Lesser Yellowlegs, Solitary, Spotted, and Least Sandpipers, Long-billed Dowitcher, and American Pipit. At the proper time this may be the best place to see a variety of shorebirds in the eastern interior, including Killdeer that have nested here.

On the north at Milepost 1309.2 the state-owned Tok River campground ($10/night) offers pull-in and pull-through campsites, a picnic area, a small-boat launch, and nature trail. Great Horned Owls often nest in this area along the river and a Yellow-shafted Flicker family usually nests in a cavity in an old sign pole across the river from the camp.

Scan the spruce snags carefully on the way into Tok for perching raptors. The first building on the south side of the highway in Tok, Milepost 1312.8, is the dogmushers' hall, where European Starlings have nested. A track and grassy field here should be scanned closely in spring for American Golden-Plover and Upland and Buff-breasted Sandpipers. Inspect the shrubs for Yellow Warbler and Gambel's White-crowned Sparrow.

Tok is a full-service community with all necessary visitor services and amenities. Visit the Alaska Public Lands Council (APLIC) Visitor Center and the Tok Community Visitor Center on the northeast corner of the junction for tourist information, maps, and local conditions. At Milepost 1314.2 the Glenn Highway's Tok Cutoff (Route 1) heads south to Glennallen (see page 180). The Alaska Highway continues west 108 miles to its end at Delta Junction.

In the Alaska Range and portions of the Yukon-Tanana Uplands' alpine-tundra and tundra-shrub habitats, there are opportunities to find Upland Sandpiper, Whimbrel, and Timberline Sparrow (Gold Hill in the Alaska Range, see page 183). 40-Mile Air based in Tok offers scenic flights and charters, giving birders a means of reaching some of the more remote birding locations. Ask at 40-Mile Air about less-costly seats on mail runs to bush villages such as Chisana.

West of Tok the highway traverses 11 miles of predominantly spruce forest. Just past Milepost 1318 on the north is a large field cleared for agriculture. In the early hours of the day during spring and fall migration this is a good spot to see grazing Sandhill Cranes and Canada Geese. Look for a pair of nesting American Kestrels on the utility poles next to the field.

Continue west to Milepost 1324.6 and turn north for 1.6 miles to the Tanacross airstrip, used during World War II when the U.S. shuttled aircraft across the Arctic to Russia. Today, the airstrip is used in summer as a tanker base for wildland firefighting. Its grassy margins attract shorebirds and others during spring migration—look for Northern Harrier, Sandhill Crane, American Golden-Plover, Semipalmated and Pectoral Sandpipers, American

Pipit, and Lapland Longspur. At the north end of the airstrip is the Tanana River. Here the river often is ice-free earlier in the spring than much of the river in the Upper Tanana Valley. When it is ice-free you might find Common and Red-breasted Mergansers and other waterfowl.

The spruce forest opens up into Black Spruce woodland and muskeg at Milepost 1325. Scan the treetops for Northern Hawk Owl and Great Gray Owl. North of Milepost 1327, stands of aspen bordering a small lake might have nesting Western Wood-Pewees. Shrubs in these muskeg habitats hold Lincoln's Sparrow, while Wilson's Snipe winnow overhead. A gravel-pit lake on the south at Milepost 1327.3 is an excellent spot in spring for migrant shorebirds (Lesser Yellowlegs, Semipalmated, Least, and Pectoral Sandpipers, and Long-billed Dowitcher) and waterfowl (Green-winged Teal, Bufflehead, and Barrow's Goldeneye). Several pairs of Mew Gulls usually attempt to nest on an island. Walk 0.2 mile west along the highway to another gravel-pit lake on the north for similar species and to view an active Beaver lodge.

Heading west, the highway traverses more Black Spruce muskeg before climbing the lower slopes of the Alaska Range. At the summit, stop at a pullout on the north (Milepost 1330.1) to scope the lakes below for Trumpeter Swan, Gadwall, Blue-winged Teal, scoters, and goldeneyes. Early morning hours are an excellent time to see Moose grazing in the meadows surrounding these lakes.

Beautiful Moon Lake State Park campground (Milepost 1331.9; $10/night) is another excellent spot for spring Trumpeter Swans, waterfowl, and shorebirds. Gadwall and Blue-winged Teal have both been spotted in recent years. Moose usually graze on the banks in the early morning. A canoe or kayak is useful for exploring. During summer the lake serves as a base for floatplanes and locals use it for water skiing.

The road west continues along the north side of the Alaska Range. At Milepost 1347.2 a trailhead leads west to Forest Lake that is stocked with Rainbow Trout. The 6-mile-long trail gets extremely muddy (wear rubber boots) during summer due to ATV use. Typical boreal forest birds—Boreal Chickadee, Myrtle Warbler, and Slate-colored Junco—can be found as the trail winds through spruce and aspen.

The highway crosses glacial Robertson River at Milepost 1347.5. Scan the cliffs along the river for Golden Eagle and Peregrine Falcon. Another lake stocked with Rainbow Trout has a trailhead on the north at Milepost 1348.1. The 0.3-mile trail goes through spruce and aspen forest.

At Milepost 1353.6 turn north onto a 0.5-mile dirt road ending at a parking lot with boat launch for Jan Lake. A hike around this lake and up the hill on the south shore is another good opportunity to find boreal-forest birds. Search for Townsend's Solitaire on the well-drained, open, aspen-woodland south slope of the hill that overlooks the Alaska Range.

At Milepost 1357.3 is a paved pullout on the northwest side of Bear Creek. The habitat here is a mixture of spruce, aspen, and birch forest where one might find Spruce Grouse, Downy and Hairy Woodpeckers, Hammond's Flycatcher, Boreal Chickadee, Ruby-crowned Kinglet, Swainson's Thrush, Myrtle Warbler, Slate-colored Junco, and Common Redpoll.

Dot Lake community (Milepost 1361) has a lodge with gas station, grocery, and campground. Park at the lodge and walk west along the highway a short distance to scout the lakes on both sides of the road. The lakes are fairly boggy and are surrounded by willows, good spots to look for migrating Trumpeter Swans, waterfowl, and shorebirds in spring and fall.

Continuing west to Delta Junction the highway winds through spruce, aspen, and birch forest with patches of Black Spruce muskeg. Sears Creek at Milepost 1374.3 marks the beginning of the area on the north called Dry Lake. Turn into a large gravel parking area at Milepost 1376. Do not drive the small dirt road leading down to the lake; the road is often muddy. This large lake bed is usually full during spring migration and dries up in the summer. Only occasionally during peak summer flooding does the lakebed have water in July, August, or September. The lake is surrounded with Quaking Aspen and Balsam Poplar with tall willow shrub; the center is grassland. During spring the lake is good for geese, waterfowl, shorebirds, and Sandhill Cranes. In summer breeding Alder Flycatchers, Swainson's Thrushes, Orange-crowned and Yellow Warblers, and Savannah Sparrows abound. During fall migration large flocks of Sandhill Cranes stop over and lots of raptors—Northern Harrier, and Red-tailed and Rough-legged Hawks—hunt the lake bed. Arctic Warbler and Palm Warbler were recorded at Dry Lake in fall. This is also an excellent area to find landbirds during spring and fall migration.

From Dry Lake to Delta Junction the road drops into and continues along the Tanana River valley. Johnson River, glacial in origin, is crossed at Milepost 1380.5. Although Moose can be anywhere along—or on—the highway from the Johnson River to Delta Junction, this is a notorious stretch where many collisions have occurred.

At Milepost 1381.5, a 0.9-mile trail leads south to Lisa Lake, and at Milepost 1383.3 you can walk south to Craig Lake on a 0.5-mile trail. Both small lakes are stocked with Rainbow Trout and both trails pass through spruce, birch, and aspen forest, giving you a chance to stretch your legs and look for boreal-forest birds. Another pair of stocked lakes can be accessed by trail from Milepost 1391.1. Use the pullout on the south and walk to Big Donna (3.5 miles) or Little Donna Lake (4.5). Both trails traverse spruce and aspen forest and are often muddy.

The highway crosses the glacial Gerstle River at Milepost 1392.7; on the southwest side of the bridge the rest area has a nice stand of Balsam Poplar and plenty of tall willow-shrub habitat. As you drive the rest of the way to Delta Junction, watch for Bison and Sharp-tailed Grouse along the highway.

A few miles past the Gerstle River patches of burned spruce forest open up to the south, good places to search for Northern Hawk Owls perched on snags. At Milepost 1403.9 Sawmill Creek Road departs to the north into the Delta Agricultural Project fields (see sidebar, page 173).

Delta Junction, Milepost 1422, is the end of the Alaska Highway. Continuing northwest the road becomes the Richardson Highway to Fairbanks (page 100) and to the south the Richardson Highway to Valdez (page 107), meeting the Glenn Highway to Anchorage (page 185). Delta is another full-service community with all the services a visitor might expect and need.

Logistics

The area code for all telephone numbers is 907 unless otherwise indicated. Tourist and travel services (accommodations, restaurants, attractions, etc.) not listed below can be found in the latest edition of The Milepost. *Statewide travel and birding information services are listed under Logistics in the* Introduction, *page 15.*

Tok Alaska Public Lands Information Center — Milepost 1314 Alaska Highway, Tok, AK 99780, 883-5667.

Primitive Camping: Tetlin National Wildlife Refuge maintains campgrounds at Deadman's and Yarger Lakes (64 and 57 miles east of Tok respectively). Alaska State Parks maintains a campground 4 miles east of Tok at the Tok River on the Alaska Highway 8 miles west of the Taylor Highway. Another campground is located 17 miles west of Tok Junction at Moon Lake.

Hunting and fishing information, special permits, and regulations can be obtained at the Alaska Department of Fish and Game office in Tok (883-2971). Licenses can be purchased at a variety of locations in Tok.

USGS maps of the local area can be purchased from any USGS map dealer. The Eagle, Nabesna, and Tanacross (1:250,000 scale) quadrangles would be most useful. For hiking on Mount Fairplay the Tanacross C-3 1:63,000 quad map and for hiking at Gold Hill, Nabesna A-2 and A-3 1:63:000 quad maps are necessary.

Call Yukon-Charley National Park at 574-2234 in Eagle or 474-7722 in Fairbanks for more information about floating the Yukon and Charley Rivers.

Contact Tetlin National Wildlife Refuge at 883-5312 for information about the refuge, campgrounds, public-use cabins (require chartering floatplanes in summer), and general information.

40-Mile Air, 883-5191, offers regional charter flights.

Acknowledgements: Terry Doyle reviewed the chapter and added many bird-sighting notes.

DELTA AGRICULTURAL PROJECT

Steve DuBois

The Delta Agricultural Project is a large area that stretches along the north side of the Alaska Highway for some 20 miles, starting about 10 miles east of Delta Junction. (See maps on pages 103 and 168.) The project is generally not visible from the highway. The main access is on Sawmill Creek Road at Milepost 1403.9. Turn north and after about 3 miles Sawmill Creek Road intersects east-west, gravel Barley Way that runs the length of the project. By driving along these two roads you can explore a wide area, but please bird from the roads because the fields are private property.

From mid-March through mid-April look for Snow Bunting, the first migrant passerine to return to the area. Sharp-tailed Grouse commonly use the gravel roads for display grounds during the lekking season. Look for them from mid-April to mid-May by driving along the dirt roads in early morning or evening.

The project is one of the most reliable places in Alaska for Mountain Bluebird, although numbers are small. Look for them on farms with livestock. Summer-resident Upland Sandpipers prefer short-grass fields. During migration scan fields and power lines for raptors, including Northern Harrier, Harlan's Hawk, Rough-legged Hawk, American Kestrel, Merlin, Short-eared Owl, and occasionally Peregrine Falcons that nest along bluffs on the Tanana River to the north. The project provides one of the best opportunities for finding Northern Hawk Owl in the Interior, primarily along Barley Way, where forested greenbelts parallel the road. An occasional Snowy Owl is reported during winter. Large numbers of geese, swans, and puddle ducks stop during spring and fall migration to feed primarily on barley and oats left in the fields, but their springtime numbers are somewhat dependent on the amount of snowmelt forming temporary ponds. Thousands of migrant Sandhill Cranes feed in the fields in fall. A Common Crane was observed 15–20 September 1998.

Agricultural development in the Delta Junction area began with homesteading in the 1950s and expanded with the development of the Delta Agricultural Project in 1978, when large parcels of land north of the Alaska Highway were sold. There are currently 85,000 acres of land in the project, and 130,000 acres under cultivation in the Delta Junction area. Principal products include barley and oats, hay, potatoes, grass seed, and straw as a by-product.

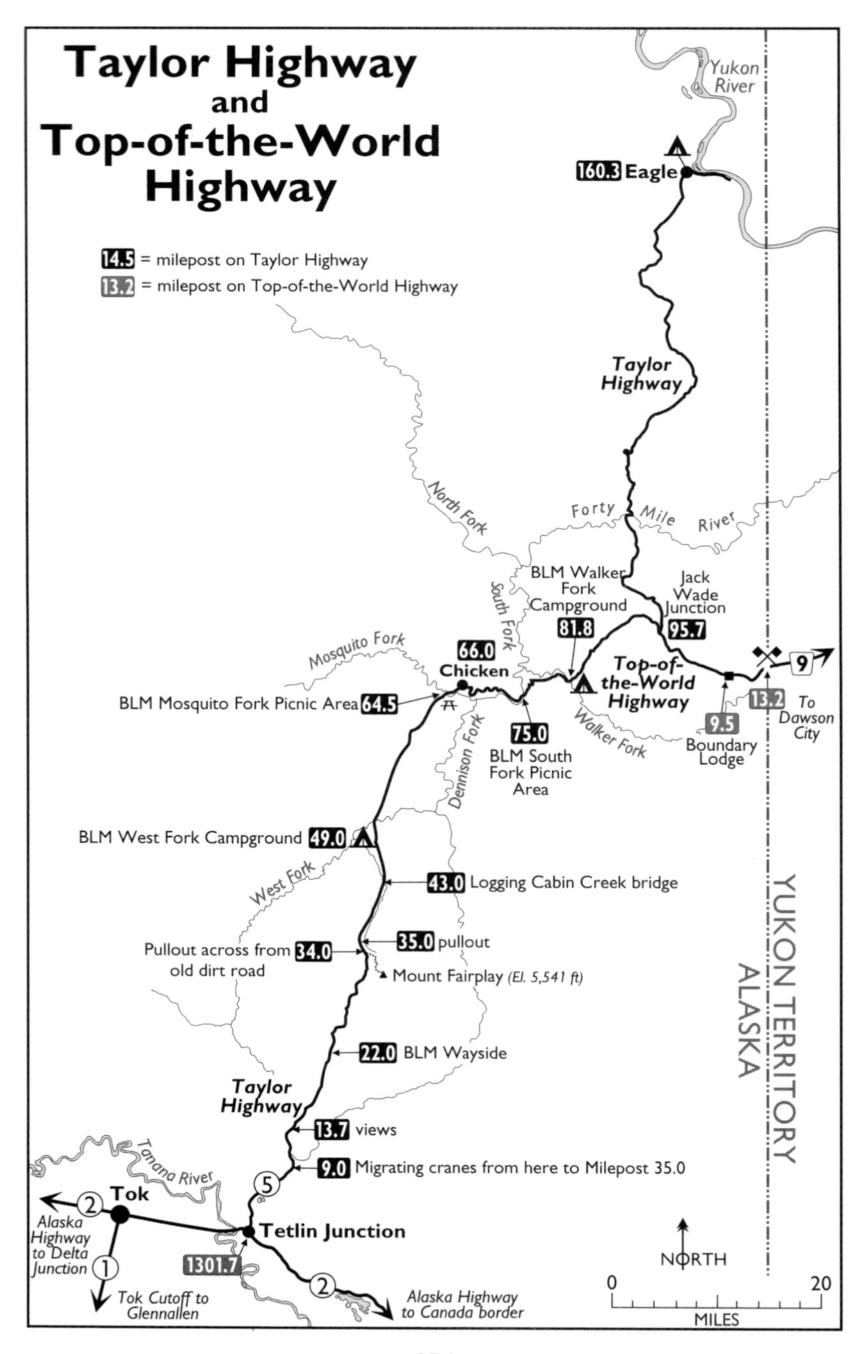
Taylor Highway
and
Top-of-the-World
Highway
14.5 = milepost on Taylor Highway
13.2 = milepost on Top-of-the-World Highway
Yukon River
160.3 Eagle
Taylor Highway
North Fork
Forty Mile River
BLM Walker Fork Campground
81.8
Jack Wade Junction
95.7
South Fork
Mosquito Fork
66.0
Chicken
Top-of-the-World Highway
9
13.2
To Dawson City
BLM Mosquito Fork Picnic Area 64.5
75.0
BLM South Fork Picnic Area
Dennison Fork
Walker Fork
9.5
Boundary Lodge
BLM West Fork Campground 49.0
West Fork
43.0 Logging Cabin Creek bridge
YUKON TERRITORY
ALASKA
Pullout across from old dirt road 34.0
35.0 pullout
Mount Fairplay (El. 5,541 ft)
22.0 BLM Wayside
Taylor Highway
13.7 views
9.0 Migrating cranes from here to Milepost 35.0
Tanana River
5
Tok
2
Alaska Highway to Delta Junction
1
Tetlin Junction
1301.7
Tok Cutoff to Glennallen
2
Alaska Highway to Canada border
NORTH
0
20
MILES

Taylor Highway

Keith Larson

The Taylor Highway (Alaska Route 5) begins at Tetlin Junction on the Alaska Highway and ends in Eagle on the banks of the Yukon River. This intermittently paved two-lane road is officially open only between 15 May and 15 September, the dates when the U.S. Customs station is open (8 AM to 8 PM ADT). Locals use the highway whenever it is snow-free. It is wise to fill up with gas in Tok Junction prior to beginning this trip due to the high cost of gas at the few gas stations along the highway. Make sure to take a good spare tire.

Along the road there are spectacular views of the Yukon-Tanana Uplands boreal spruce forest, the rugged Alaska Range to the south, and the Ogilvie Mountains to the northeast. There are countless pullouts, gravel pits, and waysides where you can pull off to rest, picnic, or do some birding.

Turn north on the Taylor Highway at Alaska Highway Milepost 1301.7 (12.7 miles east of Tok Junction or approximately 80.2 miles from the Yukon border). Traveling north, the road transitions from the Upper Tanana River Valley to the Yukon-Tanana Uplands and the Fortymile watershed that drains into the Yukon River. The Wild and Scenic Fortymile River system (check with BLM office in Tok Junction for details) is noted for its Peregrine Falcons and occasional Golden Eagles nesting along the bluffs and cliffs. This is the most reliable place in the state to find Yellow-bellied Flycatcher and, perhaps, Townsend's Solitaire.

The first six miles of road cuts through hillsides of glacial loess deposited by strong winds during the last ice age when much of the Upper Tanana Valley and Yukon-Tanana Uplands was ice-free. These dunes were stabilized by vegetation 4,000–6,000 years ago. Above the loess and below the soil is a layer of fine white ash that was deposited by a volcanic eruption in the Saint Elias Range almost 2,000 years ago.

At Milepost 13.7 you will have good views of Mount Fairplay to the north (5,541 feet) and Prindle Volcano (4,580 feet) to the northeast. Birds in these boreal spruce forests include Northern Goshawk, Spruce Grouse, Three-toed Woodpecker, Yellow-shafted Flicker, Gray Jay, Common Raven, Boreal Chickadee, Ruby-crowned Kinglet, Bohemian Waxwing, American Robin, Varied Thrush, Myrtle and Townsend's (rare) Warblers, Slate-colored Junco, White-winged Crossbill, and Common Redpoll.

Huge flocks of migrating Sandhill Cranes can be seen during September on hills and ridge tops between Mileposts 9.0 and 35.0. The peak of the flight is from 10–15 September. Trumpeter Swans are typically found later in the month as lakes in the interior valleys begin to freeze. During the fall Sandhill Cranes use alpine tundra as stopover habitats.

Along this stretch of highway check the numerous stands of burned spruce for Northern Hawk Owl, Three-toed Woodpecker, or stop to pick Morel mushrooms. At Milepost 22.0 a BLM wayside interprets the Fortymile Caribou herd's ecology. This pullout is ringed by Black Spruce where one might find Boreal Chickadee, Ruby-crowned Kinglet, Myrtle Warbler, and Slate-colored Junco.

Continuing north to Mileposts 28.3 through 35.8 the spruce forest transitions into alder-willow shrub, alpine tundra, and shrub tundra (typically Dwarf Birch). Alder-willow shrubs and alpine shrub tundra are some of the most productive bird habitats in this region. Stop at any pullout to look for Alder Flycatcher, Gray Jay, Ruby-crowned Kinglet, Gray-cheeked and Swainson's Thrushes, American Robin, Orange-crowned, Myrtle, and Wilson's Warblers, American Tree, Fox, Lincoln's, and Gambel's White-crowned Sparrows, Slate-colored Junco, and Common Redpoll. Other possibilities include Yellow-bellied Flycatcher, Northern Shrike, Blackpoll Warabler (rare), Golden-crowned Sparrow (rare), and Hoary Redpoll.

At Mileposts 32.8 and 35.0 there are pullouts to access Mount Fairplay on the east side of the highway. There are no trails, but hiking a short distance through the brush takes one into the alpine tundra. At Milepost 34.0 an old dirt road leaves the east side of the highway heading up into the tundra several hundred yards before it peters out. Opposite the old road is a large pullout on the west side of the highway. This is the best spot to begin a hike. Sturdy hiking boots are a must. During the summer months, Bellflower, Hairy Lousewort, and Mountain Avens are a few of the alpine wildflowers encountered. Birds you might see while hiking on Mount Fairplay include Northern Harrier, Golden Eagle, Willow and Rock Ptarmigan, American Golden-Plover, Surfbird, Short-eared Owl, Northern Shrike, Townsend's Solitaire, American Pipit, American Tree and Savannah Sparrows, Smith's Longspur, and Gray-crowned Rosy-Finch. On clear days spectacular views include prominent Mount Sanford (16,237 feet) to the south and Mount Hayes (13,832 feet) to the distant southwest.

Pull off at Milepost 35.7 to visit the BLM's boreal wildlife and Caribou interpretive display. The highway now begins to descend into the Fortymile River watershed. At Milepost 37.8 you enter the spruce forest again. Continuing north at Milepost 43 the highway crosses Logging Cabin Creek with roadside fishing access. The valley floor is reached at Milepost 44 and the road continues through open spruce woodlands, wetlands, and muskeg with stands of birch and alder. Along this stretch of the highway are several old burns.

The BLM West Fork Campground is on the banks of the West Fork, Fortymile River, at Milepost 49. It is surrounded by tall shrub habitat where Solitary and Spotted Sandpipers, Gray-cheeked Thrush, Orange-crowned, Yellow, Blackpoll, and Wilson's Warblers, and American Tree and Gambel's White-crowned Sparrows might be found.

North to Milepost 64.5 the highway crosses the Mosquito Fork, where there is a day-use BLM picnic area. Both sides of the river are tall shrub and Balsam Poplar-spruce woodland. Look for Harlequin Duck, Common and Red-breasted Mergansers, Spotted Sandpiper, Alder Flycatcher, American Dipper, Swainson's Thrush, and Yellow Warbler.

The highway now winds through the uplands, dropping into and climbing out of river valleys. From here to the junction to the Top-of-the-World Highway, expect to find Alder, Hammond's, and occasional Yellow-bellied Flycatchers, Gray Jay, Gray-cheeked, Swainson's, Hermit (in deciduous forest), and Varied Thrushes, American Robin, Yellow, Myrtle, and Wilson's Warblers, Northern Waterthrush, Fox, Lincoln's, and Gambel's White-crowned Sparrows, and Slate-colored Juncos. Other possibilities include Northern Goshawk, Merlin, Olive-sided Flycatcher, Say's Phoebe, Boreal Chickadee, Ruby-crowned Kinglet, Townsend's Solitaire, Bohemian Waxwing, Pine Grosbeak, White-winged Crossbill, and Common Redpoll.

Chicken, Milepost 66, is the only community encountered between Tetlin Junction and Eagle. This is an historic gold-mining district where small-scale mining and scars of past large-scale mining efforts are found everywhere. In some areas the tailings are being revegetated with early successional alder and willow shrub habitats. These can be especially good places to find flycatchers and warblers. The community has a bar, restaurant, store, gas station, post office, and RV campground.

As you leave Chicken the road climbs again before dropping down to a BLM day-use area at the South Fork bridge, Milepost 75. On the river's edge, picnic tables, a boat launch, and outhouses are available. The river is lined with White Spruce, Balsam Poplar, aspen, and alder-willow shrubs.

As the road winds along these uplands, it narrows—drivers should use caution due to heavy summer use by tour buses, RVs, and semi-trucks. At Milepost 81.8 the highway crosses the Walker Fork, where the BLM maintains a campground.

As the road continues to climb, it parallels Jack Wade Creek, where past dredging and hydrologic mining exposed deposits of Pleistocene megafauna mammal bones in the riverbanks. At Milepost 92.0 the habitat transitions from spruce forest to spruce woodland and eventually into alpine tundra. The Taylor Highway forks at Milepost 94.2, where a left takes you north to Eagle (65 miles) and a right turn leads east to Dawson (78 miles) on the Top-of-the-World Highway.

Between Mileposts 92.0 and 108.0 the Taylor follows high ridge tops in predominately alpine tundra with widely dispersed, stunted spruce. Search in this habitat for Gyrfalcon, Willow Ptarmigan, Long-tailed Jaeger, Horned Lark, Black-billed Magpie, Northern Wheatear, American Pipit, and Gray-crowned Rosy-Finch.

The Top-of-the-World Highway (sidebar on next page) intersects the Taylor Highway at Jack Wade Junction, 95.7 miles from Tetlin and 64.6 miles south of Eagle, leading to Dawson, Yukon, 78.8 miles to the east.

The Taylor descends into narrow rocky canyons lined with White Spruce, aspen on well-drained south-facing slopes (where Townsend's Solitaire is likely to be found), and Balsam Poplar with alder-willow shrub adjacent to rivers. At Milepost 160 you reach the town of Eagle on the Yukon River. Here the BLM maintains historic Fort Egbert, including a campground (no services) with outhouses and water. The US Army built Fort Egbert as the end point of the Valdez-to-Eagle trail and telegraph line in 1900. The area around the fort is primarily open grassy lawns, White Spruce, Balsam Poplar, aspen, and alder-willow shrub.

John McPhee's *Coming into the Country* (1976) made the community of Eagle famous. This full-service community offers a post office, grocery store, gas station, restaurants, motel, and B&Bs. There are daily riverboat trips to Dawson. A National Park Service ranger station and visitor center serve as a gateway to Yukon-Charley National Park.

Along the Yukon River at Eagle, Herring Gulls can be seen circling about with Violet-green and Bank Swallows. The occasional Belted Kingfisher might be perched on an over-hanging limb. Hermit Thrushes and Gambel's White-crowned Sparrows are heard singing along the shores of the river. A Eurasian Wigeon was found here one summer.

LOGISTICS

The area code for all telephone numbers is 907 unless otherwise indicated. Tourist and travel services (accommodations, restaurants, attractions, etc.) are listed in the The Milepost. *Statewide travel and birding information services are listed under Logistics in the* Introduction, *page 15.*

All necessary traveler services are available in Tok Junction, Eagle, and Dawson. Check the listings in *The Milepost* for a variety of commercial and primitive campgrounds on the Alaska, Taylor, and Top-of-the-World Highways.

Contact the BLM office (883-5121) in Tok about campgrounds, the Fortymile Wild and Scenic River Corridor, and historic Fort Egbert in Eagle.

Hunting and fishing information, special permits, and regulations can be obtained at the Alaska Department of Fish and Game office in Tok (883-2971). Licenses can be purchased at a variety of locations in Tok Junction and Eagle.

Maps of the local area including, the Mount Fairplay area, can be obtained from any USGS maps dealer. The Eagle and Tanacross (1:250,000 scale) quadrangles would be most useful. For hiking on Mount Fairplay the Tanacross C-3 1:63,000 should be useful.

Call Yukon-Charley National Park (574-2234) in Eagle or (474-7722) in Fairbanks for more information about floating the Yukon and Charley Rivers.

ACKNOWLEDGEMENTS: Terry Doyle reviewed this section and added many birding notes.

TOP-OF-THE-WORLD HIGHWAY

From Jack Wade Junction at Milepost 95.7 of the Taylor Highway the Top-of-the-World Highway climbs for 13.2 miles before reaching the U.S.-Canada border. At Milepost 9.5, Boundary Lodge has rooms, gas, restaurant, and store. Pullouts at Mileposts 11.7 and 12.7 offer spectacular views of the Yukon River Valley and the Ogilvie Mountains to the northeast. At Milepost 12.7 you will find outhouses and an observation deck. From here you can easily walk through alpine habitats to look for birds.

The U.S.-Canadian Customs station at Poker Creek is situated at Milepost 13.2. The border is open from 8 AM to 8 PM daily (ADT) during the summer months. These 13.2 miles of road are all in alpine tundra habitat and are noteworthy for the wildflowers and birds as mentioned for previous alpine habitats.

This road continues another 65 miles to the Yukon River crossing at Dawson. There is no bridge there, but a ferry operates continuously during the summer months. On the south side of the river opposite Dawson is a nice campground on the river where Peregrine Falcons can be scoped on the river bluffs. Each summer Dawson hosts a music festival which draws world-renowned musicians. See *The Milepost* to be tempted by the area's other historical and natural attractions.

LOGISTICS

Services, accommodations, and other helpful information is listed above in the *Logistics* section of the Taylor Highway chapter.

Tok Cutoff and Glenn Highway:

Tok to Glennallen and Palmer

George West

The Tok Cutoff and Glenn Highway (Alaska Route 1) is the most direct overland route to Anchorage from the Alaska Highway at Tok. The road heads southwest along the Tok and Little Tok Rivers to Slana, then along the northern boundary of the Wrangell-Saint Elias National Park and Preserve. The boundary of the park is the Copper River that runs south into Prince William Sound east of Cordova. The Tok Cutoff ends after 125 miles at Gakona Junction on the Richardson Highway that starts in Valdez and runs north to Delta and Fairbanks. To reach the Glenn Highway, you must go south on the Richardson for about 14 miles and turn west (right) at Glennallen. The Glenn Highway continues southwest for 189 miles through alpine country with views of several glaciers to Palmer (page 185), an agricultural community about 45 miles northeast of Anchorage. A divided four-lane highway continues into downtown Anchorage. This 328-mile route can be driven in one day if you do not stop too often to bird. The road is completely paved, but in recent years it has been undergoing continuous reconstruction as frost heaves play havoc with the pavement each spring and early summer. Watch for humps and depressions in the roadbed, especially along the Tok Cutoff, and especially if you are driving or towing an RV.

Scenery along these highways is spectacular, with views of the Wrangell and Chugach Mountains and their impressive glaciers. Magnificent Matanuska Glacier is easily viewable from the Glenn Highway and is well worth a visit (fee) in its own right. The Glenn runs through miles of spruce forest with braided glacial rivers, clear streams, and many ponds and small lakes. Birding can be very good, especially on the Tok Cutoff and along the eastern, wooded section of the Glenn Highway. You should readily find the following species: Lesser Yellowlegs, Mew Gull, Arctic Tern, Alder Flycatcher, Gray Jay, Common Raven, Swainson's Thrush, American Robin, Varied Thrush, Myrtle Warbler, Northern Waterthrush, Savannah, Lincoln's, and Gambel's

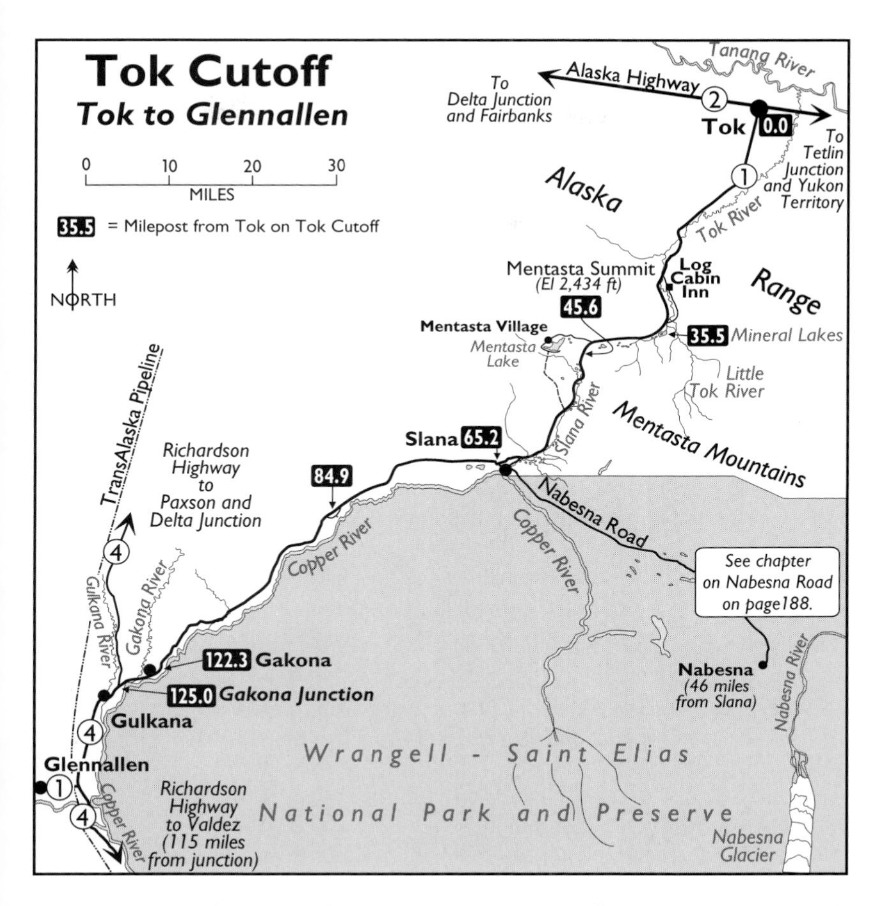

White-crowned Sparrows, Slate-colored Junco, and Common Redpoll. With a little effort you can add Merlin, Solitary Sandpiper, Violet-green Swallow, Boreal Chickadee, Bohemian Waxwing, Red-winged and Rusty Blackbirds, Pine Grosbeak, and White-winged Crossbill. There is a chance to get into good alpine country just east of Palmer by taking a side road to Hatcher Pass (see page 41).

Note: The first map for this chapter (above) and the text that describes the route from Tok to Gakona Junction give mileages from Tok. The second map (page 184), showing the route from Glennallen to Chickaloon (36 miles east of Palmer on the Glenn Highway), gives mileages from Anchorage. If you get confused, the mileages provided in *The Milepost* correspond with those in this guide's text and maps.

BIRDING FROM TOK TO GLENNALLEN

Take Alaska Route 1 south from the Alaska Highway in Tok. (For details of birding the Tok area, see Alaska Highway–Yukon Border to Delta Junction, page 169.) There are several campsites along the road in the first 15 miles. The road crosses the Little Tok and Tok Rivers in several places from here to Milepost 34. Arctic Grayling and Dolly Varden (trout) can be caught in these rivers by using a small spinner (Mepps 0) or a wet or dry fly. Mineral Lakes at Milepost 35.5 is a good place to scan for waterfowl, including Tundra and Trumpeter Swans, as are other lakes and ponds in both directions from here. At Milepost 45.6, the road crosses Mentasta Summit at 2,434 feet elevation and then drops along the Slana River that feeds the Copper River. Slana (Milepost 65.2) is at the junction of the Nabesna Road that runs 45 miles to Nabesna (see page 188) and access to Gold Hill (sidebar on next page), where you can find Timberline Sparrows. There are good views of the Wrangell Mountains off and on from here to Glennallen. Check the tops of spruce trees all along this road for resident Northern Hawk Owls. While more easily seen in winter, they breed throughout this region and can be found in summer as well. Waterbird potential diminishes as the highway parallels the Copper River to Gakona Junction, although Cliff Swallow, Ruby-crowned Kinglet, Gray-cheeked Thrush, Orange-crowned and Wilson's Warblers, Fox Sparrow, and White-winged Crossbill become more likely.

The text covering the Glenn Highway between Glennallen and Palmer continues on page 185. If you are headed for Valdez on the Richardson Highway, turn to page 132.

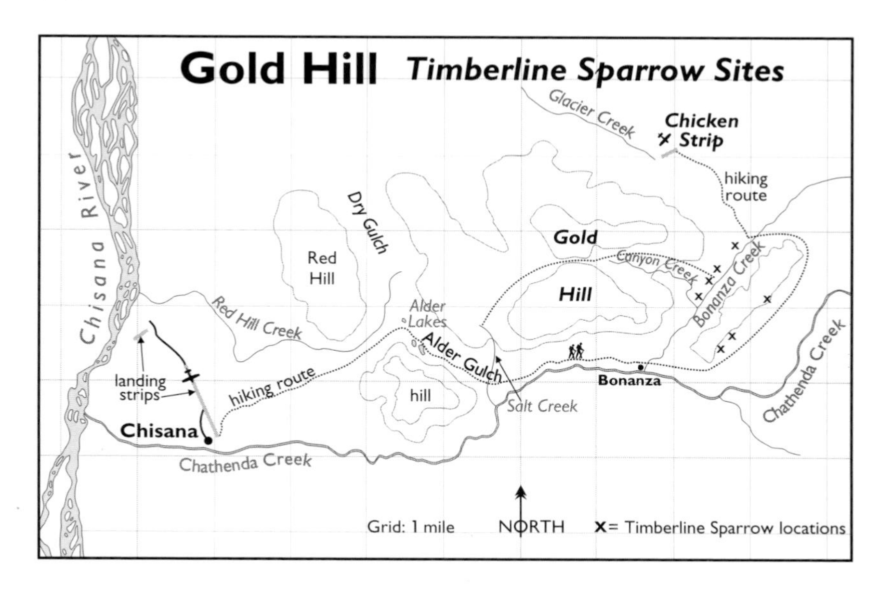

GOLD HILL TIMBERLINE SPARROW

Terry Doyle

Timberline Sparrow (*Spizella breweri taverneri*), a subspecies of Brewer's Sparrow, is found regularly in Alaska only at Gold Hill in the Nutzotin Mountains northeast of the small community of Chisana. Late June to early July is the most reliable time to find Timberline Sparrows at Gold Hill as the birds do not arrive until mid-June and song activity diminishes rapidly by mid-July. This is also a good time of the year to find the regular alpine and subalpine breeders such as Upland Sandpiper, Say's Phoebe, Horned Lark, Townsend's Solitaire, American Pipit, Orange-crowned and Wilson's Warblers, American Tree, Savannah, and Gambel's White-crowned Sparrows, and Smith's Longspur.

There are two ways to get to—less difficult and more expensive or more difficult and less expensive. The less-difficult but more-expensive alternative is to charter a plane into the Chicken Strip, a 1,300-foot gravel runway located in Caribou Pass (see map). The Chicken Strip is a convenient camping location, as well. From there the closest sparrows can be found 1.5 miles SSE (bearing 160 degrees) from the east end of the runway. Hike up and over the low ridge until you come to the 3-to-5-foot-high scattered willows on the southeast-facing slope. The sparrows prefer the transition between the alpine and subalpine zones along this narrow band of open thickets of low-to-medium shrubs. Walking SW along this band should yield several singing males that sound superficially similar to the nominate race of Brewer's Sparrow. The next-best location is the SE slope on the next ridge to the SE (between Bonanza and Chathenda Creeks), about another mile as the raven flies.

Be sure to fly with an experienced pilot as there is only one way in and out of this short runway. In Tok, contact 40-Mile Air. There are also experienced bush pilots in Chisana that may fly into the airstrip.

The more-difficult but less-expensive alternative is to fly the regularly scheduled flight from Tok to Chisana on 40-Mile Air and hike the 7–8 miles uphill from there. There is a wet ATV trail that leads from the Chisana airstrip to at least Salt Creek via Red Hill Creek and Alder Gulch. This hike will take most of a day to accomplish, so be prepared to camp and bring a good USGS topographic map of the area. Waterproof or water-resistant boots are recommended and good ankle support is required. Another alternative is to fly the regularly scheduled flight from Tok to Chisana on 40-Mile Air and charter a flight from Chisana to the Chicken Strip. Good luck!

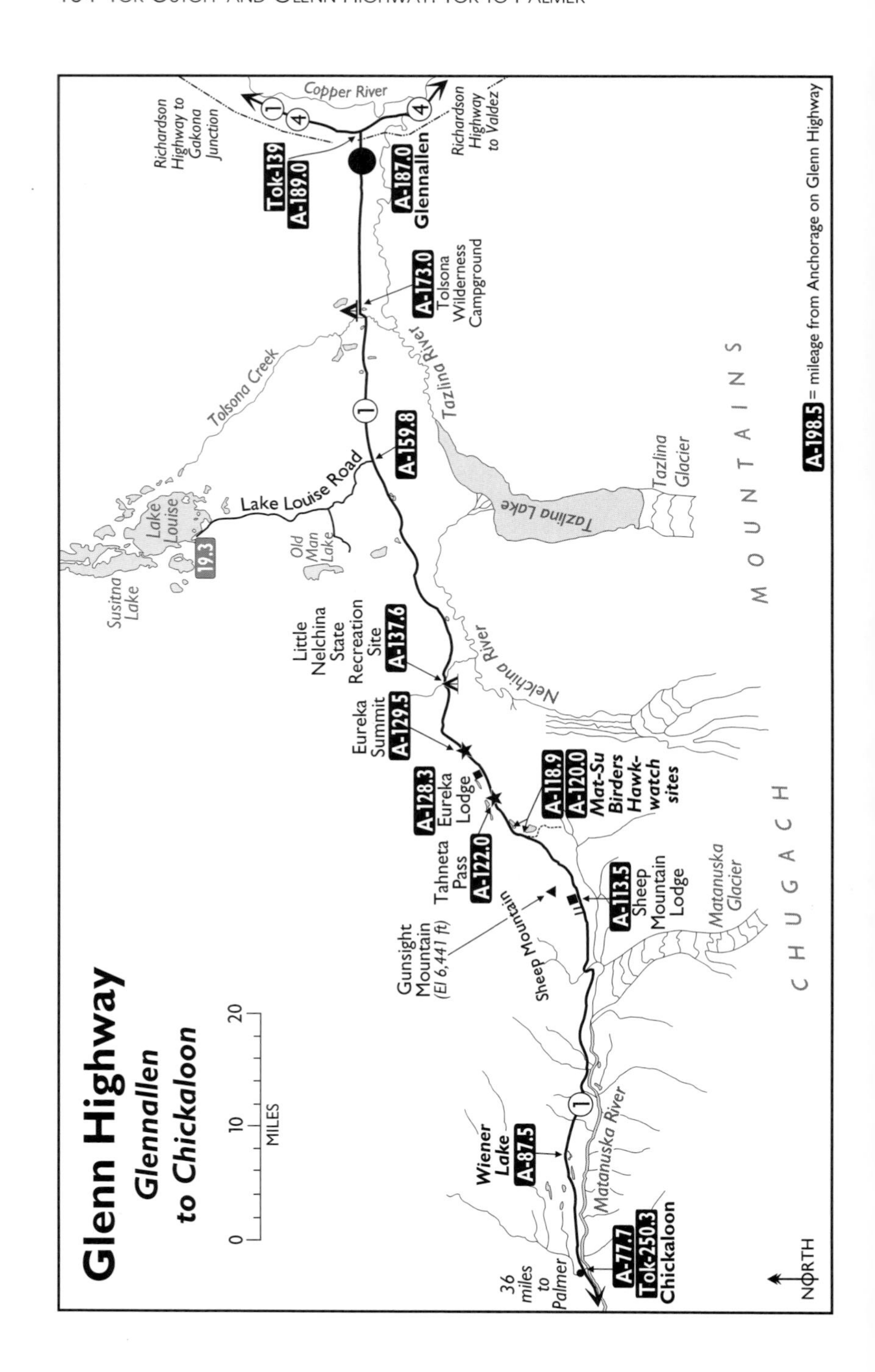

Glenn Highway
Glennallen to Chickaloon
0
10
20
MILES
NORTH
36 miles to Palmer
A-77.7
Tok-250.3
Chickaloon
Wiener Lake
A-87.5
Matanuska River
Sheep Mountain
Gunsight Mountain (El 6,441 ft)
A-113.5
Sheep Mountain Lodge
Matanuska Glacier
Tahneta Pass
A-122.0
A-128.3
Eureka Lodge
A-118.9
A-120.0
Mat-Su Birders Hawk-watch sites
Eureka Summit
A-129.5
Little Nelchina State Recreation Site
A-137.6
Nelchina River
C H U G A C H   M O U N T A I N S
Susitna Lake
Lake Louise
19.3
Old Man Lake
Lake Louise Road
A-159.8
Tazlina Lake
Tazlina Glacier
Tolsona Creek
Tazlina River
A-173.0
Tolsona Wilderness Campground
Tok-139
A-189.0
A-187.0
Glennallen
Richardson Highway to Gakona Junction
Copper River
Richardson Highway to Valdez
1
4
A-198.5 = mileage from Anchorage on Glenn Highway

BIRDING FROM GLENNALLEN TO PALMER

Turn left onto the Richardson Highway (Alaska Route 4) to go to Anchorage or Valdez. You will cross the Gakona River as it joins the Copper River, both silt-laden glacial streams. There are several places to eat, buy gasoline, and stay in the Gakona and Glennallen areas if you do not want to go all the way to Anchorage in one day. Continuing south along the Richardson takes you across the Gulkana River, a favorite salmon and Rainbow Trout fishing river with annual runs of large King and Red Salmon. Turn right at the junction of Alaska Route 1 to continue into downtown Glennallen and on to Palmer and Anchorage.

All of the boreal forest species can be found along the Glenn Highway, but the following are some of the better places to stop and search. Tolsona Wilderness Campground is 0.75 mile north of the highway at Milepost 155 from Tok (173 miles from Anchorage, or A-173). Boreal Chickadee, Pine Grosbeak, and White-winged Crossbill all occur along the gravel road leading into the campground. Great Gray Owls nested there in 2002, and Three-toed Woodpeckers might be abundant in the area. At Milepost 168 (A-159.8) the gravel road to Lake Louise leaves the highway to the right. You may find the first part of this road less traveled and easier to bird, if you have the time, than the paved Glenn Highway. The only known colony of Double-crested Cormorants in central Alaska nests on the island just offshore in Lake Louise. This is also a good place to see other waterbirds and Blackpoll Warbler. At Milepost 196 (A-132) is a good view of Nelchina Glacier in the Chugach Mountains to the south.

You are now approaching Eureka Summit (elevation 3,322 feet) in the alpine at Milepost 198.5 (A-129.5). This is one area to look for Arctic Warbler nesting in the willow brush near the summit. They arrive and sing their trilling song in mid-June and remain through mid-August. They also occur commonly in the taller areas of willows right by the roadside near Gunsight Lodge (may be closed) and Tahneta Pass at Milepost 206 (A-122). Pull off the highway (left, downhill side of Gunsight Mountain) here and note some small ponds to the east. The warblers are in the willow brush along the pullout; Willow and Rock Ptarmigan, Northern Wheatear, and Blackpoll and Wilson's Warblers occupy the alpine on Gunsight Mountain.

One of the best sections of the highway is between Mileposts 199 and 213 (A-129 and A-115), where several roadside lakes are good for waterfowl. Lesser Scaup is the dominant species, but a good variety of dabbling and diving ducks occurs. White-winged Scoter and Barrow's Goldeneye are possibilities and, if you are very lucky, you may see Trumpeter Swans. Some shorebirds occur, mostly Lesser Yellowlegs and Wilson's Snipe. Although there are lakes all along the highway, these seem to have the highest concentration of birds.

EUREKA HAWKWATCH

Cecily Fritz

There is a regularly manned spring raptor-migration site located near Eureka. If you are coming from Anchorage on the Glenn Highway, drive to Milepost 120. Just beyond is a large pulloff on the south with ample parking space. Observers watch from the far end of the pulloff, scanning the valley to the northeast for approaching raptors that generally parallel the road as they fly in a southwesterly direction—even in spring migration. On a few occasions, depending on wind conditions, observers may instead be at Milepost 118.9, a right pulloff about a mile west of Milepost 120. On the third weekend of April, Anchorage Audubon conducts a hawkwatching field trip to the Milepost 118.9 site.

Hawkwatching season runs from approximately the last week of March through early May, with adult Golden Eagles (breeding birds) returning first. The best daily flight of adult Golden Eagles was 54 individuals (1 April 1983). Golden Eagles continue to come through in reduced numbers throughout the season. Other species do not arrive in significant numbers until mid-April, with peak flights of Northern Harrier, Harlan's Hawk, and Rough-legged Hawk occurring in the last half of April. Also seen somewhat regularly, but in lesser numbers, are Bald Eagle, Sharp-shinned Hawk, Northern Goshawk, Merlin, Gyrfalcon, and a variety of Red-tailed Hawk color morphs other than the typical dark Harlan's subspecies. Osprey, Swainson's Hawk, and Peregrine Falcon, seen a time or two in past years, may prove to be regular migrants through the area. A great day during peak season can number 200–300 birds.

Other birds commonly seen at the hawkwatch include Northern Hawk Owl, Gray Jay, Boreal Chickadee, and Common Redpoll. Expected migrants include Trumpeter and Tundra Swans, Greater White-fronted and Canada Geese, American Robin, Varied Thrush, Lapland Longspur, and Snow Bunting.

Discovered by Bob Dittrick and Ted Swem in the early 1980s, this raptor migration site has been monitored for several days each spring. Since 1999, hours of observation have increased, with the 2001 and 2002 seasons logging over 100 hours of observation and tallying around 1,000 raptors each year. Weather permitting, the site is manned every weekend and generally two or three days during the week, with a goal of increasing coverage for future seasons (volunteers are welcome). Data collected include hourly weather conditions, raptor species, sex, age, and subspecies and morph when possible. Data compiled over time will help contribute to a better understanding of Alaska's raptor populations and their migratory behavior. In recent years this all-volunteer effort has been conducted primarily by members of Mat-Su Birders. Experienced observers on-site are available to assist with identification. Anyone wanting further information, with questions on weather conditions, or to see if the site will be manned on a specific day, can contact Cecily or Paul Fritz by email (*gulogulo@alaska.net*) or by phone (907-746-1299).

You can reach more of them by driving south off the highway on a gravel road at Milepost 209.4 (Anchorage 118.6).

The Eureka Hawkwatch site (sidebar on previous page) is located at Milepost 208 (A-120) and is worth a stop when counts are in progress. The ridge running above the north side of the highway is worth scanning for raptors, with Golden Eagle appearing frequently. Bald Eagle, Northern Harrier, Sharp-shinned Hawk, Northern Goshawk, and Red-tailed and Rough-legged Hawks are seen, as well. There are several paved pullouts along this section of the highway, some with restrooms. A pair of Merlins has nested for several years behind Sheep Mountain Lodge at Milepost 216.5 (A-113.5). Ask the lodge owners for a list of recent bird, mammal, and wildflower sightings in their area (645-5121). From Milepost 217 (A-113) to Milepost 222 (A-106), keep an eye to the ridge and slopes on the north side of the road for Dall's Sheep. Golden Eagle can often be seen here and there is evidence of them nesting on the cliff face at Milepost 222 (A-106).

Matanuska Glacier is close to the road near Milepost 226 (A-102) and can be accessed through the Matanuska Glacier State Recreation Area at Milepost 227 (A-101), but the birding is not good. You might see Gray Jay, Black-capped and perhaps Boreal Chickadee, and Wilson's Warbler. Again, watch the spruce and utility poles for Northern Hawk Owls that breed in this area.

As the road drops through twists and turns toward Palmer, birding doesn't pick up until you reach some of the lakes such as Wiener Lake at Milepost 240.5 (A-87.5). This is worth checking for species like Pacific Loon and Barrow's Goldeneye, especially during spring migration in May. Continuing down the mountain, you will parallel the silty Matanuska River on your left as it runs into Knik Arm east of Anchorage. At Milepost 278.5 (A-49.5) is the junction of the Hatcher Pass road that leads into the alpine north of Palmer and Wasilla and extends west to the Parks Highway north of Willow. See page 41 for details of the Hatcher Pass area.

LOGISTICS

Gas and food are available all along the road. There are a few lodges where you can stay overnight, but don't expect plush accommodations. There are several campgrounds, and if you have an RV and wish to dry-camp, you can usually overnight in a gravel pit or paved pullout. See *The Milepost*, the Alaska Highway chapter on page 172 for logistics in Tok, the Anchorage chapter page 35 for logistics in Anchorage, and the Glenn Highway, page 40, for logistics in Palmer.

ACKNOWLEDGEMENTS: Cecily Fritz reviewed the chapter, and Terry Doyle added birding information. Birding notes from Tim Schantz are appreciated. Some birding information from Lethaby (1994).

NABESNA ROAD:

WRANGELL-SAINT ELIAS NATIONAL PARK AND PRESERVE

Keith Larson

The Nabesna Road is one of the best-kept secrets for finding birds and other wildlife in Alaska. It traverses the northwest side of Wrangell-Saint Elias National Park and Preserve, the largest national park in the country at 24 million acres. From the Nabesna Road visitors can view many of the tallest peaks in North America.

Wrangell-Saint Elias National Park and Preserve has an impressive avian checklist totaling 221 species. The majority of birds are typical of the interior boreal forest and include many northern specialties such as Gyrfalcon, Rock Ptarmigan, Long-tailed Jaeger, Northern Hawk Owl, Gray Jay, Boreal Chickadee, Northern Shrike, Timberline Sparrow, Rusty Blackbird, and Gray-crowned Rosy-Finch. Mammals you might encounter are Caribou, Moose, Dall's Sheep, Black and Brown Bears, and Wolf. Encounters with humans are few.

The Nabesna Road enters the park from the Tok Cutoff (page 180), 65.2 miles southwest of Tok Junction and about 75 miles northeast of Glennallen. The road is 46 miles long and is open to automobiles and RVs only during the summer months. The gravel road follows the several rivers and creeks, passing through Black Spruce muskeg, mixed Black and White Spruce woodlands, alpine shrub tundra, and alpine tundra habitats. Along this route there are numerous backcountry trails and plenty of primitive campsites and picnic spots, all excellent for birding. *There are no mile markers along the road, and all mileages in this text are measured from the Tok Cutoff junction.*

Only the first four miles of the road are paved and the remainder is gravel. Most cars will do well until Mile 29.0, where a series of gravel stream-crossings makes traveling in spring or wet conditions rough. The last four miles of the road are not maintained by the state and are deeply rutted. Creek crossings may be a trickle on cool mornings and raging torrents on warm afternoons. It is strongly recommended that visitors check in at the Slana Ranger Station at Mile 0.2 to inquire about conditions prior to travel.

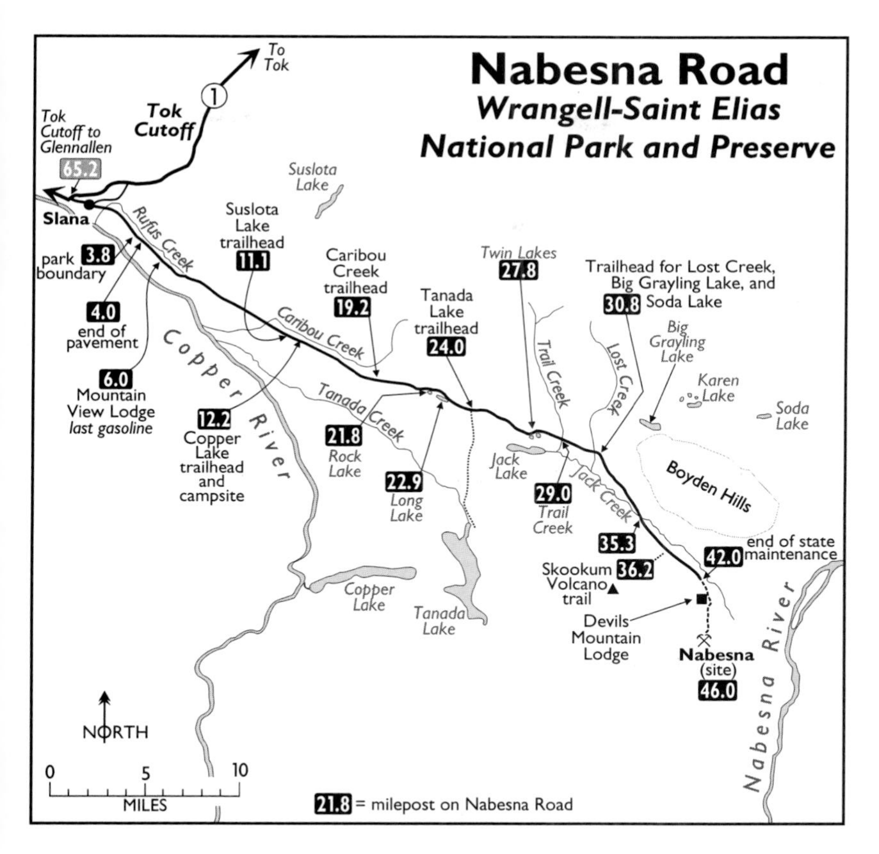

At Mile 0.8 is the Slana Post Office and a public telephone. Cross the Slana River bridge at Mile 1.5. There are primitive campsites and access for the Slana River at Mile 1.7. The road passes through Black Spruce muskeg, spruce forest, and mixed-spruce woodlands. Views to the southwest include Mount Sanford (16,237 feet), Mount Drum (12,010 feet), and the enormous, active, shield volcano Mount Wrangell (14,163 feet). Search for Mew Gulls around the Slana River and Olive-sided and Alder Flycatchers, Gray Jay, Boreal Chickadee, Ruby-crowned Kinglet, Gray-cheeked, Swainson's, and Varied Thrushes, Myrtle and Wilson's Warblers, Savannah and Gambel's White-crowned Sparrows, and Slate-colored Junco along the roadsides. Upland Sandpiper can be found at scattered locations where there is open tundra near the road.

The park boundary is at Mile 3.8 and the road becomes gravel at Mile 4.0. The Copper River parallels the road on its descent from headwaters at Copper Lake. No gas is available after Mile 6 at the Mountain View Lodge. A

Myrtle, Townsend's, and Wilson's Warblers (males)

primitive campsite at Mile 6.1 on Rufus Creek offers good shrub habitat for warblers and sparrows, and the creek has Rainbow Trout and Dolly Varden.

At Mile 11.1 a gravel parking area on the south lies opposite the Suslota Lake trailhead. This multiple-use (ATV) trail provides a 12-mile round-trip through spruce forests, muskeg, and alpine shrub tundra. Most of the trails here are traditional ATV trails, and you can expect to find wet, muddy, and uneven hiking conditions.

The Copper Lake trailhead and campsite are reached at Mile 12.2. Great views, camping, and picnic tables are available from pullouts at Miles 16.6 and 17.8. On the north at Mile 19.2 is the Caribou Creek trailhead.

There are pullouts and campsites at Rock Lake (Mile 21.8) and Long Lake (Mile 22.9). These lakes are good spots for scaup, Surf Scoter, Common and Barrow's Goldeneyes, and Red-necked Phalarope. Another multiple-use trail leading south to Tanada Lake is at Mile 24. Alder Flycatcher, Gray-cheeked Thrush, Orange-crowned, Yellow, Blackpoll, and Wilson's Warblers, and Gambel's White-crowned Sparrow inhabit the shrubs around the lakes and creeks of this region.

At Mile 24.7 the road crosses a subtle divide (3,320 feet) between the Copper River watershed that empties into the Gulf of Alaska and the Yukon River watershed that empties into the Bering Sea. A nice pullout with picnic spots and campsites at Twin Lakes is available at Mile 27.8. The lakes and their shrubby margins are great for waterfowl, shorebirds, warblers, and sparrows.

Trail Creek (Mile 29) is a good place to turn around if conditions or low vehicle-clearance make a series of creek crossings dangerous. The trailhead for Lost Creek, Big Grayling Lake, and Soda Lake is on the north at Mile 30.8. This is an excellent hike up the gravel bed of Lost Creek to a beautiful alpine lake in shrub tundra and finally up to Soda Lake where Dall's Sheep are found. Olive-sided Flycatchers sing from the tallest spruce trees along the creeks, and nesting Bald Eagles and Surf Scoters are found at Big Grayling Lake. A nice side-trip with spectacular views in all directions is to continue from Big Grayling Lake and hike to the ridge of the Boyden Hills to the southeast.

At Mile 35.3 you can easily explore the spruce woodlands and alpine shrub tundra from an excellent primitive campsite at Jack Creek. Hiking anywhere upslope to the tree line where alpine shrub tundra takes over would be an appropriate place to look for Willow and Rock Ptarmigan. The mile-long trail to Skookum Volcano (Mile 36.2) is an interesting place to explore the geology of this region.

Mile 42 is the end of the state-maintained road. From this point there are many opportunities to hike and explore the headwaters of the Nabesna River. Devil's Mountain Lodge owns the property on both sides of the road and parking is limited. Four miles up the road is the historic Nabesna Mine. Driving past Mile 42 is not recommended.

From the end of the road, experienced wilderness backpackers might consider a trip up to Jaeger Mesa and beyond to glacier-covered peaks and to explore the tundra for birds. During summer look for Golden Eagle, Gyrfalcon, Willow and Rock Ptarmigan, American Golden-Plover, Upland Sandpiper, Whimbrel, Long-tailed Jaeger, Say's Phoebe, Horned Lark, Northern Wheatear, Townsend's Solitaire, American Pipit, Smith's Longspur, and Gray-crowned Rosy-Finch.

LOGISTICS

The area code for all telephone numbers is 907 unless otherwise indicated. Tourist and travel services (accommodations, restaurants, attractions, etc.) are listed in the The Milepost. *Statewide travel and birding information services are listed under Logistics in the* Introduction, *page 15.*

There are plenty of primitive campsites along this road, several B&B establishments, and lodges. Gas stations are available only on the Tok Cutoff and at Mountain View Lodge located at Mile 6 on the Nabesna Road.

The Slana Ranger Station is an excellent source of information on accommodations, backcountry permits, bear reports, camping, road conditions, and trails. Purchase detailed USGS and *Trails Illustrated* maps before hiking anywhere in the park. Wrangell-Saint Elias National Park and Preserve Slana Ranger Station can be reached at 882-5238. The station is open from June to September, 8 AM to 5 PM.

Air taxis in Tok Junction and Nabesna offer access to the alpine tundra habitats of the region. Inquire with 40-Mile Air in Tok Junction at 883-5191 or Ellis Air Service 822-3368 on the Nabesna Road for air taxi information. The Upper Cheslina on the north side of the mountains and the Gold Hill area to the east of Chisana are likely places to encounter the Timberline Sparrow (page 183).

ACKNOWLEDGEMENTS: Terry Doyle reviewed this chapter and added bird sightings from his earlier Breeding Bird Surveys.

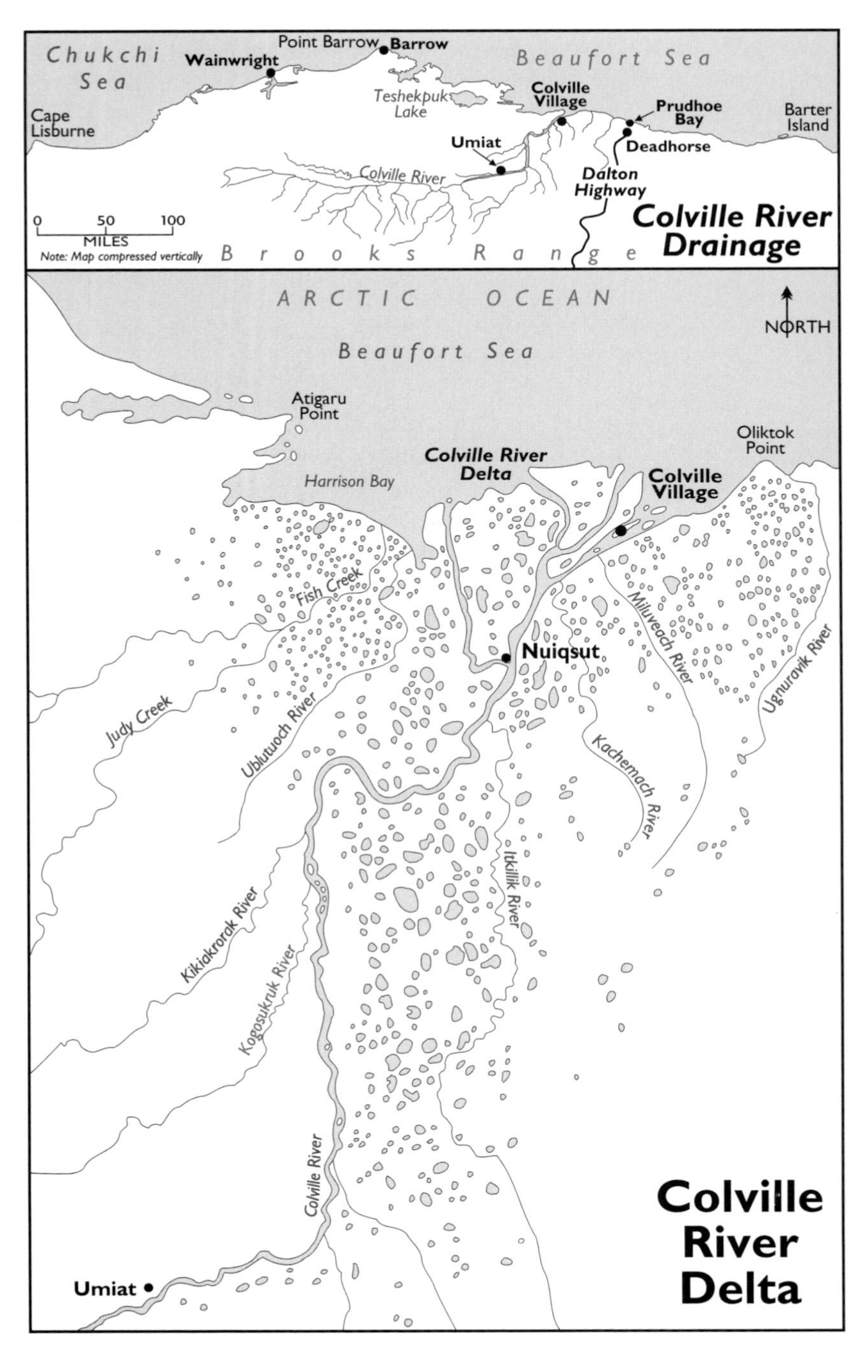
Chukchi Sea
Point Barrow
Barrow
Wainwright
Beaufort Sea
Teshekpuk Lake
Colville Village
Prudhoe Bay
Barter Island
Cape Lisburne
Umiat
Deadhorse
Colville River
Dalton Highway
Colville River Drainage
0 50 100
MILES
Note: Map compressed vertically
Brooks Range
ARCTIC OCEAN
NORTH
Beaufort Sea
Atigaru Point
Oliktok Point
Colville River Delta
Harrison Bay
Colville Village
Fish Creek
Nuiqsut
Miluveach River
Ugnuravik River
Judy Creek
Ublutuoch River
Kachemach River
Itkillik River
Kikiakrorak River
Kogosukruk River
Colville River
Umiat
Colville River Delta

Colville River Delta

James W. Helmericks

Most birders traveling to the north coast of Alaska fly to either Barrow (page 197) or Prudhoe Bay. (Prudhoe Bay is also reached by driving the Dalton Highway, page 91). In visiting only these places, they miss one of the more unique and diverse areas on the North Slope, the Colville River delta.

The Colville River watershed drains nearly 30 percent of the Arctic North Slope. This high-volume flow, with its heavy sediment load during spring break-up and summer rains, has created a dynamic delta of over 200 square miles, made up of complex and diverse wetlands. Deep-water channels and meandering side-channels with their associated system of tapped lakes are a prominent part of the delta. Other features include high- and low-centered polygons, both shallow- and deep-water polygon ponds, deep-water lakes, sand dunes, willow meadows, and the saltmarsh-mudflat ecosystem of the outer face of the delta.

This ecological diversity attracts some of the highest concentrations of many bird and fish species across the North Slope. During both spring and fall migration, the Colville delta provides important habitat needed for the survival of many migrants. The polygon and wet-sedge system that covers much of the delta is excellent nesting habitat for many species of waterfowl, shorebirds, and passerines. Some of the more-common birds using the delta are Red-throated, Pacific, and Yellow-billed Loons, Greater White-fronted Goose, Black Brant, Tundra Swan, Northern Pintail, Greater Scaup, Spectacled and King Eiders, and Long-tailed Duck. Both Willow and Rock Ptarmigan nest in the delta, as do Black-bellied Plover, American Golden-Plover, Bar-tailed Godwit, Ruddy Turnstone, Semipalmated, Western, Pectoral, and Stilt Sandpipers, Dunlin, Long-billed Dowitcher, Red-necked and Red Phalaropes, Pomarine and Parasitic Jaegers, Glaucous and Sabine's Gulls, Arctic Tern, Savannah Sparrow, Lapland Longspur, and Snow Bunting.

Unless you fly in or charter your own small airplane, your options for visiting the Colville River delta are limited to traveling with Golden Plover Guiding, a professional guide service operating from Colville Village on Anachlik Island on the eastern side of the 18-mile-wide delta face, about 1.5 miles inland from the edge of the Arctic Ocean. (See *Logistics*)

This tour/lodge operator will pick you up at Deadhorse Airport and transport you to and from Colville Village in a Cessna 206, giving you an aerial view of the Prudhoe Bay oil field, the TransAlaska Pipeline, and the Arctic Ocean with its barrier-island system and vast expanse of pack ice to the north.

The basic birding trip of four days and three nights includes room and board at the lodge and transportation from and return to Deadhorse. Also included is a half-day boat trip, either upriver or out to the Arctic Ocean (weather permitting). Other optional trips are described below. Groups wanting more independence can rent a guesthouse and do their own cooking and housekeeping. Food and transportation are not included in the guesthouse rental price, so you need to bring your own food and arrange the charter flight in and out with Golden Plover Air.

Once you arrive at Colville Village you can bird locally on foot or by canoe, or choose from several optional day-trips. Traveling upriver by boat or plane lets you visit a greater variety of habitats, going from the wet sedge of the coastal area to riparian brush and high bluffs. These trips depend a lot on the season and whether you want to see more breeding birds or hatched young not found in the delta. If you want to see male eiders, plan to arrive before 20 June. In some years Spectacled males are gone by 16 June, while a few male Kings can be seen for another week. The main brood-hatching time starts the last week of June for shorebirds, while the geese start hatching the first of July. The eiders start hatching out around 10 July, and the loons closer to the middle of the month. July also sees the start of the fall migration, when many shorebirds move south. In balance, an ideal time to visit the Colville would be between the third week of June through the second week of July in order to coincide with some of the best weather, the largest number of birds, herds of caribou moving through the delta as the mosquito season starts up, and the plant life in full growth, with prolific flower displays.

The Black Brant colony surrounding the lodge contains nearly 1,000 pairs, the largest concentration of breeding Black Brant on the North Slope. From the lodge deck you can see and hear Red-throated, Pacific, and Common Loons, Black Brant, Northern Pintail, King Eider, Long-tailed Duck, Semipalmated Sandpiper, Dunlin, Sabine's Gull, Lapland Longspur, and Snow Bunting, all of which nest around or near the lodge. Snowy Owls are usually seen every season, but nest infrequently in the delta. During high lemming years, there are many Snowy Owls, though most are non-breeders. Rarities that have been recorded, but should not be expected, include Steller's Eider, Red-necked Stint, Sharp-tailed and Buff-breasted Sandpipers, Ruff, Thayer's, Slaty-backed, Ross's, and Ivory Gulls, Arctic Warbler, Bluethroat, and Siberian Accentor.

From the lodge, you may take guided birding trips away from the local area by boat, either half-day or overnight trips depending on how far up the river you want to go. Or you can take a one-day trip and fly to Umiat, a small community 90 miles upriver from the coast, for a half-day of birding in the willow brush for Bluethroats and other more-inland species.

The shortest boat trip takes you seven miles up the Colville River to its confluence with the smaller Kachemach River. Here the tundra is much drier and full of tussock grass, pingos, and flowers not seen closer to the coast. Nesting birds in this area include Red-necked Grebe, American Golden-Plover, Whimbrel, Bar-tailed Godwit, and Long-tailed Jaeger; mammals summering here are denning Arctic Fox, Red Fox, Muskox, Brown Bear, and at times, large herds of Caribou. During the summer bug season it is hard to predict the movements of the Caribou since their trekking is dependent on each day's wind direction and temperature.

The overnight trip takes you over 30 miles up the Colville River to the start of the high bluff system that runs along the west side of the river for over 60 miles and increases from 50 feet high at the northern end to over 500 feet high near Umiat. Up on top of the bluffs is dry tussock-heath tundra, while along the river is riparian willow brush at the edges of extensive gravel bars. The most interesting birds in this area are the nesting raptors—Rough-legged Hawk, Gyrfalcon, and Peregrine Falcon. Arctic Warblers and Bluethroats are often seen flitting around in the willow bushes. Animals you might expect are Caribou, Muskox, Moose, Red Fox, Brown Bear, Spotted Seal, and perhaps a Wolf or Wolverine.

The airplane trip to Umiat gives one a better feel for the vastness of the land as you fly up the Colville along the bluffs. At Umiat you have both dwarf shrub and tall riparian brush along the river and up to the foothills where the tussock-heath starts. Here you can look for nesting Gyrfalcon, Peregrine Falcon, Willow Ptarmigan, Arctic Warbler, Bluethroat, and Yellow and White (rare) Wagtails.

LOGISTICS

Golden Plover Guiding / Golden Plover Air, Colville Village, via Pouch 340109, Prudhoe Bay, AK 99734; 659-2622; *jwhgpa@astacalaska.com*; *http://www.alaskaone.com/goldenplover/*; *http://astacalaska.com/~jwhgpa*.

ACKNOWLEDGEMENTS: A thorough review by Ed Clark and Judy Dearborn is greatly appreciated.

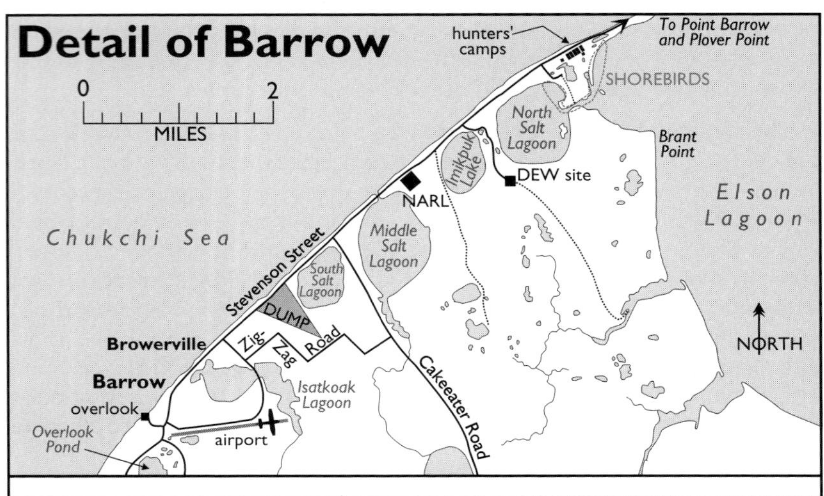
Detail of Barrow
0
2
MILES
hunters' camps
To Point Barrow and Plover Point
SHOREBIRDS
North Salt Lagoon
Brant Point
Imikpuk Lake
DEW site
NARL
Elson Lagoon
Chukchi Sea
Middle Salt Lagoon
Stevenson Street
South Salt Lagoon
DUMP
Zig-Zag Road
Browerville
Barrow
overlook
Isatkoak Lagoon
Cakeeater Road
NORTH
Overlook Pond
airport

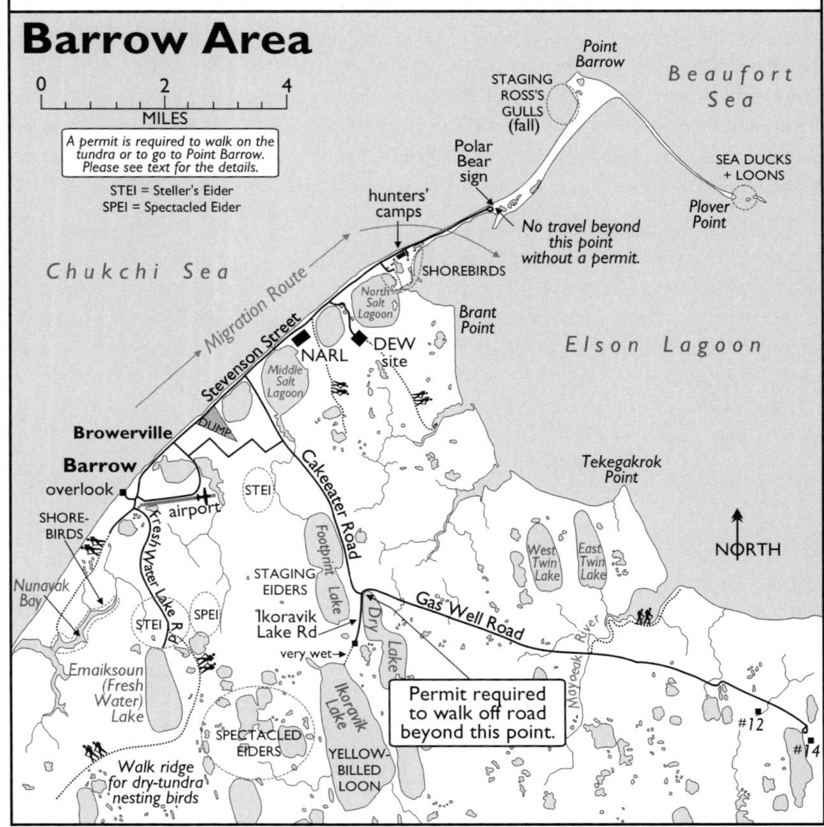
Barrow Area
0
2
4
MILES
A permit is required to walk on the tundra or to go to Point Barrow. Please see text for the details.
STEI = Steller's Eider
SPEI = Spectacled Eider
Point Barrow
STAGING ROSS'S GULLS (fall)
Beaufort Sea
Polar Bear sign
SEA DUCKS + LOONS
hunters' camps
No travel beyond this point without a permit.
Plover Point
Chukchi Sea
Migration Route
SHOREBIRDS
North Salt Lagoon
Brant Point
Stevenson Street
NARL
DEW site
Elson Lagoon
Middle Salt Lagoon
Browerville
DUMP
Barrow
Tekegakrok Point
overlook
STEI
airport
Cakeeater Road
SHORE-BIRDS
Fresh Water Lake Rd
Footprint Lake
West Twin Lake
East Twin Lake
NORTH
Nunavak Bay
STAGING EIDERS
Gas Well Road
STEI
SPEI
Ikoravik Lake Rd
Dry Lake
Mayoeak River
very wet
Emaiksoun (Fresh Water) Lake
Ikoravik Lake
Permit required to walk off road beyond this point.
#12
SPECTACLED EIDERS
#14
YELLOW-BILLED LOON
Walk ridge for dry-tundra nesting birds

BARROW

Judy Dearborn, Ed Clark, and George West

The predominantly Native village of Barrow is situated on the western shore of the peninsula that separates the Chukchi Sea to the west from the Beaufort Sea to the east. At 71°20'N, Barrow is the most northerly town in Alaska and, for birders, the most accessible place to reliably find some of the high-arctic specialties that breed in the area. In addition, Barrow's position at the northernmost point of Alaska makes it an excellent place to observe migration, especially in fall.

The best time to visit Barrow is during the first three weeks of June, unless you are coming to see Ross's and Ivory Gulls, which are more reliable from late September to late October (see *Fall Birding* below). Many of the breeding species, including Steller's and Spectacled Eiders, do not arrive in Barrow until the beginning of June, and after mid-June the male eiders begin to leave the tundra ponds to molt. Since the eiders aren't present until the first few days of June, if you come during the second week of June you will have allowed for a late thaw and will have a better chance of seeing the eiders. As the thaw progresses, the character of any individual location will change rapidly from day to day. For example, an area that was initially good for shorebirds can change within a few days to an extensive lake with eiders and Long-tailed Ducks.

In addition to the town itself, there are three other birding areas that you could cover, depending on the season, your physical condition, and your means of transportation. (See *Logistics* below for vehicle rental and local guide information.) The best birding road south of town is Gas Well Road, leading 12.3 miles into the polygon tundra, far past the gas well that supplies natural gas to Barrow. Even though vehicular travel is allowed on the road past about Mile 4.5, you will need a permit to walk on the tundra anywhere beyond this point. To the southwest you can follow the Chukchi Sea coast past the airport to Fresh Water Lake. To explore farther in that direction, you can charter a small plane to reach the Will Rogers and Wiley Post Memorial (1935 crash site) 13 miles southwest of Barrow, but you will probably not see any species there that you cannot find more easily around Barrow. To the northeast, Stevenson Street will take you from town through Browerville and past the old Naval Arctic Research Laboratory (NARL) buildings to the base of Point Barrow. You may continue for about 4 miles onto the point itself, either on foot or on a rented ATV, but neither is recommended because of the potential danger from Polar Bears. For safety, you should go with a tour operator (see *Logistics*).

If you plan to bird away from town—past NARL toward the point, on the point itself, south of Fresh Water Lake, or south of the south gas field complex—you may need a permit that can be obtained from the Ukpeagvik Inupiat Corporation (see *Logistics*).

SPECIAL CONSIDERATIONS

Birders visiting Barrow should read the section on Alaska Native Cultures in the *Introduction*, page 10. Drive only on the gravel roads and do not attempt to drive on the tundra. You will sink into the boggy vegetation, causing long-term damage to the tundra, not to speak of possible damage to your rental vehicle and disappearance of your birding time. Read the Bear Cautions in the *Introduction*, page 17. Polar Bears are very dangerous carnivores, and all those TV specials and adorable photographs should not desensitize you to this fact. Ask for and then take local advice about current bear conditions. At the other end of the size scale, mosquitoes are not often a major problem in Barrow because the prevailing winds usually keep them down. However, as you move south of the coast into areas where shorebirds nest along Gas Well Road, be prepared for mosquitoes to become a nuisance.

THE BIRDS

Barrow is a good place to see loons—Red-throated, Pacific, and Yellow-billed all breed in the general vicinity, although not in areas accessible from the road system. They are easiest to see from July onward, when the sea is no longer frozen. The best way to see Yellow-billed Loons is to look for birds flying by on their commute between breeding lakes and the coast, or feeding on Elson Lagoon or on the sea. They also stage on Ikoravik Lake before the inland lakes thaw and you can walk to see them if you have hip waders. During August and September, loons may be seen migrating over the base of Point Barrow. Most have passed by mid-September, but it is still possible to see a few individuals as late as October.

You should find all four species of eider if you visit Barrow in the first part of June, even though both Steller's and Spectacled have declined in recent years. Small numbers of Steller's, Spectacled, and King Eiders occur on the tundra melt ponds. You will usually see only Common Eiders flying over the area on migration. The peak time for the spring migration of King and Common Eiders is mid-May, although flocks are still passing through into June. Most of the migration takes place along the edge of the ice that still extends several miles from the shoreline in June. You are not allowed to walk over this shorefast ice by yourself and it would be extremely dangerous to do so without the assistance of a local guide. Even then, it is highly unlikely that you can obtain permission to walk on the shore ice at any time and certainly not during whaling season, when no one but local Native whalers is allowed on the ice.

The southward eider migration begins in mid-July, with breeding-plumaged males predominating until early August. After this date, adult females and then young-of-the-year predominate, making identification difficult, because you typically see them only in flight. Variety and numbers tend to decrease during September and, after mid-month, only King Eiders and Long-tailed Ducks are frequent, although Spectacled Eiders have been recorded into October. The best place to watch for these migrant flocks is a group of buildings known as the Shooting Station (Pigniq) at the base of the point.

During breeding season, other waterfowl include Greater White-fronted and Snow Geese, Tundra Swan, American Wigeon, Northern Shoveler, Northern Pintail, Green-winged Teal, and Long-tailed Duck. Only the last species is present in good numbers.

Large numbers of shorebirds, often displaying in bright breeding plumage, are one of the highlights of birding at Barrow. Several species—Western, White-rumped, Stilt, and Buff-breasted Sandpipers—are at the northern edge of their range and occur in somewhat fluctuating numbers. The common species are American Golden-Plover, Semipalmated, Baird's, and Pectoral Sandpipers, Dunlin, Long-billed Dowitcher, and Red-necked and Red Phalaropes. A few Black-bellied and Semipalmated Plovers, Ruddy Turnstones, Sanderlings, and Wilson's Snipes also occur. A number of Asian shorebirds have been recorded at Barrow, some of which breed at least occasionally. Although you shouldn't expect to see them on a short visit, the most likely are Red-necked Stint and Curlew Sandpiper. Additionally, Mongolian Plover, Eurasian Dotterel, Wood Sandpiper, Gray-tailed Tattler, Bar-tailed Godwit, Little Stint, Sharp-tailed Sandpiper, and Ruff have all been recorded. Since the shorebirds are scattered widely across the tundra in summer, finding a rare one depends on persistence and luck.

Sabine's Gulls and Arctic Terns are regular breeders, but are not easily found until July when the sea ice disappears. Ivory Gulls are often seen in early May at the base of the point. Point Barrow and Elson Lagoon are good areas to look for these species. During fall migration in late August, large numbers may congregate around the tip of the point. Black Guillemots nest under boxes and other debris along Point Barrow, arriving to breed in mid-June. This species is difficult to see until the sea opens up in July.

At this latitude, passerine variety is very limited. Lapland Longspurs are abundant on the tundra, and Snow Buntings breed wherever there are buildings. Villagers put up nest boxes for the buntings since they are said to bring good luck. Common Redpolls may be numerous, while Hoary Redpolls are usually present in small numbers, although both can be abundant in good seed years. A few are found regularly around the UICC-NARL buildings. A small number of other passerines overshoot from the south. These are mostly species that breed a little farther south, such as Northern Wheatear, Mountain Bluebird, Varied Thrush, and Brown Thrasher. However, several interesting North American and Asian species have turned up, so be aware that something odd could occur.

FALL BIRDING

Barrow is an excellent place to observe the migration of Ross's and Ivory Gulls. Ross's Gulls initially move north into the Beaufort Sea starting about mid-September. From mid-October they begin to move south again, and can be seen even into November. Ross's Gulls can often be seen flying along the shoreline or cutting across the base of the point. You can look for them from town or at the Shooting Station at the base of the point. They also congregate in numbers at the tip of the point.

Ivory Gulls are dependent on the formation of sea ice in fall, so later in fall (late September) or in early winter (the first ten days of October) is the best time to find this species. Their numbers fluctuate somewhat from year to year and their presence here is not reliable. If the Bowhead Whale hunters are successful, they generally leave the carcass at the point to attract Polar Bears that might otherwise wander into town. Ivory Gulls are attracted by these mammal carcasses, as well, where they feed on insect larvae in the rotting flesh.

If you come to look for Ross's or Ivory Gulls in late September and October, you will not see many other species. Fall migration is dependent on weather and ice conditions so, as at any good migration spot, you should plan to stay for a few days.

BIRDING IN AND AROUND TOWN

Birding in town can be productive, especially on Pisokak Street to the west of the airport. A ravine here courses by some houses just before reaching Apayauk Street. This low, wet area is worth checking for both shorebirds and passerines.

The section of South Salt Lagoon closest to Stevenson Street (locally known as Coast Road or Ocean Road) and Cakeeater (or Cake Eater) Road is one of the first bodies of water to be ice-free in spring.

Large numbers of Glaucous Gulls forage at the landfill and should be checked for Vega Herring Gull, Thayer's Gull (rare), and Slaty-backed Gull. You can reach the landfill from Stevenson Street (see map). The landfill is being "cleaned up" and may eventually be reestablished on Gas Well Road.

Ahgeak Street (Zig-Zag Road) is one of the more productive roads to bird in Barrow. It begins at about Mile 1.5 on Cakeeater Road, passing through wet and dry tundra and by shallow and deep-water lakes. At 0.65 mile there are views of the landfill and wet tundra if you stand up on the roadside snow berms. Curving left you will pass Qaiyaan Road at 1.0 mile; Uula Street is reached at 1.1 mile. The hummocky tundra to the left is good for Snowy Owls. Yugit Street is at 1.25 miles and the road curves to the right and intersects A Avenue. Proceed on A Avenue to C Avenue and follow this back to Ahkovak Street between Isatkoak Lagoon and the airport. Continuing left along this road will bring you back to town. The condition of the tundra changes daily as the thaw proceeds in spring, making this a good route to check daily for shorebirds.

BIRDING SOUTH OF BARROW

During June, the tundra ponds along Cakeeater Road are the best areas for most of the breeding shorebirds. Cakeeater Road heads south from Stevenson Street and runs for 12.3 miles to Gas Well #14 in the South Gas Field. It leaves Stevenson Street between Middle and South Salt Lagoons about 2.5 miles from the center of town. If you have not yet visited the landfill by its Stevenson Street entrance, you can scope it from a pullout at about Mile 0.7 on this road. Stop at another pullout 0.1 mile farther along to scope for Red-throated, Pacific, Common, and Yellow-billed Loons, all four species of eiders, and nesting shorebirds.

At Mile 1.5 you reach the intersection with Ahgeak Street (Zig-Zag Road). A pullout where you can scope Footprint Lake is at Mile 3.2. Check this lake and Dry Lake to the south in spring for Spectacled Eider. There is a stop sign at 4.2 miles at Gas Well #4, the main South Field gas complex of buildings and the official end of Cakeeater Road. Do not walk on the tundra beyond this point without a permit (see below).

The road makes a short left and then a right turn as it goes around the buildings. It is now named Gas Well Road and continues south an additional mile to an unnumbered gas-well pumphouse and deep-water Ikoravik Lake, where you can find nesting Yellow-billed Loons. Hip-boots are necessary to walk around and to the margin of this lake. Gas Well #6 is at Mile 5.75, where the tundra is drier and may hold Curlew Sandpiper, Buff-breasted Sandpiper, or Ruff. After about Mile 6.7, the drier tundra is a good place to look for

Ross's Gull

nesting Snowy Owls. In peak lemming years, both Snowy and Short-eared Owls can be very common.

At Mile 8.25 you cross the Mayoeak River over some large culverts. From here you can walk (permit required) north on the east side of the river about a mile across the tundra (water levels permitting) to an embayment of Elson Lagoon to look for eiders and geese. At Mile 11.3 you reach a T-intersection; turn left and then go right around the buildings. Gas Well #13 is at Mile 11.7, and the Gas Well Road ends at Mile 12.3 at well house #14. There are two lakes worth scoping here: one is a short walk of a few hundred yards to the northeast and the other is one-quarter mile to the southwest. Remember to have your permit when venturing away from the road onto the tundra. Gas Well Road is best for finding all three jaegers, although the lemming population cycle determines their relative and actual abundance. Pomarine Jaeger is the earliest to arrive, and can be extremely common in a lemming year. Return to town by the same way you came out.

BIRDING TO THE SOUTHWEST

Fresh Water Lake Road is an extension of Apayauk Street in town and runs southwest from town for 2.7 miles along the Chukchi Sea coast to Fresh Water (Emaiksoun) Lake. At about 1.5 miles from the center of town, you will reach the intersection of Pisokak and Apayauk Streets. Drive south for 0.2 mile to a turnoff to the right and drive a short distance to the top of a bluff overlooking the Chukchi Sea. This is a good seawatch spot for pelagic species during stormy weather and for waterfowl and gulls during migration. At Mile 0.7 a right turn onto Nunavak Road leads, in 0.6 mile, to the beginning of a very rough trail. Park here and walk this wet trail—good for Black Brant and Greater White-fronted Geese—for two miles to Nunavak Bay, a spectacular place for viewing shorebirds. The area along this trail is very good for the usual nesting shorebirds and a good place to look for White-rumped and Curlew Sandpipers.

Back on Fresh Water Lake Road, at Mile 1.0 from the starting point in town, you will come to a very short track to the right leading to an aircraft radar facility that looks like a bowling pin. Park on the main road and walk this sometimes very soft roadway to look for nesting shorebirds. You'll pass the Barrow Cemetery at Mile 1.25 (please do not enter), where you can look from the road for Short-eared Owls. The road ends at Fresh Water Lake (Mile 2.7), where you can look for loons and eiders. A one-half-mile walk to the east through very wet tundra (hip-boots needed) takes you to an elevated ridge where you can scope to the south; this is one of the better places to find nesting Spectacled Eiders. Look for Buff-breasted Sandpipers on the drier ridges. Don't forget your permit when venturing onto the tundra.

NORTHEAST TO POINT BARROW

Past its intersection with Cakeeater (Gas Well) Road, Stevenson Street follows the Chukchi Sea shore for about three miles to the base of the point. (From downtown Barrow to the Polar Bear sign, it's 7 miles.) As you drive past Middle and North Salt Lagoons, check both for waterfowl and shorebirds. At the former NARL facility you might find an unusual passerine in the lee of the buildings—Eastern Kingbird, Varied Thrush, and Yellow Wagtail have occurred here. Merlin is occasional. Farther out the road you will pass Point Barrow (NARL) airfield. Next is a strung-out collection of hunting camps known as Shooting Station (Pigniq). Just beyond, Stevenson Street ends in a cul-de-sac featuring a warning sign about Polar Bears. Do not proceed beyond the warning sign without a permit. This is a great spot to spend some time—between the Chukchi Sea on the left and Elson Lagoon on the right—during spring and fall migrations.

With a permit in hand and careful preparation, it is possible, *but not advisable*, to continue out to Point Barrow on foot, a four-mile (one-way) walk on loose sand, where you have the added danger of a possible encounter with Polar Bears. The bears are attracted to the point by the rotting whale and seal carcasses purposely dumped there at the end of hunting season (May) by the Natives in an effort to keep the bears from wandering into town in search of food. When the sea ice melts, however, any bears already at the point are pretty much stuck there from June until freeze-up in October. Therefore, it is not advisable for you to make this hike. Instead, you may choose to rent an ATV ($100 per day) and drive out yourself if you trust your ability to handle it when you are being chased by a Polar Bear! We recommend that you sign up with a guide service that goes out to the point (see *Logistics*).

At the base of the point, small buildings offer some shelter from the wind. However, the tip of Point Barrow—the farthest-north land in the United States—has only a 2-to-3-square-yard patch of beach, surrounded by a sea of ice or water, that seems to form a natural vagrant oasis. The carcasses along the spit attract gulls as well as bears, and should be checked for Ivory Gulls that occasionally show up in spring. The base of the point is best during spring migration and in late fall and early winter.

LOGISTICS

The area code for all telephone numbers is 907 unless otherwise indicated. Tourist and travel services (accommodations, restaurants, attractions, etc.) for Barrow are ***not*** *listed in the* The Milepost. *Statewide travel and birding information services are listed under Logistics in the* Introduction, *page 15.)*

Access: Scheduled daily flights run from Fairbanks and Anchorage to Barrow. Charter service is available from Barrow to several other places in northern Alaska (Kotzebue, Wainwright, Point Hope, Deadhorse, and Barter Island, for example).

Accommodations and Food: Make reservations at least six months in advance of your planned stay. In 2000 prices ranged from $115 to $175 per night. Following are some suggestions:

King Eider Inn (some kitchenettes) — 852-4700 or 888-30-EIDER; *www.kingeider.net.*

Ilisagvik College at NARL Hotel — 852-7800.

Top of the World Hotel (some kitchenettes) — 852-3900 or 800-882-8478 (within Alaska 800-478-8520); *tow@asrc.com;* web site *www.alaskaone.com/topworld/.*

Airport Inn — 852-2525.

Arctic Hotel (some kitchenettes) — 252-7786.

There are at least six restaurants in the area; ask your hotel for locations and recommendations. If you have a kitchenette unit, you can buy groceries at the

Alaska Commercial Company at the corner of Ahkovak Street and C Avenue, where the selection is good and the prices high. *Barrow is dry—no alcoholic beverages of any kind are allowed.*

Vehicle rentals: A vehicle is essential in June unless you are a very strong walker. Since some of the roads can be muddy, four-wheel drive is advisable. In fall, a vehicle would not be necessary if you stayed at UICC-NARL, which is only a mile from the migration-watch point. However, you may appreciate a vehicle's ability to keep you warm, as temperatures dip well below freezing at this time of year. There is one vehicle (as of 2000) available to rent if you are staying at the King Eider Inn. Otherwise, you will have to rent a vehicle from the UICC rental fleet in the Cape Smyth building at the airport (852-2700, *uicc@alaska.net*). An extended-cab four-wheel-drive pick-up cost $115/day in 2000, and gasoline went for over $2.75/gallon.

Tours: Alaskan Arctic Adventures Barrow (John Tidwell, 852-3800) charged $60/person for a trip out to the point (no Native permit fee required) in 2001 for about two hours minimum of birding.

Clothing: The tundra is very wet in summer, making knee-high rubber boots essential for birding. You may wish to wade out into the tundra melt ponds to get better views of the birds, but be careful as you might drop into a soft spot and end up waist deep in icy water. Warm clothes are needed whenever you visit, especially in fall when the temperature falls well below freezing and you will be standing in a cold wind for long periods. A warm hat, gloves, long underwear, and waterproof boots, including knee-highs and hip waders, are essential if you wish to get far from the road.

Permit: If you wish to walk to the point, or drive your rented ATV there (not recommended), inquire about the necessity of having a permit ($50/person in 2001) by contacting the Ukpeagvik Inupiat Corporation at 852-7439 or 800-852-8845, *edonovan@ukpik.com*. You will also need this permit for birding past Mile 4 on the Gas Well Road and at Fresh Water Lake south and southwest of town.

ACKNOWLEDGEMENTS: Birding and logistic notes from Jim and Nancy DeWitt are appreciated.

Sabine's Gull

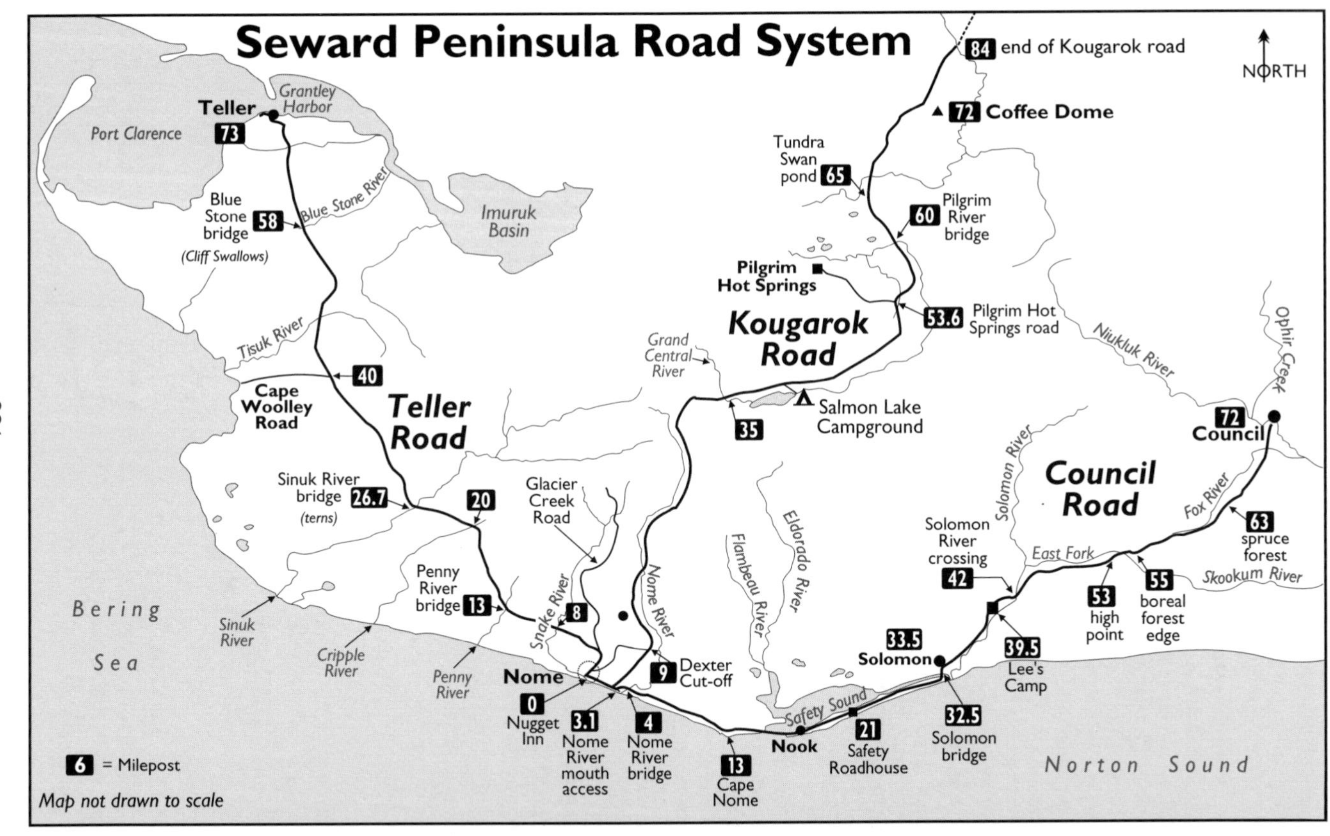
Seward Peninsula Road System
84 end of Kougarok road
NORTH
72 Coffee Dome
Teller
Grantley Harbor
Port Clarence
73
Tundra Swan pond 65
60 Pilgrim River bridge
Blue Stone bridge 58
Blue Stone River
Imuruk Basin
(Cliff Swallows)
Pilgrim Hot Springs
53.6 Pilgrim Hot Springs road
Kougarok Road
Tisuk River
Grand Central River
Niukluk River
Ophir Creek
40
Cape Woolley Road
Teller Road
Salmon Lake Campground
35
72 Council
Solomon River
Council Road
Sinuk River bridge 26.7
(terns)
20
Glacier Creek Road
Flambeau River
Eldorado River
Solomon River crossing
42
East Fork
Fox River
63 spruce forest
Skookum River
Penny River bridge 13
Snake River
8
Nome River
53 high point
55 boreal forest edge
Bering Sea
Sinuk River
Cripple River
Penny River
Nome
0 Nugget Inn
3.1 Nome River mouth access
4 Nome River bridge
9 Dexter Cut-off
33.5 Solomon
39.5 Lee's Camp
Safety Sound
13 Cape Nome
Nook
21 Safety Roadhouse
32.5 Solomon bridge
Norton Sound
6 = Milepost
Map not drawn to scale

NOME AND THE SEWARD PENINSULA

Lana Creer-Harris

Nome is one of Alaska's prime birding destinations. If you are not planning to visit either Gambell on Saint Lawrence Island (page 235) or Saint Paul Island in the Pribilofs (page 247), be sure to come to Nome. Some of the rarer Alaskan species, such as Bristle-thighed Curlew, Bluethroat, and White and Yellow Wagtails, often can be found here, and you might pick up an Asian stray, as well, although they are not to be expected on every several-day visit. You will need at least four days to cover Nome and the Seward Peninsula in spring and early summer; in late summer and fall, two or three days will suffice. Since all flights to Gambell depart from Nome, you might be able to arrange two-day stays in Nome on both ends of your Saint Lawrence Island adventure.

The best time to come to Nome is in late spring and early summer when the sea-ice breaks up and snow begins to melt; the first two weeks of June are best for migrants, Asian strays, and displaying shorebirds. On the other hand, late summer and early fall are not to be ignored. Many of the breeding birds stay well into August, with a few lingering into September before heading south. For example, in September a major migration of Sandhill Cranes comes through, comprised mostly of birds heading east from Siberia. Although most landbirds have stopped singing and are harder to find in late summer and early fall, you can usually kick up a few mixed-species groups of warblers, sparrows, and redpolls in the streamside willow-and-alder thickets. Going far inland, such as driving the Kougarok road to its end, is usually not productive this late in the season.

SPECIAL CONSIDERATIONS FOR VISITING NOME

Seward Peninsula roads are narrow, surfaced with gravel, and are tough on tires, especially if you drive too fast. While there may be some stores open on roads out of town, don't count on getting gas or food once you leave Nome. You must carry water, food, a change of warm clothing, rain gear, and insect repellent.

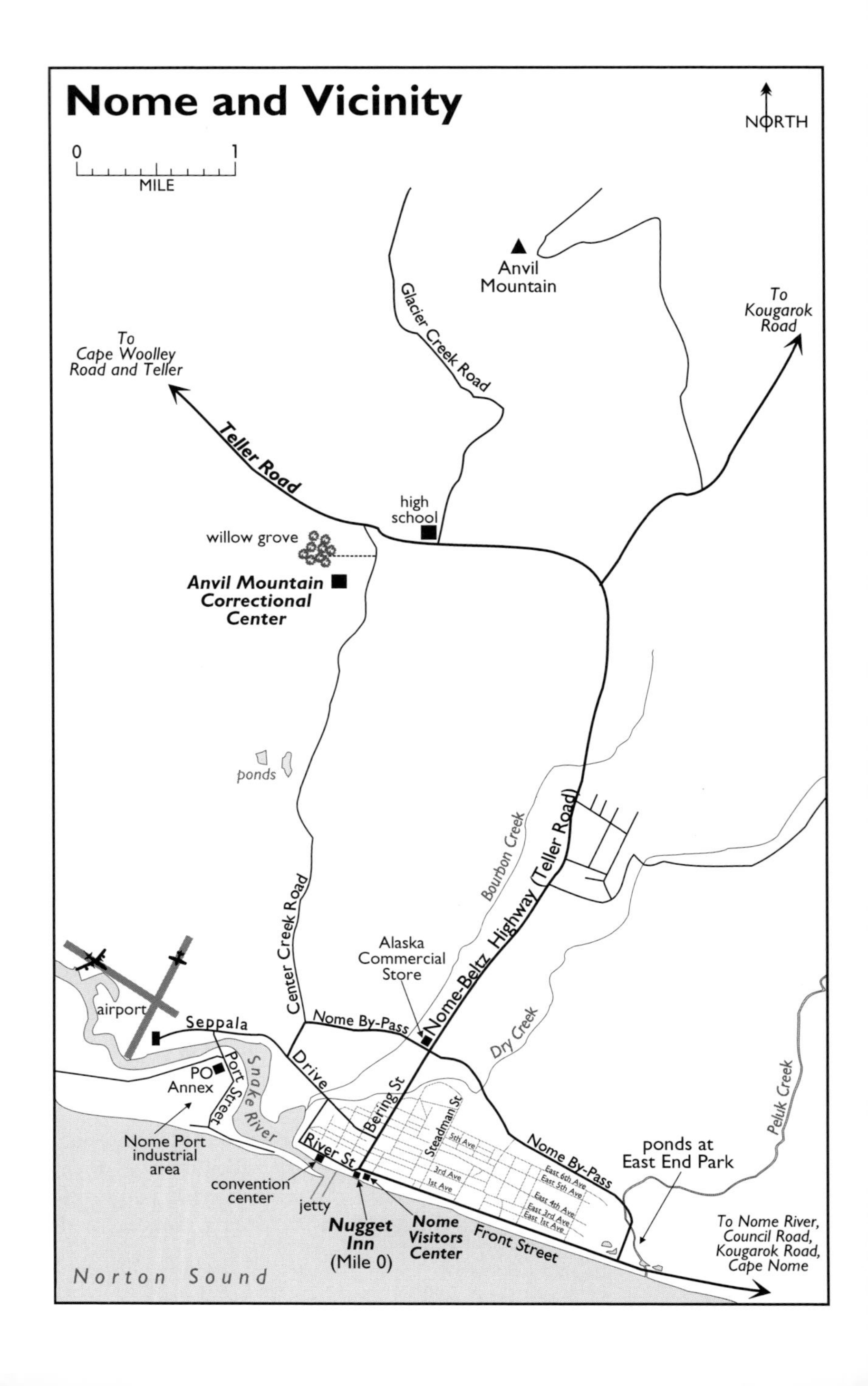
Nome and Vicinity
NORTH
0
1
MILE
Anvil Mountain
Glacier Creek Road
To Kougarok Road
To Cape Woolley Road and Teller
Teller Road
high school
willow grove
Anvil Mountain Correctional Center
ponds
Center Creek Road
Bourbon Creek
Nome-Beltz Highway (Teller Road)
Alaska Commercial Store
airport
Seppala
Nome By-Pass
Dry Creek
Drive
PO Annex
Port Street
Snake River
Bering St
Steadman St
5th Ave
3rd Ave
1st Ave
River St
Nome By-Pass
East 6th Ave
East 5th Ave
East 4th Ave
East 3rd Ave
East 1st Ave
Peluk Creek
ponds at East End Park
Nome Port industrial area
convention center
jetty
Nugget Inn (Mile 0)
Nome Visitors Center
Front Street
To Nome River, Council Road, Kougarok Road, Cape Nome
Norton Sound

When you are on foot in the brush, speak in normal tones and make a fair amount of human noise. You might lose sight of a few birds by doing so, but you will also warn the Brown Bears of your presence. Bears are not the only dangerous local mammal—Moose, especially cows with calves, are every bit as troublesome. Even the placid-looking Muskox will charge if it feels threatened or is defending breeding territory. Last, but not least, Reindeer herds are guarded by bulls that often do not take kindly to strangers. Please read the safety and bear cautions in the *Introduction* to this guide, page 17.

The Seward Peninsula is a patchwork of Native corporation (i.e., private), federal, and state holdings. Subsistence villages or areas at Fort Davis, Nook, Cape Woolley, the top of Anvil Mountain, Solomon, and Teller are all Native-owned. Although there are public road easements on Native property into Cape Woolley and up Anvil Mountain, you may not trespass on Native lands. Fortunately, in both places birding from the road is productive. Inupiat residents often are occupied with the subsistence activities important for assuring their winter food supply. They catch and dry fish and seal meat, and gather greens and berries depending on the time of year. It is hard work and serious business. Please respect their activities. Parking along the road easements is allowed, but walking through camps or photography is not appreciated and not permitted. Read about Native Cultures in the *Introduction*, page 10.

BIRDING CLOSE TO NOME

After you arrive in Nome, a useful first stop is at the Nome Convention and Visitors Bureau on Front Street. Ask the staff about the latest sightings of the birds you are looking for, as well as for any sort of information you need about the town, the condition of the roads, and birding. If you are not already part of a birding tour group, you will maximize your birding time and have more options by arranging well in advance to rent a vehicle (see *Logistics*). Be forewarned that tour groups book years in advance for the best vehicles and most comfortable accommodations. But you can and should do that, too!

Following are directions for a short loop-tour of some good birding spots close to town. (Other productive close-in sites are covered in detail at the beginning of the Council road section, page 213.) Begin this half-day loop-trip at the Nugget Inn on Front Street. Drive north on Bering Street for several blocks to Seppala Drive and turn left toward the airport. In less than a mile turn right (north) onto Center Creek Road. Pause at some ponds to the west (2.5 miles from the Nugget Inn) to check for Northern Shoveler, Northern Pintail, and Red-necked Phalarope. Just past Anvil Mountain Correctional Center, in another one-half mile, a dirt road leads to the left into a large grove of willows. Here, and in the vicinity of the Center Creek Road/Nome-Beltz Road junction just ahead, you could expect to find passerines such as Alder

Flycatcher, Gray-cheeked Thrush, Yellow Wagtail, and Orange-crowned, Myrtle, and Blackpoll Warblers. Dog-lot owners and home-owners along the Nome-Beltz Road report Snow and McKay's Buntings, as well as both Common and Hoary Redpolls, in their lots or at feeders in early spring (mid-March to mid-May), and Red Fox, Gambel's White-crowned, and Golden-crowned Sparrows throughout the summer.

Turn right at this major intersection to complete the birding loop and head back toward Nome. The access road to Anvil Mountain will be on your left in about one mile. The hill is topped with large radar antennae from the former White Alice radar site. You may drive up the road for a mile, staying clear of the posted antenna site at the top. This whole area is owned by the Sitnasuak Native Corporation, and you are allowed to park only on the public road easement and must do your birding by walking along the road. You should be able to find Northern Wheatear and both redpolls on the upper slope. The higher, drier slopes harbor American Golden-Plovers, while the lower, wetter areas might yield Pacific Golden-Plovers and Long-tailed Jaegers. Red-throated Pipits have been found on the back side of this hill, but not in recent years.

Following are excerpts from the Sitnasuak Native Corporation Land Use Policy: *The public may use Sitnasuak's land at Anvil Mountain for recreation following these stipulations: After parking within 60 feet of the road easement people may walk on the mountain for sight seeing and non-destructive recreation. No motorized vehicles, bicycles, teams of animals, skiing or parking of motorized vehicles, including recreational vehicles, is permitted on the mountain. No commercial activities including: tours, photography, motion pictures, or picking flora is permitted. To protect the resources there will be no picking of flowers or other vegetation.*

Continue driving east and then south on the Nome-Beltz Road, turning left (east) onto the Nome By-Pass Road at the major Alaska Commercial Store junction. Heading back to the city on the by-pass gives you a chance to check for puddle ducks, Black-bellied Plover (rare), Pacific Golden-Plover, and all three jaegers. The by-pass curves north of Nome, ending on the Safety-Council Road at East End Park. Two very good birding ponds flank the road here. Tree and occasional Cliff Swallows feed over the water. A right turn here onto Front Street takes you back into Nome city center.

The seawall and rocks along Front Street are not particularly good birding spots because of human activity, but the Nugget Inn has a viewing-platform on the rocks behind the hotel—and large windows in the cozy bar overlooking Norton Sound. From the outdoor platform, birders can look out to the jetty, the oldest part of Nome Port and a veritable gull magnet. You can also view the jetty from behind the Convention Center on River Street.

As you head west along River Street from the Convention Center, and then north on West F Street to Seppala Drive—turn left to the airport—the Snake River will be to your left. When you can find a good vantage point, stop to check for Common and Spectacled (rare) Eiders that have been seen on the river near the port and below the post office annex (see map).

The next road to the left (unmarked) takes you across the Snake River bridge (one mile from the Nugget Inn) and cuts through the busy industrial/port area. White Wagtails have been seen among the piles of rusty barrels and old buildings, but sightings are few in recent years. Don't forget to mind the traffic if the port is open when you visit. Ephemeral ponds lie to the right of the road, where an old fuel-tank farm once stood. These ponds have produced all four stints, but they are rare to casual here at best. At the end of the road, the rock groin of the port toes into Norton Sound. At present the port is closed to entry by the public, but that situation might change in coming years if the new security regulations are relaxed. When you arrive in Nome inquire at the Nome Convention and Visitors Bureau about the current situation. White Wagtails nested near the bridged water-pass under the port facility for most of the mid-1990s. Deep-water ducks, Pelagic Cormorants, murres, and other seabirds might be found along the rocks. Early morning and evening are good times for fly-bys of Spectacled (rare), King, and Common Eiders, and Sabine's Gulls (rare).

If gulls are your passion, the best spot to check them out, especially in late summer and fall, is the Nome landfill, about three miles up the Kougarok road. Also see page 214 for a discussion of gulls. Muskoxen are often behind the landfill.

In addition to the sites around town, the three main roads out of Nome offer good birding: the Kougarok road, the Council road, and the Teller road. (A fourth road, the Glacier Creek road, is not maintained and does not provide access to any birds not found along the other three roads.)

THE TELLER ROAD

(73 miles one way)

In spring and early summer, allow one full day to drive the road to Teller, an Inupiat village on Grantley Harbor. Sometimes overshadowed by Nome's more popular birding destinations, the Teller road is under-rated for birding according to the professional tour leaders. Starting at the Nugget Inn (Milepost 0), head north on Bering Street, which becomes the Nome-Beltz Highway. In about 4 miles the highway curves to the northwest, passes the high school, and at Milepost 4.2 the pavement ends.

At Milepost 13, look for Spotted Sandpiper on the gravel banks along the Penny River, and Arctic Warbler, Gray-cheeked Thrush, and Common and Hoary Redpolls in the willows. Park in the wide pulloff just beyond the bridge. Be careful in thick willows here and elsewhere, and don't *pish* to attract birds—you are in Brown Bear country. (Note: Although Arctic Warblers are generally scarce during the first ten days of June, they might be found as early as 5 June. The most reliable site for them in very early June has been along the Nome River around Milepost 11 of the Kougarok road. These birds become much more plentiful everywhere during the second week of June, and all depart around mid-August.)

Search the rocky canyons on the way to Teller, good habitat for Northern Harrier, Rough-legged Hawk, and sometimes for Golden Eagle and Gyrfalcon. All three jaegers patrol this road; Parasitic and Long-tailed nest here. In years when lemming and vole populations are high, a Snowy Owl might nest on grass hummocks here. Arctic and Aleutian (occasional) Terns nest on gravel river banks—the Sinuk River, Milepost 25, is a good place to look for both species. Bluethroats can lurk in water-filled, brushy draws, and Red-throated Pipits (rare) have nested one-half mile off the road past the Cape Woolley turnoff. Check first at the visitor center to find out if the pipits are nesting here when you are in Nome. If they have been seen there, you may walk around to find them as long as you do not go near the Native camps.

Cape Woolley Road, Milepost 40, is the most reliable place in the Nome area to find nesting Black-bellied Plovers. There are sometimes only two or three pairs, but they invariably show up along this road. Nesting Pacific Golden-Plovers are here, too. Northern Wheatears can sometimes be found near the start of the road. The short side-road is a public-easement corridor through private King Island Native Corporation land, ending at Woolley Lagoon near the shore of Norton Sound at the King Islanders' summer subsistence camp. Birding within 50 feet of the road is permitted, but you must not stray beyond that limit. Please do not bird near the village or the lagoon.

Blue Stone Bridge, Milepost 58, supports a colony of Cliff Swallows in most years. Scan the ravines and rocks here for raptors and Northern Wheatear. Bluethroat is usually reliable toward the top of the hill leading down to the bridge. A nesting pair of Northern Shrikes can usually be found at the bottom of the hill close to the creek. Say's Phoebe, rare on the Seward Peninsula, has been nesting around the bridge since about 1999.

At Milepost 73 you reach Teller, where at least one pair of White Wagtails has nested just below the cemetery for six out of the last eight years (the exceptions were 2001 and 2002). Do not enter the cemetery. Grantley Harbor is a good place to look for Pelagic Cormorant, Common Eider, Pigeon

Guillemot, and Horned Puffin. The spit is private property; do not drive out onto the sandy area.

Along the coast note the fish racks in camps that are used to dry salmon and seal meat for winter meals. Please do not enter or cut through these camps. Reindeer herding is another important industry on the Seward Peninsula. One of the herds is centered in Teller, so you may see Reindeer near the road. A family group of Muskoxen and an occasional lone bull often feed along the Teller road.

In late summer and fall, the Teller road can be good for the first 40 to 50 miles (at least to the turnoff for Cape Woolley Road) for Rough-legged Hawk, Golden Eagle, Gyrfalcon, Peregrine Falcon, and Northern Wheatear. You can also expect to see Willow and Rock Ptarmigan. At this time of year the Rock Ptarmigan are found around the higher, rockier passes, and not lower and closer to the coast where they are found in late spring. Also, they will be in breeding plumage, making them harder to spot compared to late spring when they are still mostly white. A Snowy Owl or two turns up sporadically in late summer and early fall, but they are absent more years than present.

The road is well-traveled. Taxi companies operate between Teller and Nome. If you have car trouble, raise the hood and wait for help. There are good restrooms at the laundry, which is located between the town hall and the school. Many of the local children hanging out around the basketball court know of the White Wagtail and might be willing to help you search for one (for a modest tip).

THE COUNCIL ROAD

(72 miles one way)

The road from Nome to Council, a 1900s-era mining town on the Niukluk River at the edge of the boreal forest, takes you through every habitat type found on the Seward Peninsula. There is great birding on this road from spring through fall. From the Nugget Inn (Milepost 0), drive east on Front Street. The road parallels the beach and provides ample space for you to pull off to bird. Roadside dredge ponds (Milepost 1.4) are used routinely by Red-throated Loon, Green-winged Teal, and Greater Scaup. Semipalmated Plover, Semipalmated and Western Sandpipers, and several other species of shorebirds can be found on the pond margins. Arctic Terns often fish around the Swanberg Dredge, an abandoned 1920s-era gold dredge at the third pond you'll encounter.

The Nome River bridge, Milepost 4, has acquired a reputation over the years as a hot spot for rarities. Nome's only Ruff was seen here, and Mongolian Plover, Terek Sandpiper, and Great Knot have been found in this area, but like the Ruff, they are very rare and not to be expected. As you approach the bridge, watch for a small road (Milepost 3.1) leading to the mouth of the river; you'll see it just as the highway begins to curve to the left. The small road is passable, but since it ends in soft beach sand, travel with caution. There are private Native camps in this area; please respect any posted areas. Walk to the mouth of the river to scan for loons, seabirds, ducks, wading birds, gulls, and terns. Various gulls use the mudflats—Mew, Herring, Slaty-backed, Glaucous-winged, Glaucous, and Black-legged Kittiwake. Check the beach for Surfbird and Red-necked Stint. Rarities here include Killdeer, Buff-breasted Sandpiper, and Great Knot.

If you are here in late summer or fall, check the Nome River mouth right after dawn for a movement of hundreds of shorebirds heading east down the coast for the first hour or so of light. The most common species will be Pacific Golden-Plover, Western Sandpiper, and Dunlin, but small groups of Bar-tailed Godwits and other species are often involved. Staging waterfowl here include good numbers of Tundra Swans, small numbers of Black Brant, and lots of ducks. Gulls are good in late summer. Slaty-backed Gulls are regular then, in contrast to late spring when they are rare, and it is not unusual to see as many as 12 or so in a day in August and early September. Vega Herring Gull is even more numerous, with up to 40 in a day. The best gull spot is certainly the Nome dump (see page 211), but numbers of birds are spread out all along the coastline (e.g., in the harbor area and at the Nome River mouth), and additional birds are inland, upstream on some of the major streams and rivers, feeding on spawned-out, dying salmon.

After crossing the Nome River, you'll find the next few miles along the Council road can produce ptarmigan, Whimbrel, Bar-tailed Godwit, jaegers, and, in some years, Aleutian Tern. There are a few late-summer records of Bristle-thighed Curlew from here, as well. The road crosses Hastings Creek at Milepost 9 and then Golden Gate Creek; both have brushy ravines that should be scouted for passerines. Short-eared Owls occasionally are seen along the road all the way out to Solomon Bridge.

Cape Nome at Milepost 13 is a granite outcropping that has been quarried. Rock from the quarry has formed a pier where barges dock. If the quarry is not operating, you can walk out on the rocky pier to scan for deep-water ducks and gulls. In spring, check for Harlequin Ducks and Surfbirds that sometimes hang out on the rocks at waterline. Peregrine Falcons might be on the cliffs above. Fall storms cause deep-water ducks to shelter near the rocks; check then for Steller's and Spectacled Eiders (both rare) and all three scoters. The shoreline grasslands of Nook open up just past Cape Nome. Yellow Wagtails and Lapland Longspurs nest in good numbers in the grass from Cape Nome to the Safety Roadhouse. Red-necked Stints are annual on the mudflats between Mileposts 15 and 19 and probably nest there in very small numbers. They are usually found with the far more numerous nesting Semipalmated and Western Sandpipers. If Safety Roadhouse is open (Milepost 21), you can stop to buy snack food or to use the public restroom.

SPRING BIRDING AT SAFETY SOUND

Nobody can predict what rarities will turn up here. A Whooper Swan once appeared in the midst of a mixed flock of regular-though-scarce migrant Tundra Swans, Emperor Geese, and Steller's and King Eiders. Mongolian Plover occurs in many years, but Long-toed and Temminck's Stints are considered accidental. A group of seven Ross's Gulls was once recorded in this area, and individuals are seen from time to time. As the sea-ice on Norton Sound melts in early June, mudflats appear close to the road. In past years, mudflats between Mileposts 23 and 25 have been especially productive for rare shorebirds. During fall migration (July and August) Bristle-thighed Curlews (rare) have been found in these grasslands; check also for Bar-tailed Godwit (regular) and Sharp-tailed Sandpiper (rare).

You have two choices upon entering the Safety Sound area—you can drive straight through and bird your way back toward town, or you can thoroughly bird Safety as you continue eastward, hoping that there will enough time left for you to get to Council. If you have the time, you can easily spend a full day birding your way from the Nome River bridge through Safety Sound to Solomon, especially during late May or early June. The drive to Council can then be made the following day in a more leisurely fashion, giving you more time for birding the boreal forest.

Whatever your birding plan might be, a stop at Safety Sound bridge (Milepost 21.5) is recommended. The parking area is on the left across the bridge, where a boardwalk provides you with a stable platform for close examination of nearby shorebirds and gulls. Be alert for migrant Arctic Loons— rarely, one is discovered (and, rarely, correctly identified) among the many Pacific Loons. In spring look for Red-necked Stint. In late summer a few Common Loons, Red-necked Grebes, and Black Brant are reported from here.

You might see Aleutian Terns in flight, and if you carefully scope the spit to the right (as you are pointed east) at the mouth of Safety and Norton Sounds, you can usually find Aleutian Terns mixed in with the much more numerous Arctic Terns resting on the sand. If you're specifically looking for Aleutian Tern, one of the best places to find them is about 10 miles farther out the road—starting in the 200–300 yards to the west of the Solomon Bridge through to the Bonanza Bridge. Aleutian Terns nest on islands in Safety Sound, near the Bonanza Bridge, and to the northwest just before the Solomon Bridge. Do not walk out into any tern colony.

LATE SUMMER AND FALL BIRDING AT SAFETY SOUND

The end of July and the first three weeks or so of August can be excellent for large numbers of birds along the coast, especially along Safety Sound. Shorebirds stage throughout the month, and waterfowl stage late in August and well into September. During August, mixed flocks of Pacific Golden-Plover, Whimbrel, and Bar-tailed Godwit feed in the coastal tundra —especially at Safety Sound, and sometimes at the Nome River mouth. However, the tundra just east of the Nome River and along the beginning of the Kougarok Road are often the better spots. Also, in very late August and early September, a very small number of Sharp-tailed Sandpipers may sometimes be found. Records of the rarer Asian shorebirds are few—but that might reflect a lack of birder coverage in late summer and fall rather than actual abundance. There is at least one recent late-August record of Mongolian Plover near Safety Sound. Bristle-thighed Curlews have been seen a few times along or very close to the coast between late July and early September, but are not to be expected there. Do not expect to find them at their inland nesting sites this late in the season, either.

Between 1997 and 2001, up to five adult Arctic Loons were found regularly during August (and even in late July) and early September in Safety Sound between Mileposts 25 and 28. Aleutian Terns, if they have bred successfully, remain until about the beginning of the fourth week of August, and then abruptly depart. At this time of year one can sometimes see the little-known juvenal plumage of this species. Parasitic and Long-tailed Jaegers and Arctic Terns are also present at this same time, but are gone soon thereafter. A small number of Sabine's Gulls is sometimes seen. Gyrfalcons occur in ones and twos along the coast in late summer and early fall—almost anywhere is fair game—and you can usually expect to see one per day. Rarely, a Steller's or a Spectacled Eider is seen in August or September, particularly off the Nome harbor or around Cape Nome. A few Emperor Geese are found sporadically in late August and early September, with Safety Sound probably the best spot to look for them. Good numbers of Yellow Wagtails are present from late July through mid-August, a few late in the month; and a few Arctic Warblers, Northern Wheatears (especially), and Bluethroats can be found during August by walking around in the coastal vegetation and grasses around Safety Sound. Several Northern Shrikes are also scattered about.

As you press on, the Council road climbs to the Native village of Solomon at Milepost 33.5. Farther east is the Solomon River, where the riparian willows are great for passerines. Lee's Camp, named for the mining family that settled the area and left behind the gold dredge, is at Milepost 39.5. This abandoned piece of machinery often holds raptor or Common Raven nests. Green-winged Teal have fed in the shallows around the dredge, and White Wagtails have been seen at the camp and in the willows. If your goal is boreal species, drive on. The road crosses the Solomon River at Milepost 42, then winds up to the highest elevation reached by any road in the area, at about Milepost 53. As you pass through canyons, watch for Golden Eagle, Willow and Rock Ptarmigan, American Golden-Plover, other tundra-nesting shorebirds, and the local passerines. From the high ridge above Skookum Pass, the road descends into the boreal forest edge, Milepost 55. Fox River's spruce forest, beginning at Milepost 63, and the forest beyond could produce Spruce Grouse, Gray Jay, Black-capped and Boreal Chickadees, Varied Thrush, and Myrtle and Blackpoll Warblers, and Pine Grosbeak. Muskox, Brown Bear, Reindeer, Red Fox, and Beaver often are seen in this region.

The road ends at Council. Most of this community is situated across the Niukluk River, but rather than attempting to negotiate the tricky ford, scan for Osprey and Bald and Golden Eagles instead, and then head back toward Nome unless you've made a reservation to overnight here (see *Logistics*).

THE KOUGAROK ROAD

(84 miles one way)

Stalking the elusive Bristle-thighed Curlew is the main reason for birders to drive to the end of the Kougarok (or Taylor) road. The curlews arrive in early June and, in some years, they depart within a few weeks due to nest failure; in other years they may be present into July. There are two known curlew nesting areas reached from this road, and both require you to make a moderately strenuous hike. Before heading out, inquire at the Nome Convention and Visitors Bureau to make sure the road is open—in some years heavy snows and spring runoff close the road some distance short of the curlew nesting area.

You can look first for this scarce and easily frightened bird around Coffee Dome, a dark-colored hilltop at Milepost 72. Try to arrive by 8 AM, before 9 AM at the latest. Park at the highest point on the road adjacent to Coffee Dome. The curlews typically gather on the ridge on the opposite side of the road from the dome. Some lucky birders have seen curlews flying across the road in this area, vocalizing as they pass close to the visitors and their vehicles. If you're not this fortunate, you can hike the one-half mile distance over the tundra to the ridge top in about 30 minutes. If the birds are not there, continue along the ridge in either direction, remembering that you have to hike back again whether you find the curlews or not.

The other known nesting area is near the end of the road, Milepost 84. Here the gravel Kougarok road meets a four-wheeler track that leads some 25 miles to Taylor, the Tweet mining families' summer community. The first part of this track is often used as a hiking trail by birders in search of curlews. Unless you are in top-notch condition, though, looking for the curlews at the

Bristle-thighed Curlew

end of the road is not advised. The hike up through the tussocks to ridges where the curlews (usually bachelors) congregate can involve three to six miles of arduous hiking through very active bear country. In general, Bristle-thighed Curlews are hard to find, since brooding birds do not flush, so not every trip up the Kougarok yields the curlew. Many birders choose to seek this species with the aid of professional guides or with birding tour groups.

Much easier to find are Bluethroats. Look for them along the last miles of the Kougarok road in any of the many water-filled, brushy draws that this skulking passerine prefers. Other good areas for Bluethroat include the flat, willowy areas around Milepost 25, and between the Grand Central Bridge and Milepost 43. Bluethroats favor the low, shrubby willows, while Arctic Warblers tend to occur in the mid-level willows, although both can sometimes be found together.

There are many nesting pairs of Tundra Swans on this drive. One good place to check is the pond at Milepost 65, 19 miles from the end of the road.

Another interesting place to stop is the primitive camping area nestled in the cottonwoods, as the locals call them—actually Balsam Poplar—at Milepost 60 at the Pilgrim River bridge. The broad-leaved trees here are uncommon in this part of the Seward Peninsula, and this habitat attracts a variety of tree-nesting species. This is one of the few places American Robins can build tree nests; elsewhere on the peninsula they use buildings because trees are so scarce. Alder Flycatchers and Blackpoll Warblers are also found. These trees lack a thick understory and, therefore, this riparian habitat is not as attractive to birds as that at Pilgrim Hot Springs.

Pilgrim Hot Springs Road leads seven miles west from the Kougarok road at Milepost 53.6. The springs and the land around them are privately owned and, due to vandalism, the owners ask anyone intending to visit to contact caretaker Louie Green in Nome (PO Box 1223, Nome 99762; 907-443-5583). The road into Pilgrim Springs skirts granite tors where raptors and Northern Wheatears often are seen. At the end of the road a collection of historical buildings is the remnant of a Catholic orphanage and boarding school built to house Native children orphaned by epidemics. Again, a dense grove of Balsam Poplars provides a habitat unusual on the Seward Peninsula, where Common Goldeneye, Spotted Sandpiper, Alder Flycatcher, Tree and Cliff Swallows, Varied Thrush, Northern Shrike, and Rusty Blackbird can be found.

Check for Northern Wheatear around Milepost 51. A stop at any one of a number of Salmon Lake turnoffs (near Milepost 38)—especially at the BLM picnic ground at the north end of the lake (restroom)—is a good idea, but snow usually renders this area inaccessible until the second week of June. Bluethroats have been sighted flitting down the dirt road into the campground. Look for loons and Red-necked Grebes, as well as Long-tailed and other ducks on the lake. As you drive along, check gravel pond margins for Wandering Tattler. Grand Central River (Milepost 35) is a good stop for Harlequin Duck, Arctic Tern, American Dipper, Bluethroat, and Yellow and Wilson's Warblers. The view is fantastic. Grand Central is a favorite Brown Bear highway to nearby Salmon Lake.

Nesting Golden Eagles use the rock cliffs at Basin Creek (Milepost 16). Many people who live in Banner Creek (Milepost 12) commute year round to Nome. Some residents keep bird feeders and don't mind if birders drive into their community along the Nome River, but they do ask that you stay off private property. There are numerous sled-dog lots at Banner Creek—steer clear of sled-dog lots wherever you find them. Banner Creek is a good place for Willow Ptarmigan, nesting Whimbrels, and Yellow and Wilson's Warblers. Also watch for Yellow Wagtail, Common and Hoary Redpolls, and other passerines in the willows along the road. The pond between the main road and the community road is a place to scan for nesting gulls and Violet-green Swallows. After Banner Creek, the road heads down to Norton Sound. Birders often choose the Dexter cut-off (Milepost 9) on the return to the Nome-Beltz Highway because it passes through some good tundra areas.

LOGISTICS

The area code for all telephone numbers is 907 unless otherwise indicated. Nome is not covered in The Milepost. *Your best bet for obtaining loads of up-to-date information is to contact the Nome Convention and Visitors Bureau. For your convenience, some information about accommodations and local transportation is listed below. Statewide travel and birding information services are listed under Logistics in the* Introduction, *page 15.)*

Contact the Nome Convention and Visitors Bureau for comprehensive information packets containing extensive information about accommodations and the many Seward Peninsula attractions — PO Box 240, Nome, AK 99762; 443-6624; *www.nomealaska.org*.

Access: Alaska Airline provides twice daily jet service to Nome, with a third flight often added in summer, 800-252-7522.

Accommodations: An Ocean View B&B, 443-2133; Arctic Lodge B&B, 443-3515; Aurora Inn & Suites, 800-354-4606; Chateau de Cape Nome, 443-2083 after 5 PM; Mai's Guest House, 443-4113; Nanuaq Manor, 443-5296; No Place Like Nome, 443-2451 or 443-5869; Nugget Inn, 877-443-2323; Polar Arms, 443-2661; Polaris Hotel, 443-2000; Ponderosa Inn, 443-5737; Sweet Dreams B-n-B, 443-2919; Trails End Apartments, 443-3600; Weeks Apartments, 443-3194. In Council: Camp Bendeleben, one rental cabin with kitchen is on the west, more accessible side of the river bank; contact John and Fran Elmore at 522-6663.

Vehicle Rental: Check your rental vehicle carefully to make sure you have working brakes, wipers, fluids (oil, window-washing fluid, transmission fluid), a usable jack, and full-size spare tire. Check tire wear as well, and if the tires are bald, ask to have them replaced with better tires. You don't want to get stuck far out on the road system, especially on the Kougarok road, where it may be some time before you can get assistance.

Trucks, vans, SUVs: Alaska Cab Garage, 443-2939; Aurora/Stampede Vehicle Rental, 800-354-4606.

20-passenger Buses: Morgan Enterprises, 443-2556.

Taxis: Checker Cab, 443-5211; Nome Cab, 443-3030; Village Taxi, 443-2333.

ACKNOWLEDGEMENTS: Paul Lehman thoroughly reviewed the chapter and provided notes on late summer and fall birding as well as on general logistics. Paul Baicich and Jim Williams added valuable information in their review of this chapter. Forrest Davis added important sighting-location information. Walt Childs added some species notes. Richard Konz drove the roads and verified the locations of many species. Updates and birding notes from Jon Dunn are greatly appreciated.

WALES AND VICINITY

Paul J. Baicich

Once a significant whaling center and site for some major ornithological collecting, Wales is today a small Inuit village dependent upon subsistence hunting, fishing, and trapping. Few birders come here, so if you're looking for something entirely different, Wales is a good place to visit.

This Native village of fewer than 200 people located right on Bering Strait has been the source of some remarkable ornithological records, especially from the 1920s through the 1940s (e.g., Baikal Teal, Eurasian Dotterel, Oriental Cuckoo, and Eurasian Wryneck). Since then, there has been a smattering of important visits by researchers and birders, especially during the 1970s. Wales is not visited much these days, but it is certainly worthy of continued attention. Wales has a traditional Kingikmiut whaling culture, with ancient songs, dances, and customs still practiced.

Situated directly at the Bering Strait, and tucked between Cape Mountain (elevation 2,289 feet) and Lopp Lagoon, the village provides access to upland and coastal tundra, seacoast, and scores of ponds and lagoons. On a very clear day, you can see the Diomede Islands and even the Siberian coast across the Bering Strait. Fairway Rock, south of the Diomedes, is more often visible from the village.

At least three significant waves of Man have passed through this area from the East, beginning as early as 8,000 to 10,000 years ago (and some claim much earlier). More recently, the Birnirk culture (A.D. 500–900) left its mark here. These people were mainland-oriented, especially linked to Caribou. Birnirk sites have been found at Cape Krusenstern, Cape Nome, and other locations on the Seward Peninsula. A burial mound of the Birnirk culture near Wales is now a national landmark. Birnirk culture gave way to what we currently consider a more classic lifestyle of winter ice-hunting, kayak and umiaq (sealskin boat) open-sea hunting (especially for Bowhead Whales), dogs, and dog sleds. Extensive trading and communications networks were maintained through here for northwest Alaska, the Seward Peninsula, and into Siberia.

Vitus Bering actually reached the Diomede Islands in 1728, far earlier than his official "discovery" of the Alaskan mainland in 1741. In 1732 Mikhail Gvozdev and Ivan Federov reported seeing the village along the shore at the cape, but they did not go ashore. In 1778 the famed British explorer, Captain

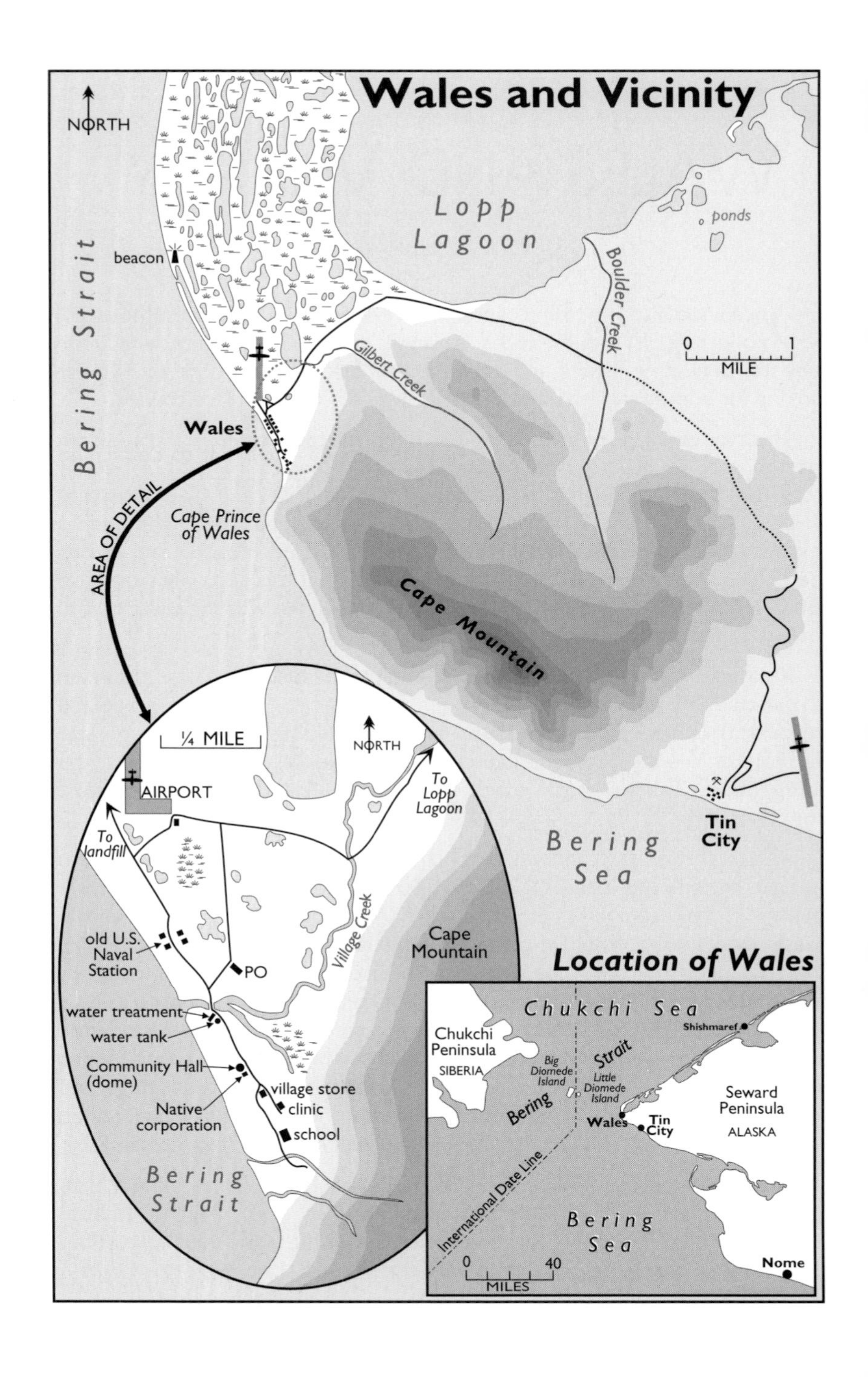
Wales and Vicinity
NORTH
Lopp Lagoon
ponds
Boulder Creek
beacon
Bering Strait
Gilbert Creek
0
1
MILE
Wales
AREA OF DETAIL
Cape Prince of Wales
Cape Mountain
Bering Sea
Tin City
¼ MILE
NORTH
AIRPORT
To Lopp Lagoon
To landfill
old U.S. Naval Station
PO
Village Creek
Cape Mountain
water treatment
water tank
Community Hall (dome)
Native corporation
village store
clinic
school
Bering Strait
Location of Wales
Chukchi Sea
Shishmaref
Chukchi Peninsula
SIBERIA
Big Diomede Island
Strait
Little Diomede Island
Bering
Seward Peninsula
ALASKA
Wales
Tin City
International Date Line
Bering Sea
0
40
MILES
Nome

James Cook, sailed along the Seward Peninsula coast in the HMS *Resolution* and gave the site its name, Cape Prince of Wales. In 1827 the Russian Navy reported on the Native villages of "Eidamoo" near the coast and "King-a-ghe" farther inland.

U.S. possession of Alaska changed the scene considerably. By 1890 the American Missionary Association established a mission at the village site on the coast by the foot of Cape Mountain. In 1894 a reindeer station was organized, and a U.S. Post Office was established in 1902. Wales became a major whaling center due to its location along migratory routes, and it became the region's largest and most prosperous village, with a population of over 500. Tragically, the world-wide influenza epidemic in 1918–1919 claimed the lives of many villagers, including many of the finest whalers.

A visit in late May through June may be best. It is difficult to determine when spring migration will be ideal through the region, since sea-ice break-up, winds, and temperatures vary from year to year. A fall visit (early September) may also be good, but we have little direct information. (However, North America's only Eurasian Wryneck was picked up on the beach at Wales on 8 September 1945.) The Bering Strait is usually ice-free from June into November. Average summer temperatures range from 40° to 50°F; winter temperatures range from -10° to +6°F. Annual precipitation is 10 inches. Frequent fog, wind, and blowing snow limit access to Wales.

Wales is reached by air and by sea only, with air being the primary access. There is a state-owned 2,600-foot gravel airstrip, and the ice on the strait is used by planes in the winter. Scheduled and charter flights are available. Flights from/to Nome are scheduled almost daily, but conditions often make them unpredictable. Round-trip cost in 2001 was about $240.

Walking the lower mountain slopes, around local ponds, and along the shoreline is the most reliable way to cover birding sites around the village. There is a 6.5-mile road to Boulder Creek, around Cape Mountain, and a fairly good road continuing on to Tin City. You can inquire in the village about renting an ATV. (In 2001 the town had a good Honda 4x4-ES to rent for $75 per day.)

Wales can be a favorable location to witness large movements of loons, sea ducks, and alcids, especially during early spring migration (late May and early June). Birders should realize that there are no nearby alcid colonies, but alcid numbers passing by can be significant in early spring (e.g., Parakeet, Least, and Crested Auklets, usually in that order of abundance), depending on wind and weather. The good news is that at this time Ivory Gulls are very possible on the remaining shelf ice, and there is a remote possibility for Ross's Gulls. The bad news is that under those circumstances there will be few birds on the frozen-over ponds and cold slope of Cape Mountain. Local wet tundra and ponds provide good habitat for shorebirds (including Semipalmated,

Western, and Pectoral Sandpipers, Dunlin, Long-billed Dowitcher, and Red-necked and Red Phalaropes). Some other uncommon and specialty birds of Wales include the following:

Arctic Loon—Look in groups of Pacific Loons offshore in spring. Also reported nesting at Lopp Lagoon.

Emperor Goose—Small spring flocks of less than a dozen are sometimes seen passing by.

Spectacled Eider—May be rare breeders "along inner margins of Lopp Lagoon" (Kessel 1989).

Pacific Golden-Plover—Breeds on tundra near the village and on lower slopes of Cape Mountain. (American Golden-Plovers are also in the vicinity.)

Mongolian Plover—Has been seen here in early June; unlikely.

Common Ringed Plover—Semipalmated Plovers are common; Common Ringed Plover has been seen and collected a few times; unlikely.

Eurasian Dotterel—Found consistently at Cape Mountain in June (including two pairs in 1972); very rare.

Wood Sandpiper—A few have been seen from late May to early June; unlikely.

Bar-tailed Godwit—Fairly common in tussocks at the edge of coastal flats, wet meadows, and the edges of ponds and lagoons; local breeder.

Red-necked Stint—A few pairs breed here (Kessel 1989) and sometimes can be found after diligent searching.

Slaty-backed Gull—Uncommon, but increasing in frequency since the late 1970s. Sometimes, they are found in late May on the remaining ice, occasionally, and later on, in small numbers. Watch for Vega Herring Gulls that are far more common in early spring.

Bluethroat—They do not nest here (try roads out of Nome), but pass through, occasionally in numbers during the early spring (up to a dozen per day in the last days of May). (Arctic Warblers pass through, too.)

Northern Wheatear—Numbers have been observed crossing the strait and passing through in late May. There are multiple nesting records for Cape Mountain.

Yellow Wagtail—Migrants pass through in early May and some remain to nest in nearby low shrub thicket habitat.

White Wagtail—Regular nester most years near or around the village. (The earliest hatching is in the fourth week of June.)

Red-throated Pipit—A number of birds in passage have been observed in late May on the slopes of Cape Mountain. Probably is a regular nester on the slopes of Cape Mountain (young hatch in late June). Apparently, the largest populations occur on nearby Little Diomede Island (Kessel 1989).

LOGISTICS

The area code for all telephone numbers is 907 unless otherwise indicated. Wales is not covered in The Milepost. *For your convenience, information about accommodations and transportation is listed below. Statewide travel and birding information services are listed under Logistics in the* Introduction, *page 15.)*

Accommodations might be arranged by renting a trailer from the Wales Native Corporation, PO Box 529, Wales AK 99783; 664-3641, or more likely, for the room at the City of Wales dome building. This "city apartment" has a kitchenette (with refrigerator and microwave), two beds, shower, and toilet. Contact the City of Wales, PO Box 489, Wales AK 99783; 664-3501; the cost in 2001 was $50 per person per night. Wales has recently received federal funding to construct a multi-purpose center that will include office space, small conference room, kitchen, bathroom, and four single rooms for overnight guests.

Pete and Lena Sereadlook have modest accommodations available (a single bedroom for guests and floor space to camp, as well as a bathroom with a honey bucket). They also own a small cabin that could sleep four people comfortably. The cabin has a bathroom/honey bucket and a heater. They will cook for guests at either site. You can write to them at PO Box 503, Wales Alaska 99783, or leave a message with their daughter Peggy Tokeinna at her house in Wales, 664-0055. Other villagers may have places to stay and might assist with local transportation.

Water comes from Gilbert Creek during the summer, and residents haul treated water from a 500,000-gallon storage tank at the "washeteria" (where a laundromat and showers are available). Some villagers will use untreated water from Village Creek. Almost all residents use honey buckets, and very few homes have plumbing. The school, clinic, and city dome building are connected to a piped water and septic system.

There is a fairly well-stocked village store where you can buy food, and a couple of villagers run small stores selling snacks, soft drinks, and some staples.

Advice and warnings: Dress warmly—the wind can be fierce. Regardless of what arrangements you've made for accommodations, bring a sleeping bag. The sale or importation of alcohol is strictly banned in the village. Be prepared to boil or treat your water. The villagers survive through subsistence hunting. If this makes you squeamish, please stay home. Consider sending food ahead by USPS mail, in care of your host. Because the place is so remote and the weather potentially troublesome, flights can be very unpredictable. It is advisable to be patient and build in a few spare days into your schedule. Read the statement on Native Cultures in the Introduction, page 10.

ACKNOWLEDGEMENTS: James Huntington and Joseph Swertinski helped collect vital information on-site. Nancy Anderson of Anchorage and Emma Anungazuk of Wales contributed important details.

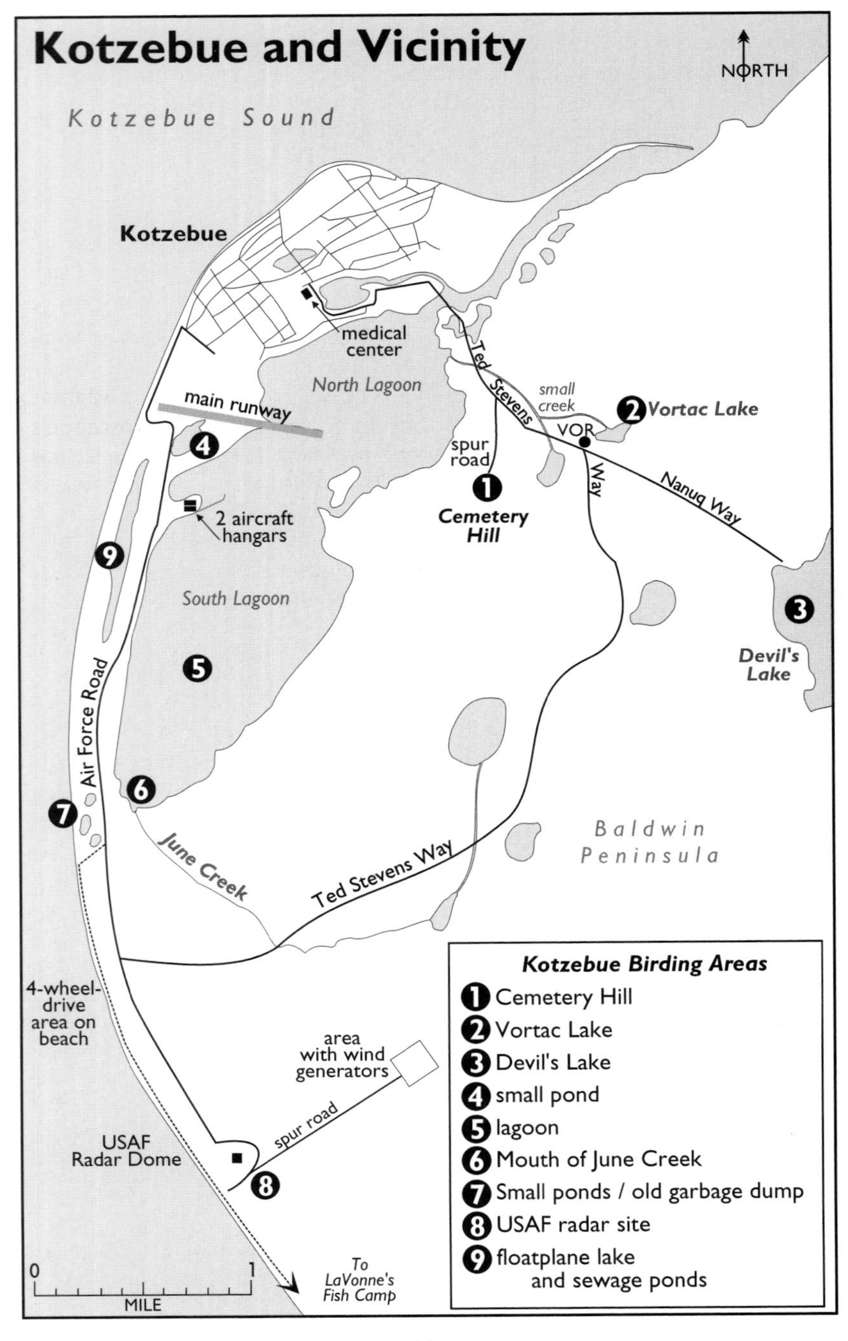
Kotzebue and Vicinity
NORTH
Kotzebue Sound
Kotzebue
medical center
North Lagoon
main runway
Ted Stevens
small creek
Vortac Lake
VOR
spur road
Cemetery Hill
Way
Nanuq Way
2 aircraft hangars
South Lagoon
Devil's Lake
Air Force Road
Baldwin Peninsula
June Creek
Ted Stevens Way
4-wheel-drive area on beach
area with wind generators
spur road
USAF Radar Dome
0
1
MILE
To LaVonne's Fish Camp
Kotzebue Birding Areas
1 Cemetery Hill
2 Vortac Lake
3 Devil's Lake
4 small pond
5 lagoon
6 Mouth of June Creek
7 Small ponds / old garbage dump
8 USAF radar site
9 floatplane lake and sewage ponds

KOTZEBUE

John Puschock and Randy Meyers

Kotzebue, one of Alaska's largest Native communities, is located 33 miles north of the Arctic Circle at the end of the Baldwin Peninsula. Many species of interest, such as Arctic Loon, Pacific Golden-Plover, Parasitic and Long-tailed Jaegers, Bluethroat, Yellow Wagtail, and Common and Hoary Redpolls can be found around Kotzebue, but fewer breeding and vagrant species are found here compared to the Nome region due to Kotzebue's geographic location, low habitat diversity, and lack of an extensive road system. Birders with limited time who are interested in building their lists will be better off visiting Nome. On the other hand, many flights to Nome pass through Kotzebue, and you may want to stop to look for several species, notably Arctic Loon and Hoary Redpoll, that may be easier to find here. Kotzebue also serves as the starting point for birders seeking Gray-headed Chickadee at the Kelly Bar, located north of Kotzebue at the confluence of the Kelly and Noatak Rivers (see page 232).

The greatest number of species occurs during spring migration from the second half of May (many songbirds don't arrive until early June) through mid-June. Snow Buntings and a few McKay's Buntings migrate through Kotzebue earlier in the spring (mid-March to mid-April). They can be found where there are bare patches of ground near the coast and occasionally in town. Most breeding species are present from mid-June to mid-August. Hoary Redpolls are easiest to find before Common Redpolls arrive during the second week of June (when hordes of mosquitoes first appear), but Arctic Loons and Bluethroats are best looked for later. July is probably the best time for Bluethroats, but loons can be found through September. Southbound shorebirds occur in large numbers in August.

Keep in mind that northwest Alaska receives little birding attention and that the distribution of many species is still poorly known. Use range maps in field guides only as a general guide. For example, some field guides show Yellow-billed Loon, Emperor Goose, Spectacled Eider, and alcids occurring at Kotzebue, but these and other marine species are not found here. This is due to the probable influence of fresh water from the Noatak and Kobuk Rivers and the shallow water surrounding the town. Kittiwakes and alcids nest on islands only at the southern end of the Baldwin Peninsula. On the other hand, visitors probably will find many duck and songbird species that are not shown to occur in this region.

Two roads extend out of town into the surrounding tundra. Birding along both is excellent. Birders looking for Arctic Loon should take Ted Stevens Way to the VOR (FAA navigational aid) and Vortac Lake, and continue east on Nanuq Way to Devil's Lake. This road begins in town on the north side of the medical center. It first passes the north floatplane lagoon. Scan the lagoon for loons and ducks, and the shoreline and adjacent saltmarsh for plovers and sandpipers. You may spot a Red-throated Loon, Pacific Golden-Plover, Hudsonian Godwit, or Black Turnstone. Eurasian Wigeons have also been seen here. Continue up into the tundra to an area known as Cemetery Hill (**1**). Alder Flycatcher, Gray-cheeked Thrush, American Tree, Fox, and Gambel's White-crowned Sparrows, and a number of warblers nest in the surrounding alders and willows. Bluethroats are found here some years, and Yellow Wagtails are common. Wilson's Snipe often are seen in display flight. You might see a Willow Ptarmigan, but they are more often heard calling. The tall white VOR structure and Vortac Lake (**2**) are on your left. Arctic Loons have bred here recently, so check every loon carefully, because the similar-looking Pacific Loon also occurs on tundra lakes. Keep in mind that Arctics often hold their bills upward as do Red-throated Loons.

Glaucous Gull

Nanuq Way continues for several miles to Devil's Lake (**3**). Long-tailed Jaegers and Lapland Longspurs are common along this stretch. Parasitic and occasional Pomarine Jaegers occur in small numbers, especially during spring migration. Pacific Golden-Plovers are possible, and Short-eared Owls can be seen during the low-light periods of an arctic summer "night." At the end of the road, scan Devil's Lake for loons, Red-necked Grebes, ducks, and Arctic Terns. More adventurous birders may want to explore the tundra, but walking over this terrain is difficult. You might be able to follow four-wheeler tracks around the north side of the lake. A group of eight Arctic Loons once was found on a small lake in the Devil's Lake area.

The other road out of Kotzebue begins at the west side of the airport and heads south as Air Force Road toward the U.S. Air Force radar dome. It runs between the main runway and Kotzebue Sound. Make sure no aircraft are taking off or landing before passing this spot. Look for shorebirds on the small pond (**4**) on your left just to the south of the runway. Semipalmated Sandpipers are the most common peep during the breeding season, but large numbers of Western Sandpipers pass through in fall migration. Other common shorebirds include Semipalmated Plover, Pectoral Sandpiper, Long-billed Dowitcher, Wilson's Snipe, and Red-necked Phalarope. Lesser Yellowlegs, Ruddy Turnstone, Least Sandpiper, and Dunlin are found in small numbers. Upland Sandpiper, Bar-tailed Godwit, Red Knot, White-rumped, Baird's, Sharp-tailed, and Stilt Sandpipers, and Ruff all have been reported. You will see a barren area between this pond and the two aircraft hangars farther down the road. Check here for Northern Wheatear in spring migration. Aleutian Terns formerly bred here, but a worker from the medical center used to regularly take his dog for walks through the colony. Both the terns and the man are now gone.

Continue south along the road. During spring migration, almost any duck species is possible on South Lagoon (**5**) to your left. American Wigeon, Mallard, Northern Shoveler, Northern Pintail, Green-winged Teal, Greater Scaup, and Long-tailed Duck are common throughout summer. American and Pacific Golden-Plovers commonly are found in the wet area on the west side of the road during fall migration. Since Pacific Golden-Plovers tend to begin their post-breeding molt earlier than Americans, any golden-plover with very little black on its underparts in July and early August is likely to be a Pacific.

June Creek (**6**) empties into the lagoon at its southern end. Many of the species found at Cemetery Hill also occur here. Bluethroats may be here when they aren't at Cemetery Hill, and Arctic Warblers have been seen during migration in mid-June. If you haven't seen a Hoary Redpoll yet, check here, but be careful as some male Common Redpolls can look very pale. The most well-known field mark of Hoary Redpoll, the unstreaked undertail coverts, is usually difficult to see. If you find a likely candidate, check its bill shape—a Hoary will have a short and stubby bill. The backs of Hoary Redpolls also look gray or silver, while those of Commons appear brown.

Several small ponds and the old garbage dump (**7**) are on the side of the road opposite June Creek. This area is good for shorebirds, particularly Pacific Golden-Plover. Red Phalaropes occur in fall migration. The dump is now closed, so gull-watching probably isn't as productive as it once was, but Herring, Slaty-backed, and Glaucous-winged Gulls are still possible along with the common Mew and Glaucous Gulls. Four Steller's Eiders were found just offshore at this spot in August 1998.

If you have time, you may want to continue south to the radar site on top of high ground overlooking Kotzebue Sound (**8**). There is a nice view, but you may not add much to your list. At the summit, a 0.75-mile spur road (hiking only) leads southeast through tussock tundra to 11 wind-generator towers. Whimbrel, Long-tailed Jaeger, Short-eared Owl, Yellow Wagtail, Lapland Longspur, both redpolls, and various warblers and sparrows are possible here. Just past the summit and radar dome, the road heads steeply down to the narrow sand-and-gravel beach. Late-lying snow often blocks vehicle access to the beach well into July on this west-facing slope. A four-wheel-drive vehicle, a four-wheeler, or hiking are recommended for the soft surface. Gulls congregate at the mouth of Sadie Creek several miles south of LaVonne's Fish Camp (an Elderhostel site). During fall migration, you're most likely to find Whimbrel and Snow Buntings along this section.

You can return to town by four different routes: a) by retracing your steps, b) by taking the four-mile link described below (the continuation of Ted Stevens Way), c) by going back along the shoreline, or d) by going back along the shoreline and around the sewage lagoons (**9**). There is an irregular network of small dirt ATV trails between the floatplane lake/sewage ponds and Kotzebue Sound. Most of the common duck species can be found on the lagoons, and Yellow Wagtails are particularly numerous in this area. Wandering Tattler, Black Turnstone, Surfbird, Sanderling, and Red Knot can be found on the shore during migration. You also may see migrant Common Eiders, Pomarine Jaegers, and Black-legged Kittiwakes offshore during spring. Lone migratory juvenile Sabine's Gulls have been observed following the coastline in fall. Before getting back to town, you will see a floatplane lake between the shore and the north-south gravel runway. Depending on water levels, shorebirding here can be outstanding. During fall migration, Merlin and Peregrine Falcon are occasionally drawn in by shorebird concentrations at the lagoon/sewage pond complex.

A third gravel road completed in late summer 2001 extends Ted Stevens Way as a four-mile link to Air Force Road. It can be accessed by turning south on Ted Stevens Way at the tall white VOR structure. The road winds through typical tussock tundra dotted by small lakes interspersed with patches of willow and alder. It joins Air Force Road near the new municipal landfill, about two miles south of the east-west runway. The habitat and birding opportunities here are very similar to those found along Ted Stevens and Nanuq Ways, but without the lagoon and brackish saltmarsh habitat.

LOGISTICS

The area code for all telephone numbers is 907 unless otherwise indicated. Kotzebue and Kelly Bar are not covered in The Milepost. *For your convenience, information about accommodations and local transportation is listed below. Statewide travel and birding information services are listed under Logistics in the* Introduction, *page 15.)*

Accommodations: There are several B&Bs and one hotel in Kotzebue. Nullagvik Hotel, 442-3723; Drake's Camp, 442-2736; Lagoon Bed and Breakfast, 442-3723; Sue's Bed and Breakfast, 442-3770 or 442-2758; Bayside Restaurant has a few rooms for rent, 442-3600; LaVonne's Fish Camp (Elderhostel), 276-0976 (1 September–15 June), 442-6013 (16 June–31 August).

Transportation: Two pilots provide air charter service in the Kotzebue area. Arctic Air Guides, 814-698-2409 (October–May) or 442-3030 (June–September); Northwestern Aviation, 442-3525.

Other air taxi operations provide daily scheduled flights between Kotzebue and outlying villages: Baker Aviation, 442-3108; Bering Air, 442-3943; Cape Smythe Air Service, 442-3020; Hageland Aviation, 442-2936; and Village Aviation, 442-3535.

Vehicles may be rented from Arctic Auto and Maintenance, 442-2474; Kikiktagruk Inupiat Corporation (KIC), 442-3165; Roger Mauer, 442-3268.

Wandering Tattler

KELLY BAR

FOR GRAY-HEADED CHICKADEE

John Puschock

Kotzebue serves as the jump-off point for trips to the Kelly Bar, traditionally one of the best places in North America to find Gray-headed Chickadees (however, several recent birding expeditions have failed to find them). Kelly Bar is located 90 miles north of Kotzebue in Noatak National Preserve. Birders visiting here will have a true adventure! This area is accessible only by chartered flight, and you will have to camp once you get there. Brown Bears can be common, so exercise caution—make noise so the bears know you're there, and don't go crashing through thick willow, a favorite resting spot for the bears. Bears are sound sleepers and don't like to be surprised! (See Bear Cautions in the *Introduction*, page 17.) Bad weather (more likely in August) can prevent your pilot from picking you up, so you need to be prepared to stay longer than planned. There is a National Park Service ranger station on the north shore of the Noatak River at the upstream end of the Kelly Bar. It usually isn't staffed, but there is a radio in one of the walled tents that can be used in case of emergency.

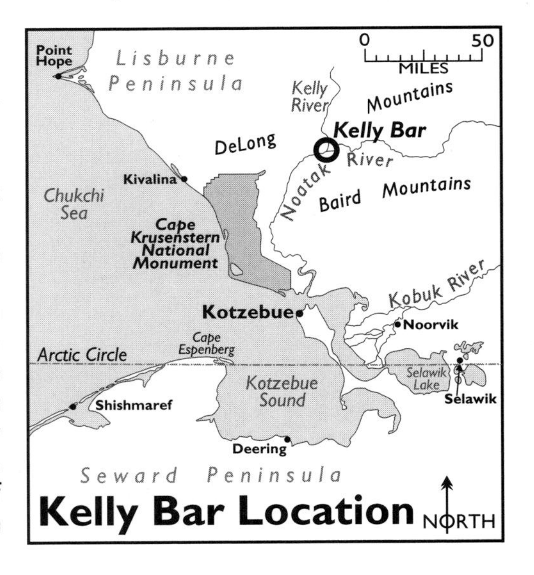

Most birders visit Kelly Bar in late August or early September, based on the theory that the chickadees will be easier to find once the young have fledged because there will be more birds flying around. However, it is likely that the young fledge earlier than late August—young chickadees have been found as early as late July—so earlier visits that would yield a greater number of other species might be more successful. High water-levels earlier in the summer usually prevent aircraft from landing on Kelly Bar, so you may need to charter a floatplane if you go before late July. The chickadees are not always easy to locate, so plan on staying several days.

Gray-headed Chickadees can be found anywhere along the Noatak River between the ranger station and the Kelly River. They have been seen in both willow and spruce woods. One birder who saw many of them recommends looking in the mixed spruce/willow zone along the bank of the Noatak. Boreal Chickadees are very common, so make your identifications with care.

Other interesting species occur in the area. Spruce Grouse, Northern Hawk Owl, Three-toed Woodpecker, Northern Shrike, Gray Jay, Gray-cheeked and Varied Thrushes, Bohemian Waxwing, Blackpoll Warbler, Pine Grosbeak, and White-winged Crossbill can be found in the spruce and willows along the river. Arctic Warblers breed on the tundra on the hills behind the ranger station. Red-throated and Pacific Loons, Glaucous Gull, and Arctic Tern can be seen on the Noatak. Rough-legged Hawk, Golden Eagle, Gyrfalcon, and Peregrine Falcon nest along high bluffs farther upriver and atop ledges on occasional rocky outcrops inland from the Noatak River.

Don't forget to bring a fishing pole (remember to purchase a license)—the Kelly River offers world-class fishing. Arctic Grayling are easy to catch, and Arctic Char fishing is excellent. Finally, birders who have become jaded with the "typical" Alaskan birding experience may want to consider a rafting trip along the Noatak. Gray-headed Chickadees might be possible anywhere along the river, and the area is mostly *terra incognita* for the birding world. Who knows what you might find?

LOGISTICS

See *Logistics* for Kotzebue, page 231.

There have been several published articles about Gray-headed Chickadee (Siberian Tit) expeditions. With the understanding that these are now some years out of date, you can find them by searching on Chickadee, Gray-headed in the *Birding* Index at *www.americanbirding.org*.

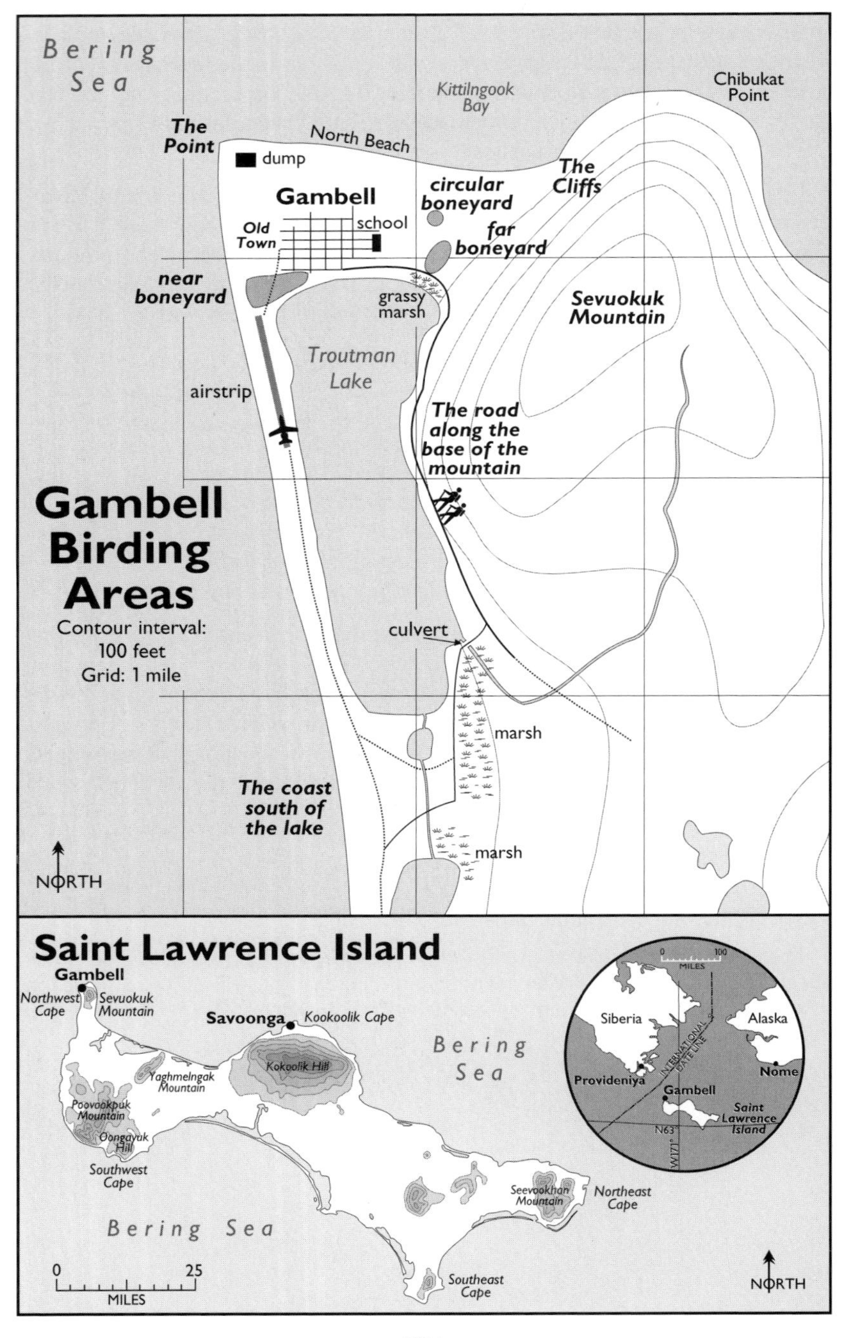

Bering Sea
Kittilngook Bay
Chibukat Point
The Point
North Beach
dump
Gambell
circular boneyard
The Cliffs
school
Old Town
far boneyard
near boneyard
grassy marsh
Sevuokuk Mountain
Troutman Lake
airstrip
The road along the base of the mountain
Gambell Birding Areas
Contour interval: 100 feet
Grid: 1 mile
culvert
marsh
The coast south of the lake
marsh
NORTH
Saint Lawrence Island
Gambell
Northwest Cape
Sevuokuk Mountain
Savoonga
Kookoolik Cape
Bering Sea
Kokoolik Hill
Yaghmelngak Mountain
Poovookpuk Mountain
Oongayuk Hill
Southwest Cape
Seevookhan Mountain
Northeast Cape
Bering Sea
Southeast Cape
0
25
MILES
NORTH
0
100
MILES
Siberia
Alaska
INTERNATIONAL DATE LINE
Provideniya
Nome
Gambell
Saint Lawrence Island
N63°
W171°

GAMBELL

SAINT LAWRENCE ISLAND

Paul Lehman and Jim Williams

The village of Gambell, located on the northwest tip of Saint Lawrence Island in the northern Bering Sea, is some 190 miles west-southwest of Nome. It is a place unique in North America for its sheer numbers of birds combined with the opportunity for rarities. Mountains on the coast of Siberia, only 40 miles away, are clearly visible from Gambell on a day when fog or rain do not obscure the view. Gambell, and its companion village Savoonga, are Siberian Yupik communities.

Today, Gambell is a homely collection of buildings scattered across a gravel peninsula. There are houses old and new, and buildings to accommodate the services that any community needs—grocery stores, laundromat, post office, school, municipal services. There is a paved airstrip for the small twin-engine planes that link the island with the mainland.

Gambell is home to about 700 people. Their forebears left traces in the area that date to at least 1500 B.C. Saint Lawrence Islanders were fully dependent on subsistence hunting until recently, and hunting continues today.

At the end of this chapter under *Logistics* you will find a great deal of information to help you plan your trip to Saint Lawrence Island, whether you are traveling independently or as part of an organized birding tour.

BIRDING GAMBELL IN THE SPRING

One of the good things about spring is that the season is concentrated in a period of just several weeks; the fall season is more protracted. A few lingering winter birds overlap with the spring seabird push, which, in turn, largely overlaps the peak rarity season for most groups of birds.

The seabird migration in late May and early June, combined with the movements of locally nesting birds to and from feeding grounds, can provide a million birds per day for you to watch. They fly along the shore past the Northwest Cape (The Point) in flocks, endless lines of birds 24 hours a day—a blizzard of alcids. Asian strays find the island in spring with impressive regularity. The list of rarities here is almost as impressive as that for Attu.

And the regular visitors aren't bad, either. Here is a partial survey of the rarity potential in spring.

Shorebirds—The common local breeders include Western Sandpiper, Dunlin, and Rock Sandpiper. Small numbers of migrant Pacific Golden-Plovers and Long-billed Dowitchers are seen. Just about annual in ones or small numbers are Common Ringed Plover (be careful, Semipalmated Plovers are regular!), Mongolian Plover, Wood Sandpiper, Gray-tailed Tattler, Bar-tailed Godwit, and Red-necked Stint. Seen some years but not every year are Eurasian Dotterel, Common Greenshank, Eurasian Whimbrel, Terek and Common Sandpipers, Temminck's and Long-toed Stints, and Ruff. There are a few records of Black-tailed Godwit, Great Knot, and Little Stint. Accidental are Green Sandpiper and Little Curlew. There is also a single record of an Oriental Pratincole. A few errant North American mainland shorebirds have occurred, as well.

Eurasian Wigeons are rare, Eurasian Green-winged (Common) Teal are regular in small numbers.

Casual waterbirds have included Taiga Bean Goose (careful again, Greater White-fronted Geese occur), Whooper Swan, and (Eurasian) Common Tern.

"Trans-Beringian" landbirds heading back from Asia into western Alaska to nest (some possibly to breed locally on the island) include Arctic Warbler (June), Bluethroat (scarce), Northern Wheatear (regular), Yellow Wagtail (regular), White Wagtail (breeds on the island and formerly around town, but has become more difficult the past couple of years), and Red-throated Pipit (fairly regular). Of the Asian landbird vagrants, only Brambling is annual. But if a birder visits for several days or more, he or she can hope to be rewarded with at least one or two additional strays. Species that have occurred in some years include Common Cuckoo, Sky Lark, Eyebrowed Thrush, Black-backed Wagtail, Olive-backed and Japonicus American Pipits, and Rustic Bunting. Rarer still are Siberian Rubythroat and Eurasian Bullfinch. Ultra-rarities have included Brown Shrike, Dusky Warbler, Asian Brown and Red-breasted Flycatchers, Stonechat, Dusky Thrush, Fieldfare, Tree Pipit, Pallas's Bunting, and Hawfinch. A few Alaska mainland passerine strays occur in spring, but fewer than in fall.

Birders are advised to arrive no earlier than 20 May. The height of the spring season runs from around 25 May to 8 or 10 June, which is when most of the tour groups visit. Obviously, arrival of vagrants is not scheduled. In general, earlier is better for Ivory Gulls and possibly for McKay's Buntings, later for some of the landbirds. Arctic Warblers don't arrive until around 10 June, to give a particularly late example. Very few birders have ever remained in the village beyond the second week of June. Some experts believe that mid- and late June—although past peak for most migrants—would be very good for mega-rarities. There are already a few late-June and early-July gems, including Oriental Cuckoo, Middendorff's Grasshopper-Warbler, and Yellow-breasted Bunting, and that's with essentially no coverage.

Be prepared for cold weather. Temperatures average in the 30sF. It is often windy. Light precipitation may occur in any of several forms. Standing at The Point conducting a seawatch for an hour or more can become bone-chilling if you are unprepared. Proper footgear is also imperative—be ready for lots of walking, for possible snow, and for standing water.

SPRING BIRDING SITES

Seawatching at The Point — Alcids and other seabirds stream by 24 hours a day from mid-May onward. Migrant seabirds will be done by mid-June. The alcids that nest on the island come and go as they feed, and their numbers hold strong until fledging time in late August and September. The most abundant alcids are Crested and Least Auklets, followed by the other common nesting species—Common and Thick-billed Murres, Pigeon Guillemot, Parakeet Auklet, and Horned and Tufted Puffins. A few Black Guillemots can be seen from The Point, as can the rare Dovekie. Overall, birds are on the wing, on the water, and sometimes can be seen loafing on chunks of sea-ice drifting by. It is possible to see four species each of loons and eiders. Small numbers of Arctic and Yellow-billed (mornings) Loons pass by most days. Steller's and Spectacled Eiders are seen in numbers almost every year; some years they are relatively easy to see. In other years, observers must put in a long time before seeing both and, rarely, one or the other can be missed. Northern Fulmar and Pelagic Cormorant are common. Small groups of Emperor Geese and Black Brant are likely. Black and White-winged Scoters and Harlequin and Long-tailed Ducks can be seen. Red-necked and Red Phalaropes and all three species of jaegers migrate through. Glaucous Gull and Black-legged Kittiwake are common; Vega Herring Gulls are fairly common. Sabine's Gull is an uncommon migrant. Ivory Gull is present most years in May (and earlier in spring), sometimes even at the end of the month, and perhaps into early June if there is substantial sea-ice (less and less frequent in recent years). Ross's Gull is quite rare in late spring. There are a few records of Black-headed Gull, two records for Black-tailed Gull, and a small but regular number of Slaty-backed Gulls. Mew Gull is casual. *Note*: there are no records or only single records of Red-faced Cormorant, Red-legged Kittiwake, and Aleutian Tern.

Birders should find a place to sit on shore, facing the sea, to rest and to watch. As close as possible to The Point and out of the wind are usually best. The beach gravel may be damp. Find a scrap of cardboard or bring a cushion to sit on. Whatever site you choose, just sit and watch. There is value at Gambell in letting the birds come to you. The larger flights of Least and

Crested Auklets—often in the hundreds of thousands—typically pass by late in the day. In the fall, the best variety of seabirds often will be found in the morning. However, any time of day can be good in both spring and fall.

The Cliffs — A mile east of The Point is Sevuokuk Mountain, 400 feet tall. You can walk to its juncture with the sea, look up, and watch nesting alcids race back and forth between rock and water. In the mountain's nooks and crannies and on its cliffs nest thousands of pairs of the eight common species. With a little luck, one or two pairs of Dovekies also can be seen here.

The Boneyards — In earlier times the subsistence hunters of Gambell tossed the butchered carcasses of marine mammals into middens that exist today as migrant traps called boneyards. You cannot miss these three large boneyards scattered around the village. They also are the scene of excavation when the ground is suitable for digging, as village residents search to recover long-buried ivory (for carving), as well as other artifacts. Visitors to the island may not scavenge for such items. In a part of the world where plants grow sparsely, the animal matter in the boneyards nourished the soil. Although in late spring it is too early for there to be much new vegetation, this disturbed ground is still very attractive to migrant birds prospecting for food and cover. Look for Bluethroats and pipits of several species. Watch also for Northern Wheatear, Yellow Wagtail, and Hoary Redpoll. White Wagtails have nested at Gambell, but in recent years sightings have become fewer and the species has been harder to pin down; try Old Town and near the dump for this species. Many of the best Asian passerine strays found at Gambell have been discovered in one of the boneyards. In spring, small meltwater pools here may attract shorebirds. The largest of these middens—referred to by birders

Least Auklets

as "the near boneyard"—lies between the airstrip and the village proper. Two more boneyards are located to the east between the village and the mountain, beyond the school building—the larger one is at the base of the mountain ("the far boneyard") and a smaller one lies immediately to the northwest in the gravel field ("the circular boneyard"). Birders patrol these three sites through the day, all day, slowly, methodically. You never know what might be seen.

Old Town — Birders also work Old Town, which is the western edge of the village, between the top of the runway and the village dump that is just short of The Point. Old Town has patches of enriched, disturbed soil, and thus some vegetation (lush later in the summer and early fall), and large whalebones. This area can be good for both regular and vagrant passerines, and for a few shorebirds.

The road along the mountain — At the foot of the mountain, a firmly-surfaced dirt road leads south above the shore of Troutman Lake to the lake's far end and to the tundra beyond. Snow Buntings are seen here. McKay's Bunting is a distinct possibility, but is irregular; it has also been seen elsewhere near the village, such as in Old Town. Lapland Longspurs, the most abundant passerine on the island, are here, along with courting Red-throated Pipits (rare but regular). Eurasian Bullfinches were seen two springs (they've also been seen in the boneyards). Other rarities seen along this walk include Alaska's only Little Curlew, several Common Cuckoos, and Eyebrowed Thrush. Western and Rock Sandpipers flutter in courtship flights here. Northern Wheatears are possible, and may be numerous in late summer.

Troutman Lake and beyond — This large lake is still frozen in May, but when open it is a loafing place for gulls and puffins. A small number of shorebirds work its margins, and there usually is some open water along the edges from late May onward. Watch the grassy marsh at the northeast corner of the lake near the far boneyard, the larger marshes immediately below (beyond) the lake, and any small puddles and pools for a variety of shorebirds. Mongolian Plover and Common Ringed Plover have been seen where a culvert brings drain water into the far end of Troutman Lake. White Wagtail has been seen on numerous occasions near the culvert. The water drains from a series of pools that back up into the tundra for a mile or more. A Far Eastern Curlew once was found at one of those ponds, and the open water here often is good for waterfowl. Later in the season, roosting gulls frequently gather on the adjoining shorelines and gravel fields.

The walk from the village to the far end of Troutman Lake and the marshes beyond is long, bordering on five miles round-trip. It can be very tiring. Plan accordingly.

The coast south of the lake — With the standard land-crossing permit in hand (see *Logistics*), you can go to the first rocky headland about two miles south of the lake (that includes the ponds and marshy areas discussed previously). This territory includes a stretch of ocean shoreline where there are a couple of semi-protected coves that might be good for loafing gulls and idling seabirds. The headland can be good for small flocks of eiders and Harlequin Ducks from spring through fall.

The mountain top — Again, with an extended permit (see *Logistics*), some birders walk the road along Troutman Lake, then climb the far slope of Sevuokuk Mountain to gain the upper ground, where Eurasian Dotterel has sometimes been found (in early summer, but no earlier than the first week of June). This species also has been seen within the village on several occasions. Caution is urged when on the mountain. The villagers bury their dead here; some of the ground is off-limits to visitors.

BIRDING GAMBELL IN THE FALL

Groups of birders have visited Gambell in late spring annually since the late 1970s. In contrast, coverage during the late summer and fall began only in the early 1990s, with most such visits taking place during late August and early September and of no more than a week's duration. Only since 1999 have birders stayed for longer periods (up to six weeks) and as late as the beginning of October. Patience is the name of the game in the protracted fall season, but those with time have been rewarded. Some superb seabird concentrations, a variety of Asian shorebirds, a good passage of trans-Beringian passerines, and a few high-quality Asian strays (as well as a good selection of North American mainland wanderers) are the autumn's highlights.

The seabird spectacle continues as the days shorten. Alcid numbers (hundreds of thousands daily) and variety (some eight species) pass The Point through August in numbers as impressive as in late spring. Dovekie is only casually seen in fall, however, and Black Guillemot is sporadic until late September. The auklets start thinning out near the end of August (although a few juveniles may be found crash-landed around town), followed in early and mid-September by the murres, and finally the puffins in late September. A few rare visitors, such as Kittlitz's and Ancient Murrelets (and Fork-tailed Storm-Petrel) have been seen on multiple occasions.

Clearly one of the most spectacular events is the concentration of Short-tailed Shearwaters that resides off the island at this season, with numbers peaking at a half-million or more per day between late August and mid-September. Concentrations of up to 40,000 Red Phalaropes have been noted in September. There is a steady passage of all three jaegers (sometimes including major flights of Pomarines), and small numbers of Yellow-billed

Loon, Emperor Goose, Black Brant, Sabine's Gull, and Arctic Tern are seen. (Arctic Loon is, at best, only casual in August/September.) All four eiders may be seen, with Steller's occurring singly or in small groups some days. One or two Spectacled Eiders may pass by sporadically until its numbers (and those of Yellow-billed Loon) increase in late September. Unfortunately for some birders, all early fall eiders are in eclipse plumage. Other waterfowl that occur in small numbers include Snow Goose and Eurasian Wigeon.

Shorebirds are fairly numerous, including good numbers of Pacific Golden-Plover, Western Sandpiper, Dunlin, Pectoral Sandpiper, and Long-billed Dowitcher, plus a few Rock Sandpipers. Juvenile Sharp-tailed Sandpiper is regular from late August through at least mid-September, with up to 40 to 50 seen during a single season. Rainy weather produces the most individuals. Rarer Asian species occur as well, with Red-necked Stint being regular in very small numbers in August, and Mongolian Plover and Gray-tailed (and Wandering) Tattler annual in late August and early September. There are several August records of Common Ringed Plover, though Semipalmated Plover is more numerous. American Golden-Plover is rare but regular. Rarer species seen only once or twice include Wood and Terek Sandpipers, Eurasian Whimbrel, Bristle-thighed Curlew, Great Knot, Temminck's and Long-toed Stints, and Common Snipe.

The best places to search for fall shorebirds include the grassy marsh at the northeast corner of Troutman Lake, the marshes below the lake (typically not quite as interesting in fall as in late spring, however), the grassy areas just north of the runway, and just about any rain puddle. Visits to Gambell earlier in August (earliest birder arrival to-date is only 20 August) would likely produce a larger overall number and variety of shorebirds, and probably additional rarities.

Gulls are numerous, and among all the Glaucous there are good numbers of Vega Herring Gulls and small numbers of Slaty-backed and Glaucous-winged Gulls. Casual visitors have included Black-headed, Kamchatka Mew, Herring, and Thayer's.

Trans-Beringian landbird migrants—those species that nest in western Alaska but return to Asia (and even Africa for the wheatear!) for the winter, such as Arctic Warbler, Bluethroat, Northern Wheatear, Yellow Wagtail, and Red-throated Pipit—occur in moderate but variable numbers during August and early September. They are more numerous at this season than during spring. Late August is probably peak for most of them. Earlier is better for Yellow Wagtail, slightly later perhaps for Red-throated Pipit. Poor weather grounds the largest numbers of birds. The boneyards and Old Town are, again, the best places to search. Getting good looks at a Bluethroat or a pipit may take some running after a bird that is periodically flushed from (what is considered on the island) lush vegetation. Many trans-Beringian and Asian passerines are true skulkers! White Wagtail has become hard to find during the past several years. Gray-cheeked Thrushes migrating from nesting areas in Siberia back into North America are also found in small numbers. Only a few autumn McKay's Buntings have been seen to date, with your chances likely improving the later you visit.

Asian landbirds are found periodically during the fall. The bad news is that they simply do not occur every day or two...or seven! The good news is that the list of stragglers includes a number of species that are exceptionally rare in North America, several of which are not found in spring. Some of the fall highlights between 1992 and 2001 include Oriental Cuckoo, Fork-tailed Swift, Sky Lark, Flava Horned Lark, Asian Barn Swallow, Middendorff's Grasshopper-Warbler, Dusky Warbler, North America's first Yellow-browed Warbler, Siberian Rubythroat, two Siberian Accentors, several Japonicus American Pipits, Olive-backed Pipit, a total of four Little Buntings, two Common Rosefinches, and multiple Bramblings.

It should be emphasized again that the majority of days in fall produce no Asian landbirds. Although these avian waifs are relatively few, they tend to be of high quality. Anytime from late August (possibly earlier?) onward seems to be fair game, with perhaps the second half of September being peak. Weather likely plays an important role. The best places to look are the same as for the regular migrants: the three boneyards, Old Town, and the lower slopes of the mountain. In addition, fall is a good time to find North American strays—it is much better than spring in producing such species. Small numbers of Seward Peninsula and other mainland Alaska species turn up, and additionally such far-flung wanderers as Least and "Western" (Pacific-slope/Cordilleran) Flycatchers, Tennessee and five other species of warblers, multiple Chipping and several other species of sparrows, and Brown-headed Cowbird have turned up.

Gambell's appearance in late summer and early fall is different from that in late spring, the time when most birders visit. There is no ice or snow (until late September or later). Pack ice does not reappear until late November or December. Daytime temperatures in late August average in the mid-40sF, dropping to the upper 30s by late September. Be prepared for damp conditions some days (more likely than in spring), with periodic mist and showers. Always be ready for wind. A few days are calm and very comfortable. A chilly north-northeast wind may set up for a number of days in a row and can be good for seawatching and for some trans-Beringian landbirds, but may not be helpful otherwise. In late August sunrise is not until around 7:30 AM, but the sun does not fully set until almost 11 PM. Given the loss of six minutes of daylight per day, by the end of September one cannot go birding until almost 9:30 AM, and it is dark before 8 PM. The boneyards are covered in a mint-like vegetation that grows to a height of a foot. Patches of this vegetation are also found in Old Town, particularly around large whalebones and other areas of disturbed ground. Migrant passerines concentrate in this relatively lush vegetation, making some of them difficult to dig out. Troutman Lake is open, though fairly sterile overall. Its shoreline is dotted with a few shorebirds, good numbers of Horned Puffins loaf on the lake itself, and a daily afternoon gull roost sets up along the northeastern shore. Overall, the season provides for the study of many species in interesting and challenging plumages.

The lodge is rarely crowded during the late summer and fall, though occasionally it is close to full for a few days with the periodic arrival of groups of government and other workers. August and early September generally have more visitor use than late September and October. In any case, except for a regular late-August tour group, only a few of the visitors have been birders. The deli is open for lunch and dinner most days, and the two food markets have their regular hours.

So, when to visit Gambell in fall? Compared to spring, such a decision is not easy. A visit during the last week of August and first week of September combines high seabird numbers and diversity, good shorebirding, near-peak numbers of trans-Beringian landbirds, and a chance for an early Asian landbird stray or two. Slightly earlier in August may be best for peak shorebird numbers and also might be near-peak for some early trans-Beringian passerines. Late-August rarities have included Middendorff's Grasshopper-Warbler, Dusky Warbler, Little Bunting, and Common Rosefinch. The first half of September has produced single Olive-backed Pipit, Little Bunting, and Common Rosefinch. Later visits, during the second half of September, are good for a different mix of seabirds and probably afford better chances for Asian landbird strays. That period has produced Sky Lark, the Yellow-browed Warbler, Siberian Rubythroat, two Siberian Accentors, and two Little Buntings. But by then some of the alcid species have departed, and, given that the trans-Beringian migrants are also gone (as are almost all of the locally breeding Lapland Longspurs!), there are not many landbirds to look at except for the resident ravens, a few Snow Buntings, and some redpolls. Any landbird found then other than those few species may well be a rarity! Gyrfalcon may become somewhat regular by late September, or even earlier.

No birder has visited Gambell beyond early October. Local residents report seeing "strange little birds" seeking shelter in the boneyards and around and even inside buildings during harsh weather during October and early November. Who knows what odd-ball species might be occurring then! Also, according to local residents, during late October and early November there is a substantial flight of Spectacled Eiders and a small passage of Ross's Gulls past The Point.

SAVOONGA

The other village on Saint Lawrence Island is almost unexplored for birding. It is accessible by regular air service. Many flights to Gambell stop at Savoonga, which is located farther east along the north shore of the island. Birds are evident near the runway even during brief stops. Shorebirds can be seen in puddles and pools. The village does not have the advantage of the western cape location that Gambell has (so will likely host far fewer Asian strays), nor the latter's seabird cliffs. Savoonga is on the coast, however, with unknown potential. The few interesting records here to date include Baikal Teal (July 1937), Common Merganser, Mongolian Plover, Slaty-backed Gull, Tree Swallow, Slate-colored Junco, and McKay's Bunting. Birders who have visited Savoonga suggest that additional interesting areas to bird may be found outside of the village, including perhaps an hour's trip south into the interior. They also suggest that guides and ATVs would be less expensive here than at Gambell.

LOGISTICS AND TRIP PLANNING

The area code for all telephone numbers is 907 unless otherwise indicated. Saint Lawrence Island is not covered in The Milepost. *For your convenience, complete information about accommodations and transportation is listed below. Statewide travel and birding information services are listed under Logistics in the* Introduction, *page 15.)* Gambell is in the same time zone as the rest of Alaska, one hour earlier than Pacific Coast time.

Getting there — You can fly one of two airlines serving Gambell, Bering Air (443-5464) and Cape Smythe Air (443–2414). Both make two round-trips daily from Nome. Weather is highly variable and there are no instrument landings, so flight schedules vary with the weather. You may check in and stand by, to wait and wait and wait. It is a simple flight of about an hour if you go straight to Gambell with no stop at Savoonga. A round-trip ticket cost about $300 in 2002.

Necessities — A "land-crossing permit" is required by the Native corporation (Sivuqaq, Inc.) that owns Saint Lawrence Island for general access to the village itself and to the land surrounding it. In 2002 it cost $50 and was valid for one year. If you wish to venture farther, including exploration of the land atop the 400-foot mountain on the east border of the village (where Eurasian Dotterel has occasionally been seen in June), the fee increases to $100 (in 2002). It is important to discuss just where one can and cannot go. Visitors must be certain to avoid town burial sites on the mountain. Purchase your permit upon arrival.

You also will need accommodations at Gambell. Birders have flown in for 24 hours, expecting to bird round the clock, as daylight at high birding season—late May and early June—lasts nearly forever. The same birders, cold and wet, have later been seen knocking on residents' doors, looking for a warm place to dry-off and nap. Budgeting so little time there also can present problems if flights are delayed. And, because rare birds are not present every day, the longer you stay, the more you will see.

The village itself now rents rooms. The best place to stay is a lodge-like village building (the Sivuqaq Inn) built in the early 1990s to house the construction crew that erected the new school. There are simple but comfortable single and double rooms there, toilets, showers, hot water, washer/dryer, a kitchen (shared with a take-out deli operation), and a common room. The cost per room was $90 per night in 2001, single or double. There are other village accommodations as well, none as comfortable as the lodge, but all serviceable. Individual families also provide rooms and sometimes food. The village personnel who manage tourism can provide information about the opportunities available. Most of the rooms—and certainly the best ones—are booked far in advance by the birding tour groups that visit during the springtime birding rush in late May and early June.

Birders should plan to bring their own perishable food. The two stores in the village are usually reasonably well stocked with microwave foods, canned foods, and dry goods. Some birders ship everything wanted or needed ahead of time using USPS parcel post or UPS services. Inquire about cooking facilities and the availability of microwaves, utensils, pots and pans, dishes, and silverware. There also is a take-out deli operating in the lodge. Visitors can purchase burgers, chicken, pies, soft drinks, etc. It usually is open for lunch and dinner, but it may be closed some days and the schedule can be sporadic, so one should not rely on it. The village has a modern water system.

Because of these varied inconveniences, it is generally much easier (although more expensive) to book a trip with one of the birding tour companies visiting Gambell than to plan a trip on your own or with a few friends. There is value in numbers of people when you are combing a site for one specific Asian passerine. For groups, it is useful to bring the small two-way radios known as "family" or "FRS" radios in order to communicate with other members of your group.

The island is dry; no alcoholic beverages of any kind are allowed. Read the statement on Native Cultures in the *Introduction*, page 10.

There are no motor vehicles on the island beyond four-wheel all-terrain runabouts (ATV) and snowmachines. You will bird on foot or perhaps rent an ATV once the snow melts. The gravel surface that dominates the village makes walking tiresome. You quickly learn the walking routes that avoid some of the worst gravel. The distance from the lodge to The Point is about one mile. The distance from the lodge to The Cliffs is also about a mile. The distance to the marshes and ponds at the far end of Troutman Lake is over two miles. The boneyards within the village can be one-half mile from your bed. Ideally, you visit many of these birding places more than once each day. Some birders believe that they get the most from their trip investment by renting an ATV so they can visit more birding spots more often. The cost of an ATV can range from $75 to $100 per day. All carry two persons. All rentals are privately made from village residents. Lodge personnel can help find ATV owners willing to rent.

The village person who handles Gambell accommodations and land-crossing permits can be reached at 985-5826. Those visitors staying at the lodge have use of a guest phone for placing and receiving calls—985-5335.

ACKNOWLEDGEMENTS: Paul Baicich, Shawneen Finnegan, Evan Obercian, Michael O'Brien, and Louise Zematis reviewed and added information to the text.

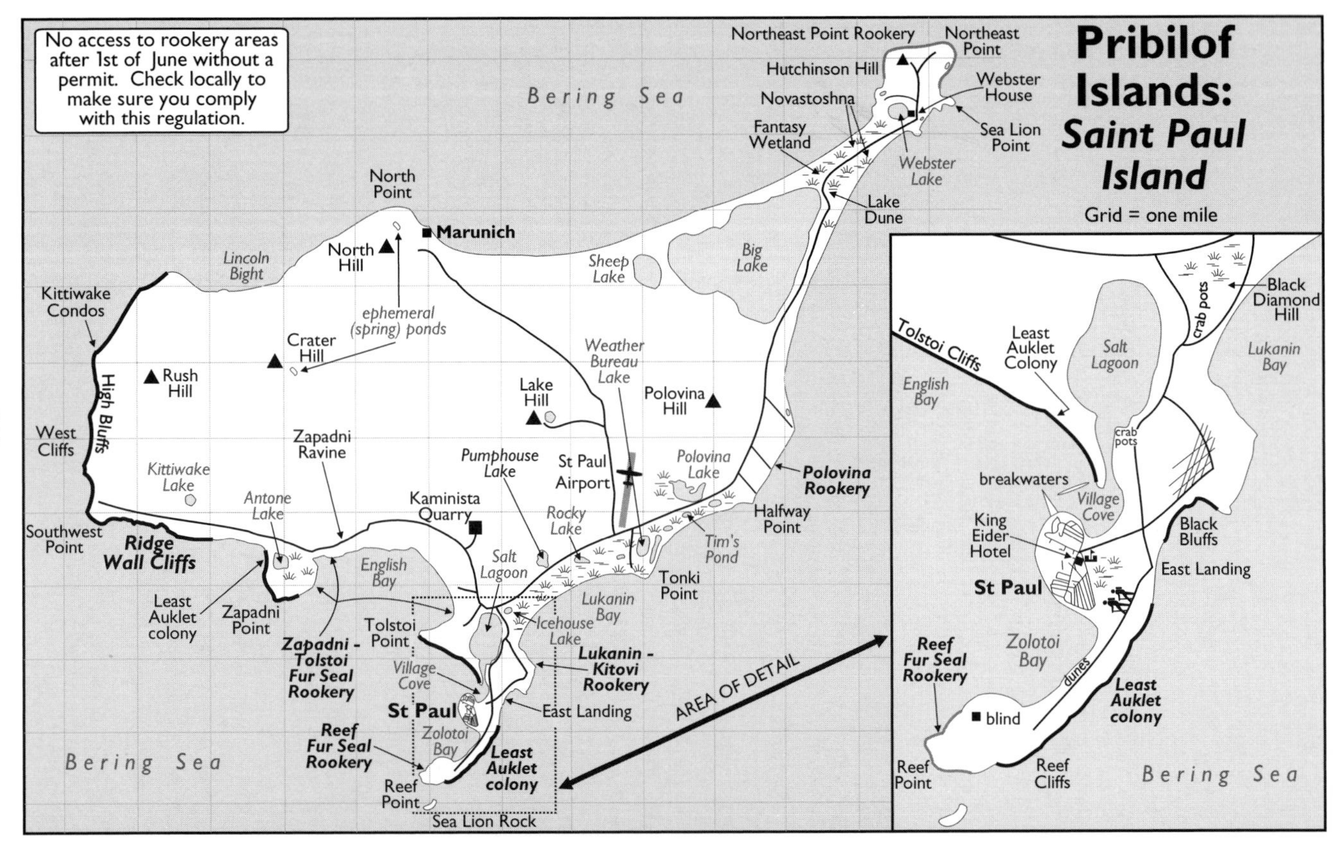

Pribilof Islands: Saint Paul Island
Grid = one mile
No access to rookery areas after 1st of June without a permit. Check locally to make sure you comply with this regulation.
Bering Sea
Northeast Point Rookery
Northeast Point
Hutchinson Hill
Webster House
Novastoshna
Sea Lion Point
Fantasy Wetland
Webster Lake
Lake Dune
North Point
Marunich
North Hill
Lincoln Bight
Sheep Lake
Big Lake
Kittiwake Condos
ephemeral (spring) ponds
Crater Hill
Rush Hill
Weather Bureau Lake
Lake Hill
Polovina Hill
High Bluffs
West Cliffs
Zapadni Ravine
Pumphouse Lake
St Paul Airport
Polovina Lake
Kittiwake Lake
Polovina Rookery
Antone Lake
Kaminista Quarry
Rocky Lake
Halfway Point
Southwest Point
Ridge Wall Cliffs
Salt Lagoon
Tim's Pond
English Bay
Tonki Point
Lukanin Bay
Least Auklet colony
Zapadni Point
Tolstoi Point
Icehouse Lake
Zapadni - Tolstoi Fur Seal Rookery
Lukanin - Kitovi Rookery
Village Cove
St Paul
East Landing
AREA OF DETAIL
Reef Fur Seal Rookery
Zolotoi Bay
Least Auklet colony
Bering Sea
Reef Point
Sea Lion Rock
Black Diamond Hill
crab pots
Tolstoi Cliffs
Least Auklet Colony
Salt Lagoon
Lukanin Bay
English Bay
crab pots
breakwaters
Village Cove
King Eider Hotel
Black Bluffs
East Landing
St Paul
Reef Fur Seal Rookery
Zolotoi Bay
dunes
Least Auklet colony
blind
Reef Point
Reef Cliffs
Bering Sea

THE PRIBILOF ISLANDS

Sean Smith

The Pribilof Islands, part of the vast Alaska Maritime National Wildlife Refuge, support the largest number of nesting alcids and seabirds in Alaska. The Pribilof's murres, auklets, and puffins—along with other seabirds, including cormorants, fulmars, gulls, and Red-legged Kittiwake—are easily accessible for both birders and photographers.

Saint Paul and Saint George Islands, strategically located in the south-central Bering Sea, lie nearly 300 miles from both the western Alaska mainland and the Aleutian Islands. Each year during spring and fall migration shorebirds and passerines veer off course on their way to and from their breeding and wintering grounds. A number of the lucky ones find the Pribilofs and land there to feed and rest up before continuing on. Small numbers of North American and Asiatic vagrants appear annually.

The chance of encountering rare Asian species admittedly adds spice to birding on these islands. Some of these species—Wood Sandpiper for instance—are more likely to be found here than in any other currently accessible location in the state. However, even at the peak of migration, a short stay is unlikely to yield more than one or two vagrant birds. Even then, these accidentals may be from the "wrong" side of the Bering Sea for North American birders. Other than the seabirds, migrants—even the expected ones—will occur in very low numbers. The lists of rarities included in this account are meant to illustrate the possibilities of birding here, but even if rare birds are scarce, the seabird spectacle will ensure that you won't regret your visit to one of the most remote and exciting birding and natural history destinations in Alaska.

The islands are rocky, treeless, windswept, wet, and cold in summer. To enjoy birding here, you must bring warm clothing as well as full rain gear and knee-high rubber boots. For your initial visit, consider joining a tour group to ease the logistical problems of independently arranging shelter, meals, and transportation (see *Logistics* below).

WHEN TO COME

Most birders visit the Pribilofs in late spring—from mid-May until mid-June—when the greatest numbers of breeding birds and migrants arrive or pass through during a relatively short period. In recent years, the best time to see Asian migrants has been the last week of May. It can be quite cold in May, but this is practically the only drawback to visiting at that time, unless seeing large numbers of Northern Fur Seals is a priority. Most birding groups and individuals, however, visit during June. Early June can deliver some unexpected vagrants. If this is your Alaska birding trip of a lifetime, make late spring your first choice.

By late June the breeding seabird activity is beginning to peak. Although mid-summer is a great time to enjoy birding the Pribilofs, with the added attractions of wildflowers and seal pups, it is not generally a good time to see migrants. Nevertheless, some rarities have occurred in July, including Eurasian Hobby, Terek and Curlew Sandpipers, Oriental Turtle-Dove, Oriental and Common Cuckoos, Common House-Martin, and Middendorff's Grasshopper-Warbler. Although hardly regular, Common Greenshank, Wood and Common Sandpipers, and adult Red-necked Stints have been found several times in July.

Similarly, August promises many birding treasures. Juvenile Red-necked Stints are expected by the second week in August, and young Temminck's Stints are possible in late August, with several records since the mid-1990s. Juvenile Wood Sandpipers are almost annual during late August, just as adults are in spring. Remarkable single records of Fork-tailed Swift and Common House-Martin have occurred in late August in recent years. Both Northern Wheatear and Yellow Wagtail are annual in late August. Unfortunately, late summer all but lacks the auklet species so numerous just a few weeks earlier.

Songbird migration begins in September, although passerines are even tougher to find than waders. In early September northeast winds sometimes bring many migrant North American warblers and sparrows off the Alaska mainland. However, most autumn records of Siberian vagrants have occurred much later, however—late September, October, and November. Red-flanked Bluetail, Gray Wagtail, Olive-backed Pipit, Brambling, and Hawfinch have all been documented in fall. But with the prolonged nature of fall migration, the unpredictable weather, and the possibility that you might be the only birder on the islands, this type of birding is suitable for only the hardiest. The potential for exciting discoveries, however, remains high.

BIRDING THE PRIBILOFS

Most of the migrants encountered on the Pribilofs will be seabirds and shorebirds. The most obvious breeding shorebird is the nominate race of Rock Sandpiper (*Calidris ptilocnemsis ptilocnemsis*) that is commonly found on the upland tundra of Saint Paul, Saint George, and Otter Islands. At one time this species was known as Pribilof Sandpiper—it is larger and paler than the other subspecies of Rock Sandpiper.

The Pribilofs are also known for their non-avian summertime residents. The bulk of the world's Northern Fur Seal (*Callorhinus ursinus*) population breeds on Saint Paul and Saint George. Hundreds of thousands of these pinnipeds effectively take over much of the exposed shoreline in congested rookeries. Arctic Foxes patrol both the seal rookeries and the bird cliffs. In summer, exquisite arctic wildflowers saturate large expanses of the islands' interiors.

The Pribilofs provide birders with many opportunities to observe and photograph seabird species from only a few feet away. As the easiest island to reach and get around on, Saint Paul is the most accessible location in Alaska where one can see nesting Northern Fulmar, Red-faced Cormorant, Red-legged Kittiwake, Parakeet, Least, and Crested Auklets, and Tufted and Horned Puffins. The best locations to see and photograph seabirds on Saint Paul are Reef Point, Zapadni Cliffs, and Ridge Wall.

Both Native villages of Saint Paul and Saint George are modern, but Saint Paul has an improved runway and airport, as well as a more extensive road system than Saint George. This larger, more northerly island with its extensive wetland areas and greater variety of habitats attracts a greater number of migrants—and birders who make use of the local tours (see *Logistics*).

Nevertheless, it is Saint George where spectacular numbers of seabirds nest amidst magnificent scenery. Although all the same species occur on Saint Paul in much smaller numbers, it is the vastness of Saint George's cliff faces that attracts the greatest biomass of nesting seabirds in Alaska. For some, this spectacle is worth the extra time and expense. Ideally, both islands should be visited. In reality, almost all visitors elect to stay only on Saint Paul. Because of this, and due to the more intensive history of birding there, this chapter focuses predominately on the birding opportunities on Saint Paul.

Black-backed Wagtail

SAINT PAUL ISLAND

SAINT PAUL VILLAGE ENVIRONS

For most visiting birders, home base will be within the village of Saint Paul, (population 800 in 2001). Several good birding areas are within easy walking distance of the village. Northern Wheatear, Yellow Wagtail, Rustic Bunting, Hawfinch, Siberian Rubythroat, and Red-throated Pipit have all occurred in town. Birders should be aware, however, that Asiatic songbirds are extremely rare at any time and that North American passerine strays are more likely to be found.

There are only four common breeding songbirds on the Pribilofs. Snow Buntings nest in ancient rocky lava flows and Lapland Longspurs may be found in grassy tundra. The insular races of the pale, long-billed Winter Wren (*Troglodytes troglodytes alascensis*) and the large Gray-crowned Rosy-Finch (*Leucosticte tephrocotis umbrina*) are especially interesting. The rosy-finches nest under the eaves of many houses and buildings in the village. The wrens are infrequently seen on the seabird cliffs of Saint Paul, but are common on Saint George.

Directly downhill from the old King Eider Hotel and adjacent to the school is a marshy area that in May and early June might have Northern Shoveler, Northern Pintail, North American Green-winged Teal, or Common Teal. Wood Sandpiper, possible in any freshwater wetland on the islands in May, June, and August, has been seen here on several occasions, as has Black-headed Gull.

The harbor, known as Village Cove, often contains summering Harlequin Ducks near shore in the morning. In early spring, females and immature drake King Eiders, Long-tailed Ducks, or even Steller's Eiders might be found along the rocky shorelines and breakwaters. Most adult drake King Eiders, common winter residents, have flown north by mid-May.

The breakwater that adjoins some short cliffs west of Village Cove and just opposite the large fish-processing building is good in the morning for Parakeet, Least, and Crested Auklets. Offshore from here Black Guillemot has been identified twice in recent years.

East Landing is a 20-minute walk from the hotel and Reef Point is twice the distance. Take the first right on the main road that leads from town. Two hundred yards along is East Landing, marked by rock piles and a crumbling concrete dock. During storms from the south and the east, this is an especially productive spot from which to scan the water. At these times, and when fish-processing waste is emitted from the outfall line, large flocks of

Northern Fulmars, Black-legged and Red-legged Kittiwakes, and, sometimes, Short-tailed Shearwaters are observed. Interspersed with these species could be Fork-tailed Storm-Petrel, any of the jaegers, or even a Sabine's Gull. Later in the summer, huge flocks of Red Phalaropes might be spotted from this vantage point.

If cormorants are nesting on Black Bluffs, immediately to the north of East Landing, you can get good comparisons between Red-faced (common) and Pelagic (relatively rare). To the south, and stretching toward Reef Point along the beach boulders, is a Least Auklet colony. In spring, Least Auklets, or *chuuchkies*, as they are known locally, can be seen best during the early part of the day or very late in the evening. All three auklet species fledge their young quickly and abandon terrestrial life without delay. By mid-August it is very difficult to see auklets on cliffs or rocks, and views of them at sea are distant.

Almost one mile south from the center of town, past the Least Auklet colony, a series of low cliffs begins on the left. If you choose to cross the marshy area mentioned above to access the road, take extra care not to disturb birds or seals in this area. Reef Fur Seal Rookery, (off limits from 1 June–15 October), is adjacent to the dunes on the right. Do not cut through these dunes if you are hiking back to the hotel. It is illegal to disturb marine mammals at any time. Disturbance of birds or seals is taken very seriously here, and there is no reason why a careful, conscientious observer cannot enjoy the sights without causing undue stress to the wildlife. Murres are especially vulnerable to disturbance. A mass exodus of them from the cliff is known as a "dread flight." Arctic Foxes, not over-anxious birders, should be the cause of dread flights. Seabirds often will allow a close approach if it is done with patience and stealth.

At the gate near the Reef Fur Seal Rookery, a half-hour walk from town, you can get great looks at many of the Pribilof seabirds. These short cliffs are usually best in the morning for Black-legged Kittiwake, Thick-billed Murre, all three auklet species, Horned and Tufted Puffins, and Winter Wren. Photographic opportunities are outstanding at this location. With a proper permit (see *Logistics*), or with a local tour guide, you can visit the Fur Seal Rookery blind a short distance away. Be sure to scan the waters in front of the blind for rarer alcids, such as Ancient and Marbled Murrelets.

Salt Lagoon is another good birding location close to Saint Paul village. Check the mudflats and lagoon waters every time you pass by for ducks, shorebirds, and gulls. Any crab-pot stacks should be checked for migrant passerines. Salt Lagoon provides a unique tidal habitat within the Pribilofs and is a resting, feeding, and staging area for many birds. Shorebirds favor the extensive muddy flats at low tide. Fall migration is especially productive here, with Rock Sandpipers in various plumages, as well as Ruddy Turnstones, both sometimes numbering in the hundreds during late July and August. Juvenile

Gray-tailed Tattlers and Red-necked Stints are annual on Salt Lagoon during this period. Red-necked Stints typically appear in fall on the mudflats and on any dried-up freshwater ponds on both islands. Wandering and Gray-tailed Tattlers occur in fall migration, but Wanderings are always more numerous. On the Pribilofs either species can occur on rocky or muddy shorelines, even inland on fresh water. Final determination of the identification of tattler species should be based on voice as well as on plumage.

Salt Lagoon frequently has a mixed flock of gulls and kittiwakes resting on mudflats. This is one of the best places to see Black-legged and Red-legged Kittiwakes side-by-side. Scope all gulls carefully for Black-headed, Vega Herring, Slaty-backed, and Sabine's. In spring, the mudflats often appear devoid of shorebirds. If you are very lucky, a Terek Sandpiper, Far Eastern Curlew, or Great Knot will appear, but you are more likely to find Bar-tailed Godwits, sometimes in substantial flocks. Don't ignore the back (north) end of Salt Lagoon, especially the area opposite Ice House Lake. This spot is good for tattlers in fall; spring rarities have included Common Greenshank and Common Sandpiper.

The sheltered area created by the crab pots and the low hills seems to be attractive to vagrant songbirds. In spring 2001, Hermit Thrush, Eyebrowed Thrush, Olive-backed Pipit, Gambel's White-crowned Sparrow, and Brambling were found here, along with breeding Hoary Redpolls, a first Pribilof nesting record. Short-eared Owls often forage over the hills in this vicinity. From here it is a half-hour walk back to town and twice that to the airport.

Red-legged Kittiwakes

THE SOUTHWEST ROAD

All mileages in the text start at the old King Eider Hotel. You will not find many mile-marker signs on the roads, so remember that any miles mentioned will be the distance from the hotel. An occasionally productive location for migrant birds is Kaminista Quarry. After turning left onto the Southwest Road at the base of Telegraph Hill (Mile 1.7), take the first right into the exposed rocky area. (Don't go here if quarry workers are present.) Check here early in the morning or later in the evening. Take the first left going through the rock piles and park where the road opens up a little.

The best spot to bird is around the pile of crab pots. Since 1997, many exciting discoveries have been made here, including Eyebrowed Thrush, Myrtle Warbler, Yellow Wagtail, American Tree Sparrow, Rustic Bunting, and Hoary Redpoll. However, the weather events that bring such exotic birds to these island outposts are few and far between.

The area behind the quarry itself and all of the inland tundra north of the Southwest Road provide breeding habitat for Lapland Longspurs and Snow Buntings. These beautiful, but rocky, meadows are difficult to navigate on foot, but many years ago they supported one or two breeding pairs of McKay's Buntings. Considerable time is needed to thoroughly cover such a wide area, and such forays are not advisable in foggy conditions because it is too easy to become disoriented and lose your way. Purebred nesting McKay's have not been found on Saint Paul for some years, and migrants are infrequent. Since few birds other than longspurs, buntings, and rosy-finches will be found on such strenuous treks, birders with limited time on the island might best focus their energies elsewhere.

Farther down the Southwest Road, Zapadni Fur Seal Blind (Mile 4.7) is on the left. From the blind scan the bay for loons, eiders, jaegers, and alcids. By making the short, but steep, walk up the hill opposite the blind, you reach Zapadni Ravine, another vagrant hot spot that should be checked daily between mid-May and mid-June and in late August and September. In recent years, Common Cuckoo, Siberian Rubythroat, Eyebrowed Thrush, Olive-backed Pipit, Brambling, and Common Rosefinch have all occurred.

Antone Lake (Mile 5.3) is an excellent location for shorebirds. Although probably less productive than in the past when water levels were higher, this area is still an essential stop and should accompany a morning spent at the Ridge Wall seabird cliffs. Check the lake, the slough that snakes through the former marsh, and a tiny pond hidden on the back side of the marshy area. Common Greenshank, Wood Sandpiper, Common Sandpiper, Gray-tailed Tattler, and Red-necked Stint have all been found here multiple times. Both Common Snipe and Wilson's Snipe can sometimes be flushed from Pribilof marshes in spring or fall. Brackish Antone Lake, although usually without waterfowl, has spring records of Eurasian Wigeon, Falcated Duck, Tufted Duck, and Smew. An influx of juvenile shorebirds in August makes exploring these and other Pribilof wetlands especially worthwhile.

Antone Lake is bordered to the west by a rocky causeway where Least Auklets have a small colony. Most sightings of Dovekies have been in the vicinity of these *chuuchkie* breeding sites. At the far end of the causeway a short but very steep climb leads to the Zapadni bird cliffs. For those who have difficulty climbing, the same birds are usually present only a few steps off the road at Ridge Wall. Again, great care should be taken to not disturb birds or seals. In spring 1998, Sky Larks were found inland and just northeast of the causeway.

In spring, the fog-shrouded cliffs of Ridge Wall host all of the locally breeding seabirds. Horned and Tufted Puffins jostle for space on the tightly packed cliff face. Directly across from the vantage point you will have side-by-side comparisons of Red-legged and Black-legged Kittiwakes and Common and Thick-billed Murres. The facial ornamentation of all three auklet species can also be easily viewed. The kittiwakes and murres are mostly responsible for the cacophony of sound that surrounds you. Although they frequently shift their semi-communal nesting sites, Red-faced Cormorants will likely be incubating eggs or feeding chicks near Ridge Wall when you visit. Northern Fulmars will soar by, following the contours of the cliffs as they perform their own reconnaissance for nesting crevices. Ridge Wall is 7.0 miles from the King Eider Hotel. Park on the gravel pad on the right and take the short path toward the cliff.

If it is not foggy and you don't mind a brisk hike, the walk inland from the gravel pad can be pleasant. The low ridge ahead shelters a small pond, Kittiwake Lake, that Red-legged Kittiwakes particularly favor, as well as a lava tube and natural arch where a male hybrid Snow x McKay's Bunting paired with a Snow Bunting has nested for the past several years. The area below this ridge has been a traditional location to look for pure McKay's Buntings. Very few have been found in recent years, but such searches have occasionally yielded vagrant Asiatic passerines. Chances are that during this walk your attention will be diverted by the many wildflowers present, including louseworts, saxifrages, and even Arctic Forget-me-not.

During southwest and northwest winds, Southwest Point is another excellent place from which to conduct a sea watch. From the point you can look north toward the beehive of activity at the peak of High Bluffs, where hordes of seabirds circle and call. If time allows, and especially if you are not visiting Saint George, the real flavor of the Pribilof bird cliffs can be fully experienced by walking from Southwest Point to the top of High Bluffs. Allow several hours for this walk so that you can enjoy the wildflowers and vistas along the way. Be sure to watch for the area known as Kittiwake Condos, where nesting Red-legged Kittiwakes are particularly numerous.

THE NORTHEAST ROAD

A series of freshwater wetlands beginning at the base of Telegraph Hill and extending past the airport should be checked daily during migration. Many of these lakes and ponds will have breeding ducks such as Northern Pintail, Common Teal, and Long-tailed Duck, as well as nesting Red-necked Phalarope. Most of the Green-winged Teal breeding on the Pribilofs are Common Teal, but you may see the more familiar North American race as well as hybrids and backcrosses between both forms.

The shallow waters of Pumphouse (Mile 2.4) and Rocky (Mile 2.7) Lakes are also good places to find Rock Sandpipers and some of the rarer shorebirds. First, scan these ponds and then walk around them to discover any secretive migrants. Such "pond tromps" can be exhausting and are not for everyone. Compared to the Alaskan tundra in other areas, however, Pribilof walks are relatively easy.

The entire range of small Asiatic stints—Red-necked, Little, Long-toed, and Temminck's—have been found at these Saint Paul hot spots. Wood Sandpiper, Common Sandpiper, Gray-tailed Tattler, and Black-tailed Godwit have also been seen here in spring. In fall, an influx of juvenile shorebirds means a relatively greater number of shorebirds can be expected in the wetlands. Sharp-tailed Sandpipers and Ruffs are regularly encountered during August and September. Adult Pacific Golden-Plovers are uncommon on Pribilof uplands after mid-July. Mongolian Plovers are sporadic in their occurrence, yet almost annual in spring or fall.

After checking Rocky Lake, drive past the Saint Paul airport (Mile 3.8) and turn right just before the Weather Service building complex to scan Weather Bureau Lake from the cul-de-sac. From late May into September a flock of kittiwakes, many of them Red-legged, rest and bathe on this lake. This spot is often the first place visited by the local tour bus after the plane arrives. Jaegers, especially Parasitics, regularly harass the kittiwake flocks. Watch for Long-tailed Duck, Bufflehead, and Common Goldeneye. Common Pochard, Tufted Duck, and Smew have occurred in recent springs, but are not to be expected. Slaty-backed Gulls have been found here more than once.

A sandy road extends from Weather Bureau Lake to Tonki Point and leads to a series of unnamed wetlands that snake through the dunes almost to Polovina Point. Many of the aforementioned species might be flushed here or from the marshy west side of Polovina Lake. The flat tundra between the airport and Polovina Lake had breeding Sky Larks in the spring of 1995.

See sidebar on next page for a possible side-trip from this location.

If you have extra time and if it is before 1 June, back on the Northeast Road turn right at Mile 5.1 and park where this track forks to the right. Walk

SIDE-TRIP TO MARUNICH

A possible side trip from the airport area is the 5-mile-long road to Marunich and the North Point area. Begin at the intersection of the road leading to the airport terminal (3.6 miles from town on the Northeast Road; see map). It is a 30-minute drive from here to North Point, if you don't get lost in the confusing maze of tracks in the center of the island. It is best to obtain a local map (the aerial pictures hanging in the hotel might help) or to get directions from locals, and to travel only on well-defined roads. The road to Marunich changes from crushed volcanic scoria gravel to sand, making four-wheel drive advisable.

Along the way, Lake Hill can be a pleasant but often birdless stop. A small, privately-owned cabin marks the end of the road at Marunich. The tiny pond below the cabin is always worth checking. On the nearby coast Pelagic and Red-faced Cormorants are often found on the bare lava promontories. Carefully check the kelp beach here for shorebirds—southbound Ruddy Turnstones often are found at this spot during the first week of July. A long beach hike in either direction may yield tattlers. Scan the sea for loons, grebes, eiders, scoters, and alcids. North Point is an excellent place to sit and wait for jaegers to pass by.

For adventurous hikers, the half-day walk from Marunich to Southwest Point takes you past some of the most beautiful and remote areas on Saint Paul. Most birders prefer to travel this route from west to east after visiting the High Bluffs during the earlier part of the day. Try to arrange to be picked up at whichever spot you plan to finish your hike.

toward Polovina Point, where you can do a sea watch or explore the intertidal area. The best viewing is at low tide, when the exposed basalt provides a resting place for eiders, occasional shorebirds, and gulls. Storm-tossed driftwood just south of this point—or anywhere on the Pribilofs—might shelter songbirds.

Past Polovina Point the Northeast Road traverses several miles of fairly nondescript tundra. The peninsula that juts to the northeast past Big Lake (Miles 7.9–9.4) is one of the best places to search for vagrants during migration. Just past the end of the lake and up the hill on the left is Fantasy Wetland (use the pullout at Mile 9.9). The thick growth of rushes requires a thorough reconnaissance (wear your rubber boots); even then the birds, usually Common Teal and a variety of shorebirds, will probably flush before you can get a good look at them. Wood Sandpiper and Ruff are possible in late August. In mid-May 1998, a Taiga Bean Goose was seen here. Both subspecies of Bean Goose are possible on the Pribilofs.

Around the corner an interesting dune formation dominates on the right. In spring, and after heavy rains, the ephemeral pool created below here can attract shorebirds, kittiwakes, and other gulls. Semipalmated Plovers and

Least Sandpipers have been regular breeders in this area during recent years and often can be heard and seen displaying.

Carefully check both sides of the road between Fantasy Wetland and Webster House for migrants during spring and fall. From 15 May to 15 June, depressions here may hold water that attracts shorebirds. This narrow isthmus is known as Novastoshna, Russian for "new land," and it is an excellent area in which to observe the waterfowl and jaegers that pass over this bridge of sand or stop to rest. Drivers beware—both sides of the road along this stretch consist of soft sand that can quickly bury a vehicle to its axles. In late June almost the entire isthmus is carpeted in the small white-flowered Rock Jasmine.

On the morning of 18 May 1998 birders traveling this road witnessed a truly impressive fallout of Asiatic birds. Scores of Wood Sandpipers and dozens of Long-toed Stints lifted off from Fantasy Wetland and Novastoshna to fight the strong southwest wind. Several Bramblings were flushed from the road en route to Webster House. In Webster Lake were Eurasian Wigeons, Common Pochards, and Tufted Ducks, and three Common Greenshanks circled and called. On the way to Hutchinson Hill an Eyebrowed Thrush was seen. At the top of the hill, a Sky Lark sang and displayed. This area has proven to be the most consistent place to find rare birds on Saint Paul Island. If you are determined to squeeze in one more hour of birding before leaving Saint Paul, check this area on your final morning on the island.

Although good for sea-watching, Northeast Point is not particularly productive for alcids in late spring and summer. Prior to 1 June, however, good movements of eiders, murres, and auklets can be observed. There is a small Least Auklet colony at the outermost point. In winter, large daily and seasonal movements of Crested Auklets and Common Murres sometimes occur on northeast and east winds; the passing swarms occasionally number several thousand birds per minute.

Turn left after traversing Novastoshna and park beside Webster House (Mile 11.0). From late July into October, Red Phalaropes in various stages of molt rest and feed in Webster Lake. Occasionally several hundred to a few thousand join the locally-breeding Red-necked Phalaropes. Scan the lake, then walk around it. Shorebirds such as Wood Sandpiper or Long-billed Dowitcher may be on the back side of the lake during spring and fall, and both American and Eurasian Wigeons can remain out of sight in the partially submerged vegetation. All of Saint Paul's rare ducks have occurred here, including a pair of Falcated Ducks in 1995, Common Pochards in 1998, and Smew on several occasions. Greater Scaup and Bufflehead sometimes oversummer here, and in early spring King Eiders may rest on the rocks on the far shore. In short, Webster Lake is the best spot on Saint Paul for waterfowl.

The area immediately around Webster House has reliably yielded vagrant passerine species over the years. At least six records of Siberian Rubythroat have occurred in this area. Eurasian cuckoo species, Hermit Thrush, Olive-backed and Red-throated Pipits, Yellow Wagtail, Savannah Sparrow, Brambling, and Hawfinch have been seen in the past decade. Regardless of which side of the Bering Sea such vagrants may have originated, observers should report all unusual sightings to both local guides and state compilers.

A short, winding path leads across the road and dune opposite Webster House to an excellent seabird scanning point. On 1 June, when the seal rookery and most of Northeast Point are closed to public access, this is often the best spot to look for loons, grebes, and eiders. Yellow-billed Loons in various plumages are frequently sighted here from 20 May into June. Harlequin Ducks are always present off the rocky point. Interesting gulls, especially Slaty-backed, and jaegers might be seen flying by or resting on the beach during spring and fall migrations.

Before 1 June, when a barrier is erected on the road just beyond Webster House, there are a couple options as one travels toward the point. Turning right at Mile 11.7 onto a non-maintained road leads to a small bay and Sea Lion Neck, a narrow point of rocks where local hunters may sometimes be found on weekend mornings in spring. (Do not go to the point if hunters are present.) Local hunting generally ceases at the same time rookeries are closed at the beginning of June, however, Aleuts do this voluntarily and in deference to visitors, not because they are required to.

The wide bay here may have loons, grebes, or if you are very lucky, Steller's Eiders. From here you may walk (15 October–31 May) about one-half mile east toward another hunting blind in the midst of a small Least Auklet colony. You can also drive to that point and have a pick-up at the other end. En route a wet swale could hold resting shorebirds in spring. This entire windswept plain can be good for Bristle-thighed Curlew and Snowy Owl during May. Spreading out your party usually helps to flush any birds camouflaged in the brown vegetation and field of *poochkie* (Wild Celery – *Angelica lucida*). Such strategy turned up a stunning male Siberian Rubythroat on 31 May 1994.

Keep in mind that even before 1 June many male fur seals, especially large dominating ones (beachmasters), arrive on beaches almost anywhere on the islands. These seals are dark, and when wet they are almost the color of rocks in the vicinity. After a long winter of pelagic existence, they are usually sleeping and hence not moving. Although encountering a seal usually results in both seal and human quickly retreating in opposite directions, a true beachmaster may stand his ground. Over rocky territory they can move much faster than you can for short distances. You will not forget your first encounter with these magnificent animals! Because they are on the federally endangered species list, any disturbance of the seals' natural behavior could result in severe penalties.

By taking the first left beyond Webster House, you will reach the seal rookery on the north side of the point. After less than one-quarter mile, veer to the left at the fork and look toward your right. During early spring another wet swale here can hold shorebirds and ducks. Bean and Greater White-fronted Geese have been seen here in late May. A tight cul-de-sac loop is your turnaround. From here you could walk up Hutchinson Hill, or you could drive up by returning to the main road, turning left, and then taking the next left that goes about one-quarter mile up the hill. Again, these are options only before 1 June or after 15 October. During summer, a permit may be obtained (see *Logistics*) to view seals both here and at Reef Point. Seal rookery boundaries are signed, and conservation officers are vigilant about intruders. Basically, if a seal can see you, you've gone too far.

Hutchinson Hill barely qualifies as a hill, but it does offer a panoramic view of the entire Northeast Point. This is a great spot for sea watching to the north and to the east and for rarities in any season. During summer the area is lush, green, and frequently carpeted in wildflowers. This promontory has also compiled an impressive record of vagrant passerines—from 1993–2001 the

Lesser Yellowlegs

list included Common Cuckoo, Red-breasted Flycatcher, Siberian Rubythroat, Red-flanked Bluetail, Eyebrowed Thrush, Yellow Wagtail, Brambling, and McKay's Bunting, not to mention many North American species, from Ruby-crowned Kinglet to Wilson's Warbler. Almost all of these birds were first spotted in the small turnaround at the end of the road just before it reaches the top of the hill. If you drive here, it is wise to either get out of your vehicle before reaching this point and walk, carefully peering around the corner and "into" the hill, or to drive up very slowly, looking to the left for any movement. Walk to the top of the hill—a very short distance—marked by a lone sailor's grave. The headstone is a favorite perch for migrating Snowy Owls in early spring. Scan the sea, the seal rookery, and the wooden catwalks, and walk around the hilltop to discover any hidden birds. Again, how far you can walk depends on the date. By mid-summer, young seals have pushed almost to the top of the hill.

Go back down the hill, turn left, and walk or drive the remainder of the road as it turns toward the southeast. In May, a flock of Pacific Golden-Plovers frequents the area, sometimes joined by Ruddy Turnstones and Dunlins. Again, watch for Bristle-thighed Curlews. Although both the North American and the Eurasian races of Whimbrel are still the expected curlew, Bristle-thighed occurs sporadically every few years on the Pribilofs, sometimes in numbers. Both species respond to even feeble imitations of their calls, so it can't hurt to try this method if a bird is flying away.

The end of this road is usually muddy, so stop well in advance. This is another good spot for sea watching, and the rock blind built by Aleut hunters testifies to its strategic location. If no one is hunting, proceed to the shore. During mornings in May you will be joined by chattering flocks of Least and a few Parakeet Auklets nervously alighting not far from you. In winter the vantage point here can be amazing, with huge Crested Auklet flocks resembling giant bee swarms coalescing in loose balls and stringing out in seemingly infinite lines. If you have not already done so, the walk to Sea Lion Point lies one-half mile to the southwest.

Snowy Owl

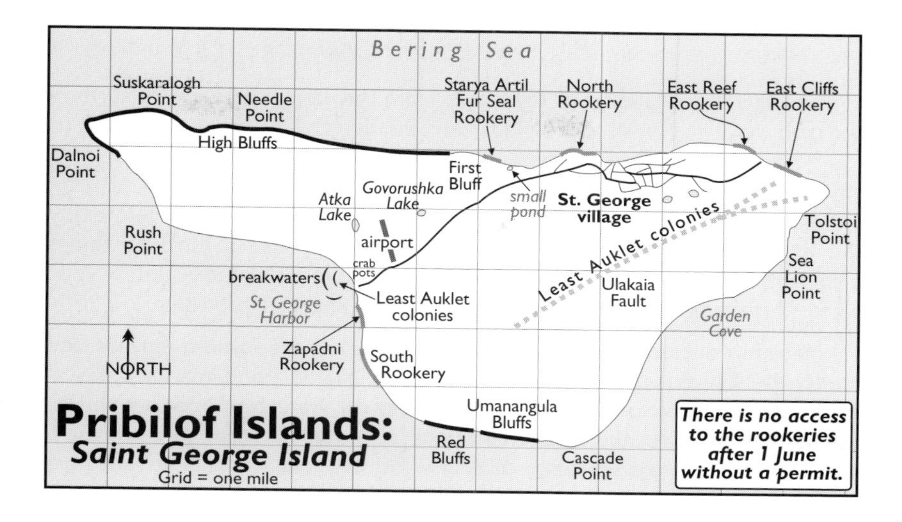

SAINT GEORGE ISLAND

Saint George Island is summer home to the greatest biomass of seabirds nesting in Alaska, due primarily to the huge colonies of Thick-billed Murres that number over one million. Saint George is smaller, higher, and geologically older than Saint Paul. The island is dominated by boulder-strewn tundra and steep cliff faces. Sandy beaches, frequently encountered on Saint Paul, are at a premium here. Basically only a single 7-mile road bisects Saint George, so birders should be prepared for strenuous, but rewarding hiking.

At the west end of this road is the airport (no phone or facilities) and harbor area. The picturesque village of Saint George, at the east end of the maintained road, features a small grocery store and the quaint Aikow Inn.

Getting to the southernmost Pribilof Island can sometimes be an ordeal. The runway is shorter and has a more difficult approach. Be prepared for delays getting to and getting off the island, often to the tune of waiting days, not just hours.

Saint George offers one of the greatest seabird spectacles in the world. A hike up the High Bluffs towards Needle Point can be a birder's dream come-true, with the circling flocks of fulmars and kittiwakes, the shoulder-to-shoulder masses of murres, and the clouds of auklets set amidst a magnificent seascape of towering 1,000-foot cliffs.

BIRDING LOCATIONS

To reach Saint George's High Bluffs from the village, take a right turn off the main road just west of the old airport buildings. This short road leads to the Starya Artil Fur Seal Rookery. Alternatively, you could walk north from any point along the main road as it traverses the island's central plateau. Either option requires at least half a day, and preferably a full one, to fully enjoy the experience. Bring some food, water, and in case fog makes things disorienting, a compass. Dress in layers and let someone in town know your plans. Arranging for a vehicle pick-up may help shorten your hike.

Many birders ascend the bluffs via Starya Artil, where some steep hills lead up to the highest cliffs. A small, driftwood-ringed pond marks the seal rookery itself and provides a sheltered refuge for waterfowl and shorebirds. Remember to give any seal rookery a wide berth from June through mid-October. The abundance of driftwood may occasionally attract rare passerines and other birds. A male Great Spotted Woodpecker drummed on storm-tossed logs here in May 2001. At any rate, enjoy your last look at birds near sea level—the next few hours will be spent high above. Also, remember that despite the multitudes of seabirds and the impression of a healthy ecosystem, many of these species, including Red-legged Kittiwakes and both murres, have been in a population decline since the mid-1970s.

Least Auklets arrive en masse in April, often flying over, around, and through town on route to Ulakaia Ridge. Here, one mile from the sea, they breed on the talus slopes of the island. To reach Ulakaia Ridge, walk behind the village and follow the flocks of auklets inland. At the base of the ridge tens of thousands of chattering auklets create an almost ear-splitting crescendo. Individual flocks of hundreds of birds lift off to perform aerial pirouettes, only to land again, sometimes quite close to you. In late spring and early summer, auklets frequent remnant patches of snow where breeding displays featuring "take-downs" and "tumble-rolls" can be enjoyed.

By hiking directly uphill on the ridge across to the south side of the island, you can experience another lovely day-trip. You will traverse much Snow Bunting habitat—remember to check for McKay's and hybrids. One of the few spots on Saint George that offers a sandy beach is Garden Cove. Both this hike and the hike up High Bluffs will require much more exertion than most seabird watching found on Saint Paul.

Other places to check on Saint George include any ponds and lakes, especially those directly behind the village and Govorushka Lake. Any of the rarer shorebirds is possible, but Wood Sandpiper, Gray-tailed Tattler, Bar-tailed Godwit, and Sharp-tailed Sandpiper are, in season, the most-expected Asiatics. Even though some Palearctic and Holarctic species are more likely to occur in the Bering region than are North American species, birders should carefully eliminate all possibilities before jumping to conclusions.

Govorushka Lake is undoubtedly the most inviting body of fresh water on Saint George for waterfowl and waders. Red-legged Kittiwakes can also be found loafing on the gravel pad adjacent to the lake—this artificial pad was constructed specifically for the kittiwakes in order to entice them away from roosting on the airport runway.

Driftwood areas at East Cliffs Rookery and adjacent to the harbor should be thoroughly checked. Least Auklets have adopted the boulder breakwaters in the harbor as suitable nesting habitat. Most Dovekies observed on the Pribilofs have been with *chuuchkie* flocks, and colonies should be scrutinized accordingly. Saint George harbor hosted a Falcated Duck in June 1986. Carefully examine the crab pots here for skulking passerines.

Despite the extra time and expense, Saint George Island is one of the most delightful and remote birding experiences in Alaska. It has a very different atmosphere than "busy" Saint Paul Island. If at all possible, try to visit both islands, but if only one can be included in your Alaska tour, Saint Paul is the logical choice—for accessibility, amenities, and overall birding opportunities. Nonetheless, if it is sheer numbers and a seabird spectacle that you are after, then go to the cliffs of Saint George.

Northern Fur Seal beachmaster

LOGISTICS

The area code for all telephone numbers is 907 unless otherwise indicated. The Pribolofs are not covered in The Milepost. *For your convenience, extensive information about accommodations and local transportation is listed below. Statewide travel and birding information services are listed under Logistics in the* Introduction, *page 15.)*

The Pribilofs are part of the Alaska Maritime National Wildlife Refuge and all seabird nesting cliffs and colonies are administered by the U.S. Fish and Wildlife Service. The islands also make up the Seal Islands National Historic Landmark, the official designation given to them by the National Oceanographic and Atmospheric Administration (NOAA). This affiliation with the Department of Commerce is a telling one, for it has been the seals that have provided a source of great income for governments and private companies over the years, but only a meager one for the Aleut Pribilovians themselves. NOAA Fisheries, along with island stewards, administer and regulate the seal rookeries.

Human economic activity has continued to negatively impact the region into the 21st century. When visiting the seal rookeries during the summer, you must either be accompanied by a registered NOAA guide or you must obtain a permit (see below). Access to the bird cliffs is not regulated. Dogs are not permitted on the Pribilofs. Isolation, wind, and climate prevent biting insects such as mosquitoes from breeding. And, for obvious reasons, there are no bears present.

Land holdings away from the villages, bird cliffs, and seal rookeries are owned almost entirely by the Native Aleut village corporations. On Saint George the corporation is Tanaq; on Saint Paul, Tanadgusix (TDX) Corporation runs the Saint Paul Island Tour as a small part of its business ventures. Whether or not you are on this or any other tour, visitors are welcome to explore the islands' natural and cultural heritage. There is no fee imposed for walking on the tundra. Aleuts are friendly and willing to share information. Nevertheless, common courtesy and respect for all the local inhabitants will only increase the enjoyment of your visit. Read and follow the guidelines about Native Alaskan Cultures in the *Introduction*, page 10.

Most major birding-tour companies and some smaller ones include Saint Paul in their Alaskan itineraries, often as an extension before or after their mainland component. It's not difficult to arrange a trip to the Pribilofs on your own. TDX Corporation packages their Saint Paul Island Tour with regional airlines. As well as round-trip airfare, this package includes hotel, ground transportation, guide services, and generally everything but meals (usually easily obtained on Saint Paul), as part of the price. Organized groups, birding-tour companies, and individual birders all take part in this tour. Bird-location information is shared, and every effort is made to ensure that everyone sees rarities. The guides hired to lead visiting birders on these trips are usually experienced with the local birds. If you time your visit for migration, most others on the tour will be ardent birders hoping to see not only the regular Pribilof specialties, but also any Asiatics.

Basically, you have three choices: 1) go with an organized commercial tour, 2) purchase the same TDX tour as an independent birder (many do), or 3) organize a group through your local bird club. A group of 10 or more often gets to set its own itinerary while on the island. Call 877-424-5637 or fax 278-2316 to ask for a brochure and a free bird list. In 2002, this packaged tour cost $1,361 for 3 days/2 nights and $1,570 for 4 days/3 nights. Check the website at *www.alaskabirding.com* for current information.

If you go on your own, remember that primitive tent-camping is permitted, but only near the wind-swept and precarious cliff edges managed by the U.S. Fish and Wildlife Service.

Saint George does not have any organized tour set-up and you must visit there on your own. This requires reserving a long, interesting plane trip during which the itinerary might change according to weather, mail, weight, and other matters that are sometimes never fully explained. Patience and a good book will make your trip much more enjoyable. You will also need to make hotel and truck-rental (if available) reservations for Saint George. Call Tanaq Corporation at their Anchorage number, 272-9886, or fax them at 272-9855. There are kitchen facilities at the Aikow Inn and a small grocery store in town. Saint Paul also has a grocery store as well as an ATM machine. Many birders have made their own Pribilof itineraries and have had a great time.

Transportation: As of late 2001, Peninsula Airways was the only commercial airline with regular passenger service to the Pribilofs. This trip runs around $830 round-trip from Anchorage. The fare for flying between the islands is $70. Contact them at 800-448-4226; *www.penair.com*. Local PenAir phone numbers are 546-2460 on Saint Paul and 859-2239 on Saint George. Also inquire about their tours and charters.

Accommodations: Hotel costs on the islands range between $100–200 per person, per night.

Saint Paul — King Eider Hotel (546-2477 or 546-2312).

Saint George — Aikow Inn, contact Tanaq (272-9886).

Vehicle Rental: Rental trucks are sometimes available from the Native corporations and range over $100/day.

Saint Paul — TDX (546-2477); Biff Baker (546-2420).

Saint George — Tanaq (859-2255 in Saint George; 272-9886 in Anchorage).

Permits to view seals at Reef Fur Seal Rookery and Northeast Point Rookery on Saint Paul are free with a lecture from Ecosystem Conservation Office (546-2641).

NOAA Fisheries — 546-2626.

Weather Service — 546-2215.

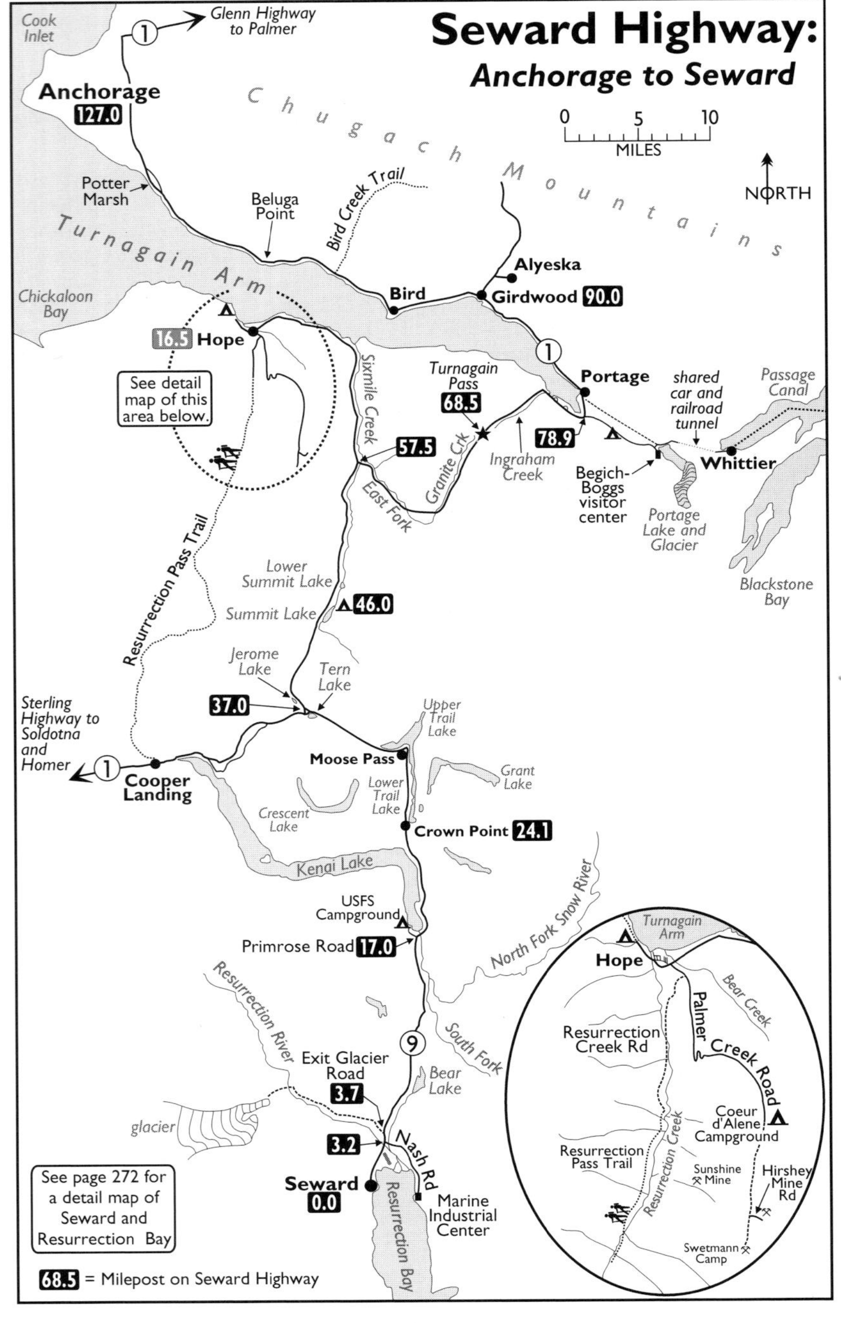

Seward Highway:
Anchorage to Seward
0 5 10
MILES
NORTH
Cook Inlet
Glenn Highway to Palmer
Anchorage
127.0
Chugach Mountains
Potter Marsh
Beluga Point
Bird Creek Trail
Turnagain Arm
Chickaloon Bay
Alyeska
Bird
Girdwood 90.0
16.5 Hope
See detail map of this area below.
Sixmile Creek
Turnagain Pass
68.5
Portage
shared car and railroad tunnel
Passage Canal
57.5
78.9
Ingraham Creek
Granite Crk
East Fork
Begich-Boggs visitor center
Whittier
Portage Lake and Glacier
Blackstone Bay
Resurrection Pass Trail
Lower Summit Lake
Summit Lake
46.0
Jerome Lake
Tern Lake
37.0
Upper Trail Lake
Sterling Highway to Soldotna and Homer
Moose Pass
Grant Lake
Cooper Landing
Lower Trail Lake
Crescent Lake
Crown Point 24.1
Kenai Lake
USFS Campground
Primrose Road 17.0
North Fork Snow River
Resurrection River
South Fork
Exit Glacier Road
3.7
Bear Lake
glacier
3.2
Nash Rd
Seward
0.0
Resurrection Bay
Marine Industrial Center
See page 272 for a detail map of Seward and Resurrection Bay
68.5 = Milepost on Seward Highway
Turnagain Arm
Hope
Bear Creek
Palmer Creek Road
Resurrection Creek Rd
Coeur d'Alene Campground
Resurrection Pass Trail
Resurrection Creek
Sunshine Mine
Hirshey Mine Rd
Swetmann Camp

KENAI PENINSULA

George West

The Kenai Peninsula is a microcosm of Alaska, including all habitats except high-arctic tundra. If you have limited time or a tight travel budget, a few days to a week on the Kenai is a good way to enjoy a taste of birding in Alaska. Perhaps the most profitable way to spend time birding here is along the coast, either at Seward or Homer. Both have excellent opportunities to get out on the water to find seabirds and marvel at the glaciers, fjords, and mountain scenery these venues have to offer.

From Whittier, Seward, or Homer you can catch one of the Alaska state ferries to reach other places in southcoastal Alaska, from Cordova to Dutch Harbor (page 323), and one ferry will take you from Seward down to Juneau (page 453).

If you are heading to Seward from Anchorage, you can either fly, drive, or take the Alaska Railroad. Although you can fly directly from Anchorage to Seward, Kenai, and Homer, you will miss a lot of the birding and scenery the road system has to offer. The train makes two daily round-trips between Anchorage and Seward. It also makes a side-trip from Portage to Whittier. Be sure to make reservations for the train in advance. The train is slow but gives you a nice overview of the habitats from Anchorage through Girdwood, along Turnagain Arm past the Portage area, and over the pass into Seward. You can get off about anywhere you wish and then get back on again going either north or south (remember that trains pass by only a few times a day).

Both the Seward and Sterling Highway milepost markers start in Seward (Milepost 0). The Seward Highway leads north 127 miles to Anchorage (Milepost 127). The Sterling Highway runs north to Tern Lake (Milepost 37), west to Soldotna (Milepost 126), then south to Homer (Milepost 174).

ANCHORAGE TO PORTAGE

After leaving Anchorage on the Seward Highway (Alaska Route 1), be sure to stop at Potter Marsh to scan for grebes, geese, ducks, gulls, and Rusty and Red-winged Blackbirds (page 34). Around Turnagain Arm, check Beluga Point for Beluga Whales and the rocks across the highway for Dall's Sheep that frequently come to the roadside to a mineral source. You can tell if sheep are present—there will be a line of cars and RVs parked in the pullout to the right and people with cameras crossing the road. Stop at the bridge over Indian Creek (Milepost 103) to look for American Dippers under the bridge and in the fast-flowing stream. At Girdwood, Milepost 90, you may turn left into the Alyeska resort area and ride the chair lift to the top of the ski area, or you can try to find locally very rare Chestnut-backed Chickadees. The Girdwood area is the farthest northwestern extent of the Pacific coastal rain forest, the habitat preferred by Rufous Hummingbird and Chestnut-backed Chickadee. In summer, look also for Steller's Jay, Red-breasted Nuthatch, Townsend's Warbler, Pine Grosbeak, and White-winged Crossbill (irregular). Note the avalanche chutes on the north side of the Seward Highway from here to Seward. Avalanches are common in winter and spring when the snow softens.

There are numerous ponds and flats along the highway to Portage. Turn left (east) at Milepost 78.9 (48.1 miles from Anchorage) to visit Portage Glacier and the Begich-Boggs Visitor Center (operated by Chugach National Forest). You can view icebergs on the lake, look for Harlequin Ducks and Common Mergansers in the salmon streams along the road, or scan for Golden Eagles along the ridge tops. There are several hiking trails here; inquire at the visitor center.

Whittier

The road to Whittier on Prince William Sound leads east from the junction of the road to Portage Glacier. You may have to wait in line up to 45 minutes to drive through the one-way car/railroad tunnel, the only overland access to Whittier. The tunnel is 2.5 miles long and the entire road to Whittier is only 5.5 miles. The only accommodation in Whittier is the Anchor Inn, and there are no camping sites available.

There is little point in driving to Whittier unless you plan to take one of the State ferries, either the *Tustumena* to Valdez (page 132), or the *Bartlett* to Valdez and Cordova (page 373). Check the State ferry office for schedules (see *Introduction*, page 15).

Portage to Tern Lake

As you continue on the Seward Highway around the end of Turnagain Arm, note the dead spruce trees on both sides of the road. The largest earthquake recorded in North America (9.2 on the Richter scale) hit Valdez and Seward in March 1964 with severe damage to all coastal communities, including Anchorage. Here it caused Turnagain Arm to subside several feet, allowing the influx of saltwater that killed the trees. Between Mileposts 78 to 75, scan the grass and tidal flats on the right (north) for spring-migrating geese, swans, and cranes. Trumpeter Swans have nested here in recent years. Scan the shallow ponds on the south for grebes, swans, ducks, gulls, and Arctic

Terns. Traffic can be very heavy, so if you pull off to the side of the road, keep clear of traffic, but do not drive off the gravel shoulder. You can use the two pullouts along the straight stretch of highway toward its west end.

The highway crosses Ingram Creek and climbs a long hill to Turnagain Pass (elevation 988 feet; Milepost 68.5), almost in the alpine zone. In winter, when snow depths can exceed 12 feet, the large parking area on the west is heavily used by snowmachiners and the one on the east side by cross-country skiers. Birding is generally slow here, but rarely Willow Ptarmigan are present. No formal trails lead from here into the high country, but hiking is fairly easy. It may be better to go to Hope, however, if you wish to hike into the alpine.

At Milepost 64, you will begin to see dead spruce trees that have been killed by Spruce Bark Beetles. Since 1992 these beetles have devastated the whole Kenai Peninsula. Most of the mature spruce trees have been killed, although the younger trees have proven to be more resistant.

HOPE

If you wish to drive into the alpine or explore an old gold-mining village, turn north onto the Hope Highway that exits to the right at Milepost 57.5 (69.5 miles from Anchorage). The road follows Sixmile Creek north to Turnagain Arm. The creek once supported a profitable gold-mining operation in the late 1800s and early 1900s. Amateur prospectors still take their portable dredges, sluice boxes, and gold pans to search for gold among the boulders and fast water in this creek. The old village of Sunrise City is at Mile 7, but is barely discernible. From here, the highway turns west along Turnagain Arm, passing several pullouts between Miles 9 and 11. You may look for the Beluga Whales that sometimes cruise the shoreline during summer, but do not walk out on the mudflats (see Cautions in the *Introduction*, page 19). At Mile 16, just past Bear Creek (and the store, motel, and RV park), turn left at the sign for Resurrection Pass Trailhead. This gravel road (Palmer Creek Road) runs south and makes a sharp right turn after about a mile onto Resurrection Creek Road. At the turn, the smaller road that continues straight ahead is the continuation of Palmer Creek Road leading to Coeur d'Alene campground (tents and picnics only).

Palmer Creek Road is a 6.4-mile winding, narrow, gravel road with several hairpin turns that takes you into the alpine between the Sixmile Creek valley to the east and the Resurrection Creek valley to the west, the most accessible alpine habitat on the Kenai Peninsula. The road is not recommended for trailers or larger RVs. An unmaintained gravel road continues about five miles past the campground and in good weather it can be driven with a regular car for about four miles; four-wheel drive is recommended if you wish to drive the last mile. Once above tree line, you may climb the steep hills on foot to look for alpine birds (and flowers). Near the end of the road watch for Hirshey Mine road zig-zagging up the hill to the left immediately beyond the Palmer Creek crossing. This jeep road provides relatively easy access to the alpine, where you might find all three species of ptarmigan, possibly Golden Eagle, American Pipit, Northern Wheatear, Wilson's Warbler, American Tree Sparrow, Golden-crowned Sparrow, Common Redpoll, and others. Look for Willow Ptarmigan at lower elevations in alder, willow, and grass/sedge habitat; Rock Ptarmigan will be higher in rocky slopes; and White-tailed prefers the highest elevations. The Hirshey Mine is located near the top of the ridge. Its 1911 discovery set off the major gold rush in this area, and it was the most consistent lode-gold producer of the Kenai Peninsula.

There are a few informal campsites on the road and good views of Beaver activity in Palmer Creek below the road. There is extensive willow and alder brush, lots of Mountain Ash and Pacific Red Elder, some stands of High-bush Cranberry, and many species of wildflowers in July.

Return to the junction of Palmer Creek and Resurrection Creek Roads. If you turn left, the rough gravel road leads about 4.5 miles to Resurrection Creek where you may pan for gold and visit tourist attractions or start a 38-mile hike from the Resurrection Creek Trailhead over the mountains to Cooper Landing. Back at the junction of Palmer Creek Road and the Hope Highway, turn left to explore the old mining town that has several buildings constructed in the 1890s. Hope was the first gold-rush town in Alaska, established in 1889, years before Dawson or Nome, when a man named King found gold nuggets in Resurrection Creek. Hope had a population of over 3,000 before Anchorage even existed. Now the population is fewer than 200.

You can reach the shore of Turnagain Arm at "Main Street" (unmarked), which is the last north-south gravel street to the west before Resurrection Creek. Turn right (north; past a cafe, general store, social hall) and park before getting your vehicle near the slimy mud that borders Turnagain Arm. Scan from a grassy area for cranes and waterfowl or hike along the edge of the fields. Do not walk on the mud. There is a clean campground across Resurrection Creek at the end of the Hope Highway (17.8 miles from the junction with the Seward Highway) and two trails from the campground.

Return to the Seward Highway, turn right (south), and drive up the hill to the broad pass that holds first Lower, then Upper Summit Lakes. These shallow lakes may have loons and a few ducks or swans. At Milepost 46 stop at Tenderfoot Campground to look at a Bald Eagle nest in one of the large cottonwood trees near the lake. Summit Lake Lodge has a good restaurant on the lake. Continue south along the pass with boggy lakes and creeks, looking for the trailhead sign to the Devil's Pass trail on the right (west) just north of Jerome Lake. A hike across Quartz Creek and up the trail paralleling Devil's Creek about 10 miles to Devil's Pass (Forest Service cabin at the top) may yield nesting Wandering Tattler and Northern Wheatear. Back on the highway, check Jerome Lake for goldeneyes or fish for stocked Rainbow Trout. Then continue to the junction of the Sterling Highway to the right (Alaska Route 1 to Soldotna and Homer) with the Seward Highway straight ahead (Alaska Route 9 to Seward). If you miss the turn to Homer, you can still turn right at the bottom of the hill at Tern Lake.

TERN LAKE TO SEWARD

South of Tern Lake (Milepost 37, Anchorage 90; described on page 279), the Seward Highway passes through steep-sided mountains (avalanche danger in spring), along Upper and Lower Trail Lakes, and through the villages of Moose Pass and Crown Point on its way to Kenai Lake. Along this route many trails lead into the mountains on both sides of the road. The Trail Lakes and their feeder streams provide the main source of glacial water for Kenai Lake and the Kenai River. There are many salmon-spawning streams that drain into Kenai Lake, but salmon fishing is prohibited in the entire Kenai Lake system. Birding on Kenai Lake is discussed in the section on the Sterling Highway (page 279). The Alaska Railroad parallels the Seward Highway from Moose Pass south to Seward. The Snow River empties into Kenai Lake under the bridge between Mileposts 17 and 18. Just past the bridge on the right (west) is an access road to Primrose Campground and Trailhead, a good place to camp for exploring this area.

At Milepost 12.7 a scenic pullout on the east has views of the North and South Forks of Snow River. During summer, Olive-sided Flycatchers nest in the clearcut below the pullout. The highway climbs to about Milepost 12 and then drops into the Resurrection River valley through steep-sided mountains covered with Sitka Spruce and Western and Mountain Hemlocks—part of the northernmost extent of the Pacific coastal rain forest.

The turnoff to Exit Glacier (Kenai Fjords National Park) is at Milepost 3.7. A 10-mile gravel road parallels the Resurrection River, ending at a trailhead, where you can walk to the face or onto the tongue of the receding glacier. Western Screech-Owl (rare in southcoastal Alaska) is sometimes heard along this road, although Great Horned, Boreal, and Northern Saw-whet Owls are the more common species. Owl nest-boxes have been placed every half-mile from the national forest boundary to the Resurrection River bridge. At the bridge, you could find nesting American Dippers.

Return to the highway and continue toward Seward. Turn left (east) onto Nash Road (Milepost 3.2), which leads 5.5 miles to the Marine Industrial Center on Resurrection Bay. In recent years a pair of Hooded Mergansers has frequented a pond at this intersection. As you drive along, scan the marshes and ponds for ducks and, in migration, geese and swans. Stop at a

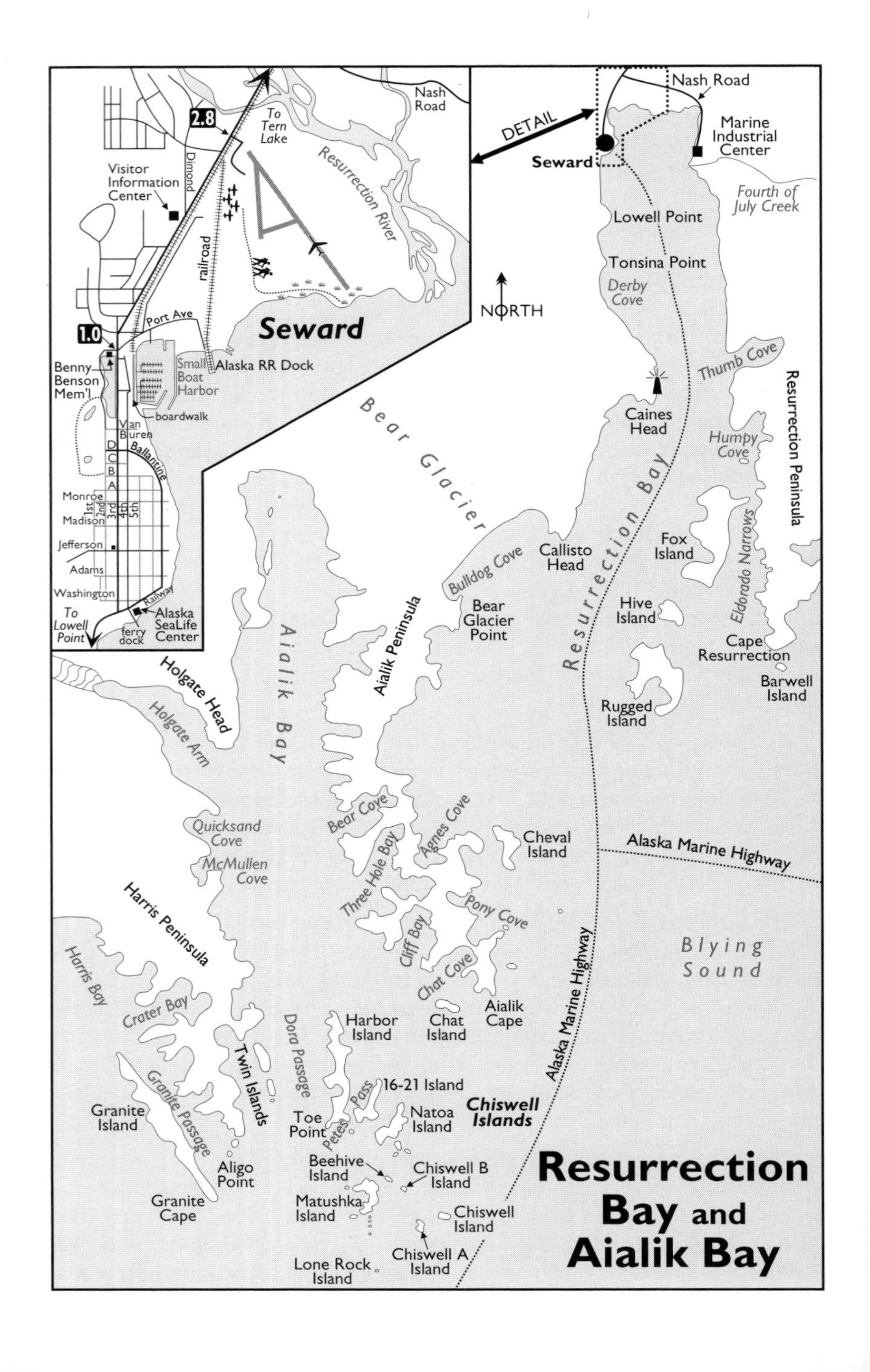
Resurrection Bay and Aialik Bay
Seward
DETAIL
NORTH
Nash Road
Marine Industrial Center
Fourth of July Creek
Lowell Point
Tonsina Point
Derby Cove
Thumb Cove
Caines Head
Humpy Cove
Resurrection Peninsula
Resurrection Bay
Fox Island
Eldorado Narrows
Callisto Head
Hive Island
Cape Resurrection
Barwell Island
Rugged Island
Bear Glacier
Bulldog Cove
Bear Glacier Point
Aialik Peninsula
Aialik Bay
Holgate Head
Holgate Arm
Bear Cove
Agnes Cove
Three Hole Bay
Cheval Island
Alaska Marine Highway
Quicksand Cove
McMullen Cove
Harris Peninsula
Pony Cove
Cliff Bay
Chat Cove
Blying Sound
Harris Bay
Crater Bay
Aialik Cape
Harbor Island
Chat Island
Dora Passage
Twin Islands
16-21 Island
Granite Passage
Petes Pass
Chiswell Islands
Natoa Island
Toe Point
Granite Island
Aligo Point
Beehive Island
Chiswell B Island
Granite Cape
Matushka Island
Chiswell Island
Chiswell A Island
Lone Rock Island
To Tern Lake
Resurrection River
2.8
Dimond
Visitor Information Center
railroad
Port Ave
1.0
Alaska RR Dock
Small Boat Harbor
Benny Benson Mem'l
boardwalk
Van Buren
Ballantine
D
C
B
A
Monroe
1st
2nd
3rd
4th
5th
Madison
Jefferson
Adams
Washington
Railway
Alaska SeaLife Center
To Lowell Point
ferry dock

pullout 2.4 miles from the highway to scope the bay for diving ducks and mergansers. You may find Harlequin Duck, Barrow's Goldeneye, and, in winter into spring, all three scoters, Long-tailed Duck, Common Goldeneye, and Common Merganser, with King or Steller's Eiders possible, though only in winter. Driving farther on Nash Road takes you past the lumber mill and the road to the state prison (Mile 4.8), and finally to the Marine Industrial Center. The road is gated at this point, but you may be able to drive along the fence to the east among the many dry-docked boats until you can see the beach. If the area is restricted when you get there, ask at the office if you can walk or drive to the beach near Fourth-of-July Creek. Find a place to park near the beach as far south as you can drive (around Mile 5.5); then walk along the beach (at lower tides) east (left) to Fourth-of-July Creek near the far rocky shoreline. Here you might find the diving ducks you missed farther up the road, plus Horned and Red-necked Grebes, shorebirds (Killdeer has been seen here in winter), Snow Bunting, and, in winter, possibly a Yellow-billed Loon or a King Eider. Access for birders to this area might end in 2002—please respect any no-trespassing signs you encounter.

Return to the Seward Highway and continue toward town. At Milepost 2.8, you will notice the Seward airport runway to the left and some airport buildings. You may turn here; drive past the airport buildings to the end of the fenced area where small airplanes are parked Park outside the fence, put on rubber boots, and walk across the taxi strip at the end of the runway in front of you. Turn right to the dirt road leading through the marshy area to the head of Resurrection Bay at the end of the main runway. In spring, search the wetlands for dabbling ducks, including Eurasian Wigeon, migrating shorebirds, including Marbled Godwit (uncommon southcoastal Alaskan migrant and rare in Seward), Caspian Tern (rare), and "beach" birds such as American Pipit, Horned Lark, and Lapland Longspur. There may be Snow Buntings here in winter; McKay's Bunting has been found once. The peak of the waterfowl migration is 15 to 30 April; shorebird migration peaks from 1 to 14 May. There is a Mew Gull and Arctic Tern colony near the end of the runway, so please avoid walking along the beach grass in this area during their summer nesting season. Return to the Seward Highway and continue south.

SEWARD

Seward is a small city of about 2,900 that supports commercial fishing, shipping (southern terminus of the Alaska Railroad and access to ocean shipping), lumber, sportfishing, and tourism. The city enjoys an annual average of 64 inches of precipitation, including over six feet of snow. At sea level much of the snow melts rapidly, however, and the harbor is ice-free year round. From May through September, Seward can be very appealing, especially on sunny days when the surrounding mountain peaks and glaciers are in full view.

There is good birding here at any season, but especially in winter, so if you find yourself in Anchorage with a short time to bird, head for Seward, a 127-mile, 2.5-to-3.5-hour drive, depending on weather and stops. The annual Christmas Bird Count averages 53 species, one of the highest in the state. In summer, Seward's big draw is its accessibility to seabirds in the Chiswell Islands, Cape Resurrection, Barwell Island, and surrounding fjords and islands of Kenai Fjords National Park. Other outstanding attractions include the new (1998) Alaska SeaLife Center near the ferry dock; the center features a large aquarium with some seabirds and marine life exhibits. Or you can visit the small historical museum (at Jefferson and Third Avenues) that specializes in the history of Seward, including the effects of the 1964 earthquake—a submarine landslide first destroyed the waterfront and that major subsidence triggered a tidal wave that then destroyed much of the old town.

Stop at the Chamber of Commerce Visitor Center on the right at Milepost 2 for a Seward bird checklist and information about activities and services in the town. Proceed another mile and turn left (east) at Milepost 1 onto Old Airport Road leading to the Alaska Railroad dock. If there are no barges or cruise ships present, you should be able to walk out on the dock. This is an excellent vantage point from which to check the head of Resurrection Bay for Double-crested, Red-faced (rare), and Pelagic Cormorants, gulls, Common Murre, Marbled Murrelet, and, in winter, loons, several species of diving ducks (including flocks of Barrow's Goldeneyes and Common Mergansers), Rock Sandpiper, Dunlin (rare), and Sea Otter. To the east is the mouth of the Resurrection River, accessible through the airport (see map).

Almost directly across the highway from the Old Airport Road turnoff is Government Road (which may not be marked, but you'll see a sign for Benny Benson Memorial Park); pull in here to check the lake between Government Road and the Seward Highway. From November through January, there may be many Bald Eagles feeding on salmon in the small lake. Up to 100 eagles roost in the dead trees at the north end of the lake in winter. This is also a good place to get close looks at Barrow's Goldeneye and basic plumaged Rusty Blackbird. Government Road becomes Second Avenue to the south and will lead you through town to the bay. First, however, it is best to go back to the Seward Highway and drive north a short distance to the small-boat harbor.

Kenai Fjords National Park headquarters is on the boardwalk fronting the small-boat harbor. This 580,000-acre park was created to protect the Harding Ice Field, a remnant of the last glacial epoch, and the marine life that depends on the waters in the myriad glacier-carved fjords that form the ragged coastline of the southern Kenai Peninsula. Although you can hike to the ice field, you could also charter a small plane from Seward or Homer to reach this flat area of glacial ice and snow with its nunataks of rock projecting through the surface.

Check the small-boat harbor—sometimes birds of interest come close to the docks. Northwestern Crows are common year around. In summer, sort through the larger gulls around fish-cleaning stations for possible Glaucous-winged X Herring Gull hybrids. In winter there are usually goldeneyes, mergansers, perhaps a locally rare Thayer's Gull, Common Murre, and sometimes Steller's Sea Lions in the harbor. Just outside the entrance to the harbor you might find Red-throated, Pacific, Common, and Yellow-billed Loons, and possibly King and Steller's Eiders as well as Common and Barrow's Goldeneyes, and Common and Red-breasted Mergansers.

Often the best winter birding is at Seward's backyard feeders, which occasionally attract unusual species such as White-throated Sparrow (only a few records), Brambling (very rare), Rusty Blackbird, and Hepburn's Gray-crowned Rosy-Finch (uncommon). Rosy-finches arrive once snow covers the peaks and remain throughout the winter. They used to be more regular before the 1964 earthquake, but then weren't recorded for over 20 years. Mountain Ash and Chokecherry ornamental trees along First Avenue provide food in early winter for Bohemian Waxwings, American Robins, and occasionally Varied Thrushes. Two Cedar Waxwings were seen here in December 1993, the first record for Seward.

Drive through town and for several miles out Lowell Point Road, south past the ferry dock, to scan for seabirds (Marbled Murrelet) along Resurrection Bay. Watch for Black Oystercatchers in the exposed shallows during low tide. The road ends at a residential area and a campground where you can ask permission to check the bay and the shoreline. In nearby tall spruce and hemlocks look for Rufous Hummingbird, Three-toed Woodpecker, Chestnut-backed Chickadee, Red-breasted Nuthatch, Brown Creeper, and Townsend's Warbler.

SEWARD BY SEA

Resurrection Bay and the waters of the Gulf of Alaska just outside the bay can be extremely dangerous for unskilled and inexperienced boaters. Water temperatures are scarcely above freezing, even in summer, and it takes only a few minutes to numb one's extremities and a few more minutes to induce hypothermia. If you plan to boat, read the Cautions in the *Introduction* on page 19, listen to the marine weather forecasts, and pay attention to any changes in wind on the water. South winds can create a good chop on Resurrection Bay in minutes. It is best to do your birding with an experienced boater, from the state ferries, or from one of the many tour ships operating out of the small boat harbor. As in all coastal situations, be aware of the tides. Seward tides range from plus 12 feet to minus 3 feet at the extreme, but are usually less than this 15-foot range. Nevertheless, hiking on tidal flats at low tide requires careful attention to the rise of water between you and the shoreline.

Black-legged Kittiwake

KENAI FJORDS AND THE CHISWELL ISLANDS

In Alaska, so much depends on the weather. There is no exception to this rule when planning your trip to Kenai Fjords National Park and the Chiswell Islands group (part of the Alaska Maritime National Wildlife Refuge, with headquarters in Homer). Although the large tour vessels operating daily in summer can safely negotiate rough water, your chances of easily observing seabirds will be limited in bad weather and rough seas. If possible, plan to go out on a relatively calm day. However, at certain times of the summer, you may not be able to get on a boat at the last minute and will be forced to make reservations well ahead of your trip to Seward. Check with the Chamber of Commerce for information on tour boats currently operating.

There are both large and small ships that offer tours, and birding is best from one of the smaller boats with pilots who are experienced birders themselves and will stop to allow you to look for birds along the way and at the Chiswell Islands. All the tour companies have offices on the boardwalk at the small-boat harbor. In good weather, most boats follow approximately the same route—heading out past Aialik Cape and into Aialik Bay, one of the major fjords in the park. Most boats then usually go up into Holgate Arm to the foot of Holgate Glacier, as this is the first glacier encountered that calves icebergs into tidewater. From there, they motor to the Chiswell Islands and then back to Resurrection Bay. Trips take from five to nine hours depending on the speed of the boat and number and length of the stops. Most tours start between 8 and 11:30 AM and try to be back by 5 or 5:30 PM. Kittlitz's Murrelet is one of the most-sought-after species in the Kenai Fjords. They may be seen at Holgate Glacier, but are more likely to be near Northwestern or Aialik Glaciers.

Half-day tours may also be available that take you to Cape Resurrection and Barwell Island on the southeastern limit of Resurrection Bay. The seabird colonies there are impressive, because the precipitous cliffs rise vertically from the sea, but the bird abundance and diversity are not as great as around the Chiswell Island group.

Seabirds encountered on a trip to the Chiswells vary with season, but you will certainly find enough variety to keep you occupied. Tours generally exit Resurrection Bay along the west side and pass inside of Cheval Island where there are colonies of Double-crested and Red-faced Cormorants, Glaucous-winged Gull, and Horned and Tufted Puffins. After rounding Aialik Cape, you will enter Aialik Bay. Between Aialik Cape and Holgate Arm is a good place to see flocks of Rhinoceros Auklets. After visiting a tidewater glacier, your tour should take you south to the Chiswell Island group. This group of about 10 islands and rocky pinnacles has been extensively studied by scientists after the *Exxon Valdez* oil spill in March 1989, when the oil slick passed through this archipelago where large numbers of seabirds nest.

This is what you can expect at the Chiswells: Northern Fulmars nest on Lone Rock Island, but you probably will not sail that far. Nevertheless, you should see several of these birds on your return trip. Sooty and Short-tailed Shearwaters are both present but are hard to differentiate. Compare relative sizes of head and bill (see illustration on page 345) and look for the usually bright-white underwing linings of the larger Sooty Shearwater. Shearwaters are most common when the seas are at their worst. This possibility offers a positive note to the potential impact of rough seas with large swells on the status of your stomach. Double-crested, Pelagic, and Red-faced Cormorants are easily found. Bald Eagles should be on the islands or perched in a tall Sitka Spruce anywhere along the shoreline. Peregrine Falcons nest on the islands and feed on seabirds. When you see large numbers of murres dive from the cliff, a raptor may be nearby. You might find a Black Oystercatcher along the rocky shores of the islands. Pomarine, Long-tailed, and sometimes Parasitic Jaegers, Arctic and rarely Aleutian Terns, and Marbled, Kittlitz's, and Ancient Murrelets are often seen on your return trip. Watch for Cassin's Auklet if you are near Granite Island. Mew Gulls are common near shore; Glaucous-winged Gulls and Black-legged Kittiwakes are abundant on the islands. Common Murres are on most islands, and there is a small colony of Thick-billed Murres on Chiswell A Island. Both Horned and Tufted Puffins are common and conspicuous around the islands.

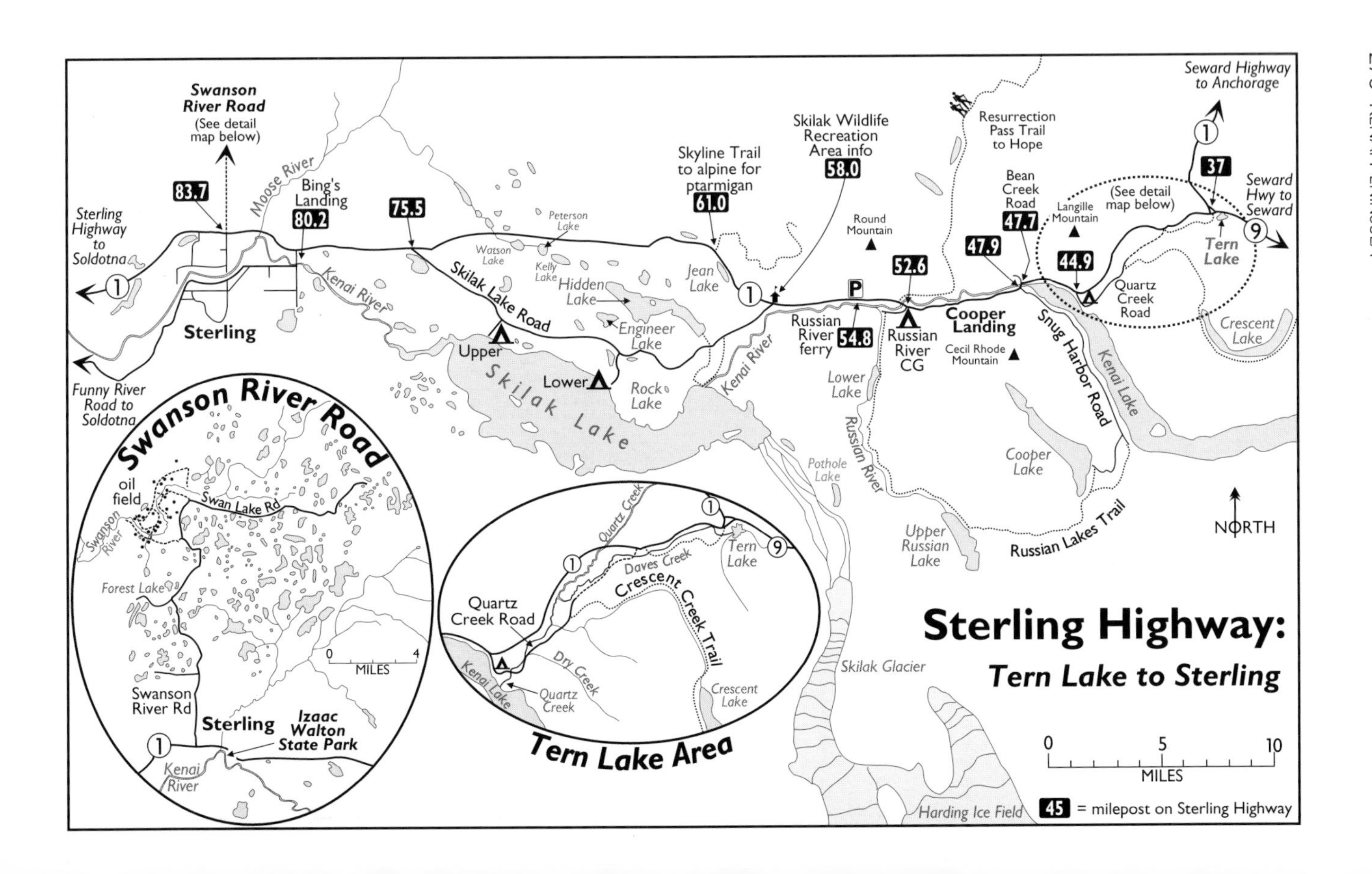

Sterling Highway:
Tern Lake to Sterling
Swanson River Road
(See detail map below)
83.7
Moose River
Bing's Landing
80.2
75.5
Sterling Highway to Soldotna
Sterling
Funny River Road to Soldotna
Kenai River
Skilak Lake Road
Watson Lake
Peterson Lake
Kelly Lake
Hidden Lake
Engineer Lake
Upper
Lower
Skilak Lake
Rock Lake
Jean Lake
Skyline Trail to alpine for ptarmigan
61.0
Skilak Wildlife Recreation Area info
58.0
Round Mountain
Russian River ferry
54.8
52.6
Russian River CG
Cooper Landing
Cecil Rhode Mountain
Lower Lake
Russian River
Pothole Lake
Upper Russian Lake
Cooper Lake
Russian Lakes Trail
Resurrection Pass Trail to Hope
Bean Creek Road
47.7
47.9
Langille Mountain
44.9
(See detail map below)
Quartz Creek Road
Snug Harbor Road
Kenai Lake
Seward Highway to Anchorage
37
Seward Hwy to Seward
Tern Lake
Crescent Lake
NORTH
Skilak Glacier
Harding Ice Field
0
5
10
MILES
45 = milepost on Sterling Highway
Swanson River Road
oil field
Swan Lake Rd
Swanson River
Forest Lake
0
4
MILES
Swanson River Rd
Sterling
Izaac Walton State Park
Kenai River
Tern Lake Area
Quartz Creek
Daves Creek
Tern Lake
Crescent Creek Trail
Quartz Creek Road
Dry Creek
Kenai Lake
Quartz Creek
Crescent Lake

Parakeet Auklets, although nesting on three of the islands, are not found on each trip. There is a colony of Rhinoceros Auklets on Matushka Island, but they are usually away from the colony during daylight hours and return to their nesting burrows only at night. Although both Fork-tailed and Leach's Storm-Petrels (a few of which nest on Beehive Island) nest in the Chiswell group, they leave and re-enter their burrows only at night. They are often far from the nesting colony during daylight hours and are usually not encountered on the tours.

Most of the passengers on the larger tour boats are not birders but tourists interested in the grandeur of the scenery, in the numbers of birds, especially the puffins, and, of course, the marine mammals. It is common to see Sea Otter, Harbor Seal, numbers of Steller's Sea Lions, Dall's Porpoise, the occasional Harbor Porpoise, often Humpback Whale, and sometimes Killer Whale. If you are looking for a particular bird species, ask a crew member to inform the captain who will try to find what you are looking for from personal knowledge of the area and his vantage point from the bridge. Remember that these boats go out almost every day in summer to the same locations and often a captain can pinpoint certain species. Also, the boats from the various tour companies are in constant radio contact and inform each other of unusual sightings. For an all-around scenic Alaskan adventure for families or the serious birder, a tour of the Kenai Fjords is hard to beat.

For an extended ocean trip out of Seward, you can take the state ferry *Tustumena* as it returns to Homer or Kodiak along the south side of the Kenai Peninsula, in the Gulf of Alaska. You can expect to see the same species that you encountered out of Seward or those seen on the ferry from Homer to Kodiak. In late summer there will be more shearwaters and perhaps an occasional albatross—Black-footed is the most common, although Laysan is sometimes seen. Every few years, a Short-tailed Albatross (usually an immature bird) is reported in the deeper waters. Or you can schedule a ferry trip on the *Kennicott* across the Gulf of Alaska to Juneau (see page 453), where the rarer pelagic species are more likely to be found.

TERN LAKE TO STERLING: COOPER LANDING AND SKILAK LAKE

Drive north on the Seward Highway to Tern Lake (37 miles from Seward, 95 miles to Soldotna, 137 miles to Homer), which lies at the junction of the Seward and Sterling Highways. Like most of the small lakes in the middle and northern parts of the Kenai Peninsula, Tern Lake is shallow, with emergent vegetation that sometimes creates islands for birds to nest on out of the reach of many mammalian predators. Arctic Terns may be here in mid-summer, but are gone by the first week in August. Some dabbling ducks, occasional diving ducks, and Mew Gulls are common around the lake. Common Loons nest here annually, and sometimes there is a Pacific Loon. In early-to-mid-May, you might find a few shorebirds around the lake, including Greater (nests) and Lesser Yellowlegs, Solitary Sandpiper, Wandering Tattler, Whimbrel, Pectoral Sandpiper, and Short-billed Dowitcher. Alder Flycatchers nest across the Seward Highway in the avalanche chute at the east end of the lake. There is a pleasant picnic ground at the west end of the lake with a viewing area for observing spawning Red (Sockeye) Salmon in Daves Creek, which drains the lake. From the parking area next to the viewing platform, you can walk a degraded gravel road westward for over five miles through old burns (some managed, some accidental) and forest to connect with Crescent Creek Road out of Cooper Landing. As with all places in Alaska where spawning salmon are present, be alert for bears. There are several side roads and trails that have been used recently to remove downed timber from Spruce Bark Beetle-killed trees. This might be a good place to see Spruce Grouse, find woodpeckers, including Three-toed and (rarely) Black-backed, see Olive-sided Flycatcher or Western Wood-Pewee, and see Orange-crowned, Yellow, Myrtle, and Wilson's Warblers, and several species of sparrows, such as Lincoln's, Sooty Fox, Golden-crowned, Gambel's White-crowned, and Slate-colored Junco.

From Tern Lake to Cooper Landing (eight miles), the Sterling Highway parallels Quartz Creek, which supports a good run of Dolly Varden (trout) as well as Red Salmon and Rainbow Trout. There are pullouts on the south side of the road where you can park to listen for birds.

Cooper Landing (population about 260) begins at Milepost 45 of the Sterling Highway and continues intermittently to about Milepost 50. Scattered along the way are many tourist-oriented businesses, such as gift stores, fishing, rafting, and hunting guide operations, motels, campgrounds, and general stores that can supply you with groceries, gas, hardware, fishing tackle, and other necessities. As the highway reaches Kenai Lake, you can turn left (south) onto Quartz Creek Road to a campground at the mouth of Quartz Creek on Kenai Lake, or follow the road across Quartz Creek for about 3 miles to its terminus at the Crescent Creek trailhead. This is a good location to listen for Northern Saw-whet and Boreal Owls on a spring evening. From here, the old gravel "road" continues eastward for about a mile, encountering Daves Creek trail to the Tern Lake campground. The road has extensive water-filled depressions after a rain and is underlain with "corduroy," logs that have been placed crosswise to the road and covered with dirt and now gravel. The logs are evident after about one-half mile and could tip up and damage the underside of a car, so driving this road is not recommended. Note the mixed stands of spruce and hemlock on the rocky slope. This is a good spot to compare the extensive stands of birch that in this area are a mixture of the white Paper Birch (*Betula papyrifera*) of interior Alaska and the duskier-barked Kenai Birch (*B. kenaica*) that is common throughout the southern Kenai Peninsula. These two species probably hybridize.

At the west end of Kenai Lake the road crosses the head of the Kenai River, which runs 82 miles to Cook Inlet at the town of Kenai. Kenai Lake is fed by glaciers in the Kenai Mountains and supports many species of fish, including King, Red, Silver, and Pink Salmon, Dolly Varden, and Rainbow and Lake Trout. The blue-green color of the lake, as well as the Kenai River and Skilak Lake, is caused by glacial flour suspended in the water. Mew, Glaucous-winged, and Glaucous-winged x Herring Gull hybrids are common here, and there may be flocks of Mallards or Common Mergansers in the quiet water near the bridge, especially in winter. Search for other ducks here; American Wigeon and Northern Pintail are found regularly in winter. Bald Eagles are present downstream for several miles feeding on spent salmon, especially in fall and winter.

At the east end of the Kenai River bridge, Bean Creek Road (Milepost 47.7) on the north leads two miles to the Princess Tours lodge on a bluff overlooking the Kenai River. Northern Saw-whet Owls have been heard along this road in spring.

Just past the bridge, you may turn left onto Snug Harbor Road (Milepost 47.9) and drive about eight miles on a sometimes rough gravel road along the south shore of Kenai Lake, where Western Screech-Owls (rare) have been heard in winter. Even though the road is above the lake and there is no easy access to the lakeshore, the area is good for observing wintering ducks. In about eight miles you can turn right onto a three-mile-long gravel road that rises from the lake (about 500 feet elevation) to 1,300 feet elevation on the shore of Cooper Lake in the Kenai Mountains. A delightful short trail to Clever and Rainbow Lakes crosses a tiny sedge meadow filled with wildflowers (Burnet, gentians, Tundra Rose, Dwarf Birch, Bunchberry, Bog Candle, Pink Daisy, and Mountain Ash) and goes through a stunted stand of Mountain Hemlock to the lakes. A trail from south of Cooper Lake leads to the Russian Lakes trails to the west and the Resurrection trail to the south. There is a colony of hybrid gulls nesting at the south end of Cooper Lake.

The Sterling Highway continues past Cooper Landing along the scenic Kenai River for 10 miles, crossing the river just before its confluence with the Russian River. Russian River Campground is on the left at Milepost 52.6. You can take a float trip down the Kenai River in this area with a guide from one of several operations out of Cooper Landing. The mountains to the north often have Dall's Sheep on their slopes (scan Langille Mountain above Kenai Lake and Cooper Landing or Round Mountain above the Russian River ferry). The mountains to the south are more likely to support Mountain Goats (those on

Cecil Rhode Mountain were transplanted there). This area of the Kenai River is prized for sportfishing for King, Red, and Silver Salmon and Rainbow Trout. One of the most popular fishing areas is the mouth of the Russian River, where you can observe or participate in combat-style fishing, with anglers standing shoulder to shoulder, flailing the water with single-hook flies, trying to land the prized Red Salmon (tastiest of all salmon species). These fish do not feed or take lures, so you have to maneuver your line so that it floats into the fish's mouth, then pull in the line so the hook catches the corner of the fish's mouth. King Salmon arrive in June and early July, Red Salmon in June and July, and Silvers from early August into December. Rainbow Trout, although resident, provide the best fishing in fall, when they feed on salmon eggs.

Just downstream from the Russian River mouth is a small passenger ferry (fee) that will take you to the south side of the Kenai River, where you can fish along the bank or walk the river's edge looking for birds. Mew and Glaucous-winged Gulls, along with Common and Red-breasted Mergansers, are abundant on the river. Look for American Dipper in the rapids. In winter, when the fishermen leave, you'll find Bald Eagles (feeding on spawned-out salmon), Harlequin Ducks, and Common and Barrow's Goldeneyes. Numerous hiking trails lead into the mountains, some taking you rapidly up into the alpine. Watch for bears on any of the trails along the Kenai River.

At Milepost 58 (37 miles to Soldotna) is a small visitor information station for the Skilak Wildlife Recreation Area. Stop and check maps for trails and campgrounds here and ask about the bear situation before hiking. Rangers advise carrying a rifle of at least .30-06 caliber in Brown Bear country. It may be prudent not to hike if bears have been seen along the trails in this area. At this point, paved Sterling Highway continues west, while gravel Skilak Lake Road loops south, returning to the Sterling Highway after 19 miles (see map).

If you follow the Sterling Highway, you will pass by Jean Lake on the south, and just beyond, at about Milepost 61, Skyline Trail leading north to the alpine. On it you might find all three species of ptarmigan. Continuing west on the Sterling, you will pass through some old burns and large areas of boggy sedge-meadows interspersed with shallow bog-lakes filled with water lilies. Some of the larger and deeper lakes (Watson, Kelly, Peterson) have Common Loon and Trumpeter Swan, and there are populations of Rainbow Trout in these lakes, too. During winter, watch for Northern Hawk Owls perched on the tops of Black Spruce trees on the flats between Mileposts 65 and 72.

For better birding during summer and access to two improved campgrounds, take gravel Skilak Lake Road from Milepost 58. After only two miles you will pass through the Pothole Lake burn—note the charred aspen and spruce trees to the south. The fire started at Pothole Lake, some 10 miles south of the road, on 19 May 1991, and spread to this location on 26 May. Burns such as this are usually not controlled unless they threaten private property or economically important forests, but are left to burn. This creates better Moose browse, since the young trees reoccupy the area previously in spruce-birch climax forest. Kenai National Wildlife Refuge was once Kenai National Moose Range and the area was managed primarily for Moose. Over the past 50 years there have been many burns between here and Sterling. This burned habitat is excellent for Olive-sided and Alder Flycatchers and Western Wood-Pewee.

Hidden Lake, on the north side of Skilak Lake Road 3.6 miles from the turnoff, also has Common Loons, populations of Rainbow and Lake Trout, Dolly Varden, and Kokanee (land-locked salmon), and a paved campground. This and some of the other larger lakes require a boat with a motor for adequate exploration. There are several trails leading to Skilak Lake—the Hidden Lake trail takes you on a three-mile round trip to where the Kenai River pours into Skilak Lake.

Skilak Lake is approachable by road at two campgrounds—Upper and Lower Skilak Lake Campgrounds. This large lake is potentially dangerous to small boats since wind comes up quickly and may prevent boaters from returning to the launch ramps at the campgrounds. Heed the warning signs at the boat launches if you are heading out on the cold glacier-supplied water. There are several small islands in the lake, one easily visible from the boat launch or picnic area of Upper Skilak Lake Campground. This rocky island supports some Double-crested Cormorants and a colony of hybrid Herring x Glaucous-winged Gulls that are seen throughout this area and commonly as far south as Homer. Herring Gulls are more common in the Anchorage area and Glaucous-winged Gulls farther south in Cook Inlet, but most of the gulls here are hybrids and have some black on the wing tips with white windows and dark eyes, rather than the light eyes of the Herring Gull. Juveniles, seen in early August, are darker than Glaucous-winged first-year birds and will be difficult to distinguish from Herring Gulls. Islands at the entrance of the Kenai River into the lake also have gull colonies and probably nesting Double-crested Cormorants. Numbers of Pacific and Common Loons cruise the lake along with some Red-throated Loons. Red-necked Grebes may be abundant.

Skilak Lake Road passes through a glacially scoured landscape; there is evidence of massive ice sheets that have retreated to the Kenai Mountains to the east and the Harding Ice Field. Barrow's Goldeneyes nest near Rock Lake and can often be found on that lake, Great Horned Owls are often heard, and a Boreal Owl was once encountered near Engineer Lake. Olive-sided and Alder Flycatchers are common; Western Wood-Pewee is present, as are both Gray-cheeked and Swainson's Thrushes, Orange-crowned and Myrtle Warblers, Northern Waterthrush, and Gambel's White-crowned Sparrow. Slate-colored Juncos are abundant.

The Kenai River begins again below Skilak Lake, but there is no road access to the outlet where there may be Osprey, uncommon on the Kenai Peninsula. The river is heavily fished for King Salmon from the lake to its mouth in Cook Inlet in June and July. The best access to this portion of the Kenai River is at Bing's Landing on the south at Milepost 80.2, some 1.5 miles before Sterling. A gravel road leads 0.75 mile to a boat landing and small campground. Most of the other roads leading to the river terminate in private property. From the west end of Skilak Lake Road, the Sterling Highway continues seven miles to the town of Sterling (Milepost 81; Soldotna 14).

King Salmon

STERLING TO SOLDOTNA

Sterling is a small community with a dispersed population of almost 4,000 that specializes in supporting the sportfishing industry. There are restaurants, gas stations, motels, campgrounds, grocery and general stores, as well as guiding services here. This is one of the best places in Alaska for salmon and trout fishing.

Izaac Walton State Park is on the southeast side of the Moose River bridge at the west end of Sterling. Here you can walk to the confluence of the Moose and Kenai Rivers to scan the water. Approximately 1.3 miles west of this bridge the Swanson River Road leads north (Milepost 83.7). This rough gravel road traverses taiga forests dotted with small lakes to reach several oil-field drill sites and, more pertinent to your birding interests, to the Swanson River and Swan Lake canoe-trail system in the Kenai National Wildlife Refuge. Shuttle service from Sterling to the Swan Lake canoe-trail system is available because the terminus of the trail is on the Moose River. Although there are hundreds of lakes in this area, only a few are visible from the road. You can hike to several more, but a canoe is required to really explore the area. If you have time and enjoy wilderness camping, short and long trips in this system can be rewarding in getting close-ups of birds such as loons and Trumpeter Swan, or for fishing for Rainbow Trout, Dolly Varden, and stocked Silver Salmon. Get a map and information at the Refuge headquarters on the south end of Soldotna before starting out in your canoe.

The best time to drive the 12.6-mile Swanson River and Swan Lake Road is early morning in June when the birds are nesting. Common Loons breed on most of the lakes and you'll find occasional breeding Pacific Loons. Trumpeter Swans usually nest in lakes with less disturbance, so they're harder to find. A few Sandhill Cranes also nest in the area. In spring, Boreal Owls are sometimes heard south of Forest Lake—from Mile 8 to 10 of the Swanson River Road. Three- toed Woodpeckers are present in most spruce stands, especially those with diseased or dying trees. Olive-sided and Alder Flycatchers are relatively common. All five thrushes on the Kenai may be found here—Gray-cheeked, Swainson's, Hermit, Varied, and American Robin.

Bohemian Waxwings have been seen here in June. Myrtle Warblers are abundant, and you'll also find Orange-crowned, Yellow, and Blackpoll Warblers, and Northern Waterthrush. Slate-colored Juncos are abundant; Pine Grosbeaks and White-winged Crossbills (irregular) are found in the spruce. Do not trespass on oil-and-gas roads; they are usually marked with closed gates. Return to the Sterling Highway and drive on to Soldotna, about 10.5 miles.

SOLDOTNA

Kenai-Soldotna is often referred to as "twin cities" because of their proximity and sharing of resources. Soldotna is the more recent of the two, established in 1947, and now with a population of about 3,700. It provides services along the heavily traveled Sterling Highway and supports the sportfishing activities on the Kenai River. The section of the Kenai River that runs between Skilak Lake and its mouth in Cook Inlet has the best run of large King Salmon anywhere in the world, along with often-staggering numbers of Red Salmon. Guiding services, fish camps, boat rentals, and fishing charters are big businesses on the Kenai River and attract many thousands of tourists each summer. It is hard to hear birds along the river because of the constant roar of outboard motors from early June through July when the Kenai Kings are running. On and near the river there may be diving ducks such as goldeneyes (especially in winter) and mergansers, Spotted Sandpiper, Bonaparte's and Mew Gulls, Arctic Tern, and Rusty Blackbird. Tree and Violet-green Swallows are common over the river. Cliff Swallows nest under the Sterling Highway bridge and Bank Swallows dig their nests in the bluffs of the river bank. Ruby-crowned Kinglet, all the thrushes, Orange-crowned,

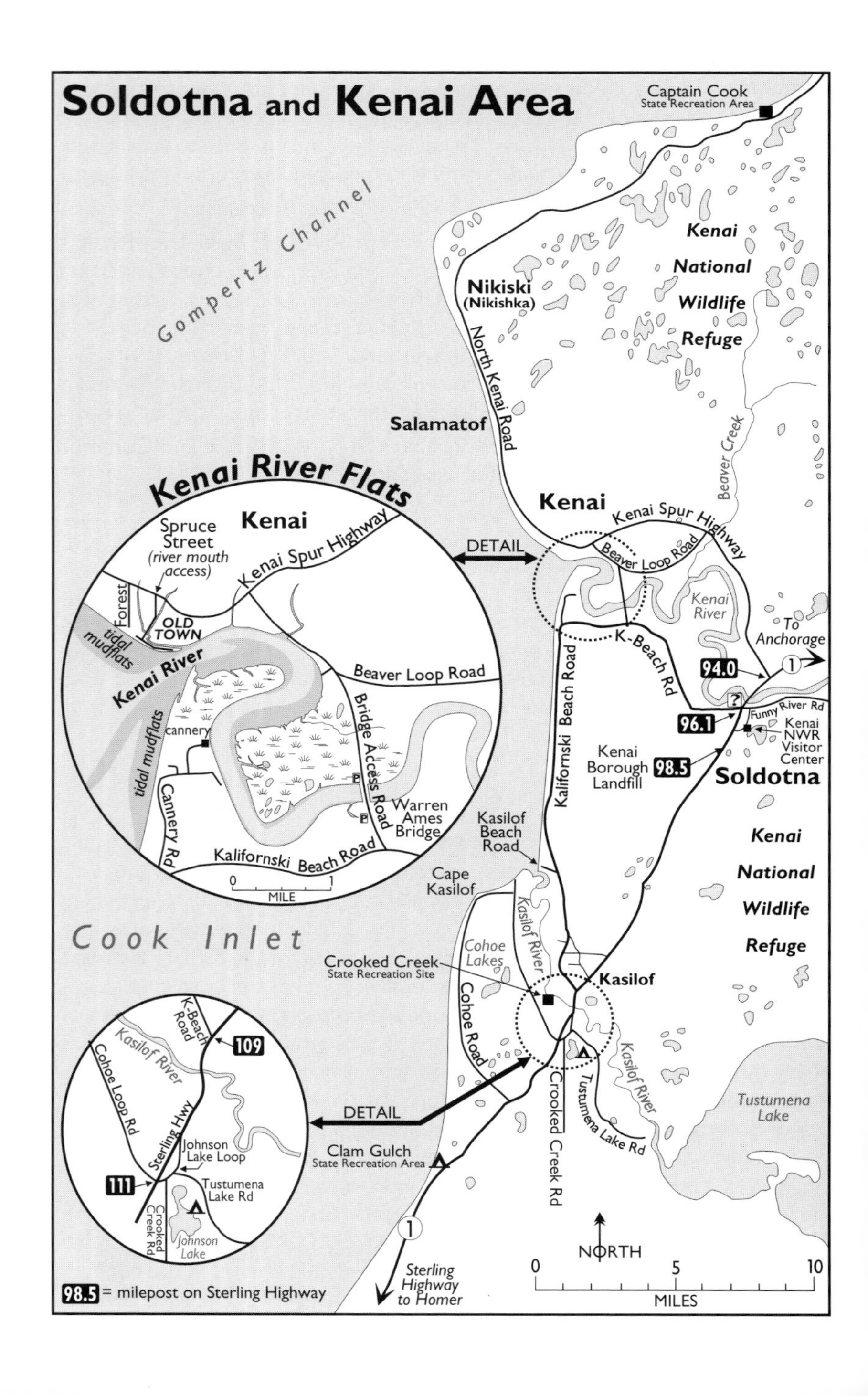
Soldotna and Kenai Area
Captain Cook State Recreation Area
Gompertz Channel
Kenai National Wildlife Refuge
Nikiski (Nikishka)
North Kenai Road
Salamatof
Beaver Creek
Kenai
Kenai Spur Highway
DETAIL
Beaver Loop Road
Kenai River
To Anchorage
K-Beach Rd
Kalifornski Beach Road
94.0
96.1
98.5
Funny River Rd
Kenai NWR Visitor Center
Kenai Borough Landfill
Soldotna
Kenai River Flats
Spruce Street (river mouth access)
Forest
OLD TOWN
tidal mudflats
Kenai River
cannery
Bridge Access Road
Warren Ames Bridge
Cannery Rd
Kalifornski Beach Road
MILE
Kasilof Beach Road
Cape Kasilof
Cook Inlet
Kasilof River
Cohoe Lakes
Crooked Creek State Recreation Site
Cohoe Road
Kasilof
Crooked Creek Rd
Tustumena Lake Rd
Tustumena Lake
K-Beach Road
109
Cohoe Loop Rd
Sterling Hwy
Johnson Lake Loop
111
Tustumena Lake Rd
Crooked Creek Rd
Johnson Lake
Clam Gulch State Recreation Area
Sterling Highway to Homer
NORTH
0 5 10
MILES
98.5 = milepost on Sterling Highway

Myrtle, and Wilson's Warblers, Savannah, Sooty Fox, and Gambel's White-crowned Sparrows, and Slate-colored Junco are common. Much of the river is bordered by private property and there are only a few public accesses. For more information, stop at the Kenai Peninsula Information Center operated by the Soldotna Chamber of Commerce at the south end of the bridge over the Kenai River, south of Soldotna, on the right.

Before exploring the Kenai-Soldotna area, check in at the Kenai National Wildlife Refuge Visitor Center for a bird checklist. Drive through Soldotna on the Sterling Highway, cross the Kenai River bridge, and turn left (east) at the traffic light onto Funny River Road. After about 100 feet (before Spenard Builders Supply) turn right onto Ski Hill Road leading up the hill to the visitor center. Several walking and hiking trails start at the parking lot, including a short hike to Headquarters Lake where you might find Pacific and Common Loons, ducks, and other local water-associated birds.

One excellent place to observe eagles and gulls is the Kenai Borough landfill just west of Soldotna at Milepost 98.5 of the Sterling Highway. During winter, over 150 Bald Eagles have been seen at one time. There is even an eagle nest right above the entrance to the landfill. Inform the attendant at the scale house that you are a birder and she will direct you to safe places to park and view. The landfill attracts many gulls, including an occasional Glaucous Gull from late fall to spring. With patient scoping, perhaps you will find a gull unusual for this area.

KENAI

There are two ways to drive to Kenai from Soldotna, and the better choice for birders is Kalifornski Beach Road (known locally as K Beach Road). From the road's junction with the Sterling Highway (Milepost 96.1) at the traffic light south of the Kenai River bridge, drive six miles on K Beach Road to the right turn (Bridge Access Road) that leads to Kenai. As you drop down over the Kenai River flats, pull off in a state wayside on the left just before the Warren Ames Bridge. In spring migration, thousands of Snow Geese stop here to feed. In April, one can find hundreds of Greater White-fronted and several races of Canada Geese, American Wigeon, Mallard, Northern Shoveler, Northern Pintail, Green-winged Teal, and Sandhill Crane. Also reported are Eurasian Wigeon and, rarely, Common Teal. Sometimes the geese are on the other side of the Kenai River, where there is another viewing platform.

The entire area to the west is called the Kenai River Flats. A census each spring by Alaska Department of Fish & Game biologists reveals large numbers of gulls and shorebirds as well as waterfowl, especially Snow Geese. For the past several years a pair of Parasitic Jaegers has nested on the flats from late June to mid-July. To locate the jaegers, park on the shoulder of the road on the north side of the bridge (legal if you are off the pavement) near the brown sign indicating that you are entering the Kenai River Special Management Area. Look west toward Cook Inlet. The birds are surprisingly difficult to locate initially, unless they take wing. The nest is no more than a small depression in the sparse vegetation. When the parent bird is not present, the chick(s) is amazingly exposed. The hypothetical plural chick is mentioned because we believe that one of the chicks dies or is killed. Most observations have been of one chick only, but two were observed at one time, with only one present later on. There are several records of Slaty-backed Gull in winter and one for Black-headed Gull in summer. Recently, Northwestern Crows have come to the Kenai-Soldotna area and have nested there. Another viewpoint for the flats is at the Kenai small-boat harbor and public dock on the left (west) as you continue toward Kenai from the bridge. Continuing another two miles will bring you to Kenai.

Kenai was founded in 1791 by Russian fur trappers and traders near the Kenaitze (Dena'ina Indian) village at the mouth of the Kenai River. With a population of about 6,600, it supports, with Soldotna, an area-wide population of 27,500. Most residents are employed in some manner by the petroleum industry, with commercial fishing a second source of employment. There are six large salmon-processing plants in operation near the mouth of the river. Recent and historical information about Kenai can be found at the Kenai Bicentennial Visitors and Cultural Center at 11471 Kenai Spur Highway. Kenai-Soldotna has all the services that travelers need.

To begin birding, turn left (west) from the road over the Warren Ames Bridge onto Kenai Spur Road and drive through town, watching for access to Captain Cook Park and Old Town on the left. There are several exits from the Kenai Spur Highway to this area of old buildings that comprised the original settlement of Kenai that overlooks the mouth of the Kenai River. There is a 100-year-old three-domed Russian Orthodox church here. Sometimes Beluga Whales feed in the mouth of the river, and during the commercial fishing season there are thousands of gulls waiting for cannery waste below and across the river on the flats. There will be a mixture of Herring and Glaucous-winged Gulls here, along with hybrids from the colony that breeds in Skilak Lake, and many Mew Gulls.

NIKISKI

From Kenai, you can drive north to Nikiski (also known as Nikishka), a booming community of over 2,800 people dedicated to the oil and gas industry. North Kenai Road goes past several petrochemical plants for about 28 miles to reach Captain Cook State Recreation Area on Cook Inlet. There are few other accesses to the saltwater on this road. One is at the Arness

Dock about 16 miles north of Kenai, where you can take a paved road past a school to a parking area and beach access. As with all of upper Cook Inlet, the water here is silty from glacial outflow and there is little bird life except for the possibility of gulls and shorebirds on the mudflats. In summer, the area from here south along Cook Inlet is clogged with salmon set-nets. However, on some of the lakes east of the road to Nikiski, you might find loons, swans, and Osprey. There are numerous gravel roads, beginning with Miller Road eight miles north of Kenai, that one can explore, but much of the land is private property. Do not proceed beyond closed gates on private oil or gas roads.

KENAI TO KASILOF

Return from Kenai over the Warren Ames Bridge to Kalifornski Beach Road. Turn right toward Homer. In 2.3 miles, where K Beach Road bends left, turn right onto Cannery Road. Drive 1.5 miles on Cannery Road (which becomes Bowpicker Lane as it curves right) and turn left onto Seacatch Drive toward the cannery. Stop at the corner to scan the area to the left for waterfowl and shorebirds. You can turn around at the gate to the cannery. During migration, there may be an occasional jaeger, or even a Sabine's Gull, along with American Pipit and Lapland Longspur. The marshy flats at the mouth of the Kenai River are great for spring waterfowl. In April, Snow Geese and Sandhill Cranes might be here rather than near the Warren Ames Bridge. At one hour before high tide, shorebirds may be found along the beach, including Sharp-tailed Sandpiper from mid-September into October. The water is heavily silted with glacial flour, so there are no marine birds.

Return to K Beach Road and drive south toward Homer along Cook Inlet. There are two "scenic" pullouts on the right where you can look over the bluff at the salmon set-nets and hundreds of drift-net seiners on the inlet in summer. Look for mile-markers on the left side of the road and judge when you are at about Mile 4.75. There is no road sign here, but on the right is Kasilof Beach Road that runs to the mouth of the Kasilof River. Turn onto this gravel road, drive to the gate of Cook Inlet Processing, and park next to the phone booth. From here, you can walk a few yards over the sand dune to view the river mouth. At low tide, there are extensive mudflats, where you could see many species of shorebirds as well as Bonaparte's, Mew, Herring, and Glaucous-winged Gulls, and Arctic Tern. The Kasilof supports smaller runs of salmon than the Kenai River but, as you will see, it is heavily used by fishermen. The spruce-covered benches along the north side of the Kasilof River are good for woodpeckers, including Three-toed and Black-backed, from Mile 4 to Mile 2 of K Beach Road.

KASILOF TO NINILCHIK

K Beach Road ends at the Sterling Highway near Milepost 109. Turn right toward Homer, cross the Kasilof River, and drive about 2.5 miles to a sign for Crooked Creek State Recreation Area off Cohoe Loop Road. Turn right just after crossing Crooked Creek. Access to the mouth of Crooked Creek and the Kasilof River can be found at the campground. For birding, it may be better to proceed northwest along Cohoe Loop Road. Continue straight beyond the pavement's end onto a gravel road that leads to the beach. Just before the road dips to the beach, you can turn right to check out access to the flats at the mouth of the Kasilof River. If it is dry, you can drive a winding dirt road through an extensive stand of Beach Rye grass to the river mouth; four-wheel drive may be required at some seasons. You can travel the soft sandy beach with four-wheel drive, but watch out for the tide. Again, the river mouth can be good for spring and fall shorebirds.

Return to the Sterling Highway on the paved part of Cohoe Loop Road, cross the highway, and go by the state fish hatchery (look for spawning Red Salmon in Crooked Creek) to Johnson Lake Loop. There is a nice state campground on Johnson Lake. Just beyond it is Tustumena Lake Road, a six-mile rough gravel road to the beginning of the Kasilof River, about two miles downstream from Tustumena Lake. The road borders typical dry taiga habitat that supports woodpeckers and other woodland species. The Kasilof River and Tustumena Lake are glacial and support King, Red, Pink, and Silver Salmon, Dolly Varden, and Rainbow Trout; Lake Trout and several species of whitefish are also in the lake. You may see Common Loon, Double-crested Cormorant, ducks, mergansers, and Arctic Tern on the river.

Return to the Sterling Highway and turn left toward Homer (56.7 miles). The road parallels the shore of Cook Inlet from here to Anchor Point and you can stop at pullouts to view the volcanic peaks of the Aleutian Range across the inlet. The highway passes through areas that have been severely damaged by Spruce Bark Beetles. Look for woodpeckers in stands of dying trees.

NINILCHIK

Ninilchik is a small fishing community of about 800 people founded by Russians and supported by commercial and sportfishing and the tourist industry. (See inset map on page 292.) The old village of Ninilchik with its harbor, picturesque Russian Orthodox church, and beach access is at about Milepost 135, immediately after crossing the Ninilchik River bridge. The gravel road leads right (west) along the river and forks—the right fork leads to the old town and the harbor, and the left fork leads to the beach camping area. The beach may have shorebirds and several species of gulls. You will begin to start seeing seabirds on Cook Inlet at Ninilchik, and they become more abundant as you approach Anchor Point and Homer.

Return to the Sterling Highway and drive through the town of Ninilchik and down across Deep Creek. There is a campground and picnic area on both sides of Deep Creek east of the highway. Continue up the hill and, as the road bends left, there is a marked access road on the right that leads down the hill to the beach and to a heavily used campground and boat-launch area at the mouth of Deep Creek. Both the Ninilchik River and Deep Creek contain runs of King, some Pink, and Silver Salmon, Steelhead, and Dolly Varden, and the campgrounds and river banks are often crowded with anglers. Check the river for goldeneyes, mergansers, and Spotted Sandpiper, and the mouth of Deep Creek for other shorebirds during migration. An Ivory Gull was found once in late fall. Bald Eagles are common when salmon are running. Search the coast for Merlin and Peregrine Falcon. Campground birds such as Gray Jay and Black-billed Magpie, as well as warblers and sparrows, should be in the cottonwoods and campgrounds along the river.

ANCHOR POINT

The best Cook Inlet birding from land is probably at Anchor Point (Milepost 156.9; 16 miles to Homer; see map on next page). Anchor Point (area population under 2,000) has facilities and accommodations for a comfortable stay. Drive through town until you see the school on your right, turn right in front of the Anchor River Inn, and proceed down the hill and across the Anchor River bridge on the Old Sterling Highway. Just past the bridge, turn right onto paved Anchor River Road and park in any one of several campgrounds at Anchor River State Recreation Area. The trails along both banks of the river west of the bridge and on the southwest side of the river east of the bridge can easily be negotiated in order to look for birds in the cottonwoods, willows, and alders. Here you may find Common and Red-breasted Mergansers, Greater and Lesser Yellowlegs, Spotted and Least Sandpipers, Belted Kingfisher, and most of the local songbirds such as swallows, warblers, and woodland sparrows. Patient fly fishermen sometimes watch Beaver, River Otter, Muskrat, and Mink along the bank.

Continue down Anchor River Road toward Cook Inlet (1.3 miles from the turnoff) and park at the campground or the parking lot at the end of the road. From here you can walk the beach in either direction. Occasionally you can drive on the beach to the mouth of the river, but be alert for soft sand. Scan the grassy marshes between the road, the beach, and the river as well as the braided last mile of the river for ducks, Bald Eagle, Northern Harrier, Least Sandpiper, Savannah Sparrow, and other marsh birds. Whimbrel and Baird's and Pectoral Sandpipers are regular spring and fall migrants. Scoping the nearshore waters of Cook Inlet might yield a good assortment of seabirds

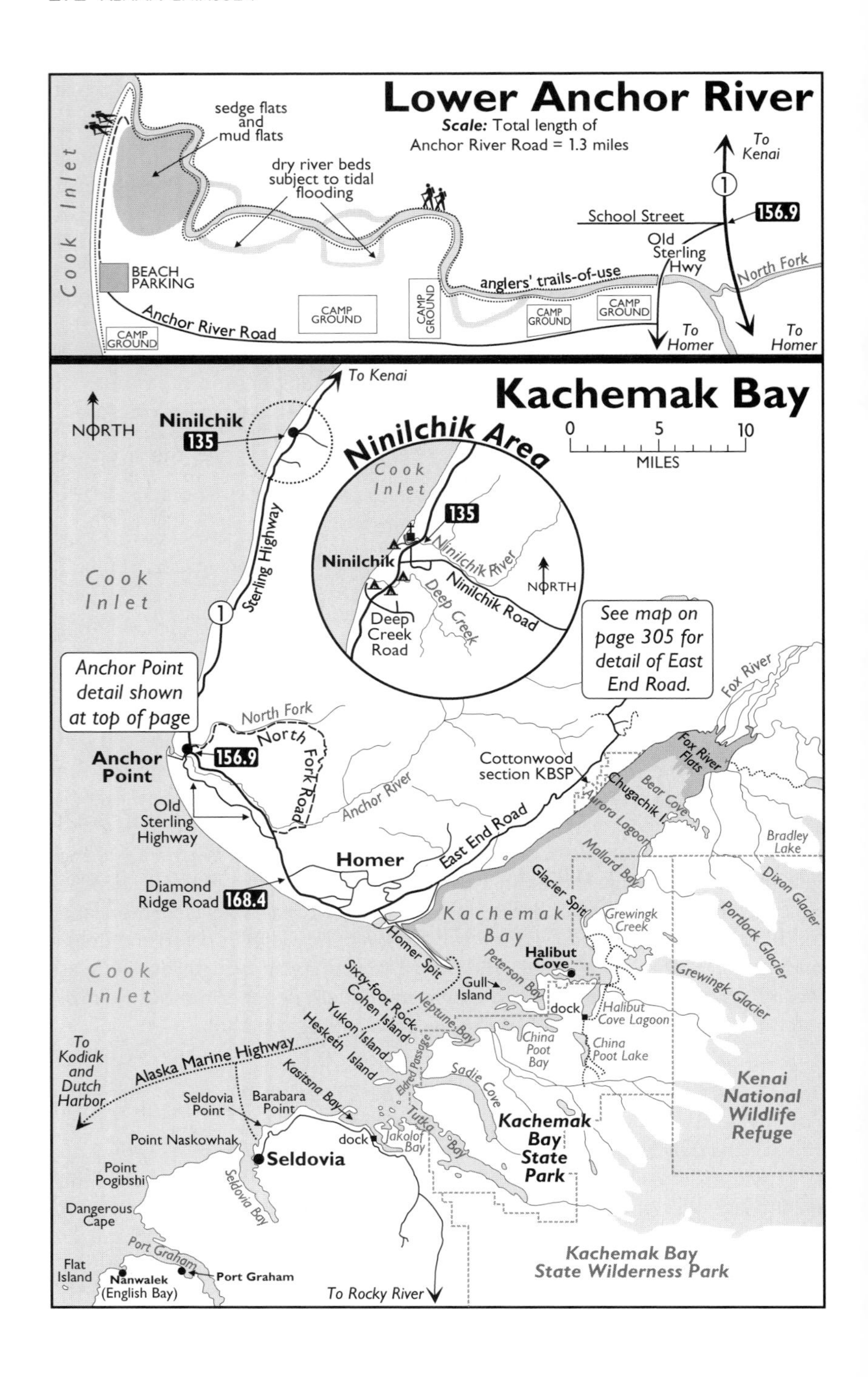
Lower Anchor River
Scale: Total length of Anchor River Road = 1.3 miles
To Kenai
1
156.9
School Street
Old Sterling Hwy
North Fork
sedge flats and mud flats
dry river beds subject to tidal flooding
Cook Inlet
BEACH PARKING
anglers' trails-of-use
Anchor River Road
CAMP GROUND
CAMP GROUND
CAMP GROUND
CAMP GROUND
CAMP GROUND
CAMP GROUND
To Homer
To Homer
Kachemak Bay
To Kenai
NORTH
Ninilchik
135
Ninilchik Area
0 5 10
MILES
Cook Inlet
135
Ninilchik
Ninilchik River
NORTH
Ninilchik Road
Deep Creek
Deep Creek Road
Sterling Highway
Cook Inlet
1
See map on page 305 for detail of East End Road.
Anchor Point detail shown at top of page
North Fork
North Fork Road
Fox River
Anchor Point
156.9
Cottonwood section KBSP
Fox River Flats
Old Sterling Highway
Anchor River
Chugachik I.
Bear Cove
Aurora Lagoon
Bradley Lake
East End Road
Mallard Bay
Homer
Dixon Glacier
Glacier Spit
Diamond Ridge Road 168.4
Grewingk Creek
Portlock Glacier
Kachemak Bay
Homer Spit
Halibut Cove
Peterson Bay
Grewingk Glacier
Cook Inlet
Sixty-foot Rock
Gull Island
Cohen Island
dock
Halibut Cove Lagoon
Neptune Bay
Yukon Island
China Poot Bay
China Poot Lake
Hesketh Island
Alaska Marine Highway
Eldred Passage
Sadie Cove
To Kodiak and Dutch Harbor
Kasitsna Bay
Kenai National Wildlife Refuge
Seldovia Point
Barabara Point
Tutka Bay
Kachemak Bay State Park
dock
Jakolof Bay
Point Naskowhak
Seldovia
Point Pogibshi
Seldovia Bay
Dangerous Cape
Port Graham
Kachemak Bay State Wilderness Park
Flat Island
Nanwalek (English Bay)
Port Graham
To Rocky River

feeding in the rapidly moving tidal flow of the inlet, including Red-throated, Pacific, and Common Loons, Sooty and Short-tailed Shearwaters, Double-crested and Pelagic Cormorants, scoters, Bonaparte's, Mew, and Glaucous-winged Gulls, Black-legged Kittiwake, Arctic and Aleutian Terns, Common Murre, Pigeon Guillemot, and Horned Puffin. Bright-plumaged juvenile Pacific Golden-Plovers are often along the beach in fall; Aleutian Terns feeding young on the beach also have been found in fall, and an Ivory Gull was seen here one spring.

ANCHOR POINT TO HOMER

Return to the Sterling Highway and proceed south toward Homer. At Milepost 160 you can turn right onto a gravel road, cross the bridge, and park to walk the riverside trails. At Milepost 161, the road crosses the river. At Milepost 164.5, the North Fork Road leaves to the left and 18.1 miles later returns to downtown Anchor Point. Continuing south on the Sterling Highway, you will come to Diamond Ridge Road on the left at Milepost 168.4. The headquarters for Kachemak Bay State Park is on the right at Milepost 169.9 and the Borough Solid Waste Disposal Facility (dump) is on the left at Milepost 170.5. The dump usually attracts hundreds of gulls and Common Ravens. Rarely, European Starlings and Brown-headed Cowbirds have also been seen here. Just around the next corner at the top of Baycrest Hill on the right a large viewpoint (restrooms) that allows you to obtain unobstructed views of Kachemak Bay from the Grewingk Glacier to Point Pogibshi, the Homer Spit, and lower Cook Inlet. From here you can look north to see the impressive volcanoes of Mount Redoubt and Mount Iliamna, look across at Mount Augustine, and look toward the southwest to Cape Douglas on the west side of Cook Inlet. On windy summer days, watch along this steep bluff face for eagles, hawks, gulls, and ravens using the updrafts for lift. Barrow's Goldeneyes nest below at some ponds and vegetation on a bench above tideline. This area is protected, because it is a jewel at the entrance to Homer. It can be reached by a very steep climb from the bluff or from the beach in a long hike from Homer.

HOMER

Homer is located on the southwestern shore of the Kenai Peninsula and on the north shore of Kachemak Bay (maps on pages 294 and 308). About 9,000 people live in the city and surrounding area between Anchor Point and the head of Kachemak Bay. The bay was designated a Critical Habitat Area by the Alaska legislature and is managed by the ADF&G to maintain and enhance fish and wildlife populations and their habitats. It is a biologically diverse and rich ecosystem supporting thousands of birds, marine mammals, and fish, as

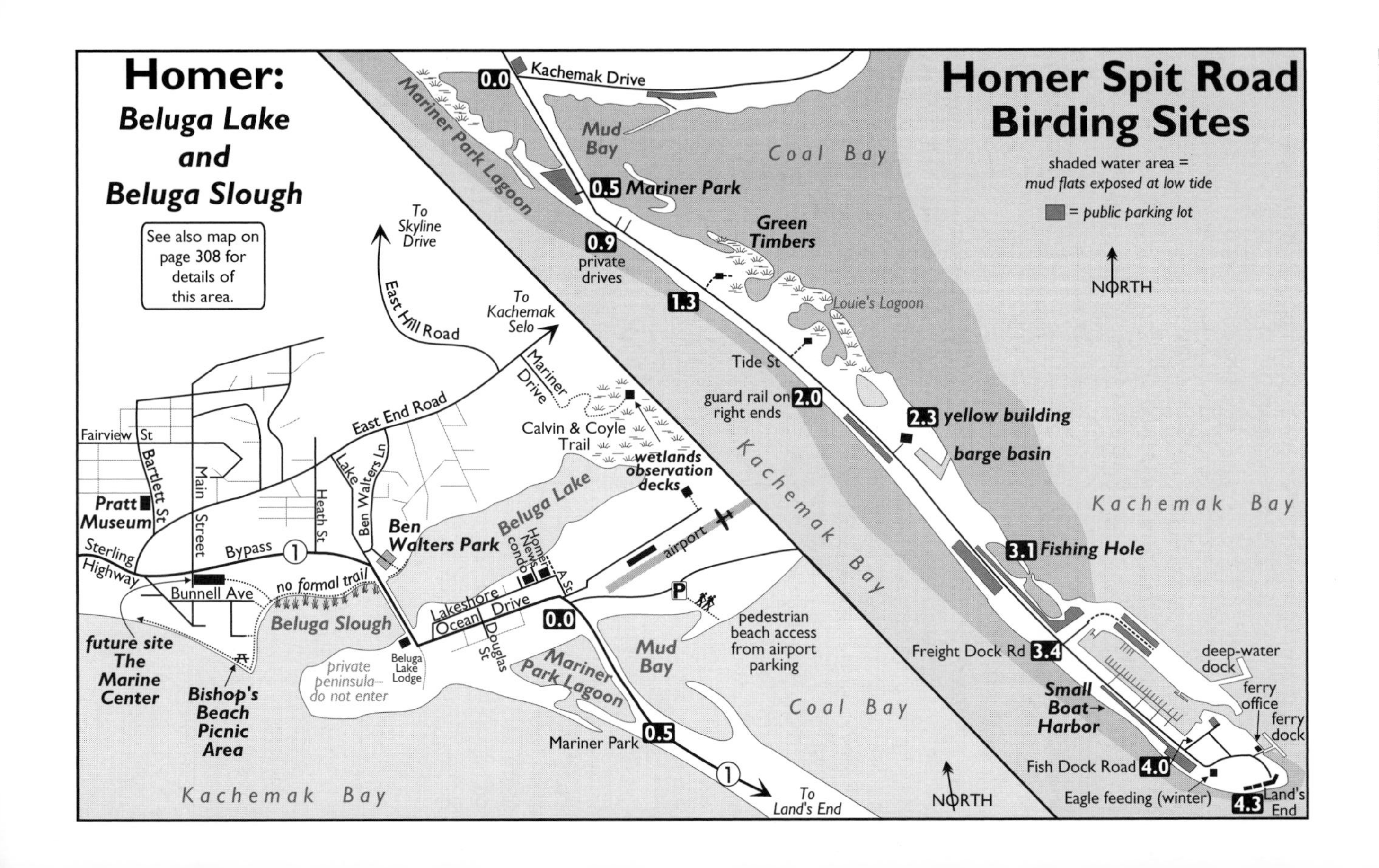
Homer: Beluga Lake and Beluga Slough
See also map on page 308 for details of this area.
To Skyline Drive
East Hill Road
To Kachemak Selo
Mariner Drive
East End Road
Calvin & Coyle Trail
wetlands observation decks
Fairview St
Bartlett St
Main Street
Heath St
Lake
Ben Walters Ln
Pratt Museum
Ben Walters Park
Beluga Lake
Homer News condo
A St
airport
Sterling Highway
Bypass
1
Bunnell Ave
no formal trail
Beluga Slough
Lakeshore Drive
Ocean Drive
Douglas St
0.0
P
pedestrian beach access from airport parking
Mud Bay
future site The Marine Center
Bishop's Beach Picnic Area
private peninsula—do not enter
Beluga Lake Lodge
Mariner Park Lagoon
Coal Bay
Mariner Park
0.5
1
To Land's End
Kachemak Bay
NORTH
Homer Spit Road Birding Sites
shaded water area = mud flats exposed at low tide
= public parking lot
NORTH
0.0
Kachemak Drive
Mariner Park Lagoon
Mud Bay
Coal Bay
0.5 Mariner Park
Green Timbers
0.9 private drives
1.3
Louie's Lagoon
Tide St
guard rail on right ends 2.0
2.3 yellow building
barge basin
Kachemak Bay
Kachemak Bay
3.1 Fishing Hole
Freight Dock Rd 3.4
deep-water dock
Small Boat Harbor
ferry office
ferry dock
Fish Dock Road 4.0
Eagle feeding (winter)
4.3 Land's End

well as shellfish and other invertebrates that form the base of the marine food chain. Any activity that could potentially harm fish and wildlife resources in the bay is thoroughly reviewed. Many activities, such as oil and gas exploration and mining, are prohibited outright; others, such as use of personal watercraft (jet skis) may be regulated in the future, and timber transport, dock construction, and mariculture require special permits.

Kachemak Bay is part of the National Estuarine Research Reserve system (see Kachemak Bay Research Reserve under *Organizations*, page 539). The Research Reserve has formed a partnership with the U.S. Fish and Wildlife Service's Alaska Maritime National Wildlife Refuge that is headquartered in Homer, and will move into a new visitor facility in 2004 (see below).

The Pratt Museum, one of the finest small museums in the country, is located on Bartlett Street just north of Pioneer Avenue. It houses interpretive exhibits of the biological and cultural features of Kachemak Bay and lower Cook Inlet, including wildlife, marine resources, geology, anthropology, archaeology, history of the Homer area, and local art. A condensed version of the nationally acclaimed traveling exhibit, *Darkened Waters: Profile of an Oil Spill,* detailing the *Exxon Valdez* oil spill in Prince William Sound in 1989, is a main attraction. There is a botanical garden, adjoining woodlands with interpretive nature trails, a gift store, and extensive collections of local fauna, flora, and cultural materials that are available by appointment to the interested researcher. In the marine room you can watch nesting birds by television from cameras mounted on Gull Island in Kachemak Bay. You can zoom in and out on various birds or areas and move the camera in all directions. Museum visitors can also see Alaska's huge Brown Bears live through the Pratt's *River of Bears* remote camera exhibit. Museum docents are on hand to answer questions or share fascinating life-history information about these bears as they are being photographed across Cook Inlet at the McNeil River Bear Sanctuary.

Homer is also headquarters of the Alaska Maritime National Wildlife Refuge that stretches along coasts and islands from Southeastern Alaska to the tip of the Aleutian Islands and north along the western Alaskan coast almost to Barrow. Its mission is the protection and study of seabirds. More seabirds nest on this refuge than on the coastline of *all the rest* of the North American continent. The refuge visitor center is temporarily located at 451 Sterling Highway until a new, large Marine Center that will include seabird exhibits is completed in 2004. The site is on the south side of the Homer Bypass between Main Street and the Homer Waste Water Treatment Plant at 95 Sterling Highway. Nature trails that lead from the site of the future visitor center to Bishop's Beach are now in place. Additional trails to Beluga Slough and the shore of Kachemak Bay are planned. The refuge and the City of Homer sponsor the annual Kachemak Bay Shorebird Festival during the first week of May at the peak of the shorebird migration. Shorebird identification workshops, guest lectures, children's programs, and field trips attract hundreds of birders to witness the arrival of shorebirds to Kachemak Bay.

Homer has a northern maritime climate. The temperatures are generally cool and the seasonal temperature fluctuations that occur inland are moderated by Homer's proximity to the ocean. The cold ocean temperatures in lower Cook Inlet and Kachemak Bay (from 40–48°F in summer and down to 32°F in winter) keep summer temperatures cool and also don't allow the winter temperatures to dip very low. The annual average air temperature is 36.6°F, and precipitation is 24 inches, with May, June, and July being the driest months. The south side of Kachemak Bay is wetter than the north side and is an extension of the Pacific coastal rain forest. Differences in air temperature between the cool water surface and the land warmed by the sun create onshore winds (day breezes) on most sunny summer days. Seas on Kachemak Bay usually kick up in the afternoon to 3–4 feet, a little much for a skiff and too rough to permit birding from a small boat. Offshore winds sweeping down from the glaciers or out of bays and passes are more dangerous. Listen to the marine weather forecast on the VHF weather band (Channel 2) or on local radio stations. Generally, winds are out of the southwest in summer and northeast in winter. The bay is generally calmest in early morning and late evening after the sun goes down, so plan your birding and boating accordingly.

One of the most significant features of Kachemak Bay and Cook Inlet is the extent of the daily tide. You will need to schedule your birding activities along the coast with the tide in mind. Tidal ranges exceed 20 feet regularly and may go from -6 to +23 feet in a six-hour period. A vertical range of 20 to 29 feet translates into miles of mudflats exposed twice daily, especially in Mud Bay on the northeast side of the Spit and in sheltered lagoons on the south side of the bay. Read the Tide Cautions in the *Introduction*, page 19.

Because of the sensitivity of the storm berms above the high tideline throughout the Homer area, driving on the beach has been curtailed. In some areas you may drive below the high-tide line as long as you do not disturb the vegetation and driftwood in the storm berms. These berms not only protect inland areas from storm tides, but also provide nesting habitat for several species of birds. If you wish to drive on the beach, please check with the local police for current laws.

HOMER SPIT AND MUD BAY

The prime location to look for birds from shore is the 4.5-mile stretch of gravel projecting into Kachemak Bay, the Homer Spit. The Spit is a result of an ancient glacial moraine and is maintained by gravels deposited by ocean currents and reinforced by humans. Generally, the current flows into the bay on its south side and circles counter-clockwise to exit along the north shore of the Spit, where silt and sand are deposited. Severe winter storms hit the southwest side of the Spit and move tons of gravel towards the end of the Spit. Erosion of the Spit and undermining of the Spit Road require constant attention and addition of riprap (large rocks) to prevent the ocean from breaking through. Erosion of the bluffs all along the north side of the bay on both sides of the Spit reveals layers of coal that were mined early in Homer's history and still provide a heating source for local residents. There is a good history of Homer and Kachemak Bay written by Janet Klein (1996).

To reach the Spit from the Sterling Highway, follow the signs to the State ferry. Drive southeast on the Sterling Highway around the south side of Homer (the Bypass), bend right across the causeway between Beluga Lake and Beluga Slough, then continue to the left on Ocean Drive, and then right again after the gas station, and you are on the Spit road.

You can park at a lot on the left at the intersection of Kachemak Drive and Spit Road (Mile 0.0). From this location a paved trail goes almost the entire length of the Spit. Birding stops below are accessible from the trail and the road, however, the described route (with trip-odometer readings) is designed to be driven. A short distance from the parking area there is a viewing platform with interpretive displays on shorebird ecology. Scan the mudflats at the head of Mud Bay and Mariner Park lagoon. You can also park in the Mariner Park area farther along on the right and walk across to the paved trail to scan the rest of the head of Mud Bay. At high tide in the first two weeks of May, thousands of Western Sandpipers, along with Dunlins and Short-billed Dowitchers, sleep here, waiting for the tide to turn. As the tide falls, these species are joined by Black-bellied and Semipalmated Plovers, Whimbrels, occasional Hudsonian and Bar-tailed Godwits, Black Turnstones, Surfbirds, Red Knots, Semipalmated (rare) and Least Sandpipers, Bonaparte's and Mew Gulls, and other species to feed on the small clams and worms in the mud. In fall, Semipalmated Sandpipers may equal or exceed the number of Westerns; there may be a few godwits, Sanderlings, and other shorebirds here. Look for Stilt Sandpipers (rare) among the dowitchers. In late fall (September–October), Pectoral and Sharp-tailed Sandpipers can be seen in Mud Bay and on the flats on the west side of the Spit road. Eurasian and American Wigeons, Mallard, Northern Shoveler, Northern Pintail, Green-winged Teal, and Sandhill Crane can often be seen in and around Mud Bay from the viewing platform. Several species of diving ducks, especially rafts of Greater Scaup and Common Merganser, are present in winter. Rock Sandpipers winter along the north side of Kachemak Bay and along the Spit from October to March, with some birds arriving in August and others not departing until mid-May. They may be anywhere in rocky and gravel habitats from Bishop's Beach to

Miller's Landing, or on the mudflats in Mud Bay in winter, often in flocks numbering over 2,000 birds. Look for Dunlins in these large flocks. The intertidal area of Mud Bay is owned by the City of Homer, but has been designated as an international site by the Western Hemisphere Shorebird Reserve Network.

At Mile 0.5 of the Spit Road, a turnout on the right leads to the beach and a camper parking lot (Mariner Park). A regular two-wheel-drive car can pull in here, but as is true with the other turnouts on the Spit, it is not wise to drive any farther than necessary to get yourself comfortably off the road. This is often a good place to scan Kachemak Bay for loons and sea ducks, including eiders, scoters, and Harlequin Duck (to the west and along Bishop's Beach). A White-winged Tern was seen feeding here for 10 days in late summer 1992. You can walk across the inlet to the lagoon at low tide (but you cannot return at high tide) or walk the storm berm to the west to find nesting Semipalmated Plovers, Spotted and Least Sandpipers, and Savannah Sparrows. The berm also provides another view of Mariner Park lagoon. When the tide is high in summer, you may see Aleutian Terns flying across the road between Kachemak Bay and Mud Bay as they return to a nesting area farther up the bay.

As you continue down Spit Road, you may pause at pair of private driveways at Mile 0.9 on the left to scan Mud Bay, but please don't park here or walk through private property. A Western Gull and a Black-tailed Gull were seen here in June 1995. Juvenile Glaucous Gulls often loaf with Glaucous-winged, Mew, and Herring Gulls on an exposed gravel bar in Mud Bay during spring and early summer. At Mile 1.3, a turnoff to the left leads to a large flat (called Green Timbers) that is dry at low tide and also at moderate high tides, although a 20-foot tide will come up almost to the bottom of the access road. This can be an excellent area for all the shorebirds mentioned earlier, especially for species that like to wander in the grassy areas, such as American and Pacific Golden-Plovers, Whimbrel, Bristle-thighed Curlew (rare), and Least, Baird's, and Pectoral Sandpipers. Hudsonian, Marbled, and Bar-tailed Godwits also have been seen here along the outer berm at high tide. These grassy areas, and others farther along the Spit, are good spots in spring and fall for migrating Horned Lark, American Pipit, and Lapland Longspur, and in winter for Snow Bunting, the rare McKay's Bunting, and Gray-crowned Rosy-Finch. A Yellow Wagtail was seen here in July 1995, and two Yellow-headed Blackbirds were reported in July 1997.

On the left are two more private driveways (Mile 1.5). Most of the rest of the area to the left has been developed, but you can park and walk the flats in some places. Along the beach Ruddy and Black Turnstones and Surfbirds often loaf at high tide in the spring. Louie's Lagoon can be accessed at Tide Street (Mile 1.8), a short gravel road down the hill on the left toward a platform. This area has a conservation easement for shorebird-habitat protection. The platform may be developed as a bird-observation spot in the future.

The guard rail along the right side of the road between Mariner Park and Mile 2.0 does not allow you to pull over to scope the bay. However, the guard rail ends at Mile 2.0 and then you can pull over, park, and scan Kachemak Bay for seabirds (good place for loons, Common Eider, Harlequin Duck, and all scoters). Black Turnstones and Surfbirds often feed among the stones here, joined in summer by occasional migrant Wandering Tattlers. Sometimes Sanderlings are here in fall, and Steller's Eiders and Rock Sandpipers in winter.

At Mile 2.3 is a large dark mustard-yellow metal building on an area developed for marine storage and a barge basin. This is private property, but you can stop briefly on the roadside to scan the adjacent flats for shorebirds (godwits and the same species as those at Mud Bay) and Kachemak Bay to the west. Do not park in the lot. On the north side of the Spit there are a few remaining tidal basins that retain water at low tide that attract migrant waterfowl, such as Black Brant and Emperor Goose (very rare in winter and spring), as well as more common species such as Northern Pintail, Mallard, Green-winged Teal, and goldeneyes.

Black-bellied Plovers

You can park on the right side of the road by the riprap from about Mile 2.5 on to scan the ocean for loons, grebes, cormorants, sea ducks, gulls, sometimes murres and murrelets, and guillemots. Watch for shorebirds such as Wandering Tattler, Whimbrel, Black Turnstone, and Surfbird in the rocks and gravel between the road and the offshore sand bars.

On the left at Mile 3.1 is the popular Fishing Hole, stocked by the ADF&G with salmon for sport- fishing. Fingerling (smolt) King and Silver Salmon from a hatchery are planted here each year, and after a time in the open sea, they return to the Fishing Hole. This area is usually crowded with campers and fishermen, who are most active on the incoming tide in the first two weeks of June when the Kings return. Silvers return in August and September. The first

Franklin's Gull for Homer was seen here with kittiwakes as it was trying to catch bait cast by fishermen into the Fishing Hole. California Gull has been seen a few times at the outlet from the Fishing Hole, and Black Brant often stop along the gravel beach from here to the west for about a mile.

At Mile 3.4, turn left onto Freight Dock Road to a 30-acre landfill resulting from dredging of the Small Boat Harbor, which is on your right. Sometimes there are birds in the harbor itself— Pacific Loon, Mew and Glaucous-winged Gulls, Black-legged Kittiwake, Common Murre, Pigeon Guillemot, Marbled Murrelet, and even Fork-tailed Storm-Petrel may be swimming among the myriad of commercial fishing and sport boats in summer. In winter there are sometimes King Eider, often Long-tailed Duck, Common and Thick-billed Murres (rare), along with Pelagic Cormorant, Mew, Herring (and their hybrids), Thayer's, Slaty-backed (very rare), Glaucous-winged, and Glaucous (rare) Gulls, Black-legged Kittiwake, and Marbled Murrelet.

The large gravel landfill here is in a state of development, so it is difficult to predict where you can and cannot go. There is a large pile of wood chips with a complicated conveyor system to the freight dock that delivers 12–15,000 tons of chips to the Orient each year, and there may be large piles of logs stored here, also on their way to foreign markets. The Deep Water Dock has restrictions to access. Some of the area may be occupied by boat trailers and campers in the summer. You can park anywhere you can find a place and walk along the north edge of the landfill outside the log barrier to scan the water for sea ducks such as Common and Steller's Eiders, Harlequin Duck, Surf and White-winged Scoters, Long-tailed Duck, and Red-breasted Merganser. You may also find loons, Red-necked Grebe, cormorants, murres, Pigeon Guillemot, murrelets, and Arctic and Aleutian Terns. Merlin and rarely Peregrine Falcon stop on the log barrier and rocky north edge of the landfill. A Black-backed Wagtail was found here in June 1990. In early spring, Bald Eagles sit on the rocks at the harbor mouth. If you are allowed to walk toward the end of this projection, you might find a large Kenai Song Sparrow (*M.m. kenaiensis*) in the rocks or just get a better view of birds in the water. In winter, a large flock of Rock Sandpipers often roosts on the rocks on both sides of the harbor mouth at high tide. In spring, large flocks of Black Turnstones and Surfbirds, with occasional Red Knot (rare), Ruddy Turnstone, and Rock Sandpiper in breeding plumage, often spend high tide on these rocks. As you return to the Spit Road along the south side of the landfill, you can scan the harbor. Harbor Seal and Sea Otter sometimes are outside the mouth of the harbor and all the way into the head of Mud Bay, especially in spring and fall. In winter, over 250 Sea Otters loaf on gravel bars in Mud Bay or on ice cakes during a cold winter. Return to the Spit Road and turn left toward the end of the Spit.

There are several places to park along the edge of the Small Boat Harbor, but it is usually crowded in summer. There are restrooms here and charter boat offices, restaurants, and gift shops. The Harbormaster's office is at Mile 3.8 on the left and restrooms are there, also. Fish Dock Road at Mile 4.0 leads to a parking area at the harbor mouth, where you can check for Bonaparte's, Mew, Herring and Glaucous-winged Gulls, and Black-legged Kittiwake. A Ross's Gull was seen here one spring. Return and head toward the end of the Spit. The Alaska Marine Highway System (ferry) office and parking lot is on the left. Continue to the parking lot adjacent to Land's End resort at Mile 4.3. From here, you can walk on the beach around Land's End to scan for birds in Kachemak Bay. Fork-tailed Storm-Petrels are often present in spring and usually come in around the ferry dock in late summer and fall. You can sometimes see Pelagic and Red-faced Cormorants, Short-tailed and Sooty Shearwaters, Red-necked Phalaropes, jaegers, and Tufted Puffins from here, as well as loons, grebes, ducks, murres, guillemots, and murrelets. Sometimes a Northern Fulmar and, rarely, Sabine's Gull can be found near the dock.

On the southwest side of the RV Park at the end of the Spit is an assemblage of permanent trailers with a fence around them. For the past 15 years (usually after Christmas until mid-April) Jean Keene who lives here has been feeding the Bald Eagles with fish scraps collected from local canneries and fishermen. In summer the eagles are mostly across the bay where they nest, but in winter, up to 600 may collect at the end of the Spit to feed around Ms. Keene's trailer along with Ring-billed (rare), Herring, Thayer's, Glaucous-winged, hybrid, rarely Glaucous, and Slaty-backed Gulls, Northwestern Crows, and Common Ravens. She also puts out seed for wintering Gray-crowned Rosy-Finches. If you are here in winter, be sure to stop to see if she is feeding the eagles. Do not leave your car; you can watch and photograph from an open car window and not disturb the eagles. With development of Land's End Resort moving along the southwest side of the Spit, it is not known how long Jean Keene will be feeding the eagles in this area.

BELUGA LAKE AND BELUGA SLOUGH

From mid-April until the end of June and again from late September into early October, Beluga Lake is an ideal place to look for migrant waterfowl. There is only one public access to the lake on its north side. To reach it, turn right on Ben Walters Lane just north of the corner of Lake Street and the Sterling Highway, go around the north side of McDonald's restaurant, and turn immediately right into Ben Walters Park. Walk the short trail to the boardwalks at the edge of Beluga Lake. In spring, look for American Wigeon, Mallard, Northern Shoveler, Northern Pintail, Green-winged Teal, Greater Scaup, Bufflehead, and Common Merganser (rare). If you are lucky, you will find Trumpeter Swan, Eurasian Wigeon, Canvasback, Redhead, and

Ring-necked Duck. American Coots have been found here a few times in fall. One pair of Common Yellowthroats nested in the reeds west of the boardwalk in 1990. Red-necked Grebe and Bonaparte's Gull are common, the former a common breeder on the lake. A Black-headed Gull was found once in summer. Sometimes Short-eared Owls patrol the edge of the lake and you might see a few shorebirds there, such as Greater Yellowlegs. Take the path heading east to look for landbirds, such as Steller's and Gray Jays, Black-billed Magpie, Black-capped Chickadee, Ruby-crowned and Golden-crowned Kinglets, Hermit and Varied Thrushes, American Robin, Orange-crowned, Yellow, Myrtle, Wilson's, and sometimes Townsend's Warblers, Savannah, Sooty Fox, Lincoln's, Gambel's White-crowned, and Golden-crowned Sparrows, Slate-colored Junco, rarely Rusty and Red-winged Blackbirds, White-winged and sometimes Red Crossbills, Common Redpoll, and Pine Siskin.

Another access to the lake on its south side (to avoid looking into the morning sun) can be reached by driving across the causeway to Ocean Drive and turning left on Douglas Street that leads to the road paralleling the lake (Lakeshore Drive). Drive east until you see a condominium complex on the left. Turn down Landings Street to the lake's edge in the condo's parking lot (Homer News is to the right of the parking lot). From here, you can scan most of the lake. Return to Lakeshore Drive and drive east to the next intersection. The road to the right leads back up to Ocean Drive; you can turn left, park, and walk down the gravel road to the margin of the lake. There is private property on both sides of this road.

Return to Ocean Drive and turn left onto the road on the north side of the airport leading to the airport terminal building. Just past the entrance to the terminal on the north side is a viewing platform that looks over the east end of Beluga Lake, its marshes, and the extensive grasslands beyond. Sometimes you can spot Greater White-fronted and Canada Geese, Trumpeter and Tundra Swans, Sandhill Cranes, as well as the ducks mentioned earlier. In early spring, the grassy flat at the upper end of the lake is prime habitat for Homer's wintering Moose population. With a scope, you might spot up to 40 Moose in early morning or at dusk.

Surfbird

To view Beluga Slough, return west on Ocean Drive and park in the Beluga Lake Lodge parking lot on the corner. Or you can drive back to Ben Walters Park or to the lower section of McDonald's parking lot. Do not park along the causeway. The pulloffs on the east side of the causeway are private for floatplane pilots and not for the public. The south side of Beluga Slough is private property, so you will have to do your viewing from the sidewalk paralleling the highway. On the north side of the slough a path connects with the Alaska Maritime Refuge Visitor Center's nature trails at the outlet of Beluga Slough and at Bishop's Beach. Currently the trail extends from the location of the future visitor center to the east side of Bishop's Beach parking lot, with exits at Bunnell Street and a small street leading to beachfront homes. The central portion of the trail floats at high tides. You can park in a small lot across from the Tesoro/ Burger King building on the Bypass and walk the trail. Other access points are at Bishop's Beach and the east end of Bunnell Street. You may walk to the mouth of Beluga Slough (no trail), but do not drive on the beach or berms.

Homer's first Western Gull and first White-winged Tern both were found on Bishop's Beach in August 1992. From Bishop's Beach, you can walk all the way to Anchor Point at low tide, if you have the time and the endurance, but watch for tides over 18 feet as the water will back up to bluffs that are over 100 feet high and cannot be scaled!

Although Beluga Slough fills completely only at tides over 18 feet, it is still a good place for dabblers (Eurasian Wigeon in spring) and some diving ducks (Bufflehead, both goldeneyes, and, rarely, both mergansers) and shorebirds during spring migration. Greater Yellowlegs are regular along the tidal channels and are joined by flocks of Western and Least Sandpipers and occasional dowitchers. Geese and Sandhill Cranes are often seen in the marsh grass on the north side of the slough. A Killdeer here was a local rarity. Look for Merlin and Peregrine Falcons hunting shorebirds. All local species of swallows may be seen over the lake and slough on quiet summer evenings. Belted Kingfishers are sometimes present. From late September to mid-October, this is an excellent location to find a Sharp-tailed Sandpiper in a flock of Pectorals.

KACHEMAK DRIVE

Kachemak Drive begins at its junction with the Homer Spit Road (Mile 0.0) and extends 3.7 miles to join with East End Road. This paved road is heavily traveled by commercial fishermen who store and repair their boats and buy supplies at businesses on Kachemak Drive. At Mile 0.6, opposite one of the airport buildings and right before the Kachemak Bay Research Reserve building, a turnoff to the right leads to the long-term parking area for the older section of the airport. If you drive straight through the parking lot, a distance of only 100 feet or so, you will see a road that dives down the hill. Although you can drive this road and turn around at the bottom, you may find it slippery with mud, so it is best to park in the lot and walk the 250 yards down the hill. From here, at moderate tides, you can walk out on a sand bar that projects into Mud Bay to scan the area for ducks and shorebirds (see Homer Spit description for species and tidal dangers). From here, you can also walk the beach of Mud Bay and Kachemak Bay to your left and, at low tide, it is possible to make it to the head of Kachemak Bay by crossing the mouths of several creeks. This is a distance of some 25 miles and is not safe at tides over 18 feet because there are steep bluffs butting against the high-tide waters. However, this is the only public access near town to the north shore of Kachemak Bay; the balance of the south side of Kachemak Drive is private property.

Return to the parking lot and drive east on Kachemak Drive. Lampert Lake is on your left at Mile 1.1, with a bog consisting of stunted Black Spruce and ericaceous vegetation extending on the north side all the way to the end of the road. Lampert Lake is only a few feet deep and usually does not have many birds of interest on its surface. However, the bog and marsh vegetation around the lake often contain nesting Bonaparte's and Mew Gulls, Greater and Lesser Yellowlegs, Whimbrel, Short-billed Dowitchers, Wilson's Snipe, Red-necked Phalarope, and several passerines such as Alder Flycatcher, Orange-crowned and Wilson's Warblers, Savannah and Lincoln's Sparrows, Rusty Blackbird (rare), Common Redpoll, and Pine Siskin. During migration American Golden-Plover, Pectoral Sandpiper, and Long-billed Dowitcher are sometimes seen here. At Mile 1.7 on the left is a warehouse and storage yard and the narrow gravel road (Airport Access Road) that leads to the former tern colony. You can drive down this road, but stop and park before the red stop sign at the broken and open gate. From here, walk another 100 yards to view the marsh.

Over 80 pairs of Arctic and Aleutian Terns used to nest on the small island mounds in June, but by 1992, Mew Gulls had all but displaced the terns. As of this time, terns are no longer nesting here, but adults of both species may be seen flying over the area in summer. Both species apparently have relocated their nesting colonies farther northeast on the hills at the far upper end of Kachemak Bay. A small colony of Aleutian Terns has been located east of the mouth of Fritz Creek, but the area is not accessible to the public. Arctic Terns also nest elsewhere around the bay in several small colonies. In summer, both species feed in the north end of the bay, but the trip to find them requires a boat. In fall, Arctic Terns accumulate on the Spit, often in the hundreds, prior to their migration.

Return to Kachemak Drive; between the road and the bluff on your right note the devastated forest of majestic Sitka Spruce that has been killed by Spruce Bark Beetles. You can park in several turnouts along the road (one on the left at Mile 2.2) to search the remaining trees for common woodland birds. The land between the road and the bluff is private property. You will encounter much alder brush and scrub-willow vegetation on the north side of

Kachemak Drive that supports Alder Flycatcher, Orange-crowned and Wilson's Warblers, Sooty (and Red *P.i. zaboria* in winter) Fox, Savannah, Lincoln's, and Golden-crowned Sparrows, and a good population of Moose from late winter to mid-summer.

Opposite the gate of Northern Enterprises Boat Yard (Mile 3.3), pull into the parking lot on your right and walk to the edge of the low bluff overlooking Miller's Landing. Scan the beaches for shorebirds such as Wandering Tattler, Whimbrel, Black Turnstone, and Surfbird, in addition to the usual ducks, eagles, and gulls. Hundreds of Greater Scaup and thousands of scoters may be found along this side of the bay in winter. Kachemak Drive ends at East End Road.

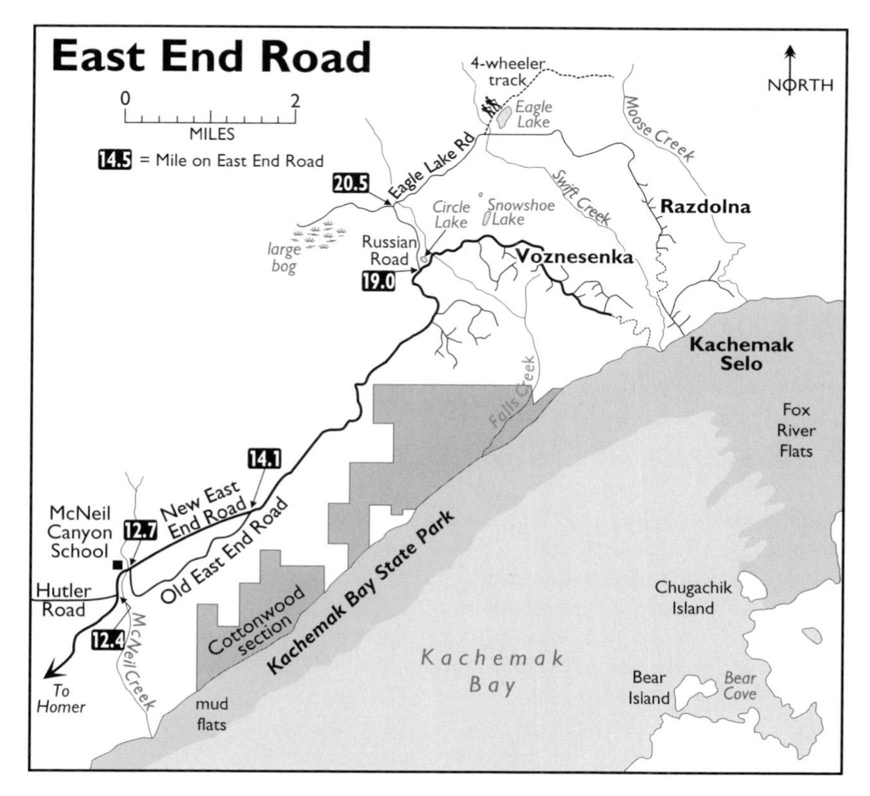

EAST END ROAD AND THE FOX RIVER FLATS

East End Road extends 23.3 miles through residential neighborhoods, fields, and heavy spruce woods to a parking area above the Russian village of Kachemak Selo. The view of the bay and the mountains just east of McNeil Canyon is worth the trip on a good day, but bird species are similar to those found closer to

Homer. There is a lot of "wild" country up on the ridge where one can hike, ride horses, cross-country ski, or snowmachine (depending on the season).

Pioneer Avenue becomes East End Road at its junction with Lake Street at the east end of Homer. Drive east on Pioneer Avenue, and at the corner of Lake Street (bowling alley on the left and blue building on the right), set your trip-odometer to 0.0 and continue straight ahead. (*Note*: You are not following actual roadside mile-markers on this birding route.) Drive east through a residential area and note the intersection of East Hill Road on your left at Mile 0.8; it provides one of three accesses to Skyline Drive (see below). The next road on your right (Mile 1.1) past the school is Mariner Drive leading to Calvin and Coyle Woodland Park. Park at the trailhead and walk the trail that circles around to a viewing platform overlooking the head of Beluga Lake. You may find many of the breeding thrushes, warblers, and other landbirds along the trail, and may see many Moose from the platform. Bring insect repellent! The trail connects to the Paul Banks school trail ending at the school's parking lot.

Continue along East End Road and note fields on both sides of the road starting at Mile 1.3 and continuing off and on most of the way out the road. Some of these fields are cultivated, some are used for production of hay, and some have returned to native vegetation. Sandhill Cranes frequent these fields in summer and can most predictably be seen at the lower end of the field east of the driveway to Seaside Farms (Mile 4.5). American Golden-Plover, Whimbrel, and Pectoral Sandpiper may be here in spring and fall. The turnoff to Kachemak Drive is at Mile 3.7.

East End Road continues through open fields and residential areas to about Mile 8.0. A Townsend's Solitaire was seen once at Mile 6 and again at Mile 8 in winter. The road drops to cross Fritz Creek at Mile 8.2. The Fritz Creek General Store, gas station, Homestead restaurant, and post office are at Mile 8.5. The road climbs gradually to the top of the ridge at about 1,300 feet above the bay. There are numerous gravel side roads that are safe to travel to search for owls, woodpeckers, Spruce Grouse, and thrushes. The uphill grade continues to McNeil Canyon (Mile 12.6). At Mile 12.4, Hutler Road enters from the left. This gravel road leads three miles west along the ridge; a branch turns north after about 1.7 miles, paralleling Beaver Creek; another side road at about 2.5 miles leads towards Bald Mountain. Drive these back roads with caution since they may be impassable with mud in early summer or with snow and ice in winter. Willow Ptarmigan and Snowy Owls are often seen around Bald Mountain in winter. East End Road passes the McNeil Canyon School and continues straight ahead.

The old gravel East End Road turns south at Mile 12.7 and is the best choice for views of the bay (near Mile 13.3). At Mile 13.8, for example, you can look up the bay and see Bear Cove, Chugachik Island, the dock and buildings supporting the Bradley Lake hydroelectric facility, and the Fox River Flats at the head of Kachemak Bay. These flats support large numbers of shorebirds and waterfowl in the spring and are the basis for establishment of the Fox River Flats Critical Habitat Area managed by the ADF&G for wildlife conservation. Directly across the bay is Aurora Lagoon and the outlet of Portlock Glacier. The road is narrow and winding and returns to the paved road at Mile 14.1.

East End Road now begins to drop and eventually turns inland through dense spruce at Mile 16.3, where you might easily find Spruce Grouse, Three-toed Woodpecker, Steller's Jay, Boreal Chickadee, Hermit and Varied Thrushes, Myrtle and Townsend's Warblers, and other forest species. At Mile 19.0, the road to the Russian village of Razdolna turns to the left past Circle Lake. Turn left on Circle (Eagle) Lake Road and continue to a fork at Mile 20.5. Stay left and go through an open gate. Continue on this gravel road through open bog and dwarf spruce vegetation, staying left again at Mile 21.8. There is a large bog on the left where Least Sandpipers, Parasitic Jaegers, Mew Gulls, and Arctic Terns nest. To view the bog, continue down the hill past Mile 21.8 and park at the pullout at the bottom. Scope the area to the left. You should find singing Wilson's Warblers and Golden-crowned Sparrows and possibly a Willow Ptarmigan. Keep alert for the call of Aleutian Terns that have been seen flying over this bog to the north carrying fish. The new nesting colony has not been discovered, however, and it is not advisable to drive farther out this road.

Return to the open gate mentioned above (at Mile 20.5) and turn sharp-left onto the road to Razdolna. Continue about one mile to a parking area on the left just before a four-wheeler track that leads up the hill. Walk up the trail to view Eagle Lake, where there is a nesting pair of Pacific Loons, and in spring, Mallard, Lesser Yellowlegs, Least and Pectoral Sandpipers, dowitchers, Red-necked Phalarope, Boreal and Black-capped Chickadees, and sometimes warblers, such as Townsend's and Blackpoll.

Wilson's Snipe

Return to East End Road. You can drive farther out this road through the Russian

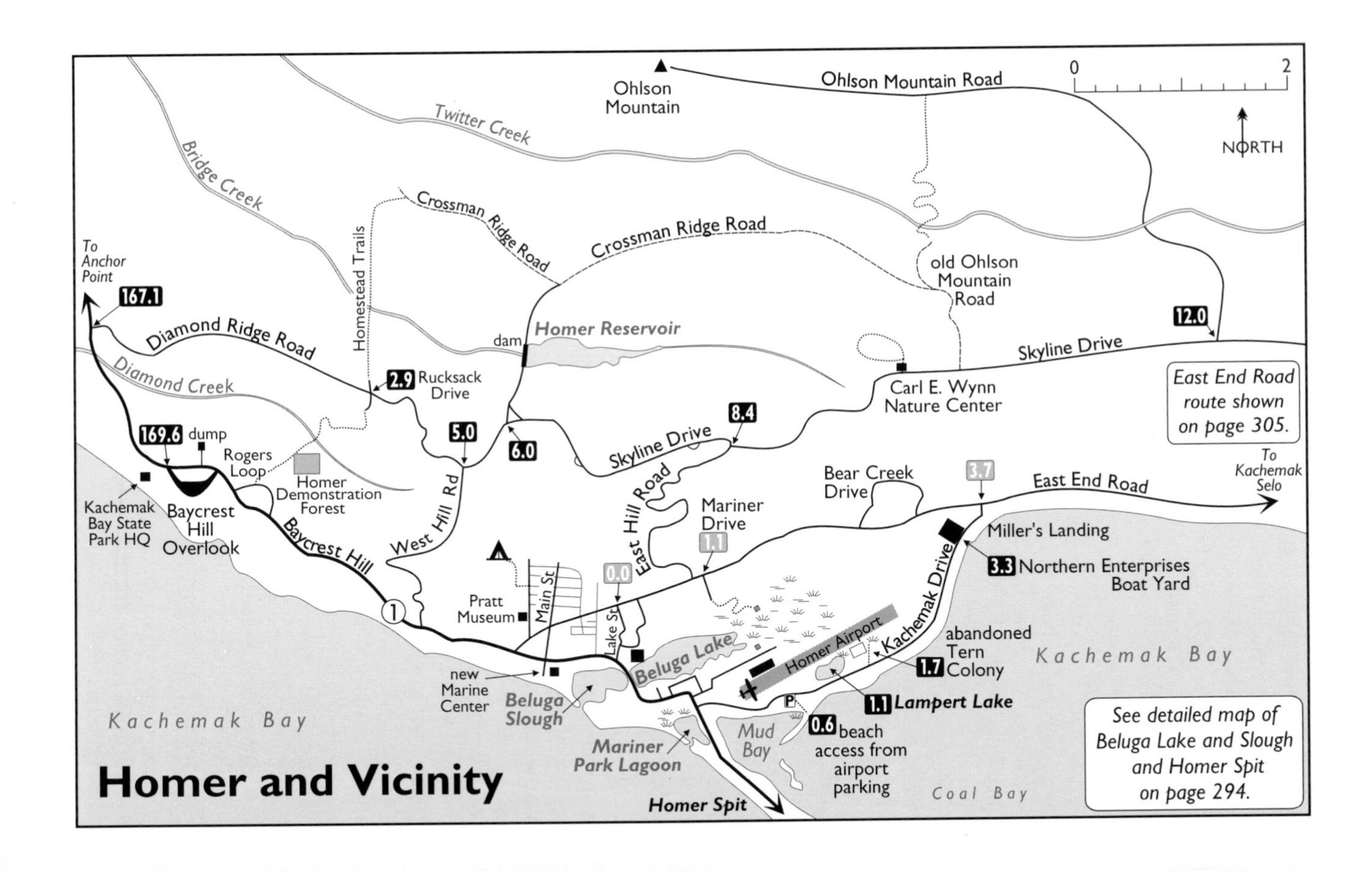
Homer and Vicinity
0
2
NORTH
Ohlson Mountain
Ohlson Mountain Road
Twitter Creek
Bridge Creek
Crossman Ridge Road
Crossman Ridge Road
old Ohlson Mountain Road
Homestead Trails
To Anchor Point
167.1
Diamond Ridge Road
Diamond Creek
dam
Homer Reservoir
12.0
Skyline Drive
East End Road route shown on page 305.
2.9
Rucksack Drive
Carl E. Wynn Nature Center
169.6
dump
5.0
6.0
Skyline Drive
8.4
Rogers Loop
Homer Demonstration Forest
To Kachemak Selo
Bear Creek Drive
3.7
East End Road
East Hill Road
Kachemak Bay State Park HQ
Baycrest Hill Overlook
Baycrest Hill
West Hill Rd
Mariner Drive
1.1
Miller's Landing
3.3
Northern Enterprises Boat Yard
Pratt Museum
Main St
0.0
Lake St
1
Kachemak Drive
Homer Airport
Beluga Lake
abandoned Tern Colony
1.7
Kachemak Bay
new Marine Center
Beluga Slough
1.1
Lampert Lake
P
0.6
beach access from airport parking
Mud Bay
Kachemak Bay
Mariner Park Lagoon
Homer Spit
Coal Bay
See detailed map of Beluga Lake and Slough and Homer Spit on page 294.

village of Voznesenka. If you stay on the main road, at its end you will find a series of parking places filled with four-wheel-drive cars, pick-up trucks, and all-terrain vehicles (ATVs). The people living in the Russian village of Kachemak Selo, to the left at the base of the bluff, drive their ATVs up the narrow switch-back trail and drive their cars into town. You can see some of their fishing boats in the water or beached on the mud from lookouts on the trail. You may walk down the trail to the beach if you wish and proceed left up the bay, passing the Russian village, to meet the Fox River Flats. There are several rivers to cross to get onto the flats. Although it is possible to reach the flats at low tide when the rivers spread out over the mud (watch for deep tidal trenches), it is not advisable.

DIAMOND RIDGE AND SKYLINE DRIVE

Diamond Ridge Road begins at its junction with the Sterling Highway north of Homer, 5.6 miles from the intersection of Pioneer Avenue with the Sterling Highway. Diamond Ridge Road continues as Skyline Drive past its intersection with West Hill Road, so these two roads are treated together along with Ohlson Mountain Road, which extends north into the hills from Skyline Drive. All of these roads are gravel and have heavy frost heaves in spring that persist well into June. Diamond Ridge Road runs from 800 to1,200 feet above sea level.

The ridge affords marvelous views of Homer, the Spit, the Kenai Mountains and glaciers across Kachemak Bay, and the volcanoes on the west side of Cook Inlet. Vegetation consists of a mixture of wet boggy meadows with tall grasses and sedges, Fireweed, intermittent stands of spruce, and clumps of alder, willow, and Pacific Red Elder. Some of the area is residential and some has been farmed.

The climate here is somewhat colder in winter than that in Homer, with more snow than at sea level; it is slightly warmer in summer. Nevertheless, with few exceptions, birds here are the same as can be found at lower elevations. Swainson's and Gray-cheeked Thrushes are more common, especially the latter, on the ridge. Spruce Grouse, Wilson's Snipe, Gray Jay, Hermit and Varied Thrushes, American Robin, Pine Grosbeak, Common Redpoll, Pine Siskin, and Sooty Fox and Golden-crowned Sparrows are common. Northern Shrike is uncommon. Occasionally there may be American Pipit, Lapland Longspur, and Snow Bunting during migration. Northern Saw-whet Owls have been heard along the bluff in spring, and you might spot Willow Ptarmigan or Snowy Owl in winter. Moose move into this area in late spring and summer, remaining until heavy snow drives them down to the Homer bench at or near sea level below. Coyotes are here, too.

Beginning at the Sterling Highway / Diamond Ridge Road junction, you will climb for about 1.6 miles and reach the top of the drive at at the radio station, 1,200 feet above sea level . Behind you are Mount Iliamna and Mount Redoubt to the north and Mount Augustine and Cape Douglas to the south. At about Mile 2.9 look for Rucksack Drive and a sign to the Homestead Trail system. Developed in 1993 this system of trails affords a great opportunity to explore the ridges, fields, and forests above Homer. You can walk to the south and west where the trail currently leads to Rogers Loop (called also Sterling Loop) on Baycrest Hill at the west entrance to Homer. This trail goes through a wet spruce forest with nesting Solitary Sandpipers and White-winged Crossbills. Sometimes there are Spruce Grouse easily visible here. To the north the trail leads down the valley and up to Ohlson Mountain Road (about three miles). Diamond Ridge Road ends after five miles at its intersection with West Hill Road, which will bring you back down a steep paved switchback road through residential neighborhoods to the Sterling Highway one mile west of Homer.

Skyline Drive (leading left from the West Hill Road intersection; see map) continues along the ridge above Homer. Turn left onto Skyline Drive and at Mile 6.0 are two left turns that form a Y leading to a single narrow dirt road that travels down about one-half mile to the reservoir for the City of Homer. Drive across Bridge Creek dam to look for ducks, loons, and swallows, or stop to fish for Steelhead Trout stocked in the lake. American Dippers may be in the outflow stream and have nested at the base of the dam. There are hiking and mountain-bike trails from the far end of the dam up on Crossman Ridge, but do not attempt to drive beyond the dam. Turn around and come back to Skyline Drive, turn left, and proceed eastward. There are good views at Miles 7.0 and at 8.0 where there is a school-bus turnaround that is a good spot to park to enjoy the view of Kachemak Bay, Beluga Lake and Slough, the Spit, and Homer. At Mile 8.4, Skyline Drive meets East Hill Road (to the right). If you wish to head back to town now, East Hill Road leads down a steep paved switchback through residential neighborhoods to East End Road, 0.8 mile east of Homer.

To continue the birding route, proceed along the rim of the bluff and note the stands of Quaking Aspen on the hillside, unusual at this elevation. The road turns abruptly left and then right. Just past the second turn is a parking lot on the left for the Carl E. Wynn Nature Center, part of the Center for Alaskan Coastal Studies (CACS). You can walk the boardwalk and trail system in an area rich in wildflowers in mid-to-late summer. A nominal fee is charged during daylight hours in the summer while naturalists are stationed at the Center, but in the off-season you may walk the trails without calling for permission.

About one-half mile farther on Skyline Drive is another parking lot next to a gravel road that runs north. This is the Old Ohlson Mountain Road, which connects via a very rough mud road to Crossman Ridge Road. It is best to park in the lot and walk the road. Where Crossman Ridge road turns left after about one-half mile, continue straight until the road turns sharply to the right to end at a private house. At the westernmost bend of the last turn, find the rough car-track slanting across the fields and down the hill to the west. You can walk this track in summer as it descends into Twitter Creek and occasionally find Spruce Grouse, Belted Kingfisher, warblers including Blackpoll, and sparrows. The track continues across the creek and up the hill to join Ohlson Mountain Road.

Return to your car at Skyline Drive and drive east until your odometer reads 12.0 (that is, 12 miles from the junction of the Sterling Highway and Diamond Ridge Road). Skyline Drive continues another four miles and ends in a turnaround. Turn left onto Ohlson Mountain Road (no sign). This road goes only five miles to an abandoned radar station (now a gravel pit) on the top of Ohlson Mountain, but is a worthwhile drive through pasture land and great Moose habitat. There is a rope tow on a ski hill and cross-country ski trails on your left at Mile 2.1; plowing in winter stops at Mile 4.3, but in summer you can drive to the top of the mountain for a panoramic view of the area. Watch for gravel trucks. Northern Shrikes sometimes sit on the power lines. Return down the hill and Ohlson Mountain Road to Skyline Drive, turn right, and continue straight ahead down East Hill Road and back to town.

KACHEMAK BAY STATE PARK

Kachemak Bay State Park and the adjoining Kachemak Bay State Wilderness Park cover almost 290,000 acres on the lower Kenai Peninsula across Kachemak Bay from Homer (map on page 292). The park extends from tidelands on Kachemak Bay, through coastal spruce forest, into alpine meadows, through glacier-covered valleys and over rocky mountain peaks, and down to saltwater on the Gulf of Alaska. There is a small section of the park at Cottonwood Creek on the north side of the bay east of Fritz Creek. Headquarters is at the top of Baycrest Hill on the Sterling Highway, four miles north of Homer (May–September hours, 8 AM–4:30 PM). Here you can pick up a map and a description of its numerous hiking trails. Because most of the park is across the bay, access is available only by boat or floatplane. Several water-taxi operators and air-charter services are permitted to take you into the park; inquire at the Homer Chamber of Commerce (235-7740) or ask at park headquarters.

The Center for Alaskan Coastal Studies maintains a field station in Peterson Bay with extensive hiking trails for those interested in birds, botany, and intertidal life. Contact their office in Homer to obtain maps and to schedule trips to the Center (235-6667). The land surrounding the CACS station is owned by the Seldovia Native Corporation (SNA) and this land borders the Park. If you wish to walk on SNA land, you should have a permit ($5) and take a water-taxi to those lands. Check with CACS for information.

Once you reach the park by boat, stop at the Halibut Cove Lagoon ranger station (open May–September) to check in. Entering and leaving Halibut Cove Lagoon however, can be accomplished only around high tide when the connecting channel is running with tidal flow. If you are in a small skiff, you should make it at a six-foot tide or greater. Stay close to the right bank all the way in to the lagoon. Private boats can moor at the dock at the head of the Lagoon. From here, you can reach some of the trailheads such as those leading to China Poot Lake, Poot Peak, and the Lagoon Trail. There are mooring buoys at other locations in the park.

The south side of Kachemak Bay is wetter than the Homer side and still has some good stands of Sitka and Lutz (hybrid of White and Sitka) Spruce and Western Hemlock in a coastal rain-forest climate with accompanying plant and animal life. Some birds are easier to spot here than on the north side of the bay, including, for example, nesting Pacific Loon, Three-toed and Black-backed (uncommon) Woodpeckers, Winter Wren, Golden-crowned Kinglet, American Dipper, Gray-cheeked and Varied Thrushes, Townsend's Warbler, Song Sparrow, and Red and White-winged Crossbills (irregular). Rufous Hummingbird and Chestnut-backed Chickadee are often seen on this side of the bay. If you hike to alpine tundra, look for Golden Eagle, ptarmigan, Horned Lark, Northern Wheatear, nesting American Pipit, and possibly Yellow Wagtail (one record in summer). Kittlitz's Murrelet nests in the rocky scree above timberline.

Kittlitz's (*left*) and Marbled (*right*) Murrelets; basic (winter) plumages above, alternate (summer) plumages below

ON THE WATER — KACHEMAK BAY AND LOWER COOK INLET

One of the biggest thrills a birder can have in the Homer area is to get out on the water and observe seabirds up close. This can be accomplished by taking the state ferry *Tustumena*, taking a chartered tour, using your own boat, or going with a friend who is knowledgeable about the birds and boating on Kachemak Bay. A current schedule for the *Tustumena* may be obtained at the State Ferry Office at the end of Homer Spit, by checking the Alaska Marine Highway System's web site, or by telephone (see page 15). Most of the summer ferry trips to Seldovia, Kodiak, and Dutch Harbor have a USFWS naturalist on board, who can advise you where to expect species of interest. The naturalist is also available to assist in identification of seabirds and marine mammals and presents informational programs about refuges and wildlife. Call the Alaska Maritime Refuge Visitor Center to find out when a naturalist will be on board the ferry.

Several charter companies and private ferries with offices located on the Spit boardwalks cater to birders and sightseers, generally from May through September. Bay Excursions has two boats, a small one for 3-4 people and a larger one for up to 12. They are captained by Karl Stoltzfus who knows where to find Kittlitz's Murrelets and Aleutian Terns and other birds around the bay. Rainbow Tours has a larger boat and makes daily trips to Peterson Bay, Gull Island, and Seldovia. In 2001 they made trips to the Barren Islands; check with them to find out if they are still making this run.

TRIPS ON KACHEMAK BAY AND COOK INLET BY CHARTER AND PRIVATE BOAT

If you take your own boat onto Kachemak Bay, take every safety precaution for yourself, your passengers, and your boat. Follow all of the Coast Guard safety rules and carry all required equipment. Let someone know where you are going and when you expect to return. Kachemak Bay can be smooth as glass one minute and an hour later have four-to-six-foot swells with chop and wind out of the southwest. You may find it calm back in a cove, but a gale can be blowing on the bay. Pay attention to the Marine Weather forecasts. In summer, your best boating (and best birding) is usually done in the morning before the day breeze kicks up. Usually you will not encounter rough seas if you plan to return to port by noon.

Most birding and sightseeing charter boats and Kachemak Bay ferries to Halibut Cove take you to Gull Island, a series of small rocks only a few miles across the water from the end of the Spit. A population of 15,000+ birds nest on Gull Island in summer. Here you should be able to find nesting Pelagic and Red-faced Cormorants, Glaucous-winged Gull, Black-legged Kittiwake, Common Murre, Pigeon Guillemot, Tufted Puffin, and usually Horned Puffin. There are thousands of kittiwakes nesting along the lower part of the rocks, and the murres occupy the middle and upper rocky sections, with both species of cormorants tucked in also. Tufted Puffins dig burrows at the top of the island and a few pairs of Horned Puffins may nest in crevices in the rocks.

There may be a Song Sparrow on the island; usually there are one or more Double-crested Cormorants and occasional shorebirds on the rocks, such as Black Oystercatcher, Wandering Tattler, Black Turnstone, and Surfbird. Watch for Brandt's Cormorant, seen only twice on Gull Island. Usually there are Bald Eagles on the island or preying on nesting birds. With luck you'll see a Peregrine Falcon. On your way to and from the island, look for loons, ducks, phalaropes, jaegers, gulls, Arctic and Aleutian Terns, and Marbled and Kittlitz's Murrelets.

Your charter-boat captain can negotiate the back (southeast) side of Gull Island from 0 to any high tide by staying about 15 to 20 feet away from the rocks all the way past the island group. Thick areas of Bull Kelp appear at low tide, there are rocks to the south of the island that are covered at higher tides, and the tide rips toward the entrance to China Poot Bay can be dangerous.

Excellent birding can be found within a mile of the Spit if you stay in about 30 feet of water and cruise the southwest side of the Spit back toward its base. Here you will find Red-throated Loon (rare), Pacific Loon (common, summer), Common Loon (common, all year), Yellow-billed Loon (rare anytime, but more likely in winter), grebes, cormorants, King Eider (uncommon, winter), Steller's Eider (common in winter), Common Eider (common, all year), Harlequin Duck (all year), rafts of Surf, White-winged, and some Black Scoters, Long-tailed Duck (late spring, early fall, winter), gulls, terns, murres, Pigeon Guillemot, puffins, murrelets, and other marine species. On the other side of the Spit in Coal Bay and Mud Bay, there may be rafts of Greater Scaup as well as some of the alcids, but watch out for shallow water. Beluga Whales are often found between the ferry dock and the head of Mud Bay when the herring are running in the spring, when the Silver Salmon are running in the fall, and sometimes in mid-winter. Killer Whales are sometimes seen from the tip of the Spit west during summer. If you go north of Miller Landing, you may find Aleutian Terns.

If you have time, ask your captain to go to the extreme north end of Kachemak Bay where you can find most species of dabbling ducks and some geese on the Fox River Flats and the common marine species in adjacent waters. Most of the area north of Chugachik Island becomes marginal at best to navigate at low tide. There is a public dock at the Bradley Lake hydroelectric facility that allows access to a road up the mountain that leads into the alpine tundra. You can reach the dock only at high tides since the dock goes dry at most low tides. You will have to tie your boat up to the dock, realizing that it will go dry at low tide, and wait until the next high tide before being able to get back out to the bay. Along the 6.5-mile-long, steep road to Bradley Lake dam, you might find ptarmigan and Golden Eagle. In migration look for Rough-legged Hawk, Horned Lark, and if you are lucky, Northern Wheatear and Yellow Wagtail. Belugas are sometimes found off the mouths of rivers in the upper part of Kachemak Bay.

Returning along the south side of the bay, Aurora Lagoon and the tidal basin behind Glacier Spit are excellent for fall waterfowl concentrations. Your captain may be able to let you go ashore on the bay side, where you can walk over the gravel and sand dunes to scan the basins. Both of these areas and the Fox River Flats have concentrations of shorebirds in spring. An excellent place to spend an hour is near the mouth of Grewingk Creek, which drains Grewingk Glacier Lake. Being careful of the shallow water, you can maneuver your boat close to the mouth where even in summer you might find a flock of Surfbirds along with a few Black Turnstones, a dowitcher, and occasionally a summer-plumaged Rock Sandpiper. Kittlitz's Murrelets prefer to fish in the silty glacial water off the mouth of the creek, where you might see up to 100 of these rare alcids from the creek mouth north to Aurora Lagoon. A slow trip all along the south side of the bay from Bear Cove to Halibut Cove will provide you with many interesting views of sea ducks, including eiders, scoters, Harlequin Duck, and goldeneyes, as well as many of the alcids.

Halibut Cove Lagoon and China Poot Bay are navigable to the uninitiated only at higher tides and even then it can be tricky. It is best to go with an experienced boater or guide. From the landings you have access to the trails of Kachemak Bay State Park. The rocky shores of Peterson Bay and China Poot Bay are excellent for studying intertidal life. A few Pigeon Guillemots and Horned Puffins nest in the rocks along the shore from Halibut Cove to Point Pogibshi. A stop near Sixty-foot Rock might yield some species not seen on Gull Island. Steller's Sea Lions and Sea Otters occasionally haul out on the rock.

After Sixty-Foot Rock, you can visit Tutka Bay and Sadie Cove, deep-water fjords. Although these fjords do not have unusual birding concentrations, sometimes you can find Mountain Goats on the hillsides of Sadie Cove. Sea Otters are often abundant around nearby Cohen, Yukon, and Hesketh Islands and in the Herring Islands near the mouth of Jakolof Bay. Eldred Passage behind Yukon Island is the preferred charter-boat route since there is more bird life and the water is protected from winds from the west. A pair of Black Oystercatchers has nested for several years on the southeast beach of Cohen Island. Do not come ashore on this private island. The oystercatchers have abandoned their nest in the past due to trespassers and their dogs. The shallow rocky waters between Yukon and Hesketh Island often contain concentrations of Marbled and sometimes Kittlitz's Murrelets. Look for Harbor Porpoise here. Horned Puffins nest on the west end of Hesketh Island. To the south, Jakolof Bay has a public dock where you can tie up and walk the road system south up into the alpine tundra and over the ridge to the Rocky River or to the west to Kasitsna Bay and Seldovia. (If you intend to walk this road and leave the right-of-way, you will be on Seldovia Native Association land, which requires a seasonal-use permit.) The best place to find auklets rare to Kachemak Bay is often in about 80 feet of water between Barabara Point and Seldovia Point west of Jakolof and KasitsnaBays. Minke and occasional Humpback Whales are sometimes here.

Proceeding southwestward on the water from Seldovia, you will come to Point Pogibshi. Usually there are increasing numbers of puffins off this point and south toward Dangerous Cape and Flat Island. In late summer and fall, you will encounter thousands of shearwaters, Northern Fulmars, hundreds of storm-petrels, and a few jaegers here in the open waters of lower Cook Inlet. If you have some bait herring, you can sometimes feed the fulmars from your hand. On a calm day you can boat south along the eastern shore of Cook Inlet and out into the Inlet itself. Your captain will watch the weather and the seas closely since there are dangerous tide rips around the islands and points in this part of Cook Inlet. Proceeding south from Point Pogibshi, stay in deep water as you near Dangerous Cape, named for its shallow, rocky reefs, which will have cormorants and kittiwakes on them at low tide. Note the large inlet on your left, Port Graham, which can be navigated by following the channel markers into the bay. The Native Alutiiq village of Port Graham is on the south side of this bay and just beyond is another Alutiiq community, Nanwalek (English Bay), easily visible from Cook Inlet.

Continue south and approach Flat Island on its eastern side (between the island and the mainland) and enter the bay, watching out for the large Bull Kelp. In summer a colony of over 200 Tufted Puffins nests on Flat Island; their burrows can be seen at the top of the rocky bluff in the grass-covered soil. One or more pairs of Black Oystercatchers and a colony of Bank Swallows also nest here. In early summer, there are sometimes a few Parakeet Auklets on the east side of Flat Island. You might also find Ancient Murrelet and Cassin's and Rhinoceros Auklets in the vicinity of Flat Island.

TRIPS TO SELDOVIA

The round-trip to Seldovia takes about six hours on the ferry *Tustumena* (3-hour layover in Seldovia), but much less on a charter boat, depending on the route taken. Most charters pass the Gull Island and Sixty-foot Rock seabird colonies, but the ferry does not. On a good day, you can see White-winged Scoters, gulls, thousands of Black-legged Kittiwakes, Common Murres, many Marbled Murrelets, as well as smaller numbers of the other seabirds such as loons, cormorants, sea ducks, eagles, jaegers, terns, guillemots, and puffins on or over the water. In late summer, the occasional Northern Fulmar, thousands of Short-tailed and Sooty Shearwaters, hundreds of Fork-tailed Storm-Petrels, and Red-necked Phalaropes can be seen. Charter operators keep close track of unusual birds, such as several species of auklet (Cassin's, Parakeet, Crested, and Rhinoceros) and Ancient Murrelets that often come into Kachemak Bay in late summer.

In Seldovia you can stroll the historic boardwalk and find the large, dark Kenai Song Sparrows, or scan Seldovia Slough for ducks, grebes, and alcids. You might find Varied and Hermit Thrushes more common on this side of the bay, as well as Chestnut-backed Chickadee, Winter Wren, American Dipper, Townsend's Warbler, and Red and White-winged Crossbills. An overnight stay would be required to walk back into the hills or the road system toward Jakolof Bay. You can get a city map and information from the chamber of commerce on boat-taxi service to Jakolof Bay and on the condition of the road and trail that lead to Rocky River and Red Mountain.

Seldovia is a quiet town, originally settled in 1800 by the Russians. It now has a population of about 300, a lovely Russian Orthodox church built in 1891, a fleet of commercial and some charter fishermen, and the headquarters of the Seldovia Native Association. A walk through town might yield Rufous Hummingbirds at feeders on Fulmore Street, diagonally across from the small-boat harbor ramp. Continue down this street, turn left on Alder Street, and then right on a dead-end street that leads to Susan Lake, where you will see

Mallards, occasional goldeneyes, and a possible Great Blue Heron. Cross the usually dry marsh to the gazebo, then angle left, following the path, to come out of the marsh on Anderson Way. Follow this street to the right until you see Seldovia Lagoon ahead and to your right. Turn right on Shoreline Drive and walk along this road as it goes up and down hills following the west bank of Seldovia Slough—look for Chestnut-backed Chickadee, as well as Steller's Jay, warblers, and many Northwestern Crows. The airport is across the slough and is reached by Airport Avenue, which crosses the slough from Shoreline Drive. You can watch stocked King Salmon swimming in the slough from the bridge deck. Continue south along Shoreline Drive to access the historic boardwalk on your left. Either the boardwalk or the road will lead you back to Main Street and the harbor. There is excellent fall berry picking near the airport.

TRIPS TO THE BARREN ISLANDS

As of 2001, there were three ways to reach the Barren Islands. One is on the state ferry *Tustumena* on its route to and from Kodiak. The ferry steams through the middle of the islands, giving birders a fleeting glimpse of the birding potential here. The second is to get on a whale-watching/birding tour with Rainbow Tours (235-7272); this tour started in 2001, so we cannot predict how long it will continue. The third way is to get on a charter fishing boat looking for Pacific Halibut around the Barrens. Ask the captain if you can get on at a lower price if you just look for birds rather than fish. You will have to be content with the locations the captain chooses to fish, however. You may be able to put together a group charter to the Barrens, but do so only with larger boats and reputable captains. Check with the chamber of commerce before asking at the charter-boat offices at the end of the Spit.

Horned Puffin

The Barren Islands are located about 50 miles south-southwest of Homer at the entrance to Cook Inlet and at the northwestern extent of the Gulf of Alaska. The islands are in an area of strong tidal currents and severe storm potential. Seas are seldom calm, as winds from the southeast have a long reach before meeting the Barrens. The rocky sea floor from which the Barrens protrude causes dangerous tide rips and, with accompanying chop and standing waves, the area can be hazardous to small boats when the tides are running into and out of Cook Inlet. The uneven sea floor and the occurrence of strong tidal currents produce upwelling of deep-sea water rich in nutrients and sea life upon which seabirds depend for food. It is not surprising that the Barrens support the largest number of breeding seabirds in the Gulf of Alaska.

There are seven named Barren Islands totaling over 10,000 acres spread over an area 15 miles east to west and 5 miles north to south. All of the islands are part of the Alaska Maritime National Wildlife Refuge system, but before being transferred to the refuge, were occupied by fox farmers who raised Red and Arctic Foxes for furs in the late 1800s and early 1900s. The foxes fed on the nesting seabirds, their eggs and young, and on Arctic Ground Squirrels the farmers imported to the islands. Thankfully, the refuge staff has eliminated the foxes from all of the Barren Islands, although ground squirrels remain and are preyed upon by Rough-legged Hawks and other raptors.

Sugarloaf Island is a rookery for the endangered Steller's Sea Lion and, as such, boats are not permitted to approach within a three-mile radius of that island. Sea lions, however, haul out on the other islands. Because most of East and West Amatuli Islands are within the three-mile restricted zone, not all of the bird colonies of the Barrens are accessible. The larger islands are vegetated with plant species that also occur on the southern Kenai Peninsula; only Ushagat has a stand of trees (Sitka Spruce).

All of the islands have populations of nesting seabirds. The vegetated islands also support breeding and migrating populations of other birds that also occur on the mainland. Numbers of nesting individuals vary greatly from year to year as does the success of breeding by each individual species. The total population of seabirds nesting on the Barrens is between 400,000 and 600,000 individuals. Because the Barrens are often difficult to reach, the number of observers is far fewer than in more accessible locations, thus knowledge of bird life here is relatively incomplete.

The largest bird colonies are on East Amatuli, but many of them are on the south side of the island, unavailable because of the restriction to access. Also, there are an estimated 90,000 to 300,000 Fork-tailed Storm-Petrels nesting in burrows on this island alone. Storm-petrels come to their burrows only at dusk and leave at daylight to feed at sea. It is rare to see any storm-petrels around the islands during daylight. Therefore counting the actual number of breeding storm-petrels would require finding each burrow to see if there was an egg or chick inside during the day, an impossible challenge. Rhinoceros Auklets that nest on Sud Island are also nocturnal and, like storm-petrels, leave the vicinity of the islands during daylight. However, usually one or two individuals can be found on a tour to the Barrens.

The *Exxon Valdez* oil spill in Prince William Sound in March 1989 reached the Barrens in April at the time when Common Murres were staging in large rafts prior to nesting. The oil killed large numbers of adult murres, but the long-term impact of the spill on breeding murres is still debated by scientists who have studied the Barren Islands' murre populations since the oil spill. In general, some colonies are doing well and others showed a delay in initiating nesting for several years. Slight changes in water temperature, such as those produced from an El Niño or La Niña year, for example, can have major consequences on survival of murres by affecting the abundance and distribution of the small fish upon which the murres depend.

LOGISTICS

The area code for all telephone numbers is 907 unless otherwise indicated. Refer to The Milepost *for information about accommodations and other traveler services. Other useful Kenai Peninsula contacts are listed below for your convenience. Statewide travel and birding information services are found under* Logistics *in the* Introduction*, page 15.)*

Access: You will need a car for the best birding opportunities on the peninsula. Homer may also be reached by the Alaska state ferry system from Seward, or by air from Anchorage or Kenai.

Accommodations: There are many accommodations in Seward, Kenai, Soldotna, and Homer, with a few places in Sterling, Cooper Landing, Ninilchik, and Anchor Point. Campgrounds are abundant. Restaurants are varied and frequent all along the road system, and other services are available in the larger towns. Check with the various chambers of commerce or refer to *The Milepost.*

Tours: Call the Seward Chamber of Commerce (see below) for the telephone numbers of current tour operators that take birders to the Chiswell Islands and into Kenai Fjords National Park. Try to find one with relatively small boats that caters to birders, rather than boats that hold 100 passengers or more. There is a tour boat out of Soldotna that runs across Cook Inlet to Duck Island where you might see murres, kittiwakes, and puffins. You are better off taking the tours out of Seward or Homer for these and other species. Duck Island is the farthest north location in Cook Inlet for nesting seabirds.

Marlow's on the Kenai runs a number of tours from Anchorage to Homer, but primarily in the central peninsula. They specialize in float trips on the scenic Kenai River and can offer you birding as well as first-class salmon fishing. There are many sport-fishing charters for salmon and trout on the Kenai River and several float charters as well that start near Cooper Landing.

In Homer, you can obtain a list of fishing charters and tour operators from the chamber of commerce or from one of the web site addresses below. Since these change regularly, only two of the charters that take birders around Kachemak Bay and one to the Barren Islands are mentioned. Rainbow Tours has a large boat that makes daily trips to Gull Island and other places on the south side of the bay. Check for their schedule of trips to the Barren Islands. Bay Excursions is a charter taxi for one to about five people who wish to go across the bay to hike, or to go up the bay to look for birds. Captain Karl Stoltzfus will help you find Kittlitz's Murrelets, Aleutian Terns, and other birds as well as take you around Gull Island or other places in the bay for birds on your wish list.

Alaska Maritime National Wildlife Refuge Visitor Center — 235-6961; *http://www.r7.fws.gov/nwr/akmnwr/akmnwr.html.*

Alaska SeaLife Center in Valdez — 800-224-2525 or 224-6300; *www.alaskasealife.org.*

Anchor Point — *www.xyz.net/~apcoc.*

Bay Excursions, Kachemak Bay — 235-7525, email *bay@xyz.net; http://bayexcursions.com.*

Center for Alaskan Coastal Studies, Homer — 235-6667 for summer program information; *www.akcoastalstudies.org.*

Homer Birding — *http://birdinghomeralaska.org.*

Homer Birding Alert Line — 235-7337.

Homer Chamber of Commerce — 235-7740; *www.homeralaska.org.*

Kachemak Bay National Estuarine Research Reserve — *www.state.ak.us/local/akpages/fishgam/habitat/geninfo/nerr/.*

Kachemak Bay Shorebird Festival — *www.homeralaska.org/shorebird.htm.*

Kachemak Bay State Park — 235-7024.

Kenai Chamber of Commerce — *www.kenaichamber.org.*

Kenai Fjords and Chiswell Island Tours — *www.kenai-fjords.com.*

Kenai Fjords National Park — 224-2132 or 224-3175; *www.nps.gov/kefj* or *www.kenai.fjords.national-park.com.*

Kenai Bicentennial Cultural and Visitor Center — 283-1991.

Kenai National Wildlife Refuge Visitor Center — 262-7021.

Marlow's on the Kenai — 800-725-3327 or 262-5218. *www.marlowsonthekenai.com* or *www.alaskabirdingtours.com.*

Ninilchik — *www.recworld.com/ncoc.*

Portage Glacier — *www.alaska.net/~design/scenes/portage/portage.html.*

Pratt Museum, Homer — 235-8635; *www.prattmuseum.org.*

Rainbow Tours — 235-7272.

Seldovia Chamber of Commerce — *www.xyz.net/~seldovia.*

Seward Chamber of Commerce Visitor Center — 224-8051 year round, 224-3094 in summer; *www.seward.net/chamber.*

Seward Birding Alert Line — 224-2325.

Soldotna Chamber of Commerce Visitor Center — 262-9814 or 262-1337; *www.soldotnachamber.com.*

ACKNOWLEDGEMENTS: Bill Shuster provided updated information for the Seward area and Randall Davis for the Soldotna and Kenai areas. Carmen Field reviewed the text and provided updates for Homer. Richard Konz field-checked most routes. Updates and birding notes from Jon Dunn are greatly appreciated.

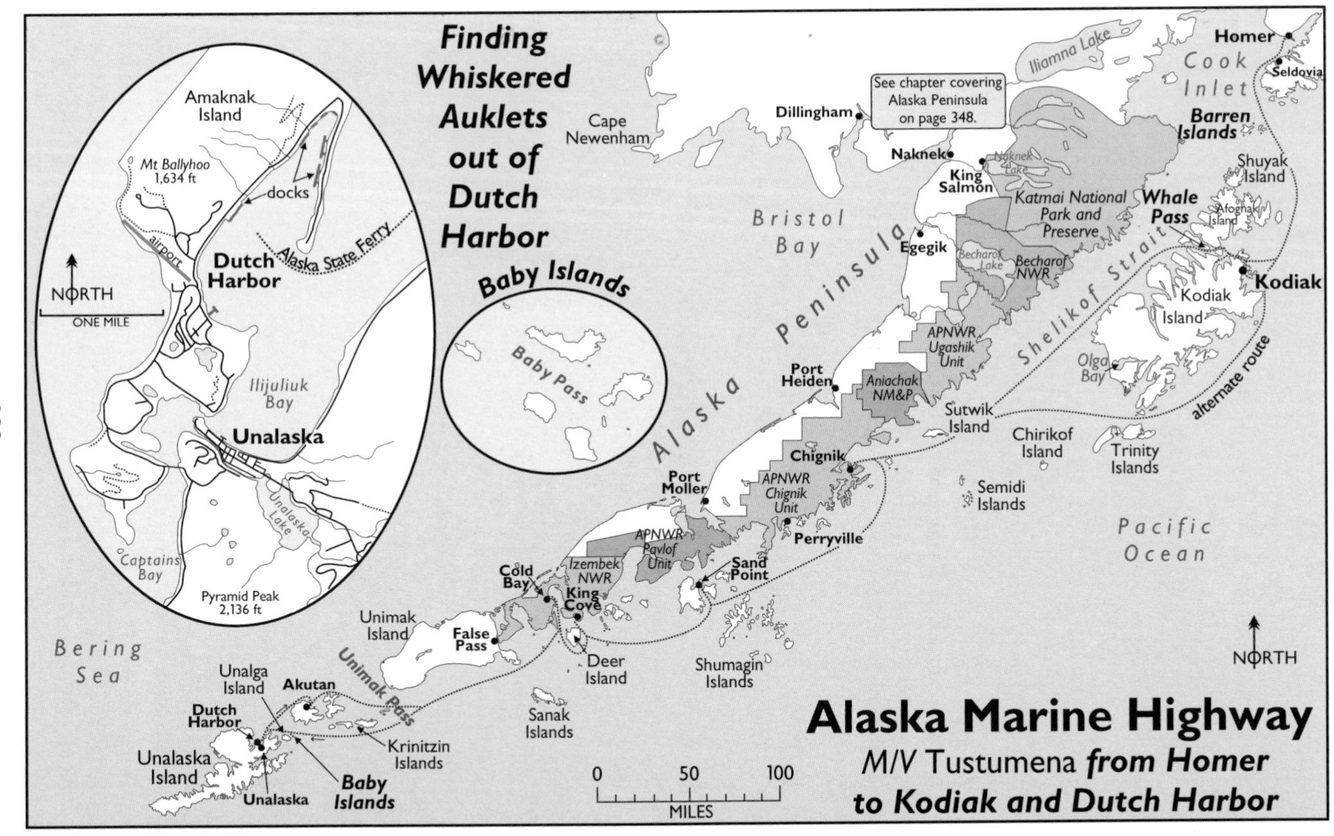

Alaska Marine Highway
M/V Tustumena from Homer
to Kodiak and Dutch Harbor
Finding Whiskered Auklets out of Dutch Harbor
Baby Islands
Baby Pass
See chapter covering Alaska Peninsula on page 348.
Homer
Seldovia
Cook Inlet
Barren Islands
Shuyak Island
Afognak Island
Kodiak
Kodiak Island
Whale Pass
alternate route
Shelikof Strait
Iliamna Lake
Katmai National Park and Preserve
Naknek Lake
Becharof Lake
Becharof NWR
King Salmon
Naknek
Egegik
Dillingham
APNWR Ugashik Unit
Aniachak NM&P
Chignik
APNWR Chignik Unit
Perryville
Port Heiden
Bristol Bay
Alaska Peninsula
Olga Bay
Trinity Islands
Pacific Ocean
Chirikof Island
Semidi Islands
Sutwik Island
Sand Point
Shumagin Islands
Port Moller
APNWR Pavlof Unit
Izembek NWR
King Cove
Cold Bay
Deer Island
Sanak Islands
False Pass
Cape Newenham
Unimak Island
Unimak Pass
Krinitzin Islands
Akutan
Baby Islands
Unalga Island
Dutch Harbor
Unalaska
Unalaska Island
Bering Sea
NORTH
0 50 100
MILES
Amaknak Island
Dutch Harbor
docks
Alaska State Ferry
Mt Ballyhoo 1,634 ft
airport
Iliuliuk Bay
Unalaska
Unalaska Lake
Pyramid Peak 2,136 ft
Captains Bay
ONE MILE

FERRY TO KODIAK AND DUTCH HARBOR

George West

The trip from Homer to Dutch Harbor/Unalaska on the Alaska Marine Highway ferry M/V *Tustumena* is a once-in-a-lifetime birding experience, with an opportunity to see hundreds of thousands of seabirds, including most species of auklet. Short-tailed Shearwaters pass by the boat in a never-ending stream, flock after flock of Ancient Murrelets and Cassin's Auklets cross in front of the bow on the way to their rookeries, and, if the ferry passes through the Baby Islands (see Dutch Harbor–Whiskered Auklets, page 328), hundreds of Whiskered Auklets, rarely seen in the dim early morning light, emerge from the darkness.

The ferry makes three trips each summer, when birding is at its best—in June, July, and August. Each round-trip takes about seven days and covers over 1,800 miles. In addition to seeing the seabirds from the moving ferry, birders will usually have time to disembark at each port and bird in the towns where the ferry docks. The ferry usually stops about eight hours in Kodiak outbound and six in Dutch Harbor/Unalaska. Unfortunately, some of the stops may be in the middle of the night when it is too dark for land birding. Similarly, some of the best ocean areas may be passed during nighttime hours. The schedule is weather-dependent and port times are frequently shortened to make up for lost time. Although none of this can be predicted, the opportunity to see tremendous numbers of seabirds will tempt you to take your chances and hope for the best. The ferry's purpose is to deliver cargo and people to ports along its route; it is not operated as a tour boat for birders or tourists. However, the captain often will make small changes in his route or schedule to increase the value of your marine birding experience.

PLANNING, WEATHER, AND GEAR

As with all trips on the Alaska Marine Highway, you should schedule your trip well in advance and make reservations, especially for a cabin, as there are few available. Opportunities for reservations usually do not open until the first week in January, and all cabins for the three-month summer trips will have been reserved by the end of that month. You can save money by camping on the upper deck in the solarium or in the forward lounge, but you will have no privacy and will get little sleep. Showers are available in the solarium. You can also bring some or all of your food with you to avoid eating in the ship's dining room. However, meals on board can cost as little as $20 per day. One option is to buy the ferry's hot breakfast and take cold lunch provisions along to save money. For current ferry schedules for all their routes and prices for passage and staterooms, call the Alaska Marine Highway System (see *Logistics*).

Plan on temperatures from 40–50°F, with many overcast days, rain, and lots of wind. The seas may be dead calm, but more likely will run from 6-to-20-foot swells. If you are susceptible to motion sickness, be prepared. If you plan to spend most of the time birding on deck, you will need to dress in layers that include a wind-resistant parka or insulated jacket with hood, warm pants, long underwear, a warm hat, gloves, rain gear, and warm shoes or boots. This is not a tour ship, so fancy clothes are not an asset.

Birding from the Ferry

Eight-power to ten-power binoculars are recommended because most small seabirds are usually at a distance from the ferry. Generally the birds fly up and away from the boat as it approaches, so your best birding position is from the bow (in good weather) to mid-ship, where the deck is covered and you can get out of the wind and rain. A spotting scope is useless from the ferry deck because of the movement of the boat and the vibration from its engines. However, you can carry a scope ashore at ports along the way to look for landbirds. The Alaska Maritime National Wildlife Refuge (AMNWR) places a naturalist on most ferry trips from Homer to Kodiak and from Homer to Dutch Harbor. Introduce yourself to the naturalist on board and mention that you are a birder. She or he will put you in touch with other birders and will be able to give you more explicit information on when and where to find particular species. The naturalist helps in spotting birds and marine mammals, assists with identifications, answers questions, presents public programs on birds and other natural history topics, and has a lending library on board.

The ferry passes by five different National Wildlife Refuges (NWR), but the largest is the Alaska Maritime NWR that extends from the Alaska border with Canada west to the tip of the Aleutians and north through the Bering Sea to Alaska's north coast. Although the ferry goes by many seabird nesting colonies, it does not slow down or go close to the dangerous rocks where seabirds nest. Non-breeding species, such as shearwaters, may occur in the millions in Unimak Pass, outnumbering local breeders in some areas. Birding hot spots include the Barren Islands in the Gulf of Alaska at the mouth of Cook Inlet, Whale Pass west of Kodiak, the Haystacks south of Sand Point, and Unimak Pass east of Dutch Harbor.

Sometimes you will be fortunate to bird not just *from* the ferry, but *on* the ferry. It is not uncommon to have seabirds land on deck or for landbirds to perch in the rigging, especially when the weather is at its worst. Bald Eagles often sit on the masts; warblers have been known to land in the rigging. On one trip, a passenger found a Cassin's Auklet that flew on board and hid behind the passenger's backpack inside the ship. Birders had a great opportunity to study this little alcid up close; it was released unharmed.

Black-footed, Laysan, and Short-tailed Albatrosses

SPECIES ACCOUNTS

LOONS—Pacific and Common Loons are common in nearshore waters from Kachemak Bay west, but become scarcer toward the Aleutian Islands. Red-throated Loon is uncommon throughout the area, and Yellow-billed Loon is very rare during the summer.

GREBES—Horned and Red-necked Grebes nest in lakes and ponds north of Kachemak Bay and are uncommon in saltwater in summer, but may be found along shore throughout the ferry route.

ALBATROSSES—Laysan Albatross may be common in Unimak Pass, sometimes south of the Krenitzin Islands southeast of Akutan, and is sometimes seen as far northeast as just southeast of Kodiak Island in the Gulf of Alaska. Black-footed Albatross is often found in Unimak Pass and south of the islands just east of Dutch Harbor. Short-tailed Albatross has been reported from the ferry and others were reported south of Kodiak Island in 1999 and 2000, indicating an increase in population in one of their original feeding areas.

FULMAR, PETREL, and SHEARWATERS—Northern Fulmar is abundant, and both light- and dark-phase birds are common all along the ferry route. Look for Mottled Petrel south of Kodiak Island, near the Shumagin Islands, and in Unimak Pass. Sooty Shearwater is common along the eastern part of the ferry route, mostly on the south or Pacific side of the Alaska Peninsula. Short-tailed Shearwater is common in Cook Inlet and becomes abundant as you travel west toward Dutch Harbor, and especially in the Bering Sea. Pink-footed and Buller's Shearwaters are possible, but are not likely to be seen from the ferry since it travels too close to shore.

STORM-PETRELS—Although over 500,000 Fork-tailed and Leach's Storm-Petrels nest along the ferry route, relatively few are seen. Fork-tails are commonly seen, but Leach's are rare. These birds feed far from their nesting islands and travel to and from their nests at dawn and dusk.

CORMORANTS—Although Double-crested Cormorant nests on islands all along the ferry route, you will see very few birds. Red-faced and Pelagic Cormorants are more abundant, feed farther from shore, and are found all along the route.

SWANS, GEESE, AND DUCKS—Trumpeter Swan, American Wigeon, Mallard, Northern Pintail, Green-winged and Common Teal may be found in ponds near villages where the ferry docks. Black Brant are rare, but could be seen anywhere along the route. Steller's Eider and King Eider have been seen near False Pass in May, but are rarer later in summer. Common Eider is uncommon, but could be near shore anywhere along the route. Harlequin Duck occurs along shore throughout the ferry route. Surf Scoter and White-winged Scoter may be seen anywhere along the route. Long-tailed Ducks may be in Kachemak Bay in May, but are gone by June. Common Merganser and Red-breasted Merganser are sometimes seen near shore or in lakes or streams near villages.

HAWKS AND FALCONS—Bald Eagle is a common nesting bird throughout the route. You might see a Rough-legged Hawk when passing the Barren Islands or on shore at Dutch Harbor. Peregrine Falcon is present at many seabird colonies and may be seen anywhere along the route.

SHOREBIRDS—Black Oystercatcher occurs all along the route and is more often heard than seen. The only small shorebirds usually seen from the ferry are Black Turnstone and Surfbird. Look for them at the harbor mouth in Homer or on rocks anywhere along the route. Thousands of Red-necked Phalaropes may be in Kachemak Bay and along the route, especially in May and August. Red Phalarope is most likely seen from Akutan through Unimak Pass.

JAEGERS, GULLS, and TERNS—Parasitic Jaeger is the most common jaeger, followed by Long-tailed and Pomarine. Parasitic and Long-tailed nest along the route and are present throughout the summer. Pomarine Jaegers are more common after mid-July. A South Polar Skua was reported once from the ferry. Bonaparte's Gull may be seen on Kachemak Bay. Mew Gull is seen near shore at ports all along the route. Glaucous-winged Gull and

Black-legged Kittiwake are abundant. Only a few Red-legged Kittiwakes have been reported from the ferry north of Akutan, but check all kittiwakes carefully in the Dutch Harbor and Akutan areas. Sabine's Gull wanders throughout the area and could be seen anywhere along the route. Both Arctic and Aleutian Terns nest all along the route, but are rare away from shore.

ALCIDS—Common Murre is abundant all along the route; Thick-billed Murre is usually seen only near Sand Point in the Shumagin Islands. Pigeon Guillemot is present at every port. Marbled Murrelet is common in Kachemak Bay, but occurs in small numbers all along the route, usually in sheltered waters. Kittlitz's Murrelet is relatively hard to identify from the ferry, and is reported rarely. It does nest throughout the area and sometimes can be seen in Cold Bay. Ancient Murrelet and Cassin's Auklet occur in vast numbers from Chignik to Dutch Harbor. There are large breeding colonies of both species on Sandman Reefs south of the entrance to Cold Bay. Parakeet Auklet is usually first seen when passing the Barren Islands, and again near the Shumagin Islands. Large colonies are on the Shumagins, the Semidis, and islands off King Cove and Cold Bay. Least Auklet is uncommon, but has been seen from False Pass and Unimak Pass to near Akutan. Whiskered Auklet is common in the Baby Islands, but this area is not often on the ferry route or is passed at night. See the following chapter for details of how best to find this species. Crested Auklet is often seen in the Shumagin Islands. Sometimes there are large flocks moving across the water, but sometimes they can be hard to find. You will be lucky to get a close look at individual birds. Rhinoceros Auklet is scarce and is usually missed. Look for them when passing the Barren Islands. Tufted Puffin is abundant and Horned Puffin can't be missed from the Barren Islands to Dutch Harbor.

LANDBIRDS—When ashore at ports along the ferry route from Chignik to Dutch Harbor, you might see the following species that have regularly been recorded by observers: Belted Kingfisher, Black-billed Magpie, Northwestern Crow, Common Raven, Tree, Violet-green, Bank, and Cliff Swallows, Winter Wren, Hermit Thrush, American Robin, Varied Thrush, Orange-crowned, Yellow, and Wilson's Warblers, Northern Waterthrush, Savannah, Sooty Fox, Song, and Golden-crowned Sparrows, Lapland Longspur, Gray-crowned Rosy-Finch, and Pine Siskin. See page 358 for birding possibilities around Cold Bay.

LOGISTICS

Alaska Marine Highway System 800-642-0066 *http://www.alaska.gov/ferry/*

ACKNOWLEDGEMENTS: Updated information was provided by Ken Russell and Steve Zimmerman. Updates and birding notes from Jon Dunn are greatly appreciated.

DUTCH HARBOR

FOR WHISKERED AUKLET

Steven T. Zimmerman

The Whiskered Auklet is the rarest alcid in Alaska. Its range is confined to the Aleutian (USA), Commander (Russia), and Kurile (Russia) Islands, with the main part of the population found in the Aleutians from Buldir Island to the Islands of the Four Mountains. In past years, birders could take the Alaska Marine Highway ferry M/V *Tustumena* from Kodiak to Dutch Harbor and possibly view Whiskered Auklets when the ferry passed through the Baby Islands east of Dutch Harbor. Unfortunately, the ferry schedule changed and the ferry now passes through the Baby Islands area during darkness (usually about 3 AM) on its way into Dutch Harbor. On the way back, the *Tustumena* travels northeast to Akutan, completely missing the Baby Islands and most of the waters that might be used by Whiskered Auklets. It is possible that this may change in the future. Recent discussions with Alaska Marine Highway staff have indicated their willingness to alter the schedule once or twice a summer to allow the *Tustumena* to travel though the Baby Islands again so that birders can look for Whiskered Auklets. No changes have been made at this time, however, and there is little probability that Whiskered Auklets will be seen from the *Tustumena* on its present schedule.

Dutch Harbor is the only sizable town in Alaska with accessibility to Whiskered Auklets. During summer there are two Alaska Airlines flights a day from Anchorage to Dutch Harbor. It is theoretically possible to leave Anchorage in the morning, fly to Dutch Harbor, charter a boat to see the auklets, and be back in Anchorage in the evening. Unfortunately, bad weather can interfere. Flights to Dutch Harbor may be canceled by weather for several days in a row, and charter boats may not be able to get to the auklets for another few days. Weather is best in the summer, and trips should be taken before September if possible.

There are several charter-vessel companies in Dutch Harbor that can take birders to the Baby Islands (see *Logistics*). Descriptions of these companies can be found on the Internet by searching for "Dutch Harbor," and then clicking on the Unalaska/Port of Dutch Harbor Convention and Visitors Bureau site. Charter costs in 2001 averaged about $165 per person for a

4-to-6-hour charter. The minimum number of people required to make the trip varies with each company—some require a minimum of two paying people, others require three or four. Also, some boats are faster than others. The one-way trip can take an hour or more for the faster boats, depending on weather. Slower boats can take up to two hours.

With regard to finding Whiskered Auklets, the most experienced charter boat company is Far West Outfitters. Owner John Lucking has been taking birders in search of these auklets since 1994. He is familiar with areas to look for Mottled Petrels (regular), albatrosses (mainly Laysan), and other seabirds of interest, and is willing to develop a cruise plan to fit special needs. Far West Outfitters has two of the faster boats and only a two-person minimum per boat.

Whiskered Auklets feed in tidal rips near their breeding islands, where they can be found year round. They are the predominant alcid around the Baby Islands. When entering the passes between the Baby Islands you will likely see large numbers of Whiskered Auklets flying away from your vessel. Because Whiskered Auklets fly away at some distance as vessels approach, it can be difficult to get a satisfying look from a moving boat. The best way to see the birds is to ask the captain to let the boat drift so you can see them popping up in the eddies and rips in the strait. Because Whiskered Auklets are very shy, they will either dive or fly as soon as they see a boat, so a brief glimpse of each bird is about all you will get. When birds are just surfacing after diving, the feathers on the head may not have time to stand up much before the bird flies or dives again. It is possible, however, to see the three white facial plumes when birds surface next to the boat. Many of the other seabirds that are common in the eastern Aleutian Islands may be seen on the way out and back.

LOGISTICS

The area code for all telephone numbers is 907 unless otherwise indicated. Statewide travel and birding information services are listed under Logistics *in the* Introduction, *page 15.)*

Unalaska/Port of Dutch Harbor Convention and Visitors Bureau, PO Box 545, Unalaska, Alaska 99685; *http://www.arctic.net/~updhcvb/main.htm*; 581-2612 or 877-581-2612.

Charters: AVI Charters — 391-7994 or 581-2615; Far West Outfitters — 581-1647; F/V *Lucille* — 581-5949 or 391-7907; Shuregood Adventures — 581-2378 or 877-374-4386; Silver Cloud Charters — 581-1348 or 866-773-3476.

Accommodations: (2001 rates) Grand Aleutian Hotel/UniSea Inn, 866-581-3844 or 800-891-1194; *www.grandaleutian.com*; $155/single, $175/double; $125 and $140 if you charter a boat. Rooms at UniSea Inn are booked through Grand Aleutian Hotel; $99/single, $110/double. Carl's Bayview Inn, 800-581-1230; $90/single, $110/double. Linda's Bunkhouse, 581-4357; $55/bed/night.

ACKNOWLEDGEMENTS: Reviewed by Dave Sonneborn and Jon Dunn.

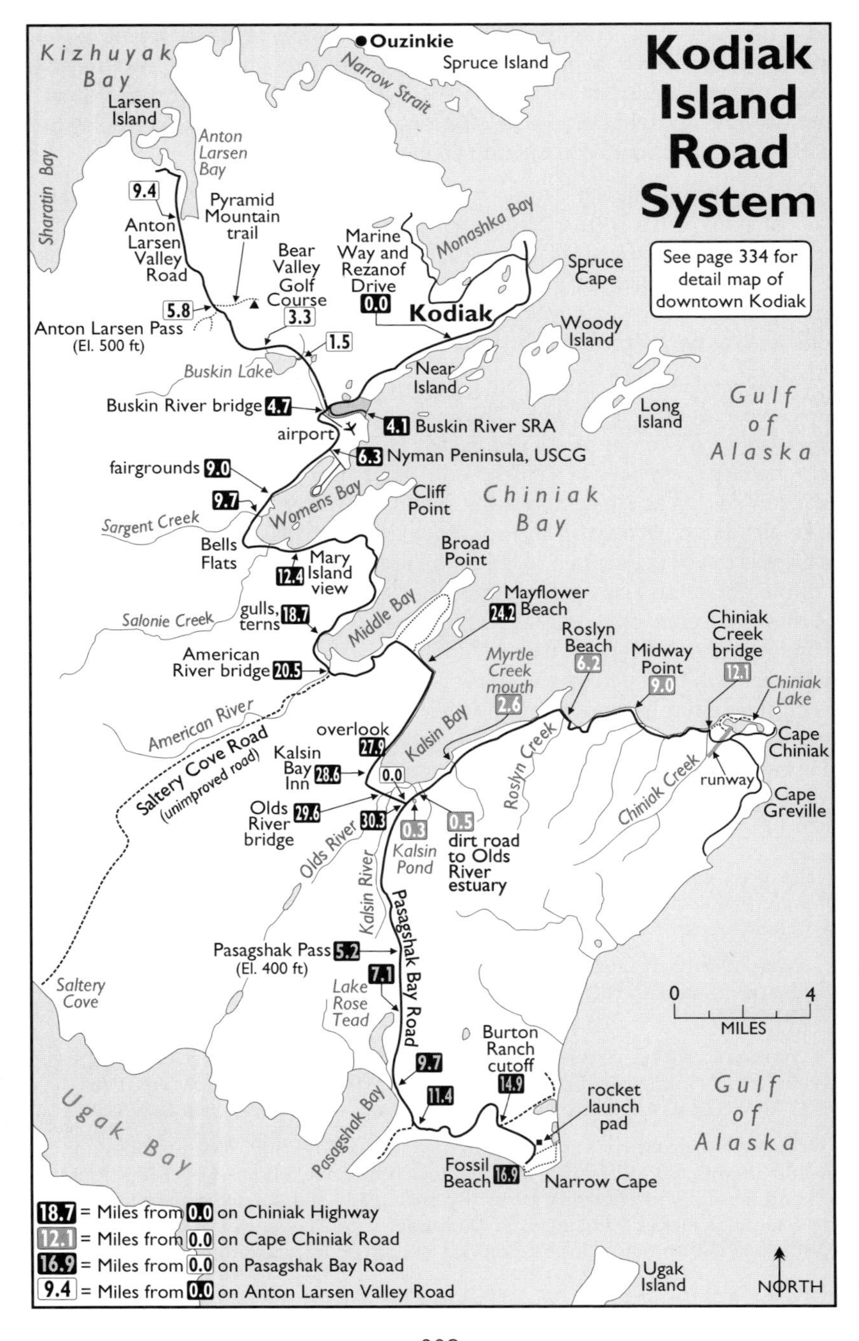

Kodiak Island Road System
See page 334 for detail map of downtown Kodiak
Ouzinkie
Spruce Island
Narrow Strait
Kizhuyak Bay
Larsen Island
Anton Larsen Bay
Sharatin Bay
9.4
Anton Larsen Valley Road
Pyramid Mountain trail
Bear Valley Golf Course
3.3
Marine Way and Rezanof Drive
0.0
Monashka Bay
Spruce Cape
Kodiak
5.8
Anton Larsen Pass (El. 500 ft)
1.5
Woody Island
Buskin Lake
Near Island
Buskin River bridge 4.7
4.1 Buskin River SRA
airport
Long Island
Gulf of Alaska
6.3 Nyman Peninsula, USCG
fairgrounds 9.0
9.7
Womens Bay
Cliff Point
Chiniak Bay
Sargent Creek
Bells Flats
12.4 Mary Island view
Broad Point
Salonie Creek
gulls, terns 18.7
Middle Bay
Mayflower 24.2 Beach
Roslyn Beach 6.2
Midway Point 9.0
Chiniak Creek bridge 12.1
Chiniak Lake
Myrtle Creek mouth 2.6
American River bridge 20.5
American River
Kalsin Bay
Cape Chiniak
overlook 27.9
Kalsin Bay Inn 28.6
0.0
Roslyn Creek
runway
Saltery Cove Road (unimproved road)
Chiniak Creek
Cape Greville
Olds River bridge 29.6
30.3
0.3
0.5
Kalsin Pond
dirt road to Olds River estuary
Olds River
Kalsin River
Pasagshak Bay Road
Pasagshak Pass 5.2 (El. 400 ft)
7.1
Lake Rose Tead
Saltery Cove
0
4
MILES
Burton Ranch cutoff 14.9
9.7
11.4
Ugak Bay
Pasagshak Bay
rocket launch pad
Gulf of Alaska
Fossil Beach 16.9
Narrow Cape
18.7 = Miles from 0.0 on Chiniak Highway
12.1 = Miles from 0.0 on Cape Chiniak Road
16.9 = Miles from 0.0 on Pasagshak Bay Road
9.4 = Miles from 0.0 on Anton Larsen Valley Road
Ugak Island
NORTH

KODIAK ARCHIPELAGO

Richard MacIntosh

The Kodiak Archipelago begins 90 miles southwest of the Kenai Peninsula and extends for more than 170 miles to the southwest in the Gulf of Alaska. Kodiak Island, the largest in the group, is the second-largest island in the United States. Thirty-mile-wide Shelikof Strait separates Kodiak from Katmai National Park and Preserve on the Alaska Peninsula mainland. The North American coniferous forest approaches its western extent in the Kodiak Archipelago. In essence, the northeastern one-third is mostly Sitka Spruce forest, while the southwestern two-thirds more closely resembles the tundra of western Alaska and the Aleutian Islands. The town of Kodiak, the archipelago's hub of travel, commerce, and government, straddles this boundary. In addition to the 12,000 residents in the region connected by Kodiak's 100-mile-long road system, six small villages on the island hold mostly Alutiiq Eskimo populations of up to 300 people each. About two-thirds of Kodiak Island and part of Afognak Island comprise 1.8 million-acre Kodiak National Wildlife Refuge, a wilderness accessible only by boat or small plane.

The Alutiiq people have inhabited the Kodiak Archipelago for more than 7,500 years. When the Russians arrived in the late 1700s, the Alutiiq numbered more than 20,000. Subsequent armed conflicts and introduced diseases wiped out entire villages. To date, more than 800 archaeological sites have been identified around the archipelago. In 1792, the Russians made Kodiak their first capital in Russian America. The colony was a major Sea Otter fur trading center for many years. After the U.S. purchased Alaska in 1867, Kodiak's economy shifted from the fur trade to the salmon trade. Canneries dotted the shoreline by the 1890s. During World War II, Kodiak became a major staging area for North Pacific military operations, and the population soared to more than 25,000. World War II bulwarks are a common sight today along the road system. Kodiak's present-day economy is fueled by rich North Pacific fisheries resources. The city is home to almost 800 commercial fishing vessels and consistently ranks as one of the top three fishing ports in the U.S. Although the salmon fishery is still large, there are other established fisheries for Pacific Herring, Pacific Cod, Sablefish, Pacific Halibut, other flatfish, and Tanner, King, and Dungeness Crabs. The nation's largest U.S.Coast Guard station is located just south of the city.

The most complete source for visitor information is the Kodiak Island Convention and Visitors Bureau (KICVB), which can answer most of your questions about travel in the archipelago.

Kodiak is best known for its winter birding (Lethaby, 1997). When the mainland is gripped by ice and snow, the island's maritime climate keeps many habitats and waters open and thus available to birds. The Kodiak Christmas Bird Count typically leads the state in number of species seen—the 10-year average is 75. In addition to the large numbers of wintering loons, grebes, cormorants, sea ducks, and alcids, Emperor Goose and Steller's Eider are near the eastern edge of their normal winter range here. Few wintering birds leave before mid-April, making March and early April a good time to visit. There are three bird checklists for the archipelago. One is published by the Kodiak NWR and covers the entire archipelago; the second is for Shuyak Island State Park at the northern end of the archipelago; and the third is for Fort Abercrombie State Historical Park, near the town of Kodiak.

Spring waterfowl migration begins with the arrival of Tundra Swans in early April and peaks in the last week of that month. Spring shorebird migration peaks in early May, but it is very small and consists mostly of species that will remain to nest. Arctic and Aleutian Terns arrive by the second week in May. The last of the breeding passerines (Gray-cheeked Thrush and Yellow Warbler) don't appear until early June. Fall shorebird migration begins in late June with the arrival of adult Western Sandpipers, and drags on until early November, when the last Sharp-tailed Sandpipers head south. Although thousands of Western Sandpipers pass through the archipelago, the numbers of most other migrant shorebirds are small. August is marked by an abundance of locally produced juvenile passerines, but by the end of the month almost all have moved south. Savannah Sparrow is the most common passerine migrant. September and October bring a surge in the number of gulls and Bald Eagles feasting on salmon carcasses at stream mouths along the coast. Wintering ducks and Emperor Geese begin showing up in late September, and the arrival of Steller's Eiders in November signals that winter has arrived.

As in most of coastal Alaska, Kodiak weather is unpredictable. Be prepared for cold, wet, and windy weather at all seasons. December temperatures average 29°F, but days no warmer than 10°F are not unusual. On occasion, roads can be very slick in winter, but usually they are in fine shape, often better than at other seasons. In general, the gravel roads on the major road system routes are good. The few places where you might want to park and walk are noted in the text. Freezing temperatures cause small coastal lakes to freeze over in November, but usually they are intermittently open throughout the winter. Although temperatures begin rising in April, high winds and rain are also an April staple. June is something short of balmy, with an average temperature of 49°F and frequent sunny, calm days.

It is best to wear the knee-high variety of rubber boots when birding here. The local boot of choice is the Xtratuf. In many places the road parallels the shoreline, so a car-window mount device for your spotting scope can be very effective, especially on rainy and windy days. The birder who will be especially happy on Kodiak is the birder who also loves to fish. An abundance of information on fishing is available from the visitors bureau and other web sites.

Perhaps the most famous inhabitant of the Kodiak area is another proficient fisherman, the Kodiak Brown Bear. The archipelago is home to about 3,000 of these, the largest bears in the world. Bears are seldom seen along the road system, but nevertheless birders must be bear-aware at all times. The Kodiak NWR and the ADF&G have a wealth of information on bear safety and options for bear viewing. Also, read the Bear Cautions on page 17 in the *Introduction* to this guide.

Birders interested in a unique cultural or wilderness experience might visit a village or wilderness lodge. At many sites, hosts provide wildlife-watching opportunities by boat. Visits to seabird breeding colonies and Bald Eagle gathering sites are the most common birding activities. The more independent traveler might want to fly or boat to one of the public wilderness cabins maintained on the Kodiak NWR or in Shuyak Island State Park. Two of the dozens of possible wilderness-birding options are discussed below.

The majority of the good birding areas along the road system are open to public access, although many are in private ownership. Obey all no trespassing signs.

THE KODIAK ROAD SYSTEM

BIRDING AROUND THE TOWN OF KODIAK

There are about eight fish-processing plants on the downtown waterfront that, when operating, can attract thousands of gulls. Stop on the bridge to Near Island, where you can view the entire waterfront to see where the gulls are concentrated. Most cannery docks are off-limits when processing is occurring, but there are other places in town and on Near Island—parking lots, roadsides, and public docks—that afford good views. City of Kodiak Pier 2 just south of downtown is one of the best observation points. The gull scene is dominated by Mew and Glaucous-winged Gulls, with Black-legged Kittiwakes from May through October, and Herring, Thayer's, and Glaucous found in small numbers from fall through spring. Slaty-backed Gull is annual, with most sightings in October and fewer from winter through spring. Much rarer are Iceland, Western, and Great Black-backed Gulls. In winter, Steller's

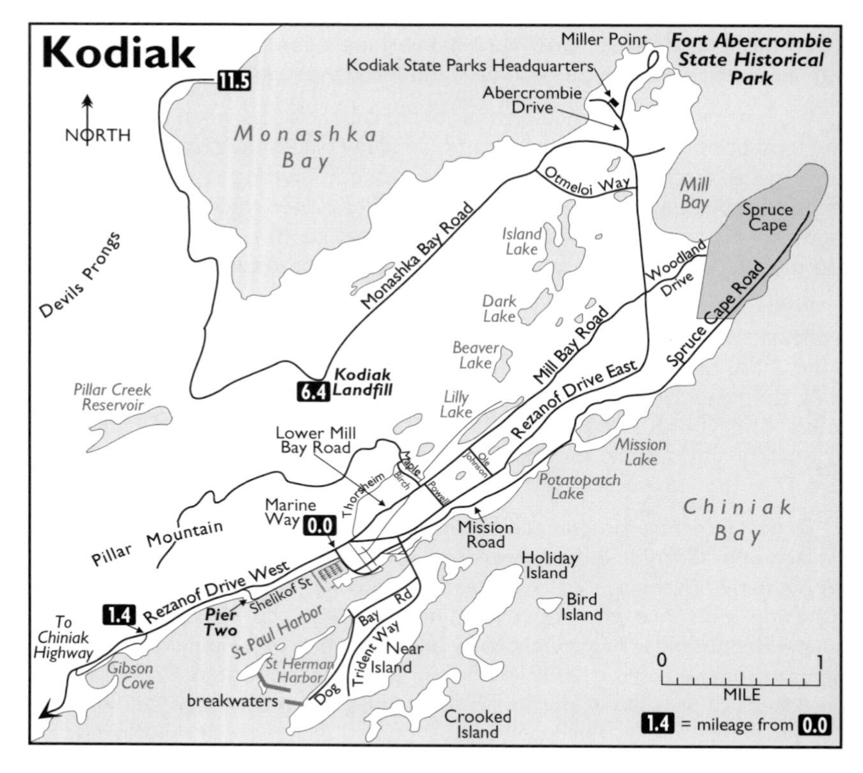

and King Eiders, Long-tailed Duck, and Common Murre are found in Saint Paul Harbor fronting the canneries, and Spectacled Eider was seen there twice.

From September through April, the rocky intertidal zone along the channel in the downtown area and the two harbor breakwaters are good places to look for mixed flocks of Black Turnstones, Surfbirds, and Rock Sandpipers. On Near Island up to several hundred Black Oystercatchers roost on the Saint Herman Harbor breakwater in winter, visible from the end of Dog Bay Road.

To reach the top of 1,400-foot-high Pillar Mountain immediately behind town, drive north from downtown on Lower Mill Bay Road. Turn left onto Birch Avenue, then right onto Thorsheim Street, then immediately left onto Maple Avenue, and follow that road up the hill. The drive is worthwhile for the view alone. Although the tundra has been degraded by ATVs, one can find breeding American Pipits by walking either north or south along the ridge. Bald Eagle, Northern Goshawk, and Merlin often soar along the flank of the mountain. In fall, both American and Pacific Golden-Plovers are regular alpine migrants, and the island's only Upland Sandpipers were found here.

Mission and Potatopatch Lakes north of downtown are good for waterfowl (look for Eurasian Wigeon in fall) and gulls. From downtown, take Mission Road north to Potatopatch Lake (1.4 miles; access through the Salvation Army parking lot) and Mission Lake (1.6 miles).

The Kodiak landfill, once voted the most scenic dump in the nation, deserves mention as a birding site, not so much for its gulls (downtown is better) as for the huge numbers of Bald Eagles that congregate there some winters. Dozens of eagles perched on baled garbage is an impressive, if not a beautiful sight. The dump entrance is on Monashka Bay Road, 6.4 miles from the downtown intersection of Marine Way and Rezanof Drive. Check for dump hours with the Kodiak Island Borough. Beyond the landfill, the Monashka Bay area is dominated by old-growth Sitka Spruce forest. Boreal Owls have been found in early spring (January–April) along Monashka Bay Road from Fort Abercrombie to the end of the road at Mile 11.5.

FORT ABERCROMBIE STATE HISTORICAL PARK

Fort Abercrombie has birds, history, 13 campsites, and beautiful scenery. From the corner of Marine Way and Rezanof Drive (the downtown stoplight) drive north 3.8 miles on Rezanof Drive, then turn right onto Abercrombie Drive. Kodiak State Park headquarters/visitor center and the Kodiak Military History Museum are located here. Pick up a bird checklist at the visitor center. Major bird habitats are old-growth Sitka Spruce forest, coastal cliffs, and nearshore marine waters (telescope looks). Walk along the 0.6-mile-long park road between the main gate and Miller Point for Three-toed Woodpecker, Red-breasted Nuthatch, Brown Creeper, Winter Wren, Golden-crowned Kinglet, Varied Thrush, and Myrtle Warbler (summer). The 1.1-mile trail around Lake Gertrude is even better. Red and White-winged Crossbills are regular, but unpredictable. In summer, campers are serenaded at dawn and dusk by Marbled Murrelets flying at treetop level and giving their high-pitched, descending *kleeer-kleeer* calls.

Miller Point itself is the site of a World War II coastal gun battery that supported two 8-inch guns originally designed for a World War I battleship. Today, the ammunition bunker is Kodiak Military History Museum headquarters. Tours are available in the summer months. Humpback Whales are commonly seen off Miller Point in summer, along with Black-legged Kittiwake, Pigeon Guillemot, and Horned and Tufted Puffins. Sea-watching with a spotting scope in late summer can yield shearwaters and jaegers. The best place to see Red-faced Cormorant from shore in winter is from the cliffs near the Piedmont Point Searchlight Bunker on the Piedmont Point Loop trail on the east side of the park. Double-crested, Red-faced, and Pelagic Cormorants often roost on the pinnacle just north of Piedmont Point.

THE CHINIAK HIGHWAY

The best Kodiak road system birding is along the Chiniak Highway south of the city. This road courses along the three large bays within Chiniak Bay—Womens, Middle, and Kalsin Bays. To help you keep better track of mileages, this route starts at the intersection of Marine Way and Rezanof Drive in downtown Kodiak (Mile 0.0) and ends at the T-intersection at Kalsin Bay (Mile 30.3). The two roads continuing on from the T-intersection will be treated separately. *Note: There are no roadside mile-markers corresponding to mileages given in this guide.*

Head south from Kodiak on the Chiniak Highway (Rezanof Drive) to Gibson Cove Road (Mile 1.4). A left turn here will take you on a short loop road that borders Gibson Cove, a small saltwater cove with a fish-meal plant and a cannery. Where the road borders the cove, look for gulls, Steller's Eider, and other winter ducks. A small wintering flock of Greater and Lesser Scaup includes a Tufted Duck in some years. In summer, the cliffs on the opposite side of the road host a few Pigeon Guillemots and Horned Puffins that approach and depart the cliff by flying low over the roof of your car. The south end of Gibson Cove loop road rejoins the Chiniak Highway at Mile 1.9.

The road to the Buskin River mouth takes off to the left at Mile 4.1. This 0.9-mile-long road, in addition to providing excellent birding, leads to the headquarters of the Kodiak NWR and to the Buskin River State Recreation Site. The refuge visitor center offers displays, films, information, and is the place to make reservations for eight public-use cabins located on the refuge. Buskin River SRS has 15 campsites and two picnic tables. From the parking lot at the river mouth you can scan Chiniak Bay in winter for loons, Horned and Red-necked Grebes, Steller's and Common Eiders, Harlequin Duck, and all three scoters. Red-faced Cormorants forage off the beach in fall. The island's only Smew was first found on the lagoon at the mouth of the river. Upstream the road runs through the campground and parallels the river, where American Dippers are seen year round.

At Mile 4.7, the Chiniak Highway crosses the Buskin River bridge. The turnoff to Anton Larsen Bay is just north of the bridge, and the turnoff to the State Airport is just south of the bridge. The road leading to the U.S. Coast Guard Support Center, the largest USCG base in the country, is at Mile 6.3. Access to the base changes from time to time, but it has some good birding, so it is worth checking at the gate to see if you can enter. On base, follow the main entrance road straight down to the beach, where you can park anywhere. Emperor Geese and Steller's and Common Eiders are often found here from fall through spring. The road around the Nyman Peninsula provides more good looks at winter ducks, with Barrow's Goldeneye easily found around the docks.

Beyond the base, the Chiniak Highway runs along the shore of Womens Bay for about seven miles. Wintering Barrow's Goldeneyes are found from the USCG base to the fairgrounds (Mile 9.0). The head of Womens Bay is the best place on the road system for Emperor Geese. They begin arriving in October, and by mid-November most of the 300 or so birds that winter here are present. In spring they usually can be found through April and sometimes into early May. Look for them anywhere along the shoreline, with the most reliable location between the mouth of Sargent Creek (Mile 9.7) and the base of Marine Hill (Mile 12.5). Here there are extensive intertidal sand and mudflats that support a variety of waterfowl, shorebirds, and gulls. Spring waterfowl migration peaks in late April–early May, with American Wigeon, Northern Pintail, and Green-winged Teal the most common migrants. In April and early May, four or five male Eurasian Wigeons per day might be found on the Chiniak Highway route. Dozens of Common Eiders nest on Mary Island at the head of the bay and can be seen all spring and summer from the beach at Mile 12.4, just before the highway climbs out of the bay. Small numbers of spring-migrant shorebirds (mostly Pacific Golden-Plover, Black Turnstone, Surfbird, Least Sandpiper, and Dunlin) are found at the head of Womens and other bays in late April and May. In fall, Western Sandpipers can number in the thousands, and many other species occur in small numbers. Rare shorebirds recorded at Womens Bay are Bristle-thighed Curlew and Temminck's Stint. In spring, Arctic and Aleutian Terns arrive in Womens Bay during the first two weeks of May, but in recent years, they have bred there only sporadically.

At the far side of Womens Bay, the road leaves the shoreline to meander through rolling alder-covered hills and, at Mile 17.4, descends toward Middle Bay. Mile 18.7, where the road first fronts the bay, is a good place to pull off to look for waterfowl and gulls. From mid-May through mid-August, hundreds of Aleutian Terns nest behind the beach on the far side of the mudflats. With hip boots, you can walk across these flats and the river mouth at low tide, but be careful not to get trapped by a rising tide. From September through November, thousands of gulls gather here to feast on salmon carcasses. Mew Gull and Black-legged Kittiwake plunge-dive for drifting salmon eggs in the American River at Mile 20.5. Just past the American River bridge, the unimproved (watch for giant potholes) road to Saltery Cove branches to the right. The wet meadow valley it traverses has breeding Greater Yellowlegs, Least Sandpiper, Short-billed Dowitcher, and Red-necked Phalarope.

Beyond the American River, the highway runs through spruce and mixed-deciduous forest. In the saddle between Middle Bay and Mayflower Beach (Mile 23.4), the large roadside spruce might hold Red or White-winged Crossbills; the two species are seldom found together. At Mayflower Beach (Mile 24.2), stop to scope the saltwater. Wintering loons, grebes, cormorants, diving ducks, and Pigeon Guillemot are common here, while

Marbled Murrelets are regular from May through October. Black Oystercatchers forage around the intertidal rocks throughout the year.

You will have a panoramic view of the head of Kalsin Bay and its drainage from the top of a steep grade at Mile 27.9. The main river below is the Olds River. Several good birding sites can be seen from here, so you might want to stop for a minute, read ahead in the text, and then locate the sites to get a feel for where they are in relation to each other. Beyond this point, the highway descends quickly into the Kalsin Bay drainage. At the base of the grade (Mile 28.6) Kalsin Bay Inn serves meals and provides overnight lodging. Arctic and Aleutian Terns nest in most years on the spit that separates Kalsin Bay from the Olds River estuary. A good access route to the spit is through the gate in the parking lot at Kalsin Bay Inn. This is a public right-of-way, but be certain to close the gate after you pass through. Once you reach the beach, park and walk to the east. You will hear the House Sparrow-like calls of the Aleutian Terns long before you reach their nesting site in Beach Rye (*Elymus arenarius*) and grasses, about one-half mile down the beach.

Back on the highway, pause to check the wet meadow on the left just before the Olds River bridge (Mile 29.6) for a nesting pair of Greater Yellowlegs. A Black-tailed Gull was found here in September 2001. The open fields and estuary toward the beach are good for Peregrine Falcon from fall through spring, and for Northern Harrier, Merlin, and Short-eared Owl in migration. This birding route ends 0.7 mile beyond the Olds River bridge, where the highway branches at the T-intersection (Mile 30.3). From here the Chiniak Highway continues northeast to Chiniak Lake and Cape Chiniak (13.1 miles), and Pasagshak Bay Road continues south to Narrow Cape (16.9 miles).

Emperor Goose

KALSIN BAY TO CHINIAK LAKE AND CAPE CHINIAK

With your trip-odometer reset to 0.0, turn left at the fork and stop a mere 0.3 mile down the highway where a culvert drains Kalsin Pond into the Olds River estuary and tidal flats. This is one of the best birding spots on Kodiak's road system. In spring migration, the pond and flats can be crowded with Black Brant and dabbling ducks. The pond is a regular stopover spot for Tundra Swans in April. In the first week of May, these flats are the best place to see Marbled Godwits on their way to join the small, isolated breeding population on the Alaska Peninsula to the west. All four of the world's godwits have been seen at this spot, with a Black-tailed present in June 1992. These flats are also one of the best places to see shorebirds during the protracted fall migration. Western Sandpipers begin to arrive at the end of June and peak in early July. Other fall migrants include small numbers of Lesser Yellowlegs and Semipalmated, Least, Baird's, Pectoral, Sharp-tailed, and Stilt Sandpipers. The sedge flats here are one of the best places to find Sharp-tailed Sandpiper on the road system. The birds like to stay in sedges that are as tall or taller than they are, and to find them you must walk out onto the vegetated flats (rubber boots required). This area is heavily grazed by livestock, and some parts of it are cropped so short that the mixed flocks of Pectorals and Sharp-tails won't use them. Look especially in the longer sedges in wet areas and on pond margins. Often, you flush birds before you spot them, but they generally land again and give you another look. Sharp-tails usually show up in early September, peak in early October, and can be found through early November.

If you go about 100 yards north from the culvert on the highway, a dirt road on the left (Mile 0.5) leads a short distance to where the Olds River estuary enters Kalsin Bay. This is a good place from which to scan for winter waterbirds and gulls, and is the first spot where you are likely to see wintering Emperor Geese of the Kalsin Bay flock. This flock is smaller than the Womens Bay flock and ranges from Kalsin Bay to Cape Chiniak. Years of sightings of collared birds suggest there is no interchange between the two flocks. All of the stops at the head of Kalsin Bay are within walking distance of each other if you are wearing hip boots and if the Olds River is not unusually high. This entire area is only about one mile across and warrants close scrutiny if you have the time. Other rarities found here over the years include Spot-billed Duck, Gray-tailed Tattler, and Curlew Sandpiper.

Beyond Kalsin Pond, the Chiniak Highway runs mostly along the rocky south shore of Chiniak Bay. This stretch of coast has many great places to stop to scan the rocky shoreline and nearshore waters for birds. Four species of loons are possible from fall through spring, although Yellow-billed s are rare anywhere in the archipelago. Mixed flocks of wintering Black Turnstones, Surfbirds, and Rock Sandpipers are regular on rocks and reefs, and the numbers of Black Oystercatchers can be staggering. The mouth of Myrtle Creek (Mile 2.6) might have a flock of resting gulls; loons, grebes, and ducks are often offshore. At Mile 5.3, the road dips down to the coast (there is a gray house perched over a small pond on the inland side), offering easy access to intertidal flats and good telescope views of offshore islands. In summer, Pigeon Guillemots and Horned and Tufted Puffins are abundant here, although not always close to the road. You can walk out to the point of land in the middle-distance by following the beach around to the right. You'll need rubber boots to cross a stream that empties a small lagoon across this beach. In winter, this area teems with loons, grebes, cormorants, Emperor Geese, Steller's and Common Eiders and other ducks, and Black Oystercatchers. Roslyn Beach (Mile 6.2) has lots of birds offshore, including Marbled Murrelets that nest in the large nearby spruce. One great place to see and hear Marbled Murrelets overhead from spring through fall is at Mile 7.4 in a patch of towering spruce, 0.8 mile beyond the Roslyn Creek bridge. Look and listen for them over the treetops at dawn and at dusk.

At Mile 9.0 a dirt track leads left about 200 yards to Midway Point. You can park by the highway or drive down this rutted road to the point. Perched along the cliff are World War II bunkers that housed an observation post. The point is a great place to scope Chiniak Bay for King and Common Eiders, and this is one of the few places where Red-faced Cormorants have roosted on rocks in winter. Wintering Black Turnstones, Surfbirds, and Rock Sandpipers feed on intertidal rocks off the point. In summer, huge flocks of kittiwakes and puffins feed offshore on Pacific Sandlance and Capelin.

Beyond Midway Point, the highway follows the coast. You could stop at the Road's End Lounge at Mile 11.7 for a great view of the waters off Cape Chiniak. Just past this restaurant/bar, a sign announces the end of state road maintenance. Although the potholes do indeed get much larger beyond this point, if you drive very slowly you can make it in any vehicle to the interesting birding areas down the road. At Mile 12.1 the highway crosses Chiniak Creek. Scan the dead trees inland for Northern Goshawks at any time of year. Birds congregate at the creek mouth, a short distance below the road. In winter, look for Double-crested and Pelagic Cormorants, Emperor Geese, Steller's, King, and Common Eiders, Harlequin Ducks, and scoters. The large, dark, beach-loving Kodiak race of Song Sparrow (*Melospiza melodia insignis*) is usually here. A rock just offshore might have a roosting Great Blue Heron (from fall through spring). Back on the road, do not be intimidated by the size of the potholes and continue to the World War II-vintage runway at Mile 12.6. Turn left onto the runway and drive to its end (Mile 13.1) where it fronts Chiniak Lake. The view is one of the most beautiful on the Kodiak road system. The lake itself is not particularly bird-rich, but in summer its margins bustle with nesting Least Sandpipers, and in some winters its small scaup flock might contain a Tufted Duck or some other locally rare diving duck. Be alert for Northern Goshawk, Merlin, and Peregrine Falcon at any season, and for Northern Harrier, Sharp-shinned Hawk, and Rough-legged Hawk in migration.

Drive or walk to the beach that separates the lake from the ocean and use it as a staging point for a hike to the easternmost point on Kodiak Island, Cape Chiniak. This complex of lake, beach, bluff, and mixed forest is birdy, beautiful, and could take half the day to fully explore. To get to the beach from here, drive back up the runway for 0.1 mile and take the gravel road to the right. This road has seen better days, but there are many places at which to turn a vehicle around if you get too uncomfortable. The road first meets the beach at 0.5 mile, but keep driving until the road comes back to the beach a second time, 1.1 miles from the runway. This beach is where you want to be. Birds abound in waters offshore. Use a scope to see Red-faced Cormorants, usually present from spring through fall. The proximity of this area to open ocean means that shearwaters are seen here in summer and fall. This is the only spot on the road system where Ancient Murrelets occur with some regularity in late summer and fall. In winter, look for Pacific Loon and King Eider in addition to all of the other coastal birds.

To walk to Cape Chiniak (1.0 mile), head east to the end of the beach (the only record of Mongolian Plover is in June from this beach), climb the bank, and continue east along the cliff to the next short beach, walk that beach, and continue east through groves of small spruce to the cape itself. Atop the cape, about 100 feet above sea level, a World War II observation post commands a panoramic view of the Gulf of Alaska. Shearwaters and Northern Fulmar (summer and fall) can often be spotted from here. Set up your scope in the concrete bunker, pointed through the same narrow concrete slit used by soldiers watching for enemy vessels in 1942. If there are strong onshore winds when you visit, you could conduct a long-shot albatross-watch from the relative comfort of this bunker. On a nice day, time spent here is hard to beat. Head back toward Kodiak or start the following route, since the habitat and road beyond the cape have little to offer.

KALSIN BAY TO FOSSIL BEACH

Another good route begins at the T-intersection at Kalsin Bay and ends at Fossil Beach, 16.9 miles down the road. Set your odometer to 0.0 and drive south toward Pasagshak Bay and Narrow Cape. Almost immediately you will pass the buildings of the Northland Ranch. The road parallels the Kalsin River for several miles before ascending to Pasagshak Pass (Mile 5.2). The pass, a lofty 400 feet above sea level, is a good place to look for Golden Eagles. Although their numbers pale in comparison to those of Bald Eagles, Goldens nest locally and can be found year round; check all birds soaring along high ridges. Beyond Pasagshak Pass, the road drops down into the Lake Rose Tead drainage. This small drainage has a late run of Silver Salmon that attracts hundreds of Bald Eagles in November and December. Most of the streams here are small, close to the road, and offer the opportunity to photograph and observe eagles and fish at point-blank range. Lake Rose Tead itself begins at Mile 7.1. The shallows along the road are a great place to watch gaudy Red Salmon spawning from July through October. Tundra Swans and the occasional Trumpeter Swan frequent the lake during migration, and Tundras would winter here if the lake did not freeze in November. When the lake is not entirely frozen in winter, it can support up to 350 Gadwalls, the largest wintering flock in the state. In some summers, Arctic and Aleutian Terns are present and may nest near the outlet of the lake. A Golden Eagle has nested on the vertical cliffs to the west.

Continuing on toward Narrow Cape, the road meets Pasagshak Bay at the mouth of the Pasagshak River (Mile 9.7). The land along the lower river is the Pasagshak River State Recreation Site, which has water, toilets, picnic sites, and 12 campsites. In winter, Pasagshak Bay attracts large numbers of Steller's Eider, Harlequin Duck, all three scoters, and Long-tailed Duck. This is the best location for winter Red-throated Loon and as good a place as any for Yellow-billed Loon. Harbor Seals are common at the river mouth and Harbor Porpoises are often nearby when the salmon are running (June–October). Pasagshak Bay opens into Ugak Bay, a 20-mile-long incision in the eastern flank of Kodiak Island. Beyond Pasagshak Bay, the road leads to Narrow Cape. At Mile 11.4, you have your first view of Narrow Cape and Ugak Island. The whole area in front of you is called the Narrow Cape area, while Narrow Cape proper is the promontory that faces Ugak Island. Most of the world's Gray Whales pass through these waters on their way to (March–May) and from (November–January) their summering grounds in the Bering Sea. They are best seen from the bluffs out on Narrow Cape itself, but from here on, the spouts usually can be seen from any spot with an ocean view. The Whalefest Kodiak festival celebrates the spring passage of whales in April. The Narrow Cape area is the unlikely location of a rocket-launching complex operated by the Alaska Aerospace Development Corporation, a quasi-public corporation sponsored by the State of Alaska. As you drive out to the end of the road at Fossil Beach, you will pass the various components of the project. Virtually all of the cape is public land and is open to public access except during very narrow time windows surrounding each movement of rocket hardware or launch. The open grassland here holds the road system's only nesting Lapland Longspurs; Savannah and Golden-crowned Sparrows abound. In fall, the area is good for Northern Harrier, Rough-legged Hawk, the occasional Gyrfalcon, Peregrine Falcon, and Northern Shrike. At Mile 14.9, a side road to the Burton Ranch (lodging available) runs 2.4 miles to a beautiful valley sandwiched between mountains and sea. Aleutian Terns have nested near the ranch buildings in recent years.

Back on the main road, continue to Fossil Beach (Mile 16.9), the end of the road. The bluffs to your right, as you face the ocean, are full of fossils that can legally be carted off as size and weight allow. Most of the fossils are mollusks, both clams and mussels. These creatures lived in the shallow seas of the Miocene about 15–16 million years ago. Many of the genera represented are still common in the Gulf of Alaska today. One of the most beautiful places on the road system is 0.4 mile to your left, up on top of Narrow Cape. To get there, walk along the beach toward Ugak Island, go up the hill on the far end of the beach, and continue in the same direction to the southwestern corner of the cape. In April, flock after flock of Black Brant pass by on their way to the Alaska Peninsula. In fall, Pacific Golden-Plover and Sharp-tailed Sandpiper can often be found in the wet sedges here. From November through April, you can scope large numbers of grebes, King Eiders, Harlequin Ducks, scoters, murres, and Pigeon Guillemots feeding in tide rips off the cape. Snow Buntings and Gray-crowned Rosy-Finches are seen atop the cape.

Pomarine, Parasitic, and Long-tailed Jaegers (*left to right*)

ANTON LARSEN BAY ROAD

At Mile 4.7 of the Chiniak Highway, Anton Larsen Bay Road heads inland toward Buskin Lake and Anton Larsen Bay. Drive this road only after you have had your fill of the others (or if you are a golfer). At Mile 1.5, turn left just before Buskin River Bridge #7, drive or walk 0.2 mile, and park at the gate near the outlet to Buskin Lake. Scoping the lake from fall through spring could yield Double-crested Cormorant, Ring-necked Duck (rare), Tufted Duck (rare), Greater and Lesser Scaup, Common Goldeneye, and Common Merganser.

Brown Bears occasionally can be seen in fall by scanning the lakeshore. Back on the main road, the island's only golf course, Bear Valley, is at Mile 3.3. Park across the road from the clubhouse and take the trail past the driving range for access to the upper end of the lake.

From Anton Larsen Pass at Mile 5.8 (elevation 500 feet) you can hike into the alpine. Trails start here and lead to both Pyramid Mountain (2,420 feet) and to the unnamed peaks on the other side of the road. See the *Kodiak Audubon Society Trail Guide* for details. Pyramid Mountain trail starts on the far side of the large gravel parking lot. Both Willow and Rock Ptarmigan can be found on the mountain's flanks. From the pass, the road drops into the Larsen Bay valley, and at Mile 9.4 it begins to parallel scenic Anton Larsen Bay.

OFF THE KODIAK ROAD SYSTEM

BIRDING FROM A BOAT

Chiniak Bay, adjacent to the town of Kodiak, has a great variety of seabirds throughout the year, with the most species present in summer and fall. Offshore trips in fall and winter often are canceled due bad weather. There are more than 25 seabird breeding colonies in the bay that contain large numbers of Pelagic Cormorants, Glaucous-winged Gulls, Black-legged Kittiwakes, Pigeon Guillemots, Horned and Tufted Puffins, and smaller numbers of Red-faced Cormorants and Common Murres. Some of these colonies are in protected waters very close to town and can be reached by kayak (kayak tours are available). In recent years, a small island on the far side of Crooked Island had many nesting Red-faced and Pelagic Cormorants. Other regularly seen summer/fall seabirds in Chiniak Bay are Sooty and Short-tailed Shearwaters (May–September), all three jaegers (May; July–September), Marbled and Ancient Murrelets, and Cassin's and Rhinoceros Auklets. Less common are Fork-tailed Storm-Petrel, Sabine's Gull, Thick-billed Murre, Kittlitz's Murrelet, and Parakeet Auklet. Winter boat-birding is possible, but the highly variable weather makes advance planning difficult. One winter bird that is rarely seen from shore, but is usually found in Chiniak Bay from November through March, is Crested Auklet. There are many Kodiak charter boats that could take birders out. These boats cater mainly to sport fishermen in summer, although whale watching, and even birding, will become an ever-increasing slice of their business. Kodiak Audubon Society sponsors a boat-birding trip in late May that finds most of the locally nesting seabirds. Currently there are no deepwater, pelagic birding trips out of Kodiak, but if there were, they would provide ready access to Laysan and Black-footed Albatrosses, Northern Fulmar, and Fork-tailed Storm-Petrel, with a good shot at Short-tailed Albatross, regular in very small numbers over the outer continental shelf.

SHUYAK ISLAND

Shuyak Island State Park encompasses an incredible maze of waterways, spruce forest, and barren headlands and peninsulas that are reminiscent of the Aleutian tundra. The island's convoluted coastline offers more protected waterways than any other part of the archipelago. In summer, this odd and intimate mix of water, forest, and tundra puts sightings of Willow Ptarmigan, Parasitic Jaeger, Parakeet Auklet, Horned Puffin, Three-toed Woodpecker, and Varied Thrush all within easy walking or paddling distance of each other. This under-birded island is best suited to summer travel by kayak or small boat. Numerous small islands and a nearshore mixing of currents result in an abundance of shearwaters, cormorants (all three local species), and alcids, not to mention whales (mostly Humpback). Arctic and Aleutian Terns both nest here. In addition to the intriguing juxtaposition of marine and upland habitats, Shuyak is also unusual in that it has no foxes. The result is higher densities of ground-nesting birds, such as loons and waterfowl, than on islands that have native or introduced populations of this skilled bird-predator. Other summer birds on Shuyak are Common Loon, Common Eider, Barrow's Goldeneye, Northern Goshawk, Black Oystercatcher, Red-necked Phalarope (marine), Gray-cheeked Thrush, Myrtle Warbler, Pine Grosbeak, and both crossbills. The 47,000-acre park is 54 air-miles north of Kodiak and 80 miles southwest of Homer. Most visitors arrive by chartered floatplane from Kodiak or Homer and either camp or stay in one of four public-use cabins. A ranger station is centrally located at Big Bay. Kayak tours are available from providers in Kodiak and on the mainland. The Shuyak Island State Park bird list was compiled in 1999 and contains only 110 species. Birding visitors stand a good chance of adding species to this list.

Sooty Shearwater (*top*) and Short-tailed Shearwater (*bottom*)

OLGA BAY—TUNDRA BIRDING AT THE SOUTHWEST END OF KODIAK ISLAND

Olga Bay is a large saltwater bay with a very constricted opening that reduces its tidal range and makes it look like a huge lake. The eastern end of the bay is surrounded by low mountains and cottonwood-lined river valleys, and the western end is surrounded by flats and rolling hills that are nearly devoid of shrubs and trees. Wet meadows and ponds are a common feature of the area and are interspersed with drier tundra habitats. This large region—extending from Cape Alitak on the south to Halibut Bay on the north—is summer home to many birds that are more characteristic of the western Alaska mainland and the Aleutians. Among waterfowl breeding here are Tundra Swan, Northern Pintail, Green-winged Teal, Greater Scaup, Black Scoter, and Red-breasted Merganser. Shorebirds are abundant, with Greater Yellowlegs, Least and Rock Sandpipers, Short-billed Dowitcher, Wilson's Snipe, and Red-necked Phalarope all breeding. Whimbrels were seen repeatedly in July 1998 and may have been nesting on the Olga Flats. Both Parasitic and Long-tailed Jaegers are common nesters. Willow Ptarmigan is abundant. Rough-legged Hawks nest on cliffs along the coast and fly inland to forage, while Short-eared Owls nest in tall grass throughout the area. Passerine diversity is low, with Bank Swallow, Savannah and Golden-crowned Sparrows, and Lapland Longspur the predominant species. Brown Bears use this area, too, so use caution. Access is by boat from the village of Akhiok or by floatplane or wheeled plane from Kodiak. Most of this land is in the Kodiak NWR and there are few facilities for visitors. Only experienced wilderness campers or those escorted by local guides should consider a stay in this beautiful and remote area.

LOGISTICS

The area code for all telephone numbers is 907 unless otherwise indicated. Refer to The Milepost *for information about accommodations and other traveler services. Other useful Kodiak contacts are listed below for your convenience. Statewide travel and birding information services are listed under* Logistics *in the* Introduction, *page 15.)*

The Kodiak Island Convention and Visitors Bureau is the best source for information about visiting the Kodiak area — 100 Marine Way, Kodiak, AK 99615; 800-789-4782 or 486-4782; email *KICVB@ptialaska.net*; web site *http://www.kodiak.org*. Ask for their annual guidebook and Kodiak Audubon Society's *Kodiak Hiking Guide*.

Kodiak Island Borough Office — The State Department of Natural Resources publishes an atlas of Kodiak land-ownership patterns if you wish to determine which lands are open to birding; 486-9363.

Access: Kodiak town can be reached only by sea or air. There are several flights daily from Anchorage via Alaska Airlines and ERA Aviation. You can arrive on the Alaska Marine Highway ferry from Seward or Homer. The local number for the Kodiak Ferry Terminal is 486-3800. For information on birding from the ferry from Homer to Kodiak see page 323 and the Barren Islands section of the Kenai Peninsula, page 318.

Accommodations: There are several hotels and many B&B establishments in the town of Kodiak. In addition, there are a few restaurants and lodgings along the Kodiak road system. The outlying villages have B&Bs, and in some cases, lodges. Many wilderness lodges are scattered throughout the archipelago. Find more information about lodging through the KICVB, the Internet, or *The Milepost*.

Car Rentals: KICVB has a list of several car rental agencies in Kodiak.

Festivals: Whalefest Kodiak, in mid-April, celebrates the spring passage of Gray Whales past the archipelago. *Http://www.koc.alaska.edu/whalefest/default.htm.*

Kodiak Crab Festival in late May features parades, carnival booths and midway, running events, golf tournament, bicycle and survival-suit races, blessing of the fishing fleet, and concerts.

Other useful contacts:

Alaska Department of Fish and Game, 211 Mission Road, Kodiak, AK 99615; 486-1880,

Alaska State Parks, 1400 Abercrombie Drive, Kodiak, AK 99615; 486-6339; *kodsp@ptialaska.net*; *http://www.dnr.state.ak.us/parks/units/ index.htm#kodiak.*

Alutiiq Museum, 215 Mission Road, Kodiak, AK 99615, 486-7004; *alutiiq2@ptialaska.net*; *http://www.alutiiqmuseum.com.*

Kodiak Chamber of Commerce, PO Box 1485, Kodiak, AK 99615; 486-5557, *http://www.kodiak.org.*

Kodiak Historical Society, Baranof Museum, 101 Marine Way, Kodiak, AK 99615; 486-5920.

Kodiak Island Borough, 710 Mill Bay Road, Kodiak, AK 99615; 486-9376;*http://www.kib.co.kodiak.ak.us/;* baler/landfill: 486-9345.

Kodiak Military History Museum; *http://www.kadiak.org.*

Kodiak National Wildlife Refuge, 1390 Buskin River Road; 487-2600; a Refuge/Archipelago bird checklist is available at *http://www.npwrc.usgs.gov/resource/othrdata/chekbird/r7/kodiak.htm.*

Beringian Seabird Colony Catalog, U.S. Fish and Wildlife Service, *http://www.asgdc.state.ak.us/metadata/vector/biologic/birds/seabird00.html.*

Kodiak Audubon Society, PO Box 1756, Kodiak, AK 99615. Trail guide information at *http://www.kodiak.org/trails.html.*

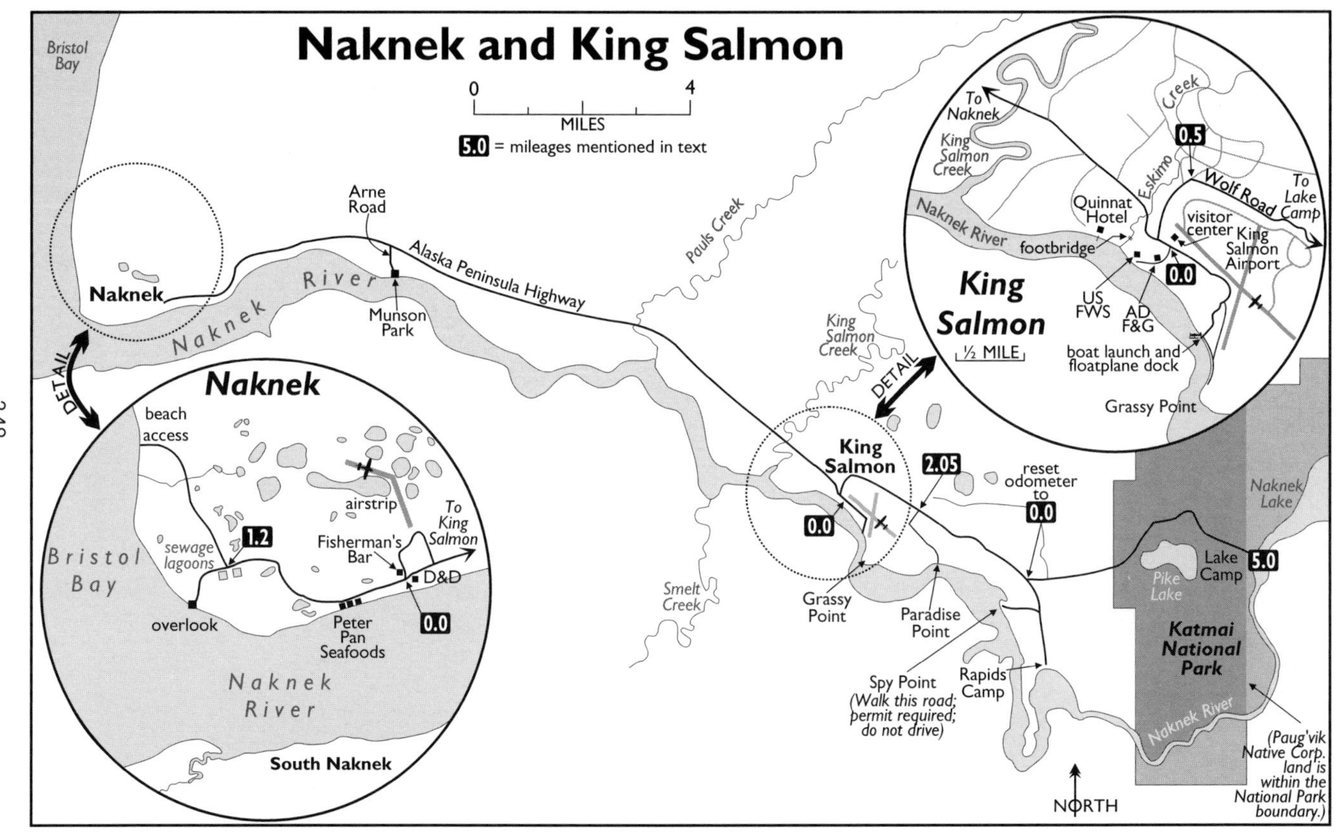

Naknek and King Salmon
0
4
MILES
5.0 = mileages mentioned in text
Bristol Bay
Naknek
DETAIL
Naknek River
Arne Road
Munson Park
Alaska Peninsula Highway
Pauls Creek
King Salmon Creek
Smelt Creek
King Salmon
0.0
Grassy Point
2.05
Paradise Point
Spy Point (Walk this road; permit required; do not drive)
Rapids Camp
reset odometer to 0.0
NORTH
Naknek Lake
Pike Lake
Lake Camp
5.0
Katmai National Park
Naknek River
(Paug'vik Native Corp. land is within the National Park boundary.)
Naknek
beach access
sewage lagoons
overlook
1.2
airstrip
Fisherman's Bar
To King Salmon
D&D
0.0
Peter Pan Seafoods
Bristol Bay
Naknek River
South Naknek
To Naknek
King Salmon Creek
Eskimo Creek
0.5
Wolf Road
To Lake Camp
Naknek River
Quinnat Hotel
footbridge
visitor center
King Salmon Airport
0.0
King Salmon
½ MILE
US FWS
AD F&G
boat launch and floatplane dock
Grassy Point

ALASKA PENINSULA:

KING SALMON TO COLD BAY

Susan Savage

The Bristol Bay Borough communities of King Salmon, Naknek, and South Naknek are the gateway to the Alaska Peninsula. Situated 300 air-miles southwest of Anchorage, King Salmon is served by jet during most of the year and by commuter planes every day except for a few holidays. (See map on page 322.) The Alaska Peninsula begins below Iliamna Lake, the state's largest lake, and arcs to the southwest for 500 miles, narrowing until it terminates at Chunak Point southwest of Cold Bay. At the end of the peninsula a visitor could look across mile-wide Isanotski Strait to Unimak Island, the first of the Aleutian Islands.

The Alaska Peninsula divides the Gulf of Alaska from the Bering Sea. The peninsula is dominated by the Aleutian Range, which forms its spine along the eastern side and gently slopes to the north and west into the Bristol Bay lowlands, a narrow coastal plain that slips into the sea. The Aleutian Range is the southwest continuation of the Alaska Range and extends from Mount Iliamna to Attu Island at the end of the Aleutian Island chain, a distance of about 1,650 miles. The range forms the northern arc of the volcanic Ring of Fire along the Pacific rim from Japan, eastern coastal Russia, across Alaska, and south along coastal British Columbia to California. The highest peaks of the Aleutian Range, reaching almost 9,000 feet above sea level, are volcanic; some remain active today, but most have collapsed. The sedimentary rock that forms the base of most of the range is intruded with granitic rocks. Volcanic rock has covered much of the basic rock structure. Pleistocene glaciers rounded off many of the peaks and carved bays on the Gulf of Alaska side of the peninsula and created basins for several large lakes on the Bering Sea side.

Naknek Lake (about 240 square miles), Becharof Lake (540 square miles), and the Ugashik Lakes (160 square miles) vie for "great lake" status; all are drained by large rivers flowing to the Bering Sea. These large lakes and rivers support a rich Pacific salmon industry. Red Salmon is the primary commercial species, although some systems support sport fisheries for Chinook (King) and Coho (Silver) Salmon. Rainbow Trout, Arctic Grayling, and Arctic Char are abundant in some of the rivers and lakes. Because of the fish, the peninsula also supports a thriving Brown Bear population. Birders can combine bear-viewing and sportfishing with their birding if they time their visit well. All precautions should be taken to avoid surprise encounters with bears and to avoid attracting bears into picnic and camping sites. See Bear Cautions in the *Introduction*, page 17.

Vegetation on the peninsula surprises most visitors. Boreal forest predominates in the northern section, but ends before Becharof Lake. From there southward a mix of shrubland, tundra, meadow, and wetland dominates the landscape, with a few Black Cottonwood woodlands found in riparian or lakeside settings. Because the avifauna follows the habitat, birders will find boreal species only as far south as King Salmon.

Before European contact the peninsula was the crossroads between Yupik Eskimo culture to the north and west and Aleut culture to the south. Prehistory presents a complex interweaving of these cultures. Native Americans have been using the peninsula for nearly 10,000 years, as evidenced by ancient archeological sites found at Brooks Camp, the Ugashik area, and Takli Island. Russian influence was prominent in several areas on the peninsula, and the fishing industry drew in fishermen from many cultures, including those of Scandinavia, Russia, and Portugal.

Land ownership is complex. Katmai National Park was established in 1918, six years after the eruption of Novarupta, which created the Valley of Ten Thousand Smokes. The passage of the Alaska Native Land Claims Settlement Act in 1971 added more land to Katmai National Park as well as creating several other federal reserves and parks. Along the southeastern side of the peninsula, south of the Katmai boundary, is Becharof National Wildlife Refuge, Alaska Peninsula National Wildlife Refuge–Ugashik Unit, Aniakchak National Monument and Preserve, Alaska Peninsula National Wildlife Refuge–Chignik and Pavlov Units, and Izembek National Wildlife Refuge. Much of the land fronting the Bristol Bay coast is state or borough land. Near each village, the local or regional Native corporation owns many parcels of land. It is the visitor's responsibility to know where the Native lands are and to check about local land ownership before going off-road. For those venturing out of the villages, most air taxis should know the land status of the destination. In the King Salmon-Naknek area visitors can buy a short-term permit at the Chinook gift shop located at the airport for access to Paug'vik lands (the Native corporation for Naknek).

Birders should be aware that during June and July the King Salmon-Naknek area bustles with commercial fishing activity. From June to September, many visitors come to visit Katmai National Park or for sportfishing. The area supports an active guided and outfitted hunting industry in May of even-numbered years and September–October of most years. If you plan to combine hunting and birding, check first, because there are many restrictions (e.g., Caribou hunting is restricted to a permit system limited to state residents). In summer, advance reservations for accommodations and vehicle rental are recommended.

BIRDING AREAS

All birding routes start from the King Salmon Visitor Center immediately adjacent to the Peninsula Air / Alaska Air terminal in King Salmon.

Naknek River at King Salmon — If you have just a short layover in King Salmon, a walk to the nearby Naknek River is worthwhile, especially in April and May. The distance is about a city block. Cross the main road and walk down the access road to the ADF&G / USFWS buildings. (Please don't venture out onto either agency's dock.) From the lawn you can watch waterfowl on the river, or at low tide you could find a few shorebirds by the boat ramp. In spring, expect to see Common Loon, Tundra Swan, Greater White-fronted Goose, Eurasian and American Wigeons, Northern Shoveler, Northern Pintail, Mallard, Green-winged Teal, Greater Scaup, Common and Barrow's (occasional) Goldeneyes, Common and Red-breasted Mergansers, Bald Eagle, Greater Yellowlegs, Hudsonian Godwit, and Short-billed Dowitcher. Bonaparte's and Glaucous-winged Gulls and Arctic Terns are also here at that time. Another treat in April (or, in late winters, into May) are the Beluga Whales and Harbor Seals that come up the river on an incoming tide to feed on smelt. Watch for Northern Shrike, Gray Jay, Black-billed Magpie, Black-capped and Boreal Chickadees, Gray-cheeked and Varied Thrushes, American Robin, Fox, Gambel's White-crowned, and Golden-crowned Sparrows, Pine Grosbeak, White-winged Crossbill (when the spruce cone crop is good), Common and Hoary (occasional) Redpolls, and toward the end of May, Orange-crowned, Myrtle, Blackpoll, and Wilson's Warblers, and Rusty Blackbird. Merlins occasionally nest in the woodlots. Local rarities, including Yellow-billed Loon or several species of eider, might be found in spring or fall. In the winter months, Snow Buntings forage in the tall grass, and a McKay's Bunting is now and again discovered in the flock.

Grassy Point — The best time to visit Grassy Point is in April and May before the floatplane traffic becomes heavy. If you have time for a longer walk, or if you have a vehicle, head east on the main road. After paralleling the main runway, the road forks at 0.7 mile. Bear right to the King Salmon boat launch (another 0.3 mile) to scan the river for the same species listed above. If you are still in the mood to walk, follow the dirt road farther east past the floatplane docks. After 0.2 mile the left loop from the first road fork rejoins this road, and you can return by that route (when you get to a new intersection at the hill, bear left to return to the original road fork). Or, you could keep following the road east to Grassy Point (another 0.3 mile). (In spring, this road can be impassable by vehicle.) If Canada Geese (usually

Cackling, but look for Aleutians and Lesser) or Black Brant are present in the King Salmon area, this is a good place to find them. You can walk out on the tundra as far as the shrubs, 200 yards farther upriver, for a better view.

Quinnat Hotel dock — Head west from the visitor center, pass the King Salmon Mall (a two-story office building that houses the bank and the National Park Service office), then cut through its parking lot, and walk between Eddie's Fire Place Inn and Antler's Inn. Ahead is a fairly rickety footbridge spanning Eskimo Creek. If you are game, you can cross the bridge and bear left past the end of the Quinnat Hotel. (You can also reach the hotel by walking up the main highway across the Eskimo Creek vehicle bridge, then turning left at the first dirt road that is marked by the hotel sign.) Across from the main entrance of the hotel is the access to their dock, but if you are not a guest, please ask permission to walk out onto the dock. This area affords another fine view of the river and the species listed above. In May, you might hear a Lincoln's Sparrow from both Eskimo Creek bridges or a Varied Thrush in the boreal forest behind the hotel.

KING SALMON TO LAKE CAMP

If you have a vehicle and several free hours, a drive to Lake Camp is a good choice. Turn right from the visitor center (Mile 0.0), and right again onto the first road that leads between the cargo companies and the King Ko Bar. You are traveling through inactive King Salmon Air Force Base, formerly "Top Cover for North America" along with bases at Galena and Anchorage; see the eight F-15 hangers to the right. Past the airport, turn right onto Wolf Road (Mile 0.5). At Mile 2.05 turn right onto a well-developed dirt road to go to Paradise Point. This road bears left after 0.4 mile to parallel the airport fence. Watch out for mudholes where you could get stuck in spring. In about a mile the dirt road ends on a bluff above the river. From late March through mid-May, this is an excellent location from which to view waterfowl. The species here might not be different from those in town, but their numbers are usually good. This vantage point is best at low tide on an overcast day (to avoid the glare off the river); take your spotting scope. Hundreds of Tundra Swans, Northern Pintails, and other species listed for King Salmon gather here, joined rarely by Canvasback, Redhead, Ring-necked Duck, and Tufted Duck. Occasionally you might see a Northern Harrier, Rough-legged Hawk, or Merlin catching the thermals off the bluff. Bald Eagles commonly perch along the banks or soar overhead.

Return to Lake Camp Road, the extension of Wolf Road. Turn right and travel 2.7 miles until the road forks. Reset your trip-odometer to 0.0. Keeping straight (right) takes you to Spy Point and Rapids Camp (read ahead before you decide where to spend your time). Bearing left takes you to Lake Camp. Along the Lake Camp Road watch for raptors, including Northern

Goshawk, Gyrfalcon, and Northern Hawk Owl (all rare). In winter, look for groups of scavenging birds, such as Bald Eagles and corvids, that may be on a carcass. In May and June listen for Wilson's Snipe, Gray-cheeked, Hermit, and Varied Thrushes, American Robin, Orange-crowned, Myrtle, Blackpoll, and Wilson's Warblers, and American Tree, Savannah, Fox, Gambel's White-crowned, and Golden-crowned Sparrows. Near Lake Camp you could hear Northern Waterthrush and Lincoln's Sparrow, too. Assuming that you have chosen the Lake Camp option, follow the road after the intersection as it climbs Pike Ridge, which has long been a source of gravel for local construction projects. From the crest you can see immense Naknek Lake and Katmai National Park. (At Lake Camp you are two miles inside the park boundary.) As you descend the ridge, Pike Lake appears on the right (best view at 2.3 miles from the Lake Camp/Rapids Camp fork; you can find a safe place to park and walk down the dirt road to the lake). It's always worth scanning the lake to see what might be there. Occasionally you'll find waterfowl, such as scoters and Bufflehead, that do not frequent the King Salmon section of river. If you happen to be here on a late-May evening during an insect hatch, you may see thousands of swallows (mostly Tree, possibly Violet-green, and also Cliff and Barn) perched on the power lines. At 4.4 miles past the fork, the view opens up on both sides. Watch for wildlife in this area, including River Otter, Brown Bear, Wolf, Moose, and Caribou.

Near Lake Camp (Mile 5.0) keep straight ahead to the end of the road at a public boat ramp. (This is a popular Rainbow Trout fishing area; however, during April–early June this section of river is closed to fishing due to trout spawning). In April and May the river level is usually low, and you can hike upstream along the riverbank for several miles. A few springs and creeks drain across the bank, so rubber boats are a plus. Look for Red-throated, Pacific, and Common Loons, waterfowl, and Sandhill Cranes on the mudflats or the tundra. Additional shorebird species could include Black-bellied Plover, Pacific Golden-Plover, and Semipalmated Plover. This is one of the buggiest locations in all of Bristol Bay—a head net is required after about mid-May.

Rapids Camp — Depending on your birding goals, the amount of time you have, and the time of year, you might want to focus on Rapids Camp rather than on Lake Camp. In late April and early May, Rapids Camp can be a magnet for waterfowl and shorebirds, but in late winters, the area might be icebound right through the prime birding time. Also, Rapids Camp is best visited at low tide. Here, the Naknek River has formed a large oxbow and a lagoon that shows its tidal influence when the river is low in spring. Rapids Camp offers excellent feed for Greater White-fronted Goose, Tundra Swan, American Wigeon, Mallard, Northern Shoveler, Northern Pintail, Green-winged Teal, Greater Scaup, several plover species, Greater and

Lesser Yellowlegs, Hudsonian, Bar-tailed (uncommon), and Marbled (uncommon) Godwits, Red Knot (uncommon), Western Sandpiper, Dunlin, Short-billed Dowitcher, and other shorebirds. Bonaparte's, Mew, and Glaucous-winged Gulls, Arctic Terns, and raptors occur, and the cottonwood-and-shrub-lined bank also supports the common passerines. There is much private land in this area, so stay on the public land, i.e., below the mean high-water line in the spring when the river is low.

Spy Point — On the way to Rapids Camp (about 0.7 mile from the Lake Camp-Rapids Camp intersection), a narrow dirt track on the right leads to Spy Point. You need a Paug'vik permit to enter this area (see *Logistics*), and you'll need to go on foot (please don't try to drive!). Park and walk the track to where it peters out after about one-half mile; bear right to reach a bluff overlooking the Naknek River. If you look to the right (downstream) toward King Salmon, you can see another bluff—Paradise Point, where you may have stopped before. This location gives another view of the mudflats. Occasionally the waterfowl are more numerous at this spot.

KING SALMON TO NAKNEK

The drive from King Salmon to Naknek is approximately 15 miles along the Alaska Peninsula Highway. The boreal forest in King Salmon thins to groves of shrub spaced between tundra and wet meadows. In late winter, early spring, and occasionally in fall, Northern Hawk Owls are spotted on the utility lines, where you should also see the more-common Northern Shrikes. In spring and summer, Northern Harrier, Parasitic and Long-tailed Jaegers, and Short-eared Owl cruise over the open meadows. During a few weeks in April, up to half a dozen Bald Eagles and crowds of Mew and Glaucous-winged Gulls concentrate on King Salmon Creek, fishing for smelt or lampreys. In April, a worthwhile stop is Munson Park (about 10 miles from King Salmon, left down Arne Road, then keep straight). From the riverbank you might see eiders, scoters, Long-tailed Duck, goldeneyes, mergansers, Bald Eagle, and Beluga Whales on an incoming tide.

Naknek — Naknek is one of the hubs of the Bristol Bay Sockeye (Red) Salmon fishery. Although the rare visitor can arrive in Naknek via commuter flight from the southern villages, Dillingham, or on a barge or fishing boat, most people drive in from King Salmon. The best times to visit are from late April through mid-September. If you happen to come in winter, check around the airport buildings for flocks of Snow Buntings that might contain an occasional McKay's. The premier birding areas in Naknek are to the west of town center—the river mouth, the sewage lagoons, and the Bristol Bay beach.

If you have come from King Salmon, drive west through town center, past the D&D Restaurant (a must stop for pizza), to the end of the pavement at

Fisherman's Bar, and bear left (zero your trip-odometer here). Continue west, bearing left past the cannery buildings, and when the road divides after Mile 0.25, angle right up a hill and past a small house to a spot with ponds on both sides of the road. Pause to check out the ponds, and then, as you crest the hill, stop to scan the tundra. Small groups of Caribou are sometimes seen in this area. Western and Least Sandpipers, Red-necked Phalarope, Bank Swallow, Savannah Sparrow, and Lapland Longspur are common. Horned Lark has been reported in spring. At Mile 0.95, you can drive to the back side of the sewage lagoons, or you can continue on to another vantage point. At Mile 1.2 is the intersection with the beach-access road (see below). For another view of the sewage ponds, go straight on the road that bears left to the far side of the ponds (1.55 miles), where there is also a viewing platform at the Naknek River mouth. In April and May you will find Northern Shoveler, Greater Scaup, Black Scoter (occasional), and Red-necked Phalarope in the lagoons. Mew, Glaucous-winged, and Glaucous (rare) Gulls may be found. In one fall, two to three Black-headed Gulls were around the ponds for months.

From the viewing platform, you can hope to see a pelagic species, but more to be expected are the waterfowl, gulls, terns, and shorebirds already listed. Parasitic and Long-tailed Jaegers, Herring Gull, Black-legged Kittiwake, and Aleutian Tern are also seen regularly. Occasional are Northern Fulmar, Sooty and Short-tailed Shearwaters, Fork-tailed Storm-Petrel, and Common Murre. In March and April, sea ducks, including Steller's (rare) and King Eiders and Long-tailed Duck, might be seen. Marine mammals could include Beluga Whale, Harbor Seal, or rarities such as Pilot Whale, Killer Whale, or Gray Whale (very rare). Bald Eagles often patrol the bluffs.

Backtrack to the beach-access-road intersection (1.2 miles from Fisherman's Bar) and drive north (left turn) to the beach. You'll find the shorebirding here best about one hour after peak high tide. Unless you are with a local expert, it is unwise to walk out on these mudflats at high tide or on an incoming peak high, because the entire beach can flood during certain tides, and some tides come in very rapidly. See tidal cautions in the Introduction, page 19. Another conflict can be commercial fishing—pay attention to opening dates. If there is a set-net opening and people are fishing on the beach (not in the river), you probably should avoid birding. The fishing activities scare away most of the birds, anyway.

At the beach, the first highlight is right at the parking area—from June through August, a small breeding colony of Aleutian Terns is present. If you are looking for shorebirds, bring your scope. The best times for shorebirds are early May (spring migration) and late June through September (with a constantly changing array of species). In May, the Naknek beach has Black-bellied Plover, Pacific and American Golden-Plovers, Bar-tailed Godwit, Black Turnstone, Western Sandpiper, Dunlin, Short-billed and Long-billed (rare) Dowitchers, and Red-necked Phalarope. In summer, you can find Whimbrel, Ruddy and Black Turnstones, Western Sandpiper, Dunlin, and abundant dowitchers. Occasionally seen are Greater Yellowlegs, Bristle-thighed Curlew, Red Knot, Sanderling, Least, Baird's, and Pectoral Sandpipers, and Sabine's Gull. In summer, sea ducks are common, and southbound Sandhill Cranes come through in late August and early September. In recent years a few Yellow Wagtails were found atop the bluff (and sometimes on the beach, from mid-June to mid-July). In fall a variety of raptors appears, including Merlin and Peregrine Falcon. At dusk Short-eared Owls fly low above the beach.

If you happen to be in King Salmon in winter, ask about river freeze-up. In some years a concentration of Common Mergansers and Bald Eagles is found at the advancing front of the Naknek River ice edge. Also in winter, if you haven't seen enough Bald Eagles or Common Ravens, there is usually a mixed gang sifting through the landfill (not open every day).

FLY-OUTS

King Salmon is the hub for air-charter companies that serve many remote lodges, hunting and fishing guides, outfit-hunters, and fisherman. If you are flying out of King Salmon to fish, hunt, or bearwatch, you might also run across some good birding opportunities. In general, as you fly over the tundra, wet meadows, and shrublands, watch for breeding pairs of Tundra Swans and Sandhill Cranes. The swans usually can be spotted from an altitude of 1,000 feet, although you won't be able to nail down a positive ID if this is your life Tundra Swan. In April and early May watch for an abundance of waterfowl, especially at the mouths of large rivers. If you are flying

Northern Fulmar

over the Aleutian Mountains, watch for cliff-nesting raptors—Rough-legged Hawk, Golden Eagle, Gyrfalcon, and Peregrine Falcon—and Harlequin Ducks in the creeks. In late summer and fall look for flocks of Willow and Rock Ptarmigan.

Brooks Camp (Katmai National Park) — Brooks Camp is world-renowned as a Brown Bear viewing area. You can stay overnight at the Brooks Lodge or in your own tent. For birding, this is one of the better boreal forests on the Alaska Peninsula. Some boreal species are more abundant here than in King Salmon, including Northern Goshawk, Three-toed Woodpecker, Alder Flycatcher, Red-breasted Nuthatch, Brown Creeper, Golden-crowned and Ruby-crowned Kinglets, and Swainson's Thrush. Occasionally, Harlequin Duck and Marbled Murrelet (rare, usually in late summer) are found on the lake, and Spotted and Semipalmated Sandpipers bob along on the beach. In some years Bald Eagle, Great Horned Owl, and Boreal Owl nest in the vicinity. Mallard and Red-breasted Merganser hens nonchalantly raise their broods among the bears. American Dippers frequent Brooks Falls. Surfbirds have been seen in June at Brooks River mouth. Visitors to Brooks can add on a bus tour to the Valley of Ten Thousand Smokes (visit the Katmai National Park web site to understand the significance of this feature). Because habitat changes drastically en route to the valley, so does the array of birds, but the bus makes few stops. If the bus stops at Margo Creek, watch overhead for Violet-green Swallows. If you arrange to hike into the Aleutian Mountains, you should encounter Rock Sandpiper, American Pipit, Snow Bunting, and Gray-crowned Rosy-Finch—all nest at the higher elevations. White-tailed Ptarmigan have also been reported in the mountains.

Alagnak Wild River — The Alagnak is one of the most heavily used rivers in this part of Alaska. Several lodges offer fishing by jet boat on the river, and several air taxis and outfitters take river rafters out for four-to-ten-day trips. This area is also more boreal than King Salmon. Although Bald Eagles nest along the river, Ospreys are more common. If you find Black-billed Magpies fussing, look for a Merlin. Northern Goshawks may be abundant. The chickadees, thrushes, warblers, sparrows, and finches should be the same species you saw in King Salmon. Watch for White-winged Crossbills in good mast years. Harlequin Duck may be spotted along the river, and Common Mergansers are common. In late summer, Bonaparte's Gull is the most common gull seen. Moose and Brown Bear are also very common.

Bristol Bay shoreline — From late March to early May, the Bristol Bay coast is an important migratory stopover and pathway for waterfowl wintering in the Aleutians, on the Pacific Coast of the Alaska Peninsula, on Kodiak Island, and points farther south. Emperor Goose, possibly Black Brant, King and Steller's Eiders, Long-tailed Duck, Marbled and Bar-tailed Godwits, Bristle-thighed Curlew, Sanderling, and Rock Sandpiper are worth looking for. If you are in a craft that can land on the beach, you might want to target Goose Point (the southern peninsula enclosing Egegik Lagoon, Ugashik Bay, Strogonof Point, or Cinder Lagoon. Some of these species may also congregate in fall, but insufficient information is available to pinpoint timing.

Pacific Coast — The rocky coast supports some colonies of seabirds and provides cliff faces for many nesting raptors. By Alaska standards, the seabird colonies are small. Species include Double-crested, Red-faced, and Pelagic Cormorants, Black Oystercatcher, Glaucous-winged Gull, Black-legged Kittiwake, Common and Thick-billed Murres, Pigeon Guillemot, and Horned and Tufted Puffins. Seabird diversity increases as you approach the end of the peninsula, and may include some of the auklets and storm-petrels. However, most of the larger colonies are found on the islands offshore (colony web site). Seabirds can be very sensitive to aircraft over-flights, so encourage your pilot to go no closer to the colonies than 1,000 feet elevation or one-half mile linear distance. Nesting Bald Eagles are common and Rough-legged Hawk, Gyrfalcon, or Peregrine Falcon nests are sometimes spotted. Please keep a respectful distance from these, as well. If you land on the Pacific coast, look for Northwestern Crow, Winter Wren, Sea Otters, Steller's Sea Lions, and Harbor Seals. Brown Bears are very common.

COLD BAY

If you take the M/V *Tustumena* state ferry from Homer or Kodiak to Dutch Harbor, you will make a stop in Cold Bay (see Ferry Trip, page 323). If you are there in fall, check for Black Brant, Emperor Goose, and eiders. The Izembek National Wildlife Refuge office has more details.

Many Asian species show up on the peninsula, island-hopping up the Aleutians from Russia. In recent years Baikal Teal, Garganey, Olive-backed Pipit, and Brambling have been seen on the peninsula. Also, a number of northern or southern North American breeders make a wrong turn and end up on the peninsula. Great Egret, Bristle-thighed Curlew, Rufous Hummingbird, Yellow-shafted Flicker, Say's Phoebe, Bohemian Waxwing, and Tennessee and Townsend's Warblers have been recorded. Your documentation of these vagrants will help us to better understand bird distribution. Please report sightings of species marked with an **N** or missing from the checklists (beginning on page 519 at the end of this guide) for Becharof NWR/Katmai NP or Izembek NWR to the King Salmon Visitor Center. Permission and possibly a permit are needed to walk or drive on the roads through Native-owned land in the Cold Bay area. Check at the Izembek NWR for details.

LOGISTICS

The area code for all telephone numbers is 907 unless otherwise indicated. The Alaska Peninsula is not covered in The Milepost. *Other useful contacts are listed below for your convenience. Statewide travel and birding information services are listed under* Logistics *in the* Introduction, *page 15.)*

The King Salmon Visitor Center (PO Box 298, King Salmon, AK 99613; 246-4250) is an interagency facility supported by the Alaska Peninsula/ Becharof National Wildlife Refuge (USFWS), Katmai National Park, and the Bristol Bay and the Lake and Peninsula Boroughs. They maintain a current list of visitor facilities and services for Naknek, South Naknek, and King Salmon as well as for the 17 villages in Lake and Peninsula Borough. The visitor center, which currently has no web site, is located at the airport and provides books and videos through the Alaska Natural Heritage Association. There is taxi service in King Salmon / Naknek.

Other useful contacts:

Alaska Peninsula / Becharof NWR, PO Box 277, King Salmon, AK 99613; 247-3339; *http://alaska.fws.gov/nwr/ap/apnwr.html; http://alaska.fws.gov/nwr/bec/index.html.*

Izembek National Wildlife Refuge, 1 Izembek Road, PO Box 127, Cold Bay, AK 99571; 532-2445; *http://www.r7.fws.gov/nwr/izembek/iznwr.html.*

Katmai National Park and Preserve, Aniakchak National Monument and Preserve, Alagnak Wild River, PO Box 7, King Salmon, AK 99613; 246-3305; *http://www.nps.gov/katm/.*

Bristol Bay Borough, PO Box 189, Naknek, AK 99633; 246-4224; *http://www.theborough.com/.* Lake and Peninsula Borough, PO Box 495, King Salmon, AK 99613; 246-3421; *http://www.bristolbay.com/~lpboro/.*

Alaska Seabird Colony Catalog *http://www.asgdc.state.ak.us/metadata/vector/biologic/birds/seabird00.html.*

Alaska Department of Fish and Game, PO Box 37, King Salmon, AK 99613; 246-4636.

In summer, you have a choice of several restaurants in King Salmon, but only one or two remain open in winter. In Naknek at least one restaurant is open year round. Both towns have grocery stores. Recommended hotels are the Quinnat Landing Hotel (246-3000; *www.quinnat.com*) and the King Ko (246-3377summer only; *www.kingko.com*), both in King Salmon. Bear Trail Lodge (246-2327; *www.beartraillodge.com*) provides quality lodging on the outskirts of King Salmon. There are several nice B&Bs in Naknek. Expect all food, lodging, and car rentals to be expensive.

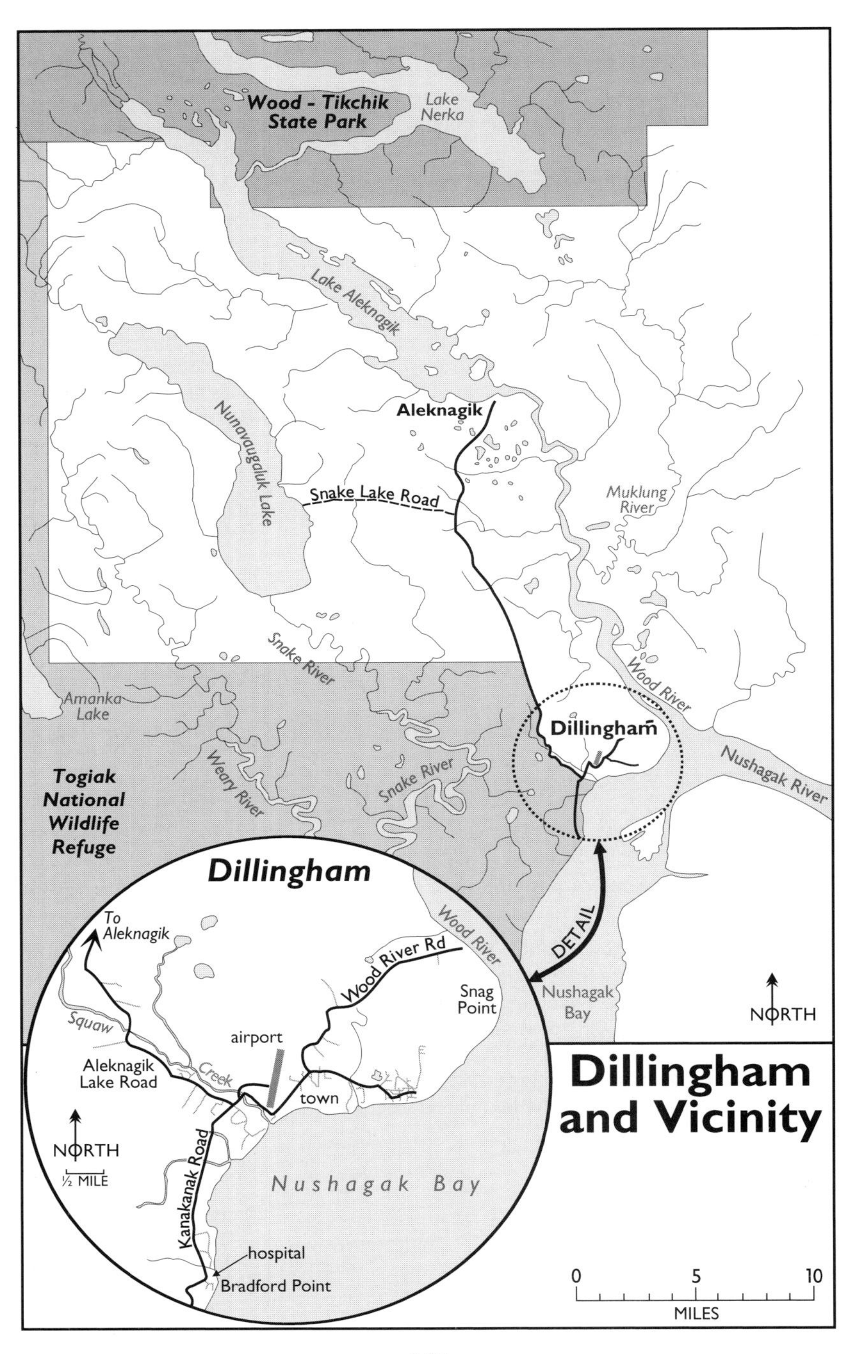
Wood - Tikchik State Park
Lake Nerka
Lake Aleknagik
Aleknagik
Nunavaugaluk Lake
Snake Lake Road
Muklung River
Snake River
Wood River
Amanka Lake
Dillingham
Nushagak River
Weary River
Snake River
Togiak National Wildlife Refuge
Dillingham
To Aleknagik
Wood River Rd
Wood River
DETAIL
Snag Point
Nushagak Bay
NORTH
Squaw
Creek
airport
Aleknagik Lake Road
town
NORTH
½ MILE
Kanakanak Road
Nushagak Bay
hospital
Bradford Point
Dillingham and Vicinity
0
5
10
MILES

DILLINGHAM

Robert MacDonald

Dillingham lies approximately 360 air-miles southwest of Anchorage. (See map on page 322 for Dillingham's location.) While most visitors are related to the salmon-fishing industry, the area should not be overlooked by birders because some 214 species of birds have been recorded here. In fall 2001 a Steller's Sea-Eagle was found here. You would be wise to check the RBAs before your Alaska trip to see whether this individual has remained in or returned to the area, as the Taku Inlet (Juneau) sea-eagle did for many years.

Dillingham, situated at the head of Nushagak Bay and at the mouth of the Wood and Nushagak Rivers, is the economic and regional hub of Bristol Bay. It is known as The Salmon Capitol of the World, supports a large commercial fishing industry, and is the largest town in the region. In 1818, Russian fur buyers established a trade center at Alexandrovsky Post, across the bay from Dillingham. The area was inhabited by Yupik Eskimos before the Russians invaded.

The Dillingham area encompasses great geographic diversity. The community sits at the edge of rolling tundra and ridges of spruce and birch trees. Rivers oxbow through the land, and pristine lakes and streams abound. To the north, rugged mountains crisscross the horizon. Dillingham is surrounded to the north by Wood-Tikchik State Park and to the west by Togiak National Wildlife Refuge. The state park—the largest state park in the United States—is known for its spectacular stair-step lakes connected by short rivers. Togiak NWR encompasses 4.7 million acres and is accessible only by plane or boat. Here, the topography includes rivers and lakes, jagged peaks, glacial valleys, tundra, cottonwood stands, spruce forests, extensive low to medium shrub communities, wetlands, rugged sea cliffs, and beaches.

Dillingham is accessible from Anchorage only by air. Alaska Airlines and Peninsula Airways provide regular flights and other airlines may operate between the two cities, so check with the Dillingham Chamber of Commerce for current information. Once you arrive, you will need to rent a car.

Dillingham weather is influenced by its near-maritime location, which means cool temperatures and moderate rainfall. Winds of 25 to 35 mph are common. Summer temperatures range from the high 30s to the high 60s°F; winter temperatures are moderate, and snowfall ranges from light to heavy.

Wind and rain are the two most predominant weather conditions that could impede your trip. Even a car trip on the road system can be severely hampered due to poor weather. Low cloud ceilings are almost to be expected. Dillingham gets about 20 hours of daylight on the longest summer day and around six hours on the shortest winter day. Residents know that the outdoors can be enjoyed all year long and in all weather conditions by dressing accordingly and being prepared.

Be on the lookout for Moose, Caribou, Brown Bear, and Porcupines on the roads, as well as for motorized traffic. Observe the Bear Cautions on page 17 in the *Introduction* to this guide. Aside from inclement weather, the biggest problem you are likely to encounter is biting insects. Mosquitoes, Black-flies, and No-see-ums can be very irritating in summer, but they are absent in winter. Bring plenty of insect repellent, a hat, long-sleeved shirt, rain gear, and hiking boots or knee-high boots. Fortunately, frequent breezes will help keep the bugs at bay.

BIRDING THE DILLINGHAM AREA

Mid-June to early July is the best time to see the most birds. Although there are 50 miles of roads for birding out of Dillingham, opportunities for observing birds are greatly increased by chartering a boat or aircraft or by striking out on foot. Winter bird enthusiasts could opt for a snowmachine trip to reach a wide array of locations and habitats. Many species uncommon to the immediate Dillingham area are common just a short distance away, where they may be accessible only by boat or aircraft.

If you rent a vehicle, make certain that it has a usable spare tire and tools for changing tires. About three-fifths of the roads are gravel and are potentially tough on tires. These roads are regularly traveled, though, and any assistance you need will not be far away. An added safety feature is the network of emergency phones that are spaced out along Aleknagik Lake Road. But, you won't find any gas stations, restaurants, or markets along the way, so carry extra food, water, clothing, rain gear, and plenty of insect repellent in case you break down.

You can bird the 50 miles of roads in about three days. More time would be needed for birders wanting to hike off the road system. Even more time may be required if you add trips using aircraft, boats, or snowmachines—modes of transportation that open up many thousands of square-miles of terrain accessible only by such means of travel. More importantly, traveling away from the immediate Dillingham area quickly puts you into areas where you won't be encountering people and you can more truly approach a wilderness experience, especially on fly-out trips.

If you have only a few hours to bird the area, you can easily explore around the airport or in town by foot or by taxi. Taxi cabs are available at the airport, three miles from town. Your best bet if you are time-limited is to walk the areas immediately near the airport. You will be able to cover open tundra, boreal forest, and a couple of creeks, especially Squaw Creek. Nushagak Bay could be reached on foot from the airport, too.

Much of the land surrounding Dillingham is a patchwork of Native Corporation, private, federal, and state holdings. Native lands are privately owned—it is permissible to bird from the road, but do not trespass where posted. Get verbal or written permission from the local Native Corporation (Choggiung Limited) to obtain access to their lands.

In your travels outside of the Dillingham area on foot or by aircraft, boat, or snowmachine, Yupik Eskimo residents are often busy with subsistence activities important for their food supply. They catch fish, big game animals, marine mammals, gamebirds, and gather berries and other resources depending on the time of year. It is important to respect Native activities and private camps scattered throughout the area. See the notes on Native Cultures in the *Introduction*, page 10.

Stop at the Dillingham Chamber of Commerce downtown, the U.S. Fish and Wildlife Service's Togiak NWR headquarters, and the Alaska Department of Fish and Game office to learn about local birds, wildlife, and trip planning. The refuge staff will be able to provide you with the latest bird sightings and suggestions about where to go on your trip.

There are three main roads for birding out of Dillingham. Kanakanak Road provides the only access from the airport to the town (5.5 miles) and to Nushagak Bay. Kanakanak Road travels through the outskirts of the boreal forest, passes through open tundra flats, and gives access to the marine environments along Nushagak Bay. It is important to have a spotting scope, especially for birding along the bay. All amenities in this small community of 2,400 are accessible from this road. Wood River Road, a spur road off Kanakanak Road, travels about five miles to the lower Wood River.

Aleknagik Lake Road begins at the midway point of Kanakanak Road and heads north for 20 miles through boreal forest, scattered open-tundra areas, small creek bottoms, and along a few small lakes to 26-mile-long Lake Aleknagik. The first seven miles are paved. You could detour through some of the residential areas and subdivisions branching off Aleknagik Lake Road to increase your birding opportunities. Aleknagik Lake Road is the site of a local federal Breeding Bird Survey that has been run since 1993. A species list from these surveys is available from the Togiak NWR office or from their web site.

Snake Lake Road is the local name for a dirt road that begins about 13 miles out Aleknagik Lake Road and which leads nine miles to Nunavaugaluk Lake, passing through boreal forest, scattered open-tundra areas, and small creek bottoms, with Snake Lake Mountain rising to the north. Although this road is marked as not maintained, it is kept in good enough condition to allow access to a sportfishing and ecotourism lodge located on Nunavaugaluk (Snake) Lake.

DILLINGHAM BIRDS

Red-throated Loons are found in small ponds or are observed flying overhead; listen for their raspy, quack-like call. Look for Pacific and Common Loons in ponds and larger lakes, such as Lake Aleknagik and Nunavaugaluk Lake. Of the 34 species of waterfowl observed in the Dillingham area, the most common species are Mallard, Northern Pintail, Green-winged Teal, Greater Scaup, Common Goldeneye, and Red-breasted Merganser. Nushagak Bay, Lake Aleknagik, Nunavaugaluk Lake, and the numerous tundra ponds in the area are all good locations for waterfowl. Other species you may see at these places are Greater White-fronted, Emperor, Snow, and Canada Geese, Black Brant, Tundra Swan, American Wigeon, Northern Shoveler, Steller's, King, and Common Eiders, Harlequin Duck, Surf, White-winged, and Black Scoters, Long-tailed Duck, Barrow's Goldeneye, and Common Merganser.

Twenty-one species of raptors have been documented, with Bald Eagle, Northern Harrier, Merlin, and Short-eared Owl being the most common. Bald Eagles are found around local water bodies, especially those containing resident fish species and anadromous salmon. The other three species are observed in the many open tundra areas along the road system. There is a chance to see Osprey, Rough-legged Hawk, Golden Eagle, Gyrfalcon, Peregrine Falcon, and Great Horned, Northern Hawk, and Boreal Owls.

Spruce Grouse and Willow Ptarmigan are common. You may hear Sandhill Cranes calling and see them flying overhead; or to get a better look, take a short hike through the shrubs or trees toward calling cranes in open areas.

Nushagak Bay is a Western Hemisphere Shorebird Reserve Network site. Look for Semipalmated Plover, Greater Yellowlegs, Whimbrel, Black Turnstone, Western Sandpiper, Dunlin, Short-billed and Long-billed Dowitchers, and Wilson's Snipe. Less-common species include Black-bellied Plover, American and Pacific Golden-Plovers, Wandering Tattler, Spotted Sandpiper, Sanderling, Least and Rock Sandpipers, and Red-necked Phalarope. The best way to see some of the 39 species of shorebirds that have been recorded in the area is a fly-out trip. This will prove most productive in August, when the shorebirds are feeding in coastal estuaries during their southward migration.

Bonaparte's, Mew, and Glaucous-winged Gulls and Arctic Tern are common. You also may find Long-tailed and Parasitic Jaegers, Herring and Sabine's Gulls, and Aleutian Terns. With a fly-out trip, you can visit some of the many seabird colonies where hundreds or thousands of seabirds nest on the coastal cliffs, with Pelagic Cormorant, Black-legged Kittiwake, Common Murre, Pigeon Guillemot, and Horned and Tufted Puffins the most common species.

Although hummingbirds are not common to the area, watch for Anna's and Rufous, the two species that have been recorded here. Belted Kingfishers are frequently observed along Dillingham's road system, especially in the Squaw Creek drainage. Downy, Hairy, Three-toed, and Black-backed Woodpeckers all occur.

Alder Flycatchers are abundant. Gray Jay, Black-billed Magpie, and Common Raven are common. Look for Northern Shrike, Horned Lark, and Tree, Bank, and Cliff Swallows. A colony of Bank Swallows nests along the shore of Nushagak Bay. You can hardly miss Black-capped and Boreal Chickadees, Red-breasted Nuthatch, American Dipper, Ruby-crowned Kinglet, Arctic Warbler, Gray-cheeked, Swainson's, Hermit, and Varied Thrushes, American Robin, Yellow Wagtail (mainly west of town), American Pipit, Orange-crowned, Yellow, Myrtle, Blackpoll, and Wilson's Warblers, Northern Waterthrush, American Tree, Savannah, Fox, Gambel's White-crowned, and Golden-crowned Sparrows, Slate-colored Junco, Lapland Longspur, Snow Bunting, Rusty Blackbird, Gray-crowned Rosy-Finch, Pine Grosbeak, and Common Redpoll.

Brown Bear

OTHER BIRDING AND TOURING OPPORTUNITIES

Although no formal bird-tour groups are presently operating in the Dillingham area, creative options may be available. Contacting local lodge owners may lead to finding someone willing to take you out birding. Local air-taxi operators are available to drop you off on a do-it-yourself trip to birding hot spots; such a trip could be coordinated through the Togiak National Wildlife Refuge. Or, contact one of the two ecotourism operations, Roberts Alaska Tours and Johnson Maritime Guide Service, to see how they can help with your birding trip.

Although birding will be your primary goal, keep in mind that many other outdoor opportunities are available, such as hunting, fishing, wildlife observation, photography, hiking, and kayaking. If you are in Dillingham in late June through late July, you may go on the free Peter Pan Seafood Cannery tour, which traces the canning process from start to finish and includes stops at the historic net loft, cold storage plant, and company store. You may choose to visit the Samuel K. Fox Museum, which houses a permanent collection of traditional Yupik Eskimo skin sewing, hunting and food-gathering artifacts, Native baskets, and artwork. You can also visit the Dillingham boat harbor, home to the commercial salmon fleet, and talk to fishermen while strolling the floating docks, or watch the boats leave for a commercial fishing opening.

A popular destination for visitors is the 4.7-million-acre Togiak NWR, one of 16 national wildlife refuges in the state. Although accessible only by aircraft, the scenery, wildlife, and birding opportunities are diverse and plentiful. There are many bird species that have been recorded on the refuge that have not been observed in the Dillingham area, so a visit would be a good way to add to your bird list. Car and boat access to Wood-Tikchik State Park is from Dillingham and the village of Aleknagik. Other than waterfowl and waterbirds, birding in the the state park will generate a species list similar to the one you create along the Dillingham road system.

Another unique option is the chance to view Pacific Walrus. Togiak NWR and the Walrus Islands State Game Sanctuary are accessible to visitors; the islands provide land-based haulouts for hundreds to thousands of walruses during the summer months. You might also see some of the large seabird colonies along the coastal cliffs, Steller's Sea Lion, Harbor and Spotted Seals, and a variety of other wildlife species. Permits to access these sites are required by Togiak NWR or Alaska Department of Fish and Game.

LOGISTICS

The area code for all telephone numbers is 907 unless otherwise indicated. Dillingham is not covered by The Milepost. *Useful Dillingham contacts are listed below for your convenience. Statewide travel and birding information services are listed under Logistics in the* Introduction, *page 15.)*

Contact the Dillingham Chamber of Commerce for information packets containing cost and availability for accommodations and any other questions about the needs for your trip: PO Box 348, Dillingham, AK 99576; 842-5115; *dlgchmbr@nushtel.com*; *www.nushtel.com/~dlgchmbr/*

Contact the U.S. Fish and Wildlife Service's Togiak National Wildlife Refuge for information on the best birding opportunities in the area: PO Box 270, Dillingham, AK 99576; 842-1063; *r7tonwr@fws.gov*; *http://togiak.fws.gov*. Contact information for Wood-Tikchik State Park: 842-2375; *dan-hourihan@ dnr.state.ak.us*; *www.dnr.state.ak.us/parks/units/woodtik.htm*.

Choggiung Limited, regional Native Corporation — to obtain access to their lands, call 842-5218.

Accommodations: Dillingham has five hotels (Bristol Inn, Dillingham Hotel, Fisherman's Hideaway, Thai-American Hotel, Whale Inn) and eight B&Bs (Alaska Cabins B&B, Aleknagik Schoolhouse Inn, Beaver Creek B&B5, Coho B&B, Hillside Haven, Thai-American Guest House, Wild Goose B&B, Lake Road Cottages B&B). Current information can be found by contacting the Dillingham Chamber of Commerce. Book your reservations well in advance of your arrival date, if possible.

Vehicle rentals: D&J Rentals is the only source for vehicle rentals and can provide pick-up trucks, vans, and cars. You can also get to birding areas in one of the many local taxi cabs or by appointment with Bill's Delivery Service.

Tours: Currently there are no formal birding tours available in Dillingham. However, you may be able to arrange assistance to reach good birding areas. Easily accessible are numerous fishing and hunting lodges with guides for hire, two ecotourism operations, numerous aircraft charter operations, and many guided float-trip operators. These operators may be willing to take you to birding sites, but keep in mind that such trips would most likely not be guided birding trips. The generally limited birding skills of the guides will vary. Some of the lodges are located north in Wood-Tikchik State Park, others are east of town along the Nushagak River, and others west of town on and adjacent to the Togiak NWR. The two ecotourism operations, Roberts Alaska Tours and Johnson Maritime Guide Service, may be better sources for your trip. The many local aircraft charter operations can take you to areas for birding on your own that would be unmatched in the immediate Dillingham area. Such charter operations give you access to remote areas by floatplane or wheel-plane, with the ability to drop you off and pick you up later in the day or on another day. In addition, there are local cab services that could take you to roadside destinations and pick you up at a later time. The complete list of commercial operators can be obtained from the Dillingham Chamber of Commerce or the USFWS Togiak National Wildlife Refuge.

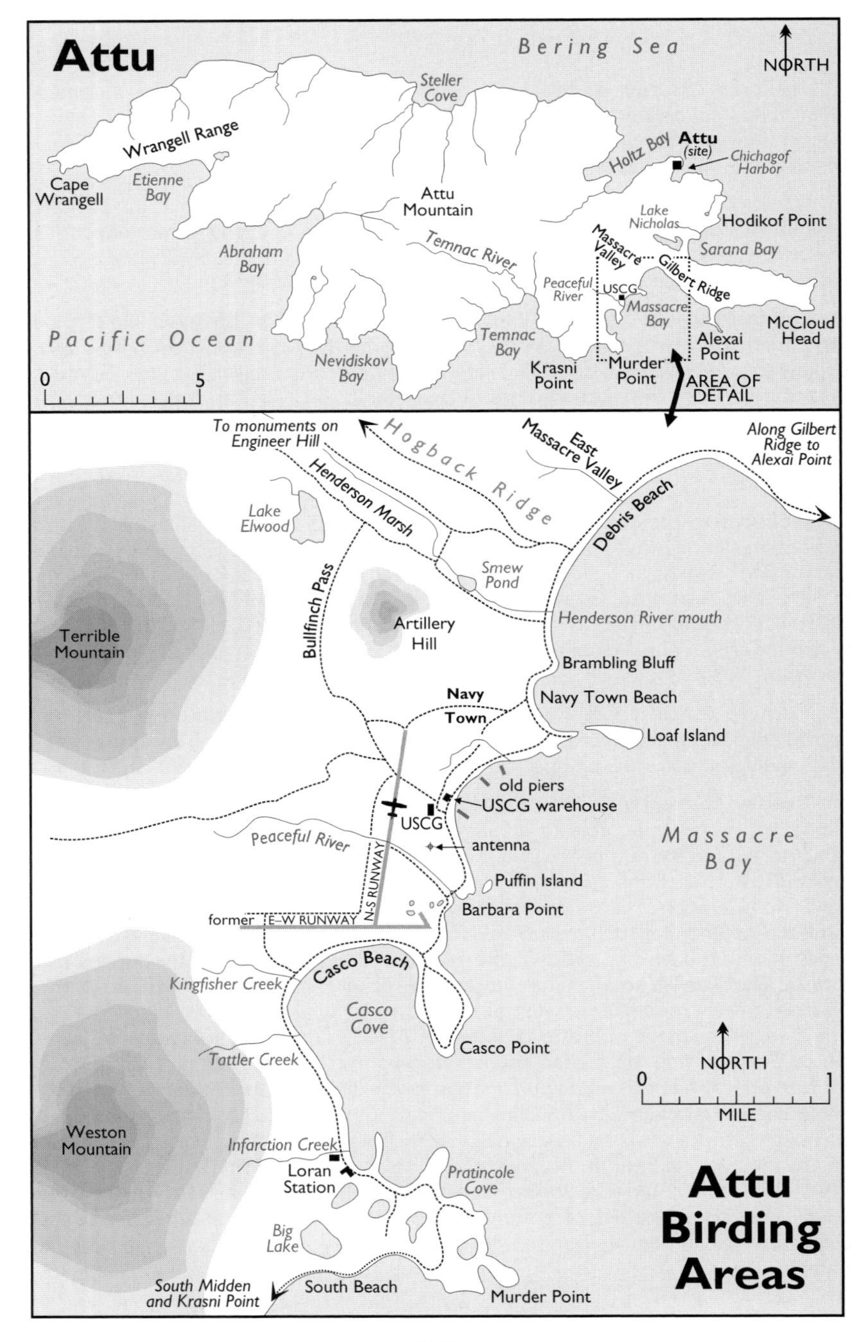
Attu
Bering Sea
NORTH
Steller Cove
Wrangell Range
Holtz Bay
Attu (site)
Chichagof Harbor
Cape Wrangell
Etienne Bay
Attu Mountain
Lake Nicholas
Hodikof Point
Massacre Valley
Sarana Bay
Abraham Bay
Temnac River
Gilbert Ridge
Peaceful River
USCG
Massacre Bay
McCloud Head
Pacific Ocean
Temnac Bay
Alexai Point
Nevidiskov Bay
Krasni Point
Murder Point
AREA OF DETAIL
0
5
To monuments on Engineer Hill
Hogback Ridge
East Massacre Valley
Along Gilbert Ridge to Alexai Point
Henderson Marsh
Lake Elwood
Debris Beach
Smew Pond
Bullfinch Pass
Henderson River mouth
Terrible Mountain
Artillery Hill
Brambling Bluff
Navy Town
Navy Town Beach
Loaf Island
old piers
USCG warehouse
USCG
Massacre Bay
Peaceful River
antenna
N-S RUNWAY
Puffin Island
Barbara Point
former E-W RUNWAY
Casco Beach
Kingfisher Creek
Casco Cove
Casco Point
Tattler Creek
NORTH
0
1
MILE
Weston Mountain
Infarction Creek
Loran Station
Pratincole Cove
Big Lake
Attu Birding Areas
South Midden and Krasni Point
South Beach
Murder Point

ATTU

Larry Balch

Now that Attour, Inc.'s organized trips to the last island in the Aleutian Island chain have ended, the most likely way for birders to visit Attu is via one of the cruise ships that travels the Bering Sea along the Aleutians, usually between Russia and Alaska. Typically, these ships stop at Attu for a few hours in June or August and ferry people to shore on inflatable boats. Following are suggestions for optimizing what you might see on such a trip.

Although a June arrival is past the peak of migration, there are often stragglers to be seen all the way until the third week or so. For example, on the morning of 12 June 2000, one small group on Attu (not from a cruise ship) found Kamchatka Mew Gull, Slaty-backed Gull, Common Cuckoo, Eyebrowed Thrush, and Hawfinch, after having spotted a Middendorff's Grasshopper-Warbler on their arrival the afternoon before. Shorebird migration is at a peak in August, as we know from Dan Gibson's work at nearby Shemya. On the one occasion (1983) when Attour personnel were on Attu in August, they saw these Asian shorebirds during the last two weeks of the month: Pacific Golden-Plover, Mongolian Plover, Wood Sandpiper, Green Sandpiper, Gray-tailed Tattler, Red-necked Stint, Temminck's Stint, and Ruff.

At any arrival time, you will want to look for resident Aleutian Terns and Black-backed Wagtails. From 1993 through 2000 (when Attour last visited), a male Spectacled Eider was also resident on Attu. The wagtails are best found near shore between the mouth of the Peaceful River and the Coast Guard Station warehouse. The Aleutian Terns will be over the bay, and the Spectacled Eider spends its time on Alexai Point and near Barbara Point. Other resident birds of interest are Red-faced Cormorant, Harlequin Duck, and—unique to Attu—the most handsome of all Rock Ptarmigan, *Lagopus mutus evermanni*. The ptarmigan are best found up Engineer Hill by the war memorial monuments.

If possible, have the cruise ship send inflatable boat parties to as many of these places as possible: Alexai Point, Casco Cove, the Coast Guard station, and Massacre Beach. It would be best if each party carried a radio so that the others could be alerted when something of interest is found. Alexai Point is the highest priority for birders. Walk the entire west, south, and east shores, and also visit the little marshy area on the stem of the point just north of the east-west arms of Alexai Point, and the small pond on the east side of the base of the stem. The cruise ship will undoubtedly send inflatables to Massacre Beach, as that is the closest landing to the road leading up East Massacre Valley to the monuments. Birders not interested in looking for ptarmigan near the monuments should, instead, take West Massacre Valley road a short way to check Smew Pond for shorebirds. (It isn't worth your while to go up the valley to the larger Lake Elwood.) If you land at the Coast Guard station, go first to check the mouth of the Peaceful River and Barbara Point, across from Puffin Island. Work your way up the beach to the warehouse. The Casco Cove party will want to look for shorebirds on the Casco Cove beach from the base of Casco Point westward. Also check the bluffs along the Casco Cove road leading to the old Loran station.

Don't be fooled by the very large and dark resident Song Sparrows, or the very dark resident Peregrine Falcons. But do be alert, because the chances for a real Asian rarity are greater on Attu than anywhere else in North America!

Your cruise ship may land you on one of the many other Aleutian Islands. Most of the islands are part of the Alaska Maritime National Wildlife Refuge, but no permit is needed to land or camp on them. However, military clearance is required to visit those islands with former or currently active military installations—Attu, Shemya, Amchitka, and Adak. If you are a passenger on a cruise ship that advertises a stop on Attu, be aware that no one will be allowed to land on the island if the vessel comes from Asia and has not cleared U.S. Customs at another port prior to arriving at Attu.

The Clipper cruise ship *Odyssey* makes trips from Nome through the Aleutians to Petropavlovsk in August. The cruises stops at several islands for birding. On the trip westward, they usually stop at Saint Lawrence, Saint Matthew, the Pribilof Islands, some of the smaller Aleutian Islands, Kiska, and Attu. In June it has stopped in the Aleutian Islands en route from Petropavlosk to Seward without going north into the Bering Sea. Passage through the Aleutians brings you close to many breeding colonies of alcids, flocks of Whiskered Auklets, millions of shearwaters, Mottled Petrels, and sometimes Short-tailed Albatross. In Russian waters, you may land on Bering Island and find some of the species that barely make it to North America at Attu. You then land on the Kamchatka Peninsula before heading to Petropavlovsk and your air trip back to Anchorage. You may contact Clipper Cruises at *www.clippercruise.com*.

MIDDLETON ISLAND

Stan Senner

Most birders will never get to Middleton Island, although this tiny island—more distant from the mainland than any other island in the Gulf of Alaska—has earned a modest reputation as a migrant trap. In the 1980s birders came in early May to search for Bristle-thighed Curlew and other northbound migrants. Most birders now visit in September, hoping to add to the list of Alaska rarities found here—Garganey, Gray-tailed Tattler, Red-breasted Sapsucker, and Tennessee Warbler. The island is only about one mile wide and five miles long, but supports significant numbers of nesting Pelagic Cormorants, Black-legged Kittiwakes, Common Murres, and Tufted Puffins. It also has nesting Rhinoceros Auklets.

You can reach Middleton Island only by chartered aircraft from Anchorage. The one-hour flight is highly weather-dependent. Most of the island is privately owned, and Audubon Alaska is working with the two private landowners and others to protect and help restore seabirds and their habitats. The island was once occupied by Chugach Natives, then homesteaded in the late 1800s, used for fox farming in the early 1900s, and as a federal military and aviation communications and radar facility in the 1950s. The military abandoned the island in the 1960s, leaving much debris and some structures now used by nesting kittiwakes. Some of the island is managed by the Alaska Maritime National Wildlife Refuge, which monitors seabird populations. The cooperative effort will try to encourage the federal government to clean up the debris and possible hazardous waste left on the island and make it more suitable for nesting seabirds.

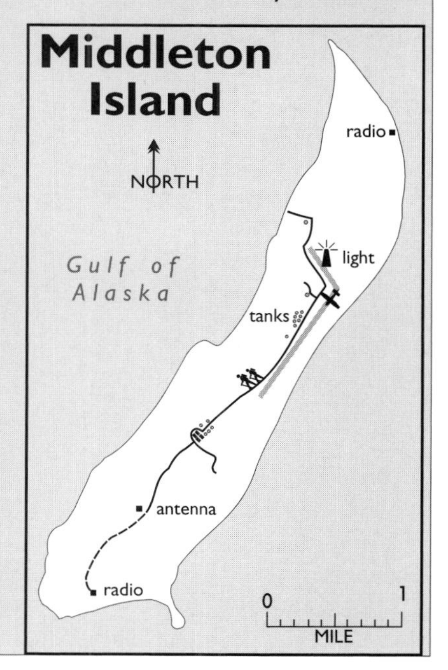

Until stewardship issues are settled, visitors are encouraged to contact the Lands and Resources Division of the Chugach Alaska Corporation (560 East 34th Avenue, Suite 200, Anchorage, AK 99503) in advance of trips to the island.

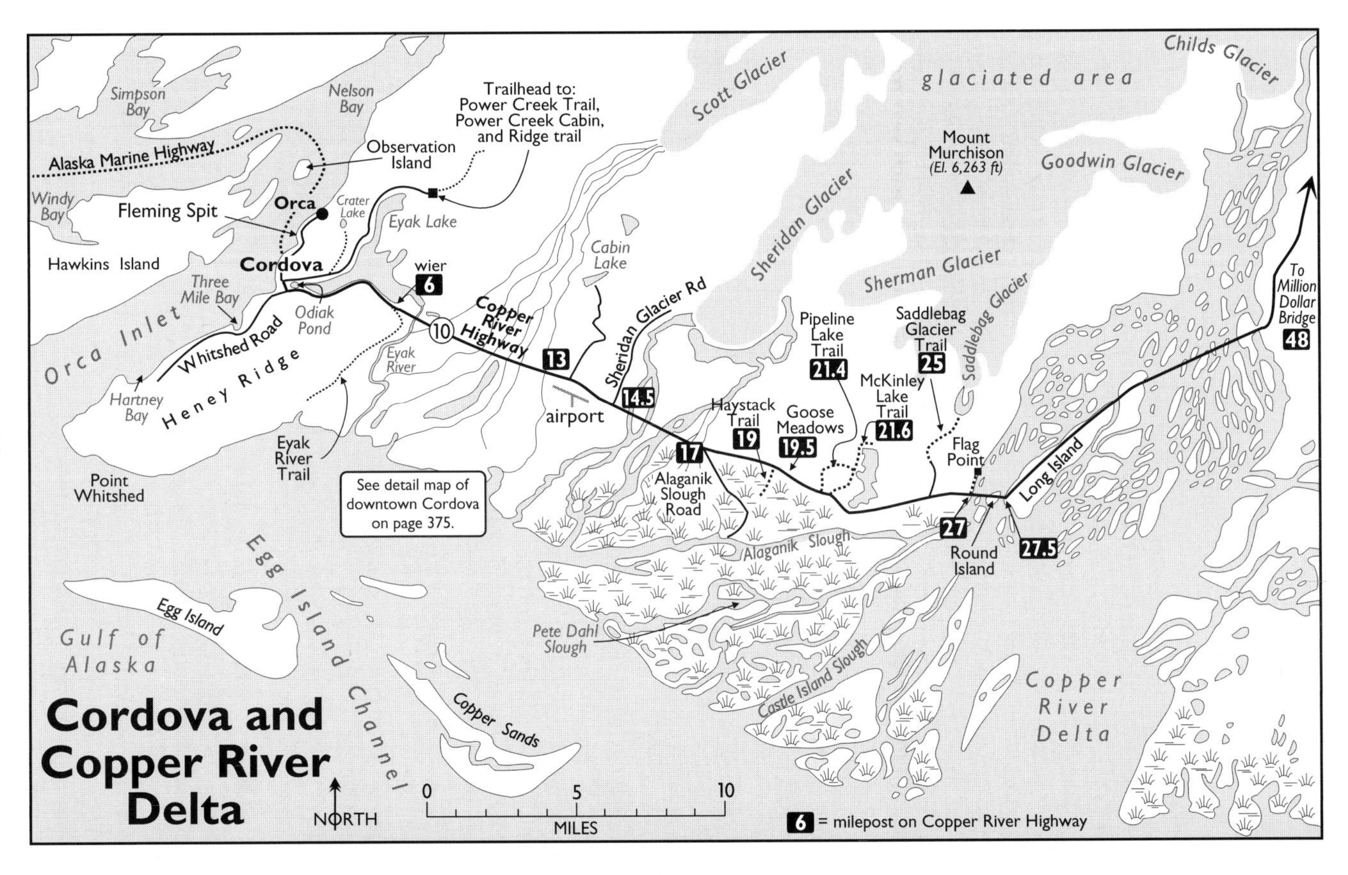

Cordova and Copper River Delta
Simpson Bay
Nelson Bay
Alaska Marine Highway
Trailhead to: Power Creek Trail, Power Creek Cabin, and Ridge trail
Observation Island
Windy Bay
Fleming Spit
Orca
Crater Lake
Eyak Lake
Hawkins Island
Cordova
Three Mile Bay
wier
6
Odiak Pond
Orca Inlet
Whitshed Road
10
Copper River Highway
Eyak River
Heney Ridge
Hartney Bay
13
airport
Cabin Lake
Sheridan Glacier Rd
14.5
Eyak River Trail
Point Whitshed
See detail map of downtown Cordova on page 375.
Scott Glacier
Sheridan Glacier
glaciated area
Mount Murchison (El. 6,263 ft)
Goodwin Glacier
Childs Glacier
Sherman Glacier
Saddlebag Glacier
Pipeline Lake Trail
21.4
Saddlebag Glacier Trail
25
McKinley Lake Trail
21.6
Haystack Trail
19
Goose Meadows
19.5
17
Alaganik Slough Road
Flag Point
Long Island
To Million Dollar Bridge
48
27
Round Island
27.5
Alaganik Slough
Egg Island
Egg Island Channel
Gulf of Alaska
Pete Dahl Slough
Castle Island Slough
Copper River Delta
Copper Sands
NORTH
0
5
10
MILES
6 = milepost on Copper River Highway

CORDOVA

Aaron Lang and George West

Cordova is the nearest town to the Copper River Delta, the site of Alaska's largest gathering of spring-migrant shorebirds. The Copper-Bering River delta system has been named a Hemispheric Site by the Western Hemisphere Shorebird Reserve Network, primarily because millions of Western Sandpipers and Dunlins, representing virtually all of the North American populations of both species, move through each year from late April to mid-May. You can expect it to be cold, windy, and rainy during the first week of May if you come to participate in the Copper River Delta Shorebird Festival, but it won't seem so bad when you are able to commiserate with hundreds of other birders in town for the experience. Although you could make an effort to find a tour boat or a fisherman to take you east of Cordova to see the greater spectacle, you will be more than impressed with the number and variety of shorebirds at Hartney Bay, a very short road trip southwest of Cordova.

Birders can reach Cordova only by ferry or by air. One option is to drive to Valdez and board the Alaska state ferry M/V *Bartlett*—with or without your vehicle—on its regular run to Cordova. On your way to Valdez you might enjoy the scenic drive over Thompson Pass with a chance to bird the alpine (see page 132). Alternatively, you could take a small commuter plane directly from Anchorage to Cordova, where you can rent a car to explore the area. Over the decades there have been numerous proposals to build a road to Cordova that would follow the old railroad grade along the west bank of the Copper River. (You can see the northern end of the grade near Chitina—see Edgerton Highway, page 137.) The old railroad crossed the Copper River on the Million Dollar Bridge, but in 1964 the third span of the bridge collapsed in the Good Friday earthquake that also destroyed the old village of Valdez and many other sites around Prince William Sound. That disaster, added to the resistance of many Cordovans to the project, has thus far forestalled construction. However, you might check to see if a road has been built when you decide to travel to Cordova!

Cordova has long been occupied by Native peoples. The Eyak lived in the area before European settlement, but their numbers today are small and their language is almost forgotten. You can visit an ancient Eyak burial site at Nirvana Park on Eyak Lake. European explorers arrived in the late 1700s as they searched for the Northwest Passage. Modern Cordova came to life at the turn of the 20th century following the discovery of massive copper deposits in the Wrangell Mountains to the north. Cordova flourished for 27 years as the terminus of the Copper River and Northwestern Railroad that ran 196 miles from the Kennicott copper mine to tidewater. When the copper mines closed in 1938, Cordova turned to the sea for its main source of income—fishing for crab, clams, salmon, herring, and shrimp. Gill-netters out of Cordova fish the Copper River Flats at the mouth of the Copper River that supports one of the largest Red (Sockeye) and King (Chinook) Salmon runs in the state. To learn more about the history of Cordova, its Native peoples, and the effects of the *Exxon Valdez* oil spill, visit the Cordova Museum on 1st Street.

Western Sandpipers

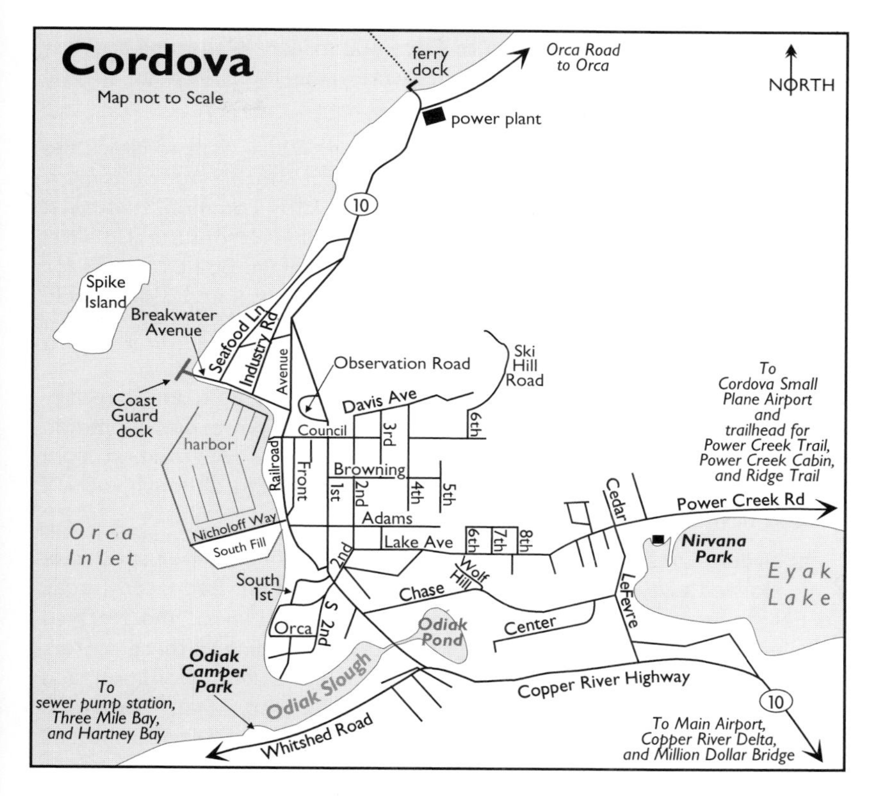

BIRDING IN AND AROUND CORDOVA

The small town of Cordova is situated on the coast in Orca Inlet. In addition to the Copper River Highway that is built on the old railroad grade, three shorter roads provide good birding year round—the Orca Road heading northeast along the coast for 2.2 miles, the Whitshed Road trending southwest for 5.5 miles to great shorebirding at Hartney Bay, and Power Creek Road that leads about 6 miles to the Power Creek Trail that you can take to explore the coniferous rain forest.

ORCA INLET AND ORCA ROAD

Cordova is an exceptional place to look for Yellow-billed Loons. In winter, you are almost certain to see them. Being a high-arctic breeder, Yellow-billed Loon lingers on its wintering grounds well into spring, and a birder looking for one in May or early June still has a slim chance of finding one. The first wintering loons usually arrive back in Orca Inlet in mid-October. To look for them, start at the Orca Road ferry dock and drive north along the coast to the site of the small town of Orca (2.2 miles). A spotting scope is essential because many of the birds, especially the loons, can be several hundred yards offshore.

Before you leave the ferry dock area, however, you'll want to check the pilings on the left just south of the terminal, a great spot to study the many cormorants that rest there. Double-crested are fairly common, Red-faced are rare in winter, and Pelagic are abundant. Great Blue Herons are also here, especially in winter. The ferry dock is a good vantage point to look for migrating Red-necked Phalaropes (late July–August) and Fork-tailed Storm-Petrels that can be forced into Orca Inlet by storms in the Gulf of Alaska (September–November).

Just north of the ferry terminal, stop at Fleming Spit, an especially productive spot. Bald Eagles, gulls, Northwestern Crows, and Common Ravens congregate here to feed on the spawned-out, dying salmon from spring through fall. American Dippers are here year round, although you will probably have to walk up the creek to find one.

By birding Orca Road in winter, you can usually find all four species of loons, Horned and Red-necked Grebes, Double-crested, Red-faced (rare), and Pelagic (most common) Cormorants, Common Murre, and Marbled Murrelet, along with a good variety of sea ducks, including all three scoters (Black is rare), many Harlequin and Long-tailed Ducks, Common and Barrow's Goldeneyes, and sometimes Steller's Eider (very rare). Cordova is the most easterly place where Steller's Eider occurs with any regularity. The birds that reach here are almost invariably females and immatures, and usually there are no more than a few birds here at one time, although a flock of 68 occurred in winter 1991–1992. The best place to look for them is Fleming Spit, but also try Odiak Slough, where the large flock spent time in 1991–1992. In summer, Black Oystercatchers forage at the end of Orca Road and on Observation Island, straight out from the old village of Orca.

Shorebirds in Cordova are generally sparse during winter, although Rock Sandpipers occur sporadically, sometimes in numbers, depending on weather. Orca Road and the harbor are the best spots to look for them.

While you are in town, it is worth checking around Cordova Harbor and Odiak Slough. The harbor and breakwater will have similar birds to those found on Orca Road. A good vantage point is the Coast Guard Dock at the end of Breakwater Avenue. This is also a great spot to watch several hundred wintering Sea Otters and occasional Steller's Sea Lions and Harbor Seals.

ODIAK SLOUGH

Odiak Slough can be a good place to bird before or after birding high tide at Hartney Bay, because the most productive birding here is at mid-to-high tides—at extreme high tides there are no mudflats available to shorebirds. You can cover the north side of the slough from South Waterfront Commercial Park (South Fill). The south side of the slough can be checked from Whitshed Road, with Odiak Camper Park being a particularly good vantage point. Both of these spots are good for ducks year round and shorebirds in spring. While the numbers of shorebirds here will be far fewer than at Hartney Bay, shorebird diversity at the slough can be high. In spring migration, Black-bellied Plover, American and Pacific Golden-Plovers, Whimbrel, godwits, and dowitchers use this area.

WHITSHED ROAD, HARTNEY BAY, AND HENEY RIDGE

The mudflats along Whitshed Road offer exceptional birding for waterfowl and shorebirds, especially during spring migration. Whitshed Road leaves the Copper River Highway between Odiak Slough and Heney Trailer Court. Shortly before the pavement ends, a pullout on the right opposite an old bridge allows you to scope Three Mile Bay. The peak passage of waterfowl occurs during the second half of April, and while the variety of species is not exceptional, local rarities such as Eurasian Wigeon is virtually annual. Five individuals were seen 22 April–11 May 2000. Eurasians have shown up at Hartney Bay, Three Mile Bay, and on ponds on the Copper River Delta, usually in the company of American Wigeons. When Greater White-fronted and Snow Geese pass through in late April and early May, Three Mile Bay and Hartney Bay are the best places to check for them.

Continue along Whitshed Road to its end at Hartney Bay, probably the best-scrutinized birding site in the Cordova area. It is the most accessible spot to watch the myriad shorebirds refuel for their northward migration. The first week of May is the best time to see them, although the shorebirds start arriving during the third week in April and late migrants push through until about the first of June. During this time most of the birds are Western Sandpipers and Dunlins, but many other species are represented, including Black-bellied Plover, American and Pacific Golden-Plovers, Semipalmated Plover, Black Oystercatcher, both yellowlegs, Whimbrel, Hudsonian Godwit, Ruddy and Black Turnstones, Surfbird, Semipalmated, Least, Baird's, and Pectoral Sandpipers, and Short-billed and Long-billed Dowitchers. Bar-tailed Godwit has been recorded here and Marbled Godwits are rare in migration. The patient birder may get a look at a Merlin or a Peregrine Falcon harassing the flocks of shorebirds. You can find the rare Caspian Tern at Hartney Bay throughout the summer, especially in late summer.

High tides of more than 10 feet, when the birds are pushed up closer to the road, are the best time to bird the flats at Hartney Bay. If you have time, it might be productive to walk out on the flats at mid-tides. A spotting scope is a must. The tide recedes for miles offshore at low tide—too far to look for shorebirds—but it is a good time to bird the wet-meadow and alder/willow thickets on the inland side of the road, especially in late April and May. Many migrant passerines take shelter and feed in the alders and willows, and in May you usually can find all the likely sparrows, as well as Orange-crowned and Wilson's Warblers. You'll need knee-high rubber boots to explore this area. In April and May, look for Horned Lark (rare), American Pipit, Lapland Longspur, and Snow Bunting along the road at Hartney Bay.

The Heney Ridge Trail begins at Hartney Bay and is a good place to bird the temperate rain forest. The trail follows Hartney Creek for about a mile. The rain forest here is usually pretty quiet, but you could find Spruce Grouse, Brown Creeper, Winter Wren, Varied Thrush, and Townsend's Warbler. When salmon are in the creek, there are several spots along this first section of trail where you can watch the Bald Eagles and gulls feed on the carcasses. If crossbills are around (which varies from year to year depending on the cone crop), the muskegs and forest openings in the trail's mid-elevations are excellent places to view both species. The trail continues up into the Heney Range and, at the top, provides panoramic views of the Copper River Delta, Prince William Sound, and the Gulf of Alaska. Willow and Rock Ptarmigan might be encountered in the alpine areas. Maps for all Cordova-area trails are available from the Forest Service (424-7661).

EYAK LAKE AND POWER CREEK ROAD

You can reach the upper arm of Eyak Lake by taking Power Creek Road, the continuation of Lake Avenue (see town map). The road is narrow and winding, so you may wish to avoid it when driving conditions are marginal, but if you can make it, you'll find good birding throughout the year. In summer, as you follow the lakeshore, watch for nesting Barrow's Goldeneyes and Common Mergansers. The common coniferous forest passerines you see might include Winter Wren, Varied Thrush, and Townsend's Warbler (easiest to locate near the end of the road). Also near the road's end is a good spot for American Dipper, and it is here that Western Screech-, Boreal, and Northern Saw-whet Owls are sometimes heard calling in March and April. Because Power Creek is a major spawning area for Coho (Silver) and Sockeye (Red) Salmon, you might run across Black and Brown Bears anywhere, especially from mid-to-late summer. Along with Eyak Weir, Power Creek usually has the only open freshwater near Cordova during winter, and this attracts a few species of waterfowl, including Trumpeter Swans. Hooded Mergansers have been recorded here in some winters.

The trailhead for the Power Creek Cabin Trail and the Ridge Trail is at the end of Power Creek Road. This trail offers good birding all summer long. Nesting species include Harlequin Duck, Semipalmated Plover, Greater and Lesser Yellowlegs, and Spotted Sandpiper; American Dipper is easy to find year round.

Birding on the Copper River Delta

OTHER GOOD BIRDING NEAR CORDOVA

The Crater Lake Trail begins just past Cordova Municipal (Small Plane) Airport on Power Creek Road. Park in the small lot next to Skater's Cabin and walk across the road to the trailhead. This is probably the best bet in the area for finding Spruce Grouse. Willow and Rock Ptarmigan may be happened upon in the tundra around Crater Lake.

On your way out the Copper River Highway, be sure to stop at the Eyak Weir at Mile 6. This is a good spot any time of year, but especially in winter when open water attracts many species of waterfowl, including the occasional Tufted Duck. As many as 100–200 Trumpeter Swans may overwinter here. The Eyak River Trail begins across the highway from the weir, following the Eyak River through muskegs and rain forest. Many of the same species common to the Heney Ridge and Crater Lake Trails are also found here. The advantage to taking this trail is that it is relatively flat, although it can be wet, so rubber boots are advised.

COPPER RIVER DELTA

The Copper River forms the largest contiguous network of wetlands on the Pacific coast of North America as it flows into the Gulf of Alaska. The delta is a tapestry of numerous shallow ponds, intertidal sloughs, and braided glacial streams. These areas are woven together by strands of sparsely vegetated mud flats, sedge marshes, alder and willow thickets, and small stands of spruce/hemlock and Black Cottonwood forest.

The delta is reached by the Copper River Highway that ends abruptly at Mile 48 at the partly collapsed Million Dollar Bridge. From spring to fall it is well worth driving all the way to the bridge. The highway is usually cleared of snow- and sand-drifts during the second week of May, although in big snow years it may not be plowed all the way to Million Dollar Bridge until early June.

The intertidal mudflats of the Copper River Delta are key stopover areas for millions of shorebirds during spring migration. Staying for only a few days, these migrants rest and refuel on the vast coastal wetlands of the delta. Unfortunately for birders, most of the migrants use the outer barrier beaches that are accessible only by boat or plane. Several local charter operations provide tours to these areas—check with the Cordova Chamber of Commerce for a list of current operators (424-7260). The best places for mudflat birding that are accessible by car are Odiak Slough (in town), Hartney Bay, and the mudflats along Whitshed Road.

If you have extra time in the area, one of the best ways to bird the delta is by canoe. Canoes can be rented from Cordova Auto Rental at the main airport (424-5982). There are several good routes that navigate the sloughs through different wetland habitats. This is the best way to find birds such as Red-throated Loon, Red-necked Phalarope, and Aleutian Tern. Check with the U.S. Forest Service/Cordova Ranger District for information on canoe routes.

The delta is a major breeding site for Aleutian Terns, which are typically difficult to see because they nest near the coast on the delta. In recent years, however, they have been seen fairly regularly in late April–early May around Odiak Slough and Hartney Bay. Caspian Terns colonized the delta in the 1980s, although no nests have been located. In August and September, Caspian Tern family groups might be seen at Odiak Slough and Hartney Bay. Arctic Terns are common on the delta, and all three species could be encountered on a short canoe trip down Alaganik Slough in May or June.

COPPER RIVER HIGHWAY

The starting point for all mileages mentioned in the following text is the Alaska State ferry dock (Mile 0.0), so don't be confused if you see one of the few old mile-markers left along this highway and it's different from your odometer reading.

After you pass Eyak Weir (Mile 6), watch for concentrations of Bald Eagles at Mile 7. Eagles usually congregate here in late winter to feed on migrating Hooligan, a small smelt that returns to fresh water to spawn. The ponds along the highway from Mile 7 to the airport are likely spots for migrant and nesting waterfowl. In late April and May, check for rarities like Pied-billed Grebe, Eurasian Wigeon, and Red-winged Blackbird. You should have no trouble finding Trumpeter Swans during the summer months—10 percent of the world's population nests on the Copper River Delta. Usually there is an easily visible pair of swans at the pond across from the interpretive kiosk at Mile 10.

At Mile 13, you will pass the airport. To look for Spruce Grouse and other forest species, try driving up either Cabin Lake Road (directly across the highway from the airport entrance) at Mile 13 or Sheridan Glacier Road at Mile 14.5. Both roads lead through coniferous forests where you should look for a variety of western and boreal species that are year-round residents—Spruce Grouse, Steller's Jay, Chestnut-backed Chickadee, Brown Creeper, Pine Grosbeak, and Red and White-winged Crossbills. In summer add Rufous Hummingbird and Townsend's Warbler. Take Sheridan Glacier Road to the trailhead for the Sheridan Mountain Trail, one of the best places to access the alpine areas. The trail is steep and rugged, but might have Willow and Rock Ptarmigan or Gray-crowned Rosy-Finch (rare) in spring and summer.

At Mile 17, turn right onto Alaganik Slough Road. The sign for the road is small and usually obstructed by vegetation, so watch your odometer to avoid missing the turn. This road provides the only vehicle access to the sedge meadow wetlands of the delta. You'll want to drive this 5-mile-long road slowly as it is almost always a productive spot. You will find a 900-foot wheelchair-accessible boardwalk, picnic tables, restrooms, and a viewing shelter at the end of Alaganik Slough Road. Stop to watch Bald Eagles feeding on migrating Hooligan in late winter. Check for Short-eared Owls at dusk in the summer months. The ponds contain numerous nesting waterfowl, including Horned and Red-necked Grebes, Dusky Canada Goose, and Trumpeter Swan. A walk on the boardwalk at the end of the road can produce various nesting waterfowl, Black-billed Magpie, Tree and Cliff Swallows, and Savannah, Fox, Song, and Lincoln's Sparrows. Be alert for Caspian and Arctic Terns, as well.

Back on the Copper River Highway check Goose Meadows marshes at Mile 19 for waterfowl, including migrant Greater White-fronted Geese (spring), and shorebirds that can be found here in migration, such as Greater

Yellowlegs and Pectoral Sandpiper. In May and June this is a good location for Red-winged (very rare) and Rusty Blackbirds. At Miles 21.4 and 21.6 you will find the trailheads for Pipeline Lakes and McKinley Lake trails, respectively. Both are level-grade, easy hiking trails through the coniferous forest. Species will be similar to those along Cabin Lake Road and Heney Ridge Trail. McKinley Lake Trail can be especially good for Spruce Grouse year round.

At Mile 25 the mile-long road to the Saddlebag Glacier trailhead leads off to the left. This is one of the better spots to look for Northern Goshawks, which have nested regularly near the trail. It may also produce Downy and Three-toed Woodpeckers. The 2.7-mile (one way) trail leads you to a splendid view of Saddlebag Glacier. In summer, you might spot Mountain Goats or a Black Bear on the hills above the glacier.

At Mile 27 a short dirt road leads north to Flag Point, a good place to scan the nearby ridge top for migrant raptors in September. Bald Eagles are the most conspicuous migrant; other regulars are Northern Harrier, Sharp-shinned Hawk, Northern Goshawk, Red-tailed and Rough-legged Hawks, American Kestrel (rare), and Merlin. Swainson's Hawks, at the extreme northern edge of their range in Alaska, have been recorded here. The road may be too rough for your vehicle, and if you decide to walk the 0.5-mile road, be aware that this area is heavily used by bears. (See Bear Cautions in the *Introduction*, page 17).

At Mile 27.5 you arrive at Long Island in the upper part of the main channel of the Copper River. Parasitic Jaegers hunt along the river on both sides of the bridge you just crossed to reach Long Island.

Long Island's many ponds attract nesting Horned Grebes, Trumpeter Swans, Red-necked Phalaropes, and Mew Gulls. This is also the most reliable location for Bank Swallows, otherwise rare on the delta. The swallows nest in the sand dunes on Long Island and hunt above the island's many ponds in mixed flocks with other swallow species. Listen for Alder Flycatcher and Swainson's Thrush (uncommon) in the shrub thickets on Long Island.

From Mile 38 to the end of the road at the Million Dollar Bridge, the habitat consists of cottonwood forests interspersed with large open areas. Much of this section is flooded and difficult to walk in, so most birding is done from the road. Merlins and Northern Hawk Owls breed here regularly and you have a good chance of seeing both, especially the owl, if you drive slowly and check the cottonwoods carefully. Peregrine Falcons are often seen along this stretch of the road in the summer.

Birding around Childs Glacier at Mile 48 can be very good in summer. From the viewpoint you can watch the toe of the glacier calve. If the glacier is active when you are there (it's most active in July and August), it's thrilling to watch the large chunks of glacial ice splash into the water. Million Dollar

Bridge is another impressive vantage point from which to watch both Childs and Miles Glaciers. In addition to the scenery, this is a great spot to look for birds that can be difficult to find elsewhere on the delta—Yellow Warbler, Swainson's Thrush (uncommon in this area), and Golden-crowned Sparrow all nest here. Northern Hawk Owls nested near this viewing area in 1998, and might be found during the summer. You can cross the Million Dollar Bridge on a footbridge spanning the collapsed section to get to a trail that leads to the terminal moraine of Childs Glacier. This short trail can produce Willow Ptarmigan, Swainson's Thrush, Golden-crowned Sparrow, and Common Redpoll in spring and summer. Bears also use this area, and it is a good idea to make lots of human-type noise as you walk through the brush.

If you visit Cordova in winter, travel on the Copper River Highway is dependent on the snow load. In most years the road is open to Mile 25, though maintenance is guaranteed only as far as the airport at Mile 13. In most winters Northern Hawk Owls and Northern Shrikes (rare) may be found just about anywhere along the highway. Willow Ptarmigan sometimes come down to the highway in winter, especially in the Sheridan and Scott River valleys. Common Redpolls are widespread residents, easily found when their large flocks forage through the delta's alders.

LOGISTICS

The area code for all telephone numbers is 907 unless otherwise indicated. Tourist and travel services (accommodations, restaurants, attractions, etc.) not listed below can be found in the latest edition of The Milepost. *Statewide travel and birding information services are listed under Logistics in the* Introduction, *page 15.)*

Access: Cordova can be reached only by sea or air. There are several flights daily from Anchorage and Seattle, via Alaska Airlines and ERA Aviation. You can take the ferry from Valdez, Seward, or Whittier. You can bring your car on the ferry from Valdez to Cordova, but be sure to make reservations well in advance of your planned travel.

Accommodations: There are a number of hotels and bed & breakfasts in Cordova. Check with the Cordova Chamber of Commerce (424-7260; *www.ctcak.net/~chamber/*) for a current list.

Car Rentals: You will need a car to bird the best areas in Cordova. Cars can be rented for about $75/day. Call the Cordova Chamber of Commerce for the current vendors.

Festival: For information on the annual Copper River Delta Shorebird Festival check the web site *www.ptialaska.net/~midtown/*.

Trail Information is available from Cordova Ranger District, 424-7661.

Prince William Sound Natural History, *www.alaska.net/~awss/pws.html*.

Prince William Sound Science Center, *www.pwssc.gen.ak.us/*.

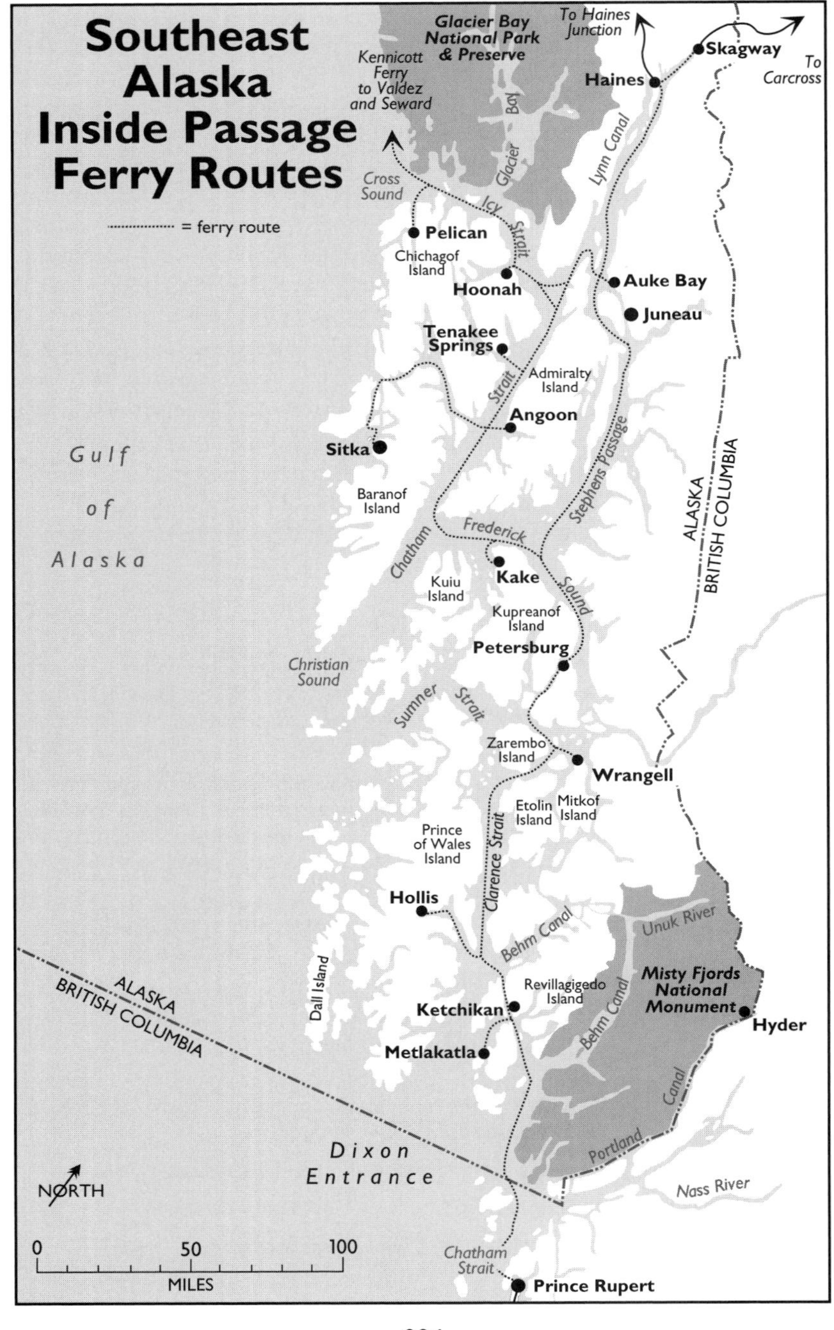
Southeast Alaska Inside Passage Ferry Routes
= ferry route
Glacier Bay National Park & Preserve
To Haines Junction
Skagway
To Carcross
Haines
Kennicott Ferry to Valdez and Seward
Glacier Bay
Cross Sound
Icy Strait
Lynn Canal
Pelican
Chichagof Island
Hoonah
Auke Bay
Juneau
Tenakee Springs
Admiralty Island
Strait
Angoon
Sitka
Gulf of Alaska
Baranof Island
Stephens Passage
ALASKA
BRITISH COLUMBIA
Frederick Sound
Chatham
Kake
Kuiu Island
Kupreanof Island
Petersburg
Christian Sound
Sumner Strait
Zarembo Island
Wrangell
Etolin Island
Mitkof Island
Prince of Wales Island
Clarence Strait
Hollis
Behm Canal
Unuk River
Dall Island
Revillagigedo Island
Misty Fjords National Monument
Ketchikan
Hyder
Metlakatla
Behm Canal
Canal
Portland
Dixon Entrance
Nass River
NORTH
0
50
100
MILES
Chatham Strait
Prince Rupert

INSIDE PASSAGE

George West

The Alaska Marine Highway System runs ferries between Bellingham, Washington, and most of the major southeast Alaska cities. The ferries can also be boarded at Prince Rupert, BC. One ferry, the M/V *Kennicott*, takes several trips each summer from Juneau across the Gulf of Alaska to Valdez and Seward (see page 453). There are several options for routes within southeast Alaska, but most people select the most direct route north. Stops along this route are in Ketchikan, Wrangell, Petersburg, Sitka, Juneau, and Haines or Skagway. Some ferries stop in some of the smaller communities as well, but these are not covered in this guide. You must make reservations well in advance for travel during the summer months, especially if you want a cabin or plan to bring a vehicle on board (see contact information below).

Several cruise ship companies ply the Inside Passage from Vancouver, BC. Some of these ships also cross the northern Gulf of Alaska and should be better for birding than the ferry through the Inside Passage (see page 455). Most cruise ships continue into Glacier Bay, sometimes Yakutat Bay, and on to Valdez or Seward. Birding from the ferry and tour boats between Bellingham and the northern ports of southeastern Alaska is limited. These ships stay in protected waters most of the time, so there is little opportunity to observe pelagic species. Birding opportunities in some of the port cities are included in the chapters that follow.

In summer you can expect to see a variety of marine species from the ferry between Bellingham and Skagway or Haines: Pacific and Common Loons, Sooty Shearwater, Fork-tailed and Leach's Storm-Petrels, Brandt's, Double-crested, and Pelagic Cormorants, Canada Goose, Harlequin Duck, Surf and White-winged Scoters, Bald Eagle, Parasitic Jaeger, Bonaparte's, Mew, Western, and Glaucous-winged Gulls, Black-legged Kittiwake, Arctic Tern, Common Murre, Pigeon Guillemot, Marbled Murrelet, Rhinoceros Auklet, and Tufted Puffin. If your ship turns out into the Gulf, you might find Laysan (rare) and many Black-footed Albatrosses, Northern Fulmar, Pink-footed Shearwater, phalaropes, South Polar Skua, jaegers, Sabine's Gull and Cassin's Auklet. If you can see the rocks along the shoreline, look for Black Oystercatcher, Black Turnstone, and Surfbird.

Because the ships run between islands all the way north, the seas are not too rough. It can be a very pleasant ride with lots of beautiful scenery depending on the weather (remember, southeast Alaska is one of the wettest places in North America!). You should see Killer Whale, Humpback Whale, Pacific White-sided Dolphin, Dall's Porpoise, Harbor Porpoise, Harbor Seal, Sea Otter, Mountain Goat, and perhaps Brown Bear, along with more Bald Eagles than you ever imagined. With guidance from the chapters that follow, you should have good birding adventures in and around the ports along the way.

LOGISTICS

The area code for all telephone numbers is 907 unless otherwise indicated. Tourist and travel services (accommodations, restaurants, attractions, etc.) not listed below can be found in the latest edition of The Milepost. *Statewide travel and birding information services are listed under Logistics in the* Introduction, *page 15.)*

Contact the State of Alaska, Marine Highway System for current schedules, which change each season (272-7116, 465-3946, or within Alaska 800-642-0066). Their web address is *http://www.alaska.gov/ferry/*.

ACKNOWLEDGEMENTS: Additional species notes were provided by Richard Ferren, Richard and Irene Flower, and Bob and Kim Hinkle.

Bald Eagle

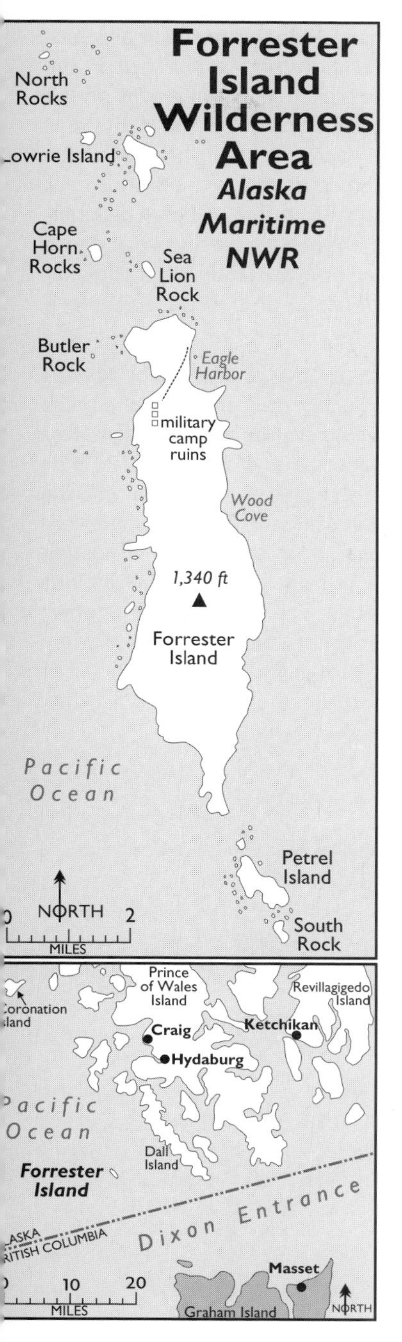

FORRESTER ISLAND

Steven T. Zimmerman

The Forrester Island Wilderness Area is home to the largest seabird colony in the eastern Gulf of Alaska. Located in the open Gulf, about 15 miles west of Dall Island and just north of the United States/Canada boundary line, the small group of islands and rocks that comprise the wilderness area provides nesting habitat for approximately 1.1 million seabirds. Forrester Island is the largest island, approximately five miles long and one mile wide. Lowrie Island to the north and Petrel Island to the south are each less than one square mile.

The islands are located near the edge of the continental shelf. Northward-flowing currents rise with the topography as they meet the islands, causing upwelling and a mix of tidal rips and eddies that bring marine life near the surface. This provides foraging opportunities for pelagic seabirds such as shearwaters, fulmars, and rarely, South Polar Skua. Jaegers, gulls, and several species of alcids will be seen feeding around the islands along with loons, cormorants, and sea ducks. This is one of the few areas in Alaska where Brandt's Cormorant can be found.

These are very rugged islands, open to the full force of storms moving east across the Gulf of Alaska. The shoreline is pounded by surf, with many sheer cliffs and large broken-boulder beaches. There are no moorages. Skiffs or kayaks can land on the few beaches on the east side of Forrester Island, but the surf can be treacherous. Landings on the other islands often must be made by jumping out of the boat as the surf recedes and then scrambling up algae-covered rocks. Because of these hazards, few people who do not have research programs on the islands ever get ashore there. Once ashore, visitors find narrow, boulder-strewn beaches, or steep-sided uplands covered with spruce-hemlock forest and very dense undergrowth right down to the water. Walking on the islands can be difficult because of abundant Devil's Club, Stinging Nettle, and loose soil. It is time-consuming and hard on the legs.

Burrow-nesting and largely nocturnal birds are the predominant species that nest on the islands. Fork-tailed and Leach's Storm-Petrels are the most common, and an estimated 780,000 nest on Petrel Island. Approximately 60,000 Ancient Murrelets, 32,000 Cassin's Auklets, and 100,000 Rhinoceros Auklets also nest in the wilderness area. Common Murres lay eggs on bare cliff edges, Horned Puffins nest in rock crevices in cliffs, and Tufted Puffins nest in burrows and are active during daylight hours near the colony. Nesting species may be seen around or on the islands during summer months, but some of the birds, especially the storm-petrels, are seldom seen during daylight hours, and can be missed if a night is not spent ashore. Approximately 135 species have been seen on or around Forrester Island (Isleib 1993). All of the passerine species that have been described there can be seen in other parts of southeast Alaska.

Tufted Puffins

LOGISTICS

The area code for all telephone numbers is 907 unless otherwise indicated. Information about Forrester Island is not included in The Milepost. *For your convenience access information is detailed below. Statewide travel and birding information services are listed under Logistics in the* Introduction, *page 15.)*

The Forrester Island Wilderness Area is part of the Alaska Maritime National Wildlife Refuge, U.S. Fish and Wildlife Service (USFWS), managed by its office in Homer (235-6546). Getting to the wilderness area can be difficult. USFWS has permitted one commercial operator, Alaska Natural Offshore Adventures (489-2233) to land tourists, via kayaks, on the southern islands. This operator offers a five-day schooner cruise (approximately noon Monday through noon Saturday between 1 May–30 September) that leaves from Craig, Alaska, and visits Coronation Island, Kuiu Island, South Prince of Wales Island, and Forrester Island. Costs for the boat trip are dependent on the number of persons on board and range from $289 per person when 4 or 5 persons are on board to $549 when only two persons are on board.

It is also possible to charter a boat to Forrester Island from Craig, although charter operators do not routinely make trips there. Getting to Forrester Island takes two hours or more, depending on the speed of the boat and the weather. The open-ocean leg can be quite rough, and weather and currents often preclude even making the trip unless winds are from the northwest. Sure Strike Charters (826-3909) has taken birders, including Peter Harrison, into the Gulf of Alaska from Craig looking for seabirds, and has indicated a willingness to set up specialty trips to Forrester Island if conditions permit.

To reach Craig, birders can either take one of the Alaska State Ferries, or they can fly to Ketchikan and take a small plane to Craig (Pacific Airways, 826-5400, and Promech, 826-3845). Air charters are also available between these communities, but they are expensive.

ACKNOWLEDGEMENTS: Reviewed by G. Vernon Byrd and Leslie Slater.

Devil's Club

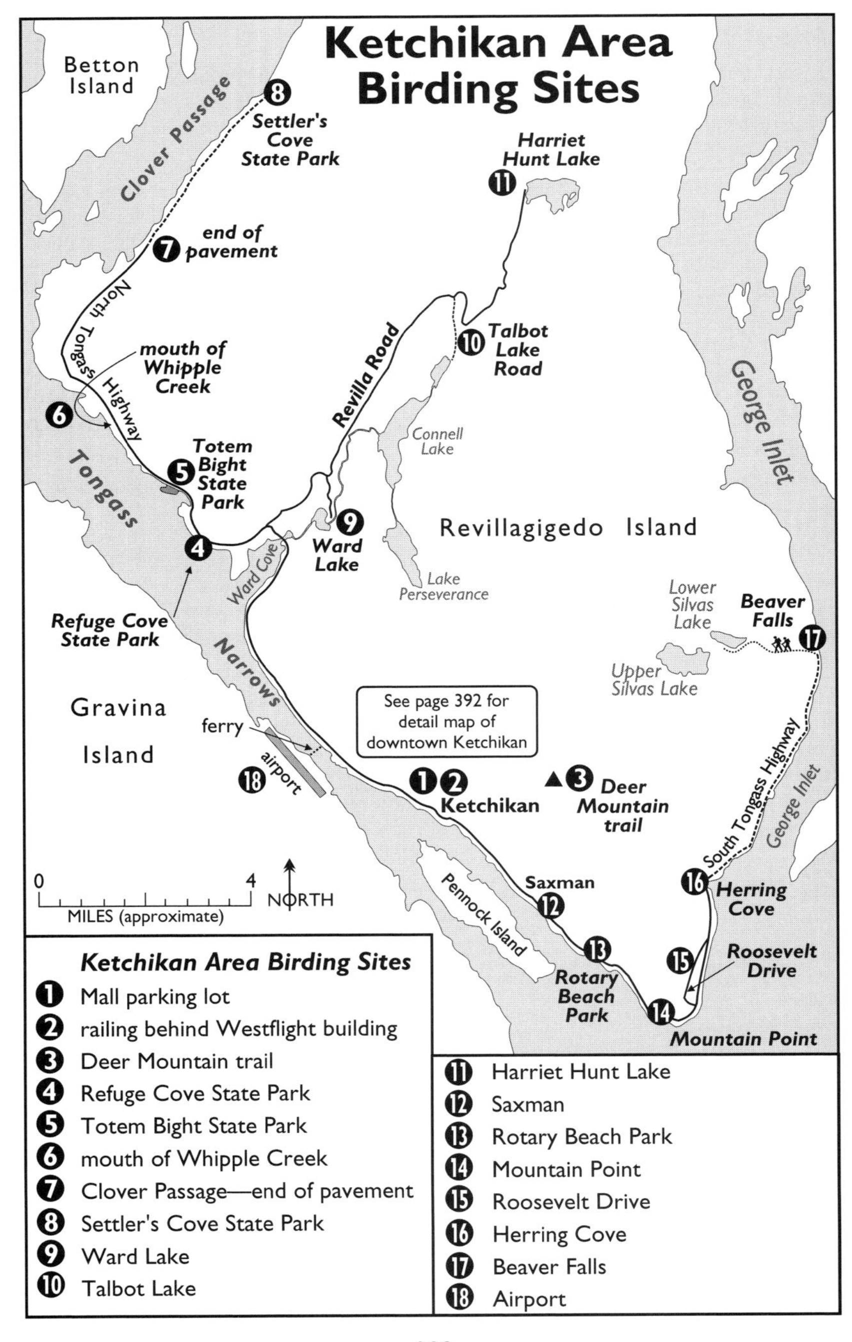

Ketchikan Area Birding Sites
Betton Island
Clover Passage
8 Settler's Cove State Park
Harriet Hunt Lake
11
7 end of pavement
North Tongass Highway
mouth of Whipple Creek
6
Revilla Road
10 Talbot Lake Road
George Inlet
Connell Lake
5 Totem Bight State Park
Tongass
4
9 Ward Lake
Ward Cove
Revillagigedo Island
Lake Perseverance
Refuge Cove State Park
Lower Silvas Lake
Beaver Falls
17
Upper Silvas Lake
Narrows
Gravina Island
ferry
airport
18
See page 392 for detail map of downtown Ketchikan
1 2 Ketchikan
3 Deer Mountain trail
South Tongass Highway
George Inlet
0
4
MILES (approximate)
NORTH
Saxman
12
Pennock Island
16 Herring Cove
13
15
Roosevelt Drive
Rotary Beach Park
14
Mountain Point
Ketchikan Area Birding Sites
1 Mall parking lot
2 railing behind Westflight building
3 Deer Mountain trail
4 Refuge Cove State Park
5 Totem Bight State Park
6 mouth of Whipple Creek
7 Clover Passage—end of pavement
8 Settler's Cove State Park
9 Ward Lake
10 Talbot Lake
11 Harriet Hunt Lake
12 Saxman
13 Rotary Beach Park
14 Mountain Point
15 Roosevelt Drive
16 Herring Cove
17 Beaver Falls
18 Airport

KETCHIKAN

Steve Heinl

More often than not it is raining and wet in Ketchikan. The people of Ketchikan enjoy an average rainfall of over 150 inches a year, although sometimes it seems like more than that. Rain gear and rubber boots are a must for birders. Ketchikan is located on Revillagigedo Island, and is accessible only by boat or plane because there are no connecting roads from the mainland to the island. There are some birding opportunities in Ketchikan within walking distance of the Alaska Marine Highway ferry terminal at the west end of town and from the cruise ship dock downtown.

The Ketchikan airport is located across Tongass Narrows from Ketchikan on Gravina Island, a two-minute ferry ride ($4 round-trip). The Ketchikan road system is limited primarily to one road, Tongass Avenue. At the east end of town the road turns into South Tongass Highway and dead-ends after approximately 13 miles. At the west end of town Tongass Avenue becomes North Tongass Highway and dead-ends approximately 16 miles from town. Revilla Road (originally a logging road) runs north from Ward Cove approximately nine miles.

The area is dominated by dense, coniferous forests of Sitka Spruce and Western Hemlock; in poorly-drained areas you will find pine/cedar muskeg bogs. Deciduous habitats are limited to the Red Alder growing along streams, the beach fringe, and disturbed areas, and Sitka Alder growing in disturbed areas. The waters adjacent to the Ketchikan road system are sheltered, relatively deep, and are lined by rocky shores.

Bald Eagle, Northwestern Crow, and Common Raven are common year round in the Ketchikan area. Other breeding birds include Red-throated Loon, Blue Grouse, Marbled Murrelet, Vaux's Swift, Rufous Hummingbird, Red-breasted Sapsucker, Hairy Woodpecker, Pacific-slope Flycatcher, Steller's Jay, Chestnut-backed Chickadee, Winter Wren, American Dipper, Golden-crowned and Ruby-crowned Kinglets, Swainson's, Hermit, and Varied Thrushes, Orange-crowned and Townsend's Warblers, Fox, Song, and Lincoln's Sparrows, Oregon Junco, Pine Grosbeak, Red Crossbill, and Pine Siskin.

Waterbirds are most numerous in the winter, from October to March, and are best viewed using a spotting scope. Common to fairly common

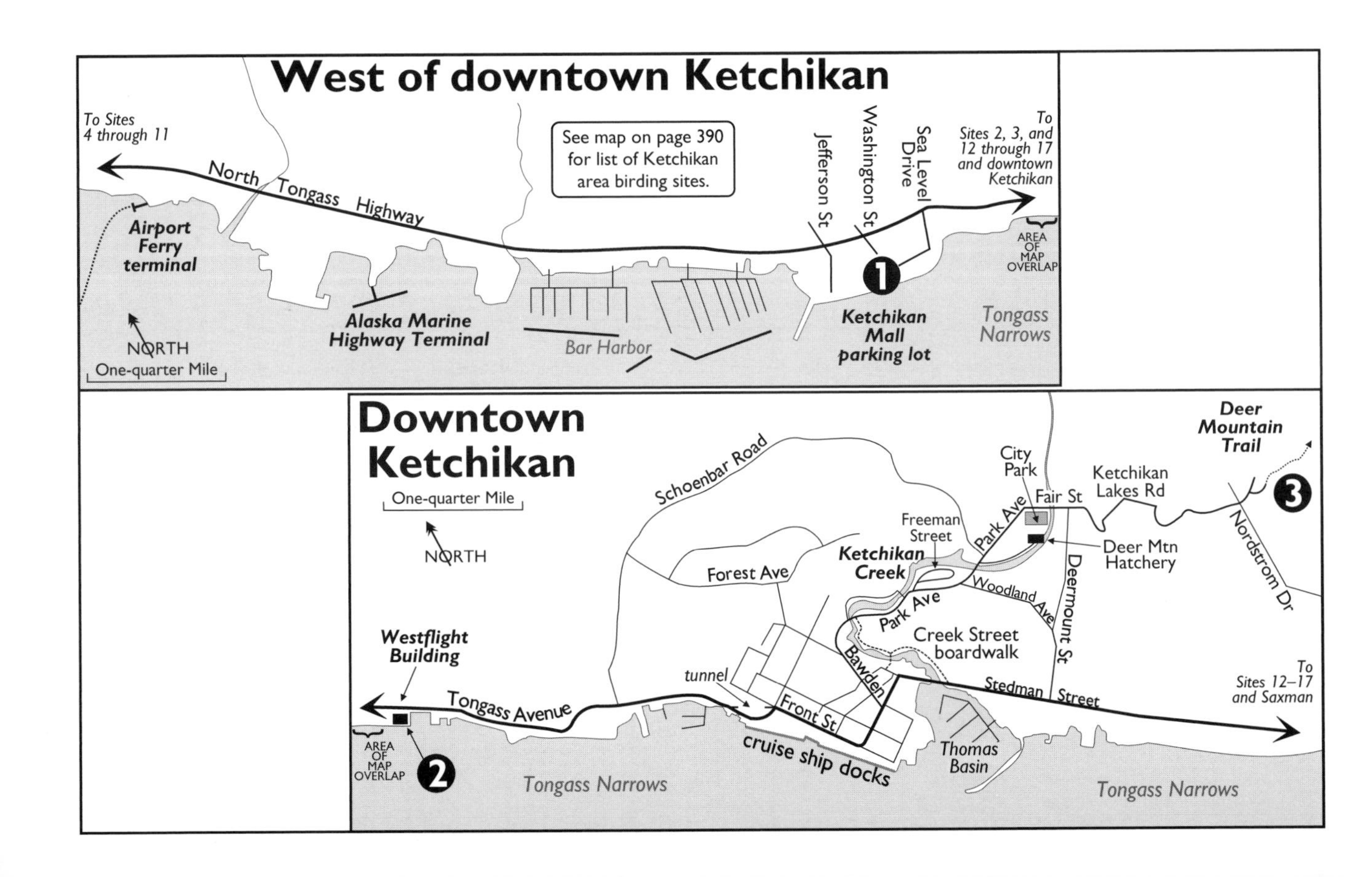
West of downtown Ketchikan
To Sites 4 through 11
North Tongass Highway
See map on page 390 for list of Ketchikan area birding sites.
Jefferson St
Washington St
Sea Level Drive
To Sites 2, 3, and 12 through 17 and downtown Ketchikan
Airport Ferry terminal
Alaska Marine Highway Terminal
Bar Harbor
Ketchikan Mall parking lot
AREA OF MAP OVERLAP
Tongass Narrows
NORTH
One-quarter Mile
Downtown Ketchikan
One-quarter Mile
NORTH
Schoenbar Road
Forest Ave
Ketchikan Creek
Freeman Street
City Park
Park Ave
Fair St
Ketchikan Lakes Rd
Deer Mountain Trail
Nordstrom Dr
Deer Mtn Hatchery
Woodland Ave
Deermount St
Park Ave
Creek Street boardwalk
Bawden
Westflight Building
tunnel
Tongass Avenue
Front St
Stedman Street
To Sites 12–17 and Saxman
AREA OF MAP OVERLAP
cruise ship docks
Thomas Basin
Tongass Narrows
Tongass Narrows

wintering birds include Western Grebe, Great Blue Heron, Harlequin Duck, scoters, Long-tailed Duck, goldeneyes, mergansers, Black Turnstone, Mew, Thayer's, and Glaucous-winged Gulls (and also Glaucous-winged x Herring Gull hybrids), Common Murre, and Marbled Murrelet. Look for Rock Sandpipers among the more common Black Turnstones, and Yellow-billed Loons among the more numerous Pacific and Common Loons.

Located at the southeastern terminus of the Alexander Archipelago, Ketchikan has hosted some unusual rarities to Alaska, such as Cattle Egret, Turkey Vulture, Western Gull, Northern Mockingbird, Western Meadowlark, Brewer's Blackbird, House Finch, American Goldfinch, Evening Grosbeak, and House Sparrow. Understandably, these species may be of slightly more interest to resident than to visiting birders!

Ketchikan's birding sites are numbered from (**1**) to (**18**) on this chapter's maps and in the following text. To reach all of the sites, a vehicle is required. Rentals are available at the airport and in town.

KETCHIKAN CREEK

Ketchikan Creek flows through downtown Ketchikan and is only five blocks from the cruise ship dock. The entire creek is visible from the streets that line it and from the Creek Street boardwalk. To get to the creek from downtown, take Bawden Street from the main road and turn right onto Park Avenue after three blocks. Park Avenue crosses Ketchikan Creek twice over the next four to five blocks and turns into Fair Street at City Park. The creek can be walked in as little time as 30 minutes. Birding is best in the spring (May) and fall (August–September) when migrant warblers and sparrows are often found in the riparian alder between Creek Street and City Park near the Deer Mountain fish hatchery. American Dippers and Warbling Vireos nest along the creek. From June to early September the creek is one of the best places in Ketchikan to look for Cedar Waxwings, and during rainy or overcast days, it is also a good place to look for Vaux's Swifts.

KETCHIKAN WATERFRONT

Two of the best places to look for waterbirds in Ketchikan are at the mall parking lot (**1**) and from the railing behind the Westflight building (**2**). Both places provide views of the water behind two seafood processors, and are easily accessible on foot from the cruise ship dock downtown (one mile), and from the ferry terminal at the west end of town (1.3 miles). If you are driving, you can park right at the water's edge in the mall parking lot and scan the water behind the processors to the southeast. At the Westflight building you must park on the street, not in the parking lot. Look for the neon Silver Lining Seafoods sign in the bottom of the Westflight building (1705 Tongass Avenue).

Walk the cement deck around to the back of the building where you can see directly behind the processors to the west. Waste from the processors attracts large numbers of gulls from late July through September, and smaller numbers through the winter. Mew, Herring, Thayer's, and Glaucous-winged Gulls are common in season. From August to October, California Gulls are common, and Ring-billed Gulls are fairly common. This is one of the easiest places in Alaska to see these two species. A total of 16 species of gulls has been recorded at this one location since 1990, including Franklin's, Little, Heermann's Black-tailed, and Slaty-backed Gulls. Afternoon is often the best time to look through the gull flocks.

From October through March large numbers of waterfowl are also attracted to the water behind the seafood processors, including hundreds of Long-tailed Ducks. During May and June Bald Eagles are common, providing an excellent opportunity to photograph eagles of all ages both in flight and resting in trees along Tongass Avenue. Often as many as 60 eagles are in the air at one time, swooping over the water to pick up small pieces of fish. From September to early November Fork-tailed Storm-Petrels occasionally appear on the waterfront after storms.

DEER MOUNTAIN

Deer Mountain (**3**) is accessible by foot from the cruise ship docks downtown. The trail begins in tall spruce/hemlock woods, breaks into scrubby subalpine habitat at about 2,500 feet, and then travels through alpine to the summit at 3,001 feet. There are a couple of overlooks on the way up. Aside from the common forest species, look for Blue Grouse and Pine Grosbeak near timberline, and Ruby-crowned Kinglet and Fox Sparrow in the scrubby patches of subalpine Mountain Hemlock and Sitka Alder near the top. The Fox Sparrows are the dark chocolate-brown race (*P.i. townsendi*). Willow Ptarmigan and American Pipit breed on the ridgeline to the north of the summit. The ptarmigan hide in dense patches of scrubby Mountain Hemlock and one must walk through the brush to find them.

The Deer Mountain trail begins as a well-groomed gravel path but turns into a dirt trail about half way up, so good footwear is required. The mountain is very steep and there are numerous switchbacks. Hikers are cautioned to stay on the trail. The distance from the parking lot to the summit is about 2.5 miles, and it may take up to two or more hours to reach the summit, depending upon the condition of the hiker. There are usually patches of snow in the alpine into early July, and even later in some years. To get to the trailhead, take Park Avenue along Ketchikan Creek until it turns into Fair Street and intersects with Deermount Street; at the intersection the road continues steeply uphill as Ketchikan Lakes Road for a few more blocks. The trailhead parking lot is about 100 feet on the right just past the intersection of Ketchikan Lakes Road and Nordstrom Drive.

NORTH TONGASS HIGHWAY

Tongass Highway extends approximately 16 miles west and north of Ketchikan. Mileages given here start at the Ketchikan airport ferry parking lot at the very west end of town. Refuge Cove State Park (**4**) is located on Sunset Drive (Mile 6.0). Turn left off of North Tongass Highway and the park is on the left only 100 feet farther. The park overlooks sheltered water and is usually productive during the winter.

Aside from having a nice collection of Tlingit totem poles, Totem Bight State Park (**5**) at Mile 7.2 is the best place in the Ketchikan area to look for Western Grebe. The grebes are nearly always found rafted up in a tight flock of 70–200 or more birds several hundred yards off the beach in Tongass Narrows. A few Western Grebes can also occasionally be found just about anywhere from the road system.

The mouth of Whipple Creek (**6**) is accessible by turning left off Tongass Highway into the Vallenar View trailer court (Mile 8.7). Follow the road down to the beach. It is best birded at low tide when there are flocks of waterfowl (Harlequin Duck, scoters, Barrow's Goldeneye), shorebirds (Black Turnstone, Surfbird, Rock Sandpiper), and gulls feeding in the shallow waters at the creek mouth. Pacific Herring spawn along Tongass Narrows near the mouth of Whipple Creek between late March and late April, attracting thousands of Surf Scoters and gulls.

The last three miles of North Tongass Highway border the sheltered waters of Clover Passage. The best places to bird Clover Passage are where the highway turns to gravel (**7**) at Mile 12.8 (wide parking area on the left; an opening in the guard rail leads to a short path down an embankment to the beach), and where the road ends at Mile 15.7 at Settler's Cove State Park (**8**). Clover Passage often hosts one or two Yellow-billed Loons, Western Grebes, and numbers of other waterbirds from late October to March, and Red-throated Loons from April through August. Marbled Murrelets are easy to find year round, and during winter hundreds or even thousands of birds may be present.

REVILLA ROAD

The turnoff to Revilla Road is found at Mile 4.3 on North Tongass Highway. The road is signed and you will see signs for Ward Lake before the turnoff. Drive 1.4 miles to the turnoff to Ward Lake (also signed), turn right, and then drive another 0.5 mile to the lake. Ward Lake (**9**) is small and has a nice, easy-to-hike gravel trail 1.3-miles long around the entire perimeter. Habitat at the lake is the classic, dense, southeast Alaska spruce-hemlock coniferous forest (there are some very large spruce trees near the parking areas), and it is an excellent place to find birds that favor this habitat, such as Blue Grouse, Red-breasted Sapsucker, Chestnut-backed Chickadee, Winter Wren, Golden-crowned Kinglet, Varied Thrush, Townsend's Warbler, and Red Crossbill. Ward Lake is one of the best places in Alaska to find a Pied-billed Grebe, and from late October through November there is one present more often than not. Small numbers of waterfowl are present from late October to May (when the lake is not frozen), including Ring-necked Duck, Barrow's Goldeneye, and Hooded Merganser. During migration the Salmonberry thickets where Ward Creek flows into the lake are sometimes full of warblers and sparrows. Ward Lake is a good place to check for Northern Rough-winged Swallow among other swallows from May to August, and the lake is also an excellent place to look for owls. Western Screech-Owls are resident in Signal Creek Campground at the end of the road. Barred and Northern Saw-whet Owls have been found after dark. Northern Pygmy-Owls are active during the day from August to October.

Beyond the turnoff to Ward Lake the road continues north through coniferous woodland and 5-to-30-year-old clearcuts. At Mile 6.1 there is a small parking space on the right. A gravel road runs down through a clearcut approximately 1.0 mile to Talbot Lake (**10**). Dense alder has grown up in the first one-quarter mile of this road, making it an excellent place to look for Vaux's Swift, Warbling Vireo, and Cedar Waxwing. Pacific-slope Flycatcher, Ruby-crowned Kinglet, Swainson's, Hermit, and Varied Thrushes, and Orange-crowned Warbler are common. This has also been the only easily accessible location in the Ketchikan area to find Alder Flycatcher and MacGillivray's Warbler, although as the clearcut grows back, those birds will stop using it. At the inlet of Talbot Lake there is a small patch of sedge and Spiraea marsh where a few pairs of Common Yellowthroats breed.

Continuing up Revilla Road, turn left at the intersection at Mile 6.6 and look for Greater Yellowlegs and Lincoln's Sparrow in muskeg bogs along the road; in wooded areas look for Pine Grosbeak and listen for the hooting of male Blue Grouse. The best bet for seeing a Blue Grouse is to drive the road just after dawn from late July through September and look for them standing alongside the road. Northern Pygmy-Owls can be found by listening for them along the road (and elsewhere in the Ketchikan area) between August and October. Revilla Road ends at Harriet Hunt Lake (**11**) at Mile 9.2. Red-throated Loons can be found here from May to August, and if you arrive early in the morning before the tour buses, you have a fair chance of watching or hearing their displays.

SOUTH TONGASS HIGHWAY

South Tongass Highway extends approximately 12 miles southeast and then north of Ketchikan. Mileages given here start in Ketchikan at the bridge over Ketchikan Creek at Thomas Basin. A bicycle path parallels the highway between Miles 0.9 and 2.0 and provides a nice opportunity for birding Tongass Narrows on foot from downtown. Good places to stop and look over the water are at Saxman (**12**; Mile 2.4 where there is another nice Tlingit totem pole park), Rotary Beach Park (**13**; Mile 3.4), and Mountain Point (**14**; Mile 5.2). One or two Yellow-billed Loons are typically found along South Tongass Highway during winter (October–March). Of interest to Alaskan birders is the fact that a few Brandt's Cormorants have recently been found among flocks of cormorants at Saxman and Mountain Point in January and February. Roosevelt Drive (**15**; Mile 6.3) is one of the best places in Alaska for Band-tailed Pigeons. Walk the road very early in the morning from April to August, and listen for their low, hooting call while you scan the tree tops close to the road. Roosevelt Drive loops back down to South Tongass Highway after 0.9 mile.

At Herring Cove (**16**; Mile 8.2) there is a fish hatchery at the head of a small bay. Large numbers of gulls are attracted to the spawning and dying salmon at Herring Cove from late July to November. South Tongass Highway turns to gravel just past Herring Cove and continues on to Beaver Falls (**17**) at Mile 13.0. At Beaver Falls there is a gated gravel road just uphill of the parking area. The road runs two miles uphill through scrubby pine/cedar habitat, then through spruce/hemlock woods, and ends at Lower Silvas Lake.

Hooded Merganser

KETCHIKAN AIRPORT

The area around the Ketchikan airport (**18**) offers interesting birding, particularly during migration (April–May; August–October), and provides an easy way to kill an hour or more if you are waiting for a flight. To bird around the airport you must first check in at the tollbooth, where you will be asked for your name, phone number, and approximate time of return. Be sure to check out at the tollbooth when you are done. A dirt road runs north along the shore for one-half mile and south along the shore for one-half mile. From each end of the road a dirt trail follows the fence line around the entire perimeter of the airport. The perimeter is about four miles long and can take from two to four hours to bird. The mouth of a small creek at the north end of the airport attracts migrant waterfowl, shorebirds, and gulls, as does the adjacent rocky shoreline. Maintenance at the airport includes regularly cutting down trees around the perimeter once they reach a certain height. The resulting brush piles, while not beautiful, are ideal habitat for sparrows and warblers.

LOGISTICS

The area code for all telephone numbers is 907 unless otherwise indicated. Tourist and travel services (accommodations, restaurants, attractions, etc.) not listed below can be found in the latest edition of The Milepost. *Statewide travel and birding information services are listed under Logistics in the* Introduction, *page 15.)*

You can request information about accommodations, travel arrangements, guiding, restaurants, etc., at the Ketchikan Visitors Bureau, 131 Front Street, Ketchikan 99901; 225-6166 or 800-770-3300; web site *www.visit-ketchikan.com* or the Southeast Alaska Visitor Center at 50 Main Street, Ketchikan 99901; 228-6214; email *akinfo/r10.ketchikan@fs.fed.us*. Ask for a city map.

There are eight hotels, at least 22 bed and breakfasts, and numerous fishing lodges, fishing charters, and sightseeing companies operating in the Ketchikan area. Many cater to tourists who are visiting for a brief, less than one-day, visit.

Campgrounds: The U.S. Forest Service maintains three campgrounds: two at Ward Lake (Three C's and Signal Creek) and one on Revilla Road 2.3 miles north of the Ward Lake turn (Last Chance). The fee is $10/night and the campgrounds are open April or May through September. Advance reservations can be made by calling 877-444-6777, or contact the U.S. Forest Service for more information at Ketchikan Misty Fjords Ranger District; 3031 Tongass Avenue, Ketchikan 99901; 225-2148. The state has a campground at Settler's Cove State Park, open from May through September for $10 per night (Alaska State Parks, 9883 North Tongass Highway; 247-8574).

Misty Fjords National Monument and Wilderness

Tim Schantz

Misty Fjords National Monument and Wilderness (2.3 million acres) is located in southeast Alaska west of Hyder, northeast of Ketchikan, and southeast of Wrangell. (See map on page 384.) The heavily forested area is broken by many creeks, rivers, waterfalls, and long saltwater fjords, and, like this part of southeast Alaska, receives copious amounts of rainfall. The monument's name comes from the daily precipitation that splatters on the needles of Sitka Spruce, Western Hemlock, and Alaska Cedar trees and creates a mist that flows from the steep hillsides into the valleys below.

The rivers at the heads of the fjords have important salmon-spawning beds for commercially harvested King, Silver, Red, Pink, and Chum Salmon, so the Alaska Department of Fish and Game sends in crews regularly to check escapement in some of these rivers.

Several records of birds rare to Alaska were made on the Chickamin River—Common Nighthawk, Cassin's, Warbling, and Red-eyed Vireos, American Crow, Magnolia Warbler, American Redstart, MacGillivray's Warbler, Western Tanager, Harris's Sparrow, and Brown-headed Cowbird.

Because of the monument's remoteness, birders are more likely to reach neighboring Hyder than to venture into the wilderness area. The species assemblage is similar for these two locations. The author recorded 98 species in Misty Fjords in 1996 and 1997.

Access is primarily by boat. Tours that allow you to sleep on the boat as you visit the monument are available out of Ketchikan and other nearby island communities . Another option is to be dropped off on shore and later to be picked up at a location of your choice. Even better, you can bring a sea kayak along to investigate the area more thoroughly. Good campsites are difficult to find because the hills are steep and heavily wooded—and because the daily tides can exceed 18 feet. Several wilderness lodges are in the area, as well as Forest Service wilderness cabins. Contact Misty Fjords National Monument, 3031 Tongass Avenue, Ketchikan, AK 99901; 225-2148.

ACKNOWLEDGEMENTS: Tim Schantz's notes were compiled and edited by George West. Tim wrote, *From early June through late August of 1996 and 1997, I was a Fisheries Technician conducting mark and recapture studies on King Salmon on the Chickamin and Unuk Rivers, two of the principal rivers in the Monument and Wilderness. This gave me ample opportunity to observe birds along these rivers.* After Tim's untimely death in May 2001, his brothers, Mike and Tom Schantz, kindly provided some of Tim's extensive notes on his Alaska birding adventures.

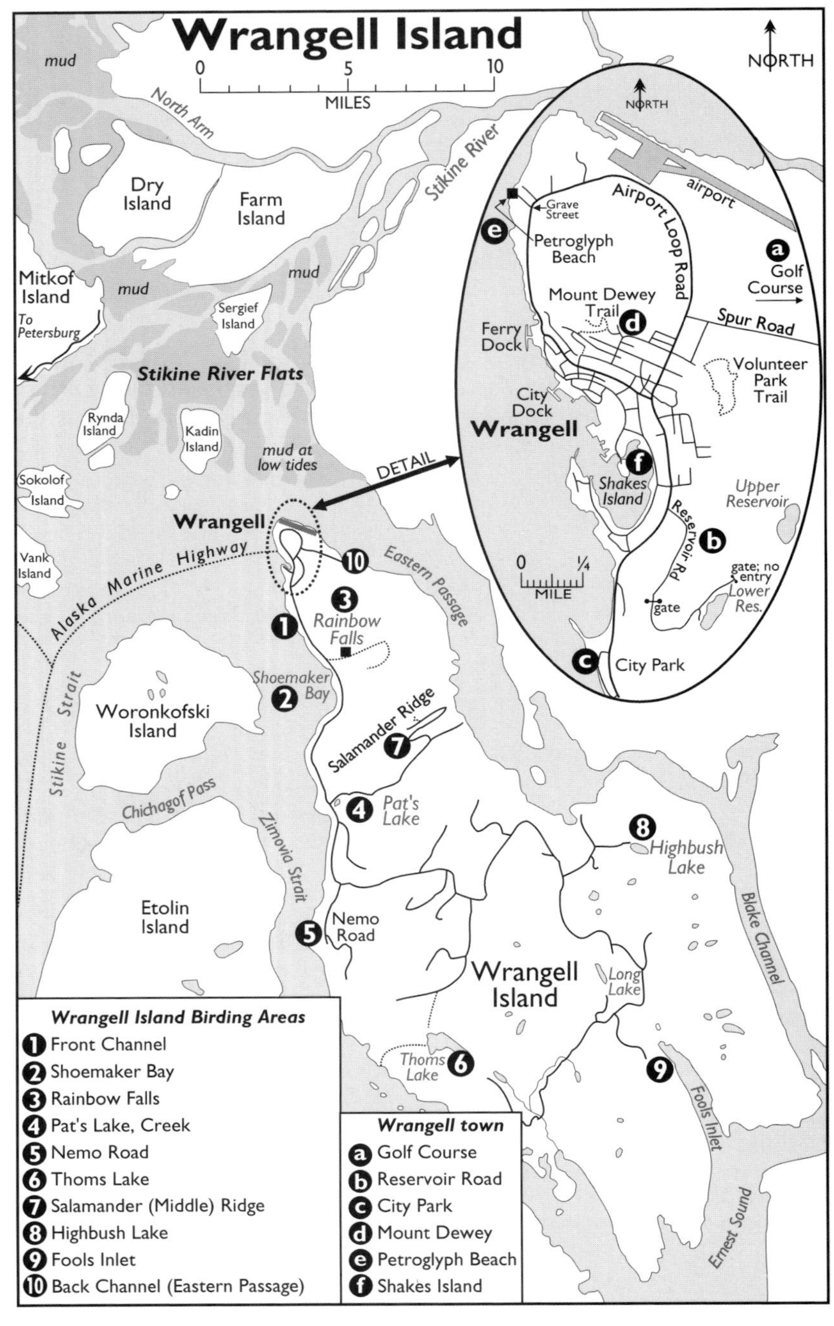

Wrangell Island
0
5
10
MILES
NORTH
mud
North Arm
Dry Island
Farm Island
Stikine River
Mitkof Island
To Petersburg
mud
mud
Sergief Island
Stikine River Flats
Rynda Island
Kadin Island
mud at low tides
Sokolof Island
Vank Island
DETAIL
Wrangell
Alaska Marine Highway
Eastern Passage
Rainbow Falls
Shoemaker Bay
Woronkofski Island
Stikine Strait
Salamander Ridge
Chichagof Pass
Zimovia Strait
Pat's Lake
Highbush Lake
Etolin Island
Nemo Road
Wrangell Island
Long Lake
Blake Channel
Thoms Lake
Fools Inlet
Ernest Sound
NORTH
airport
Airport Loop Road
Grave Street
Petroglyph Beach
Golf Course
Mount Dewey Trail
Spur Road
Ferry Dock
Volunteer Park Trail
City Dock
Wrangell
Shakes Island
Upper Reservoir
Reservoir Rd
0
1/4
MILE
gate; no entry
Lower Res.
gate
City Park
Wrangell Island Birding Areas
1 Front Channel
2 Shoemaker Bay
3 Rainbow Falls
4 Pat's Lake, Creek
5 Nemo Road
6 Thoms Lake
7 Salamander (Middle) Ridge
8 Highbush Lake
9 Fools Inlet
10 Back Channel (Eastern Passage)
Wrangell town
a Golf Course
b Reservoir Road
c City Park
d Mount Dewey
e Petroglyph Beach
f Shakes Island

WRANGELL

Peg Robertsen

Wrangell is one of the smaller towns (population 2,300) on the Alaska Marine Highway ferry route from Bellingham, Washington, to Haines and Skagway. It is located at the north end of Wrangell Island, 89 miles north of Ketchikan and about 40 miles south of Petersburg. The only way to get to Wrangell is by boat or plane. The Stikine River that flows west out of British Columbia forms a broad delta just northeast of Wrangell Island and is the main reason for birders to stop and spend some time here. The Stikine River delta is one of only a few stops for spring-migrant shorebirds traveling along the Pacific coast to Alaska. Thousands of Western Sandpipers and Dunlins come through each spring, along with Black-bellied Plovers, American and Pacific Golden-Plovers, Semipalmated Plovers, Greater and Lesser Yellowlegs, Whimbrel, Least and Pectoral Sandpipers, and Long-billed and Short-billed Dowitchers. Fall migration is less spectacular, so if you are planning a trip to southeast Alaska in spring, you may wish to stop and take a boat ride over to view the Stikine River flats at low tide in late April or early May.

Wrangell Island was occupied by Native peoples as long as 8,000 years ago and more recently by the Tlingit, who remain an important component of the present community. The area passed through Russian and British hands before it became part of the United States in 1867. After three gold rushes in the late 1800s, the economy has settled into fishing, lumber, and tourism. Wrangell is located in the heart of the Tongass National Forest, a timber source for the local lumber industry. Summer temperatures average 50–60°F and there is a moderate amount of rainfall in summer. The heaviest rains come in October and November.

STIKINE RIVER DELTA

A trip to the Stikine River delta will add another day to your stay in Wrangell, but it is well worth the time. River trips are tidally dependent. Bird viewing is best at mid-level rising tides, but access to cabins may require higher tides, so plan your day on the river carefully. Thousands of Bald Eagles congregate on the delta in April to feed on Hooligan (Eulachon), an oily fish that runs in schools from saltwater to freshwater in order to spawn. Hundreds of thousands of gulls also arrive in spring, including Bonaparte's,

Mew, Ring-billed, California, Herring, Thayer's, Glaucous-winged, Glaucous, and Black-legged Kittiwake. Thousands of Snow Geese stop to feed on the grasses and sedges on the delta's islands in spring. Also expect Greater White-fronted and several races of Canada Geese and a range of ducks, including some uncommon in Alaska, such as Blue-winged and Cinnamon Teal.

Eurasian Wigeon, Killdeer, and Spotted Sandpiper can be found on the flats in spring. You might find some rarities on the mudflats, such as Solitary and Upland Sandpipers, Marbled Godwit, Red Knot, Sanderling, and Baird's and Stilt Sandpipers. Sharp-tailed Sandpipers come through in fall. To find any of these you may need to plan several trips or an overnight stay on the flats.

There are several islands in the delta and along the lower part of the Stikine River. If you explore these islands or take a trip upriver and into some of the sloughs, you might find the following in addition to those mentioned above—American Bittern, Trumpeter Swan, Hooded Merganser, Northern Harrier, Sharp-shinned Hawk, Northern Goshawk, Red-tailed Hawk, Golden Eagle, Peregrine Falcon, Blue Grouse, Sora, Short-eared Owl, Northern Pygmy-Owl, Black and Vaux's Swifts, Rufous Hummingbird, Olive-sided Flycatcher, Western Wood-Pewee, Alder Flycatcher, Black-billed Magpie, Red-eyed and Warbling Vireos, American Pipit, Yellow, MacGillivray's, and Wilson's Warblers, American Redstart, Northern Waterthrush, Common Yellowthroat, Western Tanager, and Red-winged Blackbird.

WRANGELL ISLAND

With over 95 miles of roads and several good birding sites, it will take more than a day for you to explore Wrangell Island. You can walk around town to check several of the following sites, or better yet, rent a car and make the complete tour.

Birding areas near the city: a. **Golf Course** (*1.5 miles from ferry dock*)—Wilson's Snipe, Hairy Woodpecker, Pacific-slope Flycatcher, Tree Swallow, and Fox and Golden-crowned Sparrows. **b. Reservoir Road** (*1.0 mile from the ferry dock*)—Red-breasted Sapsucker, Red-breasted Nuthatch, Winter Wren, Bohemian Waxwing, Townsend's Warbler, and Red Crossbill. **c. City Park** (*1.5 miles from the ferry dock*)—Harlequin Duck, Barrow's Goldeneye, Chestnut-backed Chickadee, and Varied Thrush. **d. Mount Dewey** (*0.4 mile from the ferry dock*)—Swainson's and Hermit Thrushes. **e. Petroglyph Beach** (*1.0 mile from the ferry dock*)—Surf Scoter, Anna's Hummingbird, Ruby-crowned Kinglet, and Townsend's Warbler. **f. Shakes Island** (*0.6 mile from the ferry dock*)—Northwestern Crow and Black-billed Magpie.

If you have a car, you can continue south by following this chapter's map to ten additional birding sites: **1. Front Channel** (*access to the shoreline and* *saltwater at Zimovia Strait along the western side of Wrangell Island*)—Species common in winter but rare in summer include Red-throated, Common, and Yellow-billed Loons, Western Grebe, Long-tailed Duck, Parasitic Jaeger, Bonaparte's Gull, Common Murre, and Marbled Murrelet. **2. Shoemaker Bay** (*rocky beach on Zimovia Strait*)—Black Turnstone, Surfbird, and Rock Sandpiper. **3. Rainbow Falls** (*interior forest and streamside*)—Rufous Hummingbird and American Dipper.

4. Pat's Lake, Creek, and Log Transfer Facility (*freshwater and saltwater margin*)—American Dipper, Trumpeter Swan, and Sharp-shinned Hawk. **5. Nemo Road and Campsites** (*forest with clearcut openings*)—Northern Pygmy-Owl, Northern Goshawk, Band-tailed Pigeon (rare), Three-toed Woodpecker, Winter Wren, and Orange-crowned Warbler. **6. Thoms Lake** (*peat bog and lake*)—Steller's Jay and Oregon Junco. **7. Salamander (Middle) Ridge** (*peatland, alpine habitat*)—Blue Grouse, ptarmigan, and Chestnut-backed Chickadee. **8. Highbush Lake** (*freshwater lake, forest, and clearcut openings*)—Northern Goshawk, Mew Gull, and Belted Kingfisher. **9. Fools Inlet** (*saltwater beach, forest*)—Canada Goose, shorebirds. **10. Back Channel** (*Eastern Passage, the saltwater channel along the east side of Wrangell Island*)—Western Grebe, Sandhill Crane, and Red-necked Phalarope.

LOGISTICS

The area code for all telephone numbers is 907 unless otherwise indicated. Tourist and travel services (accommodations, restaurants, attractions, etc.) not listed below can be found in the latest edition of The Milepost. *Statewide travel and birding information services are listed under Logistics in the* Introduction, *page 15.)*

For information about accommodations, events, and services, check the Wrangell web site at *www.wrangell.com* or the Wrangell Chamber of Commerce at *www.wrangellchamber.org*.

For birding information contact the U.S. Forest Service, Wrangell Ranger District, PO Box 51, Wrangell, AK 99929 or stop in at 525 Bennett Street in town. Ask for the brochure on finding birds in Wrangell by Robertsen (1998). You can also obtain a brochure, *Wrangell Bike and Hike Road Map*, published by the Wrangell Senior Greeters, that has a detailed map of the north end of the island and lists eight scenic and cultural sites to visit. If you have a vehicle, the Forest Service has a detailed map of the entire island showing trails (*Wrangell Island Road Guide*) and a brochure describing recreation sites.

Tours: There are many tour companies that can take you around the island and to the Stikine River Delta. Here are four suggestions: Alaska Tugboat Tours 888-488-4386 or 874-3101; Alaska Waters, Inc. 800-347-4462 or 874-2378; Breakaway Adventures 800-385-2488 or 874-2488; and Rainwalker Expeditions 874-2549. For a complete list, check the Wrangell web site listed above.

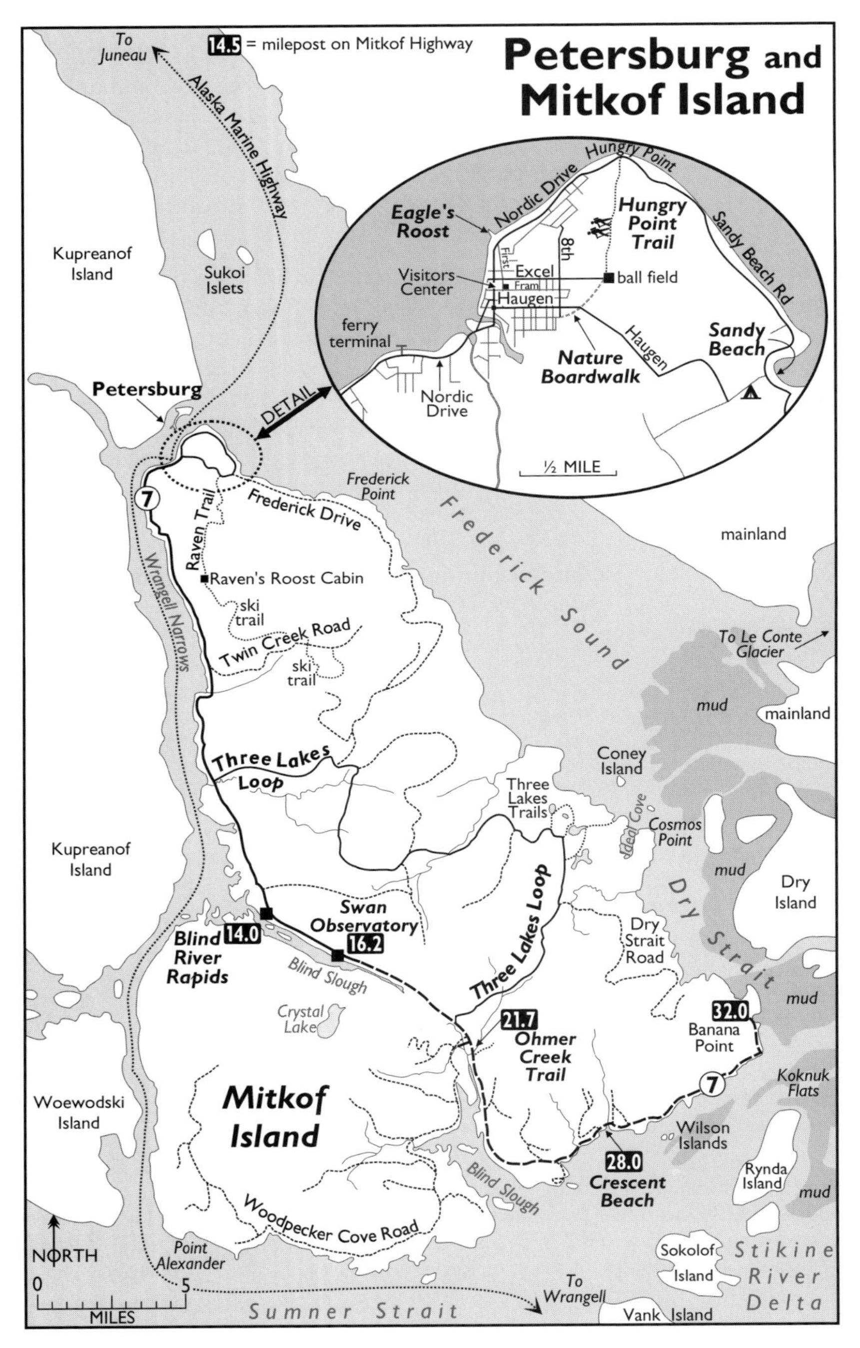
Petersburg and Mitkof Island
14.5 = milepost on Mitkof Highway
To Juneau
Alaska Marine Highway
Kupreanof Island
Sukoi Islets
Petersburg
DETAIL
Eagle's Roost
Nordic Drive
Hungry Point
Hungry Point Trail
Sandy Beach Rd
First
8th
Excel
Fram
Haugen
Visitors Center
ball field
ferry terminal
Nordic Drive
Nature Boardwalk
Haugen
Sandy Beach
½ MILE
Frederick Point
Frederick Drive
Raven Trail
Raven's Roost Cabin
ski trail
Twin Creek Road
ski trail
Wrangell Narrows
Frederick Sound
mainland
To Le Conte Glacier
mud
mainland
Three Lakes Loop
Coney Island
Three Lakes Trails
Ideal Cove
Cosmos Point
Kupreanof Island
mud
Dry Island
Dry Strait
Three Lakes Loop
Swan Observatory
Blind River Rapids
14.0
16.2
Dry Strait Road
Blind Slough
Crystal Lake
21.7
Ohmer Creek Trail
32.0
Banana Point
mud
Koknuk Flats
Woewodski Island
Mitkof Island
Wilson Islands
28.0
Crescent Beach
Rynda Island
mud
Blind Slough
Woodpecker Cove Road
NORTH
Point Alexander
Sokolof Island
Stikine River Delta
0
5
MILES
To Wrangell
Sumner Strait
Vank Island

PETERSBURG

AND MITKOF ISLAND

Melissa Cady

Petersburg is a picturesque fishing community on the north end of Mitkof Island. Located approximately 200 miles south of Juneau, Petersburg supports a thriving community of about 3,400 year-round residents. The only way to reach Petersburg is by boat or plane. Visitors can enjoy chartered sportfishing, whale-watching tours, flight-seeing tours of nearby Le Conte Glacier, hiking, biking, and sea-kayaking, in addition to birding.

Some of the most interesting birding in Petersburg is along the shoreline bordered by the Wrangell Narrows on the west and Frederick Sound on the north. You are likely to find interesting birds anywhere near these two bodies of water. Common shorebirds in the area include Greater and Lesser Yellowlegs, Spotted Sandpiper, Black and Ruddy Turnstones, and Surfbird. Other birds along the water include Red-throated, Pacific, Common, and Yellow-billed Loons, Western Grebe, Harlequin Duck, Surf, White-winged, and Black Scoters, Long-tailed Duck, Barrow's Goldeneye, Common and Red-breasted Mergansers, Bald Eagle, Bonaparte's, Mew, Herring, Thayer's, and Glaucous-winged Gulls, Common Murre, Pigeon Guillemot, and Marbled Murrelet.

PETERSBURG BIRDING SITES

Petersburg's small size means that everything in town is within walking distance. Nothing is more than a mile or so away (all distances shown are measured from the intersection of Haugen Drive and Nordic Drive downtown). There are four nice birding areas in town: **Sandy Beach Park** (*1.6 miles from downtown*) is on Frederick Sound, so any of the birds listed above may also be seen there. In addition, one can find Hairy Woodpecker, Pacific-slope Flycatcher, Chestnut-backed Chickadee, Winter Wren, and Ruby-crowned Kinglet, and you often can hear Blue Grouse in spring. **The Nature Boardwalk** (*0.8 mile from downtown*) connects the end of Excel Street to 8th Street. There you might find Steller's Jay, Orange-crowned Warbler, and Oregon Junco. **Hungry Point Trail** (*0.8 mile from downtown*) goes between the ball field and Sandy Beach Road near Hungry Point. There you might see Bald Eagle, Wilson's Snipe, and Orange-crowned Warbler. **Eagle's Roost Park** (*0.4 mile from downtown*) has Bald Eagle, Northwestern Crow, and all of the birds listed above for Wrangell Narrows.

MITKOF ISLAND BIRDING SITES

If you bring your car up on the ferry or rent a car in town, you can follow this chapter's map to check out other birding opportunities on Mitkof Island. Watch for the mile-marker signs along the road as you travel to these beautiful spots.

Blind River Rapids (*Mile 14 Mitkof Highway*)—Harlequin Duck, Bald Eagle, Belted Kingfisher, Pacific-slope Flycatcher, and Winter Wren.

Ohmer Creek Trail (*Mile 21.75 Mitkof Highway*)—Greater Yellowlegs, Red-breasted Sapsucker, Hairy Woodpecker, Pacific-slope Flycatcher, Winter Wren, American Dipper, and Yellow Warbler.

Three Lakes Trails (*Three Lakes Loop Road*)—Trumpeter Swan, Northern Goshawk, Sandhill Crane, Rufous Hummingbird, Pacific-slope Flycatcher, Steller's Jay, Chestnut-backed Chickadee, Winter Wren, Golden-crowned Kinglet, Swainson's and Varied Thrushes, Townsend's and Wilson's Warblers, Fox, Lincoln's and Golden-crowned Sparrows, and Red Crossbill.

Blind Slough Swan Observatory (*Mile 16.25 Mitkof Highway*)—Trumpeter Swan from fall through spring, Northern Harrier, Golden-crowned Kinglet, and Red-winged Blackbird.

Crescent Beach (*Mile 28 Mitkof Highway*)—The last 3 miles of Mitkof Highway have beautiful views of islands in Sumner Strait; one can also find Alder Flycatcher, Varied Thrush, and a large variety of loons, sea ducks, shorebirds, and more. The boat ramp at Banana Point (Mile 28 Mitkof Highway), at the south end of the island, provides access to the Stikine River Delta, a fantastic spot to see migrating shorebirds. Birds of the Stikine River Delta are discussed in the chapter on Wrangell, page 401.

Access to other islands and the nearby mainland is somewhat limited. Most islands do not have a well-developed road system. Many are accessible only by plane, motorboat, or kayak. If you plan to rent a boat or kayak, be aware that the waters in southeast Alaska can be unpredictable and dangerous; inquire locally for safety information and weather conditions. Birds you might find on other islands and on the mainland include all of the birds listed above, as well as Osprey, Peregrine Falcon, Willow and Rock Ptarmigan at higher elevations, Black Oystercatcher, and Black-billed Magpie.

LOGISTICS

The area code for all telephone numbers is 907 unless otherwise indicated. Tourist and travel services (accommodations, restaurants, attractions, etc.) not listed below can be found in the latest edition of The Milepost. *Statewide travel and birding information services are listed under Logistics in the* Introduction, *page 15.)*

For general information check the Petersburg Chamber of Commerce at PO Box 810, Petersburg, AK 99833; 772-4636; fax 772-3646; web site *www.petersburg.org*. There are over two dozen lodges, B&Bs, RV parks, and other overnight facilities in and around town, as well as a choice of restaurants and grocery stores. You can rent a vehicle through the Scandia House (800-722-5006) or the Tides Inn (772-4288).

For birding information contact the U.S. Forest Service, Petersburg Ranger District, PO Box 1328, Petersburg, AK 99833, or stop in at the Petersburg Visitor Information Center (772-4636) at the corner of First and Fram Streets. Information about local birding and other recreational activities is also available at the Forest Service District Office located at the corner of Haugen and North Nordic Drive.

Several tour operators offering sightseeing glacier tours, charter fishing, and whale-watching tours are based in Petersburg. Check with the Visitor Information Center for a current list.

Each May Petersburg's annual Little Norway Festival celebrates the town's Norwegian heritage with spectacular food, crafts, and performances featuring traditional dances. Information on dates and activities is available at the visitor center.

Varied Thrush

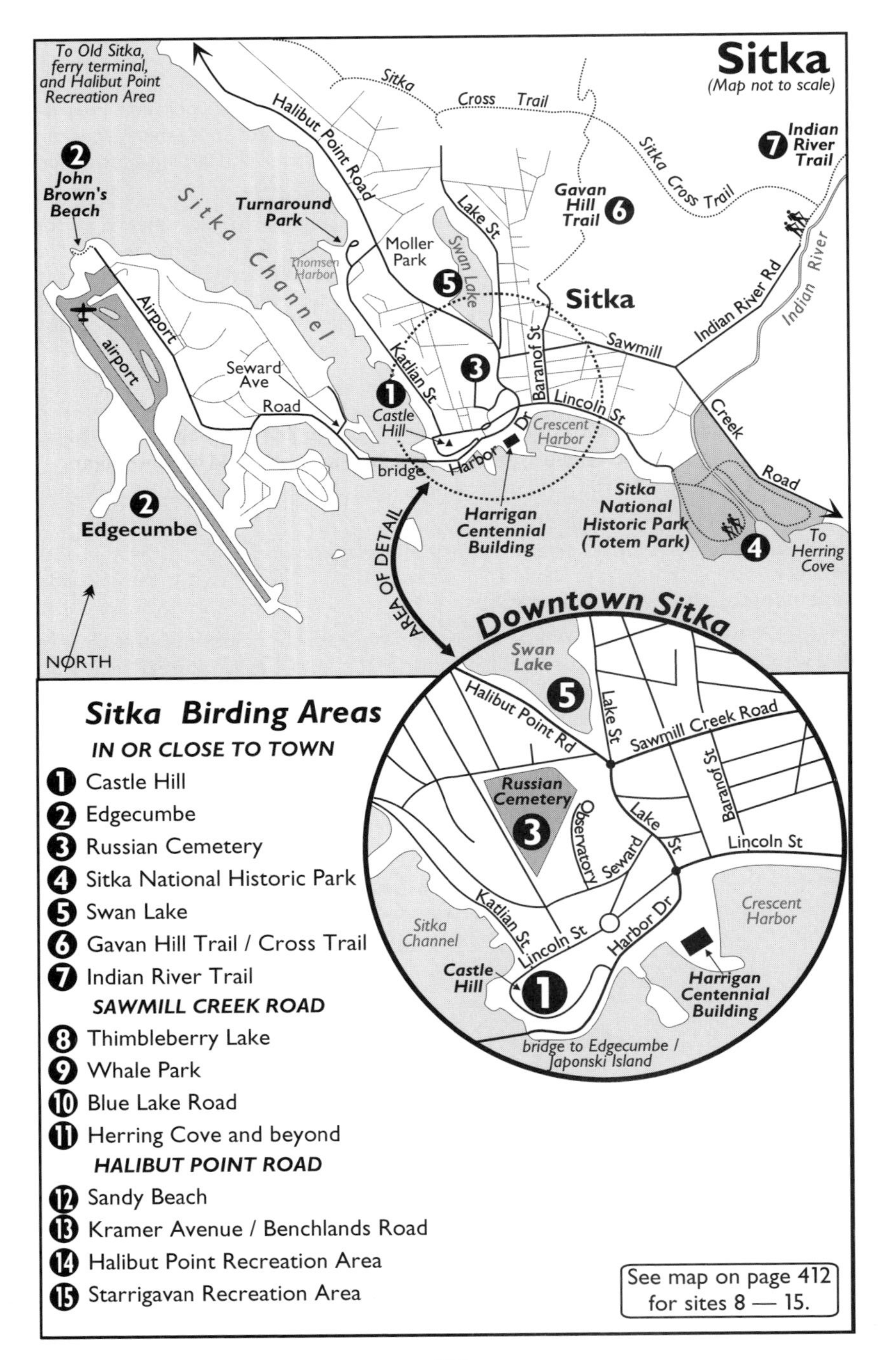

Sitka
(Map not to scale)
To Old Sitka, ferry terminal, and Halibut Point Recreation Area
Sitka Cross Trail
Halibut Point Road
Indian River Trail
John Brown's Beach
Sitka Channel
Turnaround Park
Gavan Hill Trail
Lake St
Moller Park
Thomsen Harbor
Swan Lake
Sitka
Airport
airport
Indian River Rd
Indian River
Sawmill
Baranof St
Katlian St
Seward Ave
Road
Castle Hill
Lincoln St
Crescent Harbor
Creek
Harbor Dr
bridge
Road
Sitka National Historic Park (Totem Park)
Edgecumbe
Harrigan Centennial Building
To Herring Cove
AREA OF DETAIL
Downtown Sitka
NORTH
Halibut Point Rd
Sawmill Creek Road
Russian Cemetery
Observatory
Seward
Lincoln St
Sitka Channel
bridge to Edgecumbe / Japonski Island
Sitka Birding Areas
IN OR CLOSE TO TOWN
1 Castle Hill
2 Edgecumbe
3 Russian Cemetery
4 Sitka National Historic Park
5 Swan Lake
6 Gavan Hill Trail / Cross Trail
7 Indian River Trail
SAWMILL CREEK ROAD
8 Thimbleberry Lake
9 Whale Park
10 Blue Lake Road
11 Herring Cove and beyond
HALIBUT POINT ROAD
12 Sandy Beach
13 Kramer Avenue / Benchlands Road
14 Halibut Point Recreation Area
15 Starrigavan Recreation Area
See map on page 412 for sites 8 — 15.

SITKA

Marjorie L. Ward and Marlys E. Tedin

Sitka is confined between ocean and mountains on the west coast of 100-mile-long Baranof Island on Sitka Sound, an arm of the Pacific Ocean. The town is about 75 miles west of the nearest mainland and lies at 57°N, 135°W. Surrounded by the largest temperate rain forest in the world, Sitka's climate is mild with an average temperature in January of 34°F and in July 61°F. Rainfall averages 86 inches per year, about half of that enjoyed by Ketchikan.

If you are coming north on the Alaska Marine Highway, a several-day stopover in Sitka, with its easily accessed avifauna and a chance to reach Saint Lazaria Island's seabird colonies, makes this a great opportunity for birding.

Sitka has a population of 8,700, seven National Historic Landmarks, two fine museums, several interesting cultural programs for visitors to explore, and all the necessary features and services of a small Alaskan city that will guarantee a comfortable and enjoyable stay.

The usual Alaska Bear Cautions apply in Sitka. Be sure to make enough noise, by talking or singing, to warn any bears of your presence. Remember, if you meet a bear on the trail, stop and slowly back away. Do not run. If you are with other people, stay close together and make yourself appear as big as possible with your arms up and out; spread your jacket out. Back away slowly—running triggers the predator-chase reaction. Be alert for Brown Bears anywhere in the Sitka area, including edges of residental areas. Also be aware of the tidal changes, since tides in Sitka can go from a minus 3.0 feet to a plus 12.0 feet in six hours. Read the Tide Cautions (page 19) and the Bear Cautions (page 17) in the *Introduction* before walking away from the city.

SITKA BIRDING AREAS

All of the route directions start from the Harrigan Centennial Building in the compact downtown section of Sitka. Sitka's best and most accessible birding sites are numbered **1** through **15** on this chapter's maps. You may walk to a number of these sites or rent a car to visit them all. Sites **1** through **7** are located within a 10-to-15-minute walk from the Centennial Building.

Site 1. Castle Hill. Turn left on Harbor Drive and follow the sidewalk to the right of the bridge. Castle Hill is ADA-accessible and good for spring- and fall-migrant passerines as well as giving you a terrific panoramic view of Sitka. Look for Bald Eagle, Orange-crowned and Wilson's Warblers, and White-winged Crossbill.

Site 2. Edgecumbe. (The real Mount Edgecumbe—not the same-named "suburb" of Sitka, is a 3,201-foot dormant volcanic cone located on Kruzof Island some 25 miles west-southwest from Sitka. In fine weather it dominates the view in that direction.) Stay on Harbor Drive, cross the O'Connell Bridge toward the airport, turn right onto Seward Avenue, and follow that road as it bends to the left. This places you on a large paved area on the western margin of Sitka Channel. Except during breeding season, this is an excellent spot to search for waterbirds such as Pacific and Common Loons, Horned and Red-necked Grebes, Double-crested and Pelagic Cormorants, Long-tailed Duck, Barrow's Goldeneye, Common Merganser, and, from late winter to mid-summer, many Bald Eagles. If you have time, check the various vegetated areas on the three causeway-connected islands that comprise Edgecumbe, looking for Sitka rarities such as Fork-tailed Storm-Petrel, Peregrine Falcon, Northern Shrike, Lark Sparrow, and Gray-crowned Rosy-Finch. If you are driving, continue on Airport Road beyond the airport terminal to the end of the road at the U.S. Coast Guard Air Station. A short, easy trail from the parking area leads to John Brown's Beach, excellent for fall, winter, and spring seabirds. Also, check the western end of Sitka Channel near the parking area.

On your return to Sitka from Edgecumbe, turn left at the end of the bridge and continue around Castle Hill to Lincoln Street. Then take the first left onto Katlian Street to follow the eastern side of Sitka Channel, although it is difficult to get good views of the water from the road. Continue to New Thomsen Harbor and stop at the end of the parking lot. This spot offers a good view of Sitka Turnaround Park's extensive mudflats. Shorebirds, including Spotted Sandpiper, Black Turnstone, Western Sandpiper, and Short-billed Dowitcher, are present during migration. Also, this is the best area for finding Marbled Godwit. Across Halibut Point Road at the traffic light is Moller Park, attractive to passerine migrants. Turn right onto Halibut Point Road to return to Lincoln Street and Harbor Drive, or turn left to visit Sites 12 through 15.

Site 3. Russian Cemetery. From Harbor Drive and Lake Street, turn left onto Seward Street. At the top of the hill, turn right onto Observatory Street that ends at the Russian Cemetery, a good area for passerines, especially thrushes and warblers.

Site 4. Sitka National Historic Park (local name is Totem Park). If your birding time in Sitka is limited, this is the best single site to visit due to the diversity of habitats in a compact area. From the Centennial Building, turn right onto Lincoln Street, or walk along Crescent Harbor through Crescent Park. Lincoln Street ends at Totem Park, where 0.75-mile trails on each side of the Indian River offer various habitats good for both passerines and waterbirds. Look here for Rufous Hummingbird, Red-breasted Sapsucker, Chestnut-backed Chickadee, Ruby-crowned Kinglet, Swainson's and Hermit Thrushes, American Robin, Varied Thrush, and Orange-crowned, Townsend's, and Wilson's Warblers. During migration, at medium to low tide levels, the extensive tidal flats here might hold Semipalmated Plover, Black Oystercatcher, Lesser Yellowlegs, Spotted Sandpiper, Black Turnstone, Surfbird, Sanderling, Semipalmated, Western, Least, and Rock Sandpipers, Dunlin, and Short-billed Dowitcher. Although rarities aren't mentioned here, don't forget to figure out in advance which Lower 48 species are considered rare in Alaska.

Site 5. Swan Lake. From the Centennial Building, take Harbor Drive north to Lake Street, staying on Lake Street as it follows the eastern edge of Swan Lake. A good vantage point is the peninsula jutting into the lake near the intersection with Degroff Street. Year-round residents include Great Blue Heron, Bald Eagle, Mew, Herring, Thayer's, and Glaucous-winged Gulls. Glaucous Gulls are possible in winter. Also, there might be Steller's Jay, Chestnut-backed Chickadee, Varied Thrush, and Dark-eyed Junco. Oregon Juncos outnumber Slate-colored Juncos by about 9:1 in winter. Slate-colored Juncos are unusual in summer. In migration you can expect to find Pied-billed Grebe, Double-crested Cormorant, Greater White-fronted and Canada Geese, Trumpeter Swan, Hooded Merganser, Tree and Barn Swallows, both kinglets, Swainson's Thrush, and Orange-crowned, Townsend's, and Wilson's Warblers. Ducks can include American Wigeon, Mallard, Northern Shoveler, Northern Pintail, Green-winged Teal, Canvasback, Redhead, Ring-necked Duck, Greater Scaup, and Bufflehead. By wandering through the neighborhood you might find Sharp-shinned Hawk, Wilson's Snipe, Rufous Hummingbird, Belted Kingfisher, Red-shafted Flicker, Savannah, Sooty Fox, Song, Lincoln's, Gambel's White-crowned, and Golden-crowned Sparrows, and Pine Siskin. Red-throated Loon, Ruddy Duck, Lesser Yellowlegs, American Pipit, and White-winged Crossbill are occasional.

Site 6. Gavan Hill and Sitka Cross Trail. Gavan Hill Trail is 3 miles long with the first 0.25-mile ADA-accessible. From the Centennial Building, turn right on Lincoln Street, then left onto Baranof Street for about four blocks to its end at the trailhead. This USFS trail continues on to join the Harbor Mountain Trail after intersecting Sitka Cross Trail (see map). Though it is easily accessible from downtown Sitka and offers varied habitats, birds here can be sporadic. See the current edition of *Sitka Outdoor Recreation Guide* for descriptions of this and other area trails.

Sitka Cross Trail is an easy 2.5-mile path skirting the base of Gavan Hill with varied habitats, including a large, open muskeg area and some forested sections. The trail is accessible from several places along its length, making it

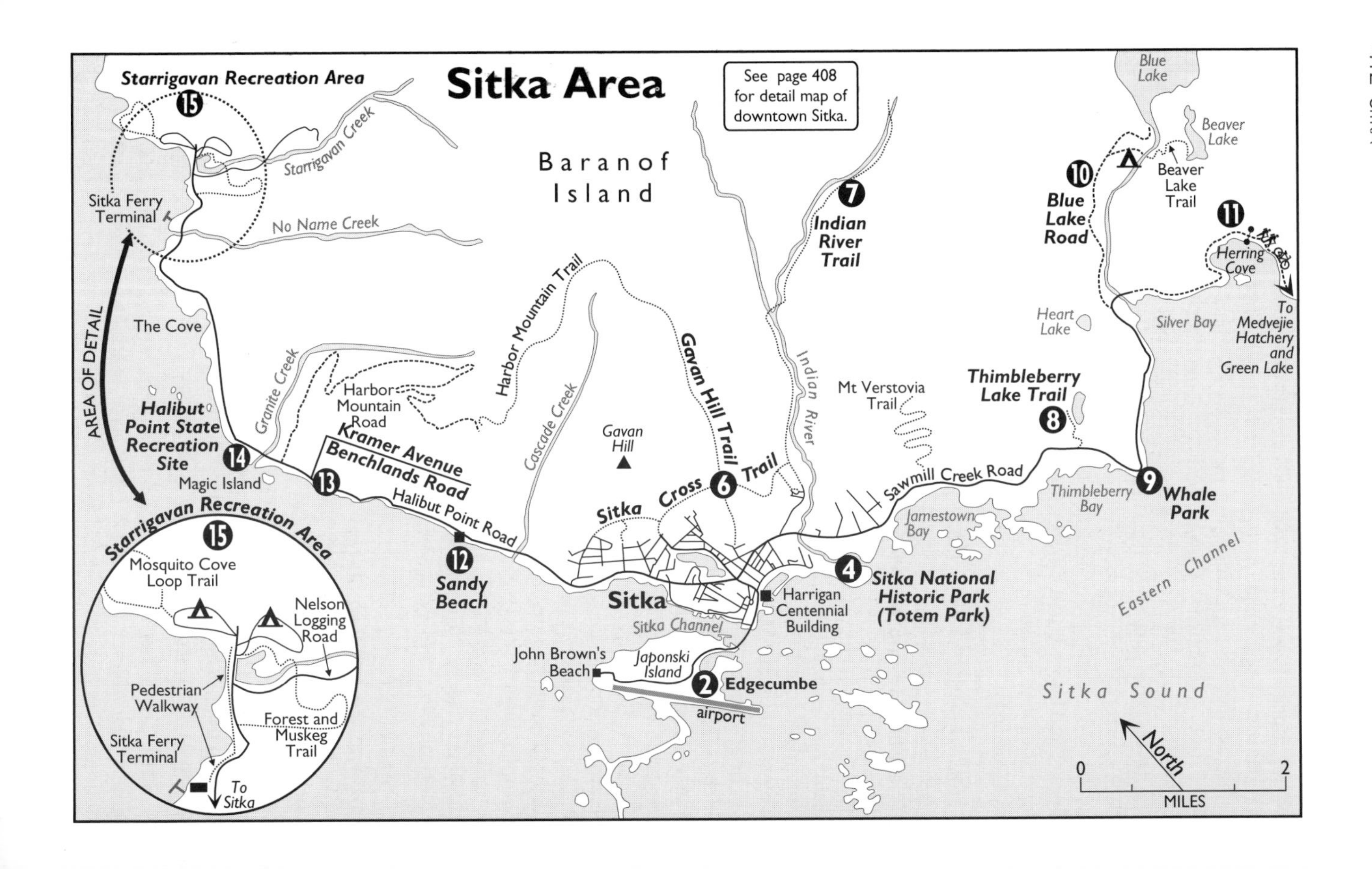
Sitka Area
See page 408 for detail map of downtown Sitka.
Baranof Island
Starrigavan Recreation Area
15
Starrigavan Creek
Sitka Ferry Terminal
No Name Creek
AREA OF DETAIL
The Cove
Granite Creek
Harbor Mountain Road
Harbor Mountain Trail
Halibut Point State Recreation Site
14
Magic Island
13
Kramer Avenue
Benchlands Road
Halibut Point Road
12
Sandy Beach
Cascade Creek
Gavan Hill
Gavan Hill Trail
Sitka Cross Trail
6
Sitka
Sitka Channel
Japonski Island
John Brown's Beach
2
Edgecumbe
airport
Harrigan Centennial Building
Indian River
7
Indian River Trail
Mt Verstovia Trail
4
Sitka National Historic Park (Totem Park)
Sawmill Creek Road
Jamestown Bay
Thimbleberry Bay
Thimbleberry Lake Trail
8
Heart Lake
10
Blue Lake Road
Blue Lake
Beaver Lake
Beaver Lake Trail
11
Herring Cove
Silver Bay
To Medvejie Hatchery and Green Lake
9
Whale Park
Eastern Channel
Sitka Sound
North
0
2
MILES
Starrigavan Recreation Area
15
Mosquito Cove Loop Trail
Nelson Logging Road
Pedestrian Walkway
Forest and Muskeg Trail
Sitka Ferry Terminal
To Sitka

possible for you to tackle short sections instead of committing to the entire distance—or you can use Cross Trail to connect to the Indian River Trail.

Site 7. Indian River Trail. A fairly easy 4.1-mile track. Follow Harbor Drive and Lake Street north to Sawmill Creek Road, go right to Indian River Road, turn left, and stay on Indian River Road to the trailhead to the left of the pump house. This heavily forested trail follows Indian River to a waterfall, passing through areas of open muskeg along the way. All Sitka-area passerines are possible here, including Red-breasted Sapsucker, Hairy Woodpecker, and American Dipper. At mile 0.4, Sitka Cross Trail departs to the left (see map).

You will need a car to reach Sites 8 through 15, located on Sitka's two 7-to-8-mile-long highways. Sawmill Creek Road runs south along the southwestern edge of Baranof Island to Herring Cove. From the Centennial Building and Lake Street, drive north and turn right onto Sawmill Creek Road at the four-way stop. At Mile 1.0, Indian River Road and trail access are to the left. A parking area on the right at Mile 1.5 leads to the back entrance to Sitka National Historical Park (Totem Park). At Mile 2.0, Eagle Way is on the right with a parking area and view of Sitka Sound.

Site 8. Thimbleberry Lake Trail and parking area are at Mile 3.75. This beautiful 0.25-mile trail is an easy walk; in fall and early winter it is possible to find Trumpeter Swans on the lake.

Site 9. Whale Park at Mile 4.25 has a boardwalk, several gazebos, and stairs that lead down to the water. Here you have an excellent view of the Eastern Channel and the entrance to Silver Bay. In late fall and winter these waters serve as feeding areas for marine mammals—Humpback Whale and Steller's Sea Lion—and seabirds, including Pacific and Common Loons, Double-crested and Pelagic Cormorants, Barrow's Goldeneye, Common Merganser, Surf, White-winged, and Black Scoters, Mew, Herring, Thayer's, and Glaucous-winged Gulls, Common Murre, Marbled Murrelet, and Rhinoceros Auklet. Glaucous Gull is possible in winter. Another parking area with good views of the channel is found at Mile 6.0.

Site 10. Blue Lake Road at Mile 7.0 is a narrow gravel road with restricted line of sight—drive slowly. (After snow accumulates in fall, and until spring avalanche danger is over, you will find the gate at the start of the road locked.) The road ascends through a mountain valley, then drops to creek level, where the USFS Sawmill Creek campground is located. Continue across the bridge to reach the Beaver Lake trailhead. The first part of this pretty one-mile gravel-and-boardwalk trail is steep. Along the way you might encounter Sharp-shinned Hawk, Northern Goshawk, Red-tailed and Rough-legged Hawks, Rufous Hummingbird, Pacific-slope Flycatcher, and various kinglets, thrushes, warblers, and sparrows.

Go back to Blue Lake Road, turn right, and drive about a mile to a parking area. (Do not drive down to the lake.) This drive offers beautiful scenery, wildflowers in season, and good birding, especially during nesting season; raptors can be seen in spring and fall. You can enjoy parts or all of this area best by walking the road and trails, which can be covered in two to three hours. (Don't climb in the rock areas unless you have climbing experience and proper gear.) Return to Sawmill Creek Road and turn left to continue the route. At Mile 7.1 from Sitka, the road crosses Sawmill Creek. Stop on the bridge beyond the industrial area to look for ducks and American Dipper. From here on the road surface is gravel.

Site 11. Herring Cove at Mile 8.0 is productive for both seabirds and passerines in season. In addition to the species found at Blue Lake, you might see Bufflehead, Barrow's Goldeneye, Common Merganser, Common Murre, and Marbled Murrelet here. The Medvejie Hatchery/Green Lake Road is closed by a gate, but walkers and bicyclists may continue on. The immediate area on each side of the road is brushy—cleared for a power line—and beyond the brush is typical southeast Alaska (Pacific coast) rain forest. To the right steep slopes fall away to fjord-like Silver Bay; to the left the mountainside rises abruptly. It is 3.4 miles to the Medvejie Hatchery and 6.8 miles total to Green Lake. The round-trip walk to power pole #53, where you can look for a Bald Eagle nest in a large tree to the left, is a mere three miles. During spring and fall migration and in nesting season you will find the birding rewarding and the scenery splendid along this road. Be sure to look seaward, where schools of Pacific Herring attract seabirds and marine mammals in winter.

North of Sitka is 7-mile-long Halibut Point Road and more good birding. From the Centennial Building and Lake Street, turn left onto Halibut Point Road at the four-way stop to follow the eastern shore of Sitka Channel. At the first left beyond the only traffic light on this road (Mile 1.0), turn in to Sitka Turnaround park to check the tidal flats, brush, and grassy areas. There are great views of Mount Edgecumbe from here, and during spring and fall migrations this an obligatory and productive birding stop. Pioneer Park and the Sea Mart parking lot are on the left at Mile 2.0, offering more good views of Sitka Sound with the added possibility of seabirds, including Harlequin Ducks, very close to the beach (except in summer). A gang of Common Ravens usually hangs out here, checking out pick-up-truck beds for food.

Site 12. Sandy Beach at Mile 2.5 might produce Pacific and Common Loons, Horned and Red-necked Grebes, and Double-crested and Pelagic Cormorants, especially during fall, winter, and spring. Look for shorebirds.

Site 13. Kramer Avenue is on the right at Mile 3.5, just before the Channel Club (2906 Halibut Point Road). You can't drive this road because the way is blocked by a very large rock beyond a parking area. Park and walk up the street to Benchlands Road, turn right, and continue on for a mile or more. This area often has passerines in season, and you might spot an active Bald Eagle nest. (Kramer Avenue is being reconfigured in 2002. When finished it will connect to, and will be the only entrance to, Harbor Mountain Road. At that time (2004) the entrance at Mile 4.25 will become a dead-end road. Check locally for the status of the construction when you visit Sitka.) Back on the highway, at Mile 4.25 and, depending on current road conditions, you might be able to drive or at least walk up the only road in Southeast Alaska that reaches the alpine—Harbor Mountain Road. Consult the *Sitka Outdoor Recreation Guide* for the latest information.

Site 14. Halibut Point State Recreation Site is accessible at Mile 4.5, with parking areas both south and north of Granite Creek, which bisects the park. This state recreation area has trails through the woods and along the beach, and at low tide you can walk to Magic Island from the south beach. (Make note of the time when the tide will turn!) Look for all three scoters, Long-tailed Duck, and Marbled Murrelet from ocean side of the island. Halibut Point has seabirds and shorebirds, including Black Oystercatchers. In the wooded areas you'll find nesting birds, including Red-breasted Sapsucker, Hairy Woodpecker, and Swainson's, Hermit, and Varied Thrushes.

Beyond Halibut Point the highway follows the shore through a less-populated area. Check out Old Sitka Rocks, a group of small islands and rocks, for seabirds except during breeding season; Black Oystercatchers are common here in summer. At Mile 5.5 a commercial area called The Cove contains marine-related businesses; in winter it's worth a stop to look for waterbirds. The road continues on through forest, with several water views to the left, to the Sitka Ferry Terminal, another good birding area during non-breeding seasons. Daytime parking at the terminal is free of charge.

Site 15. Starrigavan Recreation Area can be reached by a pedestrian walkway from the ferry terminal, or you can stay on the road which ends in less than a mile. The land beyond the ferry terminal is managed for year-round recreation use by a cooperating mix of city, state, and federal agencies. Brochures are available at kiosks to help you sort out the possibilities, which include a public boat launch, the Old Sitka State Historic Site, the Forest/Muskeg trail, Nelson Logging Road, the Starrigavan River and valley, and a USFS campground that straddles the road toward its terminus. A boardwalk with a bird-viewing deck skirts the estuary, with a spur leading to the campground. A footbridge over Starrigavan Creek connects the Estuary trail, Nelson Logging Road, and the Forest/Muskeg trail—and all of these trails connect with the pedestrian walkway at various places, allowing you to choose between short or long walks. In this area you can find many of the species mentioned above for Sitka, along with Great Blue Heron, Sharp-shinned Hawk, Northern Goshawk, Belted Kingfisher, Pacific-slope Flycatcher, American Dipper, and Lincoln's Sparrow. Birding is best here from April through September for passerines and from fall through spring for waterbirds.

At the far end of the bayside USFS campground is the start of 1.25-mile Mosquito Cove loop-trail. The first right turn takes you over a forested ridge and down a valley to Mosquito Cove. From there the trail follows the shoreline back to the campground. The alternative (and a good one) is to stay on the trail through the campground and then follow the shore. This route is easily accessible for most people, with just a few stair-steps, until you pass the first gravel beach. You will have marine views all the way to Mosquito Cove.

You can drive up Nelson Logging Road for a short distance. At about mile 1.0 is a parking area. A spur road to the right leads to the Sitka Shooting Range. On the far left of the parking area the logging road is gated, although walkers and ATVs may continue past the gate. A little over a mile beyond the gate the road forks, and if you reach this point on foot, bear right and read the following directions in reverse (the left fork is only a rough trail). A better alternative is to take a trail built for both ATVs and walkers that veers off to the right about half way between the gate and the fork. This trail crosses the river and follows an old logging path uphill. Then a new and very rough trail of shot-rock recrosses the river and connects with the right fork of Nelson Logging Road, where you can turn back to the left (north) to complete the loop. All of these trails are well-marked with USFS signposts. This is bear country, and it is important to stay on the trail and not step off into brushy areas. Observe the Bear Cautions cited above and on page 17 in the *Introduction.*

Belted Kingfisher

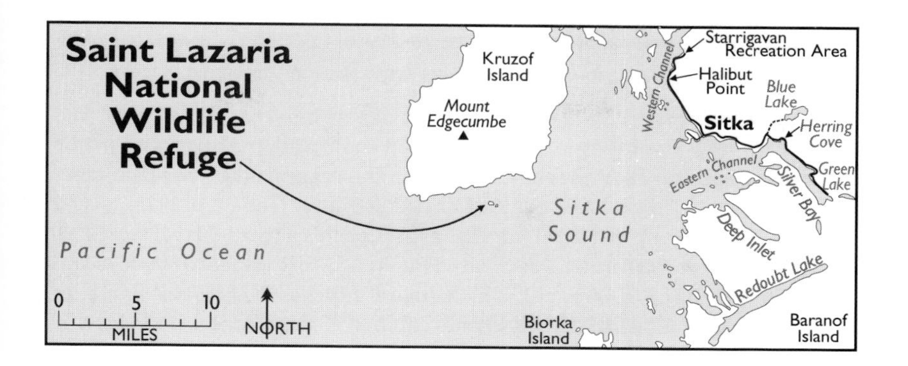

SAINT LAZARIA ISLAND

Located 15 miles southwest of Sitka off the southern tip of Kruzof Island, Saint Lazaria Island was created about 200,000 years ago by an upwelling of magma through a vent from the Queen Charlotte transform fault. The Mount Edgecumbe volcanic field (last eruption 4,000–5,000 years ago) is adjacent to it, forming most of Kruzof Island. Geologists think that Mount Edgecumbe is about 18 miles from the tectonic plate boundary on the North American side.

This exotic island has attractive lava formations, a saltwater pool with blowholes on the south end, and steep cliffs on the east, north, and west sides, rendering these areas almost unapproachable by small craft. Due to this relative inaccessibility, Saint Lazaria attracts hundreds of thousands of seabirds—mostly Leach's and Fork-tailed Storm-Petrels—to age-old breeding colonies. This important breeding area is now federally protected as part of the Alaska Maritime National Wildlife Refuge.

Due to its location at the edge of the open Pacific Ocean—with no barrier islands to moderate or deflect the incoming weather—current weather is a major factor in approaching Saint Lazaria.

It is dangerous to attempt going ashore on the island, even with experience and practice. Because the island is an ongoing research area, landing is discouraged. If you do go ashore, you must stay on the trails—wandering off-trail can cause burrow collapse and subsequent nesting failure.

On the north side is a cave where both Common and Thick-billed Murres nest; both species also use a nesting site on the southwest side. During the nesting season it is magical to anchor in the lee, turn off the boat's engines, and listen to—surprise! the songs of Hermit and Swainson's Thrushes and Fox and Song Sparrows. (You need to experience it before you realize that colonial alcids do not "sing" melodiously!) If you are lucky enough to be anchored near Saint Lazaria at night, you will find that several hundred thousand Leach's and

Fork-tailed Storm-Petrels make a heck of a racket when they return from their pelagic foraging to exchange nesting duties with their hungry mates.

Nesting seabirds arrive in early April and depart between mid-August and late September. Twenty-one species nest on the island, making this a major refuge in a region already overburdened with the responsibility for the safety of the next generation of scores of shorebird and seabird species. The numbers, taken from the 2001 survey, are: Leach's Storm-Petrel 660,000; Fork-tailed Storm-Petrel 326,000; Tufted Puffin 2,900; Rhinoceros Auklet and Common Murre 3,000 each; Thick-billed Murre 900; Bald Eagle 6; Glaucous-winged Gull 200; Black Oystercatcher 10; and Peregrine Falcon 2.

Any trip through the waters of Sitka Sound offers excellent opportunities to see the various marine mammals native to this area—Humpback, Minke, and Gray (in migration) Whales, Killer Whale, Dall's and Harbor Porpoises, Harbor Seal, Steller's Sea Lion, and Sea and River Otters.

With advance planning, it is possible to combine a visit to Saint Lazaria with a more extended pelagic trip. At the present time only one charter captain, Barbara Bingham, has the proper license to take passengers 20 miles offshore to the edge of the continental shelf. Contact her at Raven's Fire, Inc. (also the name of her boat) 888-747-4789; *www.ravensfire.com*. She offers trips to Saint Lazaria that includes an approach to Sitka Point, about two miles beyond Saint Lazaria, where there is a small colony of Horned Puffins, offering the opportunity of seeing both species of puffins. She also offers pelagic trips to the edge of the continental shelf that include Saint Lazaria and Sitka Point.

If you are able to join a boat traveling from Sitka to Saint Lazaria and then northwest along the ocean side of Kruzof and Chicagof Islands, you will travel ever-closer to the continental shelf, where the pelagic possibilities include Black-footed Albatross, Northern Fulmar, Sooty Shearwater, and a variety of jaegers, gulls, and terns.

Although you might not see any species at Saint Lazaria that are not readily found elsewhere in southeast Alaska, take a lesson from Alaskans—seize the opportunity to visit this breeding colony if the season and the weather are right rather than taking the uncertain chance of finding perfect conditions farther north.

Peregrine Falcon

LOGISTICS

The area code for all telephone numbers is 907 unless otherwise indicated. Tourist and travel services (accommodations, restaurants, attractions, etc.) not listed below can be found in the latest edition of The Milepost. *Statewide travel and birding information services are listed under Logistics in the* Introduction, *page 15.)*

Access: Sitka can be reached only by airplane or by ship. Several scheduled Alaska Airlines flights per day come in from Seattle and Anchorage. Some, but not all, of the Alaska Marine Highway ferries stop at Sitka. If you schedule an overnight or a several-day stop here and don't plan to bring your own vehicle, you can ride the shuttle buses that meet all ferries and commercial airline flights. Alternatively, rental cars from two companies are available at the Sitka Airport terminal, although advance reservations are advised during the busy summer season.

Accommodations: There are five hotels and motels in Sitka (depending on the season) and approximately 60 bed & breakfast establishments. The Sitka Convention and Visitors Bureau (303 Lincoln Street) supplies a packet of information that you can request by phone, mail, email, or download from the Internet. It includes guides to accommodations, transportation, wildlife tours, sightseeing, and much more. You may also ask for guides to visitor attractions, restaurants, shipping and services, and charter boat adventures. Contact the Bureau by phone 747-5940; fax 747-3739; email *scvb@sitka.org*; or visit the web site *www.sitka.org*. The United Methodist Church (747-8775) runs a hostel—open to all ages—June through August.

Parks and Campgrounds: There are two U.S. Forest Service campgrounds—one at the Starrigavan Recreation Area and the other on Blue Lake Road. Sitka National Historical Park (Totem Park) and three state parks are accessible from the road system; Magoun Islands, Big Bear/Baby Bear, and Sealion Cove State Marine Parks are reachable by one-day charter boat trips from Sitka. For park and trails details get a copy of the *Sitka Outdoor Recreation Guide* at the City or Visitors Bureau web sites. A brochure, *Finding Birds in Southeast Alaska—Sitka*, and a local bird checklist are available at Harrigan Centennial Hall (330 Harbor Drive) and at the Sitka Convention and Visitors Bureau. For information about parks and recreation areas, contact the City and Borough of Sitka Parks and Recreation Coordinator, 747-1852; fax 747-1856; or web site *www.cityofsitka.com*.

Sitka has a large commercial fishing fleet. Several of the nearly 60 charter boats offer wildlife eco-tours rather than sportfishing. The Sitka Charter Boat Association (747-4847) can put you in touch. Allen Marine Tours (*www.allenmarine.com*; fax 747-4819) offers wildlife tours using fast 48-passenger catamarans with two-hour trips scheduled each Wednesday, Saturday, and Sunday during tourist season. The 2001 cost was $52/person. Weather permitting, the Sunday trip visits Saint Lazaria National Wildlife Refuge to see the seabird colonies and marine mammals.

ACKNOWLEDGEMENTS: Thanks to Karla Zervos for general help and with the Swan Lake section, and to Vicky Vosberg and Barbara Bingham for their help with the Saint Lazaria and pelagic birding information.

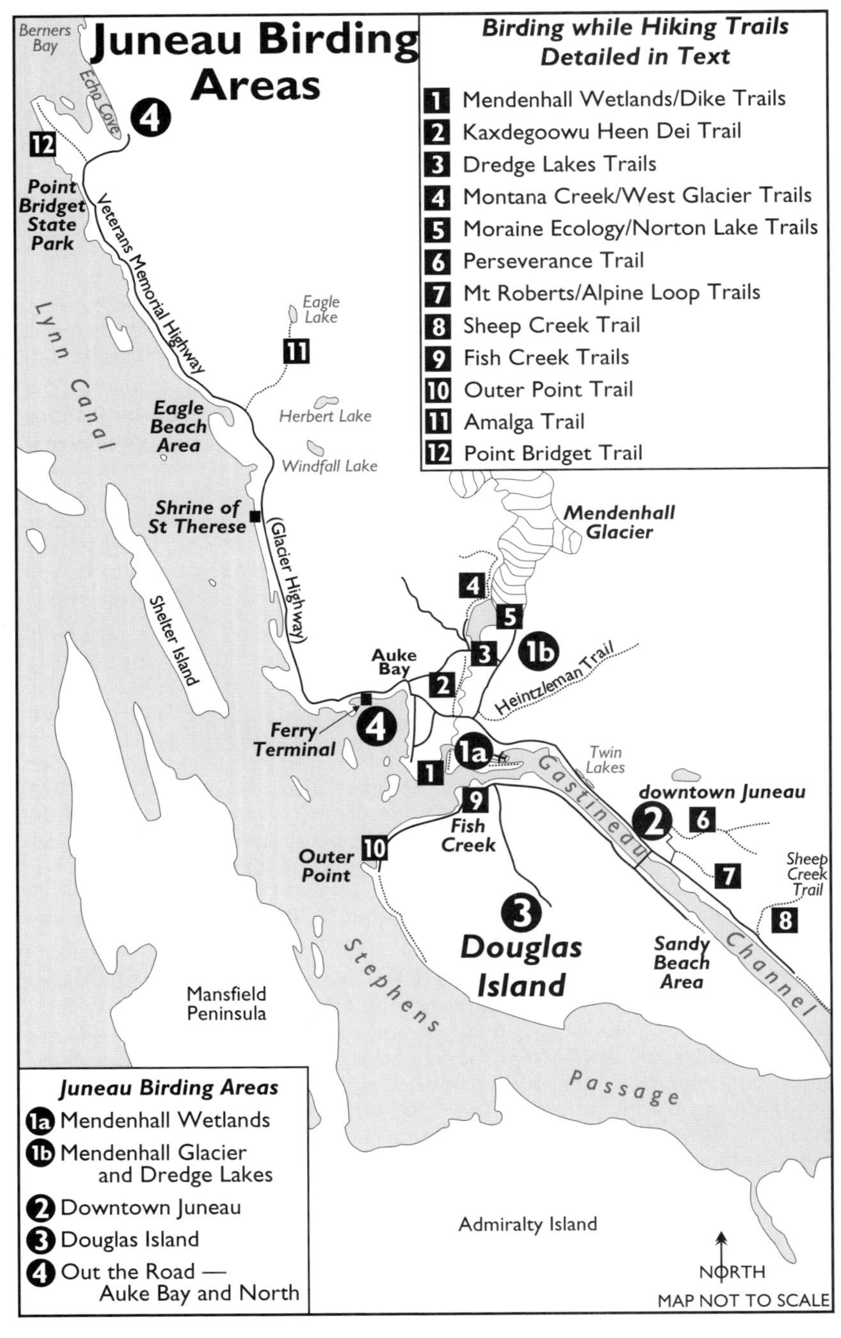
Juneau Birding Areas
Birding while Hiking Trails Detailed in Text
1 Mendenhall Wetlands/Dike Trails
2 Kaxdegoowu Heen Dei Trail
3 Dredge Lakes Trails
4 Montana Creek/West Glacier Trails
5 Moraine Ecology/Norton Lake Trails
6 Perseverance Trail
7 Mt Roberts/Alpine Loop Trails
8 Sheep Creek Trail
9 Fish Creek Trails
10 Outer Point Trail
11 Amalga Trail
12 Point Bridget Trail
Berners Bay
Echo Cove
Point Bridget State Park
Veterans Memorial Highway
Lynn Canal
Eagle Lake
Herbert Lake
Windfall Lake
Eagle Beach Area
Shrine of St Therese
(Glacier Highway)
Shelter Island
Mendenhall Glacier
Auke Bay
Heintzleman Trail
Ferry Terminal
Twin Lakes
Gastineau Channel
downtown Juneau
Fish Creek
Outer Point
Sheep Creek Trail
Douglas Island
Sandy Beach Area
Stephens Passage
Mansfield Peninsula
Admiralty Island
Juneau Birding Areas
1a Mendenhall Wetlands
1b Mendenhall Glacier and Dredge Lakes
2 Downtown Juneau
3 Douglas Island
4 Out the Road — Auke Bay and North
NORTH
MAP NOT TO SCALE

JUNEAU

Steven T. Zimmerman

Juneau is the capital of Alaska—and the only state capital that cannot be reached by road. Over 600,000 tourists arrive each summer on cruise vessels, while another 100,000 arrive on the Alaska Marine Highway System or on Alaska Airlines. What they find is a community confined to two narrow strips of land (mainland Juneau and Douglas Island) bordered by inshore marine waters and towering, 3,000- to 4,000-foot mountains. Within that area are a number of habitats, including Alaska's marine inside passage, estuarine wetlands, rocky intertidal zones, lakes, rivers, old-growth and new-growth forests, and alpine areas. Approximately 280 species of birds have been recorded in Juneau; it is the only site in Alaska where 200 species have been tallied by a single observer in one year.

Most of the birds that are regularly seen in Juneau are also found over much of the northwestern Lower 48 states and western Canada. Although an occasional Asian or Arctic vagrant may show up, Juneau is not a birder destination for such rarities. One notable exception is the Steller's Sea-Eagle that was first documented along the Taku River in 1989. This bird was regularly seen with the many nesting Bald Eagles at Swede Point until the late 1990s. Since 1997, however, it has been very difficult to locate, and although it is still occasionally seen in the Taku River area (summer 2001), few birders who have come to Juneau looking for it since 1997 have found it.

Juneau's linear road system stretches from Thane, about 5.5 miles south of downtown, to Echo Cove, approximately 38 miles northwest of Juneau. A bridge connects Juneau to nearby Douglas Island, and the road on Douglas Island extends from the town of Douglas on the southern end to Outer Point, approximately 12 miles north of the bridge. With few exceptions, birders arrive at the cruise ship docks in downtown Juneau, the Juneau International Airport, or the Auke Bay ferry terminal. Only a few of Juneau's best birding sites are accessible by public transportation, so those who do not bring their own vehicle by ferry will need to rent a car or taxi to reach the majority of sites described here. Taxis are expensive but they may be cost-effective if you want to go to only one or two sites near your point of arrival.

Like the rest of southeast Alaska, it rains a lot in Juneau. The best period to visit is from mid-April through early September when the rain is less pervasive and several sunny days may occur. March and early April, as well as mid-September through October, can be very windy and rainy. The November-through-February period is characterized by reduced daylight hours and often by freezing temperatures. Although the summer months are the mildest part of the year, travelers to Juneau at any time should come prepared for rain and temperatures in the mid-40s to low 60s° F. Rubber boots or waterproof hiking boots are a must. A tide book or the local newspaper should be consulted prior to venturing onto ocean beaches or marine wetlands. During certain times of the year the tidal range in Juneau can exceed twenty feet, and it is possible to get caught too far from the uplands with the tide coming in. See the Tidal Cautions in the *Introduction*, page 19.

Black Bears are found throughout Juneau and signs of these animals may be seen along almost any trail. Brown Bears are seen infrequently in the more-developed areas, although they occasionally may be encountered on trails away from town. Read the Bear Cautions in the *Introduction*, page 17.

JUNEAU AREA HABITATS

The primary bird habitats have been delineated by Armstrong and Gordon (1995) and can be summarized as follows.

Alpine and subalpine. Tree line ranges from 1,900 to 2,600 feet. Only a few trails lead to the alpine and subalpine areas, and consequently these are among the hardest habitats to reach. The easiest access is the aerial tramway from downtown to the upper slopes of Mount Roberts. If you would rather walk, the well-marked Mount Roberts Trail begins at the upper end of 6th Street and leads you to the same area by a 2-mile walk with a rise of approximately 2,000 feet. Granite Creek Trail, a spur off the Perseverance Trail (see Gold Creek Basin site), is one of the more accessible ways to reach the subalpine by foot. The Heintzleman Ridge Trail that begins just beyond the highway department building at about Mile 7 on the old Glacier Highway also provides access to subalpine and alpine areas. If you wish to avoid the steep, long, and often slippery walk, Temsco Helicopters can fly you from their base across from the Fred Meyers store to the top of Heintzleman Ridge in just a few minutes. Birds in alpine areas are not abundant, but Willow and Rock Ptarmigan, Blue Grouse, Golden Eagle, and Gray-crowned Rosy-Finch occasionally are seen there. Both Mount Roberts and Heintzleman Ridge are good areas for fall hawk-watching.

Spruce-Hemlock forests. Sitka Spruce and Western Hemlock are the predominant species in much of the forested land in Juneau. Many of the trails described in this chapter pass through extensive spruce-hemlock forests. Although the region has been logged extensively during the past 120 years, there are still some stands of old-growth spruce-hemlock forest remaining. The Outer Point Trail, approximately 11 miles from the bridge on North

Douglas Highway, offers a good opportunity to walk through old-growth forest. A wooden boardwalk makes it an easy hike. A number of species breed in old-growth forests—Red-breasted Sapsucker, Chestnut-backed Chickadee, Brown Creeper, Winter Wren, Golden-crowned Kinglet, Swainson's, Hermit, and Varied Thrushes, Townsend's Warbler, and one of the sooty races of Fox Sparrow (*P.i. chilcatensis*). Marbled Murrelets also nest high up in the trees of old-growth forests and can be heard or seen flying just before dawn almost any month of the year above the Eaglecrest Ski Area Road. The turnoff to Eaglecrest is a little less than six miles from the bridge on the North Douglas Highway.

Riverine areas. Many creeks and rivers in the Juneau area support large runs of salmon during summer and fall, primarily Pink (Humpback), Chum (Dog), and Silver (Coho). King (Chinook) Salmon released as smolts return to the release areas at Fish Creek (Mile 8 North Douglas Highway) or at the Douglas Island Pink and Chum Hatchery (DIPAC) (just past Mile 4 on Egan Drive). Sockeye (Red) Salmon may be seen near the Mendenhall Glacier Visitors Center. When the salmon are running, thousands of Bonaparte's, Mew, Herring, and Glaucous-winged Gulls, and smaller numbers of Thayer's Gulls, will converge on the river banks or outwash areas in search of an easy meal. American Dippers are occasionally seen picking along the stream bottoms. Bald Eagles and Northwestern Crows gather near the rivers and forage along the outwash areas. Black Cottonwood trees, which need large amounts of water to survive, often line river banks and house a variety of passerines, such as Alder and Pacific-slope Flycatchers, Chestnut-backed Chickadee, Golden-crowned and Ruby-crowned Kinglets, Swainson's, Hermit, and Varied Thrushes, American Robin, Orange-crowned, Yellow, Myrtle, Audubon's, and Wilson's Warblers, Common Yellowthroat (occasional), Oregon Junco, and other common birds of the Juneau area.

Lakes. The largest lakes are Auke Lake (approximately Mile 10 Glacier Highway) and Mendenhall Lake, which was formed by the melting of the Mendenhall Glacier. Other lakes and ponds productive for birding include Twin Lakes along Egan Drive, Dredge Lakes near the Mendenhall Glacier, the floatplane pond at the airport, and the ponds at Fish Creek along North Douglas Highway. These and other lakes or ponds may contain Red-throated Loon, Canada Goose, several species of ducks (American Wigeon, Mallard, Northern Pintail, Green-winged Teal, Greater and Lesser Scaup, Bufflehead, Common and Barrow's Goldeneyes, Hooded and Common Mergansers), and occasionally American Coot. Along the shorelines Greater and Lesser Yellowlegs, Spotted Sandpiper, Wilson's Snipe, several species of swallow, Yellow Warbler, and Northern Waterthrush may be found.

Estuarine wetlands. Mendenhall Wetlands State Game Refuge is a large marine wetland that extends on both sides of the Gastineau Channel from

Salmon Creek near the city of Juneau to past the airport. This is the best area for viewing migrating waterfowl and shorebirds in spring and fall. Thousands of Western and Least Sandpipers feed on these wetlands during late April through mid-May. As many as 21 species of shorebirds have been seen here on one day. Horned Lark, American Pipit, Savannah Sparrow, Lapland Longspur, and Snow Bunting (winter) favor the grassy areas of the wetlands. The fringing upland areas have been extensively diked, and the trees growing on or behind the dikes provide excellent habitat for Bald Eagle, Great Horned Owl, and songbirds. Several dredge islands also provide additional habitat for migrating birds and perches for Bald Eagle, Northern Harrier, Merlin, Short-eared Owl, and Northern Shrike. Because of the high diversity of habitats, species are seen here that do not occur elsewhere in Juneau. The Mendenhall Wetlands are the most extensively birded areas in Juneau. The marine wetlands at Eagle Beach are also very productive for shorebirds and waterfowl.

Marine waters and beaches. The waters and beaches of Gastineau Channel, Auke Bay, Favorite Channel, Stephens Passage, and Lynn Canal may be viewed from many sites along the road system. Although few birds will be seen from boats that cannot also be seen from shore during summer, there are many charter boats and whale-watching vessels that can be used to access marine waters. Inshore marine waters provide overwintering habitat for sea ducks (Harlequin Duck, Surf, White-winged, and Black Scoters, Long-tailed Duck, Bufflehead, Common and Barrow's Goldeneyes, Red-breasted Merganser) as well as Pacific and Common Loons, occasional Red-throated and Yellow-billed Loons, Horned and Red-necked Grebes, Mew, Herring, and Glaucous-winged Gulls, Pigeon Guillemot, and Marbled Murrelet. Many of these species are also found in at least small numbers throughout the year. Associated rocky beaches may have numbers of Black Oystercatchers, Wandering Tattlers, Ruddy and Black Turnstones, Surfbirds, Rock Sandpipers, and Northwestern Crows. Marine mammals that are often seen from shore include Steller's Sea Lion, Harbor Seal, Humpback Whale, Harbor Porpoise, and sometimes Killer Whale and Dall's Porpoise.

PRIMARY BIRDING AREAS

The vast majority of visitors to Juneau arrive on cruise ships, and birders will not have time to visit many of the sites described below before their ship leaves. The easiest sites to get to are Mount Roberts and Gold Creek Basin, both of which can be reached on foot. It is also possible to take one of the many buses or vans that transport visitors to Mendenhall Glacier, where birders can walk the Moraine Trail and possibly the trail to Norton Lake while their ship is in port. Since Mendenhall Wetlands is one of the most diverse and birdy sites, more-focused birders getting off cruise ships could take a taxi directly to the end of Radcliffe Road.

The primary birding locations in Juneau are grouped into four geographic areas: 1a. Mendenhall Wetlands and 1b. Mendenhall Glacier and Dredge Lakes; 2. Downtown; 3. Douglas Island; and 4. Out the Road. *All routes to these sites start at the junction of Egan Drive at 10th Street where the bridge from Douglas joins Egan Drive* (see Downtown Juneau map).

The area from the Mendenhall Wetlands to Mendenhall Glacier covers approximately five miles and provides access to many of the best birding habitats in Juneau, including Mendenhall Wetlands, the Brotherhood Bridge area, the Dredge Lakes area, and the Mendenhall Glacier trails, all located near the Mendenhall River. The two best sites are the Mendenhall Wetlands and the Dredge Lakes.

1a. MENDENHALL WETLANDS

Mendenhall Wetlands State Game Refuge is the most popular place to bird in Juneau. From the Juneau-Douglas Bridge and Egan Drive, head north on Egan Drive. Continue through the traffic lights at Glacier Highway and Vanderbilt Hill Road, past the K-Mart and Fred Meyers stores, to the light just past Nugget Mall (a little over 7 miles from the bridge intersection). Turn left onto Glacier Highway and drive past McDonalds and the turnoff to the airport (Shell Simmons Drive). Take the next left onto Berner's Avenue and follow it to Radcliffe Road. Turn left and drive past the sewage treatment plant to the parking lot at the end of the street. If you rented a car at the airport, pull out of the pickup area and bear left around the parking lot until you reach Shell Simmons Drive. Turn right and continue to Glacier Highway. Turn left for one block to Berner's Avenue, and follow the directions above.

During spring and summer several large cottonwoods around the parking lot often have singing Ruby-crowned Kinglets, Orange-crowned, Myrtle, Audubon's, and Wilson's Warblers, and other songbirds. Pine Grosbeaks are sometimes seen in the trees just to the right as you pass through the gate to Mendenhall Wetlands State Game Refuge. To the right of the gate is a white picket fence that protects an airport navigational aid. Dusky Thrush, Swamp Sparrow, and Eastern Kingbird, all very rare in Juneau, were found between the trail and the picket fence.

Because of the constant roar of airplanes coming and going, birders often move quickly past the end of the runway. Take a minute, however, to scan the banks of the Mendenhall River and the slough on your right as you walk toward the end of the runway. If the tide is not high, Greater and Lesser Yellowlegs, small flocks of Least Sandpipers or Dunlins, and both dowitchers are sometimes seen feeding here. Also, quickly scan the grass between the

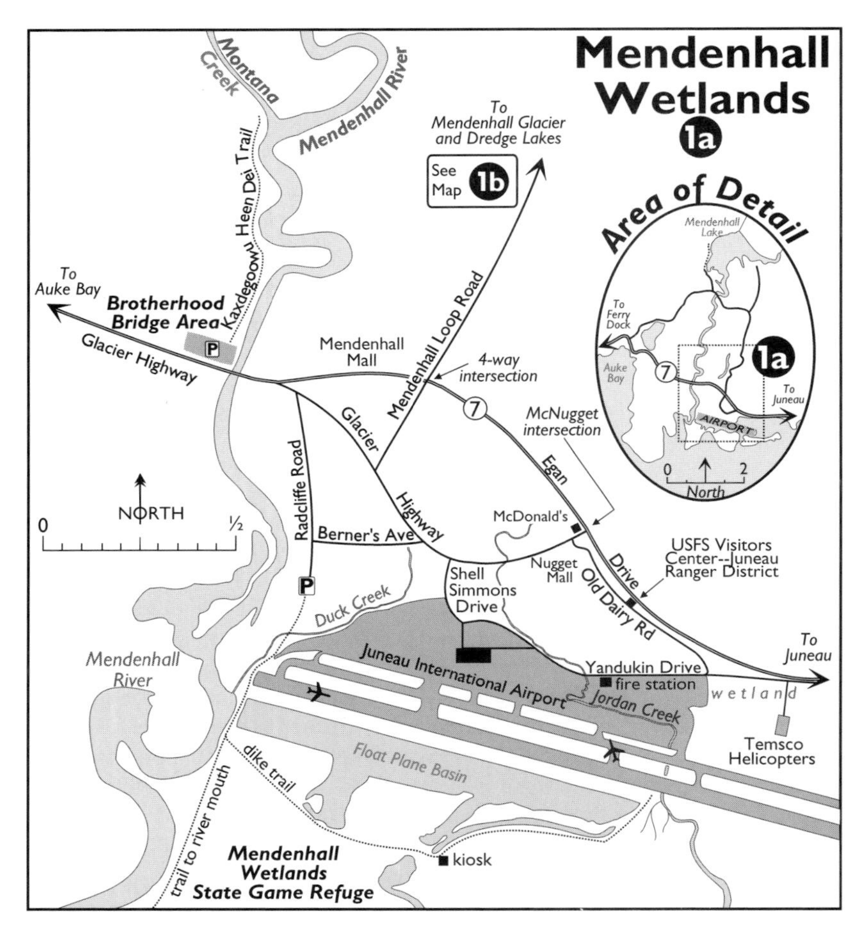

end of the runway and the fence—Pectoral Sandpipers sometimes feed here, and one of Juneau's few Buff-breasted Sandpipers was recorded at this spot.

Past the end of the runway, you have a choice of taking the Dike Trail, which soon makes an abrupt left and continues along the dike for a little more than a mile, or the Wetlands Trail, which drops off the dike and follows the Mendenhall River across the wetlands to the mouth of the river. If you don't have waterproof boots, take the dike trail, an easy one-to-two-hour hike. The Wetlands Trail is a somewhat more difficult hike, and the distance you walk is tide-dependent. Because going all the way to the river mouth can be tiring, it is best to walk the Wetlands Trail first if you have the proper footgear. The Wetlands Trail is most productive during spring and fall migrations; several of the species discussed below will not be seen during summer or winter.

Wetlands Trail. If possible, start your hike an hour or two before low tide so that you can follow the receding tide and reach the river mouth when the maximum area of mudflats is exposed. At low tide expect to spend about three hours hiking to the mouth of the river, birding there, and hiking back. Caution: On low tides, the last third or more of the hike will cross extensive mudflats and sloughs that are slippery and sometimes very soft, which can tire your legs quickly. When you stop to view birds, look for higher, drier, and firmer places to stand. If you stand still in the wrong place, your boots may begin sinking into the mud and it might be difficult for you to extract them. Don't go to this area alone if you have not been here before—you may need help getting you and your boots out of the mud. Although no birders have been lost to the mud, some have found themselves in precarious positions and have needed help to get free. See Tide Cautions in the *Introduction*, page 19. Make sure that you head back to high ground before the tide starts in since the sloughs fill in quickly and you may have to slog through deep water to reach high ground. Take a spotting scope with you because large flocks of shorebirds and rafts of ducks might be just beyond good binocular distance at the river mouth.

The trail starts down a steep bank and leads through an expansive area of grasses and sedges. In the upper grassy areas and sloughs look for American Pipit, Savannah Sparrow, Lapland Longspur, and an occasional Horned Lark. Snow Buntings may be seen in winter. American Golden-Plover (uncommon) and Least, Baird's (uncommon), and Pectoral Sandpipers prefer these higher tidal areas and sloughs, too. Vancouver Canada Geese are on these wetlands year round. During migration several additional races of Canada Geese feed here on sedges and other vegetation. In spring migration they are joined by Greater White-fronted and Snow Geese.

The trail follows the Mendenhall River before ending on the mudflats. In spring often large numbers of ducks use the river—American Wigeon, Mallard, Northern Shoveler, Northern Pintail, Green-winged Teal, Greater Scaup, Surf and White-winged Scoters, Long-tailed Duck, Bufflehead, both goldeneyes, and Red-breasted and Common Merganser are common. Uncommon or rare are Gadwall, Eurasian Wigeon, Blue-winged and Cinnamon Teal, and Lesser Scaup. When scanning from the river mouth into Auke Bay, you should look for Pacific and Common Loons, Horned Grebe, and Marbled Murrelet. Alaska's second sighting of Eared Grebe was made here in 2000. Bonaparte's Gulls and Arctic Terns are common at the river mouth, as are Mew, Herring, and Glaucous-winged Gulls. Annual sightings of California and Thayer's Gulls, Black-legged Kittiwake, Caspian Tern, and sometimes Ring-billed Gull occur. A Franklin's Gull was found in 1994, and Little Gull was seen on the Douglas side of the wetlands at Fish Creek in 2001 and 2002. If you are lucky, you might spot the Lesser Black-backed Gull that has been nesting in Juneau for several years. It nests in the gull rookery across Mendenhall Lake from the visitor center, and has been seen with other gulls on the Mendenhall Wetlands. Northern Harrier, Sharp-shinned and Red-tailed Hawks, American Kestrel, Merlin, Peregrine Falcon, Short-eared Owl, and Tree, Violet-green, Bank, Cliff, and Barn Swallows could turn up, usually during spring and fall migrations.

From the end of April through mid-May mixed flocks of Semipalmated Plover, Ruddy Turnstone, Surfbird, Western, Least, and Rock Sandpipers, and Dunlin may total many thousands. Black-bellied Plover, Whimbrel, Black Turnstone, both dowitchers, and occasional Hudsonian, Marbled, and Bar-tailed (casual) Godwits, Red Knot, Sanderling, and Semipalmated Sandpiper will be seen with the other shorebirds near the mouth of the river.

Leave the river mouth in plenty of time to cross the sloughs that will be filling as the tide returns. You can either walk directly back to the airport dike, or you may walk over to the dredge islands that will be on your right. These islands were made during the 1960s and 1970s when the Army Corps of Engineers was still dredging Gastineau Channel to maintain ship passage. Other than Savannah and Lincoln's Sparrows, passerines are not common here, but raptors use the islands for hunting. Bald Eagles commonly roost in the trees, and during migration Northern Harrier, American Kestrel, Merlin, Short-eared Owl, and Northern Shrike may be seen hunting over these islands or the nearby wetlands. Osprey, Swainson's and Red-tailed Hawks, Gyrfalcon, and Peregrine Falcon are less common. Arctic Terns have nested on one of the easternmost islands.

If you visit the dredge islands, you could continue back across the wetlands and a series of sloughs toward the wooden kiosk where the Dike Trail makes a sharp turn toward the runway. Once you reach the dike you can easily climb up to the trail and take it back to the parking area. Before doing so, check out the sloughs a little farther down the trail.

Dike Trail. This easy hiking trail is flanked by brackish marshes and ponds on the uphill side and by marine sloughs and ponds on the Gastineau Channel side. High tides can fill the sloughs, and on the highest tides of the year virtually the entire wetland on the channel side can be covered with water. As you begin the walk down the dike, note that Bald Eagles may be perching or nesting in the trees right above you. The trees are also home to many passerines, including Pacific-slope Flycatcher, Steller's Jay, Chestnut-backed Chickadee, Red-breasted Nuthatch, Golden-crowned and Ruby-crowned Kinglets, Hermit and Varied Thrushes, American Robin, Orange-crowned, Myrtle, Audubon's, Townsend's, and Wilson's Warblers, Song (*M.m. inexpectata*) and Lincoln's Sparrows, Oregon Junco, and Pine Siskin.

Northwestern Crows nest in some of these trees and Black-billed Magpies and Common Ravens are sometimes seen here. Great Horned Owls occasionally sit in the trees during the daylight hours. Species such as Barred Owl, Common Nighthawk, Belted Kingfisher, Yellow-shafted and Red-shafted (rare) Flickers, Olive-sided Flycatcher, Western Wood-Pewee, Northern Shrike, Western Tanager, American Tree, Gambel's White-crowned, and Golden-crowned Sparrows have been sighted. Several years ago a small flock of Black-crowned Night-Herons took up residence in the trees near the far end of the trail, and a Great Egret was seen for several days in 1992 feeding in the floatplane marsh.

About one-quarter mile down the Dike Trail, the trees give way to a marshy area that is connected to the airport floatplane pond. The usual puddle ducks are common, Canvasback, Redhead, and Cinnamon Teal are rare, and Ruddy Duck is casual. During spring migration Semipalmated Plover, both yellowlegs, Western and Least Sandpipers, Dunlin, and both dowitchers occur.

On the Gastineau Channel side of the trail you can usually add Northern Shoveler, Bufflehead, and Common and Barrow's Goldeneyes to the above list, along with an occasional Eurasian Wigeon or Blue-winged Teal. Great Blue Herons sometimes feed in the ponds, and Trumpeter and Tundra Swans might come by in spring or fall. A wide variety of shorebirds stop over during migration—this is one of the few areas in Juneau where Stilt Sandpiper and Wilson's Phalarope have been seen.

You can continue for several hundred yards past the Boy Scout kiosk to the end of the trail at an airport fence. Going the extra distance lets you check a few more marine sloughs. If you climb the dike you can look for any activity on the slough that lies along the back side of the dike.

1b. DREDGE LAKES

The Dredge Lakes Area is part of Mendenhall Glacier Recreation Area, managed by the U.S. Forest Service. Stop at their visitor center to pick up a free map (8645 Old Dairy Road; see Mendenhall Wetlands 1a map).

Seven small freshwater lakes comprise the Dredge Lakes, some man-made gravel pits and others the result of glaciation. The existence of these lakes, along with large numbers of relatively mature deciduous trees (willow, cottonwood, and alder), makes this one of the most diverse habitats in the Juneau area. Local rarities such as Wood Duck, Cassin's Vireo, Blackpoll and Black-and-white Warblers, and Brown-headed Cowbird have been found here. Warbling Vireo and American Redstart, seldom found elsewhere in Juneau, are annual here. It is also one of the best places to look for Western Tanager and Northern Waterthrush. Because Beavers have

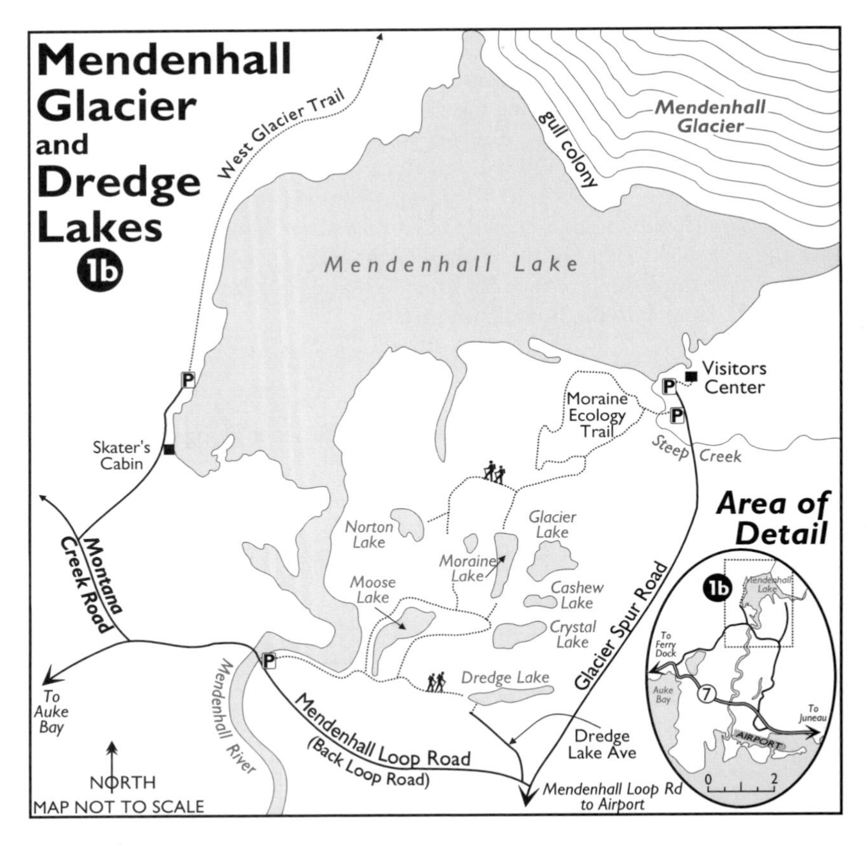

flooded part of the area, it is no longer possible to cover the whole Dredge Lakes site from one trail, so the southern area is covered below, and the northern part will be described in the Mendenhall Glacier section.

The lakes and small ponds breed large numbers of mosquitoes and other irritating insects—wear a long-sleeved shirt and long pants and use insect repellent. Black Bears use the area.

To reach Dredge Lakes from downtown, travel about 8 miles on Egan Drive from the Douglas Island bridge and turn right onto Mendenhall Loop Road. If you are returning from Mendenhall Wetlands, go back along Radcliffe Road to its end at Glacier Highway, turn left, and drive a short distance to the extension of Egan Drive. Turn right and drive about one-half mile to the large, four-way intersection, where you will turn left onto Mendenhall Loop Road. If you are coming from the airport, drive around the parking lot, following the signs for Mendenhall Valley and take a right at Shell Simmons Drive. At Glacier Highway turn left and stay on Glacier Highway until it meets

Mendenhall Loop Road, where you bear right and continue across Egan Drive on your way to Mendenhall Valley. (See Mendenhall Wetlands 1a map for all of these options.)

Drive up the Loop Road toward the glacier for about two miles, staying on the Loop Road when it makes a left turn toward Auke Bay. Locals refer to this stretch as the Back Loop road. Drive about a mile to the Mendenhall River bridge and park on the right just before the bridge. Covering the Moose Lake and Crystal Lake areas will take about an hour, but if you want to visit all of the lakes accessible here, it can take considerably longer.

The trail begins on the right side of the parking lot and follows the Mendenhall River for about one-third mile. To the left is a great view of the glacier, and to the right you might hear a Northern Waterthrush singing from a very wet area. Townsend's Warblers also could be heard along this stretch, and Spotted Sandpipers are sometimes spotted bobbing along the riverbank.

As the trail enters a woody area, it climbs a dike that contains a fish weir. Once on the dike, turn left and walk down the long, straight dike trail as it parallels Moose Lake on the right. American Redstarts are here annually in small numbers by early June, and Warbling Vireos have been found several times along this part of the trail.

After a few hundred yards you leave the dike to enter a more open area with many trails. There is no "right" way to go here, so it is best to listen and look for songbirds such as Gray-cheeked Thrush, Northern Waterthrush, Common Yellowthroat, Western Tanager, and other species that are not commonly found in Juneau. Since the lakes can contain Red-throated Loon, Trumpeter and Tundra Swans, Canvasback, Redhead, Ring-necked Duck, Hooded Merganser, and very rarely Pied-billed Grebe, Wood Duck, and American Coot, it is also worthwhile to check the larger and more accessible water bodies if you have time. Carefully note your route so you can find your way back to the trail by the river. If you get lost, remember that the area is bordered by the Mendenhall River on the west and the highway to the glacier on the east; Mendenhall Glacier is to the north.

One relatively quick route to follow after entering the more open area is to walk straight ahead (east) on the widest trail to Crystal Lake (500 yards distant). Scan Crystal Lake, then turn right (southwest) and follow the long, wide, and straight dirt road that takes you back toward Moose Lake. In a few hundred yards you will see Moose Lake on your right through the trees. Bear left and continue walking along the same road for another few hundred yards to another well-worn road that takes off to the right just before a culvert passes under the road. If you go to the right, you will walk past the end of Moose Lake and up onto the dike where you started. If you do not turn right, you can continue along the road, reaching Dredge Lake in about five minutes.

Red-throated Loons are sometimes seen on Dredge Lake, and American Redstarts are found here. After scanning Dredge Lake, retrace your steps to the trail by the culvert and return to your car. If you want to save a little walking time, you can view Dredge Lake from the end of Dredge Lake Avenue—the turnoff is on Back Loop Road just after it heads toward Auke Bay (see map).

Montana Creek Road. You can reach another productive birding area from the Back Loop Road. Drive across the bridge and continue toward Auke Bay for a little less than one-half mile. Turn right onto Montana Creek Road, which forks at about one-third mile. The right fork takes you past Mendenhall Lake Campground on the west shore of the lake. Skater's Cabin is a great place for a photo stop. The West Glacier Trail begins from the north end of the parking lot at the end of the road and leads through a mixed forest of cottonwood, alder, willow, Sitka Spruce, and Western Hemlock. After several minutes of walking, the trail climbs over a rocky area and the forest opens up as you approach the west side of the glacier. In spring and fall the bare rocky areas near the edge of the glacier are possible places for White-tailed Ptarmigan. Although you can actually walk onto the glacier at this point, doing so is not recommended.

The left fork on Montana Creek Road takes you past the Juneau Gun Club and the Community Garden, and soon breaks out into an open marshy area with several dead trees. Montana Creek is on your left. Check the marshy area for Red-breasted Sapsucker, Common Yellowthroat, and Rusty Blackbird. MacGillivray's Warbler has been heard here, as have the other more common warblers. The road continues up a hill and passes a rifle range on the right. The next one-quarter mile has been one of the better places in Juneau to look for Tennessee Warbler.

1b. MENDENHALL GLACIER

Mendenhall Glacier is one of Juneau's best-known landmarks. To reach it from Egan Drive, turn onto Mendenhall Loop Road and continue directly to the glacier in 3.5 miles. At the end of the road, park in the first paved lot on the left as you approach the visitor center. From there you can walk down past the visitor center to Mendenhall Lake. There is a gull colony across the lake on the rocky slope to the left of the glacier. A Lesser Black-backed Gull has taken up residence here for the past several years and, if you have a spotting scope, the gull might be picked out among the Herring and Glaucous-winged Gulls. There is a small Arctic Tern colony on the sand island that can be seen from the Photo Point Trail in front of the visitor center. Vaux's Swift is sometimes seen in this area.

The Moraine Ecology Trail leads into the trees from the far edge of the first parking lot. Many of the local kinglets, thrushes, warblers, sparrows, and other passerines will be found along this trail. Also, it is one of the better areas to look for Warbling Vireo, Western Tanager, and Chipping Sparrow. Walk down the steps and across the bridge over Steep Creek (heavily used by Sockeye Salmon in the summer). In about 25 yards the trail appears to split three ways. The trail leading left presently has a wooden bench where it branches off and is not heavily birded. The middle trail will take you clockwise around the Moraine Ecology Trail. The trail heading right will take you counterclockwise around the same trail. The Moraine Ecology Trail is an easy 1.5-mile, 30–45-minute loop that can be walked in either direction through early successional growths of mixed stands of alder, willow, cottonwood, spruce, and hemlock that developed as the glacier retreated. Some areas along the trail have been ice-free longer than others and those stands are denser and taller. Regular species here are Ruby-crowned Kinglet, Hermit and Varied Thrushes, American Robin, Orange-crowned, Yellow, and Wilson's Warblers, Lincoln's Sparrow, and Oregon Junco. Warbling Vireo, Swainson's Thrush, and Northern Waterthrush are occasional. Chipping Sparrows are rare in the more open areas. When you reach the part of the trail paralleling Mendenhall Lake, take one of several side-trails down to the beach to look for Semipalmated Plover, Killdeer, Spotted Sandpiper, and Arctic Tern.

The trail to Norton Lake. Norton Lake is one of the birdiest locations in Juneau, with regulars such as Yellow, Myrtle, and Audubon's Warblers, Northern Waterthrush, American Redstart, and other passerines. Species found here that are otherwise uncommon or rare include Wood and Ring-necked Ducks, Hooded Merganser, Olive-sided Flycatcher, Northern Rough-winged Swallow, Cedar Waxwing, Blackpoll Warbler, Common Yellowthroat, and Brown-headed Cowbird. Juneau's only Black-and-white Warbler was discovered here, and locally uncommon Rusty Blackbird is a possibility. It is worth a trip to Norton Lake if you have an hour or so and waterproof boots. To get there start out on the part of the Moraine Ecology Trail that leads clockwise around the loop. After 5 to 10 minutes of walking you reach a signpost with arrows pointing to the parking lot and to the Moraine Ecology Trail. At this junction take the trail heading to the left over a marshy area with planks to walk on. Bear right when you come to a branch off the trail and continue walking for 10 to 15 minutes. Continue past the trail to Moraine Lake on your left and continue several hundred yards to a more open area where three or four trails appear to meet. Take the trail to the left that forks after about 50 yards. Either fork takes you through a wet area that may require wading. The trail then becomes wide, and more-or-less dry, for about 200 yards. Then it gets very wet again for several hundred yards. There is a path along the right edge of this part of the trail that reduces the need for slogging through water. About 200 yards into this section of the trail you will find a narrow muddy trail that takes off to the right. This trail takes you toward a flooded area where many of the trees have died. Northern Waterthrush can often be heard singing in the upper parts of the dead trees in May and June. Continuing on this trail will take you to Norton Lake. There are a couple of paths through the vegetation that will give you vantage points to view the lake.

BROTHERHOOD BRIDGE

To reach Brotherhood Bridge from the Douglas bridge, travel west on Egan Drive past the intersection with Mendenhall Loop Road (see map 1a). A few hundred yards past Mendenhall Mall on the right, cross over Brotherhood Bridge and pull into the large parking area immediately on your right.

Looking north toward the glacier you will see a large meadow. Paved and well-marked Kaxdegoowu Heen Dei Trail (Tlingit for "going back to the clearwater trail") crosses this meadow and heads into a stand of trees about one-quarter mile away. Before starting down the trail, check the trees on the west side of the parking lot for warblers and the occasional flycatcher. Keep an eye on what might be flying overhead—during summer Vaux's Swifts and several species of swallows feed over the meadow and the river. Bank Swallows nest in some areas of the river bank. One of Juneau's rare sightings of a Northern Rough-winged Swallow was from here. During migration, this is a good location for Northern Harrier. Wilson's Snipe, Savannah and Lincoln's Sparrows are common in the meadow.

As the trail heads into the woods, check a small grove of willow and alder on the left for Alder Flycatcher, Warbling Vireo, and Cedar Waxwing, along with some of the more common passerines. A very rare Willow Flycatcher was seen here several years ago, and a Cassin's Vireo was here in May 2002. The trail parallels the river through mixed deciduous/coniferous forest until it meets Montana Creek about one mile (15–20 minutes) from the parking lot. Along the way, walk out onto the large footbridge over the river to scan upstream and downstream for views of the feeding swallows. The confluence is a good place to look for Alder Flycatcher and Common Yellowthroat. One of Juneau's few sightings of Magnolia Warbler was nearby.

After reaching Montana Creek, the Kaxdegoowu Heen Dei Trail continues along the Mendenhall River all the way to River Road, about two miles from the parking lot. Although this is not a particularly birdy area and the round trip is a long one, Western Tanagers may sometimes be heard singing along the trail as it nears River Road. Other birds might include Merlin, Downy and Hairy Woodpeckers, Chestnut-backed Chickadee, Winter Wren, both kinglets, American Robin, Varied Thrush, and the common local warblers.

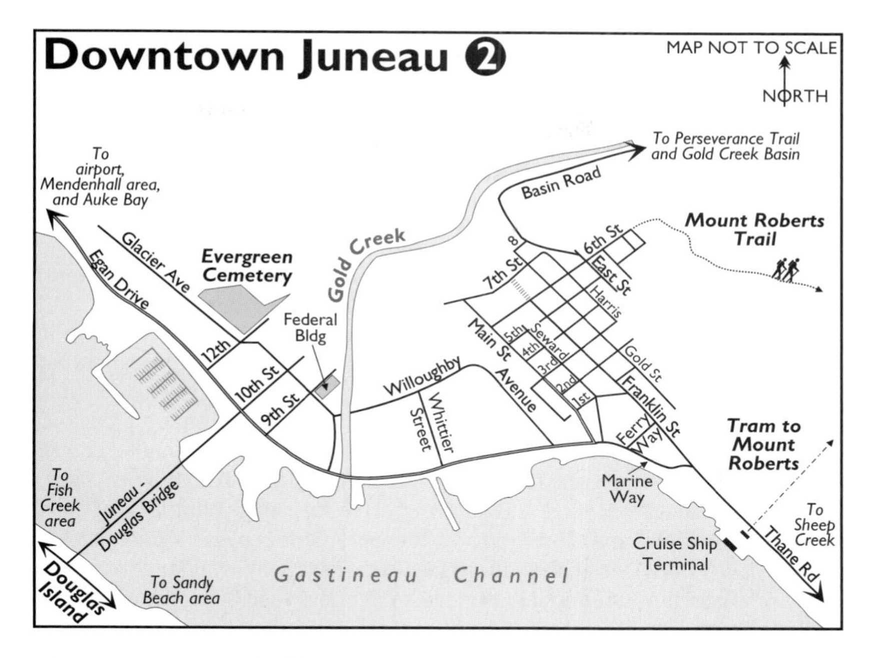

2. DOWNTOWN JUNEAU

Airport to downtown. Exit the airport on Yandukin Drive which merges into Egan Drive, following signs for downtown. Before merging, and just past the fire station on the right, is a wetland area that has been partially filled by Temsco Helicopters. (See Mendenhall Wetlands map.) In spring this is worth a stop to look for Mountain Bluebird. Also seen are the occasional Northern Harrier, Red-tailed Hawk, American Kestrel, Merlin, Short-eared Owl, and, rarely, Swainson's and Rough-legged Hawks, and Gyrfalcon.

Another place to scan along the way to town are the two small lakes that comprise Twin Lakes. Turn left at the Vanderbilt Hill Road traffic light, drive a few hundred yards to Glacier Highway, and turn right. Both lakes can be seen well from pullouts along Glacier Highway. In fall and spring migration Mallard, Greater Scaup, and Common Merganser are here daily, with American Wigeon and Green-winged Teal less regular. Redhead and Ring-necked Duck are occasional; Ruddy Duck is rare. These ponds are one of the best places to look for Hooded Merganser and American Coot.

Glacier Highway eventually crosses Salmon Creek to intersect with Egan Drive at a traffic light. For an interesting stop cross over the expressway onto Channel Drive and make a quick right into the radio-station parking lot. From the far end of the lot you have a close view of the mouth of Fish Creek, where large numbers of ducks and gulls congregate during salmon season. When you leave the parking lot you can either return to Egan Drive or continue your fish-watching side-trip by turning right to follow Channel Drive to the fish hatchery. When the salmon are returning to spawn, the hatchery is a very active place and you can learn much about the life cycle of salmon there. If you are heading out from downtown, turn right at the Glacier Highway traffic light to get to Twin Lakes, or turn left onto Channel Drive to visit the mouth of Salmon Creek.

Downtown. Downtown Juneau is an historical area that developed following the discovery of gold in 1880. Most of the local, state, and government employees who live in Juneau work there. It is also the arrival point for hundreds of thousands of cruise-ship tourists. Although most downtown areas are very built-up, species such as Glaucous-winged Gull, Rock Dove, Northwestern Crow, Common Raven, Chestnut-backed Chickadee, and European Starling live here year round. In summer many of the common passerines are found in yards or on the surrounding hillsides. Gastineau Channel provides a wintering area for large numbers of Surf Scoters, Buffleheads, and Common and Barrow's Goldeneyes. Winter flocks of Bohemian Waxwings and Pine Grosbeaks occasionally wander through in search of Mountain Ash berries. American Dippers feed along Gold Creek, most regularly where it passes in back of the Federal Building on 9th Street. Evergreen Cemetery and 12th Street provide some easy inner-city birding for a variety of birds—Hermit Thrush, American Robin, Varied Thrush, Bohemian Waxwing, Pine Grosbeak, and Pine Siskin. A rare Mountain Chickadee visited a feeder on 12th Street several years ago.

Gold Creek Basin. Gold was discovered in 1880 in Gold Creek, and for several decades thereafter the Gold Creek Basin above Juneau was filled with mining buildings and equipment. In the 60 or so years since hard-rock mining petered out, this formerly bustling area has recovered somewhat from human impact. The old mining area is now covered with trees, including some of the densest stands of deciduous species in Juneau. The preponderance of willow, alder, and cottonwood, along with a very dense understory of broadleaf vegetation, makes this a great place to look for passerines. For visitors with limited time, particularly those who come by cruise ships, this is a quickly accessible area. A short taxi ride or a half-hour walk (uphill) will take you to birdy areas along Basin Road.

Here, MacGillivray's Warblers may be found, and rarities such as Tennessee Warbler and Palm Warbler turn up occasionally among the more common local warblers. Warbling Vireo, Gray-cheeked Thrush, American Robin, Hermit, Swainson's, and Varied Thrushes, Winter Wren, Sooty Fox Sparrow, and Oregon Junco are all found here. Western Screech-Owls are heard some nights. The best months to bird the basin are May and June, when many of the birds are singing.

To reach Gold Creek Basin take Franklin Street or Main Street from the waterfront up the hill to 6th Street and turn right. Continue to East Street and take a left. East Street becomes Basin Road and continues uphill past several homes and across a long plank bridge. Basin Road ends in a parking area about a mile from the bridge. Perseverance Trail begins at the parking lot, by an old pelton-wheel air compressor. The trail is wide and well-maintained, so hiking boots or rubber boots are not necessary. Biting flies and mosquitoes are sometimes a problem, however.

After you climb for about 200 yards, you reach a wider trail. Bearing left here leads downhill to Basin Road, where another left brings you back to the parking area, a loop trip of about a mile. Many of the birds that occur in Gold Creek Basin can be found along this loop, and a more extensive walk in the basin will not necessarily add new birds to your list.

If you turn sharply right where the trails meet, you can continue along Perseverance Trail for almost 3 miles—it's about a mile to Ebner Falls, 2 miles to the Granite Creek trailhead, and about 3 miles to the end of Perseverance Trail. Several lookout points showcase panoramic views of Gold Creek and the surrounding mountains. Ebner Falls is reached in about 20–30 minutes. A trail to the top of Mount Juneau branches off to the left after you pass Ebner Falls. Soon after passing the Mount Juneau trailhead you walk through a narrow stand of spruce and then break out into an area with many low willows and a dense cover of Indian Rhubarb. Here you should pause to look for MacGillivray's Warblers and other passerines. One of Juneau's few Palm Warblers was seen here. The trail continues along for another mile, crossing Gold Creek three times and passing through an area dominated by alder, willow, and cottonwood. Granite Creek Trail, taking off to the left, is narrow and relatively steep, about 1.75 miles long, and leads to the subalpine. Rock Ptarmigan and occasional White-tailed Ptarmigan are seen along this trail. Golden Eagles sometimes soar overhead. Granite Creek Trail can be muddy, with patches of snow persisting into early summer some years.

Mount Roberts. The tramway to the 1,800-foot level of Mount Roberts offers the easiest access to the subalpine in Juneau. Located on Franklin Street where the cruise ships dock, tram cars leave every few minutes between 9 AM and 9 PM from May through September. In 2002 a round-trip cost $21.95.

Once you get off the tram, head for the nature center to check the blackboard listing recent sightings of birds and mammals. Naturalists working in the center might be able to help you find the locations where these sightings were made.

Half-mile-long Alpine Loop Trail that departs the nature center is popular with cruise-ship tourists in summer. The trail quickly passes through the forest to the subalpine meadows that characterize much of the area above timberline. There are interpretative signs along the trail and spectacular views of Gastineau Channel. Both Rock Ptarmigan and Blue Grouse have been seen with chicks above timberline along this trail. It's also a good place to find Hermit Thrush, Golden-crowned Sparrow, and Gray-crowned Rosy-Finch, as well as the more-common American Pipit and Savannah and Fox Sparrows. About half way around the loop, a side-trail leads to Father Brown's Cross (one-half mile) and on to Gastineau Peak (two miles) and Roberts Peak (3.1 miles). Most people stop near the cross, but you should continue about 50 yards beyond the cross to an outcrop that is one of the best fall hawk-watching spots in Juneau. Bald Eagle, Northern Harrier, Sharp-shinned and Red-tailed Hawks, American Kestrel, and Merlin are the most frequently seen species flying near the ridge tops. Northern Goshawk, Rough-legged Hawk, Golden Eagle, Gyrfalcon (rare), and Peregrine Falcon also have been recorded.

Near the upper tram terminal a branch off the Alpine Loop Trail takes you down the Mount Roberts Trail to Juneau. The trail is about two miles long and takes about 90 minutes to cover. Though part of the trail has been improved with planks, steps, and bridges, there are several muddy areas and tree roots that make the trail somewhat difficult to walk. Hiking boots or rubber boots are needed even in good weather. Although not particularly birdy, Mount Roberts Trail offers an opportunity to walk through the spruce-hemlock forest that characterizes much of southeast Alaska. The lower end of the trail is at the end of 6th Street, a 15-minute walk from the waterfront. By walking down 6th Street and then down Gold Street to 5th Street, you will be able to walk by Saint Nicholas Russian Orthodox Church. The Alaska Capitol Building is on 4th Street a block down and a couple of blocks farther on.

Sheep Creek Valley. Sheep Creek Valley is home to many passerines that are not common in Juneau. It is probably the best place to find MacGillivray's Warbler. Because the valley trends east toward the interior of Canada, and is rimmed by high alpine areas, it is also the best place in Juneau to look for Golden Eagle. To reach Sheep Creek Trail travel south from the Mount Roberts Tramway on Thane Road for a little over three miles. Turn onto a dirt road, park just beyond the trail sign, and walk across the dirt road to the trailhead.

It takes about 45 minutes to climb from the road through a dense forest to the area where the trail starts down into Sheep Creek Valley. The climb is steep, often muddy, and can pass close to edges where it is possible to fall some distance if you lose your footing. People who do not like to take moderately difficult trails probably should avoid this trail.

As you crest the trail the valley opens up before you and the trail descends toward Sheep Creek. Start to listen and look for MacGillivray's Warbler. The next 1.5 miles traverse very birdy areas where you may see or hear an assortment of the locally common flycatchers, thrushes, warblers, and sparrows. Keep an eye on the sky for Golden Eagle, Sharp-shinned Hawk, and other raptors that may suddenly appear. Listen for hooting Blue Grouse. Scope the upper levels of the surrounding hillsides for ptarmigan flying about. Other species that might be seen in the valley include Osprey, American Dipper, American Redstart, and possibly Blackpoll or Tennessee Warblers. Sheep Creek Valley was named for the Mountain Goats found in this valley, a misidentification by Joe Juneau and Richard Harris, Juneau's founders.

After about 1.5 miles the trail begins a steep climb to the subalpine. Many birders choose not to continue the hike, and if you don't go on, the round-trip takes about three hours. If you continue, add another two to three hours to your planned hiking time. Up in the alpine it is sometimes possible to find Rock and White-tailed Ptarmigan.

When you get back to your car, drive south for a short distance to the mouth of Sheep Creek, where there is a fish hatchery. During summer and fall, when salmon are returning, gulls abound. Ring-billed, Thayer's, Slaty-backed, and Glaucous have occurred among the myriad more-common gulls that gather here to stuff themselves.

Least Sandpiper

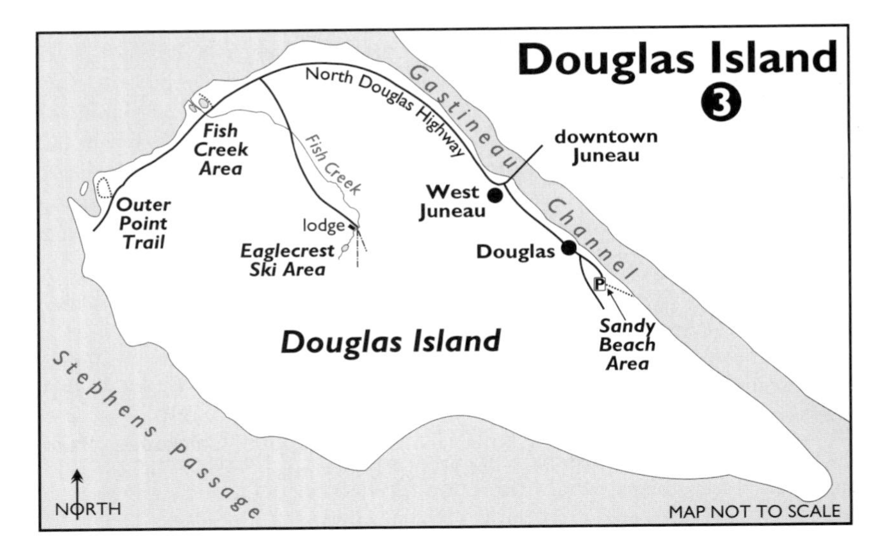

3. DOUGLAS ISLAND

Douglas Island is separated from mainland Alaska by the narrow marine waters of Gastineau Channel. Cross the bridge from the intersection of Egan Drive and 10th Street. Turn left for a little over two miles on Douglas Highway to the town of Douglas. (If you turn right you can drive almost 12 miles along North Douglas Highway to the road's end near Outer Point.) Note that the mileage signs along both highways are not measured from either end of the bridge. Distances on Douglas Island are measured from the point where traffic turns off the bridge onto either Douglas Highway or North Douglas Highway.

Sandy Beach. To reach Sandy Beach, and also to visit the town of Douglas, turn left at the end of the Juneau-Douglas Bridge. You can stop along the way to scan Gastineau Channel for sea ducks. The first stop is just over the bridge at the Breeze-In Grocery, and the second is in a little over one-half mile farther, where there is a pullout with stairs that lead part way down to the beach. Stop at the library in Douglas if you want a free copy of the map and historic guide to the Treadwell Historic Trail which starts at Sandy Beach. Continue through Douglas and bear left to Douglas Boat Harbor when the road forks at about Mile 2. At the end of the road turn right and park near the public shelters at Sandy Beach.

A paved trail begins on the uphill side of the shelters and soon enters a woody area just past the Treadwell Historic Trail sign. Several different trails lead through the forest, weaving past interesting relics of Douglas' mining history. Many local birders stay on the uphill trails all the way past the cave-in (site 15 on the map and historic guide) until they reach the beach after a 25–30-minute walk. To follow this route stay on the main trail for one-quarter mile until it rises to intersect a trail coming down from the right. Turn left onto that trail and stay on it for 200 to 300 yards. Bear left, staying on the main trail wherever the trail forks. The trail will parallel the beach, some distance above it until it reaches a concrete overlook above the cave-in area. Up to this point the trail has been very wide and possibly smooth enough to allow wheelchair access. The trail continues downhill for several hundred yards until it crosses an area of blue clay and ends at the beach.

The woods along the trail system are very lush, with many tall alder and cottonwood trees and a diverse, dense understory, where you will find many of the common passerines. Also look for Sharp-shinned Hawk, Northern Goshawk, Downy Woodpecker, MacGillivray's Warbler, and Western Tanager. Rarities such as Boreal Owl, Black-capped Chickadee, Palm Warbler, Ovenbird, and Black-headed and Rose-breasted Grosbeaks have been found here.

North Douglas Highway. North Douglas Highway parallels Gastineau Channel for about eight miles as it heads north from the Douglas-Juneau bridge. There are a couple places to pull off to scan the channel for ducks or other waterbirds—the mobile-home park at Mile1.5 and a pullout at Mile 2.5.

Eaglecrest Ski Area. The turnoff to the ski area is almost six miles from the bridge, where a left turn will take you five miles to the ski lodge. Waterproof boots are needed if you plan to do much hiking in the alpine meadows. The paved road begins its ascent to the lodge by passing through a large muskeg area where Blue Grouse might sometimes be seen feeding along the road. Red-breasted Sapsuckers nest in some of the dead trees. If you pull off the road at higher elevations just before dawn, Marbled Murrelets can be heard—and sometimes seen—almost any day of the year as they fly back and forth between their nesting area in the forest and nearby marine waters.

To the left at about Mile 4.5 planked Treadwell Ditch Trail heads out across a patch of muskeg. Although muskeg is not used by many birds, a short walk down this trail will give you an opportunity to examine a type of habitat widespread throughout southeast Alaska. Muskegs are wetlands that develop over very long time periods in poorly drained areas. They are dominated by peat mosses that are often a foot or more thick. The wet, nutrient-poor soils that develop in muskeg do not support rapid growth of plants, thus, the stunted Shore Pines and other conifers you see growing bonsai-like on the higher hummocks may be over 100 years old! Greater Yellowlegs is one of the few muskeg-dependent birds, nesting in the mosses on the ground.

After a few hundred yards the planks end and the trail enters a spruce-hemlock forest. Look along the muskeg/forest ecotone for

Orange-crowned and Wilson's Warblers. The trail continues for another 12 miles to meet the Dan Moller Trail leading into the town of Douglas. Birders will want to turn around a few hundred yards after entering the spruce-hemlock forest.

The ski area does not operate during the summer, but hikers are free to walk wherever they wish. Open alpine meadows under the ski lifts lead to ridges above the lodge where Willow Ptarmigan are sometimes seen, but most of the meadows are wet and solid trails do not exist for more than a few hundred yards. The area around the lodge is not particularly birdy, although eagles and ravens can be seen overhead, and Lincoln's Sparrows are common. Blue Grouse, Hermit and Varied Thrushes, Orange-crowned Warbler, and Oregon Junco can be heard. Be alert for small flocks of Red or White-winged Crossbills and listen also for Pine Siskins. You might spot raptors such as Sharp-shinned Hawk, Northern Goshawk, or Merlin; both Western Screech-Owl and Great Horned Owl have been reported and Townsend's Solitaire has put in a rare appearance.

Fish Creek. Fish Creek flows under the North Douglas Highway at about Mile 7. There are two old dredge ponds, one on each side of the creek. The pond on the east side by the parking lot is contained; the other has been breached so that tidal waters flow in and out. During July and August Fish Creek and the west pond are filled with returning Chum and Pink Salmon. Coho Salmon and hatchery-released King Salmon also return to Fish Creek. Below the ponds, the mouth of Fish Creek widens into an estuary with salt marshes, sloughs, and a large area of intertidal flats.

There are trails along each side of Fish Creek that lead to Gastineau Channel. Because of the diversity of habitats here, both trails traverse good birding areas. If you have limited time, it may be best to drive over the bridge and pull off onto the highway shoulder so you can walk the trail on the west side of the creek first. Walking to the end of this trail takes about 15 minutes. The trail starts at a gate, passes through a mixed stand of trees for about 100 yards, and then breaks out into the open as you begin to approach the west pond. Pacific-slope Flycatcher, Chestnut-backed Chickadee, Orange-crowned, Myrtle, and Audubon's Warblers, Song and Lincoln's Sparrows, and Oregon Juncos are common; Gambel's White-crowned and Golden-crowned Sparrows are here in migration; Warbling Vireo and Red-breasted Nuthatch are occasional; in winter 1999 a Brambling spent several days on the upper end of the trail. In addition, Bald Eagles are frequently seen in the tall spruce; Northern Pygmy-Owls are rare. The pond holds Bufflehead and Barrow's Goldeneye in winter and spring and Belted Kingfishers year round.

The trail skirts the left side of the pond, then passes through a stand of alders. Before entering the trees walk a few yards to the left to check out the slough that parallels the trees. When the grasses have grown up, this slough is not very evident, so it is a good hiding place for ducks and the locally very rare Swamp Sparrow that spent the summer there in 2000.

Follow the trail through the trees for about 200 yards until it breaks out again near the end of the west pond. During summer Northwestern Crows nest in the trees by the pond and can be very vocal, perhaps unintentionally attracting Northern Goshawks that sometimes snag crows for lunch in this area. The trail continues over a tidal slough and up onto a dike that was constructed to hold the northwest end of the pond. This is a good vantage point. Listen for singing Common Yellowthroats as you walk up onto the dike to check out the salt pond on your right, a good area for yellowlegs and other shorebirds. To the left you have a good view of the adjacent marine waters, where several species of ducks can be seen almost any time of year and shorebirds sometimes feed along the beach.

The trail continues a couple hundred yards—marine waters on the left and an estuary possibly full of hundreds of resting or feeding ducks on the right. The trail circles around Entrance Point with its large stand of trees and superb views of the western end of Gastineau Channel. On lower tides large numbers of gulls and ducks feed here, Caspian Terns among them on occasion. An adult Little Gull was seen here in 2001, and an immature bird was seen in 2002. Juneau's only Black Tern was here in 2002.

While you are at Fish Creek, check out the freshwater pond on the east side of the bridge. In addition to the more-common species, Redhead and Ring-necked Duck are sometimes here, and Pied-billed Grebe and American Coot are very rare. The stand of alders between the large east side parking lot and the river sometimes holds Alder Flycatcher, Warbling Vireo, or Western Tanager. Red-breasted Sapsuckers also use this area, and Vaux's Swifts and several species of swallows may feed overhead.

The trail along the east side of Fish Creek begins at the east end of the parking lot and passes through a dense stand of trees where you can find the usual warblers, including Townsend's, singing in the conifers. Golden-crowned Kinglets are often in the conifers, just before the trail breaks out onto the intertidal flats. Take a moment, before you lose your cover, to scan the flats, particularly in the morning when the sun will be at your back.

Because Fish Creek is easily accessible and has such a diverse number of habitats, local birders visit it frequently. Although most trips do not turn up any great rarities, the area has gained a reputation as a vagrant trap. In addition to the birds mentioned above, some of the local rarities that have been found over the years include Cooper's Hawk, Western and Eastern Kingbirds, Black-capped Chickadee, Palm Warbler, and Evening Grosbeak.

When you leave Fish Creek, continue out the highway to the North Douglas Boat Launch a little past Mile 8. For the next two miles the road hugs the shoreline, with spectacular views of Mendenhall Glacier, the mouth of the Mendenhall River, and Auke Bay. Look along here for marine birds—Pacific, Common, and Yellow-billed Loons, Horned and Red-necked Grebes, Greater Scaup, Surf and White-winged Scoters, Long-tailed Duck, Bufflehead, Common and Barrow's Goldeneyes, Common and Red-breasted Mergansers, Bonaparte's, Mew, Herring, and Glaucous-winged Gulls, Pigeon Guillemot, and Marbled Murrelet.

From fall through early spring, the area inshore from the boat landing could have large rafts of Mallards with smaller numbers of American Wigeon, Northern Pintail, Green-winged Teal, and an occasional Eurasian Wigeon.

Outer Point Trail. Outer Point Trail, located at a large pullout area about Mile 11 North Douglas Highway (approximately one-quarter mile past the 12-mile marker), provides one of the best opportunities in Juneau to walk through a variety of habitats, starting with old-growth spruce/hemlock forest, passing through a muskeg area, and then reaching the beach. The old-growth forest has many towering, mixed-age Sitka Spruce and Western Hemlocks, with a well-developed understory of Devil's Club, blueberry/huckleberry, and ferns. The first one-quarter mile (don't take the right turn a few yards down the trail) takes about 10 minutes to walk and passes by a very pretty pond with lily pads, and then climbs slightly to an open muskeg area. The trail continues across the muskeg and drops down to the beach near the mouth of Peterson Creek. Although this is not a particularly birdy route, it's a good place to see and hear Red-breasted Sapsuckers drumming, or to find Pacific-slope Flycatcher, Chestnut-backed Chickadee, Winter Wren, Golden-crowned Kinglet, the usual thrushes, and Fox Sparrow. The protected waters near the mouth of Peterson Creek are heavily used by waterfowl, especially in winter.

The rest of the Outer Point Trail meanders northeast (away from Peterson Creek) along the beach and then loops back into the forest for about 0.75 mile, where it eventually meets the trailhead. There is not a lot new to see along this segment of the trail, and many birders return to their cars by backtracking through the muskeg. The entire trail is maintained and all of the forested segments are planked for easy walking.

Over the years the Outer Point Trail became heavily used by tour companies. This led to some conflicts with local trail users. During summer 2001 the City of Juneau constructed an alternative trail for commercial use—the Rainforest Loop Trail—so that the Outer Point Trail could be returned to local users. The new trail is located about one-quarter mile before the Outer Point Trail (the parking area straddles the 12-mile marker). It has several segments, some of which are still being completed. Both trails go through similar habitat and should produce similar birds.

4. OUT THE ROAD

Juneau residents often refer to the area north of Auke Bay as "out the road." Auke Bay is a small residential area about 2.5 miles west of the four-way intersection where the Mendenhall Loop Road meets Egan Drive (about 10.5 miles from the Juneau-Douglas Bridge). Distances "out the road" will be given from this intersection unless otherwise noted.

Traveling northwest on Glacier Highway, you soon pass the Brotherhood Bridge parking area after one-half mile (see page 434). At about Mile 2 you will see Auke Lake on your right. This large lake often has good numbers of geese and ducks, especially in the fall when hunting on the Mendenhall Wetlands drives waterfowl to areas where hunting is not permitted. Scan the lake from the pullout or from vantage points along the west end of Mendenhall Loop Road that intersects Glacier Highway in Auke Bay.

Before you reach Auke Bay, at a little over two miles on Glacier Highway, a wide turnoff to the left leads to Fritz Cove Road and the east side of Auke Bay. The road ends at Smuggler's Cove, where you have good views of a sheltered saltwater area that is a winter home for sea ducks, primarily Surf Scoter, Long-tailed Duck, Bufflehead, Common and Barrow's Goldeneyes, and Red-breasted Merganser. Pacific and Common Loons, Horned and Red-necked Grebes, Common Murre, Pigeon Guillemot, and Marbled Murrelet are seen here occasionally and on other waters in Auke Bay.

Western Screech-Owl

Between the village of Auke Bay and the Alaska Marine Highway ferry terminal (4.5 miles on the Glacier Highway), stop along the road to scan the waters of Auke Bay. One of the better places is the Auke Bay Harbor, reached by turning left at DeHart's store as soon as you reach Auke Bay. Another good

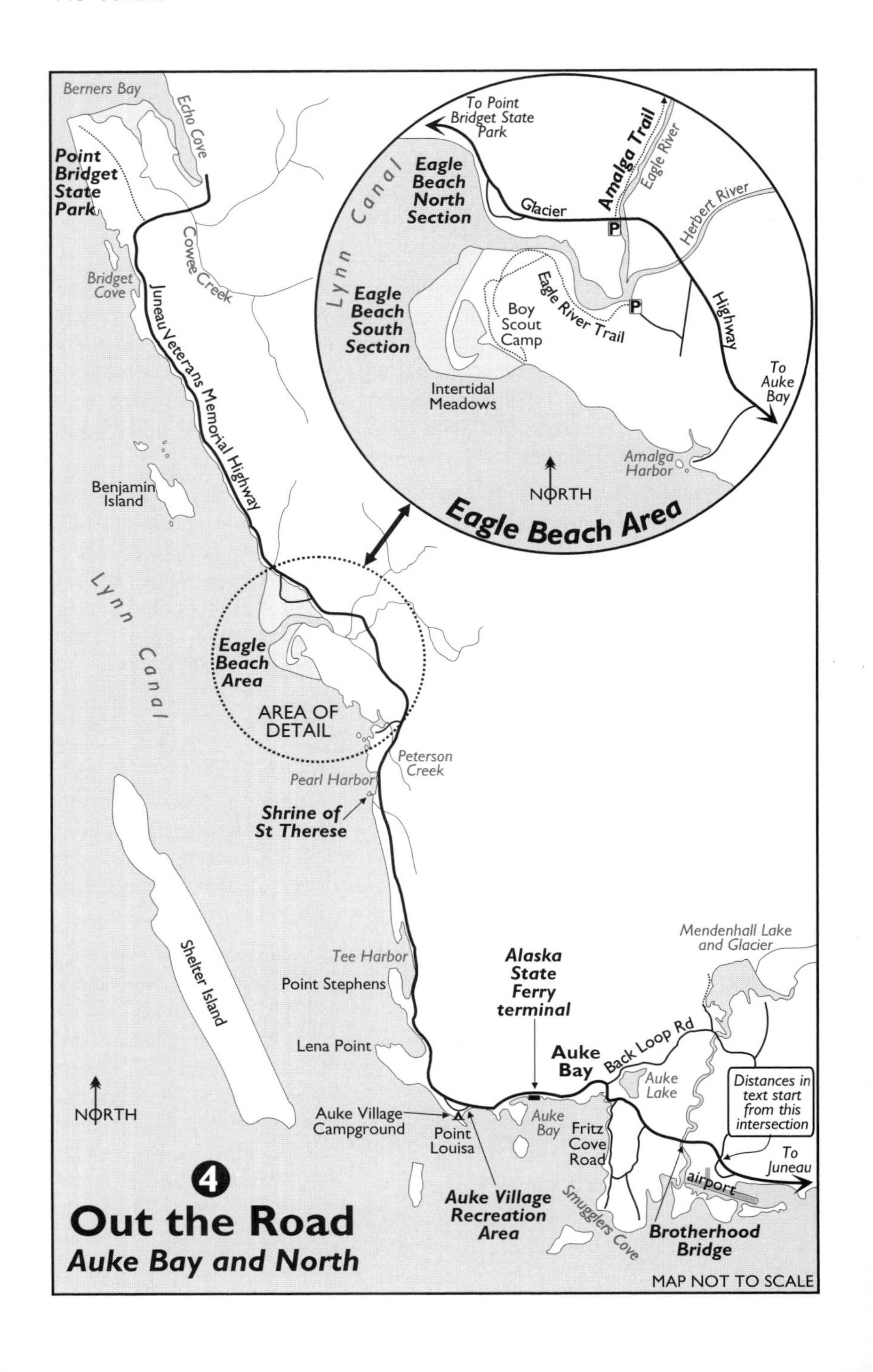

Berners Bay
Echo Cove
Point Bridget State Park
Bridget Cove
Cowee Creek
Juneau Veterans Memorial Highway
Benjamin Island
Lynn Canal
Eagle Beach Area
AREA OF DETAIL
Peterson Creek
Pearl Harbor
Shrine of St Therese
Shelter Island
Tee Harbor
Point Stephens
Lena Point
Auke Village Campground
Point Louisa
Auke Village Recreation Area
Alaska State Ferry terminal
Auke Bay
Back Loop Rd
Auke Lake
Fritz Cove Road
Smugglers Cove
Mendenhall Lake and Glacier
Distances in text start from this intersection
To Juneau
airport
Brotherhood Bridge
NORTH
To Point Bridget State Park
Amalga Trail
Eagle River
Herbert River
Glacier
Highway
Eagle Beach North Section
Eagle Beach South Section
Boy Scout Camp
Eagle River Trail
Intertidal Meadows
To Auke Bay
Amalga Harbor
Eagle Beach Area
4
Out the Road
Auke Bay and North
MAP NOT TO SCALE

area is just past the ferry terminal where the beach shallows up and becomes a wide, enclosed mudflat at low tide. Small fish often become trapped in tide pools here as the tide recedes and large numbers of eagles and gulls may use the area for feeding in the spring. It is also used by several species of ducks year round.

At about Mile 5 turn left toward Auke Village Recreation Area. Auke Village Campground is near the end of the road. Take the one-way loop through the campground, and about half way around stop at a small parking area on the right. Cross the road to a short trail that leads to Point Louisa at the end of a narrow peninsula. This is the best place in Juneau to look for Black Scoter. It is also one of the better locations for Pacific and Common Loons, Horned and Red-necked Grebes, Pelagic Cormorant, Harlequin Duck, Surf and White-winged Scoters, Long-tailed Duck, Common Murre, and Pigeon Guillemot, and the occasional Yellow-billed Loon.

The beautiful Shrine of Saint Therese, located on a small peninsula that juts into the waters of Stephens Passage, is at about Mile 13 along Glacier Highway. Look here for Harlequin Duck and other sea ducks. Since the shrine is close to the Steller's Sea Lion haulout on Benjamin Island, pods of these animals, along with Humpback Whales, can often be spotted from here.

Beginning at about Mile 14 you'll traverse a long stretch of wet meadows. If you have time, drive slowly through this area with the windows down (keeping a watchful eye on the traffic coming up behind you) so you can listen for singing birds—flycatchers, swallows, warblers, sparrows, and other passerines can often be heard. Common Yellowthroats like this habitat, and you could also spot a Red-tailed Hawk or a Barred Owl (rare).

At about Mile 14.5 (approximately 0.3 mile past the 24-mile marker) turn left to Amalga Harbor. This short road takes you over Peterson Creek and ends at a boat ramp. The harbor is very pretty and some of the common waterfowl and passerines might be around.

Eagle Beach. There are two very different sections to Eagle Beach. At the south section, reached by turning left at about Mile 17 (past the 26-mile marker, just before the Eagle River bridge), you can walk across a wide expanse of tidal meadows on the way to a protected cove where the Juneau Boy Scout Camp is located. The north section is located along the highway at Mile 18. Stop here to scope the mouth of the Eagle River and its broad tidal flats that are exposed on lower tides. Many years ago there was a bridge over Eagle River that connected these sections, and both were easily accessible, but since the bridge washed out, it has been a much longer walk to get to the broad wetland meadows.

South Section. The trail that takes you along the south side of Eagle River and out to the Boy Scout Camp is found by turning left off the highway at about Mile 17 (past the 26-mile marker, just before the Herbert River bridge). Drive to a fork, bear right, and park at the end. The trail leads you through a mile or so of spruce-hemlock forest and bogs. Eagle River will be on your right. The trail eventually breaks out of the woods into a more open area with good views of Eagle River and the waters of Lynn Canal. In spring both Mountain Bluebird and Townsend's Solitaire may occur here along with the more-common Savannah and Lincoln's Sparrows. During migration several species of puddle ducks are seen at the mouth of the river.

When the trail divides, you can walk along the dirt road that follows the river bank, or you can bear left through a stand of trees for a few hundred yards. Both routes will take you to the wide intertidal meadows and sloughs that characterize this part of Eagle Beach. Large numbers of Vancouver Canada Geese are resident, joined during migration by Greater White-fronted and Snow Geese. Migrant Northern Harriers and Short-eared Owls cruise over the meadows; American Kestrel and Merlin are occasional. Stay to the left of the meadows to follow the trail that takes you about one-half mile to the Boy Scout Camp and the wide sandy beach that extends around the point. When wildflowers are blooming, this is one of the prettiest walks in Juneau, with spectacular views of Lynn Canal and the Chilkat Mountains.

North Section. There is a campground along Eagle River at about Mile 18 (past the 27-mile marker). About 0.2 mile past the campground turnoff is a left turn into a picnic area which eventually loops back to the highway. Scan the river mouth and Lynn Canal for seabirds—loons, grebes, cormorants, Pigeon Guillemot, Marbled Murrelet, and a variety of sea ducks are all here. Thayer's Gulls are common in spring, and this is one of the best areas for Black-legged Kittiwake. California Gulls are occasional, Ring-billed Gull and Caspian Tern are rare, and one of Alaska's few Western Gull sightings came from here. From fall through spring a large flock of shorebirds, sometimes numbering more than a thousand birds, feeds during mid-to-low tides. The most common species are Rock Sandpiper and Dunlin, but large numbers of Black Turnstones and Surfbirds may be with them. A Sanderling or two may also be present. Be alert for Harbor Seal, Steller's Sea Lion, Harbor Porpoise, and Humpback Whale.

Amalga Trail. The Amalga Trail begins from a parking lot on the right at about Mile 17.5, just after Glacier Highway crosses the Eagle River. This National Forest Trail provides access to Eagle Lake and Eagle Glacier, about 7.5 miles from the highway. There is a cabin near the end of the trail that can be rented from the Forest Service. Few birders go the whole distance, which involves a round-trip of 10 to 12 hours. Instead, most venture in only about two miles to a large marshy area—probably the best place in Alaska to find Virginia Rail and also a very good spot for Sora. Although not found every year, both rails have been located during several summers since first being observed in summer 1994. If you are going to take the trail to the marsh, wear knee-high rubber boots, long pants, and a long-sleeved shirt. Leather gloves will help you work your way through the Devil's Club when you bushwhack your way to the edge of the marsh. Mosquitoes and other biting bugs can be quite annoying, and both Brown and Black Bears use this area. For these reasons, and because the walk to the marsh is a long one, it is not birded very often, leading to speculation that more-frequent visits might lead to the discovery of rarities that now go unrecorded.

The trail parallels Eagle River for more than a mile—wide and easy to walk—passing through a moss-covered spruce forest that is home to Winter Wren, both kinglets, Townsend's Warbler, Oregon Junco, and other passerines. After you walk for about 45 minutes the trail turns away from the river and begins climbing. Do not take the Yankee Basin Trail that you will pass along the way.

You are treated to about 200 yards of boardwalk where the trail turns away from the river, but when it ends the trail is much more difficult to walk and can be muddy, with rocks, roots, fallen trees, and other impediments. You will soon reach a swampy area with running water and many dead trees, usually productive for Red-breasted Sapsucker, Northern Waterthrush, and Common Yellowthroat. The trail continues around this marshy area and then climbs again. After about 25 minutes you will reach the bridge over Boulder Creek. Continue on for another 10 to 15 minutes to a very green (in summer), marshy area, covered with horsetails and grasses down the hill to your right. This area has been formed by Beaver activity, traces of which are evident on the far side of the meadow. You need to bushwhack your way down the hill to get to the edge of the marsh. There is an old, very overgrown trail along the edge of the marsh and a couple of large, fallen trees right at the edge of the marsh will give you an opportunity to sit quietly and scan the marsh for rails.

Several Red-winged Blackbirds are usually found in this part of the marsh, as are Belted Kingfisher, Red-breasted Sapsucker, Pacific-slope Flycatcher, Steller's Jay, and Song Sparrow. Solitary Sandpiper and Three-toed Woodpecker have been reported.

After coming all that distance, many birders spend an hour or more scanning the marsh and listening for rarities. If you choose to keep going, the Amalga Trail continues for several more miles to Eagle Lake.

Point Bridget State Park. The trail into Point Bridget State Park is located on the left side of Glacier Highway at about Mile 29 (just across from the 38-mile marker). This 2,850-acre park has a great diversity of habitats including muskeg, old-growth forests, streams, Beaver ponds, saltmarsh, and rocky marine beaches. One of the best birding features is the large meadow that the trail parallels for much of the way to Cowee Creek Cabin, which is situated in the meadow 2.1 miles from the trailhead. Several stands of alder and cottonwood in the meadow host a variety of species rarely seen in Juneau. Readers are cautioned that this is a high-use area for bears. Bear scat is usually seen several times along the trail. Make noise and be alert as you walk the trail (see Bear Cautions in the *Introduction*, page 17).

The trail begins on a boardwalk that passes through muskeg, then downhill through hemlock and then predominantly spruce forest. Red-breasted Sapsucker and Three-toed Woodpecker are sometimes seen in these trees as are Pacific-slope Flycatcher, Chestnut-backed Chickadee, Golden-crowned Kinglet, Steller's Jay, and Townsend's Warbler. After 10 to 15 minutes the trail levels out and much of it is no longer planked. Soon it begins paralleling the large meadow. A small pond with lily pads sometimes has Ring-necked Ducks or singing Common Yellowthroats.

After about 30 to 40 minutes be on the lookout for a survey marker that sticks up a couple of feet above the ground. There are three large spruce trees with small yellow "Bearing Tree" signs on them that are used to locate the survey marker. About 50 yards out into the meadow is a Beaver pond that cannot be seen when the grass has grown very high. Several common species of ducks can be seen here in the spring; a female Ruddy Duck was seen in 2002. About 200 yards to the left is a grove of cottonwoods. The deciduous trees in this area, particularly the cottonwood grove, have gained a reputation as vagrant traps. Such uncommon species as Olive-sided Flycatcher, Western Wood-Pewee, Hammond's Flycatcher, Warbling and Red-eyed Vireos, Blackpoll Warbler, American Redstart, Western Tanager, Brewer's Blackbird, and Brown- headed Cowbird, along with many of the more common passerines, have been seen or heard in these trees. It is easiest to bird this area in the spring or early summer, as the grass can grow to over five feet high by mid-July, making walking difficult.

After you walk steadily for about 45 to 60 minutes, the trail leaves the woods and breaks out onto the edge of the meadow. Logs have been placed to slightly block the forest trail to indicate where the trail takes this turn. Another few minutes of walking takes you to the Cowee Meadow Cabin nestled in a cozy corner of the meadow. During spring (mid-to-late April) Mountain Bluebird and Townsend's Solitaire may sometimes be seen on the tops of small spruce trees in the meadow. Northern Harrier, Red-tailed Hawk, American Kestrel, and Merlin sometimes cruise overhead. The cabin can be rented for $35 per night from the Alaska Department of Natural Resources, offering a wonderful opportunity to bird here over an extended period of time—just about the cheapest accommodations in Juneau.

The trail continues past the cabin about one-quarter mile to the beach. Red-throated and Common Loons as well as the more common species of ducks and gulls are here, and a Say's Phoebe was once seen on the rocks. You can walk the beach to the mouth of Cowee Creek (to the right), or continue on to the end of the Point Bridget Trail, about 1.4 miles farther. Most local birders go as far as the beach and then turn back. If you walk straight back without stopping you will be back to your car in about an hour.

LOGISTICS

The area code for all telephone numbers is 907 unless otherwise indicated. Tourist and travel services (accommodations, restaurants, attractions, etc.) not listed below can be found in the latest edition of The Milepost. *Statewide travel and birding information services are listed under Logistics in the* Introduction, *page 15.)*

Juneau Convention and Visitor Bureau, 1 Sealaska Place #305, Juneau, AK 99801; 586-1737 or 800-587-2201; *info@traveljuneau.com*; *http://www.traveljuneau.com*.

Birding Information: *Birds of the Juneau Area*, a checklist prepared by the Juneau Audubon Society is often available at the U.S. Forest Service Visitor Center at Mendenhall Glacier, 789-0097.

You may contact Juneau Audubon Society at PO Box 021715, Juneau, AK 99802.

There are many other places to bird in the Juneau area, and some of these are described in Armstrong and Gordon (1994). Additional trails and short walks are described in King (2000) and Tongass National Forest Juneau Ranger District (1991).

ACKNOWLEDGEMENTS: The assistance and reviews by Beverly Agler, Robert Armstrong, Deanna McPhail, and Paul Suchanek are greatly appreciated. Richard Konz drove all routes and suggested modifications.

Dunlin

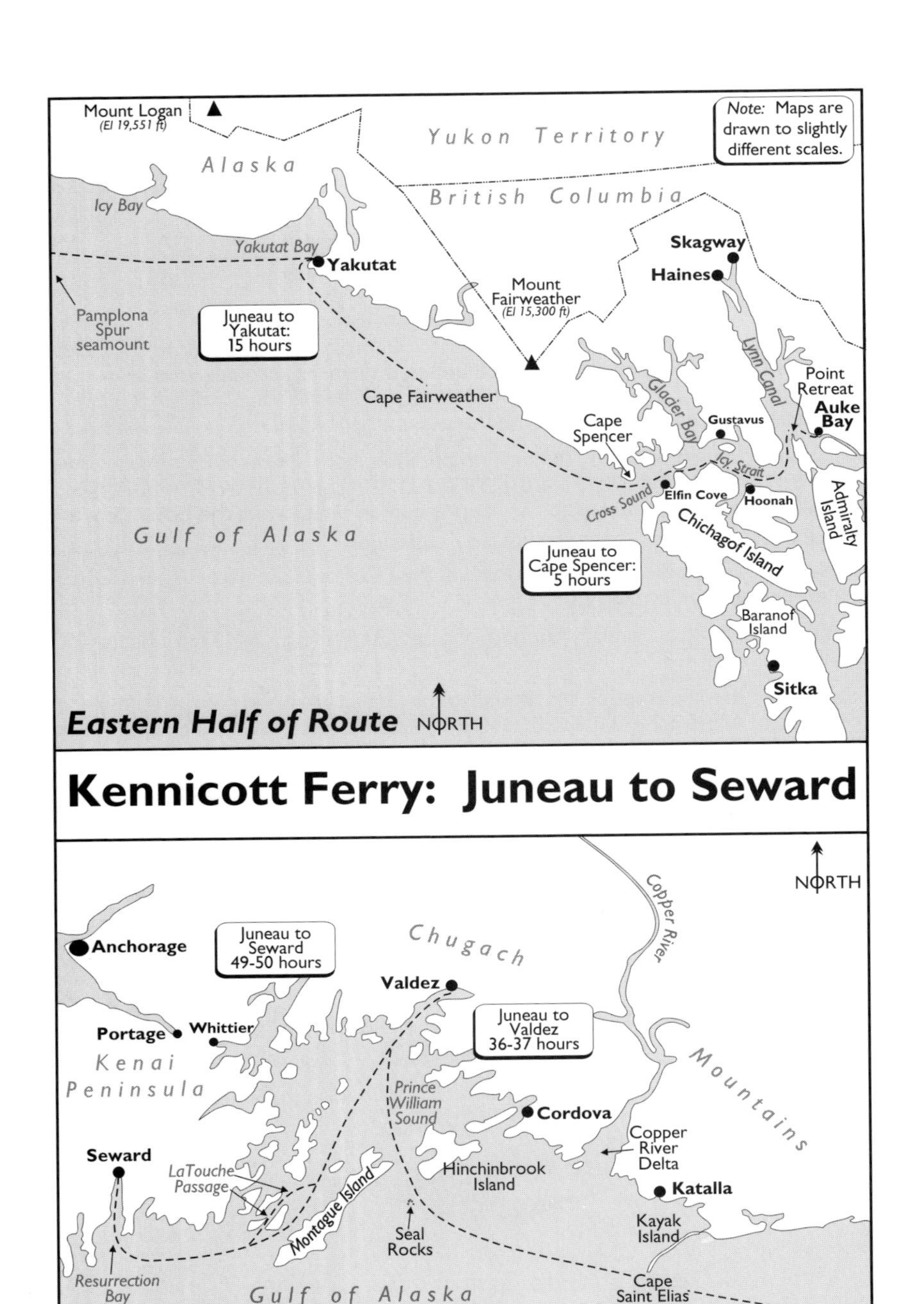
Mount Logan
(El 19,551 ft)
Yukon Territory
Note: Maps are drawn to slightly different scales.
Alaska
British Columbia
Icy Bay
Yakutat Bay
Yakutat
Skagway
Haines
Pamplona Spur seamount
Juneau to Yakutat: 15 hours
Mount Fairweather
(El 15,300 ft)
Lynn Canal
Point Retreat
Auke Bay
Cape Fairweather
Glacier Bay
Gustavus
Cape Spencer
Icy Strait
Cross Sound
Elfin Cove
Hoonah
Admiralty Island
Chichagof Island
Gulf of Alaska
Juneau to Cape Spencer: 5 hours
Baranof Island
Sitka
Eastern Half of Route
NORTH
Kennicott Ferry: Juneau to Seward
NORTH
Copper River
Anchorage
Juneau to Seward 49-50 hours
Chugach
Valdez
Juneau to Valdez 36-37 hours
Portage
Whittier
Kenai Peninsula
Mountains
Prince William Sound
Cordova
Copper River Delta
Seward
LaTouche Passage
Montague Island
Hinchinbrook Island
Katalla
Seal Rocks
Kayak Island
Resurrection Bay
Gulf of Alaska
Cape Saint Elias
Western Half of Route
Middleton Island
Pamplona Spur seamount

Gulf of Alaska by Ferry

Steven T. Zimmerman

The M/V *Kennicott*, the newest of the Alaska State ferries, is 382 feet long, and provides a remarkably stable platform for birding, even in very rough weather. In calm weather spotting scopes can be used from the bow. Since 1998 the *Kennicott* has been providing ferry service throughout southeast Alaska on runs that start in Bellingham, Washington. Once a month, from May through September, it travels from Juneau, across the eastern Gulf of Alaska to Valdez, and on to Seward. A "whistle stop" may be made at Yakutat if warranted by passenger demand. Because there are no commercial or charter vessels that routinely schedule pelagic birding trips into the eastern Gulf of Alaska, a trip on the *Kennicott* provides the only regularly scheduled platform for pelagic birding in that area.

Several seabirds that are very rare in Alaskan waters have been seen at least once from the *Kennicott,* including Short-tailed Albatross, Pink-footed, Buller's, and Manx Shearwaters, Brandt's Cormorant, and Heermann's Gull. Commonly seen species include Black-footed Albatross, Northern Fulmar, Sooty Shearwater, Fork-tailed Storm-Petrel, Double-crested and Pelagic Cormorants, Surf and White-winged Scoters as well as several other species of ducks, Pomarine Jaeger, Mew, Herring, and Glaucous-winged Gulls, Black-legged Kittiwake, Arctic Tern, Common Murre, Pigeon Guillemot, Marbled Murrelet, and Tufted Puffin. Birds that are not as common but which may be seen include Pacific and Common Loons, Laysan Albatross, Short-tailed Shearwater, Leach's Storm-Petrel, Red-necked Phalarope, Parasitic and Long-tailed Jaegers, Sabine's Gull, Aleutian Tern, Ancient Murrelet, Cassin's and Rhinoceros Auklets, and Horned Puffin. Flocks of migrating shorebirds are seen during some cruises.

The *Kennicott* leaves Juneau on its cross-Gulf run during the middle to the latter part of each month. Scheduled departure times from Juneau vary widely each year, ranging from 2:30 PM on Tuesdays in 2002 to 9:00 AM Wednesdays in 2001. These differences affect which areas are traversed in daylight, and the availability of connections to subsequent destinations. The trip from Juneau to Seward, or back, takes approximately 49 to 50 hours each way, and there is a 7-to-8-hour layover in Seward (see page 273). Persons not wanting to take the trip back to Juneau can take the train or a small plane to Anchorage, or they may connect with the M/V *Tustumena* and continue pelagic birding to Kodiak and on to Dutch Harbor (see page 323).

The *Kennicott* leaves Juneau from Auke Bay, heads north to Point Retreat, and then motors down Lynn Canal to Icy Strait. Birds seen along this part of the trip are the typical inshore species of loons, grebes, cormorants, ducks, gulls, and alcids. As the vessel enters Icy Strait, birds such as Pomarine Jaeger and Black-legged Kittiwake begin to be seen, and often there is a large concentration of these species near the mouth of Glacier Bay. By the time the *Kennicott* enters Cross Sound and approaches Cape Spencer, Sooty Shearwaters will be seen, and on some occasions many thousands of seabirds will be feeding here. The trip from Juneau to Cape Spencer, where the Inside Passage meets the Gulf of Alaska, takes about five hours.

The vessel turns northwest at Cape Spencer and travels several miles off the coast until it either reaches Yakutat or turns west toward Valdez. The farthest-offshore segments of the trip occur from Cape Spencer to the waters off Yakutat, and from there to the entrance of Prince William Sound. Northern Fulmar, Sooty Shearwater, and Fork-tailed Storm-Petrel are the most common birds along these stretches, but almost any of the seabirds that have been described from the North Pacific could turn up here. There are also long stretches where no seabirds are seen. The approach to Yakutat is a good area in which to look for Aleutian Tern and Ancient Murrelet. From Juneau the trip to Yakutat takes about 15 to 16 hours.

After leaving Yakutat, the ship heads west toward Kayak Island. The area between Yakutat and Kayak Island often provides the best opportunity for viewing albatrosses. Black-footed Albatross is the most abundant species, although a Laysan may occasionally be seen in this area. About four to five hours after leaving Yakutat, the vessel passes Pamplona Spur (59° 30' N, 142° 30' W, a little west of Cape Yakataga). This is often a very birdy area, and it was near Pamplona Spur that the only Short-tailed Albatross ever recorded from the *Kennicott* was seen. The ship sails by the southern end of Kayak Island, 8 to 15 miles offshore from Cape Saint Elias, where Black-footed Albatross will usually be seen. The *Kennicott* then travels to Hinchinbrook Entrance where it enters Prince William Sound. Brandt's Cormorants, known to nest on Seal Rocks offshore from the entrance to Prince William Sound, have been sighted on the wing in this area. The ship sails north through the sound, eventually arriving at Valdez about 36 or 37 hours from Juneau, whether it has stopped in Yakutat or not.

After a three-to-four-hour stop at Valdez, the *Kennicott* crosses Prince William Sound, exiting through Montague Strait or LaTouche Passage on its way to Seward. As the vessel approaches and enters Resurrection Bay, a concentration of seabirds will often be seen, including Pomarine Jaeger and the species that nest near the mouth of the Bay (Black-legged Kittiwake, Horned and Tufted Puffins). The stop in Seward allows plenty of time to visit the Alaska SeaLife Center and view displays of living marine birds and marine mammals before the *Kennicott* begins its return trip to Juneau.

A ticket from Juneau to Seward on the *Kennicott* cost $169 in 2002. Although it is possible to sleep in the solarium or lounges on the vessel, renting a roomette or cabin will ensure an undisturbed night's sleep. Prices range from $80 for a 2-berth roomette to $275 for a 4-berth outside cabin with facilities. Reservations may be made by calling the Alaska Marine Highway System at 465-3941, or by using that agency's web site at *www.alaska.gov/ferry*.

ACKNOWLEDGEMENTS: Reviewed by Paul Suchanek and Al DeMartini.

THE GULF OF ALASKA BY CRUISE SHIP

Capt. Ed Murphy and George West

Cruise ships often take much the same route as the State of Alaska ferry M/V *Kennicott* when they sail from Glacier Bay or Juneau west to Valdez and Seward. If you are taking a cruise ship to Alaska, you can ask the captain to let you know when you will be making the nearest approach to Pamplona Spur, the most likely place to find albatrosses. Most ships traveling from southeast Alaska to Prince William Sound and exiting at Cross Sound (Cape Spencer) would take a west-northwesterly track to a position south of Cape Saint Elias on Kayak Island and then shape a course for Hinchinbrook Entrance and Prince William Sound. These vessels would pass about 10 to 15 miles off the tip of the Pamplona Spur, where depths rise to 90 fathoms from 250 fathoms. However, there is a safety fairway outside of Prince William Sound that is used by the tankers entering and leaving Valdez. Cruise-ship captains might or might not shape their course to intercept this fairway. If they do, it would put them about 25 miles off the Pamplona Spur when passing that position. This area in the Gulf of Alaska might be your best bet for Short-tailed Albatross, uncommon shearwaters such as Pink-footed and Buller's, and for Mottled or Cook's Petrel.

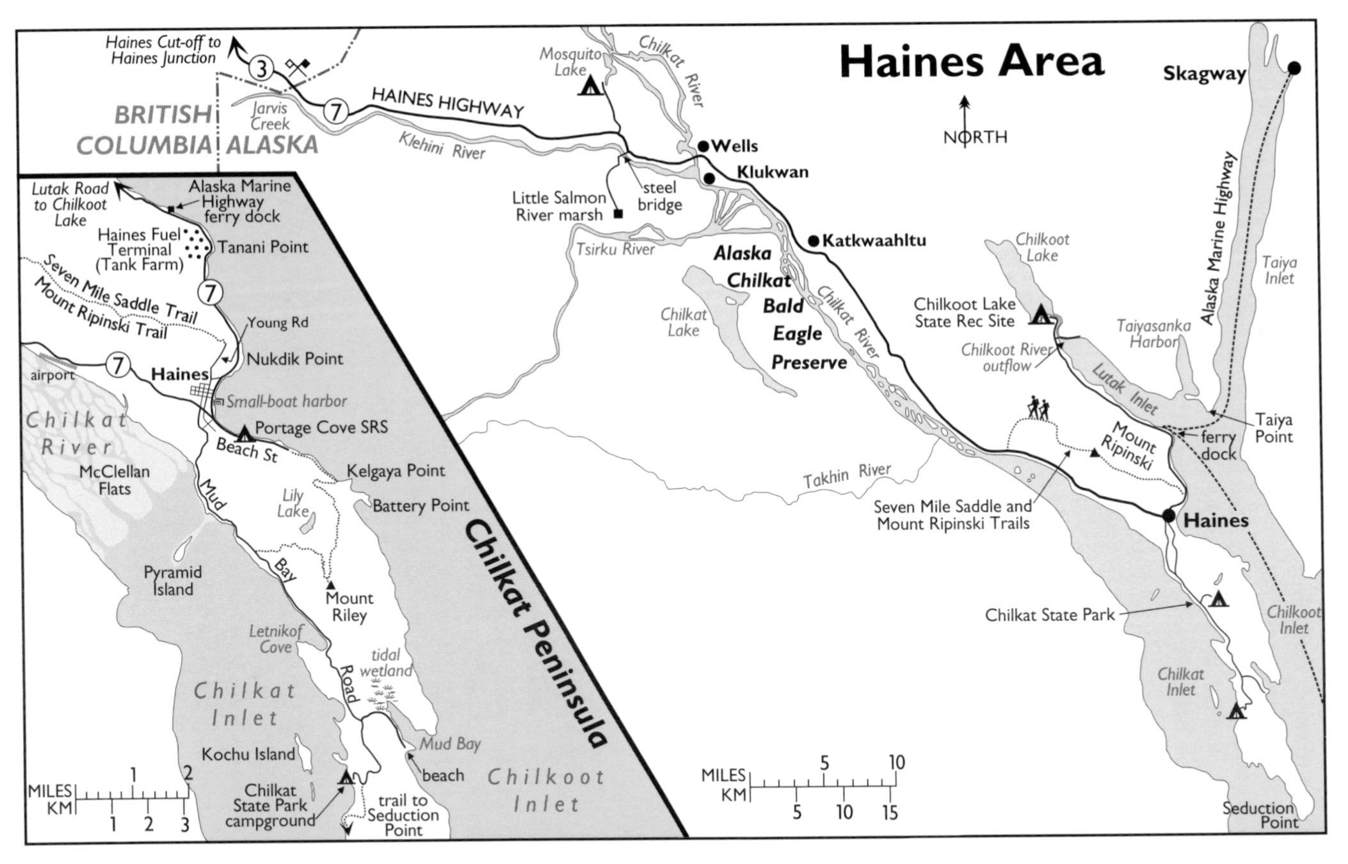
Haines Area
NORTH
Skagway
Haines Cut-off to Haines Junction
3
7
HAINES HIGHWAY
BRITISH COLUMBIA
ALASKA
Jarvis Creek
Klehini River
Mosquito Lake
Chilkat River
Wells
Klukwan
Little Salmon River marsh
steel bridge
Tsirku River
Katkwaahltu
Alaska Chilkat Bald Eagle Preserve
Chilkat Lake
Chilkat River
Takhin River
Chilkoot Lake
Chilkoot Lake State Rec Site
Chilkoot River outflow
Taiyasanka Harbor
Lutak Inlet
Alaska Marine Highway
Taiya Inlet
Taiya Point
ferry dock
Mount Ripinski
Seven Mile Saddle and Mount Ripinski Trails
Haines
Chilkat State Park
Chilkoot Inlet
Chilkat Inlet
Seduction Point
MILES 5 10
KM 5 10 15
Lutak Road to Chilkoot Lake
Alaska Marine Highway ferry dock
Haines Fuel Terminal (Tank Farm)
Tanani Point
Seven Mile Saddle Trail
Mount Ripinski Trail
Young Rd
Nukdik Point
airport
Haines
Small-boat harbor
Portage Cove SRS
Beach St
Chilkat River
McClellan Flats
Kelgaya Point
Lily Lake
Battery Point
Mud Bay Road
Pyramid Island
Mount Riley
Letnikof Cove
tidal wetland
Chilkat Inlet
Kochu Island
Chilkat State Park campground
trail to Seduction Point
Mud Bay
beach
Chilkoot Inlet
Chilkat Peninsula
MILES 1 2
KM 1 2 3

HAINES

Cameron D. Eckert

Scenic Chilkat Peninsula has a long history of occupation, from the centuries-old villages established by the Tlingit peoples throughout the Chilkat Valley to the town of Haines, established in 1881. The abundant fish and wildlife resources brought the Native peoples to this place, and the lure of gold in the 1890s attracted the ancestors of its current occupants. Today Haines has a growing tourism industry and offers a full range of attractions, services, supplies, and accommodations, including camping, lodges, cabins, and motels. The availability of some services may be limited in winter months. Haines is connected to the outside world via the Alaska Marine Highway, with ferries south to Juneau and north to Skagway, and the Haines Highway north, 152 miles, through British Columbia to Haines Junction, Yukon.

The Haines area features diverse ecosystems, including the marine waters of Lynn Canal, lush coastal forests of Western Hemlock and Sitka Spruce, impressive stands of Black Cottonwood along the Chilkat River, saltwater marshes, expansive tidal flats, subalpine Mountain Hemlock forests, and the rugged rocky outcrops and glaciers of the high alpine. Haines is located at the extreme north end of Lynn Canal where it splits into Chilkat Inlet to the west and into Chilkoot Inlet to the east. Chilkat Inlet ends at the outflow of the Chilkat River, while Chilkoot Inlet continues north and splits into Lutak Inlet to the west and into Taiya Inlet to the northeast. Lutak Inlet ends at the outflow of Chilkook Lake, and Taiya Inlet ends at Skagway and Dyea. The waters off Haines are inhabited by a variety of marine mammals including Harbor Seal, Steller's Sea Lion, Harbor Porpoise, Killer Whale, and Humpback Whale, with Dall's Porpoise seen more regularly to the south along Lynn Canal. Sea Otters are not known to occur here, although River Otters are regularly seen at the water's edge. The run of Eulachon, also known as "candlefish" and "hooligan," in the second week in May sets off a spectacular domino effect through the food chain. The mass of spawning fish concentrates a feeding frenzy of hundreds of thousands of gulls, along with King Salmon that in turn attract hungry Steller's Sea Lions and Killer Whales. Haines is not well explored by birders, and much remains to be learned about the area's birdlife.

Portage Cove: The Haines small-boat harbor, located at the foot of Main Street at Front Street, provides a panoramic view of Portage Cove,

Chilkoot Inlet, and beyond to Tongass National Forest and Mount Villard. Blue Mussels, an abundant food source for diving ducks, attract thousands of Surf and White-winged Scoters, along with a few Black Scoters, and hundreds of Barrow's Goldeneyes. Watch for four loon species, Yellow-billed being most regular in fall, Harlequin Duck, and Long-tailed Duck. This is a good place to view seabirds such as Double-crested and Pelagic Cormorants, Common Murre, Pigeon Guillemot, and Marbled Murrelet. Fork-tailed Storm-Petrels only very rarely wander north up Lynn Canal as far as Haines, although 2001 proved to be a good year for them. A Manx Shearwater was a spectacular rarity here in August 2001. The harbor's rocky breakwater should be checked for Wandering Tattler and Rock Sandpiper, the latter being most likely from late fall through spring.

Portage Cove State Recreation Site. This quiet little campground in downtown Haines offers day use and picnic tables, with tent camping limited to backpackers and bicyclists only. To reach the campground follow Beach Street for about 1.8 miles south around Portage Cove. It is a good vantage point for scanning Portage Cove and Chilkoot Inlet. Pelagic Cormorants are often seen on this side of the cove, along with Red-throated, Pacific, Common, and Yellow-billed Loons, and Harbor Porpoises.

Battery Point Trail offers a moderately-paced walk with no elevation gain through the coastal forest to a beach overlooking Chilkoot Inlet (1 mile), and across the headland to Kelgaya Point (1.2 miles). To reach the trailhead, go south around Portage Cove to the end of Beach Street, about 1.2 miles past the Portage Cove campground. While the trail is not particularly rugged, there are a few slippery sections. It offers good views of Chilkoot Inlet, particularly the beach. Barred Owl has been seen along this trail. Scan the open water for all four loons, Pelagic Cormorant, Marbled Murrelet, and passing gulls, including Black-legged Kittiwake. Watch for Steller's Sea Lion, Humpback Whale, and Killer Whale.

Portage Cove to Chilkoot Lake. To reach Chilkoot Lake follow Lutak Road north from Haines toward the ferry terminal. Lutak Road runs right along Chilkoot Inlet and Lutak Inlet. It is dangerous to stop along this road except at the frequent safe pullout areas that allow a view of the whole shoreline. Scan for loons, grebes, sea ducks, Pigeon Guillemots, and Marbled Murrelets, as well as the many gulls that regularly travel up and down the inlet, depending on the tides. Eastern Kingbird has been seen along the road at Tanani Point, and in the vicinity of the "tank farm." The songs of Chestnut-backed Chickadee, Brown Creeper, Golden-crowned Kinglet, Varied Thrush, and Red Crossbill are invariably heard from the surrounding forests. This is also a good stretch of road for owling; Boreal Owl has been heard in the vicinity of the Salmon Run campground (1.8 miles past the ferry terminal).

Chilkoot Lake is located 10 miles north of Haines at the end of Lutak Road (the road to the ferry terminal) and offers camping and a boat launch. The outflow of Chilkoot Lake into the north end of Lutak Inlet creates a coastal wetland with broad mudflats at low tides. This is perhaps the richest birding location in the Haines area. While birding is best during falling or low tides when mudflats are exposed, it remains productive at high tides when many of the birds simply move to the edge of the water or perch on the rocks along the short stretch of river between Lutak Inlet and Chilkoot Lake. The road into Chilkoot Lake State Recreation Site runs right along the river, allowing easy viewing. In spring and fall masses of birds congregate, with huge flocks of Barrow's Goldeneyes along with a good diversity of dabbling and diving ducks. Harlequin Ducks and American Dippers are often seen along the river. Shorebirds also frequent this area, particularly in spring migration. This is a wonderful place for gull enthusiasts, with especially high numbers of gulls present in spring and fall. California Gulls stage a regular fall movement into this area. Parasitic Jaegers are seen occasionally. The abundant summer and fall salmon run on the river attracts gulls, people with fishing rods, and Brown Bears that require caution and common sense (see Bear Cautions in the *Introduction*, page 17). Keep an ear to the surrounding forests for low resonant hoots of Blue Grouse, the high tooting call of Northern Pygmy-Owl, and an occasional Barred Owl. This area has proven to be a good location for rarities, with Wood Duck in July 1996, Common Teal in April 1996, and a Yellow-headed Blackbird in August 2001.

Mud Bay Road runs south from Haines to Chilkat State Park and Mud Bay. Try not to get side-tracked onto Small Tracts Road, which eventually connects with Mud Bay Road but which bypasses some of the better shoreline habitats. The good birding starts where Mud Bay Road reaches Chilkat Inlet. Explore the productive shoreline habitats and views of the lower Chilkat River. This shoreline is one of the better areas in Haines for shorebirds; Upland Sandpiper has been seen here. Large numbers of Bald Eagles and gulls congregate at low tide on the mudflats on the lower Chilkat River. Arctic Terns nest on the very distinctive Pyramid Island which was deposited by the receding glaciers.

Mud Bay is located about eight miles south of Haines. Follow Mud Bay Road toward Chilkat State Park to a fork at about Mile 6, where the right fork leads to the state park. Go left at this fork and continue for another two miles or so to an open turnaround. Beyond the turnaround the road turns into very narrow track and continues on to private residences. From the turnaround you can walk the short distance down this small road to beach access. Check the tidal wetland for dabbling ducks and migrant shorebirds just before you reach the open turnaround . Hudsonian and Marbled Godwits have been seen in spring. From the beach scan Lynn Canal for Yellow-billed Loon, an occasional Black-legged Kittiwake, as well as Steller's Sea Lion and Humpback Whale. Song Sparrows sing from the shoreline shrubs and Varied Thrushes resonate from the adjacent Western Hemlock forests. This is a good area to listen for Northern Pygmy-, Barred, and Northern Saw-whet Owls.

Chilkat State Park is located 7 miles south of Haines. Follow Mud Bay Road south along the Chilkat Inlet to a fork at about Mile 6, and continue right to the park entrance. The 6,000-acre park offers camping, a boat launch, beach access, hiking, and an interpretive center with a view across the Chilkat Inlet to the Davidson Glacier. Watch for an occasional passing Killer Whale. The birding is excellent right in the campground. The dawn chorus includes Pacific-slope Flycatcher, at the edge of its range here, Warbling Vireo, and Townsend's Warbler. Blue Grouse, Rufous Hummingbird, and Three-toed Woodpecker are also common, and MacGillivray's Warbler and Western Tanager may be seen here. A trail covering moderate terrain leads six miles (one way) to Seduction Point at the southern tip of the Chilkat Peninsula with a view south down Lynn Canal. Barred Owl has been seen at Moose Meadow, a short way down this trail, and the view from Seduction Point once yielded an Ancient Murrelet. Check at the interpretive center for detailed trail information. Nighttime in the park brings out a festival of Porcupines.

Mount Riley Trail offers a moderately-paced hike through a variety of forested habitats, culminating in a magnificent view of Chilkoot Inlet to the east and Chilkat Inlet to the west. To reach the trailhead go south from Haines on Mud Bay Road to Mile 3 and watch for the sign and parking area. The trail to the top is 2.8 miles, with an elevation gain of 1,760 feet. An alternate route to Mount Riley is from the south end of the Battery Point Trail—take the right fork just before reaching the beach. From here the trail to the top is four miles. This area is likely to be good for owls, and birders should watch for Northern Pygmy-, Barred, and Northern Saw-whet Owls. Western Screech-Owl has also been reported from the Haines area, and this would be a good area to listen for this locally rare owl. Three-toed Woodpecker, Pacific-slope Flycatcher, and Townsend's Warbler are expected.

Alaska Chilkat Bald Eagle Preserve. To explore the Chilkat River and Bald Eagle preserve go north from Haines on the Haines Highway that follows the Chilkat River. The main viewing areas with safe pullouts and walkways are between Miles 18 and 24. The 48,000-acre Alaska Chilkat Bald Eagle Preserve was created in June 1982 to protect the salmon run and the critical habitat for the world's largest concentration of Bald Eagles. Over 3,000 Bald Eagles congregate from early October through January with the highest numbers in mid-November. They are attracted to the area by availability of spawned-out Silver (Coho) and Chum (Dog) Salmon and open water. Even veteran birdwatchers cannot help being awestruck at the size of this natural event. Over 200 Bald Eagles nest in the Haines area, so that eagle viewing is good at any time of year. The annual Bald Eagle Festival in early November features the release of rehabilitated wild eagles, art exhibits, naturalist-guided tours, and natural-history talks.

Once you've recovered from the sight of 100 Bald Eagles perched in a single tree, you can cast your eyes to the impressive concentration of gulls also attracted by the salmon. Among the common Mew and Glaucous-winged Gulls, watch for the less-common species such as Ring-billed, California, Herring, Thayer's, and Glaucous. Even Ivory Gull has been found here. The variety of deciduous and coniferous habitats makes this a productive area for songbirds, as well. Listen for Hammond's Flycatcher, Warbling Vireo, MacGillivray's Warbler, and Western Tanager.

Mount Ripinsky and Seven Mile Saddle Trails. Those keen on a challenging hike can look to Mount Ripinsky. It requires a reasonable level of fitness, hiking experience, and safety planning, including an itinerary and return time left with a friend or an official in Haines. The Alaska State Troopers in Haines provide a Backcountry Explorer's Form for this purpose (see *Logistics*). These directions should be supplemented with a topo map and, if the trail becomes too vague or hard to follow, it may be best to return the way you came. Alaska Backcounty Outfitter in Haines can provide more detailed trail information. This trail through the Takshanuk Mountains has an elevation gain of 3,600 feet and traverses a wide range of habitats, eventually emerging into the alpine. There are two access points to the trail. The Mount Ripinsky trailhead is located at the edge of downtown Haines. Go to the northeast end of Young Road and bear right at the top of the hill, turning left at the water tank; the trail begins 0.5 mile down the dirt road (don't give up; keep going till you see a sign for the trail). Alternatively, go north from Haines along the Haines Highway to the Seven Mile Saddle trailhead at Mile 7. Ultimately, the two trails connect over a total distance of 9.8 miles via Mount Ripinsky. The Seven Mile Saddle trailhead appears to provide shorter yet steeper access to the alpine (3 miles). The approximate distances along the trail from the Seven Mile Saddle trailhead are as follows—1.9 miles from the trailhead to the saddle, 1.3 miles from the saddle to Peak 3920, 2.8 miles from Peak 3920 to Mount Ripinsky, 3.8 miles from Mount Ripinsky to the other trailhead. The alpine wildflower Glaucous Gentian grows on the bare rock along the trail in the vicinity of Peak 3920. Please try to watch for this delicate flower and avoid stepping on it. All that hiking won't leave much time for birding, but watch for a variety of subalpine and alpine species, such as Golden Eagle, Blue Grouse, White-tailed Ptarmigan, MacGillivray's Warbler, and perhaps Horned Lark and Gray-crowned Rosy-Finch. The possibility of Dusky Flycatcher or Mountain Chickadee could make this hike an exciting adventure.

10 Mile Marsh. This productive little marsh is located north of Haines at Mile 10 right along the Haines Highway. The white morph of Harlan's Hawk has been seen in this area in recent years. Watch for a variety of wetland species. Sora, rare in southeast Alaska, is a possibility here. A Northern Mockingbird was a rare find here a few years ago.

Little Salmon River Marsh is a favorite location among local birders, and a good place for species that are rare in southeast Alaska. To reach the marsh go north from Haines along the Haines Highway past Mile 25 and cross the bridge over the Chilkat River at Wells. Then continue about 2.5 miles and watch for a sign on the left to Porcupine. Follow this left over a steel bridge across the Klehini River. Continue another 200 yards and go left again onto a side road heading south. Continue about one mile to the Little Salmon Marsh on the right, where American Bittern has been seen and Hooded Mergansers nest. It's also a good place to look for Vaux's Swift, Common Nighthawk, Northern Pygmy-Owl, Hammond's Flycatcher, Warbling Vireo, MacGillivray's Warbler, and Western Tanager.

The Mosquito Lake road to the **Mosquito Lake State Recreation Site** is located north of Haines at Mile 27 of the Haines Highway. Mosquito Lake has camping (just 7 sites) and a boat launch. The combination of lakeshore habitats and coastal Western Hemlock and deciduous forests offers good birding. This is one of the better places for Red-breasted Sapsucker, easily located in spring by its arrhythmic drumming and raspy call. Other species to listen for include Rufous Hummingbird, Three-toed Woodpecker, Hammond's Flycatcher, and Winter Wren. Trumpeter Swans nest on the lake, and Pied-billed Grebe and Hooded Merganser have been seen. This area is generally under-birded but might be good for owls.

Haines to Skagway Boat Trip. The short (14-mile) boat trip from Haines to Skagway, south along Lutak Inlet, and then north on Taiya Inlet, provides good opportunities for whale and seabird watching. Transportation is available through the Alaska Marine Highway ferry or commercial tour companies (see *Logistics*). Alternatively, a sailing cruise, perhaps in a Wayfarer, would be an outstanding way to see the area. Watch for loons, Double-crested and Pelagic Cormorants, sea ducks, gulls, Common Murre, and Marbled Murrelet. The largest concentrations of birds are at Taiyasanka Harbor and at Taiya Point, where Chilkoot Inlet splits into Lutak Inlet and Taiya Inlet.

Haines Summit, British Columbia. Travelers headed north overland from Haines will follow the 152-mile Haines Highway to Haines Summit (elevation 3,550 feet) in British Columbia, and on to Haines Junction, Yukon (see page 156). This route passes through varied and dramatic scenery from the lush coastal forests, over the alpine tundra of the Saint Elias Range, to the interior White Spruce forests of the Yukon basin. The highway is open all year, but travelers should call (867-667-8215) for the daily, recorded road-condition report. Motorists should gas up at Haines or Haines Junction since there are no gas stations or lodging elsewhere along the highway. The weather is dynamic, and blowing snow in spring, fall, or winter can create extreme white-out conditions. Brown and Black Bears are common in the area, so use caution and good judgment. Haines Summit is an exceptional birding destination with many noteworthy species. Species regularly seen in the area include Northern Goshawk, Golden Eagle, Gyrfalcon, all three ptarmigan, Boreal Owl, Wandering Tattler, Arctic Tern, Northern Hawk Owl, Three-toed Woodpecker, Northern Shrike, Gray-cheeked Thrush, American Tree Sparrow, Golden-crowned Sparrow, Timberline Sparrow, Smith's Longspur, Snow Bunting, and Hepburn's race of Gray-crowned Rosy-Finch. The most popular birding area is at Mosquito Flats surrounding Kelsall Lake, located about 91 miles south of Haines Junction, and about 61 miles north of Haines. A rough dirt road leads east from the highway to Kelsall Lake, and travelers may have to use a more detailed topo map to locate this road. It is not a suitable for vehicles such as RVs with a limited turning radius. This is a good area in which to look for breeding Smith's Longspurs as well as Gyrfalcon, Willow Ptarmigan, and American Tree Sparrow. Gray-cheeked Thrushes and Fox Sparrows sing from the dense shrubs along creeks. Northern Wheatear has been seen. A hike up to slightly higher elevations may turn up Golden-crowned and Timberline Sparrows, as well as Rock and White-tailed Ptarmigan.

LOGISTICS

Haines has all the features and amenities of a small Alaskan town. The Mountain Market, located at 3rd Avenue and Haines Highway, serves a good espresso and provides a nice break from travel food. If a basic doughnut is more your thing, try the Chilkat Restaurant & Bakery at 5th Avenue and Dalton Street.

Haines Convention and Visitors Bureau, PO Box 530, Haines, AK, 99827; 907-766-2234 or 800-458-3579; *hcvb@haines.ak.us*; *www.haines.ak.us*.

Haines Visitor Center, 2nd Avenue, PO Box 518, Haines, AK, 99827-0518; 800-458-3579 (U.S.) or 800-478-2268 (Canada); fax 907-766-3155.

Alaska Backcounty Outfitter and Alaska Nature Tours, 120 Main Street, PO Box 491, Haines, AK, 99827; 907-766-2876; fax 907-766-2844; *aknature@kcd.com*; *http://kcd.com/aknature/about.htm*.

Alaska Marine Highway, Haines Ferry Terminal 907-766-2111.

Chilkat Cruises & Tours, (Haines-Skagway Fast Ferry; up to 26 crossings per day, 35 minutes each way; weekend service to and from Juneau), 142 Beach Road, PO Box 509, Haines, AK 99827; 907-766-2100 or 888-766-2103; fax 907-766-2101; *chilkat@klukwan.com*; *www.chilkatcruises.com/index.html*.

Alaska State Trooper, Gateway Building, Main Street, Haines, (907) 766-2552.

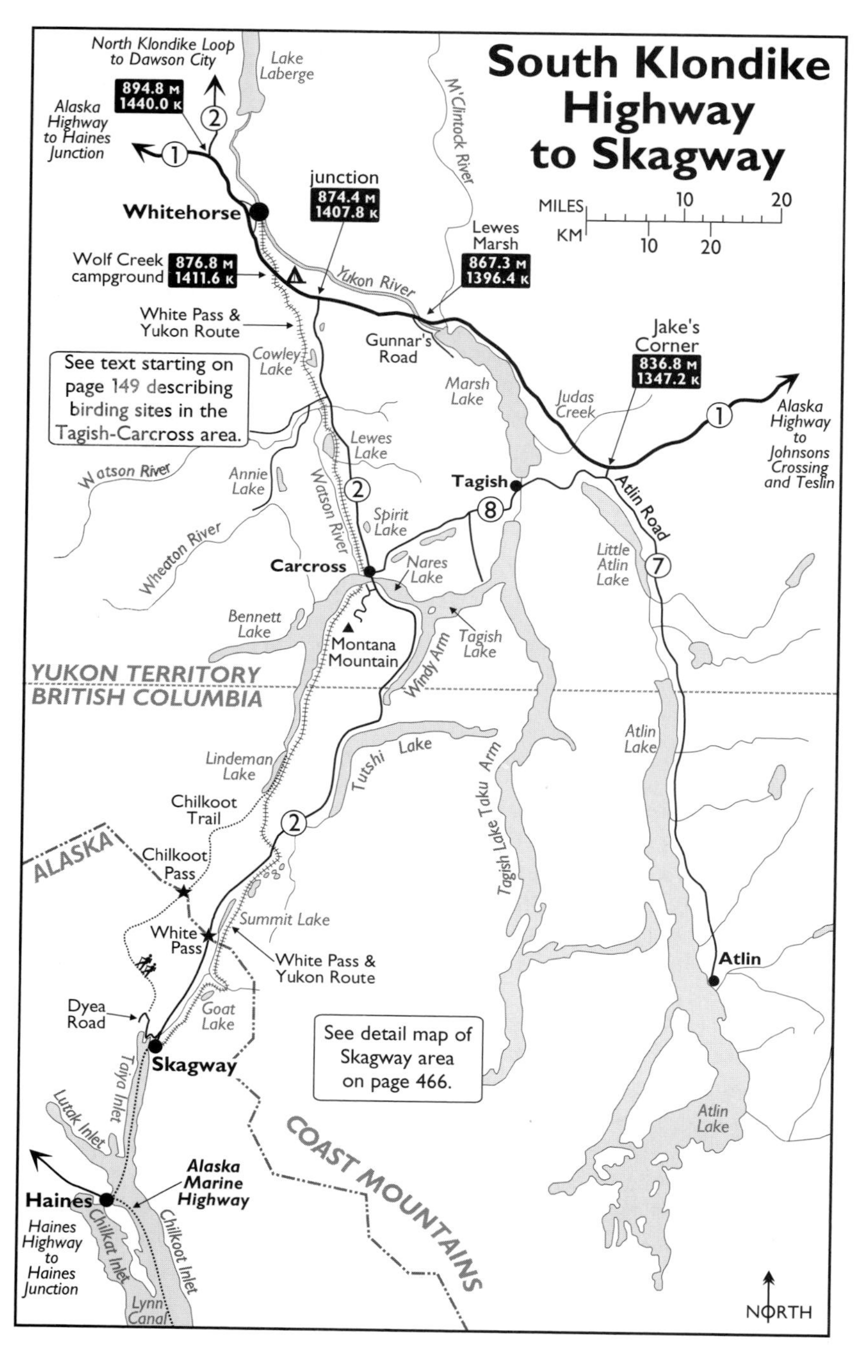
South Klondike Highway to Skagway
North Klondike Loop to Dawson City
894.8 M
1440.0 K
Alaska Highway to Haines Junction
Lake Laberge
M'Clintock River
Whitehorse
junction
874.4 M
1407.8 K
MILES
10
20
KM
10
20
Lewes Marsh
867.3 M
1396.4 K
Wolf Creek campground
876.8 M
1411.6 K
Yukon River
White Pass & Yukon Route
Gunnar's Road
Jake's Corner
836.8 M
1347.2 K
See text starting on page 149 describing birding sites in the Tagish-Carcross area.
Cowley Lake
Marsh Lake
Judas Creek
Alaska Highway to Johnsons Crossing and Teslin
Lewes Lake
Watson River
Annie Lake
Tagish
Atlin Road
Spirit Lake
Wheaton River
Watson River
Carcross
Nares Lake
Little Atlin Lake
Bennett Lake
Montana Mountain
Tagish Lake
Windy Arm
YUKON TERRITORY
BRITISH COLUMBIA
Atlin Lake
Tutshi Lake
Taku Arm
Lindeman Lake
Tagish Lake
Chilkoot Trail
ALASKA
Chilkoot Pass
Summit Lake
White Pass
White Pass & Yukon Route
Atlin
Dyea Road
Goat Lake
See detail map of Skagway area on page 466.
Skagway
Taiya Inlet
Lutak Inlet
Atlin Lake
COAST MOUNTAINS
Alaska Marine Highway
Haines
Haines Highway to Haines Junction
Chilkat Inlet
Chilkoot Inlet
Lynn Canal
NORTH

SKAGWAY

Cameron D. Eckert

Skagway is cradled in a narrow valley of the rugged Coast Mountains at the northernmost end of Lynn Canal. Its name comes from the Tlingit word, *Skagua,* "the place where the north wind blows." In July 1897 gold was discovered in the Yukon's Klondike, and Skagway became the point of entry for hordes of gold seekers. By October 1897 Skagway's population had surged to 20,000 people. Today this frontier town remains steeped in gold rush history, and its period character will appeal to visitors enthralled by the dreams of the stampeders. Skagway offers a full range of accommodations, services, and supplies during summer months, however, many businesses are closed in winter. The visitor center is located at Broadway and 2nd Avenue.

Skagway Townsite. The town of Skagway offers pleasant walking along well-treed streets, with a few shrubby and weedy patches and the odd birdfeeder. A walk around town is usually rewarded with a few interesting sightings. Watch for Northern Goshawk, Rufous Hummingbird, Steller's Jay, Cedar Waxwing, and Townsend's Warbler. Northwestern Crows nest throughout the town, usually in dense Sitka Spruce. In winter the abundant berry-laden Mountain Ash trees attract thousands of Bohemian Waxwings, as well as a few wintering American Robins. At this time of year there are also roving flocks of Chestnut-backed Chickadees, Brown Creepers, Golden-crowned Kinglets, and Oregon and Slate-colored Juncos, with a few Boreal Chickadees mixed in. The ferry dock and Skagway small-boat harbor at the south end of Broadway Street or south along Congress Way are good locations for viewing Taiya Inlet. Check the flocks of Mew and Glaucous-winged Gulls for unusual species, perhaps Black-legged Kittiwake. Bonaparte's Gulls often are seen out over Taiya Inlet, moving north or south along the inlet, depending on the tide. In some years large groups of Marbled Murrelets occur close to shore along with a few Pigeon Guillemots. During migration check the rocky shores for Harlequin Duck and Wandering Tattler.

A walk along **Pullen Creek** takes birders through a variety of habitats. In late summer and fall salmon spawn in the creek. To reach the creek from the visitor center (Broadway and 2nd Avenue), walk east on 2nd Avenue about 300 yards to Pullen Pond, which is a good place for a picnic lunch. Pullen Creek flows into the pond, so to continue birding along the creek, cross 2nd Avenue at Congress Way, and walk north along the creek or the adjacent

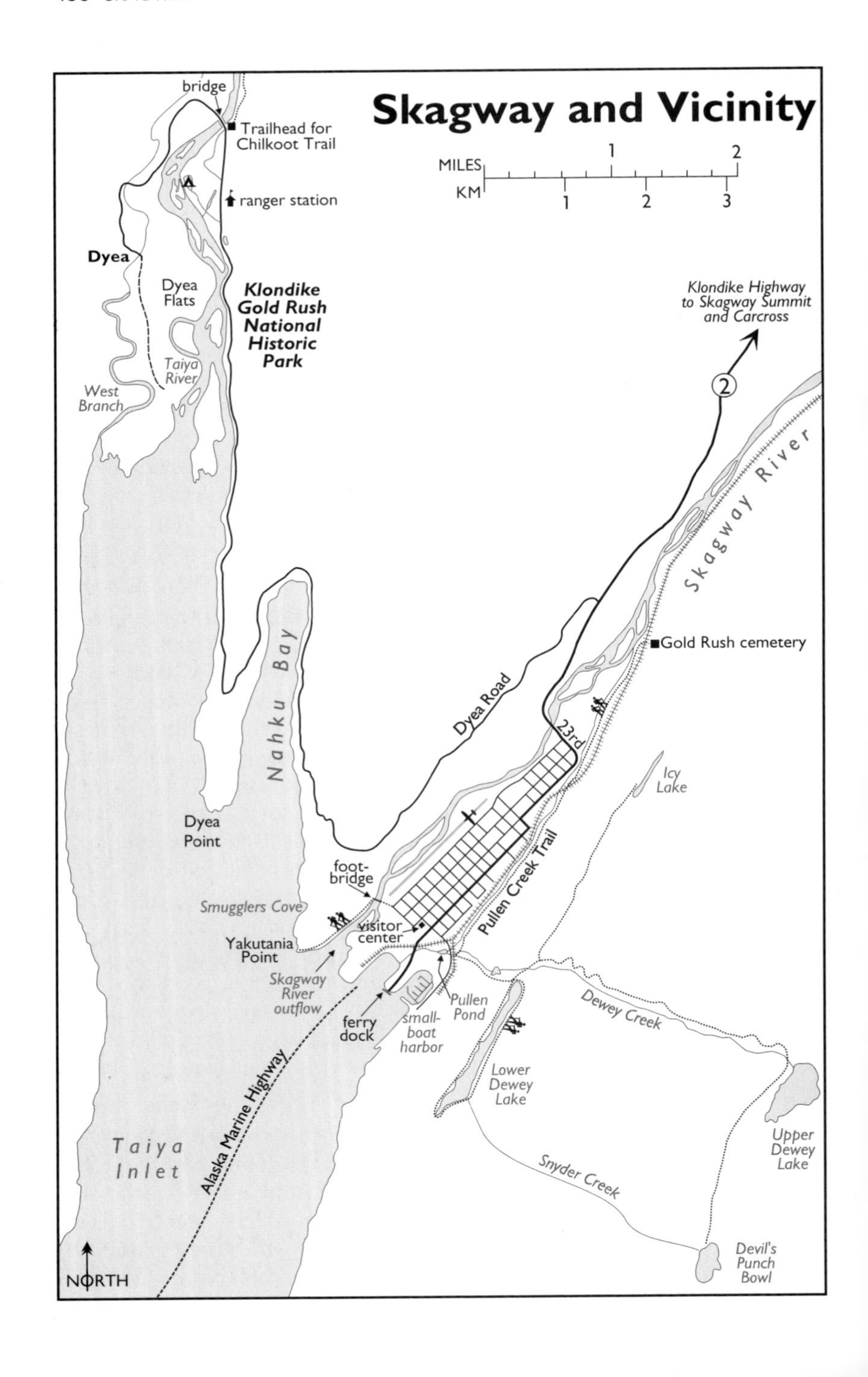
Skagway and Vicinity
MILES
1
2
KM
1
2
3
bridge
Trailhead for Chilkoot Trail
ranger station
Dyea
Dyea Flats
Klondike Gold Rush National Historic Park
Taiya River
West Branch
Klondike Highway to Skagway Summit and Carcross
2
Skagway River
Nahku Bay
Gold Rush cemetery
Dyea Road
23rd
Icy Lake
Dyea Point
foot-bridge
Pullen Creek Trail
Smugglers Cove
visitor center
Yakutania Point
Skagway River outflow
ferry dock
small-boat harbor
Pullen Pond
Dewey Creek
Lower Dewey Lake
Alaska Marine Highway
Upper Dewey Lake
Taiya Inlet
Snyder Creek
Devil's Punch Bowl
NORTH

train tracks. The trail is bounded by the creek on the east side and a steep forested hillside on the west side, and passes by the ruins of the historic Pullen House. The grand rock fireplace sitting curiously in an over-grown grassy field conjures visions of the grand parties that Harriet Pullen hosted there many decades ago. You can follow the tracks about two miles all the way to the north end of town at 23rd Avenue. To reach the Gold Rush Cemetery just continue straight along the tracks another couple hundred yards north of 23rd Avenue. Keep an eye out for trains that use these tracks on the Skagway Summit run during summer months. A short forest trail behind the cemetery leads to spectacular Lower Reid Falls. Pullen Creek is an attractive area for birds. American Dippers sing from the culvert behind Pullen Pond and may be seen anywhere along the creek. Great Blue Herons occasionally feed along the creek. During migration thrushes and warblers skirt the edges of the creek. The songs of Chestnut-backed Chickadee, Brown Creeper, and Golden-crowned Kinglet are usually heard from the forested slopes.

The **Lower Dewey Lake** trailhead is located about 300 feet north of 2nd Avenue and Congress Way along the Pullen Creek trail. The trail starts through the woods on the east side of the tracks, and after a short distance splits—you can go south to Lower Dewey Lake (or north to Icy Lake). This is a relatively easy walk through a variety of habitats with a moderate elevation gain of 500 feet. Lower Dewey Lake has a margin of alder shrubs and grasses while the mixed forests are composed of alder, birch, Sitka Spruce, Western Hemlock, and Lodgepole Pine. The distance to Lower Dewey Lake is 0.7 mile to the lake, or 2 miles around the lake. The total round-trip distance to Icy Lake is about 7 miles and covers more-rugged terrain. The area is not well explored by birders and thus lacks a list of species to lure visiting birders. It could, however, satisfy visitors who are looking to explore a new area and potentially make some interesting discoveries. Think of it as a birding frontier.

Those eager for a more challenging hike to alpine habitats can continue from Lower Dewey Lake to **Upper Dewey Lake.** Good fitness, hiking experience, and safety planning are required. Leave an itinerary and expected return time with a friend or an official in Skagway. This is a strenuous 5–6 hour, 5.6-mile round-trip hike from Lower Dewey Lake with an elevation gain of 3,100 feet. To reach Upper Dewey Lake continue on the trail at the north end of Lower Dewey Lake and go left (north) across two bridges to the trail junction. Turn right. The trail climbs steeply through a series of switchbacks along Dewey Creek and then emerges from the trees into an alpine meadow. Spectacular views span Mount Harding and Taiya Inlet. There is a cabin for public use at the southwest end of the lake which is owned by the town of Skagway. Please keep it clean and be extremely careful of fire. There is little information about what birds occur in the alpine around Skagway, but one could expect Golden Eagle, Gyrfalcon, all three ptarmigan, Blue Grouse,

Horned Lark, American Pipit, Golden-crowned Sparrow, and Gray-crowned Rosy-Finch. Now, of course, finding either Dusky Flycatcher or Timberline Sparrow would cause the Alaskan birders to sit up and take notice!

Those who are truly gripped with a passion for exploring (and an overnight hike) could continue from Upper Dewey Lake to the Devil's Punch Bowl. Take the trail south of the lake which starts near the Upper Dewey Lake cabin. This moderately-paced two-hour, 2.5-mile round-trip from Upper Dewey Lake leads south up the alpine ridge to a magnificent overlook. Rock cairns mark the footpath where it crosses boulder fields.

Skagway River Outflow and Yakutania Point. The Skagway River flows south along the west side of town and empties into Taiya Inlet. The combination of river outflow and tidal fluctuations creates a wetland that is productive at any time except extreme high tide. An easy-paced trail leads from the mouth of the Skagway River for about one mile to Yakutania Point looking out to Taiya Inlet. To reach the trailhead go west from the visitor center along 2nd Avenue for three blocks to Alaska Street, and then south (left) to the parking area at the corner of 1st Avenue. The trail starts here and runs west just below the southern edge of the Skagway airstrip to a small footbridge across the Skagway River. Go south (left) to reach Yakutania Point. Gulls often roost at the river mouth, with the most common being Mew and Glaucous-winged Gulls. Thayer's Gull occurs in early spring, fall, and winter, and occasionally a Black-legged Kittiwake may be seen. Diving ducks feeding alongside Harbor Seals at the outflow include Harlequin Duck, Bufflehead, Barrow's Goldeneye, and Red-breasted Merganser. Northwestern Crows occur in summer. The trail along Taiya Inlet is one of the better places in southeast Alaska for Boreal Chickadee. A variety of songbirds may be seen during migration.

Dyea and the Chilkoot Trail. To reach Dyea, take 23rd Avenue out of Skagway, cross the Skagway River bridge, and go north on the Klondike Highway for a few hundred yards to Dyea Road. Turn left and continue eight miles as Dyea Road swings south along the Skagway River and then follows Taiya Inlet around Nahku Bay and along the Taiya River, past the ranger station, to the Taiya River bridge. Take any opportunity to stop at the pullouts to scan Nahku Bay or the expansive mudflats at the mouth of the Taiya River. Nahku Bay is a good place from which to view Marbled Murrelets and small pods of Harbor Porpoises.

Dyea Flats offers a mix of coastal Western Hemlock and Sitka Spruce forest, open grassy flats, and expansive mudflats. To reach the flats continue north across the Taiya River bridge, then take the first left. Continue south about one mile through the forest and out onto the open grassy flats. Forest birds include the ever-present Chestnut-backed Chickadee, Brown Creeper, and Golden-crowned Kinglet, as well as Winter Wren and Varied Thrush.

Bald Eagles and various gulls congregate on the open flats. This area is not well birded and there is little information as to what birds are expected, but the habitat looks to have plenty of potential.

The Chilkoot Trail begins at Mile 8 of the Dyea Road just past the ranger station on the southeast side of the Taiya River bridge. It is a rigorous 33-mile, 3-to-5-day hike from Dyea, over the Chilkoot Pass (Elevation 3,550 feet) to the headwaters of the Yukon River at Lindeman Lake or on to Bennett Lake, both located in British Columbia. Hikers are required to reserve a place through the Chilkoot Trail National Historic Site office (see *Logistics*) in order to hike the trail. During the 1898 Gold Rush an estimated 20,000 to 30,000 people passed along the Chilkoot Trail into the Yukon. Apparently there were few birders in the crowd, since little has been published about the area's birdlife. Species expected in the area include Gyrfalcon, all three ptarmigan, Blue Grouse, American Pipit, Townsend's Solitaire, Wilson's Warbler, Golden-crowned Sparrow, Snow Bunting, Gray-crowned Rosy-Finch, and perhaps a Dusky Flycatcher or a Timberline Sparrow. Larger mammals seen along the trail include Mountain Goat, Brown and Black Bears, Caribou, Moose, Coyote, Collared Pika, and Hoary Marmot.

Travelers headed north out of Skagway will follow the Klondike Highway to the **Skagway Summit**. Visitors to Skagway who are not planning to travel farther north should take advantage of one of the tour buses up the Skagway Summit (see *Logistics*). Tour buses usually stop at a few lookout points, which allows for a bit of birding along the way. The train ride along the White Pass & Yukon Route is also a wonderful way to see this rugged landscape and ponder its gold-rush history. The low resonant hoots of Blue Grouse are usually heard on the Skagway side of the summit. The subalpine and alpine habitats are home to Gyrfalcon, Northern Hawk Owl, and Townsend's Solitaire. This is a fantastic area for lowbush cranberry and blueberry picking in fall.

LOGISTICS

Skagway offers a full range of visitor services and amenities. For information contact the Skagway Convention and Visitors Bureau, PO Box 1025, Skagway AK 99840; 907-983-2854; fax 907-983-3854; *infoskag@ptialaska.net*; *www.skagway.org*.

Chilkoot Trail National Historic Site, Parks Canada–Yukon, Suite 205, 300 Main Street, Whitehorse, Yukon Y1A 2B5; 867-667-3910 (local or overseas); 800-661-0486 (North America only); fax 867-393-6701; *whitehorse-info@pch.gc.ca*. Frontier Excursions, 7th Avenue and Broadway, PO Box 543, Skagway, Alaska; 907-983-2512; fax 907-983-3512; *frontier@aptalaska.net*, *www.frontierexcursions.com*.

White Pass & Yukon Route, PO Box 435, Skagway, AK 99840; 800-343-7373; fax 907-983-2734; *info@whitepass.net; www.whitepassrailroad.com*.

Glacier Bay National Park

George West

Glacier Bay is at the northeast corner of southeast Alaska and southcoastal Alaska. Many coastal species that are common farther south do not extend north of Glacier Bay, Haines, and Skagway (see pages 457 and 465). The bay is a beautiful area to visit, especially by ship. Over 50 tour companies schedule trips into the bay and some will land you on shore. Most of the attraction of the bay is related to its glacial history—views of glaciers calving into the bay, remaining features left by the advance of glaciers, succession of forests from bare rock and gravel uncovered by the retreating glaciers, the grandeur of the scenery with the mountains of the Saint Elias range reflected in the bay.

Smaller tour ships have the advantage of being able to cruise into narrower and shallower water, thus being able to approach some birding areas more closely than the large ships. You may get close to the South Marble Islands, where there are nesting Pelagic Cormorant, Black-legged Kittiwake, Common Murre, Pigeon Guillemot, and Tufted Puffin. Marbled Murrelets and especially Kittlitz's Murrelets are common in Glacier Bay, where some 60 percent of Alaska's breeding Kittlitz's Murrelets nest. Other areas you may visit will yield Pacific and Yellow-billed Loons, Surf and White-winged Scoters, Harlequin Duck, Bald Eagle, and Arctic and Aleutian Terns.

The bay and the forested area around Glacier Bay Lodge in Gustavus can be a good place to find additional species such as Western Grebe, American Bittern, Blue Grouse, Horned Puffin, Northern Pygmy-Owl, Northern Saw-whet Owl, Vaux's Swift, American Redstart, and Western Tanager. On a tour, you should also find Brown Bear, Mountain Goat, and Humpback Whale. See *Organizations*, page 539 for logistic information.

ACKNOWLEDGEMENTS: Vladimir Dinets provided birding information. Richard Konz added sightings and logistic information.

HYDER

Steve Heinl

Hyder is a town of fewer than 80 people located about 80 miles northeast of Ketchikan, on mainland southeast Alaska at the Alaska-Canada border. Stewart, BC, is located only a few miles away and both towns are connected by road to the Cassiar Highway and the Alaska Highway (see page 158). Thus, Hyder can be reached by motor vehicle through British Columbia or floatplane from Ketchikan. The Alaska Marine Highway system no longer provides ferry service to Hyder, although that might change in the future. There are accommodations in both Hyder and Stewart. A two- or three-day stay in June would allow plenty of time to see all of the birds of the area.

Mixed spruce/cottonwood groves and dense riparian willow thickets around town, along the Salmon River, and along Fish and Marx Creeks host many species of special interest to Alaska birders. The Salmon River valley is the easiest place in Alaska to see Black Swifts (June–August), and is the only place in Alaska where American Crows have ever been found (fairly common permanent resident). Hyder is the only place in Alaska where Magnolia Warblers are regularly found, and although they are rare, you should be able to find one with a fair amount of searching in the mixed spruce/cottonwood groves around Fish Creek. Other birds to look for include the dark subspecies of Ruffed Grouse (*B.u. umbelloides*), a different race than the one found in interior Alaska (*B.u. yukonensis*), Band-tailed Pigeon, Vaux's Swift, Hammond's Flycatcher, Warbling Vireo, Northern Rough-winged Swallow, Cedar Waxwing, American Redstart, Northern Waterthrush, MacGillivray's Warbler, Common Yellowthroat, Western Tanager, Chipping Sparrow, and Brown-headed Cowbird.

The Hyder area is generally easy to bird. Walk all of the streets around town (early in the morning is the best bet for finding a Band-tailed Pigeon). Walk the main road south out to the boat harbor (**1**) where you can see shorebirds, waterfowl, and Arctic Terns—possibly Caspian Tern in spring and summer. On the grass flats east of the road are a couple of groups of old pilings (**2**), the best place to look for kingbirds. Sort through the flocks of swallows flying over the tidal flats for Northern Rough-winged Swallows. Bird along the large windbreak of Black Cottonwoods that runs east-west across the road right at the south end of town, and walk the road out to the dump (**3**). American Crows can be found nearly anywhere in the Hyder area, but

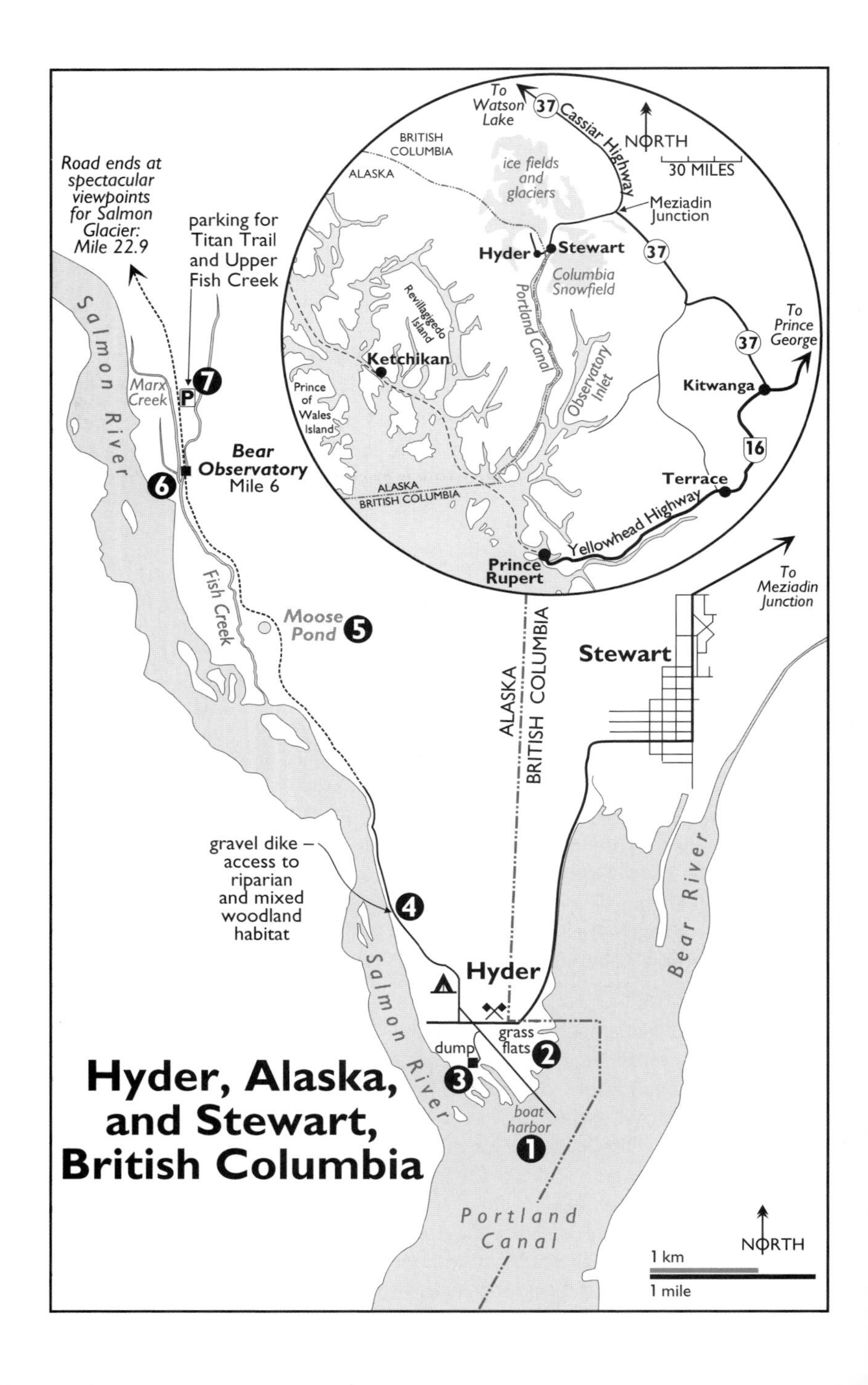
Hyder, Alaska, and Stewart, British Columbia
Road ends at spectacular viewpoints for Salmon Glacier: Mile 22.9
parking for Titan Trail and Upper Fish Creek
Salmon River
Marx Creek
P
7
Bear Observatory Mile 6
6
Fish Creek
Moose Pond
5
ALASKA
BRITISH COLUMBIA
Stewart
To Meziadin Junction
gravel dike – access to riparian and mixed woodland habitat
4
Hyder
Bear River
grass flats
2
dump
3
boat harbor
1
Portland Canal
NORTH
1 km
1 mile
To Watson Lake
37
Cassiar Highway
NORTH
30 MILES
BRITISH COLUMBIA
ALASKA
ice fields and glaciers
Meziadin Junction
Hyder
Stewart
Columbia Snowfield
Revillagigedo Island
Portland Canal
To Prince George
Ketchikan
Prince of Wales Island
Observatory Inlet
Kitwanga
16
Terrace
Yellowhead Highway
Prince Rupert

the dump is an obvious place to look. Chipping Sparrows and Brown-headed Cowbirds are found at the edges of open areas around the south end of town.

Drive the all-weather road north from town. Where the road meets the Salmon River at the north edge of town (**4**) is a wide gravel dike that runs south along the edge of the river, providing access to riparian and mixed woodland habitat. Continuing north a few miles, the road passes a sign marking the National Forest boundary, and a little farther on passes a large Beaver pond on the left named the Moose Pond (**5**). Common Yellowthroats are easy to find in the marshy areas at the pond. Checking the pond frequently during your visit could produce a Hooded Merganser. A short distance farther up the road is the Bear Observatory—a large parking area and boardwalk where the road crosses Fish Creek (**6**). American Dippers nest under the bridge. A dike runs south from the parking area. Walk the dike and walk the road. Just north of the boardwalk is another parking area on the right (**7**) that provides access to the Titan Trail and upper Fish Creek. Continue driving north, stopping where habitat looks good. The road eventually climbs up the ridge, enters British Columbia, and ends at the Salmon Glacier.

Many interesting rarities and hard-to-find species have been found at Hyder as a result of its location at the very north end of Portland Canal and its proximity to the interior of British Columbia: Yellow-bellied Flycatcher, Willow and Least Flycatchers, Eastern Phoebe, Western and Eastern Kingbirds, Cassin's and Red-eyed Vireos, Veery, Tennessee and Black-and-white Warblers, Timberline Sparrow, Black-headed Grosbeak, Lazuli Bunting, Bobolink, House Finch, and Evening Grosbeak.

A word of caution: both Black Bears and Brown Bears are common throughout the area, and some are more habituated to humans than typical wild bears. One should always be cautious and alert for bears when birding in the area. From late July to October bears gather to feed on spawning Pink and Chum Salmon in Fish Creek, where they can be observed and photographed at very close range at the Bear Observatory. During the peak of the salmon run (August–September) hundreds of tourists show up daily to view the bears, and vehicle access can be restricted, particularly in the evenings.

LOGISTICS

Information about the area's history, accommodations in Hyder and Stewart, travel, restaurants, etc., can be found at *www.stewartbchyderak.homestead.com*. Contact Hyder Community Association (250-636-9148) or USDA Forest Service in Hyder (250-636-2367) or Ketchikan (907-225-2148). Because Hyder is on the Canadian road system and most visiting tourists are Canadian, all of the businesses in town take Canadian money. Hyder is on Pacific Time, rather than Alaska Time.

ACKNOWLEDGEMENTS: Delesta Fox explored Hyder in summer 2002 and provided additional birding information.

ANNOTATED LIST OF THE BIRDS OF ALASKA

Following is a list of all species that have been reported to have occurred in Alaska as of June 2002. The basic list is derived from Gibson (1999). Most of the older information was taken from literature references (see page 560). Some of the more recent occurrences of species are from the Alaska Region section of *American Birds* and its successor, *North American Birds,* compiled by Thede Tobish, and are not listed individually in the References in this guide.

This is not an exhaustive or complete list of all sightings or occurrences, but it should serve as a general guide for planning trips to find certain species. Some of the records are from sight-reports only and have not been substantiated by specimen or photograph. Notes on these species are placed in brackets [ ].

It is practically impossible to predict where to find those species that are listed as Accidental or Casual (see definitions below) no matter when you come to Alaska. Therefore, no recommendations of specific places to find these species are given, although some of the places and dates where they have been encountered in the past are listed. Some locations are given for finding Rare, Uncommon, and Fairly Common species. Common species do not have suggested locations but only the general range and habitat where they should be found easily.

Some species are represented in Alaska by two or more subspecies. Some of these are recognizable in the field. The identification of some others may be determined by their distribution. These subspecies are mentioned in the species accounts.

For more information on locating these species, refer to the chapter that discusses birding at the specific locations mentioned in the following list.

A gazetteer of Alaska place names mentioned in the list below begins on page 549. This will assist you in locating the area(s) where these specific places are found. That chapter also gives you a pronunciation guide for some Alaska place names and words.

ABUNDANCE CATEGORIES

COMMON: Found in moderate to large numbers, and easily found in appropriate habitat at the right time of year.

FAIRLY COMMON: Found in small to moderate numbers, and usually easy to find in appropriate habitat at the right time of year.

UNCOMMON: Found in small numbers, and usually—but not always—found with some effort in appropriate habitat at the right time of year.

RARE: Occurs annually in very small numbers. Not to be expected on any given day, but may be found with extended effort over the course of the appropriate season(s).

CASUAL: Occurs less than annually, but there tends to be a pattern over time at the right time of year in appropriate habitat.

ACCIDENTAL: Represents an exceptional occurrence that might not be repeated again for decades; there are usually fewer than five records.

IRREGULAR: Represents an irruptive species whose numbers are highly variable from year to year. There may be small to even large numbers present in any one year, while in another year it may be absent altogether.

ABBREVIATIONS

ANWR = Arctic National Wildlife Refuge
E = east (ern)
Hwy = Highway
Is = Island(s)
Months are designated by the first three letters of the month, e.g., Jan, Feb, Mar.
N = north (ern)
NE = northeast (ern)
NM=National Monument
NP = National Park
NW = northwest (ern)
NWR = National Wildlife Refuge
Pen = Peninsula
Rd = Road
S = south (ern)
SE = southeast (ern)
SW = southwest (ern)
W = west (ern)
W Aleutians = almost always includes Attu Island, and usually includes Shemya and Buldir Islands.

Red-throated Loon *Gavia stellata* — Uncommon summer resident in lakes and ponds from southcentral Alaska to the N coast. Most common from the Seward Pen N and E across the arctic coastal plain into Canada, but also nests in coastal marshes in W Alaska, the Alaska Pen, on the Aleutian Is, and in SE Alaska. Best spots in summer include Cordova, Soldotna, Denali Hwy, Parks Hwy near Healy, Nome, and Barrow. Uncommon winter resident in bays and coastal saltwater from southcentral Alaska S. Uncommon in migration at Gambell and rare on other Bering Sea Is. Easy to find off the breeding grounds in marine waters in SE Alaska, Cordova, Seward, and Homer.

Arctic Loon *Gavia arctica* — Rare to casual breeder on NW coast of Alaska. In summer rare from Cape Krusenstern S to Nome on the Seward Pen, and a migrant in the far W Aleutians and on the Bering Sea Is. May be seen during spring migration from Nome, Wales, and St. Lawrence Is. Easiest to find close-up at lakes near Kotzebue where they breed, but sometimes is found with Pacific Loons at Nome in spring and at Gambell. Formerly regular at Safety Sound in Nome in June, less so recently, but has been seen there regularly in August for the past several years.

Pacific Loon *Gavia pacifica* — Fairly common summer resident in lakes, ponds, and wet tundra from southcentral Alaska and the Alaska Pen N. More common than Red-throated Loon in similar habitat, and may be found in summer nesting around Cordova, Soldotna, in lakes on the Edgerton Hwy into Chitina, and on the Glenn and Denali Hwy. Also common in saltwater in summer around Prince William Sound, Resurrection and Kachemak Bays. Uncommon to rare in the Aleutian Is. In winter common on saltwater from SE to southcoastal Alaska. Common in migration at Gambell.

Common Loon *Gavia immer* — Fairly common throughout Alaska from the Aleutians to E Norton Sound, E south of the Brooks Range into Canada, and S to all of SE Alaska. Rare at Nome except for post-breeding wanderers in August. Nests in freshwater lakes. Easily seen on any of the larger lakes along the interior road system. Winters on saltwater from southcoastal Alaska S. Rare around the southern Bering Sea Is, but not present at Gambell.

Yellow-billed Loon *Gavia adamsii* — Uncommon summer resident in lakes and ponds from the N Seward Pen N and E along the arctic coastal plain into Canada. Rare but regular in small numbers at Gambell, often uncommon in spring; casual at St. Paul. In winter rare to uncommon around Kodiak Is, and in sheltered saltwater in southcoastal and SE Alaska. Rare in Resurrection and Kachemak Bays. One sight record for the Chena Hot Springs Rd E of Fairbanks in Jun 1999. Best found at Gambell in spring and mid-autumn, Nome (rare), Kotzebue, Barrow, or the Colville River delta in summer.

Pied-billed Grebe *Podilymbus podiceps* — Casual in spring and rare in fall migration in freshwater ponds and marshes of SE Alaska. Accidental in southcoastal Alaska in summer (Anchorage, Portage) and fall (Cordova).

Horned Grebe *Podiceps auritus* — Fairly common in summer in interior Alaska where it breeds on lakes and ponds with emergent vegetation from 50 miles E of the Bering Sea coast in the Yukon River Valley E into Canada and S to Cordova. Rarely occurs in N Alaska, on the Aleutian or Pribilof Is, casual north to St. Lawrence Is. Winters in saltwater from the Aleutians and southcoastal Alaska S to SE Alaska. Easy to find in Kachemak and Resurrection Bays from fall to spring, and in lakes and ponds along the road system throughout the interior in summer.

Red-necked Grebe *Podiceps grisegena* — Fairly common summer resident throughout the state (except for SE Alaska) in lakes and ponds. Easy to find in summer on any larger lake or pond adjacent to the road system of interior Alaska and the Kenai Pen. Rare to casual on the Bering Sea Is. Winters on saltwater in southcoastal and SE Alaska. Easy to find on Kachemak or Resurrection Bay from fall to spring.

Eared Grebe *Podiceps nigricollis* — Accidental at Fairbanks in May 1998 and in Juneau in May 2000.

Western Grebe *Aechmophorus occidentalis* — Uncommon to fairly common in Ketchikan, Wrangell, Petersburg, rare in Juneau, and accidental at Skagway in SE Alaska. Large numbers winter locally around Ketchikan and can be seen there in some years as late as May.

[**Clark's Grebe** *Aechmophorus clarkii* — Accidental from sight records at Petersburg (Nov 1993) and Juneau (Eagle Beach) in Aug 1997.]

Laysan Albatross *Phoebastria immutabilis* — Uncommon to fairly common visitant from spring to early winter offshore in the Gulf of Alaska and along the S shore (locally along the N shore) of the Aleutian Is. May be seen from the Dutch Harbor ferry (Unimak Pass), and from the Juneau-Seward ferry. Possible off Kodiak Is. Casual N in the Bering Sea to near the Pribilof Is. Accidental off the Barren Is.

Black-footed Albatross *Phoebastria nigripes* — Fairly common visitant from spring to early winter offshore in the Gulf of Alaska and along the S shore of the Aleutian Is. May be seen from the Dutch Harbor ferry and from the Juneau-Seward ferry. Possible off Kodiak Is. Rare in the Bering Sea N to near the Pribilof Is.

Short-tailed Albatross *Phoebastria albatrus* — Very rare offshore in the Gulf of Alaska (over Pamplona Spur and off Middleton Is), S of Kodiak Is, S of the Shumagin Is, S of the W Aleutian Is, and in the S Bering Sea in summer N at least to St. Paul Is. Increasing in number in recent years. Has been seen from the ferry to Dutch Harbor and the ferry from Juneau to Seward. Otherwise found only from charter and commercial vessels in the Gulf of Alaska and the N Pacific Ocean.

Northern Fulmar *Fulmarus glacialis* — Common in the Gulf of Alaska offshore from Juneau to Resurrection Bay, lower Cook Inlet, around Kodiak Is, throughout the Aleutian Is, Pribilof Is, and N to St. Lawrence Is. Easy to find on most marine tours from Seward or Homer, the ferries from Juneau to Seward and Homer to Dutch Harbor, from St. Lawrence Is, and on the Pribilof Is.

Mottled Petrel *Pterodroma inexpectata* — Uncommon summer visitant well offshore in SW, SE, and southcoastal Alaska in summer and rare in the S and E Bering Sea (SW of the Pribilof Is). Very rare summer visitant nearer shore in SW, southcoastal, and SE Alaska. Casual in Amukta and Buldir Passes, but may be common south of the central and W Aleutians from Attu E to Amchitka in summer. Few documented sightings. Watch E of Chiniak Bay and S of Kodiak Is, around the Shumagin Is, in the S Bering Sea, and around Unimak Pass from the Homer-Dutch Harbor ferry. Otherwise found only from charter and commercial vessels in the Gulf of Alaska and the N Pacific Ocean.

Cook's Petrel *Pterodroma cookii* — Accidental near Adak Is in Aug 1933.

Pink-footed Shearwater *Puffinus creatopus* — Uncommon in the Gulf of Alaska and in SE Alaska well offshore. Has been found from the ferry between Juneau and Seward and around Kodiak Is.

[**Flesh-footed Shearwater** *Puffinus carneipes* — Casual in summer and fall well offshore in southcoastal (Ocean Cape below Yakutat, S of the Kenai Pen) and SW Alaska (Port Moller, Gareloi Is). One was seen inshore off Kodiak Is in Aug 1999.]

Greater Shearwater *Puffinus gravis* — Accidental off Montague Is in Aug 2001.

Buller's Shearwater *Puffinus bulleri* — Rare well offshore in late summer and early fall in the Gulf of Alaska between Middleton Is and the Fairweather Grounds and W of Kodiak Is. Very few documented sightings. One record off Sitka in Sep 1997. Best chance may be W of Kayak Is from the Juneau-Seward ferry in late summer and early fall, or from the Homer-Dutch Harbor ferry when the ferry runs S of Kodiak Is.

Sooty Shearwater *Puffinus griseus* — Common and usually in large flocks in summer from SE Alaska to the Aleutians. Casual N to the Pribilof Is. Easily found on most marine tours on Cook Inlet, Resurrection Bay, and on the Juneau-Seward and Homer-Dutch Harbor ferries.

Short-tailed Shearwater *Puffinus tenuirostris* — Common (abundant) and usually in large flocks in summer from Resurrection Bay and Cook Inlet to the Aleutians, and more common than Sooty Shearwater N of the Aleutians in the Bering Sea as far N as the Bering Strait. Easily found from the Dutch Harbor ferry and likely on tours in Cook Inlet. This species and Sooty Shearwater are usually in mixed flocks in southcoastal Alaska. Flocks often contain Northern Fulmar, as well. Flocks moving past Gambell and St. Paul in early fall can number in the hundred of thousands of birds per day.

[**Manx Shearwater** *Puffinus puffinus* — Accidental in the Gulf of Alaska in Jul 1976, lower Cook Inlet in Jun 1975, Seldovia Bay in Aug 1993, off Kodiak Is in Aug 1976, N of Cold Bay in the Bering Sea in Jun 1998, and outside Haines in Aug 2001. All the above are sight records.]

[**Little Shearwater** *Puffinus assimilis* — Accidental from sight records off Kodiak Is in Aug 1996 and outer Resurrection Bay in Oct 1997.]

Fork-tailed Storm-Petrel *Oceanodroma furcata* — Common in summer when it nests in large colonies from the Aleutian Is S to the Forrester Is. Easily seen from the Juneau-Seward and Homer-Dutch Harbor ferries and often on marine tours out of Seward and Homer. Usually can be seen from the end of the Homer Spit in spring, summer, and fall, but unpredictable. Rare in the Bering Sea N to the Pribilof Is and casual at Gambell. Accidental in Anchorage. Usually not found near its nesting area during daylight as the birds come in after sunset and leave for feeding areas before sunrise. The lighter form, *O. f. furcata,* is commonly seen from the Aleutians E to Glacier Bay. The darker form, *O. f. plumbea,* is found in SE Alaska.

Leach's Storm-Petrel *Oceanodroma leucorhoa* — Fairly common in summer when it nests on Forrester and St. Lazaria Is and in the Aleutians. May be seen from the Homer-Dutch Harbor or the Juneau-Seward ferries. Rare in the Bering Sea N to the Pribilof Is. Casual near shore in SE Alaska. Usually not found near its nesting area during daylight since the birds come in after sunset and leave for feeding areas before sunrise.

[**Brown Booby** *Sula leucogaster* — There are two records of boobies found onboard a ship in the Bering Sea, the latest in Jul 2000. Thus far these birds are not recognized as a naturally occurring species in Alaska. Photographs indicate that one bird may have been a Red-footed Booby, *Sula sula* (P. Lehman, pers. com.)]

American White Pelican *Pelecanus erythrorhynchos* — Accidental. In SE Alaska records are from one at Petersburg in spring/summer 1981, one at Klawock in Jun 1993, one at Ketchikan in Jun 1993.

Brandt's Cormorant *Phalacrocorax penicillatus* — Rare and local in SE Alaska (Forrester, Lowrie, and Hazy Is W of Coronation Is; some winter near Ketchikan) and very rare in southcoastal Alaska (small breeding colony at Seal Rocks). Accidental in Kachemak Bay.

Double-crested Cormorant *Phalacrocorax auritus* — Common summer resident and breeder along the coast from Kodiak Is into the E Aleutian Is and in many lakes in southcoastal and SW Alaska. Found along the coast from Kachemak Bay E and S to SE Alaska. Casual in spring in Anchorage and in summer N to the Pribilof Is; accidental N to Nome.

Red-faced Cormorant *Phalacrocorax urile* — Common from Resurrection and Kachemak Bays, the Barren Is, Kodiak Is, westward along the Aleutians and N to the Pribilof Is. May be seen as far N as St. Matthew Is. Winters along the coast from the Aleutians to Resurrection Bay. Easy to find on tours out of Homer and Seward, and trips to St. Paul. Hard to get decent views and to identify from the Dutch Harbor ferry.

Pelagic Cormorant *Phalacrocorax pelagicus* — Common throughout SE and southcoastal Alaska and W through the Aleutians. Uncommon to fairly common throughout the Bering Sea N at least to Cape Thompson. Easy to find on day-trips out of Homer and Seward and on visits to Gambell. Hard to get decent views and to identify from the Homer-Dutch Harbor ferry.

Magnificent Frigatebird *Fregata magnificens* — Accidental. One documented sighting off the Alaska Pen in late Aug 1985. Frigatebirds have been reported in the N Gulf of Alaska, Montague Strait, and off Kodiak Is.

American Bittern *Botaurus lentiginosus* — Rare summer visitor in the Chickamin and Stikine River valleys; casual at Juneau and Gustavus.

Yellow Bittern *Ixobrychus sinensis* — Accidental at Attu Is in May 1989.

Great Blue Heron *Ardea herodias* — Uncommon resident from SE Alaska to Cook Inlet. Easy to find along the coast or freshwater margins in SE Alaska. Rare W to Valdez, Seward, Kachemak Bay, Kenai, and Kodiak Is. Casual in interior Alaska (Tok, Chatanika River).

[**Gray Heron** *Ardea cinerea* — Accidental from sight records on Attu in Apr 1986 and from St. Paul Is in Aug 1999.]

Great Egret *Ardea alba* — Casual summer and fall visitor to SE (Sitka, Juneau, Glacier Bay), southcentral (Kodiak), and SW (Egegik) Alaska.

Chinese Egret *Egretta eulophotes* — Accidental at Agattu Is in Jun 1974.

Little Egret *Egretta garzetta* — Accidental at Buldir Is in May 2000.

[**Snowy Egret** *Egretta thula* — Accidental in Juneau from sight records in May 1957.]

Cattle Egret *Bubulcus ibis* — Casual in Nov and Dec in SE Alaska (*B. i. ibis*). A single dead bird of the Asiatic race, *B. i. coromanda*, was found on Agattu Is in Jun 1988.

Chinese Pond-Heron *Ardeola bacchus* — Accidental on St. Paul Is in Aug 1996.

Green Heron *Butorides virescens* — Accidental in Juneau in May 1983.

Black-crowned Night-Heron *Nycticorax nycticorax* — Accidental at Attu in Apr 1986 and in Juneau in summer 1987. Subsequent sight records are from Atka, Buldir, Shemya, St. Paul Is, St. George Is, Homer, and Kodiak Is.

Turkey Vulture *Cathartes aura* — Casual in interior Alaska with sightings of single birds from Delta, Northway, the Tanana, Porcupine, and Yukon River Valleys and from Cordova and Dillingham on the coast in summer. Records also from Nome in 1996, Kodiak in 1999, and Ketchikan in 1996 and 1997.

Bean Goose *Anser fabalis* — Rare spring migrant in the W and central Aleutians (Attu, Adak) and on St Paul Island; casual on St. Lawrence Is and on the Seward Pen coast (Nome). Rare on the Pribilof Is. Most birds are probably Taiga Bean Goose, *A. f. middendorffii,* but there are records from the Pribilof Is of larger birds that may be Tundra Bean Goose *A. f. serrirostris*. Best sought on St. Paul Is.

Greater White-fronted Goose *Anser albifrons* — Common in summer where it breeds along the coast from Barter Is westward (*A.a. gambelli*), southward to Bristol Bay (*A.a. frontalis*), and E into the W shore of Cook Inlet (the Tule Goose, *A.a. elgasi*). Uncommon in the interior of Alaska, where it nests in smaller numbers along major rivers such as the Yukon and Tanana. In migration, may be found in SE and southcoastal Alaska, and through the interior on their route to and from the arctic coastal plain, and at Gambell. Casual in spring and fall migration on the Pribilof Is.

Lesser White-fronted Goose *Anser erythropus* — Accidental at Attu Is in Jun 1994.

Emperor Goose *Chen canagica* — Fairly common in summer, nesting from the mouth of the Kuskokwim River N to the N side of the Seward Pen. Summer visitant E to Cordova and W to the Aleutian Is. Also occurs on the Bering Sea Is but is not known to breed there. Winters primarily in the Aleutian Is and some birds may be found E as far as Prince William Sound and even S to California. Accidental in Anchorage in Apr 2002. Best found on the Bering Sea Is in migration and around Kodiak Is in winter.

Snow Goose *Chen caerulescens* — Fairly common in migration in SE Alaska and common in migration in southcoastal Alaska, with many hundreds stopping on the Kenai River flats in spring. However, nests on the Canadian arctic islands. Some birds may be found along the NW coast of Alaska and are uncommon in fall on St. Lawrence and casual on the Pribilof Is. NW Pacific coast birds nest on Wrangel Is in NE Siberia.

Ross's Goose *Chen rossii* — Casual spring migrant in SE, southcentral, and N Alaska, usually in the company of Snow Geese.

Canada Goose *Branta canadensis* — Common resident in S Alaska and common migrant and breeder throughout the state. The following races are found in the state: *B.c. occidentalis*, the Dusky Canada Goose that breeds on the Copper River Delta near Cordova; *B.c. minima*, Cackling Canada Goose that migrates through southcoastal Alaska to the Yukon-Kuskokwim Delta; *B.c. leucopareia*, Aleutian Canada Goose that breeds on the W Aleutian Is; *B.c. parvipes*, Lesser Canada Goose that breeds throughout interior Alaska from southcoastal Alaska to N of Fairbanks; *B.c. taverneri*, Taverner's Canada Goose that breeds on the tundra of N and W Alaska (casual on the Bering Sea Is), and *B.c. fulva*, Vancouver Canada Goose that is resident in SE Alaska. Easy to find in Anchorage and throughout the state.

Brant *Branta bernicla* — Common in summer, nesting along the coast from SW Alaska N to the arctic coast and then E into Canada. May be found along the coast of southcoastal Alaska from SE Alaska to the Aleutians in migration. In winter, large numbers remain in the Aleutian Is and Alaska Pen (Izembek NWR). Common migrant around St. Lawrence Is and rare around the Pribilof Is. Most birds are Black Brant, *B.b. nigricans*, but the white-bellied form that breeds across the Canadian arctic, *B.b. hrota*, has also been reported on the Bering Sea coast.

Trumpeter Swan *Cygnus buccinator* — Fairly common to locally common summer resident from the N Kenai Pen E to N Prince William Sound, especially around Cordova. Uncommon migrant and established breeder in interior Alaska and rare in W Alaska. Winters rarely on the Kenai River and regularly in Cordova and farther S and E along the coast. Uncommon migrant and winter visitant in SE Alaska. Best found in Cordova, on the Swanson River canoe trail system near Sterling, and on small lakes along the interior road system.

Tundra Swan *Cygnus columbianus* — Common summer resident from the central Aleutians, Alaska Pen, Bristol Bay, and Kodiak Is, N along coastal W Alaska primarily along the lower Kuskokwim and Yukon Rivers through the Seward Pen and N to Wainwright and Barrow, and then E along the Beaufort Sea coast to Barter Is and into Canada. Rare on the Bering Sea Is. They migrate along the coast and through interior Alaska to winter on Pacific coasts of continental U.S. All birds are the nominate subspecies except for one record of Bewick's Swan, *C.c. bewickii,* from Adak Is in 1977.

Whooper Swan *Cygnus cygnus* — Uncommon winter visitant in the W and central Aleutian Is. Casual in spring and summer on Attu Is (successful nesting in 1996 and 1997), on St. Paul and St. Lawrence Is, and in W Alaska (Wales, Nome) N to the Noatak River Delta. Accidental in fall in southcoastal Alaska (Cordova) and in winter on the Alaska Pen (Golovin). Best found in the far W and central Aleutians in winter.

Wood Duck *Aix sponsa* — Casual migrant, summer and winter visitant in SE Alaska. Accidental in Cordova in Sep 1988 and on Kodiak Is in Nov 1994.

Gadwall *Anas strepera* — Fairly common in southcoastal Alaska on the Copper River Delta, uncommon around N Cook Inlet, fairly common on the Alaska Pen, and uncommon on the Aleutian Is. Common to uncommon migrant in SE, southcoastal, and SW Alaska and the E Aleutians. Rare migrant in SE interior Alaska and in W Alaska. Casual migrant on the Bering Sea Is.

Falcated Duck *Anas falcata* — Casual migrant and summer and winter visitant in the W and central Aleutian Is. Casual spring migrant to St. Paul Is.

Eurasian Wigeon *Anas penelope* — Very rare spring migrant in SE (Apr and May) and rare spring migrant in southcoastal Alaska, and uncommon spring and fall migrant in the Aleutian Is. Rare spring and fall migrant on the Bering Sea Is, in coastal W Alaska, and on the N coast (Prudhoe Bay). Best found during spring migration (Mar) at Cordova, Homer, or Kodiak.

American Wigeon *Anas americana* — Common spring and fall migrant in SE Alaska. Common summer resident in southcoastal Alaska from Yakutat, Prince William Sound, and Cook Inlet, N to Kotzebue and E, S of the Brooks Range, into Canada. Uncommon on the Alaska Pen and the Aleutian Is. Rare migrant on the Bering Sea Is. Common migrant and uncommon winter resident in SE Alaska.

American Black Duck *Anas rubripes* — Accidental migrant in central interior Alaska (Fairbanks, May 1972), southcoastal Alaska (Cordova, May 1975), and (Gustavus, 1969–1973).

Mallard *Anas platyrhynchos* — Common in summer throughout the state from SE Alaska to the North Slope. Rare on the Bering Sea Is. Common winter resident throughout much of SE and southcoastal Alaska and uncommon in interior Alaska where there is open water.

Spot-billed Duck *Anas poecilorhyncha* — Casual in spring on Adak Is, accidental on Kodiak Is in Oct 1977, and on Attu Is in spring and fall.

Blue-winged Teal *Anas discors* — Uncommon spring and fall migrant in SE Alaska. Rare summer resident in the Juneau area N to Glacier Bay. Uncommon migrant and rare summer visitant and breeder in E interior Alaska (Fairbanks, Tetlin NWR, Fort Yukon). Rare migrant and very rare breeder in southcoastal Alaska as far W as upper Cook Inlet (Anchorage), S on the upper Kenai Pen (Sterling) and on Kodiak Is. Accidental in the E Aleutians and at Prudhoe Bay.

Cinnamon Teal *Anas cyanoptera* — Rare spring migrant in mainland SE Alaska from Ketchikan, Sitka, and Juneau N to Gustavus. Casual spring migrant in southcoastal Alaska from Cordova to Anchorage and Kodiak Is, and casual summer visitant to central Alaska (Kenny Lake and Fairbanks). Casual in fall on Kodiak Is.

Northern Shoveler *Anas clypeata* — Fairly common migrant and breeder in the E half of interior Alaska W to Fairbanks, and locally in southcoastal Alaska including Kodiak Is. Rare to uncommon migrant and summer visitant and rare breeder in W Alaska from Bristol Bay N to the Seward Pen. Rare migrant and breeder in N Alaska along the Colville River and at Prudhoe Bay. Rare migrant and winter visitant in the Aleutian Is and SW Alaska. Rare migrant and summer visitant on the Alaska Pen, and rare migrant on the Pribilof Is. Uncommon to fairly common migrant in SE Alaska.

Northern Pintail *Anas acuta* — Common migrant through SE Alaska and common summer breeder throughout the rest of Alaska, including the Bering Sea Is.

Garganey *Anas querquedula* — Very rare spring and fall migrant in the W and central Aleutian Is. Casual spring and fall migrant on St. Paul Is.

Baikal Teal *Anas formosa* — Casual migrant and summer visitant in W Alaska from the Bering Strait N (Wainwright) and across N Alaska (Prudhoe Bay, Jun 1993). Casual migrant S of the Bering Strait on the Bering Sea coast (Wales) King, St. Lawrence (Savoonga), and St. Paul Is. Accidental on the W Aleutian Is.

Green-winged Teal *Anas crecca* — The North American subspecies *A.c. carolinensis* is a migrant and common summer resident throughout the state from SE Alaska to the Brooks Range, the Bering Sea Is, and the Aleutian Is. Uncommon on the North Slope to the Arctic coast. Uncommon winter resident from SE Alaska along southcoastal Alaska to the near Aleutian Is. The Eurasian subspecies, Common Teal, *A.c. crecca*, is a migrant and breeder on the W Aleutian Is E to Akutan and occurs rarely farther S (Haines, Juneau) and E (Kodiak Is, Kenai River flats), N in the Bering Sea to the Pribilof and St. Lawrence Is, and to the coast (Nome).

Canvasback *Aythya valisineria* — Uncommon migrant and breeder in central Alaska from Fairbanks SE into Canada. Uncommon and local breeder in southcoastal Alaska from Anchorage S and E from Homer to the Copper River Delta. Casual winter visitant to Kodiak Is. Rare to very rare spring and fall migrant and summer visitant in W Alaska from Bethel N to the Yukon-Kuskokwim River Delta. Rare migrant in Bristol Bay. Rare and local winter visitant in the E Aleutian Is. Rare spring and fall migrant and casual summer visitant to Glacier Bay and Juneau. Rare migrant to Kodiak Is and casual on the Pribilof Is. Rare north to Nome. Easy to find in summer at Potter Marsh S of Anchorage.

Redhead *Aythya americana* — Uncommon migrant and rare breeder in E central Alaska from Fairbanks SE into Canada. Rare spring migrant in southcoastal Alaska and on the Kenai Pen E to the Copper River Delta. Casual spring migrant and summer visitant to N Alaska on the Colville River and W and S along the coast (Nome) to SW Alaska. Rare spring migrant in SE Alaska from Sitka to Juneau.

Common Pochard *Aythya ferina* — Rare spring migrant in the central and W Aleutians and casual at St. Paul, Gambell, and Nome.

Ring-necked Duck *Aythya collaris* — Uncommon migrant, rare summer visitant, and very rare breeder in E central interior Alaska from Fairbanks NE through the Yukon Flats and S to Wasilla. Rare migrant and summer visitant in southcoastal Alaska from Kodiak Is, King Salmon, Homer, Sterling, Seward, and Cordova, and casual on the Pribilof Is. Casual visitant to N, W, and SW Alaska. Uncommon to rare migrant and breeder in SE Alaska from Sitka to Juneau.

Tufted Duck *Aythya fuligula* — Rare to locally uncommon spring and fall migrant and winter visitant in the central and W Aleutians. Very rare winter visitant to the E Aleutians (Dutch Harbor). Rare migrant and summer visitant on St. Paul Is and casual farther N in the Bering Sea on St. Matthew Is, at Gambell, and at Nome. Casual winter visitant to southcoastal (Kodiak, Cordova) and SE Alaska (Petersburg). Accidental in N Alaska (Barrow).

Greater Scaup *Aythya marila* — Common summer resident and breeder from the Alaska Pen N along the W coast of Alaska, the Yukon-Kuskokwim River lowlands, Seward Pen, Kotzebue Sound, and on the lower Kobuk River. Uncommon to casual N of and in the Brooks Range into Canada and on the Bering Sea Is. Also common in summer in southcoastal Alaska from the E Aleutian Is E to the Copper River Delta and on Kodiak Is. Common in winter in saltwater along southcoastal Alaska (Prince William Sound, Kachemak Bay, Kodiak) and throughout the Aleutians. Also common in winter in SE Alaska (*A.m. mariloides*). One record of the darker-backed Eurasian form, *A.m. marila,* from St. George Is in 1966.

Lesser Scaup *Aythya affinis* — Common summer resident and breeder throughout the E interior of Alaska, primarily in the Yukon and Tanana River Valleys, but also as far W as Denali NP. Rare in southcoastal Alaska, in W Alaska (Yukon-Kuskokwim River Delta), the Pribilof Is, NW Alaska (Kotzebue), and in the Brooks Range. Uncommon migrant and rare in winter in SE Alaska.

Steller's Eider *Polysticta stelleri* — Once a common breeding bird in Alaska, it is now uncommon in all areas in summer. Some pairs may still breed in coastal W and N Alaska, but the majority breeds in coastal Siberia. Non-breeders are rare in summer in the W Aleutian Is, the coast of W Alaska, and the Bering Sea Is, although it is a regular migrant at Gambell. Common in winter around Kodiak Is, the Alaska Pen, E Aleutian Is, and E to Kachemak (Homer) and Resurrection (Seward) Bays. Casual in summer in southcoastal Alaska (Homer, Seward). Casual in winter in SE Alaska. Accidental at Fairbanks (Creamer's Field, May 2002).

Spectacled Eider *Somateria fischeri* — Uncommon breeder in W and N coastal Alaska from the Yukon-Kuskokwim Delta into Canada. Best found in summer at the Colville River Delta and Barrow. Can be seen at Gambell and sometimes Nome in spring and fall. Winters well offshore in the Bering Sea. Casual spring and fall migrant around the Pribilof Is. Casual in southcoastal Alaska (Kodiak, Homer). In winter, range in the Bering Sea dependent on the extent of the sea-ice pack.

King Eider *Somateria spectabilis* — Common spring and fall migrant along the coast of W and N Alaska (Hooper Bay, Pribilof Is, St. Lawrence Is, Nome, Barrow), but only a few remain to nest in N Alaska (from Wainwright to the Canadian border). Most continue E into Canada. Winters in the E Aleutians, Bristol Bay, Alaska Pen, Kodiak Is, and rarely E to Kachemak Bay. Declining in number on the North Slope.

Common Eider *Somateria mollissima* — Common but declining summer resident and breeder in the Aleutian Is and W and N coastal Alaska from the Yukon-Kuskokwim Delta N and E into Canada. Also locally common in summer in Cook Inlet, Kodiak Is, Kachemak Bay, and rarely E to Glacier Bay. Uncommon in summer on the Bering Sea Is. Winters commonly in the Bering Sea, around the Aleutian Is, Kodiak Is, Cook Inlet, and Kachemak Bay (*S.m. v-nigra*). One record of the eastern form, *S.m. borealis,* from Barrow in 1994.

Harlequin Duck *Histrionicus histrionicus* — Common summer resident and breeder along streams in S Alaska and the Alaska Pen and from the islands of SE Alaska N to Cook Inlet. Locally common in the interior N to the Brooks Range. Rare N of the Brooks Range. Common resident around the Bering Sea Is, Aleutian Is, Kodiak Is, Kachemak and Resurrection Bays, Prince William Sound, and throughout SE Alaska.

Surf Scoter *Melanitta perspicillata* — Common summer resident on lakes and in saltwater throughout the state, but does not breed in SE Alaska. Nests most commonly along the Bering Sea coast, Beaufort Sea coast, in the upper Yukon River Valley, and in scattered locations W to Denali NP. Common in winter on saltwater in SE and southcoastal Alaska and less common along the Alaska Pen and E Aleutian Is. Casual spring and summer visitor to the Pribilof Is.

White-winged Scoter *Melanitta fusca* — Common summer resident from SE Alaska (but does not nest there) along southcoastal Alaska into the Aleutian Is, and N into interior Alaska from the upper Kuskokwim and Yukon River Valleys, E through the Koyukuk, Tanana, and Porcupine River Valleys into Canada. The center of the breeding area is away from the coast in the interior. Common winter resident throughout SE Alaska W in southcoastal Alaska to the E Aleutians, uncommon to the W Aleutians and rare around the Bering Sea Is.

Black Scoter *Melanitta nigra* — Common but declining summer resident and breeder along the coast of W Alaska. Also breeds on the Alaska Pen, rarely on Kodiak Is, at some locations in interior Alaska such as Denali NP, and E rarely to Yakutat. Rare migrant on St. Lawrence and the Pribilof Is. Common winter resident in saltwater from the Aleutians E along the Alaska Pen, Kodiak Is, southcoastal Alaska, E and S into SE Alaska.

Long-tailed Duck *Clangula hyemalis* — (formerly Oldsquaw) — Common but declining summer resident and breeder along the coast from the Alaska Pen N and then E into Canada. Easily found at Gambell, Barrow, the Colville River Delta, and Barter Is on the N coast in summer. Also common along major river valleys into the interior (Kuskokwim, Yukon, Kobuk Rivers) as far as Denali NP, Talkeetna, and Minto. Uncommon on the Aleutians, in the Brooks Range, and on the Bering Sea Is in summer. Common winter resident in open saltwater from the Bering Sea S through the Bering Sea Is, the Aleutian Is, Kodiak Is, southcoastal Alaska, and in SE Alaska.

Bufflehead *Bucephala albeola* — Common summer resident and breeder in interior Alaska from the Kuskokwim River Valley across the Yukon and Tanana River flats, and the Porcupine River Valley into Canada. Casual in summer in southcoastal (Anchorage) and W (Bristol Bay, Hooper Bay) Alaska. Common winter resident in SE Alaska, around Kodiak Is, the Alaska Pen, and the E Aleutian Is. Casual from Cordova to Homer in winter. Casual on the Bering Sea Is.

Common Goldeneye *Bucephala clangula* — Common summer resident and breeder in interior Alaska from the middle Yukon and Kuskokwim River Valleys, the Tanana River Valley, and eastward into Canada. Uncommon in southcoastal Alaska, Kodiak Is, E and S to SE Alaska. Common winter resident in the Aleutian Is, Alaska Pen, Kodiak Is, Kachemak and Resurrection Bays, Prince William Sound, S through Glacier Bay into SE Alaska. Uncommon migrant on the Pribilof Is (*B.c. americana*). One record of the Eurasian form, *B.c. clangula,* from St. Paul Is in 1914.

Barrow's Goldeneye *Bucephala islandica* — Common summer resident and breeder from southcoastal Alaska (Alaska Pen, Kodiak, Cordova, Kenai Pen, Yakutat), N through the interior (Denali NP, Minto Flats, Yukon and Porcupine River Valleys), into Canada. Common winter resident throughout SE Alaska N to southcoastal Alaska and the E Aleutians. Casual spring migrant on the Pribilof Is.

Smew *Mergellus albellus* — Rare spring and fall migrant in the W and central Aleutians; casual summer visitant in the Aleutians. Casual spring migrant at St. Paul Is, Kodiak Is, and Cordova. Best chance is St. Paul Is.

Hooded Merganser *Lophodytes cucullatus* — Uncommon resident and breeder in SE Alaska as far N as the Chilkat River and into Glacier Bay. Rare visitant any season to southcoastal Alaska (Cordova, Seward, Homer, Portage, Anchorage, Kodiak). Rare migrant and summer visitant in central Alaska S of the Alaska Range on the Parks, Denali, and Glenn Hwys, and casual in fall N of the Alaska Range (Fairbanks). Casual visitant in SW Alaska (Katmai) and on Adak, Attu, and other Aleutian Is. Accidental on the Pribilof Is in fall and St. Lawrence Is in spring.

Common Merganser *Mergus merganser* — The American subspecies, *M.m. americanus,* is common throughout SE Alaska and N to Prince William Sound (Cordova) on freshwater lakes, rivers, and streams, and in saltwater. Less common on the Kenai Pen, Alaska Pen, Kodiak Is, E Aleutian Is, and Seward Pen. Casual on the Pribilof Is. Also present in Bristol Bay N to the Kobuk Valley and E to the Tanana River at Nenana, Fairbanks, Paxson, Eagle, and Fort Yukon. Common in winter throughout SE Alaska and in saltwater in southcoastal Alaska westward to the central Aleutian Is (Umnak). The nominate race (*M.m. merganser*) is a rare migrant in the W and central Aleutian Is and casual on St. Lawrence Is.

Red-breasted Merganser *Mergus serrator* — Common throughout Alaska including the Aleutian Is along the coast and major rivers and lakes. Also occurs on islands in the Bering Sea and along the NW coast to the Kobuk and Noatak Rivers. From there E, it is casual to locally uncommon along the Beaufort Sea coast around the Colville River Delta and E into Canada. Common along the Yukon, Tanana, Koyukuk, and Porcupine Rivers as well as in lakes in the Brooks Range. Common in winter in SE Alaska and across southcoastal Alaska saltwater to the Alaska Pen. Uncommon in winter in the Aleutians. Casual on the Pribilof Is.

Ruddy Duck *Oxyura jamaicensis* — Casual migrant, summer and winter visitant, and breeder in SE central Alaska (Fairbanks, Tok). Casual on the Kenai Peninsula (Homer) and in SE Alaska. Best found along the Alaska Hwy near Tetlin and Northway.

Osprey *Pandion haliaetus* — Uncommon to rare summer resident and local breeder along larger rivers and lakes from the Brooks Range S. Casual on the Pribilof Is.

Bald Eagle *Haliaeetus leucocephalus* — Common resident along the coast from the central Aleutian Is to the Alaska Pen, Kodiak Is, and along southcoastal Alaska to Glacier Bay and S throughout SE Alaska. Less common N along the Bering Sea coast as far as Noatak and Kotzebue Sound. Rare on the N coast (Prudhoe Bay) and casual on the Bering Sea Is. Common throughout the Kenai Pen and N in the Tanana and upper Yukon River Valleys, Denali NP, and rarely to the crest of the Brooks Range. Winters commonly from the Aleutians E throughout southcoastal and SE Alaska. Easy to find at any season on the Kenai Pen at Seward or Homer as well as elsewhere in coastal Alaska.

White-tailed Eagle *Haliaeetus albicilla* — Very rare in the W Aleutians (successfully nested on Attu in 1982).

Steller's Sea-Eagle *Haliaeetus pelagicus* — Casual on Kodiak Is and in the Taku River Valley near Juneau, where a single bird could be found from 1989 to 2001, and at Attu in 1980 and 1994. A single bird was found along the Nushagak River near Dillingham in 2001.

Northern Harrier *Circus cyaneus* — Locally common migrant and uncommon summer resident throughout open country in most of Alaska. Uncommon breeder throughout interior central Alaska from the Brooks Range S to the Kenai Pen and in W Alaska. Accidental on the Pribilof Is and casual on the E Aleutians. Rare winter visitant in coastal Alaska from Adak E to Kodiak, Middleton Is, Cordova, and in SE Alaska. Casual also in central Alaska in winter.

[**Gray Frog-Hawk** *Accipiter soloensis* — (Chinese Goshawk) — Accidental from a sight record on Nizki Is in Jun 1995.]

Sharp-shinned Hawk *Accipiter striatus* — Fairly common summer resident and breeder in woodlands from Kotzebue Sound E along the S slope of the Brooks Range into Canada and S to Bristol Bay, Kodiak Is, and throughout SE Alaska. Casual in winter in the interior, uncommon in southcoastal Alaska, and uncommon to rare in SE Alaska. Most birds migrate out of the state in winter (*A.s. velox*). The darker race, *A.s. perobscurus,* breeds in SE Alaska.

[**Cooper's Hawk** *Accipiter cooperii* — Casual in SE Alaska. Many sight records for Juneau, e.g., Salmon Creek in Aug 1998, Mendenhall Wetlands in Aug and Dec 2001, and Fish Creek in Dec 1998. Also seen at Sitka, but there are no photographs or specimens.]

Northern Goshawk *Accipiter gentilis* — Common resident in forests throughout interior, southcoastal, and SE Alaska. Rarely occurs N of the Brooks Range (*A.g. atricapillus*), and accidental on the Alaska Pen, the Aleutian Is, and near Nome. The darker race, *A.g. laingi,* is resident in SE Alaska.

Swainson's Hawk *Buteo swainsoni* — Rare in summer in interior (Delta Junction, Northway, Tetlin) where it probably breeds, and along the Glenn Hwy (Glennallen, Eureka Summit) in migration. Casual in southcoastal (Homer, Cordova) and SE Alaska (Juneau).

Red-tailed Hawk *Buteo jamaicensis* — Of the several races of Red-tailed Hawk, the most common in Alaska is Harlan's Hawk, *B.j. harlani.* However, the Western Red-tail, *B.j. calurus,* has been found throughout the state and *B.j. alascensis* breeds in SE Alaska. Red-tails are uncommon in summer from the S slope of the Brooks Range S to southcoastal Alaska and in SE Alaska. Leaves Alaska in winter. It is not unusual to see dark Western Red-tails paired with Harlan's Hawks.

[**Common Buzzard** *Buteo buteo* — Accidental from a sight record on Nizki Is in 1983.]

Rough-legged Hawk *Buteo lagopus* — Uncommon summer resident and breeder in open country in southcoastal Alaska (Kodiak, Barren Is, S Kenai Pen); uncommon throughout the interior along major river valleys and the N coast (Colville River), and rare in the Brooks Range (Anaktuvuk Pass) (*B.l. sanctijohannis*). Common summer resident and breeder from the Alaska Pen and along the coast of W Alaska and the Seward Pen, and rare on the Bering Sea Is. Casual visitant in the W Aleutians (*B.l. kamtchatkensis*). Rare migrant in SE Alaska.

Golden Eagle *Aquila chrysaetos* — Uncommon to fairly common summer resident and breeder on cliffs along major rivers throughout W and central Alaska S to southcoastal Alaska. Uncommon from the Brooks Range N to the arctic coast and on the E Aleutian Is. Casual to rare migrant in SE Alaska. Accidental on St. Lawrence Is. Migrates out of Alaska in winter.

Eurasian Kestrel *Falco tinnunculus* — Casual on the W Aleutian Is and the Pribilof Is.

American Kestrel *Falco sparverius* — Uncommon summer resident in interior Alaska from Denali NP E to Paxson and Circle into Canada. Casual into the Brooks Range and accidental on the arctic coast (Prudhoe Bay). Uncommon in summer in southcoastal Alaska. Rare to fairly common migrant in SE Alaska.

Merlin *Falco columbarius* — Fairly common summer resident and breeder throughout most of the state from the tundra-taiga ecotone into continuous forest. Casual from the E Aleutians, most of N coastal Alaska, and the Bering Sea Is. Uncommon in W coastal Alaska (Nome). Most common along major river valleys in the interior and along the coast in southcentral Alaska (Homer) (*F.c. columbarius*). The darker race, *F.c. suckleyi*, is an uncommon migrant and rare breeder in SE Alaska. Migrates S of Alaska in winter.

Eurasian Hobby *Falco subbuteo* — Casual on the W Aleutian Is, on or from fishing boats in the Bering Sea N of the Aleutians, and on St. George and St. Paul Is.

Gyrfalcon *Falco rusticolus* — Fairly common resident from the E Aleutian Is, Alaska Pen, and N of the Alaska Range to the arctic coast and E into Canada. Uncommon S of the Alaska Range in summer. Uncommon anywhere in the state N of southcoastal Alaska during spring, fall, and winter, including the Bering Sea Is. Casual in SE Alaska. Best found in summer on cliffs along major river valleys as the Yukon, Tanana, Porcupine, Colville, in Denali NP, and on the Seward Pen near Nome.

Peregrine Falcon *Falco peregrinus* — Fairly common summer resident and breeder from N coastal Alaska W to the Bering Sea coast, the Aleutian Is, Alaska Pen, Kodiak Is, southcoastal Alaska, and SE Alaska. Nests on cliffs along major river valleys such as the Yukon, Tanana, Porcupine, Colville, in Denali NP, and on rocky cliffs along the coast, often in or near seabird colonies. Common in migration throughout the state. Winters S of Alaska. N and interior birds belong to the paler races, *F.p. anatum* and *F.p. tundrius*. The Aleutian and southcoastal breeding birds are mostly the darker and larger race *F.p. pealei*. Rare on the Bering Sea Is.

[**Ring-necked Pheasant** *Phasianus colchicus* — A resident feral bird in Alaska. Released in several areas on the Kenai Pen and breeds locally near Homer, but not considered an established breeding species.]

Ruffed Grouse *Bonasa umbellus* — Common throughout interior Alaska from the lower Kuskokwim River Valley E into Canada and S to the upper part of the Copper River drainage (*B.u. yukonensis*). The darker race, *B.u. umbelloides,* is uncommon in SE Alaska along major river valleys. Best found in woods between Fairbanks and Nenana and N between Fairbanks and Minto.

Spruce Grouse *Falcipennis canadensis* — Common resident in spruce forests from the Bering Sea and from the S slope of the Brooks Range through the interior S to Bristol Bay, Alaska Pen, Kodiak Is (*F.c. osgoodi*), locally in southcoastal Alaska into Canada (*F.c. franklinii*). The darker SE Alaska birds, *F.c. isleibi*, named in honor of Alaskan birder M.E. "Pete" Isleib, are found only on Prince of Wales Is and smaller islands to the west.

Willow Ptarmigan *Lagopus lagopus* — Common resident throughout N Alaska from the Yukon River N to the W and N Alaska coastline and E into Canada. Locally common in the Alaska Range (Denali NP), and the Chugach Mountains (Anchorage), W to the W extent of the Alaska Pen (Unimak Is), Kodiak Is, and locally in the mountains of southcoastal Alaska and the Kenai Pen S to SE Alaska. Easiest to find in Denali NP and Nome in summer. There are three subspecies in Alaska defined by measurements of bill, wing, and tail and color of spring males. Most of N and interior Alaska is occupied by *L.l. alascensis*. E Alaska birds are *L.l. albus* and birds of the Alaska Pen, southcoastal, and SE Alaska are *L.l. alexandrae*.

Rock Ptarmigan *Lagopus mutus* — Common resident throughout Alaska. Many races exist, especially on the Aleutian Is, as the birds are resident on each island and generally do not move to other islands. They are resident along the N coast and in the Brooks Range, on the W coast and Seward Pen, the Alaska Pen, in the interior mountains (Eagle Summit), the Alaska Range (Denali NP and the Denali Hwy), the Wrangell-St. Elias Mountains, the Chugach Mountains near Anchorage, and the Kenai Mountains. They also occur in the mountains of SE Alaska. In general, Rock Ptarmigan live at higher elevations than Willow Ptarmigan, but often retreat to lower elevations in winter. There are ten subspecies recognized in Alaska, differentiated by plumage color of summer males: *L.m. evermanni* at Attu Is; *L.m. townsendi* on Kiska; *L.m. gabrielsoni* on Amchitka and the Rat Is; *L.m. sanfordi* on the Tanga Is; *L.m. chamberlaini* on Adak Is; *L.m. atkhensis* on Atka Is; *L.m. yunaskensis* on the Is of Four Mountains; *L.m. nelsoni* on Unimak and Unalaska Is; *L.m. dixoni* around Glacier Bay; and *L.m. kelloggae* throughout the rest of Alaska. Casual also in fall on St. Lawrence Is. Island races are still vulnerable to predation by rats now that most of the imported foxes have been removed.

White-tailed Ptarmigan *Lagopus leucurus* — Common local resident on alpine summits from the Alaska Range (Denali NP) S to the Alaska Pen, the Chugach Mountains near Anchorage, the Kenai Mountains, the Wrangell-St. Elias Range, and in the higher mountains of SE Alaska into Canada.

Blue Grouse *Dendragapus obscurus* — Fairly common resident in forests of SE Alaska from Glacier Bay S to Ketchikan throughout most of the islands and mainland, and into adjacent Canada. The sooty mainland race is *D.o. fuliginosus* and the southern island race is *D.o. sitkensis*.

Sharp-tailed Grouse *Tympanuchus phasianellus* — Common resident in brush and open areas of interior Alaska from the upper Kuskokwim River Valley, and valleys of the Yukon, Tanana, and Porcupine Rivers E into Canada. Best found in the cultivated fields E of Delta Junction and at high elevations along the Richardson Hwy near Paxson.

[**Yellow Rail** — *Coturnicops noveboracensis* — Accidental in Juneau. Identified from a bird heard calling at Sunny Point in Jul 1970.]

Virginia Rail *Rallus limicola* — Casual at Klawock in 1986, at Juneau (Amalga Trail) in summer on several occasions 1994–2000, and the Stikine River in Jul 1995.

[**Baillon's Crake** *Porzana pusilla* — Accidental from a sight record on Attu in Sep 2000.]

Sora *Porzana carolina* — Rare migrant, summer visitant, and probable breeder in SE Alaska from Glacier Bay, Haines (25-mile Marsh), Juneau (Amalga Trail), Stikine River, Chickamin River, Petersburg, and Wrangell. Casual summer visitant to E central Alaska (Tetlin Lakes, Fairbanks) and S central Alaska (Portage). Rare visitor to the Palmer Hay Flats in summer 2001.

Eurasian Coot *Fulica atra* — Accidental on St. Paul Is in Oct 1962.

American Coot *Fulica americana* — Rare fall migrant and winter visitant in SE Alaska. Rare migrant and summer visitant in central Alaska from Minto Lakes to Delta and Tetlin Lakes. Casual migrant in southcoastal Alaska (Cordova, Anchorage, Homer, Kodiak). Accidental in N Alaska (Colville River Delta), SW Alaska (Pribilof Is), and the Aleutian Is (Amchitka Is).

Sandhill Crane *Grus canadensis* — Common migrant and summer resident throughout interior Alaska, primarily in the major river valleys. Common also from the Alaska Pen N along the coast of W Alaska to the Seward Pen, but less common in N Alaska and the Bering Sea Is. Also common in SE Alaska. Migrates in large flocks through the interior near Delta, along the Alaska Hwy near Tok, and from the Kenai Pen and Prince William Sound (Cordova) SE. Easy to find in summer in Nome, Fairbanks and Homer.

Common Crane *Grus grus* — Accidental in Fairbanks in Apr 1958 and in Delta in Sep 1999.

Black-bellied Plover *Pluvialis squatarola* — Locally common migrant in SE and southcentral coastal Alaska and uncommon summer breeder along the coast in wet tundra from the Yukon-Kuskokwim Delta N along the Bering Sea coast and then E along the Beaufort Sea Coast. Rare breeder and migrant in interior Alaska. Easy to find during spring migration in Juneau, Cordova, Seward, and Homer, and during the breeding season at Barrow or Nome. Rare on the Bering Sea and Aleutian Is.

European Golden-Plover *Pluvialis apricaria* — Accidental at Ketchikan in Jan 2001.

American Golden-Plover *Pluvialis dominica* — Common summer breeder on the Seward Pen, the N coast, and North Slope eastward into Canada. Migrates along the Pacific Coast throughout Alaska, intermingling with Pacific Golden-Plover in W Alaska, casual on the Aleutian Is. Rare in early fall at Gambell. Easy to find during migration at Cordova or Homer and during the breeding season at Barrow.

Pacific Golden-Plover *Pluvialis fulva* — Common summer breeder and migrant in coastal W Alaska from Hooper Bay and Nelson Is N in the Bering Sea Is to the NW coast. Intermingles with American Golden-Plover in NW Alaska and during migration. Can be found in southcoastal Alaska in spring and fall migrations and at Nome in summer. Rare in SE Alaska in fall.

Mongolian Plover *Charadrius mongolus* — Rare spring and fall migrant in the W Aleutian Is, St. Paul Is, Gambell, and casual in W Alaska (Yukon-Kuskokwim Delta, Wales, Nome). Casual summer visitant to N Alaska (Barrow) and accidental in southcoastal Alaska (Kodiak, Augustine Is).

Snowy Plover *Charadrius alexandrinus* — Accidental at Nome in May 1991.

Common Ringed Plover *Charadrius hiaticula* — Rare spring migrant and breeder at Gambell. Accidental on St. Paul Is. Casual migrant in the W Aleutian Is. Best found at Gambell.

Semipalmated Plover *Charadrius semipalmatus* — Fairly common summer resident and breeder in N SE Alaska and common throughout the rest of the state. Rare fall migrant in the central Aleutians Is and casual migrant in W Aleutian Is. Easy to find in summer in southcoastal Alaska (Homer, Kodiak, Cordova, Seward). Breeds along the coast and on river bars in the interior.

Little Ringed Plover *Charadrius dubius* — Accidental on several of the W Aleutian Is.

Killdeer *Charadrius vociferus* — Uncommon migrant, uncommon summer visitant, and rare breeder in SE Alaska. Sometimes overwinters. Rare spring migrant and summer visitant and very rare breeder and fall migrant in central Alaska. Rare migrant and summer visitant (Anchorage, Palmer, Seward) and very rare breeder in southcoastal Alaska (Anchorage). Casual spring migrant and summer visitant to coastal SW Alaska, Kodiak Is, Pribilof Is, and N to Nome, Kotzebue, Barrow, and Umiat on the Colville River.

Eurasian Dotterel *Charadrius morinellus* — Rare summer visitant and breeder on the mountains of the Bering Strait Is and Seward Pen (Nome). Best found at Wales (Cape Mountain and Ear Mountain), or on Sevuokuk Mountain at Gambell. Casual summer visitant and breeder along the coast of N Alaska (Barrow) and S into the Brooks Range (Alatna). Casual fall migrant in the W Aleutian Is.

Black Oystercatcher *Haematopus bachmani* — Common resident throughout most of southcoastal Alaska from the Forrester Is in SE Alaska to the central Aleutian Is. It is common on Kodiak Is and easy to find on trips into Resurrection Bay, Prince William Sound (Cordova, Valdez), the Barren Is, and from the ferry to Dutch Harbor. Accidental on St. Paul Is.

Black-winged Stilt *Himantopus himantopus* — Accidental on Nizki Is from May to Jun 1983.

American Avocet *Recurvirostra americana* — Accidental at Valdez in 1981 and at the Susitna River mouth near Anchorage in 2000.

Common Greenshank *Tringa nebularia* — Rare spring and casual fall migrant in the central and W Aleutian Is. Casual summer visitant and fall migrant in the W Aleutians. Casual spring and fall migrant on St. Paul Is and at Gambell.

Greater Yellowlegs *Tringa melanoleuca* — Common early spring migrant and summer breeder in S Alaska from the Alaska Range S to southcoastal and SE Alaska, also on the Alaska Pen and Kodiak Is. Casual in migration on the Seward Pen, Bering Sea Is and SW Alaska and casual on the near Aleutian Is and N of the Alaska Range.

Lesser Yellowlegs *Tringa flavipes* — Common migrant and summer breeder in wet woodlands from passes in the Brooks Range (Anaktuvuk) S to southcoastal and SE Alaska, also in W Alaska, Kodiak Is, and the Alaska Pen. In migration rarely found on the Bering Sea Is (St. Paul and St. George). Casual on the Aleutian Is.

Marsh Sandpiper *Tringa stagnatilis* — Accidental on Buldir Is in Sep 1974 and Adak Is in Aug 1999.

Spotted Redshank *Tringa erythropus* — Casual spring and fall migrant in W and central Aleutian Is, casual in fall at St. Paul Is.

Wood Sandpiper *Tringa glareola* — Uncommon spring migrant and rare fall migrant in W and the central Aleutian Is, casual spring migrant in the E Aleutians as far E as Sanak Is. Very rare breeder in the W and central Aleutians. Rare spring and fall migrant and late spring migrant to St. Paul and St. George Is. Very rare spring migrant at Gambell, casual there in fall and on the Seward Pen coast (Wales). Casual summer visitant to N Alaska (Barrow).

Green Sandpiper *Tringa ochropus* — Casual on the far W Aleutian Is and on St. Lawrence Is (1982) and St. Paul Is (1998).

Solitary Sandpiper *Tringa solitaria* — Common breeder (*T.s. cinnamomea*) throughout the taiga of central interior Alaska S to the Kenai Pen. Uncommon migrant in SE and common migrant through southcoastal Alaska, but casual on Kodiak Is. Casual visitant to N and W Alaska coasts (Barrow, Hooper Bay) and one spring record for Gambell. One record of the smaller race, *T.s. solitaria,* from N Alaska in 1914.

[**Willet** *Catoptrophorus semipalmatus* — Accidental at Minto Lakes in Aug 1961.]

Wandering Tattler *Heteroscelus incanus* — Common breeder at timberline and along streams throughout the major mountain systems of southcoastal, central, and W Alaska (Chugach Mountains and Hatcher Pass near Anchorage, Alaska Range near Paxson, Denali NP, Yukon-Tanana highlands on the Steese Hwy at Eagle Summit, Brooks Range at Anaktuvuk Pass, and on the Seward Pen). Uncommon coastal migrant in SE and common in southcoastal Alaska (Homer, Kodiak) and on the Bering Sea Is. Uncommon migrant in the central and W Aleutian Is. Rare in summer S of the breeding range.

Gray-tailed Tattler *Heteroscelus brevipes* — Rare spring and uncommon fall migrant in the Aleutian Is, Gambell, and the Pribilof Is. Casual spring migrant and summer visitant to the N coast of Alaska (Barrow) and in southcoastal Alaska (Kodiak).

Common Sandpiper *Actitis hypoleucos* — Rare spring and casual fall migrant in the W and central Aleutian Is. Very rare spring migrant in the central Aleutians, on St. Paul and St. George Is, and at Gambell. Casual on the Seward Pen.

Spotted Sandpiper *Actitis macularia* — Common migrant and breeder along lakes and rivers throughout SE, southcoastal, and interior Alaska S of the Brooks Range. Uncommon breeder on the Seward Pen and throughout the Brooks Range N into the coastal plain but becoming a casual visitor to the N coast. Uncommon local breeder in SW Alaska to the base of the Alaska Pen.

Terek Sandpiper *Xenus cinereus* — Rare migrant in the W Aleutians, casual on the Bering Sea Is (Nunivak, St. Paul, and at Gambell) and at Nome. Accidental at Anchorage in Jun 1977, Jul 1987, and Jul 1998.

Upland Sandpiper *Bartramia longicauda* — Locally uncommon breeder in the Wrangell Mountains (Nabesna), the Alaska Range (Denali Hwy, Denali NP) and the Brooks Range (along major rivers). Rare spring migrant, rare summer visitant and possible breeder, and very rare fall migrant in E central Alaska (Fairbanks, Steese Hwy, Agricultural fields E of Delta) and NW Alaska (Noatak River). Casual fall migrant in southcentral Alaska (Palmer, Anchorage), southcoastal Alaska (Seward Hwy at Summit Lake), and SE Alaska (Juneau, Metlakatla, Petersburg).

Little Curlew *Numenius minutus* — Accidental at Gambell in Jun 1989.

Eskimo Curlew *Numenius borealis* — The last documented record was in 1886 at Barrow.

Whimbrel *Numenius phaeopus* — Common migrant in southcoastal Alaska and uncommon summer breeder in coastal W and N Alaska from Hooper Bay, the Yukon-Kuskokwim Delta, Seward Pen (Nome), Noatak and Kobuk River, Barrow, Colville River mouth, Prudhoe Bay, E into Canada. Migrates through major river drainages. Also in the Brooks Range (Anaktuvuk Pass) and in the Talkeetna Mountains. In migration found in Denali NP, St. Paul and St. Lawrence Is (rare), Kodiak Is, and less commonly in SE Alaska. The uniformly-colored gray-brown-backed form, *N.p. hudsonicus,* is the common Alaska breeder. The paler Asian form, *N.p. variegatus,* is a rare spring migrant in the Aleutians, at Gambell, and on the Pribilof Is.

Bristle-thighed Curlew *Numenius tahitiensis* — Spring migrant from the central and S Pacific Is through southcoastal Alaska (casual at Kodiak and Homer, accidental at Seward), rare in SW Alaska, and the Alaska Pen N to the Seward Pen, on the Pribilof Is and casual on the Aleutian Is and at Gambell. Uncommon summer breeder in scattered locations on the Seward Pen (Kougarok Road out of Nome), in W Alaska near Hooper Bay, and the lower Yukon River (Mountain Village).

Far Eastern Curlew *Numenius madagascariensis* — Very rare spring migrant and summer visitant in the W and central Aleutian Is and at St. Paul Is. Casual spring migrant in W Alaska (St. Michaels).

[**Long-billed Curlew** *Numenius americanus* — Accidental from a sight record at the Stikine River mouth in May 1992.]

Black-tailed Godwit *Limosa limosa* — Casual spring migrant in the W and central Aleutian Is and the Bering Sea Is (St. Paul and St. Lawrence Is). One record at Prudhoe Bay in Jun 1993.

Hudsonian Godwit *Limosa haemastica* — Common migrant, uncommon summer visitant, and uncommon breeder in the Cook Inlet area (Anchorage). Uncommon migrant in southcoastal Alaska (Cordova, Seward, Homer, Kenai River Flats, Kodiak). Uncommon migrant, summer visitant, and breeder in W Alaska (Kotzebue Sound and Norton Bay from the Kobuk and Noatak River mouths S to Nelson Lagoon). Very rare summer and fall visitant in N Alaska (Barrow). Rare spring migrant in interior Alaska (Fairbanks, Circle). Rare to casual migrant in SE Alaska (Glacier Bay, Juneau).

Bar-tailed Godwit *Limosa lapponica* — Common migrant through W southcoastal Alaska (Kasilof River mouth, Homer, W to the Aleutian Is), casual in Anchorage, and common summer breeder in coastal W and N Alaska (Yukon-Kuskokwim Delta, Hooper Bay, Seward Pen, Kotzebue, Barrow, Colville River Delta, and probably farther E). Rare migrant on the Bering Sea Is and uncommon migrant in the Aleutian Is.

Marbled Godwit *Limosa fedoa* — Rare spring migrant in SE Alaska and casual spring migrant in southcoastal Alaska. Uncommon breeder in SW Alaska (Ugashik area, Bristol Bay) (*L.f. beringiae*).

Ruddy Turnstone *Arenaria interpres* — The darker-backed race, *A.i. interpres,* is a fairly common spring migrant through SE and southcoastal Alaska (Homer), the Alaska Pen, and the Aleutian Is. Common breeder from Hooper Bay and the Yukon River Delta in W Alaska N along the coast around the Seward Pen to Barrow. Also fairly common spring and common fall migrant on the Bering Sea Is (St. Paul and St. Lawrence Is). The lighter-backed race, *A.i. morinella,* breeds along the N coast to the Colville River Delta and less commonly E into Canada.

Black Turnstone *Arenaria melanocephala* — Fairly common migrant and summer visitant in SE and common in southcoastal Alaska. Fairly common breeder along the coast in W Alaska N to the Seward Pen. May be found all summer in small numbers at Homer in association with Surfbird, Ruddy Turnstone, and Rock Sandpiper. Winters in SE Alaska.

Surfbird *Aphriza virgata* — Uncommon migrant and summer visitant in SE Alaska. Common spring migrant through southcoastal Alaska along rocky coasts. Rare breeder in alpine tundra in the Chugach Mountains near Anchorage, uncommon breeder in interior Alaska (Eagle Summit, Denali NP, Alaska Range, Wrangell Mountains). Rare migrant and breeder at the base of the Alaska Pen; casual farther S on the Pen. Rare migrant on the Yukon-Kuskokwim Delta N along Norton Sound to the Seward Pen and probably farther N and rare breeder on the Seward Pen. Non-breeding birds are found in southcoastal Alaska all summer (Homer). Accidental on St. Paul Is.

Great Knot *Calidris tenuirostris* — Casual spring migrant in the W and central Aleutian Is and on the Bering Sea coast (Cape Prince of Wales, Nome) and islands (St. Paul and St. Lawrence Is). One fall record for Gambell (Aug 1997).

Red Knot *Calidris canutus* — Common spring migrant in E southcoastal Alaska (Copper and Bering River Deltas) but uncommon in W southcoastal Alaska (Homer). Birds fly overland NW from the Copper River Delta to NW Alaska and Siberia. Uncommon to rare migrant in coastal W Alaska and rare to casual on the Bering Sea Is (St. Lawrence and St. Paul Is). Uncommon breeder in the Brooks Range and the Seward Pen; rare breeder in N Alaska (Barrow). Rare fall migrant on the Alaska Pen; casual migrant and summer visitant on the Aleutian Is. Rare spring migrant in SE Alaska.

Sanderling *Calidris alba* — Uncommon spring migrant in SE and southcoastal Alaska but locally common (Copper-Bering River Delta, Cordova); uncommon spring migrant in coastal W and N Alaska; rare in the Brooks Range and interior Alaska. Very rare breeder in N Alaska (Barrow). Uncommon to fairly common fall migrant on coasts from Barrow S along W Alaska coastlines, rare on the Bering Sea Is, common through the Aleutian Is, southcoastal and uncommon in SE Alaska. Uncommon to fairly common winter visitant on the Aleutian Is; rare winter visitant on the Alaska Pen, in southcoastal and SE Alaska.

Semipalmated Sandpiper *Calidris pusilla* — Common summer breeder in tundra of W Alaska N on the Bering Sea coast then E into Canada. Nests away from the coast into the hills and mountains at least as far S as passes in the Brooks Range (Anaktuvuk Pass) but near the coast in W Alaska. It may also nest inland as at Minto

Lakes W of Fairbanks. Also nests on St. Lawrence Is and is found rarely in migration on St. Paul Is. Uncommon in migration, however, numbers appear annually in southcoastal Alaska. Casual on the Aleutians.

Western Sandpiper *Calidris mauri* — Common (abundant) migrant through SE and southcoastal Alaska in spring. Common summer breeder in coastal W Alaska (Hooper Bay) N to the Seward Pen (Nome) and St. Lawrence Is, and less commonly N (Kotzebue) and then E to Barrow. Some birds migrate E along the arctic coast into Canada in fall, but most move S along the Pacific coast to California. Casual in fall in the central Aleutian Is (Adak).

Red-necked Stint *Calidris ruficollis* — Rare spring migrant in the W and central Aleutian Is, Bering Sea Is (St. Lawrence and St. Paul), and in N Alaska (Barrow); casual as far E as the Colville River Delta. Rare summer visitant and fall migrant in the Aleutian Is, on the Alaska Pen (Cold Bay), St. Lawrence and St. Paul Is. Casual breeder on the Seward Pen (Nome) and N Alaska (Barrow). Casual fall migrant in southcoastal and SE Alaska (Homer, Seward, Cordova, Glacier Bay, Juneau).

Little Stint *Calidris minuta* — Casual in spring and fall on all the Bering Sea Is, and the W Aleutian Is. Accidental at Point Barrow and Nome.

Temminck's Stint *Calidris temminckii* — Rare spring and very rare fall migrant in the W Aleutian Is, St. Matthew Is, St. Paul and St. George Is, St. Lawrence Is; casual at Cape Prince of Wales. Casual July visitant on Buldir Is, on the Bering Sea Is, and the N coast (Barrow, Colville River Delta). Accidental in Homer (1998).

Long-toed Stint *Calidris subminuta* — Rare spring and fall migrant in the W and central Aleutian Is. Casual spring and fall migrant in the Bering Sea Is (St. Paul and St. Lawrence Is). Accidental at Wales.

Least Sandpiper *Calidris minutilla* — Common summer breeder from the E Aleutians and Bristol Bay along the coast to Kodiak, Homer, Seward, Cordova, to Yakutat Bay. Nests along the coast and inland in bogs and lake shores on the Yukon-Kuskokwim Delta. Less common farther inland and farther N (Denali NP, Chatanika, Bethel, Mountain Village, Anaktuvuk Pass, Colville River Delta). Rare breeder at St. Paul Is and casual on St. Lawrence Is. Common migrant in SE and southcoastal Alaska.

White-rumped Sandpiper *Calidris fuscicollis* — Rare migrant and breeder in northcoastal Alaska from Canada W to Prudhoe Bay, Colville River Delta, and Barrow, occasionally to Wainwright. Very rare spring migrant in central Alaska (Denali Hwy, Sheenjek River, Fairbanks, Anaktuvuk Pass). Casual migrant in southcoastal and SE Alaska (Kenai Pen, Copper River Delta, Juneau). Accidental on St. Paul Is. Best found in spring at Barrow or Oliktok Point.

Baird's Sandpiper *Calidris bairdii* — Common breeder from the Yukon River Delta (Mountain Village) N along the Seward Pen and the Bering Sea coast and then E on the Beaufort Sea coast into Canada. Less common inland on the North Slope tundra to the crest of the Brooks Range (Anaktuvuk Pass). Uncommon to rare migrant in southcoastal Alaska, SE Alaska, the Bering Sea Is, and the central Aleutian Is. Apparently most birds migrate W along the N coast from Canada in spring and return the same way in fall.

Pectoral Sandpiper *Calidris melanotos* — Common breeder along the coast of W Alaska from the Kuskokwim River mouth N (Hooper Bay) along the Seward Pen N and then E along the Beaufort Sea coast into Canada. Also breeds on the Pribilof Is and possibly in interior marshes (Minto Lakes). Uncommon in fall on the Aleutians and common to fairly common in SE Alaska. Uncommon spring and fall migrant through interior Alaska (Fairbanks, Glennallen); common fall migrant in southcoastal Alaska (Homer, Seward, Cordova).

Sharp-tailed Sandpiper *Calidris acuminata* — Rare to uncommon fall migrant on the Chukchi and Bering Sea coast and Is (Cape Seppings, Kotzebue, St. Lawrence and

Pribilof Is), throughout the Aleutian Is, E to Kodiak Is, southcoastal Alaska (Kodiak, Homer, Kasilof, Cordova), and S to SE Alaska. Casual in spring migration in W Alaska (Gambell, St. Paul, Nome, W Aleutian Is). Casual spring migrant in SE Alaska (Juneau), southcoastal Alaska (Seward), and in N Alaska (Barrow). Perhaps a rare breeder in W Alaska (Kivalina). Best found in fall at Gambell, St. Paul, outer Aleutian Is., and in the sedge flats at Kalsin and Womens Bay on Kodiak Is or southcoastal Alaska (Homer).

Purple Sandpiper *Calidris maritima* — Accidental at Barrow in Sep 1990.

Rock Sandpiper *Calidris ptilocnemis* — Four subspecies of Rock Sandpipers are recognized in Alaska. The most common are Pribilof (*C.p. ptilocnemis*) that is found on the Pribilof and St. Matthew Is and Northern (*C.p. tschuktschorum*) that breeds on the Bering Sea coast and St. Lawrence Is. *C.p. couesi* breeds on Attu Is and *C.p. quarta* breeds on Bering Is and the Commander Is (Russia). Common summer breeder from the far W Aleutian Is E to the W Alaska Pen, on the coast of W Alaska (Seward Pen and the Yukon Delta), and N on the Bering Sea Is. Common in winter in the Aleutians, E along southcoastal Alaska (Kodiak, lower Cook Inlet, Homer, Seward, Cordova). Common in spring and fall migration as well as in winter in SE Alaska. Best found in summer on St. Paul and St. Lawrence Is and in winter in Homer or Kodiak.

Dunlin *Calidris alpina* — Common summer breeder (*C.a. pacifica* with longer bill) from Bristol Bay N along the coast of W Alaska (Hooper Bay) around the Seward Pen (Wales) to N Alaska (Wainwright, Barrow) (*C.a. arcticola* with shorter bill) and E to the Colville River Delta. Uncommon to fairly common on the Bering Sea Is (St. Lawrence and Pribilof Is). Common spring migrant through SE and southcoastal Alaska (especially Cordova and the Copper-Bering River Delta, also Seward, and Homer). In winter, uncommon in SE Alaska N to Cook Inlet, where it occurs often with Rock Sandpipers. Declining on the North Slope.

Curlew Sandpiper *Calidris ferruginea* — Casual breeder in N Alaska (Barrow, Oliktok Point, Deadhorse) and casual migrant in W (Old Chevak, Nome) and N Alaska, Bering Sea Is (St. Paul, Gambell), and the Aleutian Is. Accidental on Egg Is in the Copper River Delta.

Stilt Sandpiper *Calidris himantopus* — Rare to uncommon migrant, summer visitant, and breeder in N Alaska (Barter Is, Prudhoe Bay) as far W as Barrow. Very rare spring migrant in E central Alaska (Fairbanks, Anaktuvuk Pass). Casual migrant in SE, W, SW, and southcoastal Alaska (Juneau, Cape Krusenstern, Wales, Nome, Pribilof Is, Cordova, Anchorage, Homer, Kodiak).

Spoonbill Sandpiper *Eurynorhynchus pygmeus* — Casual spring and fall migrant in N Alaska (Barrow, Wainwright), in the W Aleutians (Attu, Buldir, Shemya), and on St. Paul Is.

Broad-billed Sandpiper *Limicola falcinellus* — Casual in fall on the Aleutian Is (Adak in 1977, Buldir in 1989, and Shemya Is in 1978, 1986, and Sep 2000).

Buff-breasted Sandpiper *Tryngites subruficollis* — Rare to uncommon migrant, summer visitant, and breeder along the Beaufort Sea coast of N Alaska (Demarcation Point, ANWR, Barrow, Cape Krusenstern). Rare spring migrant in E Central Alaska and in the E Brooks Range (Eagle, Sagavanirktok River, Sheenjek River, Anaktuvuk Pass, Minto Lakes, Fairbanks). Casual summer visitant and fall migrant in NW (Pt. Hope, Cape Krusenstern, Kotzebue, Nome), W Alaska (St. Michael, Yukon River Delta, Nulato), and in SE Alaska (Glacier Bay, Juneau, Sitka). Casual fall migrant on the Bering Sea Is (St. Lawrence and Pribilof Is), Aleutian Is, and in southcoastal Alaska (Kodiak, Cordova).

Ruff *Philomachus pugnax* — Rare migrant in the W and central Aleutian Is, the Bering Sea Is (Pribilof and St. Lawrence Is), and on the Chukchi Sea coast as far N as Kotzebue Sound. Casual fall visitant in N Alaska (Barrow, Colville River mouth,

Prudhoe Bay) and fall migrant in southcoastal Alaska (Kodiak Is, Seward, Anchorage, Cordova). Accidental in spring migration in southcoastal Alaska (Homer, Seward) and SE Alaska (Juneau). Casual breeder in N Alaska (Pt. Lay) and possibly on the Seward Pen.

Short-billed Dowitcher *Limnodromus griseus* — Common spring and fall migrant in SE and southcoastal Alaska W to the Alaska Pen (Cold Bay). Common summer breeder in freshwater marshes in the same areas from Yakutat W to the Alaska Pen and N into upper Cook Inlet (Anchorage).

Long-billed Dowitcher *Limnodromus scolopaceus* — Common summer breeder from the Yukon-Kuskokwim Delta (Hooper Bay) N around the Seward Pen (Nome, Wales) to N Alaska (Barrow, Colville River Delta) and E along the coast into Canada. Also breeds on the North Slope S to the Brooks Range (Umiat) and probably migrates through passes in the Brooks Range (Anaktuvuk). Breeds inland also to Bethel in W Alaska. Uncommon to fairly common in fall on the Bering Sea Is (St. Lawrence and St. Paul); rare migrant in the Aleutian Is. Uncommon migrant in interior Alaska (Fairbanks). Common migrant in SE Alaska.

Jack Snipe *Lymnocryptes minimus* — Accidental on St. Paul Is in spring 1919.

Common Snipe *Gallinago gallinago* — Uncommon to rare migrant in the Aleutian Is, rare on the Pribilof Is, and casual N to St. Lawrence Is.

Wilson's Snipe *Gallinago delicata* — Common migrant and breeder throughout mainland Alaska in suitable wetland habitat from southcoastal Alaska to the arctic coast; fairly common migrant and rare breeder in SE Alaska and the Bering Sea Is.

Pin-tailed Snipe *Gallinago stenura* — Accidental on Attu Is in May 1984, May 1991, and May 1998.

Wilson's Phalarope *Phalaropus tricolor* — Casual spring migrant and summer visitant to SE Alaska (Juneau), southcoastal (Valdez, Anchorage, Kodiak), E central (Taylor Hwy, Kenny Lake, Fairbanks), and N Alaska (ANWR, Barrow). Very rare breeder in interior Alaska (Yukon Flats NWR).

Red-necked Phalarope *Phalaropus lobatus* — Common summer breeder throughout Alaska from southcoastal Alaska to the arctic coast and the Aleutian Is. Most numerous along the coast but also common on inland lakes and marshes and on the Bering Sea Is. Migrates in large flocks over the Gulf of Alaska and is common on saltwater, especially in fall in southcoastal and SE Alaska.

Red Phalarope *Phalaropus fulicaria* — Uncommon to common summer breeder along the coast of W Alaska (Hooper Bay), the Bering Sea coast (Wales) and Is (St. Lawrence and Pribilof Is), and N (Pt. Hope, Kotzebue) to the Beaufort Sea coast (Barrow, Colville River Delta, Camden Bay, Barter Is) and then E into Canada. Migrates primarily over saltwater but also found in passes in the Brooks Range (Anaktuvuk Pass). Sometimes common in migration at Bering Sea Is, especially in fall at St. Lawrence Is. Uncommon in migration in SE Alaska and uncommon near shore in southcoastal Alaska. Accidental in Fairbanks in July 2002.

Oriental Pratincole *Glareola maldivarum* — Accidental on Attu Is in May 1985 and on St. Lawrence Is in Jun 1986.

South Polar Skua *Stercorarius maccormicki* — Very rare summer visitant on the ocean in SE, southcoastal (Yakutat, Middleton Is, Barren Is, Kodiak Is), SW Alaska, and S of the Aleutian Is. One record from N Alaska (off Icy Cape).

Pomarine Jaeger *Stercorarius pomarinus* — Common summer breeder in N coastal Alaska from Barrow E into Canada, W to Wainwright, and less regularly S along the coast to Hooper Bay. Common in migration along the coast of W (St. Lawrence and Pribilof Is) and southcoastal Alaska (Kodiak, Kachemak Bay, Resurrection Bay, Yakutat Bay). Rare in SE and interior Alaska in migration. Least common of the three jaegers in Alaska. Best found in summer in Barrow during high lemming years, on the N end of the Dalton Hwy, or in fall at Gambell.

Parasitic Jaeger *Stercorarius parasiticus* — Common summer breeder in N coastal Alaska from Canada W to Wainwright and S along the Chukchi and Bering Sea coasts to the Alaska Pen and Aleutian Is, and E in southcoastal Alaska (Kenai, Homer) to the Copper River Delta and Glacier Bay. In migration, common over the Bering Sea (St. Lawrence and Pribilof Is), rare in the interior, fairly common through SE Alaska. Usually the most commonly seen of the three jaegers in coastal Alaska. Best found in summer at Barrow or in spring migration from Gambell.

Long-tailed Jaeger *Stercorarius longicaudus* — Uncommon breeder in N coastal Alaska from Canada W at least to Barrow but more common inland toward the Brooks Range, on the Kobuk River, Kotzebue Sound, and Seward Pen S along the Bering Sea coast to Hooper Bay and inland to Bethel. Also nests on St. Lawrence Is, St. Matthew Is, Anaktuvuk Pass, Eagle Summit, Denali NP, Denali Hwy. Found in migration over the Bering Sea, in Bristol Bay, and along southcoastal Alaska. Uncommon in the Aleutians and in SE Alaska. Best found in summer nesting in Denali NP and along the Denali Hwy.

[**Laughing Gull** *Larus atricilla* — Accidental from sight records in Ketchikan in 1976 and at Yakutat in June 2002.]

Franklin's Gull *Larus pipixcan* — Casual spring and fall migrant and summer visitant in southcoastal Alaska (Kodiak Is, Anchorage, Cook Inlet, Sterling, Homer, Cordova), SE Alaska (Juneau, Petersburg, Ketchikan), and the Bering Sea Is (St. Paul Is).

Little Gull *Larus minutus* — Casual, with scattered records from Kodiak Is, Cape Romanzof, Juneau, Anchorage, Petersburg, Hoonah, Wrangell, and Ketchikan.

Black-headed Gull *Larus ridibundus* — Rare migrant in the W and central Aleutian Is, the Bering Sea Is (Pribilof and St. Lawrence Is), the Bering Sea coast (Nome), Bristol Bay, Chukchi Sea coast (Kukpowruk River mouth), and casual in southcoastal Alaska (Cordova, Seward, Homer, Kenai).

Bonaparte's Gull *Larus philadelphia* — Common summer breeder in interior Alaska from the Kobuk River Delta S (Yukon-Kuskokwim River Deltas, Bristol Bay) throughout interior Alaska (Fort Yukon, Minto Lakes, Talkeetna, Denali NP, Chitina), and southcoastal Alaska (Anchorage, Kenai Pen, Kodiak Is). Irregular and rare in winter in southcoastal and SE Alaska. Common in migration in southcoastal and SE Alaska. Casual in the Aleutians and N in the Bering Sea to the N coast (Prudhoe Bay).

Heermann's Gull *Larus heermanni* — Casual at Ketchikan in Aug 1991, 1994, 1998, and 2001, in Sitka in Sep 1996, and offshore W of Cape St. Elias in Aug 1999.

Black-tailed Gull *Larus crassirostris* — Casual migrant in the W Aleutian Is, St. Lawrence Is, Kodiak, Homer, and in SE Alaska (Juneau, Petersburg, Ketchikan).

Mew Gull *Larus canus* — Two subpecies are recognized in Alaska. The N American Mew Gull (*L.c. brachyrhynchos*) is a common breeder throughout most of interior Alaska from Kotzebue Sound S (St. Michaels, Hooper Bay, Bethel, Yukon-Kuskokwim River Deltas) to the Alaska Pen and from the S slope of the Brooks Range S (Denali NP, Denali Hwy, Minto Flats, Talkeetna Mountains, Copper Center, Anchorage, the Kenai Pen), to SE Alaska. Casual visitor to the Bering Sea Is. The Kamchatka Mew Gull (*L.c. kamtschatschensis*) is casual in Alaska (Attu, Shemya, Buldir, St. Paul Is, and at Gambell).

Ring-billed Gull *Larus delawarensis* — Rare to uncommon visitant to SE Alaska (Ketchikan, Wrangell, Juneau), rare visitant in southcoastal Alaska (Valdez, Seward, Cordova, Homer, Kodiak), SW Alaska (King Cove), and interior Alaska (Fairbanks). Casual at Anchorage. Best found in Ketchikan.

California Gull *Larus californicus* — Rare in spring, uncommon late summer and fall visitant to SE and southcoastal (Homer) Alaska. Common in Ketchikan from Aug to Oct (*L.c. californicus*). There is one specimen record (*L.c. albertensis*) from SE Alaska.

Herring Gull *Larus argentatus* — Two subspecies of Herring Gull are recognized by birders in Alaska. The N American Herring Gull (*L.a. smithsonianus*) is the more abundant throughout Alaska and commonly breeds from SW Alaska across the interior of the state (Yukon, Denali NP, Tanana, and Porcupine River Valleys) into Canada. Also breeds in southcoastal Alaska (Upper Cook Inlet, Copper River Delta) and in SE Alaska (Glacier Bay, Forrester Is). Several colonies of hybrid Herring x Glaucous-winged Gull breed in the N Kenai Pen (Skilak Lake). Non-breeders are common throughout the interior, the Alaska Pen, Kodiak, southcoastal and SE Alaska. Rare in N and W Alaska (Nome, Gambell where casual in fall, Wainwright, Barrow). Vega Herring Gull (*L.a. vegae*) is a common visitor to Gambell and may breed on St. Lawrence Is. Rare at other Bering Sea Is (Little Diomede Is, Pribilof Is). Casual at Cape Prince of Wales, Nome, and W Aleutian Is.

Thayer's Gull *Larus thayeri* — Uncommon in northcoastal (Barter Is, Prudhoe Bay, Colville River delta, Barrow), southcoastal (Copper River Delta, Seward, Homer, Anchorage), and a common migrant in SE Alaska. Also found casually on the W coast of Alaska and the Bering Sea Is.

Iceland Gull *Larus glaucoides* — Accidental (*L.g. kumlieni*) in N Alaska (Barrow, Wainwright). There are two records for Kodiak Is. This subspecies may be combined with Thayer's Gull.

Lesser Black-backed Gull *Larus fuscus* — Accidental at Juneau, Kodiak Is, and Prudhoe Bay. Annual resident for the past several years at Juneau.

Slaty-backed Gull *Larus schistisagus* — Rare spring, summer, and fall visitant to the Bering Sea Is (St. Paul, St. Matthew, Little Diomede, St. Lawrence Is), Bering Sea coast (Nome, Wales, Kotzebue), and N Alaska. Most numerous in late summer and fall at Nome and Gambell where once rare to uncommon, more recently fairly common. Rare winter visitor to southcoastal Alaska, casual in SE Alaska, and rare visitant to the Aleutian Is from Attu E to False Pass. Accidental in summer in Anchorage and Kenai.

Western Gull *Larus occidentalis* — Casual visitant to SE, southcoastal (Homer), and SW Alaska (Bristol Bay). Many of the birds in SE Alaska are hybrids with Glaucous-winged Gull. Best found in Ketchikan.

Glaucous-winged Gull *Larus glaucescens* — Common resident and breeder from W Alaska, the Aleutian Is, E along southcoastal Alaska to SE Alaska. Uncommon to fairly common in late summer and fall on the Bering Sea Is (St. Lawrence and Pribilof Is). Hybrids between this species and Herring Gull are common from Upper Cook Inlet to the S Kenai Pen and in winter in SE Alaska.

Glaucous Gull *Larus hyperboreus* — *L.h. barrovianus* is a common breeder from Bristol Bay N to the N Bering Sea Is (St. Lawrence Is) and the Seward Pen (Nome, Cape Prince of Wales) N along the coast (Kotzebue, Cape Thompson, Cape Lisburne, Wainwright) to N Alaska (Barrow, Colville River Delta) and E (Barter Is) into Canada. Common in winter on the Aleutian Is, southern Bering Sea, southcoastal Alaska (Kodiak, Homer) and rare throughout SE Alaska. Spring, summer, and fall visitor to the Pribilof Is. The larger and paler form, *L.h. pallidissimus,* breeds on St. Matthew Is and Walrus Is.

Great Black-backed Gull *Larus marinus* — Accidental on Kodiak Is in Feb 1995.

Sabine's Gull *Xema sabini* — Common summer breeder from Bristol Bay and W Alaska (Hooper Bay, St. Michaels, Cape Prince of Wales) N along the coast (Kotzebue, Wainwright) and then E along the Beaufort Sea coast (Barrow) into Canada. Uncommon in summer in southcoastal Alaska (Homer, Cook Inlet) and along the ferry route from Homer to Dutch Harbor. Uncommon migrant on the Bering Sea Is. Fairly common in late spring at Nome. Casual inshore in SE Alaska.

Black-legged Kittiwake *Rissa tridactyla* — Common local breeder on sea cliffs and islands of the Chukchi and Bering Sea coasts (St. Lawrence, St. Matthew, and Pribilof

Is) and from Cape Lisburne S to and including the Aleutian Is and E along southcoastal Alaska (Kodiak, Barren Is, Homer, Resurrection Bay, Prince William Sound, Middleton Is), to N SE Alaska (Lituya Bay, Glacier Bay, Dixon Harbor). Common in summer and fall in the Bering, Chukchi, and Beaufort Seas. Common migrant throughout southcoastal and SE Alaska. One record from interior Alaska (George Lake).

Red-legged Kittiwake *Rissa brevirostris* — Common but declining local breeder in the Pribilof Is. Fairly common local breeder in the Aleutian Is (Unalaska to Buldir Is); casual visitor elsewhere in the Aleutians. Rare fall visitant in the Bering Sea N and E of breeding range; accidental at Gambell. Rare visitant in the N Pacific near Shumagin Is, Chignik Bay, Kodiak Is. Accidental inland below Kandik on the Yukon River.

Ross's Gull *Rhodostethia rosea* — Fairly common to common fall migrant and casual spring migrant and summer visitant in the Chukchi Sea around to Pt. Barrow. Rare fall migrant farther E on the Beaufort Sea coast. Rare migrant in the W Aleutian Is (Attu Is, Nizki Is), W Alaska (St. Lawrence Is, Wales), and casual at St. Paul Is, St. Michael, and Nome. Best found at Pt. Barrow in late fall (end of September into October) or at Gambell in spring.

Ivory Gull *Pagophila eburnea* — Fairly common pelagic migrant in the Chukchi and Bering Seas and fairly common pelagic winter visitant at the ice pack edge in the Bering Sea. Uncommon pelagic migrant on the Beaufort Sea and uncommon summer visitant on the pack ice in the Chukchi and Beaufort Seas. Uncommon to rare spring and fall migrant along shore from the Colville River mouth, Point Barrow, to Cape Prince of Wales. Rare in winter and early spring at Nome, St. Paul and St. Lawrence Is. Casual spring, summer, and fall visitant elsewhere in southcoastal Alaska (Homer, Anchorage) and SE Alaska (Glacier Bay, Skagway, Little Port Walter). Best found at Barrow in early spring or late fall or at Gambell in early spring.

Caspian Tern *Sterna caspia* — Uncommon summer visitant to SE and southcoastal Alaska (from Cordova W to Homer) and probable breeder in southcoastal Alaska (W Copper River Delta). Casual in Upper Cook Inlet at Anchorage and in interior Alaska (Central, Charley River mouth) and to the Bering Sea coast (Cape Romanzoff, Nome). Best found at Cordova in fall.

Common Tern *Sterna hirundo* — Alaska records are all of *S.h. longipennis*, the NE Asiatic race. Rare spring migrant and summer visitant in the W and central Aleutian Is and at St. Paul Is. Casual spring migrant in the N Bering Sea (Gambell) and at Nome.

Arctic Tern *Sterna paradisaea* — Common summer breeder throughout the State. Common from the N coast, the W coast, the Bering Sea Is, the Alaska Pen and the Aleutian Is, through the interior (Anaktuvuk Pass, Denali NP, Talkeetna, Mountain Village, Yukon, Porcupine, and Tanana River Valleys), southcoastal Alaska (Kodiak, Kenai Pen, Resurrection Bay, Prince William Sound, Glacier Bay) to SE Alaska (Taku Inlet, Juneau, Stikine, Salmon, and Unuk Rivers). Arrives the first week of May, departs some areas early in August, but remains later in others (Gambell until early September).

Forster's Tern *Sterna forsteri* — Accidental. One record of a bird collected in 1887 on the Yukon Delta. Gibson and Kessel are skeptical of the origin of the specimen (Gibson and Kessel 1997).

Aleutian Tern *Sterna aleutica* — Uncommon and declining local breeder along the coast of W Alaska (Cape Krusenstern, Noatak River Delta, Kotzebue, Shishmaref, Nome, Koyuk River mouth, St. Michaels, Hooper Bay, Bristol Bay, and the Alaska Pen), S to the Aleutian Is (Cold Bay to Attu), and E in southcoastal Alaska (Kodiak, Homer, Copper and Bering River Deltas, Yakutat) to N SE Alaska (Lituya Bay). Can best be found in summer at Nome or on Kachemak Bay. Departs suddenly by mid- to late August.

Sooty Tern *Sterna fuscata* — Accidental. Remains of one bird found dead at Attu in Jul 1997.

White-winged Tern *Chlidonias leucopterus* — Accidental in summer on Nizki Is in Jul 1976, at Homer in Aug 1992, and at Attu Is in May 1994.

Black Tern *Chlidonias niger* — Casual in SE Alaska (Wrangell, Juneau), two records along the Alaska Hwy in Jun 1994 and Jul 1996 (Eliza Lake, Tetlin NWR), and one possible breeding record from Fort Yukon. Two birds were seen again at Ten-mile Lake in Tetlin NWR in Jun 2001.

Dovekie *Alle alle* — Rare probable breeder in the Bering Sea Is (St. Lawrence and Little Diomede Is). Casual summer visitor to N Alaska (Barrow) and both Pribilof Is. Accidental off Kodiak Is. Best chance is at Gambell at a breeding site on Sevuokuk Mountain.

Common Murre *Uria aalge* — Common summer breeder on islands and cliffs from SE (St. Lazaria Is, Hazy Is, Forrester Is) and southcoastal Alaska (Resurrection and Kachemak Bays, Barren Is, Kodiak Is), the Alaska Pen and many of the Aleutian Is, N along the W coast (Cape Romanzof, St. Michael, Norton Sound), the Bering Sea Is (Pribilof, St. Matthew, and St. Lawrence Is), N to Cape Lisburne. Less common in winter near ice-free breeding areas. Common in winter throughout SE Alaska.

Thick-billed Murre *Uria lomvia* — Locally common summer breeder from Kodiak N to Cape Lisburne and Point Barrow (Cape Thompson, Point Hope, Kotzebue Sound, St. Michaels), the S side of the Alaska Pen, the Aleutian Is, the Bering Sea Is (Little Diomede, King Is, St. Lawrence Is, St. Matthew Is, Pribilof Is), and scattered colonies in southcoastal Alaska (Chiswell Is). Less common in winter near ice-free breeding areas. Uncommon in winter in southcoastal and casual in SE Alaska.

Black Guillemot *Cepphus grylle* — Uncommon local breeder and summer visitant on the Chukchi and Beaufort Sea coasts (Cape Thompson, Barrow E to Barter Is). Uncommon winter and spring, rare in early fall, and may be absent in summer on St. Lawrence Is. Uncommon to rare visitant throughout the year on the Beaufort and Chukchi Seas. Locally common winter visitant S in the Bering Sea to the limit of pack ice, sometimes to the Pribilof Is. Accidental in the interior near Paxson.

Pigeon Guillemot *Cepphus columba* — *C.c. columba* is common throughout coastal Alaska from the Bering Strait, Bering Sea Is (Little Diomede, St. Lawrence, St. Matthew and Pribilof Is), W Alaska (Nunivak Is), the E Aleutian Is, Alaska Pen, southcoastal Alaska (Kodiak Is, Chisik Is, Kachemak and Resurrection Bays, Prince William Sound, Glacier Bay), to SE Alaska (St. Lazaria and Forrester Is). Less common in winter near ice-free breeding areas north to the Aleutian Is, not in the central or N Bering Sea. The smaller Asiatic race, *C.c. kaiurka,* is found on the W Aleutian Is.

Long-billed Murrelet *Brachyramphus perdix* — Accidental, from remains found S of Healy in Aug 1983 and from a bird collected at Kodiak Is in 1845.

Marbled Murrelet *Brachyramphus marmoratus* — Common breeder and resident in southcoastal and SE Alaska in protected marine waters. Uncommon resident and probable breeder on the Alaska Pen and the Aleutian Is. Casual in winter at St. Paul Is, Bering Sea and accidental summer visitant to St. Lawrence Is. Best found in Kachemak and Resurrection Bays and throughout SE Alaska in summer.

Kittlitz's Murrelet *Brachyramphus brevirostris* — Locally common but declining summer breeder from the W Aleutian Is along the mountains of southcoastal Alaska (Kodiak Is, Kachemak Bay, Resurrection Bay, Prince William Sound) to Glacier Bay. Uncommon to rare N in the Bering and Chukchi Seas to Point Barrow. Casual on the Bering Sea Is. Easiest to find on Kachemak, Resurrection, and Glacier

Bays in glacial silty water in summer. Uncommon in winter near breeding areas except in the Bering Sea.

Ancient Murrelet *Synthliboramphus antiquus* — Locally common summer breeder throughout the Aleutian Is E to Kodiak Is and in SE Alaska (St. Lazaria and Forrester Is). Uncommon in southcoastal Alaska and in N SE Alaska. Casual on the Pribilof and St. Lawrence Is. Easiest to find from the Homer to Dutch Harbor ferry or in Resurrection Bay.

Cassin's Auklet *Ptychoramphus aleuticus* — Locally common summer breeder on many of the Aleutian Is, Kodiak Is, and in SE Alaska (St. Lazaria and Forrester Is). Uncommon in southcoastal Alaska. Occurs in large colonies often with Ancient Murrelets. Best found on the ferry trip from Homer to Dutch Harbor.

Parakeet Auklet *Aethia psittacula* — Locally common summer breeder from the Bering Strait, the Bering Sea Is (St. Lawrence, King, St. Matthew, and Pribilof Is), Seward Pen (Cape Prince of Wales), throughout the Aleutian Is, and in scattered colonies from Kodiak E to Resurrection Bay (Barren Is, Chiswell Is). Easiest to find at St. Paul Is, Gambell, or on the ferry trip from Homer to Dutch Harbor. Casual in the Chukchi Sea N to Barrow and to Prince William Sound. Winters at sea N to the S Bering Sea.

Least Auklet *Aethia pusilla* — Locally common summer breeder in the Bering Strait, the Bering Sea Is (St. Lawrence, St. Matthew, St. Paul, St. George), the Seward Pen (Cape Prince of Wales), and in the Aleutian Is from Koniuji Is W to Buldir Is. Easiest to see on St. Paul Is or at Gambell. Casual in the Chukchi Sea N to Barrow, and in the E Aleutians E to Kodiak Is. Winters at sea N to the S Bering Sea.

Whiskered Auklet *Aethia pygmaea* — Common but very local breeder in the Aleutian Is from Unimak Pass W to Buldir Is. Most easily found near the Baby Is on a tour out of Dutch Harbor. Casual visitant at Attu and Agattu and in the Bering Sea N to St. Lawrence Is.

Crested Auklet *Aethia cristatella* — Locally common breeder from the Bering Strait, Bering Sea Is (St. Lawrence, St. Matthew, Pribilof Is) S to Kodiak Is and the Alaska Pen and westward on many of the Aleutian Is. Casual summer visitant in N Alaska (Barrow) and southcoastal Alaska (Kachemak and Resurrection Bays). Most easily found at Gambell, on St. Paul Is, or from the ferry from Homer to Dutch Harbor.

Rhinoceros Auklet *Cerorhinca monocerata* — Common summer breeder in SE Alaska (St. Lazaria and Forrester Is), uncommon in southcoastal Alaska (Resurrection and Kachemak Bays) W to the Barren Is and into the Aleutians. Casual on St. Paul Is. Best found on tour boats to Kenai Fjords NP out of Seward or in SE Alaska.

Horned Puffin *Fratercula corniculata* — Common summer breeder from NW Alaska (Cape Lisburne, Cape Thompson) S along the Chukchi and Bering Sea coasts (Cape Prince of Wales, St. Michael) and islands (St. Lawrence, St. Matthew, Pribilof Is), throughout the Aleutian Is, then E (Bristol Bay) to Kodiak, and southcoastal Alaska (Barren Is, Kachemak Bay, Chiswell Is, Montague Is, Glacier Bay) and S to SE Alaska (St. Lazaria and Forrester Is). Easiest to see on St. Lawrence or St. Paul Is or on any boat trip in the breeding areas in summer. Winters at sea N to the central Bering Sea.

Tufted Puffin *Fratercula cirrhata* — Common summer breeder from NW Alaska (Cape Lisburne, Cape Thompson) S along the Chukchi and Bering Sea coasts (Cape Prince of Wales, St. Michael) and islands (St. Lawrence, St. Matthew, Pribilof Is), throughout the Aleutian Is, then E (Bristol Bay) to Kodiak, and southcoastal Alaska (Barren Is, Kachemak Bay, Chiswell Is, Montague Is, Glacier Bay) and S to SE Alaska (St. Lazaria and Forrester Is). Easiest to see at Gull Is in Kachemak Bay, the Chiswell Is in Resurrection Bay, on St. Lawrence or St. Paul Is, or on any boat trip in the breeding area in summer. Winters at sea N to the Aleutian Is.

Rock Dove *Columba livia* — The feral domestic pigeon is resident in Anchorage, Fairbanks, Juneau, and many of the smaller towns in southcoastal and SE Alaska.

Band-tailed Pigeon *Columba fasciata* — Rare to uncommon summer visitant and probable breeder in S SE Alaska on the mainland and on islands near the mouths of major rivers (Ketchikan, Wrangell, Stikine River mouth, Petersburg, Juneau, and Hyder). Accidental visitor to Nome.

Oriental Turtle-Dove *Streptopelia orientalis* — Accidental in summer at St. Paul Is in 1984, on board a ship near the Pribilof Is in 1986, at Attu Is in 1989 and 1996, on Chernabura Is in 1994, and at Dutch Harbor in 1995.

White-winged Dove *Zenaida asiatica* — Accidental at Skagway in Oct 1981.

Mourning Dove *Zenaida macroura* — Rare fall migrant and very rare spring migrant and summer visitant in SE Alaska. Rare fall visitant in southcoastal Alaska (Cordova, Homer, Anchorage) and casual fall visitant N of the Alaska Range (Fort Yukon) and once (prior to 1972) rare spring and summer visitant (Fairbanks, Chena Hot Springs, Circle Hot Springs). Casual fall visitant in SW Alaska (Kvichak River mouth, Dillingham). Accidental at Wales.

Common Cuckoo *Cuculus canorus* — Casual spring migrant and summer visitant in the W and central Aleutian Is, the Shumagins Is, at Gambell, and St. Paul Is. Accidental at Nome and in Anchorage (Jun 1999).

Oriental Cuckoo *Cuculus saturatus* — Accidental in May and June on Attu Is and the Rat Is, and in July and August at Gambell and St. Paul. One record on the mainland at Cape Prince of Wales in 1946.

Yellow-billed Cuckoo *Coccyzus americanus* — Accidental at Juneau in Jul 1996 and at Ketchikan in Aug 1991 and 1997. All records are of birds found dead.

Oriental Scops-Owl *Otus sunia* — Accidental. Remains found on Buldir Is in Jun 1977 and Amchitka Is in Jun 1979.

Western Screech-Owl *Otus kennicottii* — Uncommon resident in the woods of SE Alaska from Ketchikan to Juneau; rare in southcoastal Alaska (Seward, Copper Center, Sterling), and accidental farther W (Homer).

Great Horned Owl *Bubo virginianus* — Common resident from SE Alaska (*B.v. saturatus* — darker back) N to the S slopes of the Brooks Range through the wooded interior of Alaska and W through wooded southcoastal Alaska (Kenai Pen, Anchorage) (*B.v. lagophonus* — intermediate-colored back), and the coast of the Bering Sea (St. Michael) N to Kotzebue Sound (*B.v. algistus* — paler back). Casual N to Barrow.

Snowy Owl *Nyctea scandiaca* — Irruptive species breeding from the arctic coast (Demarcation Point to Barrow) S along the W coast of Alaska to Hooper Bay and probably on the Aleutian Is. Breeding density on the tundra depends on the lemming population. Easiest to find at Barrow in summer during lemming highs. Rare on the Bering Sea Is. In winter, often migrates S to the interior and southcoastal Alaska and rarely to SE Alaska.

Northern Hawk Owl *Surnia ulula* — Uncommon resident from Kotzebue Sound E along the S slope of the Brooks Range into Canada and S through the spruce forests of interior Alaska (Alaska, Richardson, Parks, Glenn, and Dalton Hwys, Denali State and NPs, on the Alaska Pen, to southcoastal Alaska (Cordova, Haines, Skagway). Casual on the Seward Pen and rare in N SE Alaska S at least to Juneau. Easiest to find near Fairbanks, along the Alaska, Glenn, and Dalton Hwy, or on the N Kenai Pen (Sterling Hwy).

Northern Pygmy-Owl *Glaucidium gnoma* — Rare resident in SE Alaska. Casual fall visitant in E southcoastal Alaska from Yakutat to Prince William Sound.

Barred Owl *Strix varia* — Rare resident in SE Alaska north at least to Haines.

Great Gray Owl *Strix nebulosa* — Uncommon resident in the deep woods of interior Alaska (Big Lake, Quartz Lake, Delta, Richardson Hwy S to Glennallen) from the Yukon River Valley S to southcoastal Alaska. Best found in Balsam Poplar stands on the Richardson Hwy between Gakona and Glennallen and near Fairbanks (Chena Hot Springs Road or in sloughs and rivers on the south side of the Tanana River).

Long-eared Owl *Asio otus* — Accidental at the Taku River in 1909 and N of Juneau in Oct 1990.

Short-eared Owl *Asio flammeus* — Uncommon (but numbers vary annually) summer breeder in open grasslands, tundra, and marshy habitats from the arctic coast S through the interior, and southcoastal Alaska. Uncommon migrant on the Aleutian Is. Uncommon spring and fall migrant and rare winter visitant in SE Alaska. Casual on St. Lawrence Is and the Pribilof Is.

Boreal Owl *Aegolius funereus* — Uncommon resident and breeder throughout wooded interior Alaska from passes in the Brooks Range S (Taylor Hwy) to the Alaska Pen, southcoastal (Sterling, Seward), and SE Alaska (Haines, Juneau) (*A.f. richardsoni*). Best found in spring when calling near Fairbanks (Chena Hot Springs Road) or in late winter (Feb and Mar) in Anchorage. Hard to find otherwise unless a nest can be located. One record of *A.f. magnus*, the larger and paler race from Siberia, on St. Paul Is in 1911.

Northern Saw-whet Owl *Aegolius acadicus* — Rare to uncommon resident and breeder in SE Alaska. Rare resident and breeder in southcoastal Alaska (Prince William Sound, Cordova, Seward, Sterling on the Kenai Pen, Anchorage, and Eagle River). Accidental in W Alaska (St. Lawrence Is and Pribilof Is).

Lesser Nighthawk *Chordeiles acutipennis* — Accidental, from an apparent window kill at the Noatak River mouth in Aug 1985.

Common Nighthawk *Chordeiles minor* — Rare fall migrant and summer visitant in mainland SE Alaska. Casual spring migrant and summer and fall visitant at scattered locations throughout the state (Barrow, Wainwright, Allakaket, Fairbanks, Cohoe, Kodiak, Cordova, Situk River). Best found near Haines along the gravel bars of the Chilkat and Klenhini Rivers and the Kelsall River, 27 miles N of Haines.

Whip-poor-will *Caprimulgus vociferus* — Accidental. One cat-killed bird found at West Petersburg, Kupreanof Is, in Nov 1972.

Jungle Nightjar *Caprimulgus indicus* — Accidental. One found dead on Buldir Is in May 1977.

Black Swift *Cypseloides niger* — Uncommon but probable summer breeder in S SE Alaska (Misty Fjords NM, Hyder, Stikine River, Juneau). Best found in the Salmon River Valley near Hyder.

Chimney Swift *Chaetura pelagica* — Accidental. One found dead in a building on St. George Is in Jun 1981.

Vaux's Swift *Chaetura vauxi* — Uncommon probable summer breeder in SE Alaska.

White-throated Needletail *Hirundapus caudacutus* — Accidental on Shemya Is in May 1974 and 1985, at Attu Is in 1978, 1984, and on St. Paul Is in Jun 1949.

Common Swift *Apus apus* — Accidental on St. Paul Is in 1950.

Fork-tailed Swift *Apus pacificus* — Casual spring and fall visitant in the W Aleutians and in SW Alaska (Pribilof Is), accidental in fall in NW Alaska (St. Lawrence Is, Sep 1993), and Middleton Is in southcoastal Alaska in Sep 1989.

Ruby-throated Hummingbird *Archilochus colubris* — Accidental at St. Michael in 1925 and at Nome in Aug 1981. One sight record from the Canning River Delta in Jun 1997.

Anna's Hummingbird *Calypte anna* — Rare fall and winter visitant in SE Alaska. Casual in summer. Accidental in southcoastal Alaska (Girdwood, Cordova, Homer).

Costa's Hummingbird *Calypte costae* — Accidental in summer and fall in Anchorage (3 records: 1989, 1994, 1998) and at Auke Bay in Oct 1992.

[**Calliope Hummingbird** *Stellula calliope* — Accidental from SE Alaska with several sight records at Juneau in May 1967 and Jun 1970. One bird was reported from Petersburg.]

Rufous Hummingbird *Selasphorus rufus* — Common migrant and summer breeder throughout SE Alaska and in southcoastal Alaska (Glacier Bay, Cordova) W at least to Kachemak Bay (Tutka Bay) and N to Girdwood in the NW extension of the Pacific Coast rain forest. Rare summer visitant in E interior Alaska (Circle, Delta, Fairbanks). There are many records of unidentified hummingbirds in central, W, and N Alaska that are probably this species or possibly Ruby-throated or Anna's Hummingbird. Accidental on St. Paul Is.

Eurasian Hoopoe *Upupa epops* — Accidental at Old Chevak in Sep 1975.

Belted Kingfisher *Ceryle alcyon* — Common summer breeder throughout most of Alaska, except the arctic coast and the Bering Sea Is, from the S slope of the Brooks Range to the E Aleutian Is, throughout W, interior, E, southcoastal and SE Alaska. Winters from Kodiak Is E along the coast.

Eurasian Wryneck *Jynx torquilla* — Accidental at Cape Prince of Wales in Sep 1945.

Yellow-bellied Sapsucker *Sphyrapicus varius* — Casual breeder in E interior Alaska near Northway and Fairbanks (2001 and 2002). Rare from Northway to the Yukon border at Scottie Creek. Accidental at Eagle in 1985, on Montague Is in 1977, and on Kodiak in 1994.

Red-breasted Sapsucker *Sphyrapicus ruber* — Common summer breeder in SE Alaska N to Glacier Bay. Casual along southcoastal Alaska W at least to Homer and N to Glennallen and Kenny Lake.

Great Spotted Woodpecker *Dendrocopos major* — Accidental at Attu Is in Oct 1985 to Apr 1986, May 1996, Sep and Oct 2000, Shemya Is in Sep to Oct 2000, St. George Is in May 2001, and on the Parks Hwy at Caswell Lake between Willow and Talkeetna from Oct 2001 to Apr 2002.

Downy Woodpecker *Picoides pubescens* — *P.p. nelsoni* (white below, undertail mostly unbarred) is a fairly common resident in the wooded interior from the limit of trees in W and N Alaska S to W southcoastal Alaska. *P.p. glacialis* (dusky below, undertail barred) ranges from Prince William Sound into SE Alaska.

Hairy Woodpecker *Picoides villosus* — Fairly common resident in the wooded interior of Alaska from the Yukon River Valley S to southcoastal Alaska (*P.v. septentrionalis* — white below, glossy black on back) and in SE Alaska (*P.v. sitkensis* — dusky below, dull black on back).

Three-toed Woodpecker *Picoides tridactylus* — Fairly common from NW (Kotzebue, Kobuk) and NE Alaska (Endicott Mountains), throughout the forested interior (Elliott Hwy, Chena Hot Springs Rd, Richardson Hwy S to Delta, Alaska Hwy) to southcoastal Alaska (Anchorage, Kodiak, Homer, Seward, Cordova) and on the Alaska Pen. Less common in SE Alaska. Best found in recent burns or beetle-killed spruce forests (Richardson and Alaska Hwys S and SE of Delta and on the Kenai Pen).

Black-backed Woodpecker *Picoides arcticus* — Locally uncommon in W and interior Alaska (Denali State Park, Parks Hwy N of Denali, Richardson Hwy S of Delta) S to southcoastal Alaska (Anchorage [rare], Eagle River) into Canada. Less common on the Alaska Pen and in N SE Alaska (Haines, Juneau). Best found in recent burns or beetle-killed spruce forests (Richardson and Alaska Hwys S of Delta and on the Kenai Pen).

Northern Flicker *Colaptes auratus* — Both races of flickers (Yellow-shafted, *C.a. auratus,* and Red-shafted, *C.a. cafer*) occur in Alaska and are highly migratory. The former is common in the wooded interior of central Alaska from the Yukon River S to southcoastal Alaska and E into Canada. The latter is common in SE Alaska from Glacier Bay S. Accidental in N Alaska and on the Bering Sea Is.

[**Pileated Woodpecker** — *Dryocopus pileatus* — Accidental at Hyder in Jun 1996. One sighting at Sitka in Nov 1992.]

Olive-sided Flycatcher *Contopus cooperi* — Uncommon and declining migrant and breeder throughout the taiga of central Alaska (Denali NP, Fairbanks, Minto Flats, Paxson) from NW Alaska (Noatak and Kobuk River Valleys, Kotzebue) eastward across the Koyukuk and Yukon River Valleys into Canada, and S on the Alaska Pen (Katmai); less common in southcoastal Alaska. Uncommon probable breeder in SE Alaska. Casual N to Prudhoe Bay; accidental at Gambell.

Western Wood-Pewee *Contopus sordidulus* — Uncommon migrant and breeder on mainland SE Alaska (*C.s. saturatus*), primarily along major river valleys and in E central Alaska (*C.s. amplus*) (Fairbanks) as far W as Denali NP, Upper Cook Inlet, and the N Kenai Pen (Sterling, Copper Center). Rare in southcoastal Alaska (Homer, Seward, Cordova), casual in W (Safety Sound) and N Alaska (Ambler, Noatak, Barrow, and Umiat).

Yellow-bellied Flycatcher *Empidonax flaviventris* — Rare summer visitant and probable breeder in E central Alaska (Tetlin NWR, Taylor Hwy, Tok, Kenny Lake, Delta, Fairbanks, Coal Creek near Woodchopper off the Yukon River) and at Petersburg, and Hyder. Casual at Juneau. Captured occasionally at the ABO banding sites in Creamer's Field, Fairbanks.

Alder Flycatcher *Empidonax alnorum* — Common migrant and breeder throughout central Alaska (Fairbanks, Delta, Paxson) S to southcoastal Alaska (Copper River Valley, Homer, Kasilof). Fairly common on the N end of the Alaska Pen, in W Alaska N to the base of the Seward Pen, the Noatak River Valley, and E in the Brooks Range, rarely N to the N coast (Barrow). Uncommon migrant and probable breeder in mainland SE Alaska. Prefers willow and alder vegetation. Latest arriving migrant in the interior and southcoastal Alaska (usually not before 1 Jun).

Willow Flycatcher *Empidonax traillii* — Casual to accidental, with only a handful of records and two specimens: (Hyder, Stikine River mouth, Juneau, Anchorage, and St. Marys). Many of the records are of singing birds.

Least Flycatcher *Empidonax minimus* — Rare in Alaska at scattered locations mostly in summer (Hyder, Juneau, Haines, Skagway, Fairbanks, Delta Junction, Kenny Lake). Casual at Anchorage. One fall record each at Middleton Is and Gambell. Check for breeding birds at Kenny Lake or Hyder.

Hammond's Flycatcher *Empidonax hammondii* — Fairly common migrant and breeder in the Yukon-Tanana uplands (Fairbanks) N to Fort Yukon. Uncommon spring migrant (through Anchorage) and probable breeder along mainland rivers in SE Alaska (Hyder, Juneau, Skagway). Accidental in N Alaska. Prefers tall deciduous woods.

Dusky Flycatcher *Empidonax oberholseri* — Accidental at Juneau in May 1992, the Stikine River mouth in Jun 1992, and at Icy Cape in Jul 1976.

Pacific-slope Flycatcher *Empidonax difficilis* — Fairly common summer breeder in SE Alaska from Glacier Bay S in the Pacific Coast rain forest to Forrester Is. There are two records of "Western" Flycatcher at Gambell.

Black Phoebe *Sayornis nigricans* — Accidental in Denali NP in Jun 2000.

Eastern Phoebe *Sayornis phoebe* — Accidental at Camden Bay in Jun 1990, Hyder in Jun 1993, and Mitkof Is in Jun 1995. Ranges as far N as the middle Mackenzie River Valley, so may be found in NE Alaska, where few birders explore.

Say's Phoebe *Sayornis saya* — Uncommon to locally fairly common migrant and breeder in the mountains and uplands of E central Alaska (Alaska Range and river valleys running out of the mountains, Paxson, Denali Hwy, Fairbanks, Steese Hwy), to the N foothills of the Brooks Range (Colville River Valley, Anaktuvuk Pass,

Bettles, Dalton Hwy), the mountains of the Seward Pen, and the mountains in southcoastal Alaska. Also found as far NW as Cape Thompson and the Noatak River Valley and E to the Canning River and Eagle. Very rare probable breeder in N SE Alaska (Glacier Bay, Juneau). Rare to casual migrant elsewhere, as in SW and southcoastal Alaska.

[**Ash-throated Flycatcher** *Myiarchus cinerascens* — Accidental from a sight record in Juneau in Jul 1999.]

Great Crested Flycatcher *Myiarchus crinitus* — Accidental on Middleton Is in Sep 1990.

Tropical Kingbird *Tyrannus melancholicus* — Casual at Ketchikan in Oct 1976, Oct 1992, and Nov 1998.

Western Kingbird *Tyrannus verticalis* — Casual summer and fall visitant in central Alaska (Susitna River bridge on the Denali Hwy, Copper River Delta) and in SE Alaska (Skagway, Hyder, Sitka).

Eastern Kingbird *Tyrannus tyrannus* — Casual summer visitant on the mainland of SE Alaska (Hyder, Stikine River mouth, Wrangell, Juneau, Gustavus, Haines). Casual summer and fall visitant elsewhere (Kodiak Is, Anchorage, Denali Hwy, Delta Junction, Nunivak Is, St. Paul Is, Nome, Cape Krusenstern, Barrow, Colville River Delta, Prudhoe Bay, Arctic Village).

[**Scissor-tailed Flycatcher** *Tyrannus forficatus* — Accidental with one sighting at Juneau and one in Gustavus in Jul 1972.]

Brown Shrike *Lanius cristatus* — Casual in spring and fall at Gambell in 1977, Shemya in 1978, Attu in 1984, Anchorage in 1983, and Sitka in 1999.

Northern Shrike *Lanius excubitor* — Uncommon to fairly common summer resident and breeder from N Alaska along the N slope of the Brooks Range, the Seward Pen, interior Alaska into Canada (Denali NP, Fairbanks, Steese Hwy), W Alaska (Nulato, St. Michael, Bethel, Mountain Village), Alaska Pen (Katmai to Unimak Is), E Aleutian Is, Kodiak, Chugach Mountains (Anchorage), Kenai Pen (Hope, Homer), E to Cordova. Fall, winter and spring records come from interior Alaska S and into SE Alaska. Casual visitor to St. Lawrence Is.

Cassin's Vireo *Vireo cassinii* — Casual at Juneau, Petersburg, and Hyder in summer and in Anchorage in Jun 1999 and May–Jun 2001.

Warbling Vireo *Vireo gilvus* — Uncommon to fairly common breeder on the mainland river valleys of SE Alaska (Hyder, Portland Canal, Chickamin River, Stikine River, Taku River, Skagway River, Chilkat River). Rare in summer at Juneau. Casual visitant to southcoastal Alaska (Anchorage). Accidental in fall at Wales. Best found at Hyder or Hot Spring Slough off the Stikine River.

Philadelphia Vireo *Vireo philadelphicus* — Casual in fall at Eagle on the Yukon River in E Alaska and in Sep 1987 at Middleton Is.

Red-eyed Vireo *Vireo olivaceus* — Rare, local, probable breeder on the mainland river systems of S SE Alaska (Chickamin River, Stikine River, Hyder). Casual at Juneau. Accidental in southcoastal Alaska (Middleton Is in Jun 1956) and Ketchikan. Best found at the Stikine River.

Gray Jay *Perisoreus canadensis* — Fairly common resident in forests along river valleys from the Brooks Range S throughout Alaska to the base of the Alaska Pen, throughout southcoastal Alaska E into Canada. Rare in SE Alaska (*P.c. pacificus*). The nominate form, *P.c. canadensis,* has a larger white forehead and comes into Alaska from Canada in NE central Alaska.

Steller's Jay *Cyanocitta stelleri* — Common resident in southcoastal Alaska spruce forests from Cook Inlet S and E along southcoastal Alaska (Homer, Seward, Cordova) throughout SE Alaska.

Clark's Nutcracker *Nucifraga columbiana* — Casual visitant with records widely distributed around the state from NW, W, and central Alaska, mostly from the summer but some records from fall. There are some winter records for Juneau.

Black-billed Magpie *Pica hudsonia* — Common resident in S Alaska from the Alaska Range S, including the E Aleutian Is, Alaska Pen, Kodiak Is, Kenai Pen, Copper River Valley to Yakutat, and Glacier Bay. Uncommon N of the Alaska Range (from Denali NP to Nenana; rare in Fairbanks). Also common in winter in SE Alaska. Casual N of the Yukon River.

American Crow *Corvus brachyrhynchos* — Fairly common summer breeder found only at Hyder.

Northwestern Crow *Corvus caurinus* — Common resident of southcoastal and SE Alaska from Kodiak Is E. Uncommon to rare N to Kenai and even rarer to Anchorage.

Common Raven *Corvus corax* — Common resident throughout the state from the Brooks Range S through all of W, central, and S Alaska to SE Alaska (*C.c. principalis*). Common summer breeder N to the Beaufort Sea coast. Casual on the Pribilof Is; locally common resident breeder on St. Lawrence Is. The larger Siberian form, *C.c. kamtschaticus,* is resident on the Aleutian Is E to Chignik and N to Cape Newenham.

Sky Lark *Alauda arvensis* — Rare spring migrant and casual summer and fall visitant in the W Aleutian Is. Casual spring migrant and summer visitant to the Pribilof Is (bred there in 1995); casual in spring and summer at Gambell and one fall record.

Horned Lark *Eremophila alpestris* — Fairly common summer resident and breeder in the foothills, mountains, and tundra of N Alaska (Arctic coast from Demarcation Point to Barrow, Anaktuvuk Pass in the Brooks Range) and interior Alaska (Yukon-Tanana Uplands at Eagle Summit, Alaska Range, Talkeetna Mountains, Denali NP, Kenai Mountains, Wrangell-St. Elias Mountains). Uncommon in N SE Alaska and casual on the Bering Sea Is. The form with a white throat and supercilium, *E.a. arcticola,* is best found at Eagle Summit and in Denali NP. The yellow-throated form, *E.a. flava,* is a casual migrant to SW, southcentral, and W Alaska including Gambell.

Purple Martin *Progne subis* — Casual spring migrant and summer visitant in central Alaska (Fairbanks), southcoastal Alaska (Anchorage, Seward), Pribilof Is, Wales, and at Wainwright and Deadhorse in N Alaska, and SE Alaska (Juneau).

Tree Swallow *Tachycineta bicolor* — Common summer breeder from the Brooks Range S throughout Alaska to Bethel, Bristol Bay, and across southcoastal Alaska and SE Alaska into Canada. Casual to rare on the Arctic coast, W coast of Alaska, and the Bering Sea Is.

Violet-green Swallow *Tachycineta thalassina* — Common summer breeder along major river valleys in interior Alaska from the Porcupine, Yukon, and Tanana Rivers S to the N end of the Alaska Pen and Bristol Bay, throughout southcoastal Alaska E into Canada. Less common in SE Alaska. Accidental in N Alaska (Barrow) and on the Bering Sea Is (St. Paul).

Northern Rough-winged Swallow *Stelgidopteryx serripennis* — Rare spring migrant, summer visitant, and breeder in SE Alaska on the mainland and on islands near mouths of major rivers (Ketchikan, Wrangell, Stikine River, Hyder, Juneau, Haines). Casual spring migrant, summer visitant, and possible breeder in southcoastal Alaska (Copper River Delta, Kamishak Bay). Accidental at Barrow.

Bank Swallow *Riparia riparia* — Common breeder throughout central Alaska, locally common NW to the Seward Pen, Kotzebue Sound, Noatak and Kobuk River Valleys, W to the Yukon-Kuskokwim River Valleys, the Alaska Pen, E Aleutian Is, and through southcoastal Alaska to Prince William Sound. Rare to casual beyond the breeding range in N Alaska (Barrow, Cape Thompson), on St. Paul Is, Gambell, and the W Aleutians. Uncommon in SE Alaska.

Cliff Swallow *Petrochelidon pyrrhonota* — Common migrant and breeder throughout central Alaska. Fairly common to rare in southcoastal Alaska, N Alaska, Seward Pen, W and SW Alaska. Rare on the Alaska Pen and in SE Alaska, and casual on St. Paul Is and the N coast (Prudhoe Bay).

Barn Swallow *Hirundo rustica* — The nearctic form, with a cinnamon belly (*H.r. erythrogaster*), is a fairly common migrant and breeder throughout SE Alaska and uncommon migrant and breeder in southcoastal Alaska (Portage) as far W as Seward. Rare at Anchorage. Casual spring migrant and summer visitant to Fairbanks, Big Delta, Tetlin Lakes, Kodiak Is, Iliamna Lake, Old Chevak, St. Lawrence Is, Nome, Wales, Colville River Delta, Barter Is. The Asian form, with a white belly (*H.r. gutteralis*), is a casual migrant and summer visitant in the Aleutian Is and Bering Sea coast. Has also been found on St. Paul and St. Lawrence Is and as far N as Barrow and Prudhoe Bay. There is at least one record of the palearctic form, *H.r. rustica,* from a bird collected in Barrow.

Common House-Martin *Delichon urbica* — Accidental, with widely scattered reports from Nome in 1974, St. Paul Is in Jun 1974, Jul 1994, and Aug 2001, from Buldir Is in 1990, St. Matthew Is in 1983, and from the Colville River mouth in 1983.

Black-capped Chickadee *Poecile atricapilla* — Uncommon to fairly common resident and breeder throughout central (Fairbanks), N (Brooks Range), W (Kotzebue Sound, E Norton Sound, S to Bristol Bay), and southcoastal Alaska (Kodiak Is, Kenai Pen, Seward, Prince William Sound). Uncommon resident and probable breeder on the Chilkat River in SE Alaska; otherwise casual there. Casual fall and winter visitant outside of breeding range in N (Barrow) and W Alaska (Wales, Nome).

Mountain Chickadee *Poecile gambeli* — Casual to rare winter visitant in SE Alaska mainland, and casual summer visitant and possible breeder N of Skagway. Also found on Mt. Ripinski near Haines.

Chestnut-backed Chickadee *Poecile rufescens* — Common resident of Pacific Coast rain forests from SE Alaska N to Glacier Bay and W along the coast through Prince William Sound, Seward, and the S shore of Kachemak Bay, Portage, and NW to Girdwood on the shore of Turnagain Arm SE of Anchorage (uncommon).

Boreal Chickadee *Poecile hudsonica* — The nominate form, *P.h. hudsonica,* is a common resident of wooded areas from NW Alaska (Kobuk) S to W Alaska and the base of the Alaska Pen, and throughout interior central Alaska. The larger and darker form, *P.h. columbiana*, is resident in southcoastal Alaska (Kenai Pen), and ranges casually into SE Alaska.

Gray-headed Chickadee *Poecile cincta* — Rare resident of N Alaska at widely distributed localities (Canning River on the ANWR, Kelly Bar N of Kotzebue, Nulato). Casual in interior Alaska (Fairbanks, Steese Hwy, Denali NP) and at Bethel. You will need a guide to find this bird in N Alaska. It is not reliably found elsewhere in the state at this time.

[**Great Tit** *Parus major* — Accidental from a sight record at a feeder on Little Diomede Is in 1988.]

Red-breasted Nuthatch *Sitta canadensis* — Rare to uncommon resident and breeder in southcoastal and SE Alaska. Some birds migrate N in the fall and numbers decline during winter. Some remain to breed as far N as Anchorage. Common on the Kenai Pen (Seward, Anchor Point, Homer, Kasilof) and in SE Alaska (Hyder, Glacier Bay). Rare S to Ketchikan. Casual breeder N of the Alaska Range (Fairbanks, Tok) where rare fall through spring. Casual on the Alaska Pen, W Alaska, and St. Lawrence Is. Best found in the spruce forests of SE (Juneau) and southcoastal Alaska (Homer, Seward, Cordova).

Brown Creeper *Certhia americana* — The paler form, *C.a. alascensis,* is a fairly common resident in southcentral (Anchorage) and southcoastal Alaska (Kodiak,

Kenai Pen, Prince William Sound, Yakutat). Rare N to Palmer and Denali NP and casual to Fairbanks. The darker and longer-billed form, *C.a. occidentalis,* is resident in SE Alaska.

Winter Wren *Troglodytes troglodytes* — Fairly common resident of southcoastal Alaska (Kodiak, Homer, Seward, Cordova, Yakutat, Glacier Bay), the Aleutian Is, Pribilof Is, and throughout SE Alaska. There are 11 subspecies identified within Alaska: *T.t. meligerus* from Attu E to Buldir Is; *T.t. kiskensis* from Kiska E to Amchitka Is; *T.t. tanagensis* in the Andreanof Is; *T.t. seguamensis* from Seguam and Anukta Is; *T.t. petrophilus* from the Fox Is; *T.t. stevensoni* from the W Alaska Pen; *T.t. semidiensis* from the Semidi Is; *T.t. alascensis* from the Pribilof Is; *T.t. helleri* from the Kodiak Archipelago; *T.t. pacificus* from SE Alaska; and *T.t. orchroleucus* from the rest of Alaska. Visible differences among these reproductively isolated populations depend primarily on gradations of the brown color from very dark to pale and gray to rufuscent.

American Dipper *Cinclus mexicanus* — Uncommon to fairly common resident along open-water streams throughout much of forested Alaska from Kobuk and the S slope of the Brooks Range S to the Aleutian Is, southcoastal Alaska, and in SE Alaska. Best found in Denali NP and along fast flowing streams throughout SE Alaska.

Golden-crowned Kinglet *Regulus satrapa* — Fairly common resident and breeder in coniferous forests throughout SE Alaska (*R.s. olivaceus*). Uncommon resident and breeder on the Kenai Pen (Kasilof, Homer), and SW Alaska at the base of the Alaska Pen (Katmai). Casual summer and fall visitant in central Alaska as far N as Denali NP, to Fairbanks (*R.s. amoenus*). Accidental on the Pribilof Is and at Wales.

Ruby-crowned Kinglet *Regulus calendula* — Fairly common migrant and breeder in the taiga forests of W and central Alaska (*R.c. calendula*), with decreasing abundance northward to the Seward Pen and the Brooks Range. Rare summer visitant and probable breeder in SW Alaska. Casual beyond the taiga (Barrow, Wales, St. Paul, Gambell). Accidental at Attu. The darker form, *R.c. grinnelli,* is casual to rare in SE and a common migrant and breeder in southcoastal Alaska W to Cook Inlet (Anchorage, Kenai Pen). Easy to find in summer in Fairbanks, Denali NP, or on the Kenai Pen.

Middendorff's Grasshopper-Warbler *Locustella ochotensis* — Casual at Nunivak Is in 1927, Attu in 1979 and 2000, Shemya in 1978, Buldir in 1990, Gambell in 1979 and 1996, and on St. Paul Is in 1984.

Lanceolated Warbler *Locustella lanceolata* — Accidental (but a total of 25 birds) on Attu Is in Jun 1984 and another record there in Jun 2000.

Wood Warbler *Phylloscopus sibilatrix* — Accidental on Shemya Is in Oct 1978.

Dusky Warbler *Phylloscopus fuscatus* — Casual in fall at Middleton Is, Gambell, St. Paul Is, and at Attu and Shemya Is. One was found onboard a ship in the central Bering Sea.

Yellow-browed Warbler *Phylloscopus inornatus* — Accidental with one record at Gambell in Sep 1999.

Arctic Warbler *Phylloscopus borealis* — Fairly common summer migrant and breeder from the base of the Alaska Pen (Dillingham) N (Bristol Bay, St. Michael, Norton Sound, Nome, Kotzebue, Kobuk) to Point Hope and E on the North Slope (Colville River Valley, Umiat, N section of the Dalton Hwy) and in interior Alaska on the S slope of the Alaska Range (Petersville Road, Denali NP, Denali Hwy, Glenn Hwy near Eureka Summit) E to the Richardson Hwy (Paxson, Summit Lake). Rare in summer N of the Alaska Range E to Fairbanks and Tok, and E to Northway on the Alaska Hwy and on the Nabesna Road. Uncommon migrant on St. Lawrence and rare on St. Matthew Is. Best found in Denali NP, Parks Hwy near Healy, Denali Hwy, Nome, Richardson Hwy, and Gambell in early fall. All breeding birds and Bering Straight migrants belong to the smaller, paler, and browner form with a smaller bill,

P.b. kennicotti. There are a few records of the larger, greenish-yellow form, *P.b. xanthodryas,* from the W Aleutian Is.

Narcissus Flycatcher *Ficedula narcissina* — Accidental on Attu Is in May 1989 and May 1994.

Mugimaki Flycatcher *Ficedula mugimaki* — Accidental on Shemya Is in May 1985.

Red-breasted Flycatcher *Ficedula parva* — Casual in the W Aleutian Is. Accidental at Gambell (Jun 1977) and on St. Paul Is (Jun 1999, Jun 2000).

Siberian Flycatcher *Muscicapa sibirica* — Casual at Attu (1986, 1990, 1999), Shemya (1977), and Buldir (1990, 1991) in Jun and Sep, and St. Paul Is in Jun 1999.

Gray-spotted Flycatcher *Muscicapa griseisticta* — Very rare spring migrant in the W Aleutian Is.

Asian Brown Flycatcher *Muscicapa dauurica* — Accidental at Attu Is in May 1985 and Gambell in Jun 1994.

[**Rufous-tailed Robin** *Luscinia sibilans* — Accidental from a sight record on Attu Is in Jun 2000.]

Siberian Rubythroat *Luscinia calliope* — Very rare spring and casual fall migrant in the W Aleutian Is. Casual in spring, summer, and fall on the Pribilof Is and at Gambell.

Bluethroat *Luscinia svecica* — Rare to locally uncommon migrant and breeder in NW and N Alaska (Wales, Nome, Kotzebue, Noatak River, Cape Thompson, Barrow, Colville River, Umiat, N end of the Dalton Hwy) E along the N foothills of the Brooks Range to the Canadian border. Rare to uncommon migrant on St. Lawrence Is, and rare on the Bering Sea coast S to St. Michael. Casual migrant in the Aleutian Is. Best found on the Kougarok Road from Nome, at Gambell, near Umiat, or on the Dalton Hwy.

Siberian Blue Robin *Luscinia cyane* — Accidental at Attu Is in May 1985.

Red-flanked Bluetail *Tarsiger cyanurus* — Casual in spring and fall at Attu, Shemya, and St. Paul Is. One sight record at Hooper Bay.

Northern Wheatear *Oenanthe oenanthe* — Fairly common migrant and breeder in rocky upland and alpine tundra areas throughout the mountain systems and highlands of W (Wales, Nome, Kotzebue) and central Alaska (Eagle Summit on the Steese Hwy, Denali NP, Denali Hwy, Taylor Hwy). Rare migrant and probable breeder in the Chugach (Anchorage) and Kenai Mountains, in N Alaska (Dalton Hwy in the Brooks Range). Fairly common migrant in W Alaska from the Bering Strait S, including St. Lawrence Is. Casual migrant in SW Alaska on the Pribilof and Aleutian Is and in N Alaska from the Chukchi sea coast N to Barrow. Casual along the N coast to the E. Casual fall migrant in N SE Alaska (Haines). Best found in summer in Denali NP, Eagle Summit on the Steese Hwy, the Dalton Hwy, Nome, and in early fall at Gambell.

Stonechat *Saxicola torquata* — Casual, with records for Gambell (Jun 1978, Jun 1985, Jun and Sep 1992), and Middleton Is (Sep 1990).

Mountain Bluebird *Sialia currucoides* — Rare summer breeder and migrant in interior Alaska (Fairbanks, Delta Junction, Eagle, Tanacross, Tok) S to the N Kenai Pen (Sterling, Copper Center). Rare in migration in southcoastal (Middleton Is) and SE Alaska (Glacier Bay, Juneau, Chickamin River). Accidental on Nunivak Is, Barrow, and Prudhoe Bay. One of the earliest arriving passerine migrants in the interior (mid-Apr).

Townsend's Solitaire *Myadestes townsendi* — Rare migrant and breeder of high open country in E central Alaska (Taylor Hwy, Fairbanks, Circle, upper Yukon River Valley) and in the major mountain systems (Wrangell-St. Elias Mountains, Denali NP and the Denali Hwy in the Alaska Range, Dalton Hwy in the Brooks Range). Very rare migrant and breeder in southcoastal Alaska (Kenai Pen, Eagle River, Cordova).

Rare migrant and probable breeder in SE Alaska (Haines, Skagway). Accidental on the N coast and at St. Lawrence Is. Best found in Denali NP.

Veery *Catharus fuscescens* — Accidental to casual at Hyder in spring and summer.

Gray-cheeked Thrush *Catharus minimus* — Common breeder in coastal W Alaska S to the base of the Alaska Pen and Kodiak Is. Nests in tall shrub vegetation at the coastal-taiga margin and adjacent to wet boggy habitats. Rare on St. Lawrence Is and casual at St. Paul. Rare to casual westward on the Alaska Pen (Cold Bay). Fairly common migrant and breeder in central Alaska S to the N Kenai Pen. Rare and local breeder farther S on the Kenai Pen, in southcoastal Alaska (Homer, Seward, Cordova), and in mainland SE Alaska (Glacier Bay, Juneau, Stikine River).

Swainson's Thrush *Catharus ustulatus* — Fairly common migrant and summer breeder in wet woods and brush from W Alaska (Nulato) along the S slope of the Brooks Range (Bettles), through interior Alaska (Fairbanks, Denali NP, Paxson) into Canada, the Alaska Pen, and southcoastal (Kenai Pen, Anchorage). Casual on St. Lawrence Is; accidental on Shemya Is (*C.u. incanus* [or *almae*] — Olive-backed Thrush). The Russet-backed Thrush, *C.u. ustulatus,* breeds throughout SE Alaska.

Hermit Thrush *Catharus guttatus* — Common migrant and summer breeder in forests of interior Alaska (Fairbanks, Denali NP) (*C.g. faxoni*), southcoastal Alaska (Kodiak Is, Kenai Pen, Prince William Sound, Yakutat) and the E Aleutian Is (*C.g. guttatus*), and throughout SE Alaska (*C.g. osgoodi* [or *nanus*]). Casual N to Barrow and W to St. Lawrence Is.

Eyebrowed Thrush *Turdus obscurus* — Rare spring and casual fall migrant in the central and W Aleutian Is, and casual in spring and fall at St. Paul and St. Lawrence Is. Accidental spring migrant in W (Wales, Nunivak Is) and N Alaska (Barrow).

Dusky Thrush *Turdus naumanni* — Casual spring and fall migrant on the W Aleutian Is and St. Lawrence Is. Accidental at Barrow, Petersburg, and Juneau.

Fieldfare *Turdus pilaris* — Accidental at Barrow, on St. Lawrence Is, and in the Brooks Range.

American Robin *Turdus migratorius* — Common migrant and summer breeder throughout the wooded interior of Alaska and from SW and W Alaska (Nome) E along the ridge of the Brooks Range into Canada (*T.m. migratorius* — with white tail corners) to SE Alaska (*T.m. caurinus* — lacking prominent white tail corners). Casual on the Bering Sea Is and N to Barrow.

Varied Thrush *Ixoreus naevius* — Common migrant and summer breeder in willow brush on the Seward Peninsula (Nome) and in deep coniferous woods from NW Alaska (Kobuk), E along the S slope of the Brooks Range into Canada, throughout interior Alaska (Denali NP, Fairbanks), in W (Yukon-Kuskokwim River Valleys), and southcoastal Alaska (Anchorage, Kenai Pen, Prince William Sound) (*I.n. meruloides*), and throughout SE Alaska (*I.n. naevius*). Casual in winter in southcoastal Alaska but sometimes common in SE Alaska. Casual N to Barrow and W to the Bering Sea Is.

Gray Catbird *Dumetella carolinensis* — Accidental at the Stikine River mouth in Jun 1996, at Cape Peirce in Sep 1998, and at Anchorage in Oct 1999.

Northern Mockingbird *Mimus polyglottos* — Casual in SE Alaska, southcoastal Alaska (Middleton Is, Anchorage), and central Alaska (Fairbanks).

Brown Thrasher *Toxostoma rufum* — Accidental at Barrow in Sep 1974, remains from Peregrine Falcon nests on the Yukon River, Fairbanks in Sep to Oct 2001, and on the Alaska Hwy near Dot Lake among several other records.

European Starling *Sturnus vulgaris* — Rare migrant and summer visitant and very rare breeder in interior Alaska (Fairbanks, Delta, Northway, Tanana, Denali NP, Palmer). Rare migrant and winter visitant in southcoastal Alaska (Kodiak, Homer, Seward, Cordova). Casual spring migrant and summer and fall visitant in W Alaska N to Kotzebue. Rare to uncommon migrant, uncommon to rare local winter visitant. Rare to uncommon resident of most SE Alaska towns; very rare away from human settlements.

[**Gray Starling** *Sturnus cineraceus* — (White-cheeked Starling) — Accidental, seen from 1–6 May 1998 at Homer; probably a stowaway on a freighter.]

Siberian Accentor *Prunella montanella* — Casual fall visitant in the W Aleutian Is, Nunivak Is, on St. Lawrence Is, and accidental at Barrow in fall 1951, Ester near Fairbanks in 1984, at Juneau in Nov 1984, and in Anchorage from Dec 1997 to Apr 1998.

Yellow Wagtail *Motacilla flava* — Common migrant and breeder throughout much of mainland W Alaska (Hooper Bay, Seward Pen, Nome, Kotzebue Sound, Cape Thompson, upper Colville River). Less common E in the Brooks Range and N (Dalton Hwy) to the N coast (Colville River mouth, Barrow). Uncommon to common migrant and rare breeder on St. Lawrence Is. Rare to uncommon spring and fall migrant in the Aleutian Is and the Pribilof Is. Casual in central Alaska and in southcoastal Alaska (Alaska Pen, Anchorage, Homer). Best found at Nome, Gambell, and on the Colville River. Breeding birds are the paler form, *M.f. tschutschensis*, while the larger and brighter form, *M.f. simillima,* is a casual migrant in the W Aleutians (only race documented in spring there) N to St. Lawrence Is and is accidental on the mainland.

Gray Wagtail *Motacilla cinerea* — Casual migrant to the W and central Aleutian Is and accidental on St. Lawrence and the Pribilof Is.

White Wagtail *Motacilla alba* — Rare breeder in coastal W Alaska (Hooper Bay), St. Lawrence Is, coastal Seward Pen (Wales, Nome), N to Cape Thompson and Cape Lisburne. Very rare in N Alaska (Barrow, Colville River mouth). Rare to casual spring migrant in the Pribilof Is. Best found in Gambell or Wales.

Black-backed Wagtail *Motacilla lugens* — Rare migrant and casual breeder in the W Aleutians, casual migrant at St. Paul and St. Lawrence Is. (Black-backed "type" birds have been observed building nests at Gambell, but there is no evidence of a successful breeding of Black-backed Wagtails there.) Casual at Nome. Accidental in southcoastal Alaska at Homer in Jun 1990, and in interior Alaska at Mile 1260 on the Alaska Highway in Jun 1990.

Tree Pipit *Anthus trivialis* — Accidental at Cape Prince of Wales in Jun 1972, and Gambell in Jun 1995.

Olive-backed Pipit *Anthus hodgsoni* — Rare to casual migrant in the W Aleutian Is; fewer records at St. Paul Is and at Gambell.

Pechora Pipit *Anthus gustavi* — Casual spring migrant to Attu Is, Buldir Is, and Gambell.

Red-throated Pipit *Anthus cervinus* — Uncommon to fairly common local breeder in the Bering Strait from St. Lawrence Is and Wales N to Cape Thompson and Cape Lisburne. Rare migrant in the W Aleutian Is and casual on the Pribilof Is. Casual in fall to Barrow and in Juneau. Best found at Gambell and at Wales.

American Pipit *Anthus rubescens* — Common migrant and breeder in drier foothills and alpine tundra throughout Alaska from N Alaska (Meade River), the Brooks Range (Anaktuvuk Pass) E to the Killik River, S on the Seward Pen (Wales, Nome), to the tip of the Alaska Pen, in the Aleutian Is, Kodiak Is, in the interior at Eagle Summit, and the high country of Denali NP and Denali Hwy, to the hills of the Kenai Pen, in southcoastal Alaska to Glacier Bay and Haines, and in the mountains of SE Alaska. The common Alaska form is *A.r. pacificus*. The more heavily streaked and darker form, *A.r. japonicus,* is a casual spring and fall visitant to the Bering Sea Is and the W Aleutian Is.

Bohemian Waxwing *Bombycilla garrulus* — Fairly common but irregular migrant and breeder throughout the taiga of central Alaska (Fairbanks). Uncommon resident and breeder in southcoastal Alaska (Anchorage, Kenai Pen, Prince William Sound,

Kodiak Is). Very rare in W Alaska, the Seward Pen, Alaska Pen, and casual on the Pribilof Is. Fairly common migrant, winter visitant, and rare breeder in SE Alaska (Glacier Bay, Hyder) (*B.g. pallidiceps*). Best found in Anchorage, Seward, and Fairbanks. The E Asiatic subspecies (*B.g. centralasiae*) is accidental, with one record from Attu in May 1989.

Cedar Waxwing *Bombycilla cedrorum* — Uncommon migrant in SE Alaska from Ketchikan to Juneau. Most common on or near the mainland. Casual winter visitant to southcoastal Alaska (Bird Creek on Turnagain Arm, Kodiak Is).

Tennessee Warbler *Vermivora peregrina* — Casual migrant in SE Alaska. Casual summer and fall visitant in central Alaska (Fairbanks, Birch Lake, Delta Junction, Scottie Creek, and on the Taylor Hwy). Casual in southcentral Alaska (Anchorage) and on the Alaska Pen (King Salmon). Accidental at Gambell (Sep 2001).

Orange-crowned Warbler *Vermivora celata* — Common migrant and breeder in central, southcoastal, SW (at the base of the Alaska Pen), and SE Alaska. Casual to the tip of the Alaska Pen and on the Pribilof Is. Fairly common to uncommon migrant and breeder in W Alaska from the Kobuk River, Seward Pen, S. Casual spring migrant and summer and fall visitant in N Alaska from Barrow to the Sagavanirktok River Delta and fall visitant to Gambell and St. Paul. The yellow form, *V.c. lutescens,* breeds in southcentral and SE Alaska and the grayer form, *V.c. celata,* breeds throughout the rest of Alaska. They come together during migration in southcoastal Alaska.

[**Nashville Warbler** *Vermivora ruficapilla* — Accidental at Middleton Is, Juneau, and other SE Alaska locations with sight records as recent as Sep 2001.]

[**Northern Parula** *Parula americana* — Accidental from a sight record on Middleton Is in Sep 1987.]

Yellow Warbler *Dendroica petechia* — Common breeder in central Alaska and fairly common in W Alaska (Seward Pen, Kotzebue Sound, Kobuk River). Uncommon in the Brooks Range from Cape Thompson E to the Sheenjek River and S to Umiat. Casual migrant to the coasts of the Beaufort and Chukchi Seas and to the Bering Sea Is (Gambell, St. Paul) (*D.p. banksi* [or *amnicola*]). Common breeder also in SW, southcoastal, and mainland SE Alaska (*D.p. rubiginosa*).

Chestnut-sided Warbler *Dendroica pensylvanica* — Accidental at Middleton Is in Sep 1981 and at Ketchikan in Jun 1997.

Magnolia Warbler *Dendroica magnolia* — Casual summer and fall visitant in SE Alaska (Hyder, Chickamin River, Petersburg, Juneau) and southcoastal Alaska (Middleton Is). Accidental in N and W Alaska (Nunivak Is and aboard ship in the Bering Sea). Best found in Hyder, where rare but annual.

Cape May Warbler *Dendroica tigrina* — Casual fall visitant in central Alaska (Fairbanks), southcoastal Alaska (Middleton Is), and SE Alaska (Haines). Accidental in N Alaska (Barrow).

Black-throated Blue Warbler *Dendroica caerulescens* — Accidental at Tee Harbor near Juneau in Nov 2001.

Yellow-rumped Warbler *Dendroica coronata* — The Myrtle Warbler, *D. c. coronata,* is a common migrant and breeder throughout the wooded interior of Alaska from NW Alaska (Kobuk), the S slope of the Brooks Range to the Porcupine River Valley, in the interior along the Koyukuk, Yukon, and Tanana River Valleys (Denali NP, Fairbanks, Delta Junction, Tok, Tetlin, Paxson), to the base of the Alaska Pen (Lake Clark), in southcentral Alaska (Talkeetna, Anchorage), and on the Kenai Pen (Homer, Seward), to Prince William Sound (Cordova). Rare to the Bering Sea coast (Nome). Casual on St. Lawrence Is N to Barrow; accidental in W and central Aleutians. Audubon's Warbler, *D. c. auduboni,* breeds in SE Alaska S of the Stikine River.

[**Black-throated Gray Warbler** *Dendroica nigrescens* — Accidental from a sight record in Petersburg in Jul 1989.]

Black-throated Green Warbler *Dendroica virens* — Accidental on Chichagof Is in Jul 1941.

Townsend's Warbler *Dendroica townsendi* — Uncommon to rare summer visitant and breeder in mixed woodlands in E central Alaska (Fairbanks). Fairly common breeder in southcoastal (Kenai Pen, Prince William Sound) and in SE Alaska. Accidental in N Alaska (Barrow) and in the W Aleutians.

[**Hermit Warbler** *Dendroica occidentalis* — Accidental, perhaps from Forrester Island.]

Prairie Warbler *Dendroica discolor* — Accidental on Middleton Is in Sep 1988 and in Ketchikan in Sep 1990.

Palm Warbler *Dendroica palmarum* — Casual in fall in scattered locations throughout Alaska (Ketchikan, Mitkof Is, Petersburg, Taku River, Juneau, Middleton Is, Ninilchik, Kodiak, Nunivak Is, Dot Lake, Brooks Range, Prudhoe Bay, Barrow). Several recent records are from Fairbanks and in the upper Tanana River Valley in fall.

[**Bay-breasted Warbler** *Dendroica castanea* — Accidental with sightings at Fairbanks in 1951, at Juneau near the Mendenhall Glacier in May 1999, and from Petersburg in 1999.]

Blackpoll Warbler *Dendroica striata* — Common but declining migrant and breeder in W (Seward Pen), SW (base of Alaska Pen), and E central (Fairbanks) Alaska. Fairly common to uncommon migrant and breeder in southcentral (Soldotna, Anchorage) and southcoastal (Kachemak Bay, Seward) Alaska. Rare spring migrant in southcoastal (Kodiak, Cordova) and SE Alaska (Chickamin River, Juneau, Glacier Bay). Casual fall visitant to St. Lawrence Is.

Black-and-white Warbler *Mniotilta varia* — Accidental on the Colville River Delta in Oct 1977, in Hyder in Jun 1992, and Juneau in May 1998.

American Redstart *Setophaga ruticilla* — Uncommon breeder on the mainland river systems of SE Alaska (Portland Canal, Chickamin River, Hyder, Stikine River, Juneau, Taku River, Skagway River, Chilkat River, Glacier Bay). Casual summer visitant to southcoastal Alaska (Anchorage, Homer) and central Alaska (Denali NP, Tok). Easiest to find at Juneau or Hyder.

Ovenbird *Seiurus aurocapillus* — Casual in Alaska, with records from Fort Yukon (no date available) and Nulato (1867), in fall at Prudhoe Bay (Sagavanirktok River delta in Sep 1981), and Fairbanks (Oct 1993, Oct 1999), and at Douglas (Jun 1997).

Northern Waterthrush *Seiurus noveboracensis* — Common migrant and breeder throughout the taiga of central Alaska (Fairbanks, Chatanika). Common to fairly common migrant and breeder in W Alaska (Noatak River, Seward Pen). Common to uncommon breeder in SW Alaska at the base of the Alaska Pen and rare out to Cold Bay. Casual in spring to St. Lawrence Is and in N Alaska (Barrow, Colville River Delta). Rare migrant and probable breeder in SE Alaska on mainland river systems.

[**Kentucky Warbler** *Oporornis formosus* — Accidental from a sight record at Beaufort Lagoon near Kaktovik in Sep 1982.]

Mourning Warbler *Oporornis philadelphia* — Accidental at Middleton Is in Sep 1987 and at Fairbanks in Sep 1992.

MacGillivray's Warbler *Oporornis tolmiei* — Rare migrant and breeder in SE Alaska (Juneau, Chickamin River, Hyder, Stikine River). Casual on Middleton Is in fall. Accidental at Barrow. Best found at Hyder.

Common Yellowthroat *Geothlypis trichas* — Uncommon to locally fairly common breeder on or near mainland river systems in SE Alaska N to Glacier Bay. Casual summer visitant in central (Harding Lake) and southcoastal Alaska (Anchorage), casual fall visitant (Cordova, Valdez) and one-time breeder (Homer) in southcoastal Alaska. The larger and paler form, *G.t. campicola,* occupies the N part of the range in Alaska, while the smaller and brighter form, *G.t. arizela,* is restricted to the S part of SE Alaska.

Wilson's Warbler *Wilsonia pusilla* — Common migrant and breeder from NW Alaska (Kobuk, Kotzebue), the S slope of the Brooks Range, S (Norton Sound, St. Michael, Hooper Bay) to the Alaska Pen (Unimak Is, Semidi Is), the E Aleutian Is, Bristol Bay, throughout interior Alaska (Denali NP, Denali Hwy, Richardson Hwy, Fairbanks, Eagle Summit, Circle, Eagle), Kodiak Is, southcoastal Alaska (Kenai Pen, Prince William Sound), and fairly common throughout SE Alaska. Casual on St. Lawrence and Pribilof Is and at Barrow.

Canada Warbler *Wilsonia canadensis* — Accidental at Barrow in Jul 1965 and Prudhoe Bay in Sep 1981.

Scarlet Tanager *Piranga olivacea* — Accidental at Barrow in Jun 1934 and Cordova in May 1977.

Western Tanager *Piranga ludoviciana* — Uncommon probable breeder on the mainland river systems of SE Alaska (Portland Canal, Chickamin River, Unuk River, Hyder, Stikine River, Juneau, Chilkat River, Skagway River). Very rare migrant and summer visitant at Glacier Bay, Petersburg. Casual at Middleton Is, Denali NP, and Fairbanks; accidental at Homer and Barrow.

Spotted Towhee *Pipilo maculatus* — Accidental in Juneau in spring (May) and winter (Sep through Jan).

American Tree Sparrow *Spizella arborea* — Common migrant and summer breeder in brush from the N coast of Alaska, the Seward Pen, through the Brooks Range and in treeline habitats S through W Alaska, the Alaska Pen, the Yukon-Tanana Highlands, the Alaska Range, and casually to the N Kenai Pen. Uncommon spring and fall migrant in SE Alaska and rare in winter. Uncommon in winter in southcoastal Alaska. Casual on the Bering Sea Is.

Chipping Sparrow *Spizella passerina* — Uncommon spring migrant and breeder in the upper Tanana River Valley of E central Alaska (Tetlin Lakes, Northway, Tok, Chicken, Big Delta, Fairbanks, Fort Yukon, N of Talkeetna). Casual migrant in southcoastal Alaska (Anchorage, Seward, Cordova). Uncommon breeder on the mainland river systems of SE Alaska. Accidental in N (Barrow) and W (Gambell) Alaska. Best found along the Alaska Hwy from the Canada Border to Tetlin.

Clay-colored Sparrow *Spizella pallida* — Casual, with records at Ketchikan, Stikine River mouth, Juneau, Haines, Tok, and Camden Bay.

Brewer's (Timberline) Sparrow *Spizella breweri taverneri* — Rare breeder in the Nutzotin Mountains in E central Alaska S of Northway (Nabesna, Gold Hill) and W of Beaver Creek, YT. Also casual at Hyder. Also breeds in subalpine brush in Canada near Carcross, Whitehorse, and Kluane Lake and on the Haines Hwy. Seen in migration in SE Alaska.

Lark Sparrow *Chondestes grammacus* — Accidental at Scottie Creek in Jul 1991 and at Sitka in Aug 1999.

Savannah Sparrow *Passerculus sandwichensis* — Common migrant and breeder in open country throughout Alaska; rare in fall in the Aleutian Is and the Bering Sea Is. Aleutian and Kodiak Is birds are larger birds with larger bills (*P.s. sandwichensis*) than the smaller birds that breed throughout the rest of Alaska (*P.s. athinus*) except in SE Alaska (*P.s. crassus*).

Fox Sparrow *Passerella iliaca* — Eight races of Fox Sparrow occur in Alaska. Seven are of the large and sooty races that occupy the Aleutian Is and S coast of the Alaska Pen through Kodiak Is, southcoastal Alaska, and SE Alaska (*P.i. unalaschcensis, fuliginosa, sinuosa, ridgwayi, annectens, townsendi,* and *chilcatensis*).The reddish Fox Sparrow (*P.i. zaboria*) is a common migrant and summer breeder from Kobuk and the S slope of the Brooks Range in N Alaska, the Seward Pen, W Alaska S to Bristol Bay, throughout central Alaska into Canada, to S of the Alaska Range. Casual on the Pribilof and St. Lawrence Is and at Barrow. Members of both red and gray races winter in southcoastal Alaska. The gray form is rare to uncommon and the red form casual in winter in SE Alaska.

Song Sparrow *Melospiza melodia* — Alaskan Song Sparrows have been divided into eight races, all of them larger and darker than Song Sparrows of the Lower 48 states. Birds in the Aleutian Is and Alaska Pen are resident (*M.m. maxima, amaka,* and *sanaka*). Others from Kodiak Is (*M.m. insignis*), Kenai Pen, and Prince William Sound (*M.m. kenaiensis*), the Gulf of Alaska coast (*M.m. caurina*), and SE Alaska (*M.m. rufina* and *inexpectata*) are partly migratory. The species is common near saltwater in southcoastal Alaska from the Alaska Pen, the Aleutian Is, Kodiak Is, N to Anchorage, on the Kenai Pen, E to Glacier Bay, and S through SE Alaska. Accidental on St. Paul Is.

Lincoln's Sparrow *Melospiza lincolnii* — Common migrant and summer breeder from Kobuk and the S slope of the Brooks Range in N Alaska, the Seward Pen, W Alaska S to Bristol Bay, throughout central Alaska into Canada; casual visitor to Gambell (*M.l. lincolnii*). Common to the S coast from the Alaska Pen through Kodiak Is, southcoastal Alaska, and SE Alaska (*M.l. gracilis*).

Swamp Sparrow *Melospiza georgiana* — Casual primarily in fall with sightings at Ketchikan, Petersburg, Juneau, Middleton Is, and Anchorage.

White-throated Sparrow *Zonotrichia albicollis* — Casual visitant at any season (Ketchikan, Sitka, Juneau, Cordova, Middleton Is, Seward, Homer, Kodiak, Fairbanks, Eagle Summit, Colville River Delta). Most reports from southcoastal Alaska are in fall and winter.

Harris's Sparrow *Zonotrichia querula* — Casual fall migrant and winter visitant in SE Alaska on the mainland and on islands near the mouths of major rivers (Juneau, Ketchikan, Chickamin River) and on Middleton Is. Casual spring migrant in N Alaska (Colville River mouth, Barrow) and casual (in winter and spring) in southcoastal Alaska (Montague and Middleton (fall) Is, Anchorage, Cohoe, Homer, Seward, Kodiak).

White-crowned Sparrow *Zonotrichia leucophrys* — Common migrant and summer breeder in brush and woodlands from Kobuk and the North Slope S to the Alaska Pen and southcoastal Alaska. Rare migrant on St. Lawrence Is. Common migrant in SE Alaska. Casual on the Pribilof Is, Wainwright, and Barrow. Virtually all records are of Gambel's White-crowned Sparrow (*Z.l. gambelii*). There is one record of the E subspecies (*Z.l. leucophrys*) taken at Anaktuvuk Pass in 1950.

Golden-crowned Sparrow *Zonotrichia atricapilla* — Common migrant and breeder in southcoastal and N SE Alaska. Common migrant and breeder in W Alaska from Wales S on the coast to the lower Kuskokwim River and on the Alaska Pen. Casual visitant on the Pribilof Is, St. Lawrence Is, and the Aleutian Is. Very rare spring migrant and summer and fall visitant in N Alaska (Barrow, Colville River Delta, Umiat, Chandler Lake). Rare migrant in central Alaska and throughout the Brooks Range. Common migrant through SE Alaska.

Dark-eyed Junco *Junco hyemalis* — Common migrant and breeder in the wooded sections of Alaska from NW Alaska across the Brooks Range into Canada and S through W, interior, and southcoastal Alaska and SE Alaska. The Slate-colored Junco, *J.h. hyemalis,* is common throughout the state but is replaced in S SE Alaska by the Oregon Junco, *J.h. oreganus*. In winter, common at feeders N to southcoastal Alaska but rarely to Fairbanks. Casual on the arctic coast, on St. Lawrence and the Pribilof Is. Accidental in the W Aleutian Is (Shemya).

Lapland Longspur *Calcarius lapponicus* — Common migrant and breeder from N Alaska, W Alaska including the Bering Sea Is, the Aleutian Is, the alpine tundra of interior Alaska mountains, E into Canada. Common in migration in SE Alaska (*C.l. alascensis*). Easiest to find at Denali NP, Gambell, St. Paul Is, Nome, or Barrow in summer. The Commander Is subspecies (*C.l. coloratus*) is accidental on Attu Is.

Smith's Longspur *Calcarius pictus* — Fairly common migrant and breeder in the E Brooks Range from Anaktuvuk Pass E into Canada. Uncommon to rare W of Anaktuvuk Pass. Casual migrant and breeder N of the Brooks Range (Dalton Hwy, Umiat, Colville River, Barrow). Uncommon local migrant and breeder in southcentral Alaska, especially along the S slope of the Alaska Range on the Denali Hwy and on the Richardson Hwy just N and S of Paxson. Uncommon migrant and breeder in E interior Alaska (Alaska Hwy, Taylor Hwy, Nabesna Road). Very rare migrant in N SE Alaska (Haines Summit, Glacier Bay, Juneau). Best found on the Denali Hwy.

[**Chestnut-collared Longspur** *Calcarius ornatus* — Accidental from a sight record in Juneau in the 1970s.]

Pine Bunting *Emberiza leucocephalos* — Accidental on Attu Is in Nov 1985 and Oct 1993.

Little Bunting *Emberiza pusilla* — Casual fall migrant in the W. Aleutian Is, on board a ship in the Chukchi Sea, and at Gambell.

Rustic Bunting *Emberiza rustica* — Rare spring and very rare fall migrant in the W and central Aleutian Is. Casual spring migrant in W Alaska (St. Lawrence Is) and in southcoastal Alaska (Kodiak, Homer, Seward). Accidental in fall at Wales and in winter at Ester west of Fairbanks in 1994 and at Petersburg in 1991.

Yellow-throated Bunting *Emberiza elegans* — Accidental on Attu Is in May 1998.

Yellow-breasted Bunting *Emberiza aureola* — Casual in Alaska, with sightings at Gambell in Jun 1978, Attu Is in May 1988 and 1996, and Buldir Is in Jun 1988 and 1990.

Gray Bunting *Emberiza variabilis* — Accidental on Shemya Is in May 1977 and Attu Is in May 1980.

Pallas's Bunting *Emberiza pallasi* — Accidental spring migrant in N (Barrow, Jun 1968), W (Gambell, May 1973) Alaska, and on Buldir Is in Jun 1993.

Reed Bunting *Emberiza schoeniclus* — Casual spring migrant in the W Aleutian Is.

Snow Bunting *Plectrophenax nivalis* — Common breeder along the coastline and in the mountains of N, W, and SW Alaska including the Bering Sea Is, Seward Pen, the Brooks Range, and the Alaska Range. Possible rare breeder in the Yukon-Tanana Highlands. Rare to uncommon breeder in the mountains of southcoastal Alaska and in N SE Alaska. Common along the coast in winter in SW and SE Alaska, but rare in winter in southcoastal Alaska. In migration, uncommon in SE, southcoastal, and E central Alaska (Alaska Hwy, Tanana River Valley) (*P.n. nivalis*). The larger race, *P.n. townsendi,* breeds on the Aleutian, Shumagin, and Pribilof Is.

McKay's Bunting *Plectrophenax hyperboreus* — Common breeder on St. Matthew and Hall Is and very rare breeder and uncommon to rare migrant on St. Lawrence Is. Uncommon to rare migrant and winter visitant along the coast of the Bering Sea (Kotzebue, Nome, St. Michael, Cold Bay, Hooper Bay). Casual winter visitant on the Aleutian Is and in southcoastal Alaska (Homer). Best found at Gambell, at feeders in W Alaska, and possibly Nome in early spring (Mar).

Rose-breasted Grosbeak *Pheucticus ludovicianus* — Accidental at Douglas near Juneau in Sep 1999; other sight records in SE Alaska.

Black-headed Grosbeak *Pheucticus melanocephalus* — Casual in SE Alaska and one record on Kodiak Is in Nov 2001.

Blue Grosbeak *Guiraca caerulea* — Accidental at Petersburg in Aug 1989.

Lazuli Bunting *Passerina amoena* — Accidental at Kake and Hyder in Jun 1992, and at Juneau in Oct 2000.

Indigo Bunting *Passerina cyanea* — Accidental in Anchorage (Sep 1973 and Aug 1991) and at Wainwright in Aug 1989.

Bobolink *Dolichonyx oryzivorus* — Accidental at Barrow in Jun 1976 and in SE Alaska at Hyder in Jun 1991 and at Ketchikan in Oct 2000.

Red-winged Blackbird *Agelaius phoeniceus* — Uncommon local breeder in the upper Tanana River Valley as far W as Fairbanks, also at George Lake, Kenny Lake, Bremner River, Northway airport. Rare migrant, summer visitant, and probable breeder in southcoastal Alaska (Anchorage, Homer, Yakutat). Fairly common local breeder in mainland SE Alaska from Glacier Bay S. Casual spring migrant and summer visitant in N (Barrow, Sagavanirktok River) and W Alaska (Cape Lisburne, Cape Thompson, Kotzebue, Wales).

Western Meadowlark *Sturnella neglecta* — Casual fall and winter visitant to SE Alaska (Auke Bay, Juneau, Mitkof Is, Ketchikan) and E interior Alaska (Tok, Scottie Creek). Accidental at Anaktuvuk Pass in Sep 1959.

Yellow-headed Blackbird *Xanthocephalus xanthocephalus* — Casual spring migrant and summer and fall visitant in scattered locations in Alaska (Hyder, Haines, Juneau, Cordova, Homer, Cohoe, Palmer, Fairbanks, Pt. Hope, Barrow).

Rusty Blackbird *Euphagus carolinus* — Uncommon to fairly common spring migrant, breeder, and fall migrant in central Alaska (Fairbanks, Denali Hwy, Palmer, Tanacross). Very rare winter visitant near Nenana, Fairbanks, and Delta Junction. Uncommon to rare migrant and breeder in SW Alaska (Chignik, Dillingham) and on the Seward Pen. Very rare spring migrant and possible breeder in N Alaska (Anaktuvuk Pass, Porcupine Lake, Canning and Utukok Rivers). Very rare spring migrant and summer and fall visitant to the coasts of the Beaufort and Chukchi Seas (Prudhoe Bay, Barrow, Colville River Delta, Wainwright) and the Bering Sea Is (St. Lawrence and St. Paul), S to the Alaska Pen (Cold Bay). Uncommon spring migrant and fairly common fall migrant through much of southcoastal Alaska (from Seward E, not at Homer and Kodiak). Rare breeder and winter visitant in southcoastal Alaska. Uncommon breeder at Kenai and in Anchorage. Uncommon migrant in SE Alaska and rare to uncommon local breeder at Glacier Bay, Taku River, Chickamin River, and Stikine River.

Brewer's Blackbird *Euphagus cyanocephalus* — Accidental at Barrow in Jun 1942 and casual in Juneau, Sitka, and Ketchikan. Several undocumented sightings from Kenai.

Common Grackle *Quiscalus quiscula* — Casual migrant and summer visitant in scattered locations in Alaska (Ketchikan, Juneau, Yakutat, Palmer, Fairbanks, Cape Thompson, Wainwright).

Brown-headed Cowbird *Molothrus ater* — Rare migrant and probable breeder in SE Alaska (Wrangell, Petersburg, Chickamin River, Juneau, Glacier Bay). Casual winter visitant in Juneau. Casual migrant and summer visitant at Fairbanks, Tok, Cordova, Copper Center, Katmai, Mineral Lakes, Kantishna, Kivalina, and Barrow. Casual fall visitant to Homer and accidental at Gambell.

[**Bullock's Oriole** *Icterus bullockii* — Accidental at Petersburg in May 1980 and Ketchikan in Apr 1996.]

Brambling *Fringilla montifringilla* — Rare to uncommon migrant in the W and central Aleutian Is. Casual in spring, summer, and fall at St. Paul Is. Rare to uncommon migrant in the W and central Aleutian Is (nested on Attu Is in Jun 1996). Casual spring migrant in W Alaska (Hooper Bay, Gambell). Casual in winter in southcoastal and SE Alaska. Accidental at Barrow.

Gray-crowned Rosy-Finch *Leucosticte tephrocotis* [or *arctoa*]— Fairly common to locally common breeder in SW Alaska from the Semidi Is and the W Alaska Pen throughout the Aleutian Is, and Kodiak Is (*L.t. griseonucha* — larger and browner). Rare breeder on the Seward Pen and the Yukon-Kuskokwim Delta; more common along the coast of W Alaska. Common breeder on the Pribilof Is (*L.t. umbrina* —

larger and blacker). Fairly common migrant and breeder at high elevations in the mountains of southcoastal Alaska, throughout the mountains of central Alaska, the Chugach Mountains near Anchorage, and in SE Alaska (*L.t. littoralis* — Hepburn's Rosy-Finch — small and gray). Uncommon local winter visitant in southcoastal (Kodiak, Homer, Seward, Cordova) and SE (Glacier Bay, Juneau, Wrangell) Alaska. Fairly common migrant and breeder in the Brooks Range (*L.t. irvingi* — small, gray and brown, named in honor of Alaskan physiologist and ornithologist Laurence Irving). Easiest to find on St. Paul Is, Arctic Valley outside of Anchorage in summer, and on the Homer Spit in winter.

Pine Grosbeak *Pinicola enucleator* — Common resident from NW Alaska across the taiga spruce woods of the Brooks Range into Canada and S throughout W, SW, and central Alaska (*P.e. alascensis*). Fairly common on the Pacific Coast from SE Alaska across southcoastal Alaska, Kodiak Is, Alaska Pen and W to the Shumagin Is (*P.e. flammula* — shorter tail and heavier bill). Casual on the Aleutian and Pribilof Is (*P.e. kamtschatkensis* — smaller with narrow, blunt, heavily hooked bill). One specimen record of *P.e. carlottae* — smallest and darkest) from Ketchikan.

Common Rosefinch *Carpodacus erythrinus* — Casual spring migrant in W and SW Alaska (Yukon-Kuskokwim River Delta, St. Paul Is, Gambell) and in the W Aleutian Is. Casual in fall at Gambell and on Shemya Is.

Purple Finch *Carpodacus purpureus* — Casual migrant and winter visitant in SE (Ketchikan, Petersburg, Juneau), central (Denali NP), and southcoastal Alaska (Homer). There is one record from Bethel.

Cassin's Finch *Carpodacus cassinii* — Accidental in southcoastal Alaska (Homer in late winter 1985 and 1992; Middleton Is in Sep 1991).

House Finch *Carpodacus mexicanus* — Accidental from Haines in Jul 1991, Hyder in Jun 1996, and Ketchikan in 1994, 2001, and 2002.

Red Crossbill *Loxia curvirostra* — Irregular and common resident and breeder throughout SE Alaska. Irregular and uncommon resident in southcoastal Alaska (Kodiak, Homer) and very rare summer visitant in SW Alaska to the limit of trees at the base of the Alaska Pen (*L.c. minor* — small with small bill). Casual summer and fall visitant on Middleton Is, E Aleutian Is, Unalaska Is, Pribilof Is, and St. Lawrence Is. There are two specimen records of *L.c. bendirei* (larger), and one of *L.c. sitkensis* (very small with heavy bill) from SE Alaska.

White-winged Crossbill *Loxia leucoptera* — Irregular and common but irruptive resident of spruce forests throughout N Alaska from the Kobuk Valley along the S slope of the Brooks Range into Canada, and S throughout central Alaska to Bristol Bay, Kodiak Is, southcoastal, and SE Alaska. Casual on St. Lawrence and Pribilof Is.

Common Redpoll *Carduelis flammea* — Common (irregular) but irruptive resident from N and W Alaska throughout the taiga forests of interior Alaska, S to the Alaska Pen. Uncommon S of the Alaska Range, the N Kenai Pen, and N SE Alaska in summer. In winter, migrates S throughout central, southcentral, and southcoastal Alaska. Rare on St. Lawrence and Pribilof Is and in the Aleutian Is.

Hoary Redpoll *Carduelis hornemanni* — Common (irregular) but irruptive resident of N and W Alaska from the N coast (Colville River, Umiat, Barrow, Nome, Wales) S to Hooper Bay, the Seward Pen, the crest of the Brooks Range (Anaktuvuk Pass) and E into Canada (*C.h. exilipes*). Fairly common in migration and in winter in central Alaska (Denali NP, Fairbanks, Circle, Fort Yukon), and decreasing in abundance southward to southcoastal Alaska (Copper River Valley). Uncommon to rare on St. Lawrence Is. Rare visitor to Pribilof Is, with first breeding recorded there in 2001. Rare in the W Aleutian Is. Best found in summer at Nome, Gambell, Barrow, Colville River Delta, Prudhoe Bay. There are many sight records and one specimen for the larger and whiter nominate race, *C.h. hornemanni*, from the Fairbanks area in winter.

Eurasian Siskin *Carduelis spinus* — Accidental at Attu Is in May 1978 and 1993.

Pine Siskin *Carduelis pinus* — Common (irregular), irruptive resident and breeder throughout SE Alaska; fairly common resident and breeder in southcoastal Alaska (Anchorage, Homer, Seward). Irregular rare summer and fall visitant, very rare breeder, and casual winter visitant in central Alaska (Fairbanks, Denali NP, Cantwell). Casual spring, summer, and fall visitant in SW Alaska, the Alaska Pen, the E Aleutian Is, Pribilof Is, St. Lawrence Is, and in N Alaska (Barrow, Chandler Lake).

American Goldfinch *Carduelis tristis* — Casual with records at Juneau, Petersburg, and Ketchikan.

Oriental Greenfinch *Carduelis sinica* — Casual migrant in the W Aleutian Is and accidental on the Pribilof Is.

Eurasian Bullfinch *Pyrrhula pyrrhula* — Casual migrant on the Bering Sea Is (St. Lawrence and Nunivak Is), NW Alaska (Cape Krusenstern), and the W Aleutian Is. Accidental in central Alaska (Nulato, Fairbanks, North Pole), in southcoastal Alaska (Anchorage), and in SE Alaska (Petersburg).

Evening Grosbeak *Coccothraustes vespertinus* — Rare winter and accidental spring and fall visitant to SE Alaska.

Hawfinch *Coccothraustes coccothraustes* — Casual migrant in the W and central Aleutian Is; accidental in the Pribilof Is, St. Lawrence Is, and on the Noatak River, 30 miles N of Kotzebue.

House Sparrow *Passer domesticus* — Accidental at Petersburg in Oct 1987, at Gambell in June 1993, and in Ketchikan in 1997, 2001, and 2002.

ACKNOWLEDGEMENTS: Dan Gibson, Dave Sonneborn, Thede Tobish, and Mark Schwann provided information and references for many species. Tom Huels, collections manager at the University of Arizona, Tucson, provided reference resources. The Tucson Audubon Society also provided access to literature references not otherwise available. Ed Clark refined some of the best places to find casual species. Jeff Bouton, Steve Heinl, Paul Lehman, and Steve Zimmerman made a complete review of the list, and made many corrections to the status and occurrence of many species. Some species notes from Tim Schantz were kindly provided by Mike Schantz.

Red Crossbill

APPENDIX A:

CHECKLISTS OF SPECIFIC LOCATIONS IN ALASKA

The following table shows the birds that may be found in various locations in Alaska during the "summer" season and should help in planning your trip. Because many checklists do not specify relative abundance, some do not specify season, and many break up the year using different date intervals, I have tried to include the possibility of making observations in late spring and early fall along with summer, i.e, about 15 April to 15 September. This should cover the period when most birders visit Alaska. The table is arranged vertically by species according to the latest *ABA Checklist* and horizontally from west to east and then north to south within six areas of the state: Northern, Interior, Western, Southwest, Southcentral, and Southeast Alaska.

Not every species found in Alaska is included because some species were found only once or twice in areas not encompassed by the checklist's defined locations. All species known to have occurred in Alaska are given in the *Annotated List*, page 474.

CATEGORIES

E = Relatively easy to find in the appropriate habitat. You should have little trouble finding these species. These include species estimated to be common and most of those considered to be fairly common.

M = Moderately easy to find in the appropriate habitat at the right time of year. If you bird the area carefully, you should be able to find all of these species. These include the uncommon and some of the fairly common species.

H = Hard to find unless you are lucky or remain long enough in the region, come at the right time of year, or look hard enough in the appropriate habitat. These include rare species.

N = Not expected to find unless you are extremely lucky or remain for a very long time (years) looking in the appropriate habitat. These are the casual and accidental species.

X = Unsubstantiated or undocumented record.

NORTHERN ALASKA

Barrow = Covers the immediate Barrow area. From a checklist available on the Barrow Birding Home Page, *www.barrowbird.org*.

Dalton Highway = Covers the Dalton Highway from Livengood to Deadhorse just south of Prudhoe Bay. From a checklist compiled in 1999 by Amy Schauer for the Bureau of Land Management, *Birds Along the Dalton Highway*. A detailed checklist may be obtained from the Arctic District Manager of the BLM, 1150 University Avenue, Fairbanks, AK 99709.

Arctic National Wildlife Refuge = The Arctic NWR covers the northeastern corner of Alaska from the coastal plain along the Beaufort Sea south into the Brooks Range to the south slope of the Brooks Range. From a *Bird List* of the refuge published by the

U.S. Fish and Wildlife Service. Details available from the Refuge Manager, ANWR, 101 12th Avenue, Room 236, Fairbanks, AK 99701; 907-456-0250.

WESTERN ALASKA

Gambell = Covers the Gambell area at the northwestern end of Saint Lawrence Island. From a checklist compiled by John Kelly in 1995 and modified by Paul Lehman, Tim Schantz and other visiting birders.

Nome = Covers the Nome area and the road system as described in this guide. Compiled by Rich and Lana Harris, modified and updated by several birders.

INTERIOR ALASKA

Denali National Park = Covers Denali National Park and Preserve in central Alaska. From *Bird Checklist for Denali National Park* compiled by K. Kertell in 1985, updated in 1999, and published by the Alaska Natural History Association (ANHA). A detailed checklist may be obtained from ANHA, 720 West 2nd Avenue, Suite 100, Anchorage, AK 99501; 907-274-8440.

Fairbanks area = The interior of Alaska or central Alaska, from the south slope of the Brooks Range in the north, the Anvik and Aniak Rivers to the west, the Alaska Range to the south, and the Canadian border to the east. From *A Field Checklist, Birds of Interior Alaska* by Brina Kessel, 1986, University of Alaska Museum, University of Alaska Fairbanks, Fairbanks, AK 99775-6960, and the Yukon-Charley River National Park and Preserve checklist provided by the National Park Service.

Tetlin National Wildlife Refuge = Includes eastern interior Alaska from around Northway to the Yukon border. From a checklist published by the refuge in 1998, *Birds: Tetlin National Wildlife Refuge and the Upper Tanana Valley*, PO Box 779, Tok, AK 99780.

SOUTHWEST ALASKA

Attu Island = From the *Attu Island Trip Bird List* compiled by Larry Balch, 1996.

Pribilof Islands = Covers the Pribilof Islands, Saint Paul and Saint George. From a *Checklist of Birds of the Pribilof Islands, Alaska* compiled by Sean Smith in 1999. A complete, detailed checklist may be obtained from TDX Corporation, 1500 West 33rd Avenue, Suite 220, Anchorage, AK 99503; 907-278-2312.

Izembek National Wildlife Refuge = Covers the Izembek NWR at Cold Bay, Unimak Island, and the Pavlof area northeast to Port Moller on the Alaska Peninsula. From a *Checklist of the Refuge* published by the U.S. Fish and Wildlife Service. For a complete checklist contact the Refuge Manager, PO Box 127, Cold Bay, AK 99571; 907-532-2445.

Becharof National Wildlife Refuge and **Katmai National Park and Preserve** = Alaska Peninsula/Becharof NWR. From a draft checklist of the refuge prepared by Susan Savage and the refuge staff in 2001, and from a checklist prepared by the National Park Service in 2001. A detailed list of the fauna of the refuge may be obtained from the Refuge Manager, PO Box 277, King Salmon, AK 99613.

SOUTHCENTRAL ALASKA

Kodiak Island = *Checklist of the Birds of the Kodiak National Wildlife Refuge and the Kodiak Island Archipelago* was compiled by Rich MacIntosh for the U.S. Fish and Wildlife Service in 1998. A detailed checklist may be obtained from the Refuge Manager, 1390 Buskin River Road, Kodiak, AK 99615; 907-487-2600.

Kachemak Bay = Covers from the Anchor River drainage south through Homer and Kachemak Bay, Kenai Peninsula. From a *Checklist of Birds of Kachemak Bay, Alaska* by

Rich Kleinleder et al. 2002, Center for Alaskan Coastal Studies, Homer. The checklist is available from the Center at PO Box 2225, Homer, AK 99603.

Kenai National Wildlife Refuge = Kenai NWR covers the northwestern corner and central portion of the Kenai Peninsula from Chugach National Forest and Harding Ice Field on the east to Cook Inlet on the west, and from Turnagain Arm on the north almost to the head of Kachemak Bay to the south. From a checklist on *Birds of the Kenai National Wildlife Refuge, Alaska* published in 1996. A more detailed checklist may be obtained from the Refuge Manager, PO Box 2139, Soldotna, AK 99669; 907-262-7021.

Anchorage = Covers the Anchorage area from the Knik River to Portage at the head of Turnagain Arm, including Girdwood. From a checklist prepared by D. DeLap, R.L. Sher, D. Sonneborn, and T. Tobish in 1993, *Birds of Anchorage, Alaska; a checklist.* A complete detailed checklist is available from Anchorage Audubon Society, PO Box 101161, Anchorage, AK 99510; 907-278-3007.

Seward/Kenai Fjords National Park = Covers Seward and adjacent Resurrection Bay from Mile 18 of the Seward Highway to the Chiswell Islands. From a checklist compiled by J. Andrew, R. McHenry, R.L. Scher, D.W. Sonneborn, and T. Tobish in 1988, *Birds of Seward, Alaska, A Checklist,* and a checklist provided by the National Park Service in 2001. A complete checklist may be obtained from the Seward Chamber of Commerce, PO Box 749, Seward, AK 99664; 907-224-8051.

Cordova = Covers areas accessible from the Cordova road system, including Orca Inlet, Nelson Bay, and the Copper River Delta. Does not cover Prince William Sound or pelagic waters adjacent to the Copper River Delta. From a checklist prepared by Ruth Fairall in 1994.

SOUTHEAST ALASKA

Glacier Bay National Park and Preserve = From a checklist provided by the National Park Service in 2001.

Haines/Skagway = From a checklist provided by Cameron Eckert, author of those chapters in this guide, and from a checklist provided by the National Park Service in 2001 for Skagway/Klondike National Historic Park.

Juneau = Covers all roads out of Juneau on the mainland from Point Bishop to Echo Cove, as well as Douglas Island, and adjacent marine waters from the mouth of the Taku River to Berner's Bay. From a checklist compiled by G. van Vliet, M. Schwan, R. Gordon, and S. Zimmerman in 1994, *Birds of Juneau, Alaska. Checklist.* A complete checklist is available from the Juneau Audubon Society, PO Box 21725, Juneau, AK 99802.

Hyder = From a checklist provided by Steve Heinl, author of the Hyder chapter.

Sitka = Covers the Sitka area, including Sitka National Historic Park. From *Birds of Sitka National Historic Park* by Marlys E. Tedin and Marjorie L. Ward, 2000, and *Bird Checklist, Sitka, Alaska area* by Marlys E. Tedin and Marjorie L. Ward, 1995.

Petersburg = Covers 240-square-mile Mitkof Island and the mouth of the Stikine River. From *Checklist of the Birds of Mitkof Island, Southeast Alaska* compiled by Peter J. Walsh in 1993, revised in 1995.

Ketchikan = Covers the Ketchikan Gateway Borough (all of Revillagigedo and Gravina Islands and adjacent bodies of water). From *Checklist, Birds of the Ketchikan Area, Alaska* compiled by Steve Heinl and Teri Goucher in 2000. A complete checklist may be obtained from Steve Heinl, PO Box 23101, Ketchikan, AK 99901.

ACKNOWLEDGEMENTS Jeff Bouton, Terry Doyle, and Steve Heinl reviewed the checklist and made many corrections. Blain Anderson, Inventory and Monitoring Technician, National Park Service, Alaska Region, provided bird checklists for Alaska's National Parks. Many of the chapter authors reviewed the locations most familiar to them. Mark Stevenson shared insights on construction and categories of the checklist.

"Summer" Checklists	NORTH			WEST		INTERIOR			SOUTHWEST				SOUTHCENTRAL						SOUTHEAST						
	Barrow	Dalton Highway	Arctic NWR	Gambell	Nome	Denali NP	Fairbanks Area	Tetlin NWR & E. Interior	Attu Island	Pribilof Islands	Izembek NWR	Becharof NWR/Katmai NP	Kodiak Island	Kachemak Bay	Kenai NWR	Anchorage	Seward/Kenai Fjords NP	Cordova	Glacier Bay NP	Haines/Skagway	Juneau	Hyder	Sitka	Petersburg	Ketchikan
Red-throated Loon	E	M	H	M	E	H	M	N	E	N	H	E	M	H	H	H	H	M	E	H	H	E	H	M	M
Arctic Loon	N			H	H				H	N															
Pacific Loon	E	E	E	E	E	N	M	E	H	N	H	E	M	E	H	M	M	E	E		H	H	H	H	M
Common Loon	N	M	H	N	E	M	E	H	E	N	H	E	E	E	E	M	E	E	E	E	H	E	E	M	E
Yellow-billed Loon	E	H	H	M	H	N	N		H	N		N	N	N			H	H	N		N		H	N	N
Pied-billed Grebe							X									N		N		H	N		N	N	N
Horned Grebe	N	H	E	N	M	M	E	E	H	N		H	M	E	E	E	E	E	H	H	N		N	H	H
Red-necked Grebe	N	M	H	N	E	H	M	M	E	H	H	H	M	E	E	E	E	E	H	H	N		H	H	H
Eared Grebe							N														N				
Western Grebe																	X	N		N	N		N	E	E
Clark's Grebe																					X			X	
Laysan Albatross									H	N	N		H												
Black-footed Albatross	N									H	N		M						N						
Short-tailed Albatross										N			N												
Northern Fulmar	N			E					H	E		H	E	E			M		M						
Mottled Petrel										N	N		H												
Pink-footed Shearwater													N						N						
Buller's Shearwater													N										N		
Sooty Shearwater										N		H	E	E			M		E				H	N	N
Short-tailed Shearwater	N		N	M			N		H	M		H	E	E			M		N						
Fork-tailed Storm-Petrel				N			N		H	H		H	E	E	N	N	H	M	H	N	N		N	N	N
Leach's Storm-Petrel									N	H	N	N	H	N		N	N		N						N
American White Pelican																								N	N
Brandt's Cormorant														N											N
Double-crested Cormorant							N	N		N	H	E	H	H	H	N	H	E	E	H	H		E	H	E

Red-faced Cormorant									E	E	H	E	M	E		N	E	E							
Pelagic Cormorant	N			E	E				E	M	H	E	E	E		N	E	E	E	E	N		E	M	E
Magnificent Frigatebird													N												
American Bittern																			N	H	N				
Yellow Bittern									N																
Gray Heron									X	X															
Great Blue Heron							N	N					H	H	N	N	H	M	H	E	M	E	E	M	M
Great Egret												N	N					N	N		N		N		
Snowy Egret																					X				
Cattle Egret																							N	N	N
Chinese Pond-Heron										N															
Green Heron																					N				
Black-crowned Night-Heron									N	N			N	X							N				
Turkey Vulture					N		N	N										N							N
Bean Goose				N					H	N	N	N													
Greater White-fronted Goose	E	E	M	N	H	H	E	M	N	N		E	N	H	H	H		E	H		H		H	M	M
Lesser White-fronted Goose									N																
Emperor Goose	N			E	H				H	H		N	H	N	N	N					N		N		
Snow Goose	E	E	H	N	N	N	N	N	N	N		N	N	N	M	H		E	N	N	N		N	H	H
Ross's Goose	N		N											N											
Canada Goose	N	E	H	N	E	N	E	M	E	H	N	H	H	N	E	E	M	E	E	E	M	E	H	E	E
Brant	N	M	M	E	E	N	H	N	N	H		N	H	H	N	N	N	M	N		N		H	N	H
Trumpeter Swan		H	N		N	M	M	M					N	H	E	M		E	H	E	H	E	H	H	H
Tundra Swan	E	M	E	H	E	H	M	M		H	E	E	H	N	H	M		N	N		N		H	N	N
Whooper Swan				N	N				N	N								N							
Wood Duck													N					N		N	N			N	N
Gadwall		H				N	H	N	H	N	H	H	H	H	N	H		M	H	H	H	H	N	H	H
Falcated Duck									H	N															
Eurasian Wigeon			N	N	H	N	H		E	H		M	H	H	H	H	H	H	H		N		N	N	N
American Wigeon	E	E	E	N	E	M	E	E	H	H		E	E	E	E	E	M	E	E	E	M	E	H	M	E

E = Easy to find M = Moderately easy to find H = Hard to find N = Not expected to find X = Undocumented

"Summer" Checklists	NORTH			WEST		INTERIOR			SOUTHWEST				SOUTHCENTRAL						SOUTHEAST						
	Barrow	Dalton Highway	Arctic NWR	Gambell	Nome	Denali NP	Fairbanks Area	Tetlin NWR & E. Interior	Attu Island	Pribilof Islands	Izembek NWR	Becharof NWR/Katmai NP	Kodiak Island	Kachemak Bay	Kenai NWR	Anchorage	Seward/Kenai Fjords NP	Cordova	Glacier Bay NP	Haines/Skagway	Juneau	Hyder	Sitka	Petersburg	Ketchikan
American Black Duck							N											N	N						
Mallard	H	M	H	N	E	M	E	E	E	H		E	E	E	E	E	E	E	E	E	E	E	E	E	E
Spot-billed Duck									N				N												
Blue-winged Teal		H				N	M	H				N	N	N	N	H	N	N	N		H	H	N	N	N
Cinnamon Teal							N	N					N		N	N		N	N	N	N		N	N	
Northern Shoveler	E	M	H	N	E	H	E	M	E	H	H	E	H	E	M	E	M	E	E	H	M	E	H	M	E
Northern Pintail	E	E	M	E	E	M	E	M	E	H	H	E	E	E	E	E	M	E	M	E	M	E	N	M	E
Garganey									H	N		N						N							
Baikal Teal				N						N		N													
Green-winged Teal	E	E	E	E	E	E	E	E	E	H	H	E	E	E	E	E	E	E	E	E	M	E	H	M	E
Canvasback	H	M	N		M	H	M	M	N	N		N	N	N	N	M		E	N		N			N	N
Redhead	H	H			N	H	M	H				N	N	N	N	H		M	N	H	N			N	N
Common Pochard				N	N				H	N				N											
Ring-necked Duck		H				H	M	M		N		N	N	N	N	M	N	M	N	H	N	H		H	H
Tufted Duck				N	N				E	H		N	N	N		N		N						N	
Greater Scaup	H	E	H	M	E	M	M	H	E	H	E	E	E	E	H	E	M	E	N	N	N		E	E	E
Lesser Scaup	N	M	E		N	E	E	E		N		N	N	N	N	M	N	M	N	N	N		N	H	H
Steller's Eider	H	H	N	E	H				H	H	N	H	H	N		N	N	N			N		N	N	N
Spectacled Eider	H	M	N	H					N	N	N	N	N												
King Eider	E	M	H	E	H		N		H	H		N	M	N			N	N						N	
Common Eider	E	M	H	E	E				E	N	N	H	H	E	N	N		N	N						
Harlequin Duck	H	H	H	E	E	M	E	N	E	E	H	H	E	E	H	H	E	E	E	E	M	E	H	E	E
Surf Scoter	H	E	H	N	E	H	E	M		N	N	E	M	E	E	H	E	E	E	E	M	E	E	E	E
White-winged Scoter	H	E	M	M	E	H	E	E	H	H	H	E	E	E	N	H	M	E	E	E	M	E	N	E	E
Black Scoter	H		H	H	E	H	N		H	H	E	M	E	E	N	H	H	E	E	N	H		N	E	M

Long-tailed Duck	E	M	M	E	E	E	H	H	H	E	H	N	H	N	N	N	H	E	N	H	N		N	H	H
Bufflehead		H	E	N	N	M	E	M	E	H		H	H	H	H	H	E	E	H	H	N	E	N	M	M
Common Goldeneye		H	N	N	H	H	E	M	E	H	N	E	M	E	M	M	E	E	N	H	N	E	N	M	M
Barrow's Goldeneye		N	N			M	E	M	N	N		H	M	E	M	M	E	E	N	E	N	E	H	M	E
Smew									H	N	N		N					N							
Hooded Merganser							N		X	N	N	X	N	N		N	N	H	N	H	H	H	H	H	H
Common Merganser	N		N	N	N	H	E	H	H	N	N	E	E	M	M	H	M	E	E	E	E	E	E	E	E
Red-breasted Merganser	N	H	M	E	E	M	E	N	E	H	N	E	E	H	H	N	M	E	M	M	H		N	M	M
Ruddy Duck							H	N						N				N		N	N		N	N	N
Osprey	N	H		N	H	N	M	H	N	N		H	N	N	N	N	N	M	N	N	N	H		H	H
Bald Eagle	N	H	H			H	E	M	N	N	H	E	E	E	E	H	E	E	E	E	E	E	E	E	E
White-tailed Eagle									N																
Steller's Sea-Eagle									N	N	N	N	N								N				
Northern Harrier	H	M	M		E	M	E	M	N	N	H	H	H	H	H	M	M	M	M	H	M	H	H	H	H
Sharp-shinned Hawk	N	H	N			H	M	M			N	N	H	M	M	H	M	M	H	M	H	M	H	H	H
Cooper's Hawk																					X		X		
Northern Goshawk	N	H	N		N	H	H	H			N	H	M	H	H	H	N	M	H	M	H	H	H	H	H
Swainson's Hawk			N			N	H	N						N		N		N	N		N				
Red-tailed Hawk	N	M				H	E	M				N	N	H	M	H	M	N	M	M	H	M	N	H	H
Rough-legged Hawk	N	M	M	N	E	H	N	H	H	N	H	H	M	N	N	H	N	N	H		N		N	N	N
Golden Eagle	N	M	M	N	E	E	M	H			H	H	H	H	H	H	N	N	H	H	H		N	N	
Eurasian Kestrel				N					N	N															
American Kestrel	N	M	H			M	E	M				N	N	N	N	N		M	N	H	N	H	N	N	N
Merlin	N	H	M	N	H	M	M	H	N			H	H	H	H	H	H	M	H	H	H	M	N	H	H
Eurasian Hobby									N	N															
Gyrfalcon	N	H	H	N		M	M	H	N	N	H	H	H	N	H	N	N	N	N	N	N		N		N
Peregrine Falcon	N	H	E	N	E	H	M	H	E	H	H	H	H	H	H	N	H	M	H	N	N		H	H	H
Ring-necked Pheasant														H											
Ruffed Grouse		H				H	E	M							H					H		H			
Spruce Grouse		M	H		N	H	E	M				E		E	E	E	E	E		H	X			N	

E = Easy to find M = Moderately easy to find H = Hard to find N = Not expected to find X = Undocumented

"Summer" Checklists	NORTH			WEST		INTERIOR			SOUTHWEST				SOUTHCENTRAL						SOUTHEAST						
	Barrow	Dalton Highway	Arctic NWR	Gambell	Nome	Denali NP	Fairbanks Area	Tetlin NWR & E. Interior	Attu Island	Pribilof Islands	Izembek NWR	Becharof NWR/Katmai NP	Kodiak Island	Kachemak Bay	Kenai NWR	Anchorage	Seward/Kenai Fjords NP	Cordova	Glacier Bay NP	Haines/Skagway	Juneau	Hyder	Sitka	Petersburg	Ketchikan
Willow Ptarmigan	E	E	M		E	E	E	M			E	E	E	H	E	E	E	E	E	H	M			H	H
Rock Ptarmigan	H	M	E	N	M	M	E	H	E		H	E	E	H	H	M	E	M	E	H	E			H	H
White-tailed Ptarmigan						H	H	N				H		N	H	M	H	H	N	H	H				
Blue Grouse																			H	E	E	E	H	M	E
Sharp-tailed Grouse		N				X	E	M							N										
Yellow Rail																					X				
Virginia Rail																					N				
Sora							N	N								N		N	N	H	N	N		N	
Eurasian Coot										N															
American Coot			N				H	N		N			N	N		N		N	N	H	N		N	N	H
Sandhill Crane	H	M	H	M	E	H	E	M	N	H	H	E	N	E	E	H	N	E	N	N	N	H	H	H	H
Common Crane							N																		
Black-bellied Plover	M	M	N	N	E	N	H	N	H	N		E	H	E	H	H	H	E	M		M		N	N	H
American Golden-Plover	E	M	H	M	E	M	E	H			N	E	H	E	H	H	H	E	H		H		N	H	
Pacific Golden-Plover				M	E			N	E	H	N	E	H	E	H	N	N	H			N			N	N
Mongolian Plover	N			H	N		N		E	H	N		N					N							
Snowy Plover					N																				
Common Ringed Plover				H					N	N															
Semipalmated Plover	H	E	M	M	E	E	E	M	N	H	E	E	E	E	E	E	E	E	E	M	M	M	H	M	M
Little Ringed Plover									N																
Killdeer	N	N	N	N		N	H	N		N			N	N	N	H	N	N	H	M	H	M	N	H	M
Eurasian Dotterel	N		N	N	N		N											N							
Black Oystercatcher										N	N	E	E	H		N	M	E	E		H		H		N
American Avocet																N									
Common Greenshank				N					H	N		N													

Greater Yellowlegs	N			N		H	H	N		N		E	E	E	E	E	H	E	E	E	E	E	H	M	M
Lesser Yellowlegs	N	H	E	N	E	E	E	E	N	H	H	H	M	M	E	E	E	E	M	H	E	E	H	H	H
Spotted Redshank									N	N	N														
Wood Sandpiper	N			H	N				E	H															
Green Sandpiper				N					N	N															
Solitary Sandpiper	N	H	E			H	E	M		N		N	H	M	H	M	N	M	H	H	N	H		H	N
Willet							N																		
Wandering Tattler	N	H	M	H	E	M	M	N	E	H	N	H	E	E	H	H	M	E	H	H	N		N	N	H
Gray-tailed Tattler	N	N		N	N				H	H			N	X			X								
Common Sandpiper				H	N				E	N															
Spotted Sandpiper	N	M	E		E	M	E	E		N		E	H	E	E	E	E		E	E	E	E	E	M	E
Terek Sandpiper				N	N				H	N						N									
Upland Sandpiper		H	M			H	M	H					N			N		N	N	N	N			N	
Little Curlew				N																					
Whimbrel	H	M	H	H	E	M	E	H	E	H	N	E	H	E	H	H	N	E	H		H	H		H	H
Bristle-thighed Curlew				N	H		N		N	H		N	N	N		N		N	N						
Far Eastern Curlew									H	N															
Black-tailed Godwit				N					H	N			N												
Hudsonian Godwit	N		N			N	H	N			N	H	N	H	E	E	H	M	N		N		N	N	
Bar-tailed Godwit	N	M	N	H	E		N		E	H		N	N	H	N	H	N	N	N		N				
Marbled Godwit												E	N	H		N	N	H	N	N	N		N		
Ruddy Turnstone	H	M	H	E	E	N	H	N	E	E	H	H	H	H	N	N	H	E	M	N	M		N	N	H
Black Turnstone				N	E	N	N	N		N		E	E	E	N	H	H	E	E		M		H	M	E
Surfbird		N	N		H	M	M	N		N		N	M	E	N	H	M	E	E		H		H	H	E
Great Knot				N	N				N	N															
Red Knot	H		N	N	E		N		N	N		N	N	H	N	N		E	N		N		N	N	N
Sanderling	H	H	N	N	H	N	H	N	N	N	N	N	H	H	N	N	N	M	H	N	N		N	N	H
Semipalmated Sandpiper	E	E	E	H	E	N	M	H	N	N		N	H	E	H	H	H	E	H	N	M			H	H
Western Sandpiper	H	M	N	E	E	N	H	N	N	H		E	E	E	H	E	E	E	E	H	E	M	M	E	E
Red-necked Stint	H			M	H				E	H				N		N		N	N						

E = Easy to find   M = Moderately easy to find   H = Hard to find   N = Not expected to find   X = Undocumented

"Summer" Checklists	NORTH			WEST		INTERIOR			SOUTHWEST				SOUTHCENTRAL						SOUTHEAST						
	Barrow	Dalton Highway	Arctic NWR	Gambell	Nome	Denali NP	Fairbanks Area	Tetlin NWR & E. Interior	Attu Island	Pribilof Islands	Izembek NWR	Becharof NWR/Katmai NP	Kodiak Island	Kachemak Bay	Kenai NWR	Anchorage	Seward/Kenai Fjords NP	Cordova	Glacier Bay NP	Haines/Skagway	Juneau	Hyder	Sitka	Petersburg	Ketchikan
Little Stint	N			N					N	N															
Temminck's Stint	N			N					H	N			N	N											
Long-toed Stint				N					E	N											X				
Least Sandpiper	H	M	E	N	H	H	E	M		H	E	E	E	E	E	E	E	E	E	E	E	E	M	M	E
White-rumped Sandpiper	M	H	N				H			N								N							
Baird's Sandpiper	E	M	H	H	H	H	M	H	H	H		N	H	H	N	H	N	H	H	N	H			N	H
Pectoral Sandpiper	E	E	E	H	H	N	M	H	H	H		N	H	H	H	H	N	E	E	E	E		M	H	H
Sharp-tailed Sandpiper	N		N	N					H	H		N	N	H	N	N	N	N		N	N			N	
Purple Sandpiper	N																								
Rock Sandpiper				E	H				E	E	E	E	M	H	N	N	H	M	N		N		M	M	M
Dunlin	E	E	H	E	E	N	H		E	H	H	E	H	E	H	N	M	E	M	M	N	M	M	M	M
Curlew Sandpiper	N			N					N	N			N					N			X				
Stilt Sandpiper	H	M	H		N		H			N		N	N	N		N	N	N			N				
Spoonbill Sandpiper	N								N	N															
Buff-breasted Sandpiper	H	M	H	N	N		H	N	N	N		N	N				N	N	N		N			N	
Ruff	N		N	H					H	H			N	N		N	N	N			N		N		
Short-billed Dowitcher								N	N	N	N	E	E	E	E	E	M	E	E	H	E		M	H	M
Long-billed Dowitcher	E	E	H	M	E	H	E	M	H	H	N	N	N	H	N	H	H	E	M	H	M			H	M
Jack Snipe										N															
Wilson's Snipe	E	E	M	H	E	M	E	E	E	H	H	E	E	E	E	E	E	E	E	E	M	E	M	M	M
Pin-tailed Snipe									N	N															
Wilson's Phalarope	N		N				N						N			N		N			N			N	
Red-necked Phalarope	E	E	E	M	E	E	E	E	H	H	M	E	E	E	E	E	E	E	E	H	H	E	H	M	E
Red Phalarope	E	E	H	E	H	N	N		H	H		N	H	N		N	N	M	N	N					N
Oriental Pratincole				N					N																

South Polar Skua													N						N						
Pomarine Jaeger	E	E	M	E	E	N	N		H	H	N	N	E	H	N		N	M	N				H	N	N
Parasitic Jaeger	E	E	H	E	E		H	N	E	H	H	E	E	M	E	N	N	E	H	N	N		H	N	H
Long-tailed Jaeger	H	E	M	E	E	M	E	H	N	H	N	E	M	H	H	N	N	M	H		N		H		N
Franklin's Gull										N			N	N	N	N		N			N			N	N
Little Gull													N			N					N			N	N
Black-headed Gull				H	N		N	N	E	H		N	N	N	N	N		N							
Bonaparte's Gull		H	H	N		M	E	E		N		E	M	E	E	E	E	E	E	E	E	E	M	E	E
Heermann's Gull																							N		N
Black-tailed Gull				N					N				N	N							X			N	N
Mew Gull	H	M	E	N	E	E	E	E	H	N	E	E	E	E	E	E	E	E	E	E	E	E	E	E	E
Ring-billed Gull							N					N	N	N	N	N	N	N		H	H	H		H	H
California Gull						X							N	N		N		N							
Herring Gull	H	N	H	E	E	N	E	M	H	H	N	N	H	M	E	H	H	E	E	H	H	H	N	H	E
Thayer's Gull	H	N	N		N								N			H	N	M	H	E	E	E	E	M	E
Lesser Black-backed Gull													N					N			N				
Slaty-backed Gull	N		N	H	H				E	H		N	N			N		N		N	N				N
Western Gull													N	N							N		N	N	N
Glaucous-winged Gull				M	H	N	N	N	E	E	E	E	E	E	E	E	E	E	E	E	E	E	E	E	E
Glaucous Gull	E	M	M	E	E	X	H	N	N	H		N	H	H	H	H	N	H	N		N			H	N
Great Black-backed Gull													N												
Sabine's Gull	E	M	H	H	H	X	N	N	N	N	N	N	H	H	N	N	N	N	N		N		N	N	N
Black-legged Kittiwake	N		N	E	E		N		E	E	N	E	E	E	H	H	E	E	E	H	H	N	H	H	E
Red-legged Kittiwake				N			N		H	E	N		N	N									N		
Ross's Gull	M		N	H	N		N		N	N	N			N											
Ivory Gull	M		N	H	N					N						N		N	N	N					
Caspian Tern					N		N						N	N		N	N	M	N	N	N	N	N	N	N
Common Tern				N	N				H	N															
Arctic Tern	E	E	H	H	E	M	E	M	N	H	H	E	E	E	E	E	E	E	E	E	E	E	N	M	N
Aleutian Tern				N	E				E	N	H	E	H	M	N		N	M	N						

E = Easy to find M = Moderately easy to find H = Hard to find N = Not expected to find X = Undocumented

"Summer" Checklists	NORTH			WEST		INTERIOR			SOUTHWEST				SOUTHCENTRAL						SOUTHEAST						
	Barrow	Dalton Highway	Arctic NWR	Gambell	Nome	Denali NP	Fairbanks Area	Tetlin NWR & E. Interior	Attu Island	Pribilof Islands	Izembek NWR	Becharof NWR/Katmai NP	Kodiak Island	Kachemak Bay	Kenai NWR	Anchorage	Seward/Kenai Fjords NP	Cordova	Glacier Bay NP	Haines/Skagway	Juneau	Hyder	Sitka	Petersburg	Ketchikan
White-winged Tern									N					N											
Black Tern							N	N													N				
Dovekie	N			H						N			N												
Common Murre	N			E	E				E	E	H	E	E	E		N	E	E	E		H		E	M	E
Thick-billed Murre	N		N	E	E				H	E		E	N	N			H	H			X		H		
Black Guillemot	M		H	M			N			N															
Pigeon Guillemot				E	E				E	H	H	E	E	E			E	E	E	E	E		E	M	E
Long-billed Murrelet						N							N												
Marbled Murrelet				N	N		N		E	N		N	E	E			E	E	E	E	E	E	E	E	E
Kittlitz's Murrelet	N			N	N				E	N	N	N	H	E			M	N	E		N				
Ancient Murrelet				N					E	H		H	H	H			M	N	N	N	N			N	N
Cassin's Auklet										N	N	H	H	N			N		H						N
Parakeet Auklet	N			E	H				N	E		H	H	H			M		H						
Least Auklet	N			E	H				N	E		N	N												
Whiskered Auklet				N					N			N		X											
Crested Auklet	N			E	H		N		H	E		N	N	N											
Rhinoceros Auklet										N		H	H	H			M		H				M		H
Horned Puffin	N		N	E	E				E	E	H	E	E	E			E		N				N		
Tufted Puffin	N			E	E				E	E	H	E	E	E			E	N	E		X		E		
Rock Dove				N			E	N				N		E		E	H			E	E		E	M	E
Band-tailed Pigeon					N																N	H		H	M
Oriental Turtle-Dove									N	N															
White-winged Dove																				N					
Mourning Dove							N						N	N	N	N	N	N	H	N	N		N	N	N
Common Cuckoo				N	N				H	N	N					N									

Oriental Cuckoo				N					N	N															
Yellow-billed Cuckoo																					N				N
Western Screech-Owl														N			H		H	N	H	H	H	H	M
Great Horned Owl		M	H		H	H	E	M				H		H	M	H	H	E	H	E	M	H	H	H	H
Snowy Owl	M	M	M	N	H	N	N	N	H	H		N	N		N	N		N			N		N	N	N
Northern Hawk Owl		M	H		H	M	M	M				H	H	H	H	H	N	M	H		N		N	N	
Northern Pygmy-Owl																			N	H	H	H	H	H	H
Barred Owl																				H	N	H		N	M
Great Gray Owl		N	H			N	H	H					N	H	N	N	N	N			N				
Long-eared Owl							X														N				
Short-eared Owl	H	E	H	H	E	M	E	M	H	H	H	H	H	H	H	N	N	M	M	H	N			N	N
Boreal Owl		N	H	N		H	M	H		N		H	M	H	H	H	N	H	H	H	N				N
Northern Saw-whet Owl				N						N		H		H		H	H	H	N	H	N	H	H	H	M
Common Nighthawk	N		N				N	N					N	N				N	N	H	N	H		N	N
Black Swift																					N	E		H	N
Chimney Swift										N															
Vaux's Swift																		N	N	H	H	E		H	M
White-throated Needletail									N																
Common Swift										N															
Fork-tailed Swift				N					N	N															
Anna's Hummingbird								N						N		N		N			N		N	N	N
Costa's Hummingbird																N					N				
Calliope Hummingbird																					X			X	
Rufous Hummingbird			N			N	H	N		N		N	H	H	N	H	H	E	E	E	E	E	E	H	E
Belted Kingfisher		H	H			M	E	M		N		E	E	E	H	M	H	E	E	E	M	E	E	M	M
Yellow-bellied Sapsucker							H	H					N			N									
Red-breasted Sapsucker								N					N	N	N			N	E	E	M	E	E	M	E
Great Spotted Woodpecker							N		N	N															
Downy Woodpecker		H	H			H	E	H				H	H	H	M	M	H	H	H	E	N	H	H	H	H
Hairy Woodpecker		M	H			H	E	M				N	N	H	M	M	H	H	H	E	H	E	H	M	E

E = Easy to find M = Moderately easy to find H = Hard to find N = Not expected to find X = Undocumented

"Summer" Checklists	NORTH			WEST		INTERIOR			SOUTHWEST				SOUTHCENTRAL						SOUTHEAST						
	Barrow	Dalton Highway	Arctic NWR	Gambell	Nome	Denali NP	Fairbanks Area	Tetlin NWR & E. Interior	Attu Island	Pribilof Islands	Izembek NWR	Becharof NWR/Katmai NP	Kodiak Island	Kachemak Bay	Kenai NWR	Anchorage	Seward/Kenai Fjords NP	Cordova	Glacier Bay NP	Haines/Skagway	Juneau	Hyder	Sitka	Petersburg	Ketchikan
Three-toed Woodpecker		H	H			H	M	M				H	H	H	M	H	H	N	H	E	N	H	N	H	H
Black-backed Woodpecker		N				H	H	M				N		H	H	N					N				
Northern (Yellow-shafted) Flicker		M	H			M	E	E		N		N	N	H	H	H	H	E	H	E	H	N			
Northern (Red-shafted) Flicker																					N	E	H	H	H
Olive-sided Flycatcher	N	H	H	N		M	E	M				H		H	H	H	H	H	H	E	N	E		H	H
Western Wood-Pewee	N					H	M	M				N		N	H	M	H	N	H	M	N	E		H	H
Yellow-bellied Flycatcher						N	N	N													N	N		N	
Alder Flycatcher	N	H	M		E	M	E	H			N	M		E	E	M	H	E	H	E	H	E		H	H
Willow Flycatcher												N				N					N	N			
Least Flycatcher				N			N	N								N						N			
Hammond's Flycatcher		H	N			H	E	H								N			N	E	N	E		N	N
Dusky Flycatcher																					N				
Pacific-slope Flycatcher				X															E	E	E	E	E	M	E
Eastern Phoebe			N																		X	N		N	
Say's Phoebe	N	M	M	N	E	M	M	M				N		H	N	N	N	H	H	N	N		N		N
Ash-throated Flycatcher																					X				
Tropical Kingbird																									N
Western Kingbird							N											N			N	N	N		
Eastern Kingbird	N		N			X	N			N			N			N		N	N	N	N	N		N	
Scissor-tailed Flycatcher																					X				
Brown Shrike				N					N							N							X		
Northern Shrike	N	H	H		E	H	M	H			H	H	M	H	H	M	M	N	N	N	N		N	H	N
Cassin's Vireo							N									N					N	N		N	
Warbling Vireo							X	N								N	X			H	H	E		H	H

Philadelphia Vireo							N																		
Red-eyed Vireo															N						N	H		N	N
Gray Jay	N	H	M		H	E	E	E				E		E	E	M	M	N		H					
Steller's Jay						N						N		E	H	M	E	E	E	E	E	E	E	M	E
Clark's Nutcracker							N												N		N				N
Black-billed Magpie		N				E	M	M			H	E	E	E	E	E	E	E	E	E	N		N	H	N
American Crow																						E			
Northwestern Crow											N	H	E	E	N	N	E	E	E	E	E	N	E	E	E
Common Raven	E	E	M	E	E	M	E	E	E	H	E	E	E	E	E	E	E	E	E	E	E	E	E	M	E
Sky Lark				N					E	N		N													
Horned Lark	H	M	M	N		E	E	H		N	N	N	N	H	H	M	N	H	H	H	N	H		N	N
Purple Martin				N			N			N						N	N	N			N				
Tree Swallow	N	H	H	N	E	H	E	M		H	H	E	E	E	E	E	E	E	E	E	M	E	E	M	E
Violet-green Swallow	N	M	H		H	M	E	E		N	N	H	E	E	E	E	E	E	E	E	H	E	N	M	M
Northern Rough-winged Swallow	N																	N		N	N	M		H	H
Bank Swallow	N	H	H	N	E	H	E	M	N	H	H	E	E	E	E	E	E	M	H	E	H	E		H	N
Cliff Swallow	N	M	M	N	E	H	E	E		H		H	N	E	H	M	E	E	H	H	N	E		H	N
Barn Swallow	N	N	N	N		N	N	N	N	H	N	N	N			N	N	M	H	E	E	E	E	M	M
Common House-Martin					N					N							N								
Black-capped Chickadee	N	E	M		N	M	E	M				E	E	E	E	E	E	E		H	N			N	
Mountain Chickadee																				N	N		N	N	
Chestnut-backed Chickadee														M		N	E	E	E	E	E	E	E	M	E
Boreal Chickadee		E	H			E	E	E				E		E	E	E	H	N		H	N			N	
Gray-headed Chickadee		N	H			X	N	N																	
Red-breasted Nuthatch				N		H	H	N			N	H	H	E	H	H	H	H	H	M	N	H	N	H	N
Brown Creeper		N				N	H	N				H	H	E	H	H	H	E	H	E	H	E	E	H	M
Winter Wren	N								E	H	H	H	E	E		N	H	E	E	E	E	E	E	M	E
American Dipper		H	H		E	H	M	H			H	M	E	E	H	H	H		E	E	M	E	E	M	E
Golden-crowned Kinglet						N	N	N		N		M	E	E	H	M	H	E	E	E	E	E	E	M	E

E = Easy to find M = Moderately easy to find H = Hard to find N = Not expected to find X = Undocumented

"Summer" Checklists	NORTH			WEST		INTERIOR			SOUTHWEST				SOUTHCENTRAL						SOUTHEAST						
	Barrow	Dalton Highway	Arctic NWR	Gambell	Nome	Denali NP	Fairbanks Area	Tetlin NWR & E. Interior	Attu Island	Pribilof Islands	Izembek NWR	Becharof NWR/Katmai NP	Kodiak Island	Kachemak Bay	Kenai NWR	Anchorage	Seward/Kenai Fjords NP	Cordova	Glacier Bay NP	Haines/Skagway	Juneau	Hyder	Sitka	Petersburg	Ketchikan
Ruby-crowned Kinglet	N	H	E			E	E	E		N		E	N	E	E	E	E	E	E	E	E	E	E	M	E
Middendorff's Grasshopper-Warbler				N					N	N															
Lanceolated Warbler									N																
Dusky Warbler				N					N	N															
Arctic Warbler	H	M	H	H	E	M	M	H	N	N						N									
Narcissus Flycatcher									N																
Red-breasted Flycatcher				N					N	N															
Siberian Flycatcher									N	N															
Gray-spotted Flycatcher									H																
Asian Brown Flycatcher				N					N																
Rufous-tailed Robin									X																
Siberian Rubythroat				N					E	N															
Bluethroat	H	H	H	M	E				N	N															
Siberian Blue Robin									N																
Red-flanked Bluetail									N	N															
Northern Wheatear	H	M	M	M	E	M	M	H	N	H	N			N	N	H	N	N			N				
Stonechat				N																					
Mountain Bluebird	N					X	H	H						N					N	N	N	H	N	N	
Townsend's Solitaire		H	H			H	M	H				N		N	N	H		N	N	N	N			N	N
Veery																						N			
Gray-cheeked Thrush	N	E	M	M	E	M	E	M		N	N	E	M	H	E	H	H	E	H	N	H	N			N
Swainson's Thrush	N	H	H	N		E	E	E			N	E	N	E	E	E	H	E	E	E	E	E	E	M	M
Hermit Thrush	N	H	H	N	H	M	E	M		N		E	E	E	E	E	E	E	E	E	E	E	E	M	E
Eyebrowed Thrush	N			N					E	N															

Dusky Thrush	N			N					H												N			N	
Fieldfare	N			N																					
American Robin	N	M	E	N	E	E	E	E		N		E	H	E	E	E	E	E	E	E	E	E	E	M	E
Varied Thrush	N	M	E	N	E	E	E	M		N	N	E	E	E	E	E	E	E	E	E	E	E	E	M	E
Gray Catbird																N									
Northern Mockingbird							N									N				N	N		N	N	N
Brown Thrasher	N						N																		
European Starling	N					N	H	N				N	H	N		N	N	H	E	E	M	E	E	M	M
Siberian Accentor	N			N			N									N					X				
Yellow Wagtail	N	M	H	M	E	X	N		E	H	N	H	N	N		N		N							
Gray Wagtail			N	N					N	N															
White Wagtail	N		N	E	E	X	N			N						N			N						
Black-backed Wagtail			N	N				N	E	N				N							X				
Olive-backed Pipit			N	N					E	N		N													
Pechora Pipit				N					N																
Red-throated Pipit	N			M	N		X		H	N											N				
American Pipit	H	M	M	M	E	E	E	H	E	H	M	E	E	M	E	E	H	E	E	E	M	E	M	M	E
Bohemian Waxwing		M	M	N		H	M	M	N	N	N	N	H	H	H	H	H	E		H	N		N	N	H
Cedar Waxwing			N				X						N			N				H	N	E	N	H	M
Tennessee Warbler				N		X	N	N				N									N	N		N	N
Orange-crowned Warbler	N	H	H		E	E	E	M		N		E	E	E	E	E	E	E	E	E	E	E	E	M	E
Nashville Warbler																					X				
Yellow Warbler	N	M	H	N	E	H	E	M		N	M	E	E	E	H	M	E	E	E	E	E	E	E	M	M
Chestnut-sided Warbler																									N
Magnolia Warbler			N													N					N	H		N	
Cape May Warbler	N						N													N	X				
Black-throated Blue Warbler																					N				
Yellow-rumped (Myrtle) Warbler	N	H	M	N	E	M	E	E	N	N	N	E	M	E	E	E	E	E	E	E	E		H	N	N
Yellow-rumped (Audubon's) Warbler																					M	M	M	H	M

E = Easy to find M = Moderately easy to find H = Hard to find N = Not expected to find X = Undocumented

"Summer" Checklists	NORTH			WEST		INTERIOR			SOUTHWEST				SOUTHCENTRAL						SOUTHEAST						
	Barrow	Dalton Highway	Arctic NWR	Gambell	Nome	Denali NP	Fairbanks Area	Tetlin NWR & E. Interior	Attu Island	Pribilof Islands	Izembek NWR	Becharof NWR/Katmai NP	Kodiak Island	Kachemak Bay	Kenai NWR	Anchorage	Seward/Kenai Fjords NP	Cordova	Glacier Bay NP	Haines/Skagway	Juneau	Hyder	Sitka	Petersburg	Ketchikan
Townsend's Warbler		H				N	H	M				N	N	E	H	M	E	E	E	E	E	E	E	M	E
Prairie Warbler																									N
Palm Warbler	N		N				N						N								N			N	N
Bay-breasted Warbler							N														N				
Blackpoll Warbler	N	H	H		E	M	M	M				H	N	H	H	M	H	N	H		N	N			
Black-and-white Warbler	N																					N			
American Redstart	N					N	N	N						N		N			N	N	N	M		N	N
Ovenbird	N						N														N				
Northern Waterthrush	N	H	H	N	E	H	E	M				H		H	H	M	H	N		H	H	E		H	
Kentucky Warbler			X																						
Mourning Warbler							N				N														
MacGillivray's Warbler							N											N	H	H	H	M		H	H
Common Yellowthroat							N	N						N		N		N	H	H	H	M		M	H
Wilson's Warbler	N	H	H	N	E	E	E	M		H	H	E	E	E	M	E	E	E	E	E	E	E	E	M	M
Canada Warbler	N		N																						
Scarlet Tanager	N																	N							
Western Tanager	N					N	N							N					N	H	N	M	N	H	N
Spotted Towhee																					N				
American Tree Sparrow	N	M	E	H	E	E	E	M		N		E	H	N	H	H	H	H			N		N	N	N
Chipping Sparrow	N		N				M	M				N				N		N	N	N	N	M		N	
Clay-colored Sparrow			N				N	N												N	X				N
Timberline Sparrow							N	H												H		H			
Lark Sparrow							N	N															N		
Savannah Sparrow	H	E	M	H	E	E	E	M		H	E	E	E	E	E	E	E	E	E	E	E	E	M	M	M
Fox Sparrow	N	M	E	N	E	E	E	M		H	H	E	E	E	E	E	E	E	E	E	E	E	E	M	E

Song Sparrow			N			X		N	E	N	H	N	E	E	N	M	M	E	E	E	M	E	E	M	E
Lincoln's Sparrow	N			N	H	M	E	E				H	H	E	E	E	E	E	E	E	E	E	E	M	E
Swamp Sparrow																N		N			N			N	N
White-throated Sparrow			N				N	N					N					N			N		N	N	N
Harris's Sparrow	N												N		N	N					N	N	N	N	N
Gambel's White-crowned Sparrow	N	E	E	N	E	E	E	E		N	H	E	H	E	E	E	M	E	H	E	H	E	M	H	H
Golden-crowned Sparrow	N	H	N	N	E	H	E	M		H	H	E	E	E	E	E	E	E	H	E	H	E	M	H	M
Slate-colored Junco	N	E	E	N	H	E	E	E		N	N	E	H	E	E	E	E	E	M	M	M	M	E	M	E
Oregon Junco							N						N	N	N	N	N	N	M	M	M	E	E	M	E
Lapland Longspur	E	E	E	E	E	E	E	M	E	E	E	E	E	H	H	M	H	E	N	N	N		N	N	N
Smith's Longspur	H	H	M			N	M	H											N		N				
Pine Bunting									N																
Little Bunting				N																					
Rustic Bunting				H					E	N														N	
Yellow-throated Bunting									N																
Yellow-breasted Bunting				N					N																
Gray Bunting									N																
Pallas's Bunting	N			N																					
Reed Bunting									N																
Snow Bunting	E	E	E	E	E	H	M	M	E	E	M	E	E		H	H	H				N			H	N
McKay's Bunting				M	N			N		N			N												
Rose-breasted Grosbeak																					N				
Black-headed Grosbeak													N								N	N		N	
Blue Grosbeak																					N			N	
Lazuli Bunting																					N	N			
Indigo Bunting																N									
Bobolink	N																					N			N
Red-winged Blackbird	N		N			N	H	H		N			N	N		H	N	N	N	H	H	E		H	H
Western Meadowlark			N				N	N								N					N		X		N

E = Easy to find M = Moderately easy to find H = Hard to find N = Not expected to find X = Undocumented

"Summer" Checklists	NORTH			WEST		INTERIOR			SOUTHWEST				SOUTHCENTRAL						SOUTHEAST						
	Barrow	Dalton Highway	Arctic NWR	Gambell	Nome	Denali NP	Fairbanks Area	Tetlin NWR & E. Interior	Attu Island	Pribilof Islands	Izembek NWR	Becharof NWR/Katmai NP	Kodiak Island	Kachemak Bay	Kenai NWR	Anchorage	Seward/Kenai Fjords NP	Cordova	Glacier Bay NP	Haines/Skagway	Juneau	Hyder	Sitka	Petersburg	Ketchikan
Yellow-headed Blackbird	N						N							X		N		N		N	N	N			
Rusty Blackbird	N	N	M	N	E	H	E	E		N	N	H	H	H	M	E	H	M	N	H	N	H	N	H	N
Brewer's Blackbird	N																				N		N	N	N
Common Grackle							N														N				N
Brown-headed Cowbird	N		N			N	H	N				N				N		N	N	H	N	E	N	H	N
Bullock's Oriole																									X
Brambling	N			H					E	H		N	N			N	N	N					N	N	N
Gray-crowned Rosy-Finch		H	H		H	M	H	N	E	E	M	E	H	H	H	H	N	H	H	H	H		N	N	N
Pine Grosbeak		H	H			H	E	H	N	N	N	M	E	E	M	M	E	E	N	H	H	H	N	H	M
Common Rosefinch				N					N	N															
Purple Finch						X		N													N			N	N
Cassin's Finch														N											
House Finch																				N		N			N
Red Crossbill				N			X			N		N	N	H		N	H	H	E	E	M	E	M	M	M
White-winged Crossbill		H	M	N		H	E	M		N		H	H	E	M	M	E	E	H	E	H	E	M	H	H
Common Redpoll	E	M	M	H	E	E	E	M	H	H	H	E	E	E	E	E	E	E	H	H	N	H	N	H	N
Hoary Redpoll	E	M	M	M	E	N	N	H	H	N	N	N	N	H		N		N			N			N	
Eurasian Siskin									N																
Pine Siskin	N		H			H	E	H				H	E	E	E	M	H	E	E	E	E	E	E	M	M
American Goldfinch																					X			N	N
Oriental Greenfinch									H	N															
Eurasian Bullfinch				N			N		N							N								N	
Evening Grosbeak							N									N					N	N		N	N
Hawfinch				N					H	N															
House Sparrow																								N	N

Appendix B:

Organizations of Interest to Birders

The area code for all telephone numbers is 907 unless otherwise indicated.

Alaska Bird Observatory — ABO is a non-profit organization whose mission is to advance the appreciation, understanding, and conservation of birds and their habitats through research and education. ABO's programs include migration monitoring, breeding-bird surveys, habitat-selection studies, school presentations, birding workshops, nature walks, student internships, and environmental volunteerism. ABO operates a large mist-netting station at Creamer's Field Migratory Waterfowl Refuge in Fairbanks. Visiting birders are welcome to stop by the station that operates daily (weather permitting) from 6 AM to noon from 1 May–5 June and from 1 August–25 September. Birds commonly captured at the station include the region's thrushes, warblers, sparrows, and redpolls; occasionally an Arctic Warbler or Northern Shrike is caught. To obtain schedules for public bird-banding presentations and summer banding, contact the ABO office at 418 Wedgewood Drive, Fairbanks, AK 99701. Wedgewood Resort is just east of Creamer's Field Refuge. From College Road turn north on Margaret Avenue to Wedgewood Drive. The facility includes interpretive displays about boreal forest birds and a small store featuring field guides, checklists, Alaska bird song CDs and tapes, T-shirts, hats, and bird-related gifts. Visitors can also obtain current information on Fairbanks birding opportunities and enjoy one of ABO's bird walks or slide programs. For information, write Alaska Bird Observatory, PO Box 80505, Fairbanks, AK 99708; 451-7159; fax 451-7079; e-mail *birds@ alaskabird.org*; web site *http://www.alaskabird.org*. See Fairbanks, page 75, for a map.

Alaska Center for the Environment — The mission of the Center is to protect Alaska's natural ecosystems and quality of life through grassroots activism and education. Its primary area of concern is the protection of natural habitats in southcentral Alaska, from the Alaska Range to Prince William Sound and from Bristol Bay to the Wrangell Mountains. For more information contact them at 807 G Street, Suite 100, Anchorage, AK 99501; 274-3621; or visit them on the web at *www.akcenter.org*.

Alaska Maritime National Wildlife Refuge — A wildlife refuge that covers over 2,500 islands, headlands, rocks, and other nesting places for colonies of seabirds along the coast of Alaska, from the Forrester Island group in southeast Alaska to the Aleutian Islands and north to Cape Lisburne on the Chukchi Sea. Some 40 million seabirds nest in the refuge. Tours are available from Seward, Sitka, Homer, Kodiak, Unalaska, and Nome to only a few islands. The Pribilof Islands are part of the refuge. For information contact the Refuge Manager, 2355 Kachemak Bay Drive, Suite 101, Homer, AK 99603; 235-6546. A visitor center is under construction at 95 Sterling Highway (Bypass) in Homer and a temporary center is located on the same street, 235-6961. Bird walks are scheduled during summer. The hot line for bird sightings in Kachemak Bay, 235-7337, is supported by the refuge. See Kenai Peninsula, Homer, page 293.

Alaska Natural History Association — A non-profit educational organization dedicated to enhancing the understanding and conservation of Alaska's natural, cultural, and historical resources by working in cooperation with land management agencies and other educational organizations throughout Alaska. The association has established agreements with several federal and state agencies to supply educational materials such as maps, guide books, identification guides, and other educational reading material. Contact them through their mail-order services at 750 West 2nd Avenue, Suite 100, Anchorage, AK 99501; 274-8440. The web site for requesting a catalog and ordering materials is *www.alaskanha.org*.

Alaska Peninsula National Wildlife Refuge — The refuge contains one of principal locations for viewing the Alaska Brown Bear and for fishing for trout and salmon. The refuge is dominated by the Aleutian Range of volcanic mountain peaks, including the most massive volcano on record, 8,400-foot Mount Veniaminof. Access is by small aircraft; there are no roads. For information contact the Refuge Manager, PO Box 277, King Salmon, AK 99613; 246-3339. There is a visitor center in King Salmon (see page 349).

Alaska SeaLife Center — The Center was developed in the late 1990s with funds from the *Exxon Valdez* oil spill settlement. It is open to visitors (fee) so they can observe live marine birds and mammals and learn more about the marine environment of southcoastal Alaska. The Center is affiliated with the University of Alaska Fairbanks. It is located on the waterfront in Seward. Research concentrates on studies that further the restoration of injured resources from the 1989 oil spill. It also serves as a local rehabilitation center and is a developing educational institution. For more information contact the Center at PO Box 1329, Seward, AK 99664; 800-224-2525; inside Alaska at 224-6300. The web site is *www.alaskasealife.org*. See also Kenai Peninsula, Seward, page 273.

Anchorage Audubon Society — PO Box 101161, Anchorage, AK 99510. For information on field trips, monthly meetings, and position papers, see the web site at *www.anchorageaudubon.org*. For information on recent bird sightings in the Upper Cook Inlet area call 338-2473.

Arctic Audubon Society — Arctic Audubon is located in Fairbanks. Established in 1979, the chapter offers field trips, programs, newsletters, a birding hot line, education programs, and it works on conservation issues. Arctic Audubon is a unique chapter within the national organization—not only is it the farthest-north chapter, but it also covers the largest area, all of Alaska north of the Alaska Range. One goal is to help to save the last large tracts of wilderness left in the U.S. The chapter encompasses the breeding grounds for many of North America's bird species. Arctic Audubon strives to share the beauty and excitement of Alaska's birds, while helping to preserve their habitat. PO Box 82098, Fairbanks, AK 99709; web site *www.arcticaudubon.org* (under construction in 2002). You can call the birding hot line at 451-9213.

Arctic National Wildlife Refuge — The refuge is home to the 160,000-member Porcupine Caribou herd as well as to herds of Muskoxen, Dall's Sheep, packs of Wolves, and many Brown, Black, and

Polar Bears. It stretches from the coast of the Beaufort Sea to the slopes of the Brooks Range and contains breeding habitat for many thousands of shorebirds and waterfowl, as well as passerine species, including Gray-headed Chickadee. Access is by aircraft. Contact the Refuge Manager for more information at 101 12th Avenue, Box 20, Fairbanks, AK 99701; 456-0250. Tours into the refuge are available from Fairbanks. See Arctic National Wildlife Refuge, page 98.

Audubon Alaska — Based in Anchorage, Audubon Alaska is the Alaska State Office of the National Audubon Society. Audubon first opened an office in Alaska in 1977 and now employs three full-time staff members. There are about 2,300 Audubon members in Alaska and five chapters—Anchorage, Cordova, Fairbanks, Juneau, and Kodiak. Audubon Alaska's mission is the conservation of natural ecosytems, emphasizing birds and other wildlife and their habitats, for the benefit of present and future generations. This mission is pursued through: policy advocacy, emphasizing the protection of nationally and internationally significant fish and wildlife habitats on public lands; education; and proactive habitat- and species-conservation projects, such as Important Bird Areas and the Alaska WatchList of declining and vulnerable bird populations. For more information about Audubon Alaska's program or about birds in Alaska, contact Audubon Alaska, 308 G Street, Suite 217, Anchorage, AK 99501; 276-7034; web site *http://home.gci.net/~akaudubon/*.

Becharof National Wildlife Refuge — Becharof Lake is the second-largest in Alaska and occupies one-quarter of the refuge. The area supports large herds of Caribou, populations of Moose, probably the largest number of Brown Bears in the state, and thousands of seabirds and mammals along its coast on the Alaska Peninsula. The refuge is used by many guides for hunting and fishing adventures. Access is by aircraft. Contact the Refuge Manager for more information: PO Box 277, King Salmon, AK 99613; 246-3339. A visitor center is located in King Salmon. See King Salmon, page 349.

Bering Land Bridge National Preserve — Eskimo populations crossed the Bering Sea land bridge from 9,000 to 6,000 years ago and settled the north slope of Alaska and the Canadian Arctic. The Preserve, one of the most remote parks in the state, encompasses 2.7 million acres on the northwest corner of the Seward Peninsula. The area is ideal for wilderness camping and birding; the only facilities are a few cabins. There are no roads into the preserve; access is by bush plane or boat along the coast. For information contact the Superintendent at PO Box 220, Nome, AK 99762; 443-2522.

Cape Krusenstern National Monument — See Kobuk Valley National Park.

Center for Alaskan Coastal Studies — The mission is to foster responsible interaction with our natural surroundings and to generate knowledge of the marine and coastal ecosystems of Kachemak Bay through environmental education and research programs. Daily, guided, natural-history tours are available in the coastal rain forest and intertidal zone on the south side of Kachemak Bay out of Homer. Scheduled daily hikes in an upland meadow and forest habitat are also available at the Carl E. Wynn Nature Center in Homer. There is a strong emphasis on education for local school children. Other programs are given during the summer. Contact the Center at 235-6667; e-mail *cacs@xyz.net*; web site *www.akcoastalstudies.org*. See also Kenai Peninsula, Homer, page 293.

Denali National Park and Preserve - See Denali National Park, page 58.

Gates of the Arctic National Park and Preserve — The Brooks Range separates interior Alaska from the tundra of the North Slope; the center of the range is encompassed by this park. With a size of 8.4-million acres, it is four times larger than Yellowstone National Park, and lies entirely north of the Arctic Circle. Athabaskan (Native Indian) people live in the taiga forest along the river valleys in the southern part of the park, and the Nunamiut (Eskimo) people occupy passes in the Brooks range and hunt to the north for Caribou. Access is by airplane to Bettles and Anaktuvuk Pass, then by dog team, snowmachine, or foot. Charter aircraft out of Bettles could take you to any sand bar or lake in the area. For information contact the Superintendent at 201 First Avenue, Fairbanks, AK 99701; 692-5494; web site *www.nps.gov/gaar*.

Glacier Bay National Park and Preserve — The park is located in the northeast corner of the Gulf of Alaska at the dividing line between southcoastal and southeast Alaska. It is a prime tourist destination, because it is one of the most beautiful areas of the state. There are some 50 charter companies providing services in and to the park. Glacier Bay can be reached from Haines by air or by boat from Juneau. The village of Gustavus at the southeast edge of the park, a 30-minute flight from Juneau, has visitor facilities and information. For information contact the Superintendent, PO Box 140, Gustavus, AK 99826; 697-2230; e-mail *glba_administration@nps.gov*; web site *www.nps.gov/glba*. Check with tour companies for round-trip air transportation from Haines to Gustavus and a boat tour of the bay with Glacier Bay Tours and Cruises; 206-623-2417; web site *http://www.glacierbaylodge.com*. If you are coming from Haines contact Chilkat Cruises and Tours, 142 Beach Road; 888-766-210. See also Glacier Bay National Park, page 470.

Innoko National Wildlife Refuge — The refuge protects habitat along the Yukon River for thousands of nesting waterfowl and an abundance of Moose. Most of the area is dominated by Black Spruce muskeg, bogs, and marshes. Access is by aircraft or riverboat. For more information contact the Refuge Manager, PO Box 69, McGrath, AK 99627; 524-3251.

Izembek National Wildlife Refuge — The refuge near Cold Bay on the Alaska Peninsula protects the largest bed of Eel Grass in the world and is a critical habitat for migratory birds and marine life. Most of the world's population of Black Brant, along with Canada and Emperor Geese, ducks, and other birds, congregate here each fall to feed on the Eel Grass. Access is by commercial airlines and the Alaska State Ferry. There is a road to the refuge from Cold Bay, one of the stops on the ferry route to Dutch Harbor. For more information contact the Refuge Manager, PO Box 127, Cold Bay, AK 99571; 532-2445. See also Alaska Peninsula, Cold Bay, page 358; *http://www.r7.fws.gov/nwr/izembek/iznwr.html*.

Juneau Audubon Society — JAS actively promotes conservation and education programs throughout southeast Alaska. The Society organizes and leads birding field trips in Juneau each Saturday from mid-April through mid-June. Catamaran trips to Berner's Bay are scheduled during the spring Eulachon (Hooligan) run to provide opportunities for viewing the large gathering of birds and marine mammals that prey on the fish. Public meetings are held on the second Thursday of each month from September through May. A rare bird alert hot line is maintained during the spring, summer, and fall months: 586-2591. The Society publishes a checklist of Juneau birds and *The Raven* newsletter. Juneau Audubon Society, PO Box 021725, Juneau, AK 99802.

Kachemak Bay Research Reserve (KBRR) — The reserve, officially designated in 1999, is now the largest reserve in a nationwide system of protected estuaries. The National Estuarine Research Reserve (NERR) program was established in 1972 to provide opportunities for long-term estuarine research and monitoring, estuarine education and interpretation, and to provide a basis for better-informed coastal management decisions. KBRR is composed of 365,000 acres of public lands and waters and is managed by the Alaska Department of Fish and Game in partnership with the National Oceanographic and Atmospheric Administration (NOAA). The overall mission of KBRR is to *develop and implement educational and research programs that enhance our understanding of the Kachemak Bay estuary and thus help ensure that the Bay remains healthy and productive for Alaskans, the nation, and the diverse species that thrive in the estuary.* In keeping with this mission, the reserve's goals and objectives focus on taking best advantage of the programs, resources, and data in existence and building on this foundation. KBRR projects currently underway include the *Kachemak Bay Ecological Characterization Project*, a CD-ROM and Internet document published in 2001. The CD-ROM includes detailed descriptions of Kachemak Bay's ecosystem components, current resource issues, a socioeconomic profile, an annotated bibliography, research summaries, and spatial data analysis for the region using Geographic Information System (GIS) technologies. Field research projects underway include intertidal habitat mapping and kelp bed studies. KBRR education staff train teachers in student monitoring techniques and protocols, lead estuarine ecology field trips, and work with environmental education organizations and individuals around Kachemak Bay to enhance marine science learning opportunities for adults and students. For information call 235-4799. *http://www.state.ak.us/local/akpages/fishgam/habitat/geninfo/nerr.*

Kachemak Heritage Land Trust — Based in Homer, Kachemak Heritage Land Trust is a regional land-conservation organization established in 1989 to preserve land with significant natural, recreational, or cultural values by working with willing landowners across the Kenai Peninsula. Work is primarily funded by over 500 members and foundation grants. The conservation tool most commonly used is a conservation easement—a permanent legal agreement in which the landowner describes the rights they wish to allow and those uses they want restricted forever. KHLT also owns land for conservation. One good example of their work includes acquisition of significant acreage on the Homer Spit, now permanently preserved as shorebird habitat. They are proud to have established a reputation for non-controversial, professional work. For more information contact the Land Trust at PO Box 2400, Homer, AK 99603; 235-5263, e-mail *khltkbr@xyz.net*; web *www.kachemaklandtrust.org*.

Kanuti National Wildlife Refuge — The refuge provides extensive wetland habitat for waterfowl nesting in the interior boreal forest along the Arctic Circle north of Fairbanks. It supports the subsistence lifestyle of the local Athabascan Indians. Access is by aircraft and riverboat. For more information contact Refuge Manager, 101 12th Avenue, Room 226, Fairbanks, AK 99701; 456-0329.

Katmai National Park and Preserve — Originally designated to preserve the Valley of Ten Thousand Smokes that was created after a volcanic eruption in 1912, the park now concentrates on the protection of Alaskan Brown Bears. You can fly in to Brooks Camp and take a tour to the volcanic valley. Fishing, birding, and bear-viewing are excellent. Access is by plane from King Salmon. For information contact the Superintendent, PO Box 7, King Salmon, AK 99613; 246-3305 or 486-6730; web site *www.nps.gov/katm*.

Kenai Fjords National Park — The 580,000-acre park on the southeast side of the Kenai Peninsula is dominated by the 300-square-mile Harding Ice Field at the head of the many glaciers that have carved valleys into Kachemak and Resurrection Bays. The marine shores of the park support thousands of breeding seabirds that can be viewed by boat out of Seward. Exit Glacier is reached by road north of Seward. For information contact the Superintendent, PO Box 1727, Seward, AK 99664; 224-3175; web site *www.nps.gov/kefj* or *www.kenaifjords.national-park.com*. See Kenai Peninsula, Seward, page 273.

Kenai National Wildlife Refuge — The refuge covers over one million acres in the northern and central Kenai Peninsula and runs from the crest of the Kenai Mountains to the shores of Cook Inlet. It was originally established to study and preserve the large population of Moose, but now protects nesting habitat for many species of birds, including Trumpeter Swan. Access by car is from the Sterling Highway. It is a popular place for a wilderness canoe trip on the Swanson River or Swan Lakes Canoe Trails. Contact the Refuge Manager, PO Box 2139, Soldotna, AK 99669; 262-7021. See Kenai Peninsula, Soldotna, page 284 for more information.

Kobuk Valley National Park — Cape Krusenstern National Monument, Noatak National Preserve, and Kobuk Valley National Park serve together as the Northwest Alaska [Parks] Areas that encompasses over 9,250,000 acres. They include the Noatak and Kobuk Rivers, two of North America's finest waters for wilderness expeditions. The area includes the western portion of the Brooks Range, sand dunes, archaeologically significant beach ridges, and is home for part of the year to the nomadic western arctic herd of Barren-Ground Caribou, whose numbers exceed 500,000 animals. The land is little used except by local Native inhabitants. Birding can be good on the two main rivers and especially along the coast of Cape Krusenstern. The information center is in Kotzebue at PO Box 1029, Kotzebue, AK 99752; 442-3890.

Kodiak Audubon Society — Founded in 1982, the Kodiak Audubon chapter has about 150 members. It supports many conservation efforts and environmental education programs within the community that focus both on birds and on other wildlife habitat issues. It publishes a *Hiking Guide to Kodiak Island* that can be purchased at the Kodiak Island Convention and Visitors Bureau. This publication contains maps of local, unmarked trails as well as descriptions of each trail. Every weekend from May through September volunteers lead guided hikes with various natural history themes. The *Kodiak Audubon Summer Hiking Program* brochure can also be obtained at the Visitor and Convention Center, the Kodiak State Parks visitor center, and the Kodiak NWR visitor center. Special arrangements can be made for guided group hikes or bird-watching trips. A checklist for the *Birds of the Kodiak Archipelago* can be obtained from the Kodiak NWR or from Kodiak Audubon. Contact: Stacy Studebaker, President, PO Box 970, Kodiak, AK 99615; 486-6498; e-mail *tidepool@ptialaska.net*. See Kodiak Archipelago, page 331.

Kodiak National Wildlife Refuge — The refuge encompasses about two-thirds of Kodiak Island and includes portions of other islands in the archipelago. It protects habitat of the Alaska Brown Bear, but also allows for hunting and salmon fishing. Over two million seabirds inhabit the coastline. Access is by commercial airline and the Alaska Marine Highway System. For more information see Kodiak Archipelago, page 331, or contact Refuge Manager, 1390 Buskin River Road, Kodiak, AK 99615; 487-2600.

Koyukuk National Wildlife Refuge — The refuge, located along the confluence of the Koyukuk and Yukon Rivers, provides habitat for breeding ducks, geese, and cranes. It supports a large population of Moose and Black Bear that are harvested by the Native Athabascan Indians. It also contains an extensive area of sand dunes, one of two such areas in the state. Access is by riverboat or aircraft. For information contact the Refuge Manager, PO Box 287, Galena, AK 99741; 656-1231.

Lake Clark National Park and Preserve — The park and preserve encompasses Lake Clark, which is located across Cook Inlet from Anchor Point and Homer. There are thousands of acres of wilderness to the north of the lake, including two active volcanoes, Mount Iliamna and Mount Redoubt, both over 10,000 feet elevation. Fishing is good in the lake and feeder streams. Access is by plane to Iliamna, Port Alsworth, or by floatplane directly to the lake. For information contact the Superintendent, 4230 University Drive, Suite 311, Anchorage, AK 99508; 271-3751.

National Park Service — *See individual parks.* For information on all of Alaska's National Parks call the Alaska Public Lands Information Center in Anchorage at 271-2737 or visit their web site *www.nps.gov/aplic*. The National Park Service Alaska web site is *www.us-national-parks.net/state/ak/htm*.

The Nature Conservancy of Alaska — The mission of The Nature Conservancy is to preserve the plants, animals, and natural communities that represent the diversity of life on Earth by protecting the lands and waters they need to survive. In Alaska that also means protecting some of the best bird habitat in the world. From the Pribilof Islands and their spectacular seabird colonies to the Alaska Peninsula and hundreds of thousands of migratory waterfowl; from the Chilkat Bald Eagle Preserve to the Copper River Delta and its extraordinary migration of shorebirds, TNC is saving great places for birds. Contact the Alaska Chapter at 421 West 1st Avenue, Suite 200, Anchorage, AK 99520; 276-3133; web site *www.nature.org/alaska*.

Noatak National Preserve — See Kobuk Valley National Park.

Northern Alaska Environmental Center — The mission of the Center is to preserve and protect the wilderness, natural habitats, and quality of life in interior and arctic Alaska through advocacy and education. For information contact them at 218 Driveway Street, Fairbanks, AK 99708; 452-5021; e-mail *info@northern.org*; web site *www.northern.org*.

Nowitna National Wildlife Refuge — Located north of Fairbanks, the refuge borders the Nowitna River, a designated Wild River, and its confluence with the Yukon River, and provides nesting habitat for ducks, geese, and Trumpeter Swans. In addition to harboring populations of salmon, it protects one of the three resident Sheefish populations in the state. The river is good for a float trip (no whitewater). Access is by riverboat or aircraft. Refuge Manager, PO Box 287, Galena, AK 99741; 656-1231.

Potter Marsh, Friends of — Friends of Potter Marsh (FOPM) is a small non-profit that exists to protect, through education and advocacy, the integrity of Potter Marsh and the Anchorage Coastal Wildlife Refuge, and to support the future Alaska Bird Center at Potter Marsh . The state's coastal refuge extends from Point Woronzof to Potter Creek, encompassing over 32,000 acres on the south side of Anchorage. The most popular and accessible portion of the refuge is Potter Marsh, where thousands of visitors use the boardwalk every year to view birds, salmon, bears, Moose, Beaver, and many other marsh residents. The marsh and refuge are rich in invertebrates, fish, and plant life that attract and support many species of birds. FOPM helps organize the Boardwalk Naturalist Volunteers program and hosts slide shows and talks throughout the year. Friends of Potter Marsh and the Anchorage Coastal Wildlife Refuge, 3170 Marathon Circle, Anchorage, AK 99515; 349-5622; *jfeier3186@aol.com*. See Anchorage, page 34.

Pratt Museum — A nationally recognized natural-history museum in Homer that gives the visitor a well-rounded look at the cultural and natural history of the Kachemak Bay area. Contact the Museum at 3779 Bartlett Street, Homer, AK 99603; 235-8635. See Kenai Peninsula, Homer, page 293. Visit the web site at *www.prattmuseum.org*.

Prince William Sound Science Center — The Center is an independent, non-profit, research and education center located in Cordova, established in 1989 to conduct and facilitate scientific studies on the ecology of the region. The Center's programs take an ecosystem approach to research, monitoring, and management of natural resources. The education programs serve the residents of and visitors to Prince William Sound. The Science Center is located on a pier at the end of Breakwater Avenue, at the mouth of the harbor in Cordova. Check their web site for research projects and educational programs: *www.pwssc.gen.ak.us/*. See also Cordova, page 373.

Selawik National Wildlife Refuge — The Selawik River supports a resident population of very large Sheefish and is one of several Wild Rivers in Alaska. The river is good for a float trip. The area is an important breeding ground for thousands of waterfowl and includes range for large herds of Caribou. The refuge straddles the Arctic Circle at the site of the ancient Bering Land Bridge. Access is by aircraft. Refuge Manager, PO Box 270, Kotzebue, AK 99752; 442-3799.

Sitka Conservation Society — The Society is working to protect the natural environment of the Tongass National Forest and surrounding waters of southeast Alaska. SCS is an educational and advocacy group concerned with the future of southeast Alaska. Contact PO Box 6533, Sitka, AK 99835; 747-7509; e-mail *info-scs@ak.net*; web site *http://home.gci.net/~sitkawild/*.

Sitka National Historic Park — The Park, the site of the early Russian occupation of Alaska, became the capital of Russian America in 1808. It was one of the busiest ports on the Pacific coast for many years when the Russians exported millions of Sea Otter pelts as well as other marine life. There were many battles with the Tlingit (Native) Indians, the original inhabitants of Baranof Island. The park and visitor center are located east of downtown Sitka, a good birding location. For park information contact the Superintendent, 106 Metlakatla Street, Sitka, AK 99835; 747-6281. See Sitka, page 409.

Skagway National Historic Park (Klondike Gold Rush) — Stop in at the Visitor Center on Second Avenue in Skagway for information on the Chilkoot and White Pass Trails that led north to the Klondike during the 1896–1897 gold rush. You can take the White Pass & Yukon Route train ride from Skagway to Whitehorse, YT, or visit historical sites in Skagway and Dyea at the head of the Chilkoot Trail. See Skagway, page 465. For information contact the superintendent at PO Box 517, Skagway, AK 99840.

Tetlin National Wildlife Refuge — The refuge covers an extensive flat area of lake-studded land east of the Yukon/Alaska border at the headwaters of the Tanana River; it is an important nesting area for waterfowl and Sandhill Cranes. A visitor center is at Mile 1229 Alaska Highway, and access is by road (see Alaska Highway: Yukon Border to Delta Junction, page 159). For more information contact the Refuge Manager, PO Box 779, Tok, AK 99780; 883-5312.

Togiak National Wildlife Refuge — Over 4.7 million acres of land between the Kuskokwim River and Bristol Bay are preserved for fish and wildlife resources used primarily by the local Native inhabitants. The area abounds with Pacific Walrus, seals, and seabirds along the coast and thousands of ducks, geese, cranes, and shorebirds throughout the refuge. Trout and salmon fishing are popular. Access is by aircraft. Contact the Refuge Manager, PO Box 270, Dillingham, AK 99576; 842-1063.

U.S. Fish and Wildlife Service — The several offices of Region 7 dealing with migratory birds within the Fish and Wildlife Service are located at 1011 East Tudor Road, Anchorage, AK 99503. For information on their programs call 786-3909; e-mail *Chuck_Young@fws.gov*; web site *www.r7.fws.gov/mbm/*.

Unalaska Aleutian WWII National Historic Area — Unalaska Island supports Dutch Harbor, the port at the western terminus of the Alaska Marine Highway System. If you travel to Unalaska to look for Whiskered Auklet (page 328), you may wish to explore the history of the island. The island is home to Aleuts (Native peoples) who were interred during World War II when the Japanese invaded the western Aleutian Islands of Attu and Kiska. The military occupied Unalaska Island, and you can visit their gun emplacements and observation posts. Contact the Unalaska/Port of Dutch Harbor Convention and Visitors Bureau, PO Box 545, Unalaska, AK 99685; 581-2612 or 877-581-2612.

Wrangell-Saint Elias National Park and Preserve — The 13.2-million-acre park covers the Wrangell Mountain range in eastern Alaska and the Saint Elias range along the Canadian border. It adjoins Kluane National Park in Yukon Territory. The Alaska Highway through Yukon Territory gives access to Kluane Lake (page 154). Park headquarters is at Mile 105.5 of the Old Richardson Highway in Copper Center (page 132). Access by road is via the Edgerton Highway to Chitina and McCarthy (page 137), and by the Nabesna Road off the Tok Cutoff (page 188). Superintendent, PO Box 439, Copper Center, AK 99573; 822-5234; web site *www.nps.gov/wrst*.

Yukon-Charley River National Preserve — The 2.5-million acre preserve is located along and to the south of the Yukon River above Circle and below Eagle and encompassing the Charley River drainage in eastern interior Alaska. It is excellent for wilderness birding and for fishing for Arctic Grayling. Access is from Eagle or Circle by floatplane or water taxi. For more information contact the Superintendent, PO Box 167, Eagle, AK 99738; 547-2233; web site *www.nps.gov/yuch*.

Yukon Delta National Wildlife Refuge — The refuge covers several million acres of treeless wetland where the Yukon and Kuskokwim Rivers empty into the Bering Sea. Millions of ducks, geese, swans, and shorebirds nest here. The refuge also includes Nunivak Island, home to an introduced herd of Muskoxen. This is the heart of the Yupik Eskimo culture in Alaska. Access is by aircraft. For more information contact the Refuge Manager, PO Box 346, Bethel, AK 99559; 543-3151. There is a visitor center in Bethel.

Yukon Flats National Wildlife Refuge — The refuge contains wetland habitat along the Yukon River as it emerges from its confined channel in the mountains of eastern Alaska and Yukon Territory. Millions of ducks and geese breed here and reach one of the highest densities in the world. Access is by aircraft or riverboat. For more information contact the Refuge Manager, 101 12th Avenue, Room 264, Fairbanks, AK 99701; 456-0440.

APPENDIX C:

GAZETTEER AND ALASKA PRONUNCIATION GUIDE

Use the following list of names to locate places mentioned in the *Annotated List of the Birds of Alaska* and in the birding chapters of this guide. Many Alaskan place names are derived from Native languages such as Inupiaq and Athabascan or from the Russian. It is often difficult to know how to pronounce some of them, especially when asking for assistance. The following might help. Pronunciation is not given for common English names. Capitalized syllables indicate emphasis.

Adak - island in the Andreanof Island group of the central Aleutian Island chain: A-dak (A as in day; dak as in tack).
Afognak - island north of Kodiak Island: ah-FOG-nack.
Agattu - island in the Near Island group in the western Aleutian Island chain: A-gat-too (A as in cat).
Ahgeak - Zig-zag Road in Barrow: AH-gee-ahk (hard g).
Ahkovak - street in Barrow: AH-ko-vuck.
Ahtna - Native corporation in the Gulkana - Copper River area: AHT-na (aht as in caught).
Aialik - glacier and fjord in Kenai Fjords National Park: eye-AL-ick.
Akhiok - village on Kodiak Island: AUK-ee-auk.
Akutan - port and island in the eastern Aleutian Island chain: ACK-you-tan.
Alaganik - slough in Cordova: al-a-GAN-ick.
Alagnak - river on the Alaska Peninsula: a-LAG-nak or a-LUCK-nuk (closer to Native pronunciation).
Alaid Island - small island in the Semichi Islands at the western end of the Aleutian Island chain: a-LAID.
Alaska Range - continuation of the Rocky Mountain chain from Yukon Territory into and across interior Alaska and then south to the beginning of the Aleutian Island chain.
Alegnagik - village and lake in southwestern Alaska north of Dillingham: ALECK-na-gick.
Aleut - Native peoples of the Pribilof Islands and Aleutian Islands: AL-ee-oot.
Aleutian - island chain in southwestern Alaska: ah-LOO-shun.
Alitak - cape on Kodiak Island: AL-a-tack.
Allakaket - village on the Koyukuk River southwest of Bettles, west of the Dalton Highway: a-la-KACK-et.
Alutiiq - Native peoples of the Kodiak and Kachemak Bay areas: a-LOO-tick.
Alyeska - the road to Girdwood from the Seward Highway on Turnagain Arm, the mountain and ski resort there, and the name of the Trans-Alaska oil pipeline company: al-ee-YES-ka.
Amalga - birding trail near Juneau: a-MAL-ga.
Ambler - village on the Kobuk River.
Amchitka - island in the Rat Island group in the western Aleutian Island chain: am-CHIT-ka.
Amukta Island - small island at the western end of the eastern part of the Aleutian Island chain: a-MUCK-ta.

Anachlik - island in delta of the Colville River in north coastal Alaska: ah-NOCK-lick.
Anaktuvuk Pass - Nunamiut Eskimo village in the central Brooks Range: a-nuck-TOO-vuck .
Anchor Point - village on Cook Inlet on the southwestern side of the Kenai Peninsula, on the Sterling Highway north of Homer.
Anchorage - major city in southcoastal Alaska at the head of Cook Inlet.
Aniakchak - National Monument on the Alaska Peninsula: an-ee-ACK-chack.
Apayauk - street in Barrow: ap-ay-AUK.
Athabascan (also Athapascan) - Native Indians of Interior Alaska: ath-a-BASK-an.
Atka - island in the central Aleutian Island chain: AT-kah.
Attu - island in the Near Island group and the farthest west Aleutian Island: A-too (A as in after).
Augustine Island - island and volcano in western Cook Inlet.
Auke Bay - bay and village north of Juneau: AUK.
Baranof - island where Sitka is located: BARE-e-noff.
Barren Islands - a group of islands at the mouth of Cook Inlet in the northern Gulf of Alaska.
Barrow - Native community at Pt. Barrow on the Beaufort Sea in northern Alaska.
Barter Island - a small island in the northeast corner of Alaska, location of Kaktovik.
Beaufort Lagoon - lagoon at the border of northeastern Alaska with Yukon Territory, Canada.
Beaufort Sea - sea that runs across the north coast of Alaska, part of the Arctic Ocean.
Becharof - Wildlife Refuge and lake on the Alaska Peninsula: ba-CHAR-off
Bering River - major river draining the Wrangell-St. Elias range into the Gulf of Alaska.
Bering Sea - sea in western Alaska north of the Aleutian Island chain between Alaska and Russia.
Bethel - village in southwest Alaska on the Kuskokwim River.
Bettles - village in northern interior Alaska, west of the Dalton Highway, on the lower John River that forms the headwaters of the Koyukuk River.
Big Lake - lake north of Anchorage and Wasilla off the Parks Highway.
Birch Lake - lake south of Fairbanks and north of Delta Junction on the Richardson Highway.
Birnirk - ancient culture at Wales: beer-NEERK.
Bremner River - river feeding the Copper River from the east, draining the Wrangell-St. Elias Range.
Bristol Bay - bay in southwest Alaska, part of the Bering Sea, at the base of the Alaska Peninsula.
Brooks Range - range of mountains running east-west across northern Alaska separating the North Slope from the Interior.
Buldir - island in the Near Islands of the western Aleutian Island chain: bull-DEER.
Cakeeater - or Cake Eater - a road leading south to the gas wells in Barrow.
Camden Bay - bay west of Kaktovik in the Beaufort Sea in the northeast corner of Alaska, at the northern edge of the Arctic National Wildlife Refuge.
Canning River - river running north through the Arctic National Wildlife Refuge into Camden Bay.
Cape Douglas - cape at the southwestern end of the Seward Peninsula, south of Wales.
Cape Krusenstern - cape on the Chukchi Sea of northwest Alaska north of Kotzebue: CRUISE-en-stern.
Cape Lisburne - cape on the Chukchi Sea of northwest Alaska, north of Point Hope.
Cape Newenham - tip of a long peninsula into the Bering Sea forming the western boundary of Bristol Bay.
Cape Peirce - cape in Bristol Bay, just southeast of Cape Newenham.

Cape Prince of Wales - cape at the western tip of the Seward Peninsula, where Wales is located.

Cape Romanzof - cape into the Bering Sea in the Yukon-Kuskokwim Delta, where Hooper Bay is located.

Cape Seppings - cape in the Chukchi Sea north of Kivalina and south of Cape Thompson.

Cape Thompson - cape on the Chukchi Sea south of Cape Lisburne and Point Hope, north of Kotzebue.

Central - small community on the Steese Highway northeast of Fairbanks.

Chandalar - river and village on the south slope of the eastern Brooks Range: schan-de-LAR.

Chandler - river and lake on the north slope of the central Brooks Range: CHAND-ler.

Charley River - wild and scenic river draining the Yukon-Tanana Uplands in eastern Interior Alaska into the Yukon River.

Chatanika - river and village on the Steese Highway: chat-a-NEEK-a.

Chena - river that runs west from the Yukon-Tanana Uplands through Fairbanks into the Tanana River: CHEE-na.

Chernabura Island - small island in the southern Shumagin Islands, south of the Alaska Peninsula: churn-a BUR-ah.

Chevak - (and Old Chevak) - Native villages between Bethel and Hooper Bay: CHEE-vack.

Chichagof Island - large island in southeast Alaska, north of Sitka and south of Glacier Bay: CHICH-a goff.

Chickamin - river in Misty Fjords National Monument northeast of Ketchikan: CHICK-a-min

Chicken - village on the Taylor Highway, eastern interior Alaska.

Chignik - bay and village on the Alaska Peninsula: CHIG-nick.

Chilkat - river, state park, and trail near Haines and a pass on the Haines Highway: CHILL-cat.

Chilkoot - lake, river, and trail in Haines and a pass on the Klondike Highway and gold trail: CHILL-koot.

Chiniak - bay, lake, cape, and road on Kodiak Island: CHIN-ee-ack.

Chisik - island in upper western Cook Inlet: CHIZ.-ick.

Chistochina - village on the Tok Cutoff: chis-toe-CHEE-na.

Chiswell Islands - island group at the southwestern edge of Resurrection Bay out of Seward.

Chitina - village on the Copper River on the Edgerton Highway: CHIT-na.

Choggiung - Native Corporation at Dillingham: CHOG-ee-ong (Both Os as in own)

Chugach - mountains, state park, and village east of Anchorage: CHOO-gatch.

Chugachik - island in upper Kachemak Bay: CHOO-ga-chick.

Chugiak - village on the Glenn Highway near Anchorage: CHEW-gi-ack.

Chukchi Sea- sea in northwestern Alaska between Alaska and Russia: CHUCK-chee.

Chulitna - river running south along the Parks Highway from the Alaska Range to the Susitna River: chew-LIT-na.

Circle - village on the Yukon River at the terminus of the Steese Highway (south of the Arctic Circle).

Cohoe - village on the Kenai Peninsula south of Soldotna on Cook Inlet: KOH-hoe.

Cold Bay - village on the western end of the Alaska Peninsula on Izembek Lagoon.

Colville - river running from the north slope of the Brooks Range to the Beaufort Sea.

Commander Islands - Russian island group west of the Aleutian Island chain, off Kamchatka.

Cook Inlet - arm of the Gulf of Alaska stretching north to Anchorage.

Cooper Landing - community on the Sterling Highway at the western end of Kenai Lake.

Copper Center - village on the Richardson Highway south of Glennallen and north of Valdez.

Copper River - major river draining the Wrangell-St. Elias Mountains to the Gulf of Alaska east of Cordova.

Cordova - community in western Prince William Sound in southcoastal Alaska.

Coronation Islands - islands south of Baranof Island in southeast Alaska.

Craig - village on the western shore of Prince of Wales Island in southeast Alaska, south of Klawock.

Dalton - highway (haul road) that runs from the Elliott Highway north to Deadhorse (Prudhoe Bay).

Deadhorse - community at the northern end of the Dalton Highway, south of Prudhoe Bay in northern Alaska.

Delta (also Delta Junction) - community in interior Alaska where the Alaska Highway from Canada joins the Richardson Highway.

Demarcation Point - point into the Beaufort Sea at the far northeastern corner of Alaska at the Canadian border.

Dena'ina - Native Indians of the Kenai Peninsula: de-NEYE-nah.

Denali - national park and highway in interior Alaska: de-NA-lee.

Dillingham - community on the Nushugak River that runs into Bristol Bay.

Dixon Harbor - inlet on the western shore of Glacier Bay National Park, on the Gulf of Alaska.

Dot Lake - small community on the Alaska Highway between Delta and Tok.

Douglas - island across Gastineau Channel from Juneau and cape and mountain on the western shore of the entrance to Cook Inlet.

Dutch Harbor - village on Unalaska Island, western terminus of the ferry *Tustumena* route.

Dyea - old village site near Skagway: DIE-ee.

Eagle - community on the Yukon River near the Canadian border at the north end of the Taylor Highway.

Eagle Summit - one high point with alpine tundra on the Steese Highway east of Fairbanks.

Edgecumbe - mountain and college in Sitka: Edge-come.

Edgerton - highway running from the Richardson Highway to Chitina and McCarthy.

Egegik - village and river on Bristol Bay on the western side of the Alaska Peninsula: EE-ga-gick

Eielson - Air Force base south of Fairbanks on the Richardson Highway: AISLE-son.

Eklutna - Native village east of Anchorage on the Glenn Highway: ee-KLOOT-na.

Elias Island - Pinnacle Rock island at the southern tip of Kayak Island southeast of Cordova.

Elliott Highway - highway that runs from the Steese Highway in Fox to Manley.

Emaiksoun - Fresh water lake south of Barrow: (Imaiqsaun) ee-MAH-k-sown.

Endicott Mountains - mountains of the central Brooks Range west of the Dalton Highway.

Ester - village on the Parks Highway west of Fairbanks.

Eureka - small community off the Elliott Highway and a summit on the Glenn Highway between Anchorage and Glennallen.

Eyak - lake and name of Native people in Cordova: EE-yak.

Fairbanks - major city of interior Alaska at the confluence of the Chena and Tanana Rivers, and the Parks, Richardson and Steese Highways.

Fairweather Grounds - rise in the sea floor off Fairweather Point and Glacier in the Gulf of Alaska west of Glacier Bay.

False Pass - narrow waterway separating the end of the Alaska Peninsula from Unimak Island.

Forrester - island west of Dall Island in the southernmost part of southeastern Alaska.

Fort Yukon - village on the Yukon River at the junction of the Porcupine River in eastern Interior Alaska.

Gakona - village on the Richardson Highway and junction with the Tok Cutoff: ga-CONE-a.

Gambell - village on St. Lawrence Island in the northern Bering Sea: GAM-ble.

Gareloi Island - volcanic island in the Andreanof Islands in the central Aleutian Island chain: GAR-eh-loy.

Gastineau - ocean channel between Douglas Island and Juneau: GAS-tin-oh.

George Lake - lake east of the Tanana River along the Alaska Highway southeast of Delta Junction.

George Parks Highway - highway that runs from Anchorage to Fairbanks past Denali National Park.

Girdwood - community on the Alyeska Road off the Seward Highway southeast of Anchorage.

Glacier Bay - National Park in northern southeast Alaska.

Glennallen - community at the junction of the Richardson Highway and the Glenn Highway.

Glenn - highway that runs from Anchorage to Glennallen on the Richardson Highway.

Gold Hill - area in the Nutzotin Mountains near Nabesna.

Golovin - village on the southern coast of the Seward Peninsula, on Norton Sound: GAUL-oh-vin.

Govorushka - lake on St. George Island, Pribilof Islands: go-ver-OOSH-kah.

Gravina Island - island across Tongass Narrows and west of Ketchikan: gra-VEEN-a.

Grewingk - glacier from the Harding Ice Field on the south side of Kachemak Bay: GRE-wink.

Gulkana - town and river on the Richardson Highway near the junction of the Tok Cutoff: gull-CA-na (CA as in can).

Gustavus - village at the southeastern end of Glacier Bay National Park: gus-TAVE-us.

Haines - community at the northern end of the Lynn Canal in southeast Alaska, also the highway running from Haines to Haines Junction in Yukon Territory.

Hall Island - small island north of St. Matthew Island in the east central Bering Sea.

Harding Lake - lake and recreation area on the Richardson Highway south of Fairbanks.

Hazy Islands - small island group in the Pacific Ocean west of Prince of Wales Island in southeast Alaska.

Healy - village on the Parks Highway north of Denali National Park.

Hinchinbrook Island - island bordering the southeastern reach of Prince William Sound from the Gulf of Alaska.

Holgate - glacier and fjord in Kenai Fjords National Park out of Seward.

Homer - town in the southern Kenai Peninsula, on Kachemak Bay, at the end of the Sterling Highway.

Hoonah - village at the northern tip of Chichagof Island on Icy Strait, southeast of Glacier Bay National Park: HOO-nah.

Hooper Bay - village on the Bering Sea at the far western extent of the Yukon-Kuskokwim Delta in southwestern Alaska.

Hyder - community at the head of the Portland Canal on the Alaska-Canada border accessed from the Cassiar Highway.

Icy Cape - point of land on the Chukchi Sea in northwestern Alaska south of Wainwright.

Iditarod - dog sled race and village on the Yukon River: eye-DIT-a-rod.

Ikoravik - lake and road in Barrow: i-CORE-a-vick.

Iliamna - large lake near the base of the Alaska Peninsula: ill-ee-AM-na.
Ilisagvik - college in Barrow: ee-lee-SARGH-vick.
Imikpuk - lake in Barrow: im-ICK-puck
Inuit - Eskimo people of northern Alaska (also Inupiat):IN-oo-it.
Inupiaq - language of the Inupiat people: in-NOO-pee-ack.
Inupiat - Eskimo people of the North Slope: in-NOO-pee-at.
Isatkoak - street in Barrow: (Isatkuaq) - ee-SAHT-kwaaq.
Izembek - bay and refuge on the Bering Sea near Cold Bay on the Alaska Peninsula: EYE-zem-beck.
Jakolof - a small bay on the south side of Kachemak Bay: JACK-o-loff.
Japonski - island in Sitka harbor: ja-PON-ski.
Juneau - capitol of Alaska, city in southeast Alaska: JUNE-oh.
Kachemach - river tributary of the Colville River near its mouth: CATCH-e-mach.
Kachemak - bay on the east side of Cook Inlet on the Kenai Peninsula: CATCH-e-mack.
Kake - village on Kupreanof Island north of Petersburg and east of Sitka: CAKE.
Kaktovik - Native village on Barter Island in the northeastern corner of Alaska: kak-TOE-vick
Kalifornsky - (sometimes Kalifonsky) road out of Kenai-Soldotna: cal-i-FORN-ski.
Kalsin - bay on Kodiak Island: CAL-sin (Cal as in California).
Kamchatka - Russian peninsula on the Bering Sea: cam-CHAT-ka.
Kamishak Bay - bay on the western side of Cook Inlet inside of Augustine Island: KAM-i-shack
Kandik - river flowing southwest out of Yukon Territory into the Yukon River.
Kantishna - village at the western end of the Denali National Park Road: can-TISH-na.
Kanuti - National Wildlife Refuge in interior Alaska: ca-NOO-tee.
Kasilof - village on the Sterling Highway south of Soldotna: ka-SEE-loff.
Kasitsna - a small bay on the south side of Kachemak Bay: ka-SITS-na.
Katlian - street in Sitka: CAT-li-ann.
Katmai - National Park on the Alaska Peninsula: CAT-my.
Kayak - island in the Gulf of Alaska southeast of the Copper River Delta: like the boat.
Kelgaya - mountain range near Haines: kell-GAI-ya.
Kelsall River - river running south into the Chilkat River near Haines, Alaska.
Kenai - peninsula, mountain range, lake, and town in southcoastal Alaska: KEE-neye.
Kenai Fjords - National Park in western Resurrection Bay out of Seward, Alaska.
Kenai Mountains - mountain chain running north-south through the Kenai Peninsula.
Kenny Lake - small lake at the junction of the new and old Edgerton Highway.
Kennicott - name of the ferry that runs from Juneau to Seward across the Gulf of Alaska, and name of an abandoned copper mine at the end of the Edgerton Highway.
Ketchikan - community on Revillagigedo Island in southeast Alaska.
Killik River - river flowing north out of the central Brooks Range to the Colville River.
King Island - small island in the Bering Sea south of Wales and west of Cape Douglas on the Seward Peninsula.
King Salmon - community on the Alaska Peninsula.
Kingikmiut - whaling culture at Wales on the Seward Peninsula: KING-mute.
Kiska- island in the Rat Island group in the western Aleutian Island chain: KISS-ka.
Kivalina - Native village on the northwestern coast of the Chukchi Sea, north of Cape Krusenstern and south of Cape Seppings: kee-va-LEE-na.
Klawock - village on the western shore of Prince of Wales Island north of Craig: cla-WOCK.
Klehini River - river paralleling the Haines Highway draining the St. Elias Mountains into the Chilkat River near Haines: kle-HEEN-ee.
Kluktoo - Tlingit tribal village near Haines: KLUK-tu.

Klukwan - Tlingit tribal village near Haines: KLUK-wan.
Knik - river, arm, and glacier east of Anchorage on the Glenn Highway: k-NIK (sound both Ks).
Kobuk - village and river in northwestern Alaska: KO-buck.
Kodiak - island and town in southcoastal Alaska: KOH-di-ak.
Koniuji Island - small island west of Atka in the eastern Aleutian Islands: con-OO-gee (soft g).
Kotzebue - town in northwestern Alaska: KOTS-a-bew.
Kougarok - road leading out of Nome: KOO-ga-rock.
Koyuk - river flowing west into Norton Bay, an inlet of Norton Sound: COY-uk.
Koyukuk - river (southward flowing tributary of the Yukon River) and village in interior Alaska: COY-you-kuck.
Kukpowruk - river in northwestern Alaska flowing into the Chukchi Sea near Point Lay: kuck-POW-ruck.
Kuskokwim - major river in western Alaska flowing into the Bering Sea: KUSS-ko-quim.
Kvichak - river flowing into Bristol Bay: KVEE-chack (sound both the K and V) or QUE-chack.
Little Diomede Island - U. S. owned island (Big Diomede is Russian owned) in the Bering Sea off the western tip of the Seward Peninsula: DYE-oh-meed.
Little Port Walter - port at the southeastern tip of Baranof Island south of Sitka.
Lituya Bay - bay on the Gulf of Alaska on the western boundary of Glacier Bay National Park: li-TOO-yah.
Lowrie Island - small island north of Forrester Island west of Dall Island in the southernmost part of southeast Alaska.
Manley - village and hot springs at the western end of the Elliott Highway.
Marunich - birding location on St. Paul Island: mah-ROO-nick.
Matanuska - glacier and river on the Glenn Highway east of Palmer: mat-a-NOOS-ka.
Mayoeak - small river about eight miles south of Barrow: (Mayugiaq) - my-YOU-reeaq.
Meade River - small village south of Barrow.
Medvejie - fish hatchery in Sika (Russian=Bear Cove): MED-ve-chee.
Mentasta - pass on the Tok Cutoff: men-TASS-ta.
Middleton - island in the Gulf of Alaska south of Cordova.
Minchumina - village west of Denali National Park and north of Kantishna: min-CHEW-mi-na.
Mineral Lake - small lake on the Tok Cutoff along the Little Tok River.
Minto - Native village and flats on the Tanana River north of Fairbanks: MIN-toe.
Mitkof - island on which Petersburg is located: MITT-cough.
Monashka - bay on Kodiak Island: moan-ASH-kah.
Montague - strait and island bordering the southwestern reach of Prince William Sound from the Gulf of Alaska.
Mountain Village - village on the lower Yukon River in southwestern Alaska.
Nabesna - village at the end of the Nabesna Road south of the Alaska Highway: na-BEZ-nah.
Nahku - bay near Skagway: NA-koo - also known as "Long Bay."
Naknek - village on the Alaska Peninsula: KNACK-neck.
Nanwalek - Native village on Cook Inlet: nan-WALL-eck - formerly known as "English Bay."
Nelson Island - island in the southwestern part of the Yukon-Kuskokwim Delta on the Bering Sea in southwestern Alaska.
Nelson Lagoon - lagoon near Port Moller on the Bering Sea at the southwestern end of the Alaska Peninsula.
Nenana - village and river flowing north by Denali National Park to the Tanana River: knee-NA-na (NA as in gnat).

Nikiski - town on Cook Inlet north of Kenai: ni-KISS-ki (also pronounced ni-KISH-ka).
Ninilchik - town north of Homer and Anchor Point on the Kenai Peninsula: nin-NIL-chick.
Nizki Island - small island in the Semichi Islands in the Near Island group at the western end of the Aleutian Island chain: NIZZ-ki.
Noatak - river and village in northwestern Alaska: NO-a-tack.
Nome - community on the Seward Peninsula on the northern Bering Sea.
Noorvik - Native village on the Kobuk River east of Kotzebue: NOOR-vick.
North Slope - the area in northern Alaska from the crest of the Brooks Range north to the Beaufort Sea..
Northway - community south of the Alaska Highway between the Canadian border and Tok.
Norton Sound - part of the Bering Sea below the Seward Peninsula.
Novarupta - volcano on the Alaska Peninsula: Nova RUP-ta (two words).
Novastoshna - area at the northeast point of St. Paul Island, Pribilof Islands: nov-a-STOSH-na.
Nowitna - National Wildlife Refuge in western interior Alaska: no-WIT-na.
Nulato - Native village on the Yukon River just below the junction of the Koyukuk River: new-LA-toe (LA as in lad).
Nunavak - road in Barrow: NOO-na-vack.
Nunavaugaluk - lake near Dillingham: new-na-VOW-ga-luck.
Nunamiut - Eskimo people living in the central Brooks Range: NOON-a-mute.
Nunivak - large island in the Bering Sea off Nelson Island in the southwestern corner of the Yukon-Kuskokwim Delta: NOO-ni-vack.
Nushagak - river, peninsula, and bay on Bristol Bay: NOO-sha-gack.
Nutzotin - mountain range east of Nabesna in eastern interior Alaska: nut-ZO-tin.
Odiak - slough in Cordova: OH-dee-ack.
Old Chevak - see Chevak.
Oliktok Point - point into the Beaufort Sea east of the Colville River Delta in northern Alaska: oh-LICK-tock.
Palmer - town on the Glenn Highway northeast of Anchorage.
Pamplona Spur - rising of the sea floor in the Gulf of Alaska between Yakutat and Kayak Island.
Panguinque - creek on the Parks Highway near Healy: pan-GWIN-kay.
Pasagshak - bay on Kodiak Island: pa-SAG-shack.
Paug'vik - Native corporation at Naknek: PAU-vik.
Paxson - community and lake on the Richardson Highway at the junction of the Denali Highway.
Pennock Island - small island south of Ketchikan in the Tongass Narrows between Revillagigedo and Gravina Islands.
Petersburg - town on Mitkof Island in southeastern Alaska, north of Wrangell and south of Sitka.
Petersville - road and community off the George Parks Highway.
Petropavlovsk - Russian village on the Kamchatka Peninsula: petro-pav-LOVSK.
Pigniq - Native shooting station at Point Barrow: PIRGH-nick
Pingo - small hill caused by frost heaves in tundra: PING-oh:
Pisokak - street in Barrow: (Pisukkaaq) - pee-SOO-kaaq:
Pogibshi - point at the southwest corner of Kachemak Bay on Cook Inlet: po-GIB-shi.
Point Hope - village and point into the Chukchi Sea between Cape Thompson and Cape Lisburne.
Point Lay - village and point into the Chukchi Sea between Icy Cape and Cape Listburne.
Polovina - lake on St. Paul Island, Pribilof Islands: pol-o-VEEN-a.

Porcupine Lake - small lake at the crest of the Brooks Range northwest of Arctic Village in the Arctic National Wildlife Refuge.

Porcupine River - large river running west from Yukon Territory into the Yukon River at Fort Yukon.

Port Dick - bay on the south coast of the Kenai Peninsula into the Gulf of Alaska.

Port Moller - village and bay on the Bering Sea at the southern end of the Alaska Peninsula.

Portage - community on the Seward Highway at the eastern end of Turnagain Arm, road that leads to Portage Lake and Whittier, and glacier.

Portland Canal - long salt-water canal running northeast along the Alaska-Canada border in southeast Alaska that terminates in Hyder, Alaska.

Potter Marsh - wetland on the Seward Highway south of Anchorage.

Pribilof - islands (St. George, St. Paul, Otter, and Walrus Island) in the southern Bering Sea: PRIB-i-loff.

Prince of Wales - large island situated on the Canadian border and running north in southeast Alaska.

Prince William Sound - inlet to the Gulf of Alaska between Cordova and the Kenai Peninsula.

Prudhoe Bay - bay on the Beaufort Sea in northern Alaska, beginning of the Trans-Alaska oil pipeline.

Qaiyaan - street in Barrow: Q-EYE-yawn.

Quartz Lake - lake east of the Richardson Highway north of Delta Junction.

Rat Islands - island group at the western end of the central Aleutian Island chain.

Redoubt - volcanic mountain on the western shore of Cook Inlet across from Kenai.

Resurrection Bay - bay from the Gulf of Alaska headed by Seward on the Kenai Peninsula.

Revilla - road in Ketchikan: ruh-VILL-a (Spanish word pronounced in American English).

Revillagigedo - Island where Ketchikan is located in southeast Alaska: Ruh-VILLA-gi-GAY-doh (Spanish word pronounced in American English).

Rezanof - road on Kodiak Island: REZ-an-off.

Richardson - highway that runs from Valdez on Prince Williams Sound north to Fairbanks.

Ripinsky - mountain near Haines: ri-PIN-ski.

Safety - sound, lagoon, and port east of Nome.

Sagavanirktok - river on the North Slope leading from the Brooks Range into the Beaufort Sea, also parallels the Dalton Highway: sag-a-va-NIRK-tock.

Salcha - river on the Richardson Highway south of Fairbanks: SAUL-cha.

Sanak - island group south of Cold Bay at the southwestern end of the Alaska Peninsula: SAN-ack.

Savoonga - Native village on St. Lawrence Island: sa-VOON- ga.

Scottie Creek - creek running through flats at the Alaska-Canada border on the Alaska Highway.

Seal Rocks - small islands south of Hinchinbrook Entrance (to Prince William Sound and Valdez) between Hinchinbrook and Montague Islands.

Selawik - village and refuge southeast of Kotzebue in northwestern Alaska: SELL-a-wick.

Seldovia - Native village and bay on the south side of Kachemak Bay: sell-DOUGH-vee-a.

Semidi Islands - island group southwest of Kodiak Island and east of the Alaska Peninsula: sem-EE-dee.

Sevuokuk - Siberian Yupik name for Gambell, the mountain that rises above the village, and St. Lawrence Island: SE-voo-cook (Se as in settle) The Native spelling is: Sivuqaq.

Seward - city at the head of Resurrection Bay on the Kenai Peninsula.

Seward Peninsula - peninsula into the Bering Sea in western Alaska.

Sheenjek - river running south from the Arctic National Wildlife Refuge to the Porcupine River: SHEEN-jack.

Shelikof - straits west of Kodiak Island: SHELL-i-cough.

Shemya - small island in the Semichi Islands in the Near Island group at the western end of the Aleutian Island chain: SHEM-ya.

Shishmaref - Native village on the northern Seward Peninsula: SHISH-ma-reff.

Shumagin - islands south of the southwestern end of the Alaska Peninsula: SHOE-ma-gin (the g is hard).

Shuyak - island north of Kodiak and Afognak Islands: SHOE-yack.

Sitka - city on Baranof Island in southeastern Alaska: SIT-ka.

Sitnasuak - Native Corporation at Nome: SIT-na-sock.

Situk - lake and river running into the Gulf of Alaska southeast of Yakutat: SIT-uck.

Skagway - community northeast of Haines in southeast Alaska and start of the Klondike Highway that runs from Skagway north to the Alaska Highway east of Whitehorse, YT.

Skilak - lake on the central Kenai Peninsula: SKEE-lack.

Soldotna - town on the northwestern Kenai Peninsula: soul-DOT-na.

Spurr - volcanic mountain on northern Cook Inlet west of Anchorage.

Saint George - village and the southern island in the Pribilof Island group.

Saint Lawrence - island in the northern Bering Sea southwest of Nome.

Saint Lazaria - island in southwestern Sitka Sound.

Saint Marys - village on the lower Yukon River near Mountain Village.

Saint Matthew - small island in the central Bering Sea.

Saint Michael - village on the south shore of Norton Sound south of Unalakleet and north of the Yukon-Kuskokwim Delta.

Saint Paul - village and the northern island in the Pribilof Island group.

Starrigavan - recreation area north of Sitka: STAR-i-ga-van or STAR-ga-van.

Steese - highway that runs from Fairbanks east to Circle on the Yukon River.

Stewart - community adjacent to Hyder in British Columbia.

Sterling - community on the Sterling Highway east of Soldotna in the central Kenai Peninsula.

Stikine - major river out of British Columbia and flowing southeast between Petersburg and Wrangell: sti-KEEN.

Susitna - major river into Cook Inlet northwest of Anchorage: soo-SIT-na.

Swanson River - river and road on the northern Kenai Peninsula north of Sterling.

Tahneta - pass on the Glenn Highway separating drainage into Cook Inlet and Prince William Sound: ta-NAY-ta.

Taiya - river and inlet near Haines: TIE-ya.

Takshanuk - mountain range near Haines: TALK-chin-ook.

Taku - river and inlet east of Juneau: TAH-koo.

Talkeetna - community on the Parks Highway north of Wasilla on the Chulitna River: Tal-KEET-na (tal as in gal).

Tanacross - village and old air field on the Alaska Highway: TA-na-cross (TA as in tan).

Tanana - village at the junction of the Tanana and Yukon River and the major river through interior Alaska south of Fairbanks: TA-na-naw.

Taylor - highway that runs from the Alaska Highway near Northway north to Eagle on the Yukon River.

Teller - community at the end of the Teller Road out of Nome.

Teshekpuk - large lake southeast of Barrow: te-SHECK-puck.

Tetlin - National Wildlife Refuge and Native Indian culture on the Alaska Highway: TET-lin.

Tlingit - Native peoples of southeast Alaska: KLING-it.

Togiak - village and refuge in southwestern Alaska west of Dillingham: TOE-gi-yak (the g is hard).
Tok (also Tok Junction) - town on the Alaska Highway: TOAK (as in coke).
Toklat - river from the Alaska Range that runs north through Denali National Park to the Tanana River: TOE-klat.
Tolovana - river running southwest from the Yukon-Tanana Uplands across the Elliott Highway into the Minto flats and Tanana River: toe-la-VA-na (VA as in van).
Tongass - National Forest and waterway near Ketchikan: TONG-us.
Tonki - point on St. Paul Island, Pribilof Islands: TON-kee.
Tustumena - name of an Alaska ferry and large lake on the Kenai Peninsula: tuss-too-MEE-na.
Tutka Bay - fjord running north into the south side of Kachemak Bay: TUT-ka.
Ugak - bay and island on the east side of Kodiak Island: YOU-gack.
Ugashik - bay on Bristol Bay, river and lake on the Alaska Peninsula: oo-GASH-ick.
Ukpeagvik - Barrow Native Village Corporation: ook-PEARGH-vick
Ulakaia - ridge on St. George Island, Pribilof Islands: yoo-la-KAI-ah.
Umiaq - Native-made walrus or seal skin whaling boat: OO-mee-ack.
Umiat - abandoned village on the Colville River on the north slope of Alaska: OO-mee-at.
Umnak- island in the Fox Islands of the eastern Aleutian Island chain: UM-nak (U pronounced as in hum).
Unalakleet - village on the eastern shore of Norton Sound: OON-a-la-kleet.
Unalaska - island and village in the Fox Islands and the farthest east of the Aleutian Island chain: un-ALAS-ka.
Unimak - island and pass in the near Aleutian Islands: OO-ni-mack.
Unuk - river flowing south from British Columbia into Burrough's Bay in Misty Fjords National Monument: OO-nuck.
Utukok - river flowing into the Chukchi Sea between Icy Cape and Point Lay in northwestern Alaska: OO-te-cock.
Valdez - town at the southern end of the Richardson Highway, terminus of the TransAlaska oil pipeline on Prince William Sound: val-DEEZE.
Villard - mountain near Haines: vil-ARD.
Wainwright - village on the coast of the Chukchi Sea southwest of Point Barrow and north of Icy Cape in northwest Alaska.
Wales - Native community on the Seward Peninsula on the Bering Sea coast.
Wasilla - town north of Anchorage at the southern end of the Parks Highway: wah-SILL-a.
Willow - community on the Parks Highway north of Wasilla.
Wrangell - community at the tip of Wrangell Island in southeast Alaska north of Ketchikan and south of Petersburg. Wrangell-St. Elias is a National Park on the Canada border, southcentral Alaska.
Yakutat - village on the northern Gulf of Alaska at the southeastern edge of Yakutat Bay: YAK-eh-tat.
Yandukin - road in Juneau: yan-DOO-kin.
Yugit - street in Barrow: YOU-git.
Yukon River - major river running from southern Yukon Territory through Alaska to the Bering Sea: YOU-kon.
Yupik - Native Eskimos of the Alaska Peninsula and inner Aleutian Islands: YOU-pick.
Zapadnie (also Zapadni) - cliffs on St. Paul Island: zah-POD-nee or ZAP-add-nee.

ACKNOWLEDGEMENTS Pronunciation of many Native names were provided by Dr. James Kari and Dr. Larry Kaplan, Alaska Native Language Center, University of Alaska Fairbanks. Assistance from many of the chapter authors is also appreciated.

APPENDIX D:

REFERENCES AND SELECTED READING

Alaska Public Lands Information Center. 2000. Steese and Elliott Highways travel guide. *Discover Alaska's Interior.* BLM Fairbanks Office and Alaska Natural History Association. Fold-out map and brochure.

Alban, J., and J. Alban. 2000. Birding Trip to Alaska. *Kachemak Bay Bird Watch* 39:1–5.

American Ornithologists' Union. 1998. *Check-list of North American Birds.* 7th edition. American Ornithologists' Union, Washington, DC. liv + 829pp.

Andres, B.A., D.L. Brann, and B.T. Browne. 1999. *Inventory of Breeding Birds on Local Training Area of the Alaska Army National Guard.* U.S. Fish and Wildlife Service, Anchorage, AK. 104pp.

Armstrong, R., and R. Gordon. 1995. *Finding Birds in Juneau.* U.S.D.A. Forest Service, Juneau, AK. 80pp.

Armstrong, R.H. 1995. *Guide to the Birds of Alaska.* 4th edition. Alaska Northwest Books, Anchorage, AK. 322pp.

Audubon Alaska. 2002. *Alaska WatchList.* Audubon Alaska, 308 G Street, Suite 217, Anchorage, AK 99501. 8-page fold-out.

Bailey, A.M. 1948. *Birds of Arctic Alaska.* Colorado Museum of Natural History, Popular Series 8. 317pp.

Balch, L.G. 1980. Mystery Bird of the North: The Gray-headed Chickadee. *Birding* 12:126–131.

_____. 1980. The Identification and Status of Asian Species in Alaska. *Birding* 12:12–22.

Bee, J.W., and E.R. Hall. 1956. *Mammals of Northern Alaska.* University of Kansas, Misc. Publ. 8. 309pp.

Benson, A.-M., T.H. Pogson, and T.J. Doyle. 2000. Updated Geographic Distribution of Eight Passerine Species in Central Alaska. *Western Birds* 31:100–105.

Brown, J., and R.A. Kreig. 1983. *Guidebook to Permafrost and Related Features along the Elliott and Dalton Highways, Fox to Prudhoe Bay, Alaska.* Guidebook 4, Division of Geological & Geophysical Surveys, Department of Natural Resources, State of Alaska. 230pp.

Brown, T., and C. Ward. 1999. *Birding the Kenai National Wildlife Refuge.* Alaska Natural History Association, Anchorage, AK. 29pp. Habitat, trail, and bird checklist information.

Bureau of Land Management. 2000. *Discover the Dalton.* BLM, 1150 University Avenue, Fairbanks, AK 99709. 24pp. Maps and information on driving the Dalton Highway.

Burns, J. 1999. Attu Island – Closing the Circle. *Kachemak Bay Bird Watch* 38:1–2.

Burt, W.H., and R.P. Grossenheider. 1952. *A Field Guide to the Mammals.* Houghton Mifflin Co, Boston, MA. xxiii+200pp.

Carley, F.L. 1988. Finding Siberian Tits. *Birding* 20:164.

Chandler, B.W., and B.W. Chandler. 2000. Birding St. Lawrence Island. *Kachemak Bay Bird Watch* 41:1–2.

Clements, J.F. 2000. *Birds of the World: A Checklist.* Ibis Publishing Co, Vista, CA. xx + 867pp.

Cole, J. 2000. Taking a Gamble on Gambell. *Kachemak Bay Bird Watch* 41:3–5.

Cooper, J.A. 1995. Chapter 11, Alaska, *in Birdfinder: A Birder's Guide to Planning North American Trips.* American Birding Association, Colorado Springs, CO. pp. 148–167.

Crabtree, C.S. 1992. Birding the "Other" Aleutians. *Birding* 24:328–333.

Creer-Harris, L. 2000. Birding the Nome Area. *Birding* 32:30–43.

Davidson, W.S. 1986. Further Notes on The Mystery Bird [Gray-headed Chickadee]. *Birding* 18:215–219.

DeLorme Mapping. 2001. *Alaska Atlas and Gazetteer.* 4th edition. DeLorme Mapping, Freeport, ME. 156pp.

Dickerman, R.W., K. Winker, and D.D. Gibson. 1998. Sooty Tern Reaches the Aleutian Islands, Alaska. *Western Birds* 29:122–123.

Doyle, T.J. 1997. The Timberline Sparrow, *Spizella (breweri) taverneri*, in Alaska, with notes on breeding habitat and vocalizations. *Western Birds* 28:1–12.

Eckert, C.D. 2001. *Ten Great Places to go Birding in Whitehorse*. Yukon Bird Club, Whitehorse, YT. Pamphlet.

Eckert, C.D., H. Groenberg, G. Kubica, L. Kubica, and P. Sinclair. 2001. *Checklist of Yukon Birds*. Yukon Bird Club, Canadian Wildlife Service, Yukon Renewable Resources, Whitehorse, YT. Pamphlet.

_____. 1995. *A Checklist of the Birds of Whitehorse, Yukon*. Yukon Bird Club. Whitehorse, YT. Pamphlet.

Emanuel, R.P., and G. Matz. 2001. *Exploring Alaska's Birds*. Alaska Geographic, Anchorage, Alaska. 96pp.

Eschmeyer, W.N., E.S. Herald, and H. Hammann. 1983. *A Field Guide to Pacific Coast Fishes of North America*. Houghton Mifflin Co., Boston, MA. xiii+336 pp.

Ferren, R.L. 1998. Trip on the Inside Passage of British Columbia and Southeast Alaska. *Kachemak Bay Bird Watch* 32:8–13.

Finlay, J.C. 2000. *A Bird-Finding Guide to Canada*, Revised Edition. McClelland & Stewart Inc., Toronto, ON. 449pp.

Fox, D., and C. Maack. 1996. Summer Field Trip to Hyder, Alaska. *Kachemak Bay Bird Watch* 28:6.

Frisch, R. 1987. *Birds by the Dempster Highway*. Revised edition. Morriss Printing Co. Ltd., Victoria. BC. 98pp.

Gabrielson, I.N., and F.C. Lincoln. 1959. *The Birds of Alaska*. Stackpole Co., Harrisburg, PA, and the Wildlife Management Institute, Washington, DC. xiii + 922 pp.

Gibson, D.D. 1997. Inventory of the Species and Subspecies of Alaska Birds. *Western Birds* 28:45–95.

_____. 1999. *Checklist of Alaska Birds*. 9th edition. University of Alaska Museum, Fairbanks, AK.

Gibson, D.D., and B. Kessel. 1992. Seventy-four new avian taxa documented in Alaska, 1976–1991. *Condor* 94:454–467.

Gill, R.E., B.J. McCaffery, and T.G. Tobish. 1988. Bristle-thighed Curlews, Biologists and Bird Tours – A Place for All. *Birding* 20:148–155.

Graef, K.V. (Editor). 2000. *The Milepost*. Morris Communications Corp., Augusta, GA. 768pp.

Groenberg, H. 1994. *Birds of Swan Lake, Yukon*. Keyline Graphics. Whitehorse, YT. 137pp.

Guppy, C.S., and J.H. Shepard. 2001. *The Butterflies of British Columbia*. University of British Columbia Press. 414pp.

Haworth, H.W. 1996. Whiskered Auklets Revisited. *Birding* 28:100–101.

Hill, D.O. 1972. Birding in the Pribilof Islands. *Birding* 4:2–5.

Hultén, E. 1968. *Flora of Alaska and Neighboring Territories*. Stanford University Press, CA. xxii + 997pp.

Irving, L. 1960. *Birds of Anaktuvuk Pass, Kobuk, and Old Crow*. U.S. National Museum Bull. 217. viii + 409pp.

Isleib, M.I. 1993. Birds of Forrester Islands National Wildlife Refuge. *Kachemak Bay Bird Watch* 15:1–5.

Isleib, M.I., and B. Kessel. 1973. Birds of the North Gulf Coast – Prince William Sound Region, Alaska. Biol. Papers U. of Alaska No. 14. 149pp.

Jarrell, G.H., S.O. MacDonald, and J.A. Cook. 2001. Checklist to the Mammals of Alaska. University of Alaska Museum web site — *www.uaf.edu/museum/mammal/AK_Mammals/Checklist.html*.

Johnson, H. 2000. Shorebirding on the North Slope. *Kachemak Bay Bird Watch* 41:5–6.

Johnson, S.R., and D.R. Herter. 1989. *The Birds of the Beaufort Sea*. British Petroleum Exploration, Environmental and Regulatory Affairs, Anchorage, AK.

Kari, P.R. 1987. *Tanaina Plantlore (Dena'ina K'et'una)*. National Park Service, Anchorage, AK. xi + 205pp.

Kertell, K,, and A. Seegert. 1984. *Bird-Finding Guide to Denali National Park*. Alaska Natural History Association, Anchorage, AK. 32pp.

Kessel, B. 1989. *Birds of the Seward Peninsula, Alaska*. University of Alaska Press, Fairbanks, AK. x + 330pp.

Kessel, B., and D.D. Gibson. 1978. *Status and Distribution of Alaska Birds*. Studies in Avian Biology No. 1. Cooper Ornithological Society. iv + 100 pp.

Kessel, B., R.B. Weeden, and G.C. West. 1967. *Bird-finding in Interior and Southcentral Alaska*. Alaska Ornithological Society, 42pp, mimeo.

Kessler, D.W. 1985. *Alaska's Saltwater Fishes and other sea life*. Alaska Northwest Publishing Co., Anchorage, AK. xxvi + 358pp.

King, M. 2000. *90 short walks around Juneau*. Taku Conservation Society, Juneau, AK. 110pp.

Klein, J.R. 1996. *Archaeology of Kachemak Bay, Alaska*. Kachemak Country Publications, Homer, AK. ix + 94pp.

Kleinleder, R., D. Erikson, C. Field, C. Field, D. Chorman, K. Stoltzfus, and G.C. West. 2002. *Checklist of Birds of Kachemak Bay, Alaska*. Center for Alaskan Coastal Studies, Homer, AK. Foldout checklist.

Klicka, J.F., R.M. Zink, J.C. Barlow, W.B. McGillivray, and T.J. Doyle. 1999. Evidence supporting the recent origin and species status of the Timberline Sparrow. *Condor* 101:577–588.

Krakauer, J. 1996. *Into the Wild*. Doubleday, New York, NY. 203pp.

Kricher, J. 2001. From Deadhorse to Fairbanks. *Winging It* 13:1–5.

Layberry, R.A., P.W. Hall, and J.D. Lafontaine. 1998. *The Butterflies of Canada*. University of Toronto Press. 376pp.

Lethaby, N. 1994. *A Bird Finding Guide to Alaska*. Nick Lethaby, San Jose, CA. 151pp.

______. 1997. Winter Birding in Southcentral Alaska. *Birding* 29:300-308.

Lord, N. 1992. *Darkened Waters*. Pratt Museum, Homer, AK. 60pp.

Maack, C., and D. Fox. 1999. Gambell – Nome Birdathon. *Kachemak Bay Bird Watch* 38: 4-5.

Mark, D.M. 1984. *Where to Find Birds in British Columbia*, second edition. Kestrel Press, New Westminster, BC. 122 pp.

Maynard, W.R. 1989. Jewels of the North. *Birding* 21:200–204. Ross's and Ivory Gulls.

McPhee, J. 1976. *Coming into the Country*. Farrar, Straus and Giroux, New York, NY. 438pp.

McIntyre, C., N. Eagleson, and A. Seegert. 2002. *Birds of Denali, An Introduction to Selected Species*. Alaska Natural History Association., Anchorage, AK. 64pp. Illustrated by David Sibley.

Morrin, H.B. 1978. *Birding the 49th State*. American Birding Association, Colorado Springs, CO. 129pp.

Morrow, J.E. 1974. *Illustrated Keys to the Fresh-water Fishes of Alaska*. Alaska Northwest Publishing Co., Anchorage, AK. 78pp.

Moskoff, W. 2000. The Impact of Oil Spills on Birds; Looking back at the *Exxon Valdez*. *Birding* 32:44–49.

Municipality of Anchorage. 2001. *Anchorage Parks and Trails. Guide to Parks and Recreation in the Anchorage, Eagle River, and Girdwood Areas*. Anchorage Parks and Recreation Design and Development, PO Box 196650, Anchorage, AK 99519-6650, 907-343-4335; *www.ci.anchorage.ak.us*.

Naske, C.-M., and H.E. Slotnik. 1979. *Alaska, A History of the 49th State*. William B. Eerdmans Publishing Co., Grand Rapids, MI. xv + 341pp.

O'Clair, R., R. Armstrong, and R. Carstensen. 1992. *The Nature of Southeast Alaska*. GTE Discovery Publications. Bothell, WA. 254pp.

Petersen, M.R., D.N. Weir, and M.H. Dick. 1991. *Birds of the Kilbuck and Ahklun Mountain Region, Alaska.* U.S. Fish and Wildlife Service, North American Fauna Number 76, Washington, DC. 158pp.

Peyton, L.J. 2000. *Bird Songs of Alaska.* Library of Natural Sounds, Cornell Laboratory of Ornithology, Ithaca, NY. 2-CD set of 260 songs and calls.

Piston, A.W., and S.C. Heinl. 2001. First Record of European Golden-Plover (*Pluvialis apricaria*) from the Pacific. *Western Birds* 32:179–181.

Pitelka, F.A. 1979. *Shorebirds in Marine Environments.* Studies in Avian Biology No. 2, Cooper Ornithological Society, viii + 261pp.

Potter, L. 1962. *Roadside Flowers of Alaska.* Roger Burt, Hanover, NH. 608pp.

Quady, D. 1998. Trip Report to Dutch Harbor. *Kachemak Bay Bird Watch* 35:1–2.

Rising, J.D. 2002. Were Swarth and Brooks right? A look at Timberline Sparrow. *Birding* 34:70–76.

Robertsen, P. 1998. *Finding Birds in Southeast Alaska – Wrangell Island and the Stikine River.* U.S. Forest Service, Wrangell Ranger District, PO Box 51, Wrangell, AK 99929. Fold-out map and checklist.

Russell, P.N. 1991. *English Bay and Port Graham Alutiiq Plantlore.* Pratt Museum, Homer, AK, Chugach Heritage Foundation and Alaska Native Plant Society, Anchorage, AK. viii + 78pp.

Russell, P.R., and G.C. West. 2002. *Bird Traditions of the Lime Village Area Dena'ina.* Alaska Native Knowledge Network, University of Alaska Fairbanks. (in press).

Schauer, A. 2000. *Birds Along the Dalton Highway.* Bureau of Land Management, Arctic District, 1150 University Avenue, Fairbanks, AK 99709-3844. 15pp. Checklist of birds in different habitats.

Scher, R. L. 1989. Birding Resurrection Bay, Seward, Alaska. *Winging It* 1:1–5.

______. 1989. Potter's Marsh. *Winging It* 1(4)11-12.

______. 1993. *Field Guide to Birding in Anchorage.* R.L. Scher. Anchorage, AK. 78pp.

______. 2002. *Field Guide to Birding in Anchorage*, 3rd edition. P. Rennick, editor. Anchorage Chapter, National Audubon Society, Anchorage, AK (in press).

Senner, S.E. 1997. Review of *Exxon Valdez* oil spill: Fate and Effects in Alaskan Waters. *Wilson Bulletin* 109:549–555.

______. 1998. A Closer Look: Surfbird. *Birding* 30:306–312.

______. 2002. Director's View Point. *Audubon Alaska News*, Winter 2001, p. 3. Status of Middleton Island.

Shaffer, B. 2000. *The Flora of South Central Alaska.* University of Alaska, Kenai Peninsula College, Kenai, AK. A handbook for field identification of Lichens, Mosses, Liverworts and Vascular Plants.

Smith, S.D. 1999. *Checklist of Birds of the Pribilof Islands, Alaska.* TDX Corporation, Anchorage, AK. Foldout checklist.

Sonneborn, D.W. 1997. The Banana Theory of Eastern Kingbirds. *Birding* 29:438–439.

Sonneborn, D.W., and R. Dittrick. 1995. More on Whiskered Auklets. *Birding* 27:172–173.

Springer, M.I. 1993. *Birdwatching in Eastcentral Alaska.* Falco, Fairbanks, AK. 71pp.

Stebbins, R.C. 1985. *A Field Guide to Western Reptiles and Amphibians.* Houghton Mifflin Co., Boston, MA. 336pp.

Stonorov, D. 2000. *Living in Harmony with Bears.* National Audubon Society, Anchorage, AK. 27pp.

Taylor, K. 1993. *A Birders Guide to British Columbia.* Keith Taylor Birdfinding Guides, BC. 306pp.

Tedin, M., and M. Ward. 2000. *Birds of Sitka National Historic Park.* Fold-out checklist.

Tobish, T.G. (compiler). 1990–1994. Changing Seasons: Alaska Region. *American Birds.* National Audubon Society.

______. 1995–2001. Changing Seasons: Alaska Region. *North American Birds.* American Birding Association.

Tobish, T.G. 1989. Arctic Warbler, Gunsight Mountain north of Anchorage, AK. *Winging It* 1 (4):11-12.

_____. 2000. The Next New ABA-Area Birds: Western Alaska. *Birding* 32:498-505.

Tolman, G. 1979. Birding Alaska Alone. *Birding* 11:154–159.

Tongass National Forest Juneau Ranger District. 1991. *Juneau Trails.* Alaska Natural History Association. Anchorage, AK. 67pp.

U.S. Fish and Wildlife Service. 1993. Field Guide to Anchorage Wetlands. U.S. Fish and Wildlife Service and Municipality of Anchorage. 60pp. Illustrations by G.C. West.

Valencia, K. 1993. *The Alaska Wilderness Guide*. Vernon Publications, Inc., Bellevue, WA. 472pp.

van Vliet, G., M. Schwann, R. Gordon, and S. Zimmerman. 2002. *Birds of Juneau, Alaska; Checklist.* Juneau Audubon Society, PO Box 21725, Juneau, AK 99802.

Viereck, E.G. 1987. *Alaska's Wilderness Medicines, Healthful Plants of the Far North*. Alaska Northwest Publishing Co., Edmonds, WA. 107pp.

Viereck, L.A. and E.L. Little, Jr. 1972. *Alaska Trees and Shrubs*. Forest Service, USDA, Washington, DC, Agricultural Handbook N. 410. viii + 265pp.

Walsh, P. J. 1993. *Checklist of the Birds of Mitkof Island, southeast Alaska*. (Revised in 1995). Fold-out checklist. Available in Petersburg book stores and visitor center.

Ward, M., and M. Tedin. 1998. *Finding Birds in Southeast Alaska – Sitka*. Juneau Audubon Society and U.S. Forest Service. 12-page brochure.

West, G.C. 1993. *Shorebird Guide for Kachemak Bay and Homer, Alaska*. Birchside Studios, Homer, AK. 32pp. (Reprinted in 1999 by Wizard Works, Homer, AK)

_____. 1994. *A Birder's Guide to the Kenai Peninsula, Alaska*. Birchside Studios and the Pratt Museum, Homer, AK. vi + 154 pp.

_____. 1999. *Discovery Guide to Birds on the Marine Waters of Southcoastal Alaska*. The Pratt Museum, Homer, AK, and Birchside Studios, Green Valley, AZ. 64pp, illustrated by the author

West, G.C., R.B. Weeden, L. Irving, and L.J. Peyton. 1968. Geographic variation in body size and weight of willow ptarmigan. *Arctic* 23:240–253.

West, G.C., and E.P. Bailey. 1986. Rustic bunting, purple finch, and Cassin's finch in south coastal Alaska. *The Murrelet* 67:32.

West, G.C., and C.M. White. 1966. Range extensions and additional notes on the birds of Alaska's arctic slope. *Condor* 68:302–304.

White, A.W. 1976. Finding Birds on Adak. *Birding* 8:305–312.

White, H. (Editor). 1974. *Alaska and Yukon Wild Flowers Guide*. Alaska Northwest Books, Bothell, WA. viii + 219pp.

Williams, J. 2000. The Gambell Side-Trip. *Birding* 32:41–42.

Yukon Conservation Society. 1995. *Whitehorse and area Hikes and Bikes*. Lost Moose Publishing Ltd. Whitehorse, Yukon. 144pp.

Yukon, Government of. 1999. *Whitehorse Trail Map: Explore the Wilderness City*. 1999. Government of the Yukon, Department of Renewable Resources and City of Whitehorse, Parks and Recreation Department, Whitehorse, Yukon. Pamphlet.

Zimmerman, S.T. 1995. Seeing Whiskered Auklets. *Birding* 27:190–191.

Zimmerman, S.T., and I.L. Jones. 1991. Birding the Pribilof Islands, Alaska. *Birding* 23:271–280.

APPENDIX E:

MAMMALS, REPTILES, AMPHIBIANS, AND FISHES OF ALASKA

MAMMALS

Note: Mammalian taxonomy to subspecies is under review and is far from settled at this time. Bear taxonomy is particularly difficult. While some call the Brown Bear a Grizzly Bear or a Kodiak Island Bear, there is only one species of Brown Bear in the northern hemisphere, *Ursus arctos*. Likewise there is only one species of Wolf and one Caribou (that includes the domestic reindeer) despite local names that suggest otherwise.

Shrews *Soricidae*
- Glacier Bay Water Shrew *Sorex alaskanus*
- Common Shrew *S. cinereus*
- Pygmy Shrew *S. hoyi*
- Pribilof Island Shrew *S. hydrodromus*
- St. Lawrence Island Shrew *S. jacksoni*
- Dusky Shrew *S. monticolus*
- Water Shrew *S. palustris*
- Tundra Shrew *S. tundrensis*
- Barrenground Shrew *S. ugyunak*
- Tiny Shrew *S. yukonicus*

Bats *Vespertilionidae*
- Big Brown Bat *Eptesicus fuscus*
- Silver-haired Bat *Lasionycteris noctivagans*
- California Myotis *Myotis californicus*
- Keen's Myotis *M. keenii*
- Little Brown Bat *M. lucifugus*
- Long-legged Myotis *M. volans*

Canids *Canidae*
- Arctic Fox *Alopex lagopus*
- Coyote *Canis latrans*
- Wolf *C. lupus*
- Red Fox *Vulpes vulpes*

Cats *Felidae*
- Lynx *Lynx canadensis*
- Mountain Lion *Puma concolor*

Mustelids *Mustelidae*
- Sea Otter *Enhydra lutris*
- River Otter *Lontra canadensis*
- Wolverine *Gulo gulo*
- Marten *Martes americana*
- Fisher *M. pennanti*
- Ermine *Mustela erminea*
- Least Weasel *M. nivalis*
- Mink *M. vison*

Walrus *Odobenidae*
- Walrus *Odobenus rosmarus*

Eared Seals *Otariidae*
- Northern Fur Seal *Callorhinus ursinus*
- Steller's Sea Lion *Eumetopias jubatus*
- California Sea Lion *Zalophus californianus*

Hair Seals *Phocidae*
- Hooded Seal *Cystophora cristata*
- Bearded Seal *Erignathus barbatus*
- Elephant Seal *Mirounga angustirostris*
- Ribbon Seal *Phoca fasciata*
- Harp Seal *P. groenlandica*
- Ringed Seal *P. hispida*
- Spotted Seal *P. largha*
- Harbor Seal *P. vitulina*

Raccoon *Procyonidae*
- Raccoon *Procyon lotor*

Bears *Ursidae*
- Black Bear *Ursus americanus*
- Brown Bear *U. arctos*
- Polar Bear *U. maritimus*

Baleen Whales *Balaenidae*
- Bowhead Whale *Balaena mysticetus*
- Northern Right Whale *Eubalaena glacialis*

Finback Whales *Balaenopteridae*
- Minke Whale *Balaenoptera acutorostrata*
- Sei Whale *B. borealis*
- Blue Whale *B. musculus*
- Fin (Finback) Whale *B. physalus*
- Humpback Whale *Megaptera novaeangliae*

Eschrichtiid Whale *Eschrishtiidae*
- Gray Whale *Eschrichtius robustus*

Dolphins *Delphinidae*
Short-finned Pilot Whale *Globicephala macrorhynchus*
Risso's Dolphin *Grampus griseus*
Pacific White-sided Dolphin *Lagenorhynchus obliquidens*
Northern Right-whale Dolphin *Lissodelphis borealis*
Killer Whale (Orca) *Orcinus orca*

Monodontid Whales *Monodontidae*
White Whale (Beluga) *Delphinapterus leucas*
Narwhal *Monodon monoceros*

Porpoises *Phocoenidae*
Harbor Porpoise *Phocoena phocoena*
Dall's Porpoise *Phocoenoides dalli*

Sperm Whale *Physeteridae*
Sperm Whale *Physeter catodon*

Beaked Whales *Ziphiidae*
Baird's Beaked Whale *Berardius bairdii*
Stejneger's Beaked Whale *Mesoplodon stejnegeri*
Cuvier's Beaked Whale *Ziphius cavirostris*

Deer *Cervidae*
Wapiti (Elk) *Cervus elaphus*
Moose *Alces alces*
Mule Deer *Odocoileus hemionus*
Caribou *Rangifer tarandus*

Bovids *Bovidae*
Bison *Bison bison*
Muskox *Ovibos moschatus*
Dall's Sheep *Ovis dalli*
Mountain Goat *Oreamnos americanus*

Sciurid Rodents *Sciuridae*
Alaska Marmot *Marmota broweri*
Hoary Marmot *M. caligata*
Woodchuck *M. monax*
Arctic Ground Squirrel *Spermophilus parryii*
Red Squirrel *Tamiasciurus hudsonicus*
Northern Flying Squirrel *Glaucomys sabrinus*

Beaver *Castoridae*
Beaver *Castor canadensis*

Jumping Mice *Dipodidae*
Meadow Jumping Mouse *Zapus hudsonicus*
Western Jumping Mouse *Z. princeps*

Rats, Mice, and Voles *Muridae*
Southern Red-backed Vole *Clethrionomys gapperi*
Northern Red-backed Vole *C. rutilus*
Collared Lemming *Dicrostonyx groenlandicus*
Brown Lemming *Lemmus trimucronatus*
St. Matthew Island Vole *Microtus abbreviatus*
Long-tailed Vole *M. longicaudus*
Singing Vole *M. miurus*
Tundra Vole *M. oeconomus*
Meadow Vole *M. pennsylvanicus*
Yellow-cheeked Vole *M. xanthognathus*
Muskrat *Ondatra zibethicus*
Northern Bog Lemming *Synaptomys borealis*
House Mouse *Mus musculus*
Norway Rat *Rattus norvegicus*
Bushy-tailed Woodrat *Neotoma cinerea*
Forest Deer Mouse *Permoyscus keeni*
Deer Mouse *P. maniculatus*
Heather Vole *Phenacomys intermedius*

Porcupine *Erethizontidae*
Porcupine *Erithizon dorsatum*

Pika *Ochotonidae*
Collared Pika *Ochotona collaris*

Rabbits and Hares *Leporidae*
Snowshoe Hare *Lepus americanus*
Tundra Hare *L. othus*
European Rabbit *Oryctolagus cuniculus*

A complete and up-to-date list of Alaska mammals with order, family, and scientific names can be found at the University of Alaska Museum web site: *http://www.uaf.edu/museum/mammal/AK_Mammals/Checklist.html*

REPTILES

Snakes
Common Garter Snake *Thamnophis sirtalis*
Valley Garter Snake *T. s. fitchi*

Marine Turtles
Pacific Green Turtle *Chelonia mydias agassizi*
Pacific Loggerhead Turtle *Caretta caretta gigas*
Pacific Leatherback Turtle *Dermochelys coriacea schlegeli*
Pacific Ridley's Turtle *Lepidochelys olivacea*

AMPHIBIANS

Salamanders

Long-toed Salamander
Ambystoma macrodactylum
Northwestern Salamander
Ambystoma gracile
Rough-skinned Newt *Taricha granulosa*
California Slender Salamander *Batrachoseps attenuatus caudatus*

Toads and Frogs

Western (Boreal) Toad *Bufo boreas*
Tailed Frog *Ascaphus truei*
Wood Frog *Rana sylvatica*
Spotted Frog *R. pretiosa*
Pacific Tree Frog *Hyla regila*

FISHES

Following is a list of the species that you might encounter while birding (and fishing) in Alaskan salt and fresh waters and those species mentioned in the text of this guide. For more information on Alaska fishes, check the following references: Eschmeyer et al., 1983; Kessler, 1985; and Morrow, 1974.

Arctic Lamprey *Lampetra japonica*
River Lamprey *L. ayresi*
Pink (Humpy) Salmon
Oncorhynchos gorbuscha
King (Chinook) Salmon *O. tschawytscha*
Silver (Coho) Salmon *O. kisutch*
Chum (Dog) Salmon *O. keta*
Red (Sockeye) Salmon *O. nerka*
Steelhead (Rainbow) Trout *Salmo gairdneri*
Cutthroat Trout *S. clarki*
Brook Trout *Salvelinus fontinalis*
Lake Trout *S. namaycush*
Arctic Char *S. alpinus*
Dolly Varden *S. malma*
Arctic Grayling *Thymallus arcticus*
Eulachon (Hooligan) *Thaleichthys pacificus*
Capelin *Mallotus villosus*
Pacific Herring *Clupea harengus*
American Shad *Alosa sapidissima*
Northern Pike *Esox lucius*
Sheefish (Inconnu) *Stenodus leucichthys*
Whitefish (6 species)
Longnose Sucker *Catostomus catostomus*
Pacific Sand Lance *Ammodytes hexapterus*
Burbot (Lingcod) *Lota lota*
Pacific Cod *Gadus macrocephalus*
Walleye Pollock *Theragra chalcogramma*
Sablefish *Anoplopoma fimbria*
Arctic Cod *Boreogadus saida*
Kelp Greenling *Hexagrammos decagrammus*
Sculpin (29 species)
Yellow Irish Lord *Hemilepidotus jordani*
Threespine Stickleback *Gasterosteus aculeatus*
Ninespine Stickleback *Pungitius pungitius*
Pacific Halibut *Hippoglossus stenolepis*
Yellowfin Sole *Limanda aspera*
Arctic Flounder *Liopsetta glacialis*
Starry Flounder *Hippoglossoides stellatus*

ACKNOWLEDGEMENTS Steve Zimmerman, Gordon Haas, and Bruce Wing provided information on occurrence of reptiles and amphibians in Alaska. Gordon Jerrell provided information on the current taxonomic status of mammals.

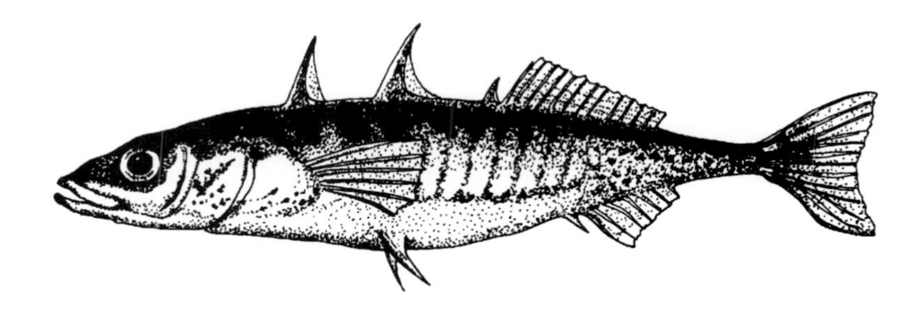

Threespine Stickleback

OTHER GUIDES IN THE ABA SERIES

A Birder's Guide to Metropolitan Areas of North America
Paul Lehman

A Birder's Guide to the Bahamas
Anthony R. White

A Birder's Guide to Idaho
Dan Svingen and Kas Dumroese

A Birder's Guide to Virginia
David Johnston

A Birder's Guide to Colorado
Harold R. Holt

A Birder's Guide to Florida
Bill Pranty

A Birder's Guide to New Hampshire
Alan Delorey

Birdfinder: A Birder's Guide to Planning North American Trips
Jerry A. Cooper

A Birder's Guide to Southeastern Arizona
Richard Cachor Taylor

A Birder's Guide to Arkansas
Mel White

A Birder's Guide to Eastern Massachusetts
Bird Observer

A Birder's Guide to Churchill
Bonnie Chartier

A Birder's Guide to the Texas Coast
Harold R. Holt

A Birder's Guide to Wyoming
Oliver K. Scott

A Birder's Guide to the Rio Grande Valley
Mark W. Lockwood, William B. McKinney
James N. Paton, Barry R. Zimmer

A Birder's Guide to Southern California
Brad Schram

American Birding Association Sales
PO Box 6599, Colorado Springs, Colorado 80934
Phone: 800/634-7736 or 719/578-0607
Fax: 800/590-2473 or 719/578-9705
www.americanbirding.org

Join American Birding Association

When you become a member of the American Birding Association, you join thousands of birders who share the passion and joy of birding, and are eager to improve their knowledge and skills to get the most out of their field birding experiences.

- Network with friends and share the passion of birding.
- Learn about birds.
- Access workshops, conferences, and tours.
- Expand your birding "tool box".
- Receive full-color magazines and monthly newsletters.

You don't have to be an expert birder to be a member of the American Birding Association. You're qualified simply by having a desire to learn more about birds, their habitats, and how to protect them.

ABA membership offers you opportunities to improve your skills. These include internationally attended conferences and conventions, Institute for Field Ornithology workshops, specialized tours, and volunteer opportunities where you'll meet and learn from experts and get to know others who share your passion.

Your membership also includes resources such as newsletters, our award-winning, full-color magazine, *Birding*, directories, and catalogs to help you develop your interest individually and expand your knowledge.

Sign Up Today!

❑ New Membership ❑ Renewing Membership (Member #__________________)

Name____

Address____

____

City____________________State__________Zip__________

Country__________________Phone__________________

E-mail____

Each level entitles members to certain benefits. Visit *<www.americanbirding.org/memgen.htm>* or call 800-850-2473 to find out more.

- ❑ Individual .... US$40
- ❑ Joint .... US$47
- ❑ Student[b] .... US$20
- ❑ Int'l/Canada Individual[a] .... US$50
- ❑ Int'l/Canada Joint[a] .... US$58
- ❑ Int'l/Canada Student[ab] .... US$30

[a]*Canadian dues include GST, which is paid to the Canadian government*

[b]*Please include your birth date, school name, and graduation date*

Select one of these levels, and you will become a Century Club member and increase your support of ABA's outstanding education and conservation programs:

- ❑ Hooded Merganser .... US$140
- ❑ Hooded Merganser Int'l .... US$150
- ❑ Mountain Plover .... US$300
- ❑ Violet-crowned Hummingbird .. US$500
- ❑ Painted Bunting .... US$1,000
- ❑ White-throated Swift .... US$2,500

Subscription to *North American Birds* magazine

- ❑ Member .... US$28
- ❑ Member Int'l/Canada .... US$33
- ❑ Non-member .... US$30
- ❑ Non-member Int'l/Canada .... US$35

Payment

Membership: US$__________

Additional Contribution: US$__________

❑ Education ❑ Conservation ❑ Unrestricted

NAB Subscription US$__________

Total US$__________

Check or Money Order payable to American Birding Association.

Charge to ❑ VISA ❑ Mastercard ❑ Discover

Card #____________________

Expiration Date____________________

Signature____________________

Send this form to **ABA Membership, PO Box 6599, Colorado Springs, CO 80934-6599**.

You may also join by phone, fax, or web:
Phone: 800-850-2473 • Fax: 719-578-1480
www.americanbirding.org/memgen.htm

AK/02

INDEX

A

B

ABBREVIATED TABLE OF CONTENTS

ABBREVIATED TABLE OF CONTENTS

H

I

ABBREVIATED TABLE OF CONTENTS

J

K

L

M

ABBREVIATED TABLE OF CONTENTS

P

ABBREVIATED TABLE OF CONTENTS

ABBREVIATED TABLE OF CONTENTS

ABBREVIATED TABLE OF CONTENTS

Y

ABBREVIATED TABLE OF CONTENTS